D1061242

Contents Table of Contents

Teacher's Edition

Student's Text

Unit and chapter titles are listed below. For a complete table of contents including lesson titles, tests, and features, see pages viii–xiii in the student's text which follows after page T48.

Emphasis on Skills

Units and chapters organized around basic skills, *page T3*

Skills broken down into specific problem types, *pages iv–v*

Problem types in teaching examples keyed to exercise sets and to items on pretests and posttests, *pages iv–v*

Clear, concise teaching examples, *pages 84, 156*

Plenty of practice in exercise sets and in applications, *pages 18–19, 96–97, 266–267*

Continued skills maintenance, *pages 63, 127*

Comprehensive treatment of computational skills as well as informal treatment of measurement, probability, statistics, algebra, and geometry, *pages viii–xiii*

Consumer and Career Applications

Practical consumer lessons that focus on uses of mathematics in everyday life, *pages vi, 78–79, 225*

Interesting career lessons that focus on uses of mathematics in a wide variety of jobs, *pages 210–211, 358–359, 420–423*

Visual appeal and motivation through realistic photographs, *pages 13, 58–59, 336–337*

Extensive use of metric measures in applications, *pages 36–37, 250–251*

Geared for Student Success

Minimum amount of reading, *pages 33, 76–77*

Skills lessons and problem types paced for continuous success, *pages 21–32*

Teaching examples that are easy to follow, *pages 6, 236*

Exercise sets with exercises of the same type in each set, *pages 70–71, 304–305*

Simple system of keying test items to examples and exercise sets, *pages iv–v*

Easy, relevant applications, *pages 80–81, 118–119*

Answers to odd-numbered exercises, *pages 386–416*

Easy for Teachers to Use

Consistent organization within chapters for easy management, *page iii*

Lessons adaptable to individual or group instruction, *page T8*

Built-in testing program, *pages T8, T28–T40, 259, 270, 276*

Maintenance and enrichment features, *pages 128, 157, 191*

Answers, objectives, and notes overprinted on the student's page, *pages T6–T7*

Lessons and tests keyed to objectives, *pages T10–T15*

Supplementary materials for testing and individualizing, *pages T5, T8*

Program Materials

Teacher's Edition

496 pages including reproduced student's pages with answers and notes overprinted plus 48 teacher pages at the front of the book.

Student's Text

448 pages including answers to odd-numbered exercises

Supplementary Materials

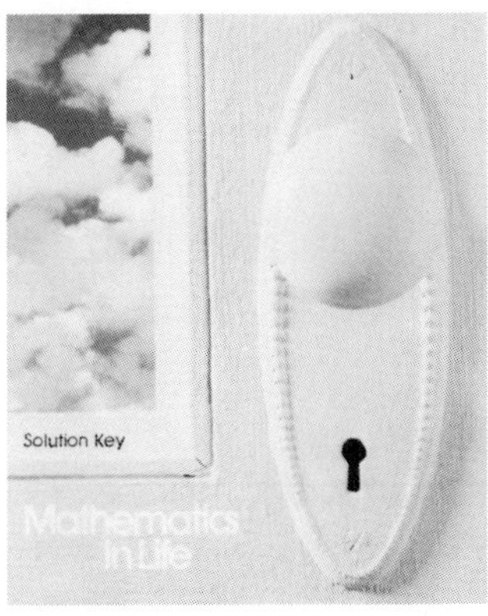

Solution Key

Contains answers for all exercises in the student's text. Steps needed to obtain answers are shown for selected exercises. The key can be used by the students.

Tests and Record Forms: Duplicating Masters

84 duplicating masters including an alternate form of each of the 18 chapter tests in the student's book and the 6 unit tests, mid-book test, and end-of-book test in the front of the teacher's edition.

Also included are two record forms for use with tests in the student's book or tests in the masters. The Criterion Referenced Individual Record Form shows test results for an individual student for the entire year. The Class Test Record Form shows test results for a class. Both record forms key test items to objectives and to text pages.

Features of the Student's Text and Teacher's Edition

Student's Text

For explanations and examples of many of the features listed below, see pages iii–vii of the student's text which follows after page T48.

Units

Chapters

Lessons
Skills lessons
Consumer lessons
Career lessons

Tests
Pretest
Posttest
Chapter Test

Maintenance
Skills Tune-up

Enrichment
Break Time
Calculator Exercises

End-of-book
Answers to Odd-numbered Exercises
Tables
Careers Chart
Glossary
Index

Teacher's Edition

Teacher pages T1–T48

Reference Charts A reference chart for each unit keys objectives to text pages, to pretest and posttest items, and to chapter test items. See pages T10–T15.

Notes Notes and activities for each unit include additional information and teaching suggestions. See pages T16–T27.

Tests Six unit tests, a two-part mid-book test, and a three-part end-of-book test are provided. See pages T28–T40.

Answers and lesson notes

① **Answers** Answers printed on a full-size replica of the student's page.

② **Objective** A brief statement of the objective for the lesson. The same objective appears in the Reference Charts on pages T10–T15.

③ **Problem type** An indication of the specific problem type that is taught in the example.

page 218

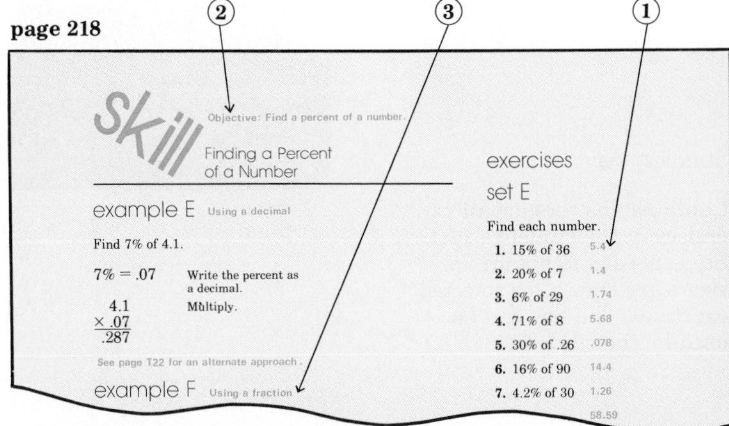
②
③
①
Skill
Objective: Find a percent of a number.
Finding a Percent of a Number
example E Using a decimal
Find 7% of 4.1.
7% = .07 Write the percent as a decimal.
4.1
× .07
.287 Multiply.
See page T22 for an alternate approach.
example F Using a fraction
exercises
set E
Find each number.
1. 15% of 36 5.4
2. 20% of 7 1.4
3. 6% of 29 1.74
4. 71% of 8 5.68
5. 30% of .26 .078
6. 16% of 90 14.4
7. 4.2% of 30 1.26
58.59

④ **References to applications** References at the end of some skills lessons indicating when the student has had the skills needed to do certain applications in the chapter.

page 347

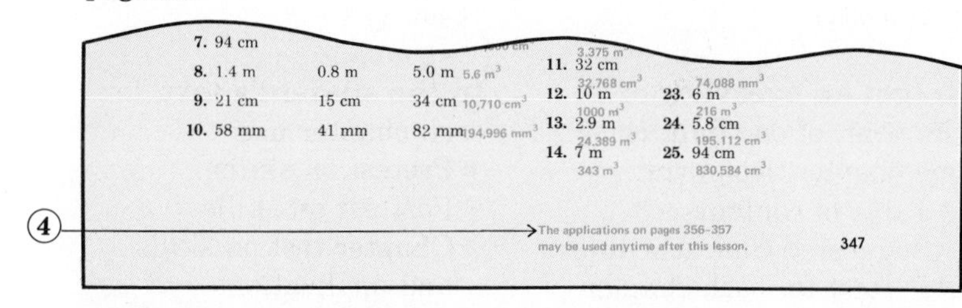

7. 94 cm
8. 1.4 m 0.8 m 5.0 m 5.6 m³
9. 21 cm 15 cm 34 cm 10,710 cm³
10. 58 mm 41 mm 82 mm 194,996 mm³

3,375 m³
11. 32 cm
32,768 cm³
12. 10 m
1000 m³
13. 2.9 m
24.389 m³
14. 7 m
343 m³

74,088 mm³
23. 6 m
216 m³
24. 5.8 cm
195.112 cm³
25. 94 cm
830,584 cm³

④ → The applications on pages 356–357 may be used anytime after this lesson.

347

⑤ **Materials** A list of materials (other than paper and pencil) that are needed by the student to do the lesson.

⑥ **Notes** Helpful information and teaching suggestions.

page 310

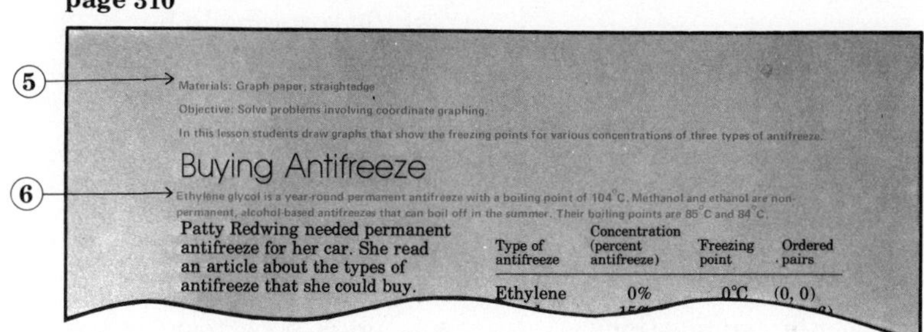

⑤ → Materials: Graph paper, straightedge

Objective: Solve problems involving coordinate graphing.

In this lesson students draw graphs that show the freezing points for various concentrations of three types of antifreeze.

Buying Antifreeze

⑥ → Ethylene glycol is a year-round permanent antifreeze with a boiling point of 104°C. Methanol and ethanol are non-permanent, alcohol-based antifreezes that can boil off in the summer. Their boiling points are 85°C and 84°C.

Patty Redwing needed permanent antifreeze for her car. She read an article about the types of antifreeze that she could buy.

Type of antifreeze	Concentration (percent antifreeze)	Freezing point	Ordered pairs
Ethylene	0%	0°C	(0, 0)

⑦ **Scoring table** A table to convert raw test scores to percentage scores on each pretest, posttest, and chapter test.

⑧ **References to problem types** A letter next to a chapter test item indicating the skills problem type being tested.

page 40

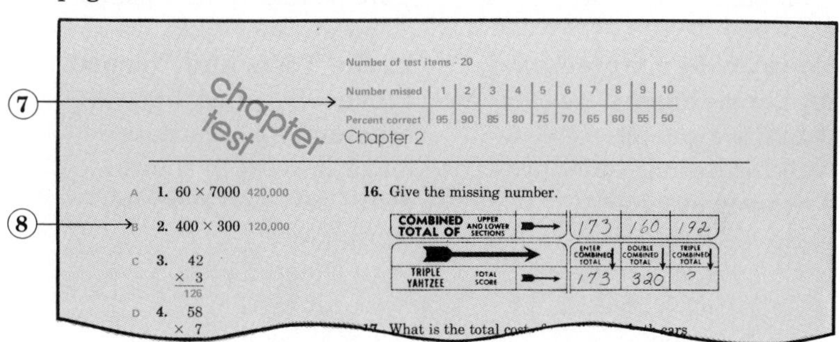

Number of test items - 20

Number missed	1	2	3	4	5	6	7	8	9	10
Percent correct	95	90	85	80	75	70	65	60	55	50

chapter test

Chapter 2

A 1. 60 × 7000 420,000

B 2. 400 × 300 120,000

C 3. 42 × 3 126

D 4. 58 × 7

16. Give the missing number.

17. What is the total cost ... cars

⑨ **References to additional tests** References to tests in the teacher's edition and in the *Tests and Record Forms: Duplicating Masters.*

page 126

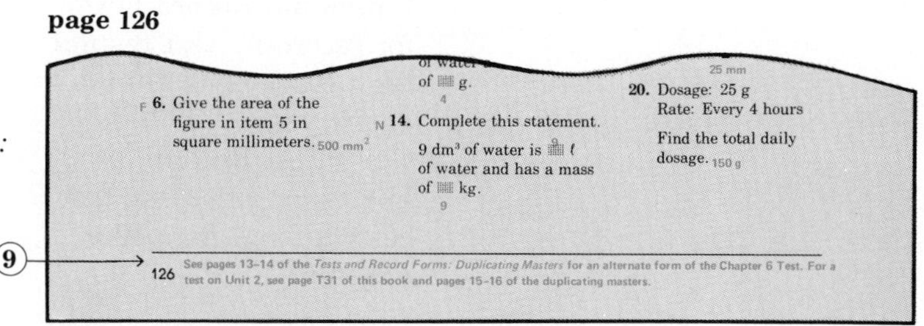

of ▒ g.
4

F 6. Give the area of the figure in item 5 in square millimeters. 500 mm²

N 14. Complete this statement.

9 dm³ of water is ▒ ℓ of water and has a mass of ▒ kg.
9

25 mm

20. Dosage: 25 g
Rate: Every 4 hours

Find the total daily dosage. 150 g

⑨ → 126 See pages 13–14 of the *Tests and Record Forms: Duplicating Masters* for an alternate form of the Chapter 6 Test. For a test on Unit 2, see page T31 of this book and pages 15–16 of the duplicating masters.

Planning, Testing, and Individualizing

Planning

To get an overview of the year, of one unit, or of one chapter, look over:
- Table of contents
- Suggested time schedule
- Pretest for each chapter
- Chapter tests

To plan daily lessons, use:
- Teaching examples in skills lessons
- Worked-out problems in consumer and career lessons
- Teaching suggestions overprinted on the page
- Additional notes found on pages T16–T27

To provide maintenance and enrichment, use:
- Skills Tune-up
- Skills exercises not previously assigned
- Break Times
- Calculator Exercises
- Activities suggested in teacher's notes

Testing

In the student's text, for each chapter use:
- Pretest on skills
- Posttest on skills
- Chapter test on skills and applications
- Teacher-constructed skills tests made by choosing one exercise from each lettered set

In the teacher's edition, use:
- 6 unit tests
- 1 mid-book test
- 1 end-of-book test
- Reference Charts that key objectives to test items and to text pages

In the Tests and Record Forms: Duplicating Masters, for alternate forms of tests in the student's text and teacher's edition, use:
- 18 chapter tests
- 6 unit tests
- 1 mid-book test
- 1 end-of-book test
- Criterion Referenced Individual Record Form for recording test results for a student for the entire year
- Class Test Record Forms for recording test results for a class on a chapter

Individualizing

To diagnose students' needs for a year, one unit, or one chapter, pretest using:
- Tests in student's text
- Tests in teacher's edition
- Tests in masters

To prescribe individual assignments, use:
- ABC system of keying test items to exercises in the student's text
- Reference Charts in the teacher's edition
- Record forms in the masters

To instruct individuals or small groups, use:
- Student self-teaching through examples in the text, answers to odd-numbered exercises, and *Solution Key*
- Teacher demonstration of problems in the text

To evaluate progress for a year, one unit, or one chapter, posttest using:
- Tests in student's text
- Tests in teacher's edition
- Tests in masters

Suggested Time Schedule

The suggested schedule given below is a general guide to allocating periods of time to chapters within each unit. The schedule is based on a school year of 170 days.

	Chapter	Pages	Title	Days
Unit 1	1	3-20	Adding and Subtracting Whole Numbers	8
	2	21-40	Multiplying Whole Numbers	9
	3	41-62	Dividing Whole Numbers	12
Unit 2	4	67-82	Adding and Subtracting Decimals	7
	5	83-104	Multiplying and Dividing Decimals	12
	6	105-126	The Metric System	10
Unit 3	7	131-150	Multiplying and Dividing Fractions and Mixed Numbers	11
	8	151-170	Adding and Subtracting Fractions and Mixed Numbers	11
	9	171-190	Probability	9
Unit 4	10	195-212	Ratio, Proportion, and Similarity	8
	11	213-232	Percent	11
	12	233-254	Statistics	9
Unit 5	13	259-276	Positive and Negative Numbers	8
	14	277-298	Expressions and Equations	10
	15	299-318	Graphing	8
Unit 6	16	323-340	Perimeter and Area	8
	17	341-360	Surface Area and Volume	10
	18	361-382	The Pythagorean Rule and Trigonometry	9

Unit 1 Whole Numbers

Objectives	*Text pages*	*Pretest, Posttest items**	*Chapter Test items*
Chapter 1 Adding and Subtracting Whole Numbers, Pages 3–20			
1. Add whole numbers.	4–5	A, B, C, D	1, 2, 3, 4
2. Subtract whole numbers.	6–7	E, F, G	5, 6, 7
3. Compute following order of operations including addition and subtraction.	8–9	H, I	8, 9
4. Solve addition and subtraction equations.	10–11	J, K	10, 11
5. Solve problems involving addition and subtraction of whole numbers.	13–19	– – –	12–18
Chapter 2 Multiplying Whole Numbers, Pages 21–40			
6. Multiply multiples of powers of 10.	22–23	A, B	1, 2
7. Multiply whole numbers with a one-digit multiplier.	24–25	C, D, E, F	3, 4, 5, 6
8. Multiply whole numbers with a two-digit multiplier.	26–27	G, H, I, J	7, 8, 9, 10
9. Multiply whole numbers with a three-digit multiplier.	28–29	K, L, M	11, 12, 13
10. Compute following order of operations involving addition, subtraction, and multiplication.	30–31	N, O	14, 15
11. Solve problems involving multiplication of whole numbers.	33–39	– – –	16–20
Chapter 3 Dividing Whole Numbers, Pages 41–62			
12. Divide whole numbers with a one-digit divisor.	42–43	A, B, C, D, E	1, 2, 3, 4, 5
13. Divide whole numbers with a two-digit divisor.	44–45	F, G, H, I	6, 7, 8, 9
14. Divide whole numbers with a zero in the quotient.	46	J, K	10, 11
15. Divide whole numbers with a three-digit divisor.	47	L, M	12, 13
16. Compute following order of operations involving addition, subtraction, multiplication, and division.	48–49	N, O	14, 15
17. Solve multiplication and division equations.	50–51	P, Q	16, 17
18. Solve problems involving division of whole numbers.	53–61	– – –	18–22

* Lettered Pretest and Posttest items correspond to lettered examples and exercise sets in the skills lessons.

Unit 2 Decimals and the Metric System

Objectives	Text pages	Pretest, Posttest items	Chapter Test items
Chapter 4 Adding and Subtracting Decimals, Pages 67-82			
19. Write and compare decimals.	68-69	A, B, C	1, 2, 3
20. Add decimals.	70-71	D, E, F, G	4, 5, 6, 7
21. Subtract decimals.	72-73	H, I, J, K	8, 9, 10, 11
22. Solve problems involving addition and subtraction of decimals.	75-81	---	12-16
Chapter 5 Multiplying and Dividing Decimals, Pages 83-104			
23. Multiply decimals.	84-85	A, B, C	1, 2, 3
24. Divide a decimal by a whole number.	86-87	D, E, F	4, 5, 6
25. Multiply or divide a decimal by 10, 100, or 1000.	88-89	G, H, I, J	7, 8, 9, 10
26. Divide decimals.	90-91	K, L, M	11, 12, 13
27. Round decimals.	92	N, O, P	14, 15, 16
28. Round quotients.	93	Q, R, S	17, 18, 19
29. Solve problems involving multiplication and division of decimals.	95-103	---	20-25
Chapter 6 The Metric System, Pages 105-126			
30. Estimate and measure the length of a segment to the nearest centimeter or millimeter.	107	A, B	1, 2
31. Choose sensible measures and do conversions involving metric units of length.	108-109	C, D	3, 4
32. Find areas of figures and do conversions involving metric units of area.	110	E, F	5, 6
33. Find volumes of figures and do conversions involving metric units of volume.	111	G, H	7, 8
34. Choose sensible measures and do conversions involving metric units of capacity.	112	I, J	9, 10
35. Choose sensible measures and do conversions involving metric units of mass.	113	K, L	11, 12
36. Write measures for given amounts of water using related units of volume, capacity, and mass.	114	M, N	13, 14
37. Choose sensible measures involving metric units of temperature.	115	O, P	15, 16
38. Solve problems involving metric units of measure.	118-125	---	17-20

Unit 3 Fractions, Mixed Numbers, and Probability

Objectives	*Text pages*	*Pretest, Posttest items*	*Chapter Test items*
Chapter 7 Multiplying and Dividing Fractions and Mixed Numbers, Pages 131-150			
39. Write fractions and mixed numbers.	132-133	A, B	1, 2
40. Rename fractions and mixed numbers.	134	C, D, E	3, 4, 5
41. Write a fraction as a decimal.	135	F, G	6, 7
42. Multiply fractions.	136-137	H, I, J, K	8, 9, 10, 11
43. Multiply mixed numbers.	138-139	L, M, N, O	12, 13, 14, 15
44. Divide fractions and mixed numbers.	140-141	P, Q, R, S	16, 17, 18, 19
45. Solve problems involving multiplication and division of fractions and mixed numbers.	143-149	– – –	20-24
Chapter 8 Adding and Subtracting Fractions and Mixed Numbers, Pages 151-170			
46. Find common denominators.	152	A, B	1, 2
47. Compare fractions and mixed numbers.	153	C, D, E	3, 4, 5
48. Add fractions.	154-155	F, G, H	6, 7, 8
49. Subtract fractions.	156-157	I, J, K	9, 10, 11
50. Add mixed numbers.	158-159	L, M, N, O	12, 13, 14, 15
51. Subtract mixed numbers.	160-161	P, Q, R, S, T	16, 17, 18, 19, 20
52. Solve problems involving addition and subtraction of fractions and mixed numbers.	163-169	– – –	21-25
Chapter 9 Probability, Pages 171-190			
53. Find probabilities and make predictions.	172-173	A, B, C	1, 2, 3
54. Find probabilities using tree diagrams.	174-175	D, E	4, 5
55. Find probabilities involving independent events using multiplication.	176-177	F, G	6, 7
56. Find probabilities involving dependent events using multiplication.	178-179	H	8
57. Use experiments to make predictions.	180-181	I, J	9, 10
58. Solve problems involving probability.	183-189	– – –	11-15

Unit 4 Ratio, Percent, and Statistics

Objectives	*Text pages*	*Pretest, Posttest items*	*Chapter Test items*
Chapter 10 Ratio, Proportion, and Similarity, Pages 195-212			
59. Write ratios and lists of equal ratios.	196-197	A, B	1, 2
60. Find a missing number in a proportion by using cross-products.	198-199	C, D	3, 4
61. Identify similar figures and name corresponding angles and sides.	200-201	E, F	5, 6
62. Find missing dimensions in similar triangles by using proportions.	202-203	G, H	7, 8
63. Solve problems involving ratio, proportion, and similarity.	205-211	---	9-12
Chapter 11 Percent, Pages 213-232			
64. Write percents as decimals and decimals as percents.	214-215	A, B	1, 2
65. Write percents as fractions and fractions as percents.	216-217	C, D	3, 4
66. Find a percent of a number.	218-219	E, F, G	5, 6, 7
67. Find what percent one number is of another.	220-221	H, I	8, 9
68. Find a number when a percent of it is known.	222-223	J, K	10, 11
69. Solve problems involving percent.	225-231	---	12-17
Chapter 12 Statistics, Pages 233-254			
70. Find the mean for a set of statistics.	235	A	1
71. Find the median and the mode for a set of statistics.	236-237	B, C	2, 3
72. Read and make a bar graph.	238-239	D, E	4, 5
73. Read and make a line graph.	240-241	F, G	6, 7
74. Read a circle graph.	242-243	H, I	8, 9
75. Make a circle graph.	244-245	J, K	10, 11
76. Solve problems involving statistics.	248-253	---	12, 13

Unit 5 Algebra

Objectives	*Text pages*	*Pretest, Posttest items*	*Chapter Test items*
Chapter 13 Positive and Negative Numbers, Pages 259–276			
77. Write, compare, and order positive and negative numbers.	260–261	A, B, C	1, 2, 3
78. Add positive and negative numbers.	262–263	D, E, F, G	4, 5, 6, 7
79. Subtract positive and negative numbers.	264–265	H, I, J, K, L, M	8, 9, 10, 11, 12, 13
80. Multiply positive and negative numbers.	266–267	N, O, P, Q	14, 15, 16, 17
81. Divide positive and negative numbers.	268–269	R, S, T, U	18, 19, 20, 21
82. Solve problems involving positive and negative numbers.	271–275	– – –	22–29
Chapter 14 Expressions and Equations, Pages 277–298			
83. Evaluate expressions.	278–279	A, B, C, D	1, 2, 3, 4
84. Evaluate expressions involving order of operations.	280–281	E, F	5, 6
85. Solve addition and subtraction equations involving integers and decimals.	282–283	G, H	7, 8
86. Solve multiplication and division equations involving integers and decimals.	284–285	I, J	9, 10
87. Solve two-step equations.	286–287	K, L	11, 12
88. Combine like terms to solve equations.	288–289	M, N	13, 14
89. Solve problems involving equations.	291–297	– – –	15–18
Chapter 15 Graphing, Pages 299–318			
90. Give ordered pairs for points, and locate points for ordered pairs.	301	A, B	1, 2
91. Read a graph on a grid, and draw the graph of an equation.	302–303	C, D	3, 4
92. Give ordered pairs of integers for points in four quadrants, and locate points for ordered pairs of integers.	304–305	E, F	5, 6
93. Read a graph on a four-quadrant grid, and draw the graph of an equation on a four-quadrant grid.	306–307	G, H	7, 8
94. Solve problems involving coordinate graphing.	310–317	– – –	9–12

Unit 6 Geometry and Right-Triangle Relations

Objectives	*Text pages*	*Pretest, Posttest items*	*Chapter Test items*
Chapter 16 Perimeter and Area, Pages 323-340			
95. Find the perimeter of a geometric figure.	324-325	A, B	1, 2
96. Find the circumference of a circle.	326-327	C, D	3, 4
97. Find the area of a rectangle, a square, and a parallelogram.	328-329	E, F, G	5, 6, 7
98. Find the area of a triangle and a trapezoid.	330-331	H, I	8, 9
99. Find the area of a circle.	332-333	J, K	10, 11
100. Solve problems involving perimeter and area.	335-339	– – –	12-14
Chapter 17 Surface Area and Volume, Pages 341-360			
101. Find the surface area of a rectangular prism.	343	A	1
102. Find the surface area of a cube.	344	B	2
103. Find the surface area of a cylinder.	345	C	3
104. Find the volume of a rectangular prism and a cube.	346-347	D, E	4, 5
105. Find the volume of a cylinder.	348-349	F, G	6, 7
106. Find the volume of a pyramid and a cone.	350-351	H, I	8, 9
107. Find the volume of a sphere.	352	J, K	10, 11
108. Solve problems involving surface area and volume.	355-359	– – –	12-14
Chapter 18 The Pythagorean Rule and Trigonometry, Pages 361-382			
109. Find powers of numbers by using positive exponents, and find square roots of numbers by trial and error.	363	A, B	1, 2
110. Find squares and square roots of numbers by reading a table.	364-365	C, D, E	3, 4, 5
111. Find the length of a side of a right triangle by using the Pythagorean Rule.	366-367	F, G	6, 7
112. Write the tangent, the sine, and the cosine of an angle as a ratio and as a decimal.	368-369	H, I, J	8, 9, 10
113. Give the tangent, the sine, and the cosine of a given angle by reading a table.	370-371	K, L, M	11, 12, 13
114. Find the length of a side of a right triangle by using trigonometric ratios.	372-373	N, O, P	14, 15, 16
115. Solve problems involving the Pythagorean Rule and trigonometry.	376-381	– – –	17-19

Chapter 1 Adding and Subtracting Whole Numbers, Pages 3-20

pages 4-5 For remedial students, you will want to review numeration, place value, and addition and subtraction basic facts before beginning whole-number computation.

pages 6-7 Problems with zeros in the minuend are not included in set E, but are in sets F and G. You may wish to review several examples using zeros. Encourage students to check their answers by adding mentally.

pages 8-9 In this lesson, we are dealing with the operations of addition and subtraction used together. Therefore, the order or grouping of the numbers in the problem might change the answer. You may wish to discuss the commutative and associative properties for addition.

You could give students some more difficult problems such as these:
(55 – 17) – (3 + 29) [6]
28 – [(4 + 17) – 3] [10]

page 13 The Home Economics Department or the library may have references that give calorie and carbohydrate counts for various foods. These could be used to generate several exercises, such as those in the lesson.

pages 14-15 You may wish to discuss with your class the advantages and disadvantages of the various forms of transportation. If possible, obtain current schedule and fare information, and have students plan their own trip.

pages 16-17 After students have correctly completed the table on page 17, you might use it to discuss questions such as this: "Your gross income last year was $13,000. You receive a $1000 raise in salary for this year. How much does your net income increase?" [$721] "Your real buying power this year will be how much more or less than your net income last year?" [$437 less]

pages 18-19 The degree days and temperatures are given in degrees Celsius. In order to have students become familiar with this scale, try to obtain an outside thermometer and note temperature in degrees Celsius.

Some Sunday papers publish the number of degree days for the week in the weather section.

Chapter 2 Multiplying Whole Numbers, Pages 21-40

pages 24-25 To provide more practice, write the digits 6, 4, 7, 9, and 3 on the chalkboard. Ask students to put the digits in these boxes to form the greatest possible product.

■■■■
× ■ [9 × 7643 = 68,787]

pages 26-27 In example H, you might use these two problems to explain why the final step is to add.

```
 36      36      36
× 8     ×20     ×28
288     720     288←8 × 36
                720←20 × 36
               1008
```

pages 28–29 To provide more practice, have students complete self-checking puzzles like this. Answers are shown in brackets.

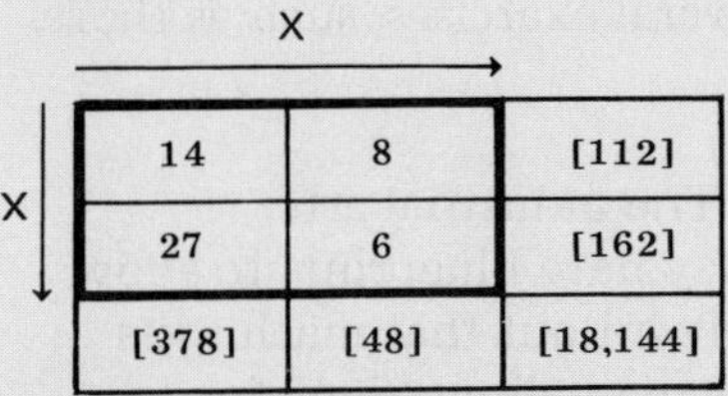

page 33 You might have some students play the game. An inexpensive set of score cards can be purchased and used with 5 dice. Each player rolls 5 dice. The player may pick up some or all of the dice and roll those again. This happens a third time. Then the player must record the final results in one of the spaces on the score card. A zero indicates the player could not fill the space.

pages 36–37 One thousand square meters is about one-tenth of the area of a football field. You might also mention that a metric ton, which is 1000 kilograms, is about the weight of a subcompact car.

Chapter 3 Dividing Whole Numbers, Pages 41–62

pages 42–43 Review the terms *dividend*, *divisor*, *quotient*, and *remainder*. Students who have trouble with set A may need a review of division basic facts.

In discussing example A, you might point out that sometimes it is better to express an answer as a quotient with a remainder rather than as a mixed number or decimal. If the problem were how many \$7 books can be bought for \$38, an answer of 5 books with \$3 left over would make more sense than an answer in mixed-number or decimal form.

You might demonstrate short division with a problem like the one below. In each step, students multiply and subtract mentally and then write the remainder in front of the next digit in the dividend.

$$\begin{array}{r} 4\ 2\ 6\ \text{R1} \\ 7\overline{)2\ 9\ {}^{1}8\ {}^{4}3} \end{array}$$

page 53 Students could divide the weekly salary by 40 to find the hourly salary, ignoring all remainders.

If students are interested in salaries for jobs in various parts of the country, they can find information in the *Occupational Outlook Handbook* in the library or in the guidance office.

pages 54–55 To add realism to the lesson, have students do similar problems from local newspaper ads.

For problems involving just basic facts, such as 3 for 22¢, an alternate method is to round the price up to the next multiple of 3 and then divide. $24 \div 3 = 8$.

pages 60–61 Inventory turnover rate is an indication of how fast goods are being sold. However, it does not indicate the store's profit. Profit depends on other factors as well such as overhead costs and mark-up on items.

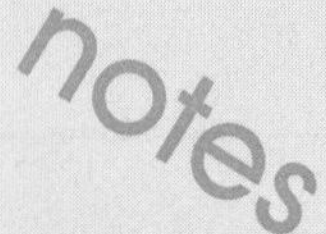

Chapter 4 Adding and Subtracting Decimals, Pages 67–82

pages 70–71 You may wish to have less able students write zeros when adding ragged decimals such as this:

$$8.625 + .3 \longrightarrow \begin{array}{r} 8.625 \\ +\ \ .300 \\ \hline \end{array}$$

pages 72–73 You can use this device to reinforce addition and subtraction computation of decimals. Answers are shown in brackets.

(+ across →, + down ↓)

[.09]	1.3	1.39
.28	[2.6]	[2.88]
.37	3.9	[4.27]

For the activity in the Break Time, Harvey can light the 9 original candles, the 3 candles from the stubs of the original candles, and 1 candle from the stubs of the three candles he made, thus lighting 13 candles in all.

page 75 Because discount stores are basically a warehouse, they have a low overhead and usually charge lower prices than retail outlets. However, be sure to mention that discount catalog stores are not always cheaper because special sales at retail outlets sometimes feature lower prices. You may wish to have students use the discount catalog and newspaper ads to compare prices.

pages 78–79 You may wish to take a field trip to a bank for further information on banking services. If possible, obtain some sample checks. These could be used to generate several exercises, such as those in the lesson.

pages 80–81 The industrial arts department may have blueprints to show to your class. Point out that machinists must often calculate dimensions from blueprints.

Chapter 5 Multiplying and Dividing Decimals, Pages 83–104

pages 84–85 In example A, some students may profit by using the "looping method" to count the number of decimal places in the product. 3 7.2 8 1 ⟵3 decimal places

Throughout this chapter, and in several other chapters, you may wish to have students check their work by using calculators. Ample practice has been provided, so you might choose to assign some of the exercises to be done on the calculator.

pages 86–87 Show students how to check division problems by multiplying and adding or by using a calculator.

page 95 Use the grocery advertisements in the newspaper to discuss differences in prices of various cuts of meat, as well as differences in prices from store to store.

pages 96-97 The data for this lesson was based on a talk by Betty Pelerkin of the Consumer and Food Economics Institute. The complete speech can be obtained from the U.S. Department of Agriculture, Agricultural Research Service, Washington, D.C. The lesson shows that even families with a low or moderate income can eat well-balanced meals.

pages 98-99 Point out that when buying a car it pays to shop around to find the best financing. Interest rates and loan payments will be dealt with in further detail in Chapter 11.

pages 100-101 Have students use their families' electric bills to find the rate charged for electricity in your area. Then have them work exercises 1-15 using that rate.

pages 102-103 To find the effect of a $.25 per hour raise, have students compute the gross income for each employee in exercises 1-10, increasing each hourly rate by $.25.

Chapter 6 The Metric System, Pages 105-126

pages 108-109 Relating metric abbreviations to a place value chart might help some students remember their meaning.

thousands	hundreds	tens	ones	tenths	hundredths	thousandths
kilo-	hecto-	deka-		deci-	centi-	milli-

To convert from one unit to another, count how many places the second unit is from the first on the chart and in which direction and then move the decimal point accordingly.

page 113 The force of gravity on an object as measured on a bathroom scale is different on the earth than on the moon. This force is referred to as "weight." The amount of substance in an object as measured on a balance scale is the same everywhere. This is referred to as "mass" but is also called "weight" in common usage. The U.S. Bureau of Standards has stated that for everyday purposes, *weight* and *mass* can be used interchangeably.

page 114 You might use the ideas on the page in the following experiment to find the volume of a rock. Measure the level of water in a graduated cylinder, say 27 ml. Submerge the rock. Record the new height of the water, 38 ml. Subtract. The rock displaced 11 ml of water, so it has a volume of 11 cm^3.

pages 120-121 The International Standard Organization (ISO) is developing a system for standardizing clothing sizes throughout the world. Tags with pictures will be attached to all garments and will show dimensions of garments in centimeters.

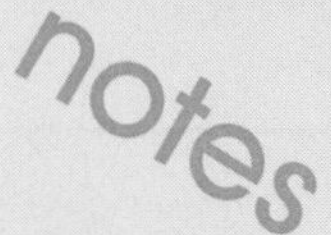

Chapter 7 Multiplying and Dividing Fractions and Mixed Numbers, Pages 131–150

pages 132–133 If reinforcement is needed, students may be asked to draw figures similar to those shown.

page 134 Point out that the process of reducing a fraction does not actually reduce the *fraction*; it only reduces the *terms* of the fraction.

pages 138–139 To find the answer to the Break Time, students can first think, "$\frac{2}{3}$ of what number is 12?" By trial and error, they find the answer and know there were 18 posters that were not faded. This is $\frac{1}{3}$ of the total posters to begin with, so there were 3 × 18, or 54 posters.

page 143 This lesson may be extended by giving various lengths of the track, such as 400 meters. Students could then compute distances when given numbers of laps, or find the number of laps for a run of a certain distance.

pages 144–145 The "C" clamp is similar to the more precise micrometer. Bring a micrometer to class, and have students compare the two measuring devices.

pages 146–147 Build on this lesson by having the students construct the scale drawings on grid paper. Also, provide the students with copies of other simple scale drawings, and have students draw the objects in actual size.

pages 148–149 The craft of decoy carving began as a functional part of the sport of duck and goose hunting. Many decoys were placed in the water around the hiding place of the hunter to lure ducks to that location. These were called "working decoys" and were actual size. The decorative decoys, mostly in demand by collectors, are more brilliantly and accurately painted. Some are carved using special wood lathes, but those that are hand-carved are more valuable.

Chapter 8 Adding and Subtracting Fractions and Mixed Numbers, Pages 151–170

page 153 You may wish to show students how to use cross-products to compare fractions.

$\frac{3}{8} > \frac{2}{7}$ $\qquad$ $\frac{3}{4} < \frac{7}{9}$

$3 \times 7 > 8 \times 2$ $\qquad$ $3 \times 9 < 4 \times 7$

pages 154–155 Have more able students group addends to help them find answers more quickly in problems such as these.

$\frac{2}{8} + \frac{3}{8} + \frac{6}{8} = (\frac{2}{8} + \frac{6}{8}) + \frac{3}{8} = 1\frac{3}{8}$

$\frac{1}{7} + \frac{3}{7} + \frac{6}{7} = (\frac{1}{7} + \frac{6}{7}) + \frac{3}{7} = 1\frac{3}{7}$

pages 160–161 Have students work several problems like example Q under your supervision before assigning set Q.

You may wish to use this method with less able students. Have them add the same fraction to both the minuend and the subtrahend so that the subtrahend is a whole number as shown in this example.

$$
\begin{array}{r}
8\frac{1}{4} + \frac{1}{4} = 8\frac{2}{4} \\
-\ 5\frac{3}{4} + \frac{1}{4} = 6 \\
\hline
2\frac{2}{4} = 2\frac{1}{2}
\end{array}
$$

pages 164-165 Be sure students are aware that a net change such as $-2\frac{3}{8}$ indicates that the last price paid per share was $2\frac{3}{8}$ dollars lower than the last price paid the day before.

Point out that money not only can be earned in the stock market but can be lost as well. You may wish to have students choose a stock and follow it for a period of several weeks to see if the final result is a gain or loss.

In addition, you could use the newspaper to generate exercises such as those shown in the lesson.

pages 166-167 Point out that a fraction of a cent can make a tremendous difference in profit on an item that is mass produced. $\frac{7}{8}$ cent per item on one million items is $8750.

Be sure students understand that all expenses, such as salaries, overhead, and so on, must be deducted from gross profit to determine net profit.

Chapter 9 Probability, Pages 171-190

pages 172-173 Discuss situations where probability of an outcome is 0 and others where it is 1. Have students find the probability of drawing the queen of hearts from a regular deck of playing cards. [$\frac{1}{52}$]

pages 176-177 In exercise 6, the nine favorable outcomes are 10, 20, 30, 40, 50, 60, 70, 80, and 90.

In exercise 10, the list of nine favorable outcomes begins with 100 and ends with 900.

In exercise 13, the list of ninety-nine favorable outcomes begins with 100 and ends with 9900.

In exercise 16, the list of ninety-nine favorable outcomes begins with 1000 and ends with 99,000.

pages 178-179 In the Break Time, each figure is a traversable network because it has 0 or 2 odd vertices. Have students start tracing these figures at an odd vertex. A vertex is odd if an odd number of paths meet at that point.

pages 180-181 Have students do this experiment and compare their results with the one shown in the book.

pages 184-185 To diagnose skills and concepts needed for this lesson, you should work the exercises beforehand.

You may wish to have students work exercises 1-6 as a class activity because these results are used in exercises 7-25.

page 192 In the Calculator Exercises, have students look for patterns found when writing equivalent decimals for fractions with a denominator of 9. A denominator of 99. A denominator of 999.

Notes and Activities for Unit 4

Chapter 10 Ratio, Proportion, and Similarity, Pages 195–212

pages 196–197 Point out that ratios apply to a variety of situations. For example, the exercises in set A deal with gasoline consumption, measurement conversion, mixtures, speeds, prices, maps, scale models, and so on.

pages 198–199 To describe similarity, you might say that if a figure is enlarged or reduced and then rotated and/or flipped, the resulting figure has the same shape of the original figure and is therefore similar. You might move the overhead projector to demonstrate this. Point out that figures that have the same size and shape, congruent figures, are also similar.

You might have students draw a figure on a grid with small squares and then draw an enlargement of the figure on a grid with larger squares.

In set F, students can check for corresponding parts by placing a tracing of one triangle over the other triangle.

pages 202–203 You can demonstrate that the measures of corresponding angles in similar triangles are equal by drawing similar triangles on separate acetates and then sliding an angle of one triangle over the corresponding angle in the other triangle.

page 205 You might have students use road maps to plan other trips. Students can use the rates given in the lesson to find driving time, liters of gasoline, and food and motel expense for their own trips.

pages 206–207 Other problems of this type can be found in scouting manuals and in other camping books.

pages 210–211 Mention that the problems in this lesson apply only to photographs taken in a vertical line to the ground.

Chapter 11 Percent, Pages 213–232

pages 218–219 For set F, if students cannot remember the fraction equivalent for a percent, they could multiply the number in the percent by $\frac{1}{100}$. For example, to find $33\frac{1}{3}\%$ of 60, follow these steps:

$$33\tfrac{1}{3}\% \times \frac{1}{100} \times 60 = \frac{\overset{1}{\cancel{100}}}{\underset{1}{\cancel{3}}} \times \frac{1}{\underset{1}{\cancel{100}}} \times \frac{\overset{20}{\cancel{60}}}{1} = 20$$

The three types of percent problems can also be solved using proportions. For example, to find 7% of 4.1, follow these steps:

$$\frac{7}{100} = \frac{n}{4.1}$$
$$7 \times 4.1 = 100 \times n$$
$$28.7 = 100n$$
$$.287 = n$$

pages 220–221 For students having difficulty with the equation method, proportions can be used. For example: 7 is what percent of 35?

$$\frac{n}{100} = \frac{7}{35}$$
$$n \times 35 = 100 \times 7$$
$$35n = 700$$
$$n = 20$$

pages 222–223 Proportions can be used for these problems also. For example: 22 is 40% of what number?

$$\frac{40}{100} = \frac{22}{n}$$

$$40 \times n = 100 \times 22$$

$$40n = 2200$$

$$n = 55$$

page 225 Point out the advantages of buying items on sale. Use local newspapers to generate problems involving amount of discount and sale price.

pages 226–227 Discuss the importance of investigating various sources before borrowing money. Assign students to contact banks and savings and loan companies to gather information.

pages 228–229 Discuss interest rates and hidden charges involved in buying on credit.

Chapter 12 Statistics, Pages 233–254

pages 236–237 Have more able students find the median in a set of data such as: 80, 73, 68, 65, 62, 41. Since there are two middle numbers, students then find the mean of the two middle numbers, 68 and 65. The median is 66.5.

Before assigning set B, have students find the modes of a set of data that is bimodal such as: 17, 17, 16, 14, 12, 12, 11. [17 and 12]

pages 238–239 Discuss how choices of different values for the vertical scale can affect the appearance of a graph and vary its impact. To emphasize this point, you may wish to have students construct the graph in example D using a vertical scale ranging from 0 to 62.

pages 242–243 Point out that a circle graph is used to highlight a division of a whole part rather than to show trends.

pages 248–249 The graph shows an increase in expenses during the winter months because this home was heated with electricity. The dramatic overall increase in 1975 was caused by the energy crisis.

You may wish to have students make a bar graph to show the same information and then generate questions such as: "What type of graph best shows trends and comparisons?" [Line graph]

pages 250–251 A world almanac contains information that can be used to generate additional exercises such as those in the lesson.

pages 252–253 Hydrocarbons are solid particles found in the air that reduce visibility. They are usually a result of open burning and poorly burned fuel. Carbon monoxide decreases the amount of oxygen in the air. It is odorless and colorless and is caused by incomplete combustion of fuels. Ozone is a mixture of hydrocarbons and nitrogen oxides. It is generally known as smog.

Chapter 13 Positive and Negative Numbers, Pages 259–276

pages 262–263 In an addition magic square, the sum for each row, each column, and each diagonal is the same. Have students tell which of these are magic squares and give the magic sum.

$^-2$	2	3
6	1	$^-4$
$^-1$	0	4

Yes. [3]

$^-7$	0	$^-8$
$^-6$	$^-5$	$^-4$
$^-2$	$^-10$	$^-3$

Yes. [$^-15$]

$^-5$	8	$^-1$
5	1	$^-3$
3	$^-7$	7

No.

pages 264–265 Use a device such as this to reinforce addition and subtraction of integers. Each answer is shown in brackets.

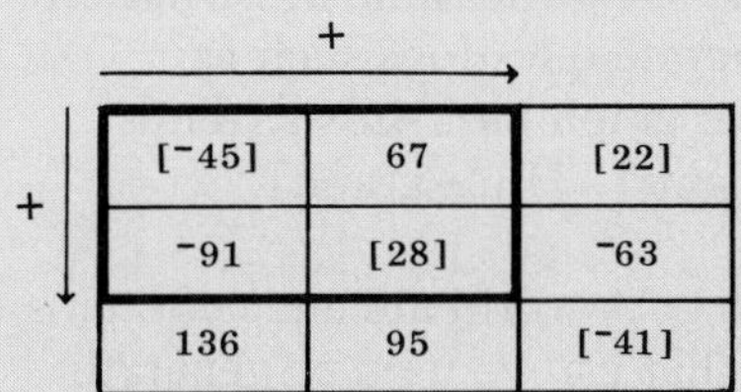

+	→	
[$^-45$]	67	[22]
$^-91$	[28]	$^-63$
136	95	[$^-41$]

pages 266–267 Have students tell which of these are multiplication magic squares and give the magic product.

$^-3$	36	2
4	$^-6$	9
18	1	$^-12$

Yes. [$^-216$]

24	18	$^-4$
2	$^-12$	72
$^-36$	8	3

No.

pages 268–269 Use a device such as this to reinforce multiplication and division of integers.

×	→	
10	$^-8$	[$^-80$]
$^-4$	$^-12$	[48]
[$^-40$]	[96]	[$^-3840$]

page 271 There are several versions of pinochle. Have students consult the encyclopedia for further information.

pages 274–275 The apparent magnitude of a star is related to both its distance from Earth and the amount of energy it produces. The brighter a star appears to us, the lower its magnitude.

Have students consult references in the library for further information.

Chapter 14 Expressions and Equations, Pages 277–298

pages 278–279 In examples A-D, have students evaluate each expression using other values for the variables.

As an additional activity, have students find all values of n for which the value of the expression $\frac{240}{n}$ is a whole number. Remind students that zero is not a possible replacement for n. [1, 2, 3, 4, 5, 6, 8, 10, 12, 15, 16, 20, 24, 30, 40, 48, 60, 80, 120, 240]

pages 286–287 For students having trouble with these problems, you might try this procedure for finding n.

$4n + 12 = 32$

n is multiplied by 4.	M 4
12 is added to n.	A 12
To solve, do the opposite.	
Subtract 12.	S 12
Then divide by 4.	D 4

page 291 Fuses or circuit breakers are used to protect electrical equipment. You could extend the lesson to solve problems such as this: "How many watts can be used in a 110-volt circuit with a 20-amp fuse?"

$W = EI$

$W = 110(20) = 2200$

[2200 watts can be used.]

pages 294–295 The practice of sinking piles is common in building homes in resort areas near beaches where the ground is sandy and there is flooding. Students may be most familiar with the piles that are used to support boat docks. Also mention that other supporting structures, such as steel beams imbedded in concrete, are often used for very tall buildings.

pages 296–297 The VASCAR instrument contains a timer, an odometer, and a calculator. The operator must qualify to use VASCAR, and must demonstrate the ability to determine speeds within a very small range for error.

Chapter 15 Graphing, Pages 299–318

pages 302–303 To extend set C, have students take an informal look at equations in the general form $y = \blacksquare x + \blacksquare$. Ask what is true about the graph when the first number is positive. [The line slopes upward from left to right.] Negative? [It slopes downward from left to right.] What happens as the second number increases? [The line slides up.] Decreases? [The line slides down.]

pages 304–305 Point out that by convention the four quadrants are labeled I, II, III, IV counterclockwise starting with the upper right quadrant.

You might have students write four ordered pairs, plot the four points, and connect them. Then ask what happens to the figure when the sign of the first number in each pair is changed. [The figure is flipped over, or reflected, in the y-axis.] What happens if the sign of the second number in each pair is changed? [The figure is flipped over the x-axis.]

pages 314–315 A geophone is a small microphone. Either many geophones are placed in the ground at one time, each at a different depth, or one geophone is placed at different depths at different times. When a charge of dynamite is set off, compression waves travel through the rock. The faster the travel, the more dense the rock. So, different rates of travel (different slopes on the graph) indicate different layers of rock. The information from the geophones is displayed above ground on a seismograph.

pages 316–317 Point out that different slopes on the graphs indicate different speeds. Notice that train B had to change speed after it met train 1 at the first siding in order to arrive at the other siding at the same time as train 2.

Notes and Activities for Unit 6

Chapter 16 Perimeter and Area, Pages 323–340

pages 326–327 To develop the concept of pi, use a circle that has a 21-cm diameter. Then use a 21-cm string, marked in seven equal segments, to show that it takes $3\frac{1}{7}$, or 3.14, diameters to "wrap around the circle," or measure the circumference.
$\pi = \frac{C}{d}$

pages 328–329 Have students draw a parallelogram on grid paper, cut the figure in two pieces—making the cut perpendicular to the bases, and rearrange the pieces to form a rectangle. $A = bh$

pages 330–331 Have students draw a triangle on grid paper, cut the figure in two pieces—making the cut parallel to the base at the midpoint of the height, and rearrange the pieces to form a parallelogram. Multiply its base (base of triangle) times its height (one-half the height of triangle). $A = b(\frac{1}{2}h)$

Have students draw a trapezoid on grid paper, cut the figure in two pieces—making the cut parallel to the bases at the midpoint of the height, and rearrange the pieces to form a parallelogram. Multiply its base (top base plus bottom base of the trapezoid) times its height (one-half the height of the trapezoid). $A = (a + b)\,\frac{1}{2}h$

pages 332–333 Have students cut a circle into 16 equal pie-shaped pieces. Then arrange pieces side-by-side to form a figure that looks like a parallelogram. Multiply its base (one-half the circumference) times its height (radius). $A = \frac{1}{2}C(r)$. Since $C = 2\pi r$, $\frac{1}{2}C = \pi r$. So $A = \pi r^2$.

page 335 Have students find the cost of carpeting a room in their homes choosing carpeting from catalogs or newspaper advertisements.

pages 336–337 Be certain students understand that they must always round answers *up* to the next whole number, or they would not buy enough fertilizer.

Chapter 17 Surface Area and Volume, Pages 341–360

page 343 Some students have difficulty visualizing surface area. You might cut apart a box to form a net. Then color the faces having like dimensions the same color. Through discussion, show how the formula is derived. If necessary, some students can find the area of each face and then find the sum.

page 345 Students might have trouble seeing that the length of the rectangle is the circumference of the base. Cut apart a salt box or other cylinder-shaped container, and demonstrate how the rectangle "wraps around" the circular base. For some students, provide exercises in which the diameter, rather than the radius, is given.

pages 346–347 For a review of cubic units, refer to the lesson on page 111.

pages 350–351 Using plastic models and sand or water, demonstrate that the volume of a rectangular prism is three times the volume of a pyramid with the same length, width, and height. The volume of the pyramid is then $\frac{1}{3}$ the volume of the prism. Use a similar approach to show the cone-cylinder relationship.

page 355 Hobby stores often have price lists that include candle molds, dies, wicks, and scents. Have students obtain such lists and then compute the cost of making various candles.

pages 356–357 In exercise 13, the conversion given is 1 m^2 = 1,000,000 mm^2. The metric unit commonly used for measuring concrete blocks is the millimeter. However, if this conversion is too difficult for your students, have them use the centimeter. 1 m^2 = 10,000 cm^2.

pages 358–359 This lesson might stimulate a discussion on automobile repair and maintenance. More information concerning the piston engine should be available from the Driver Education Department in your school.

Chapter 18 The Pythagorean Rule and Trigonometry, Pages 361–382

pages 366–367 To develop the Pythagorean Rule, have students use grid paper to draw right triangles with legs of lengths 5 and 12, 7 and 24, 3 and 4, 8 and 15. Students can use a strip of the grid paper as a ruler to measure the length of each hypotenuse. They can square the lengths of the sides in each triangle to discover that the sum of the squares of the legs equals the square of the hypotenuse. You might also have students actually draw squares on the sides of the triangles. The sum of the areas of the squares on the legs equals the area of the square on the hypotenuse.

pages 368–369 You might have students use a grid to draw three similar right triangles with sides of 3, 4, and 5; 6, 8, and 10; and 9, 12, and 15. A strip of the grid paper can be used to check the length of each hypotenuse. Then choose an acute angle in one triangle and identify the corresponding angle in each of the other triangles. These corresponding angles have the same measure. Have students write the tangent, the sine, and the cosine of each of the three angles as ratios and as decimals. Conclude that any angle of that same size will have the same tangent, sine, and cosine, regardless of the size of the right triangle that contains the angle.

pages 370–371 Emphasize that the numbers in the table are only approximations.

pages 378–379 Demonstrate why the run is one-half the diagonal in a 30°-60°-90° triangle by showing the triangle as half of a 60°-60°-60° triangle.

pages 380–381 You might have students make a scale drawing of the garden using just string and a ruler.

Information and Answers

Information about the tests

On the following pages, you will find a test for each unit, a mid-book test, and an end-of-book test. Each of these tests may be copied and reproduced for classroom use. The answers to the tests are given below.

Each unit test consists of 25 items (20 items relate to skills and 5 relate to applications). Notice that the items relating to applications have been placed at the end of each test. Each objective in a unit is related to at least one item on the test corresponding to that unit.

The items on the mid-book test and the end-of-book test relate to the skills' objectives of the various chapters. There are 90 items on the mid-book test (Part A: 50 items and Part B: 40 items) and 140 items on the end-of-book test (Parts A and B: 50 items and Part C: 40 items).

An alternate form of each of these tests is included in *Tests and Record Forms: Duplicating Masters.*

Answers for Unit 1 test

1. 761 **2.** 693 **3.** 3041 **4.** 52 **5.** 58 **6.** 75 **7.** 320,000 **8.** 2268 **9.** 1064 **10.** 3450 **11.** 238,464 **12.** 15 **13.** 62 R1 **14.** 53 **15.** 164 R7 **16.** 503 R3 **17.** 6 R2 **18.** 15 **19.** 15 **20.** 108 **21.** $347 **22.** 918 liters **23.** 6020 cases **24.** $985 **25.** 29¢

Answers for Unit 2 test

1. .400 **2.** 14.92 **3.** 6.71 **4.** 3.542 **5.** .0744 **6.** .036 **7.** 1230 **8.** .423 **9.** 45 **10.** 1400 **11.** 12.4 **12.** .38 **13.** Estimates will vary. 21 mm **14.** 10 m **15.** 6 cm^2 **16.** 3 cm^3 **17.** 130 ml **18.** 80 kg **19.** 6; 6 **20.** 6°C **21.** $429.82 **22.** $3.98 **23.** $154.38 **24.** $145.25 **25.** 480 ml

Answers for Unit 3 test

1. $\frac{3}{5}$ **2.** $\frac{3}{4}$ **3.** $\frac{20}{3}$ **4.** .6 **5.** $\frac{1}{3}$ **6.** $2\frac{2}{3}$ **7.** $3\frac{1}{8}$ **8.** $6\frac{2}{3}$ **9.** $\frac{7}{15}$ **10.** $\frac{10}{15}$, $\frac{12}{15}$ **11.** $4\frac{2}{3} < 4\frac{5}{6}$, or $4\frac{5}{6} > 4\frac{2}{3}$ **12.** $1\frac{1}{8}$ **13.** $\frac{7}{24}$ **14.** $8\frac{1}{2}$ **15.** $3\frac{7}{8}$ **16.** $\frac{1}{6}$ **17.** $\frac{2}{4}$, or $\frac{1}{2}$ **18.** 8 **19.** $\frac{2}{12}$, or $\frac{1}{6}$ **20.** $\frac{1}{30}$ **21.** 18 minutes **22.** 12 **23.** $50\frac{3}{5}$ seconds **24.** $2\frac{1}{4}$ dollars **25.** 200

Answers for Mid-book test, Part A

1. 8613 **2.** 948 **3.** 353 **4.** 7338 **5.** 144 **6.** 65 **7.** 4000 **8.** 160,000 **9.** 1863 **10.** 3595 **11.** 3440 **12.** 1675 **13.** 78,213 **14.** 667,100 **15.** 518,544 **16.** 413,592 **17.** 52 R2 **18.** 259 **19.** 17 R4 **20.** 85 **21.** 205 **22.** 270 R15 **23.** 8 R41 **24.** 56 R87 **25.** 7 **26.** 160 **27.** .800 **28.** .37 **29.** 23.85 **30.** 5.19 **31.** 3.633 **32.** 1.773 **33.** 1.536 **34.** 9.024 **35.** .01736 **36.** .00432 **37.** 2.61 **38.** .032 **39.** 93.67 **40.** 800 **41.** .18 **42.** .0452 **43.** 2.5 **44.** 945 **45.** 540 **46.** 78.4 **47.** 52.4 **48.** 8.63 **49.** .31 **50.** 15.3

Answers for Mid-book test, Part B

1. 150 cm **2.** 5 m **3.** 40ℓ **4.** 500 ml **5.** 125 mg **6.** 50 g **7.** 40°C **8.** 37°C **9.** $\frac{2}{5}$ **10.** $5\frac{2}{5}$ **11.** $\frac{11}{3}$ **12.** $\frac{8}{21}$ **13.** $\frac{2}{15}$ **14.** $6\frac{2}{3}$ **15.** $1\frac{1}{8}$ **16.** 24 **17.** 6 **18.** $2\frac{3}{4}$ **19.** $\frac{1}{4}$ **20.** $\frac{8}{9}$ **21.** $\frac{2}{49}$ **22.** $\frac{3}{8}$ **23.** $12\frac{1}{2}$ **24.** $5\frac{1}{3}$ **25.** $\frac{2}{9}$ **26.** $2\frac{1}{10}$ **27.** $\frac{4}{5}$ **28.** $\frac{20}{24}$, $\frac{21}{24}$ **29.** $1\frac{2}{7}$ **30.** $\frac{7}{8}$ **31.** $5\frac{1}{18}$ **32.** $6\frac{11}{12}$ **33.** $\frac{1}{2}$

34. $\frac{1}{12}$ **35.** $4\frac{1}{7}$ **36.** $4\frac{2}{3}$ **37.** $\frac{1}{6}$ **38.** 2 **39.** $\frac{1}{4}$ **40.** 36

Answers for Unit 4 test

1. 6/9 **2.** 10 **3.** 2 **4.** side KF **5.** 15 **6.** .86 **7.** $\frac{7}{20}$ **8.** 40%
9. 11.2 **10.** 2 **11.** 60% **12.** 84% **13.** 40 **14.** 370 **15.** 80
16. 6 **17.** 1970 **18.** March **19.** 50% **20.** See graph at right.
21. \$216 **22.** 9 hours **23.** \$6 **24.** \$30 **25.** 91

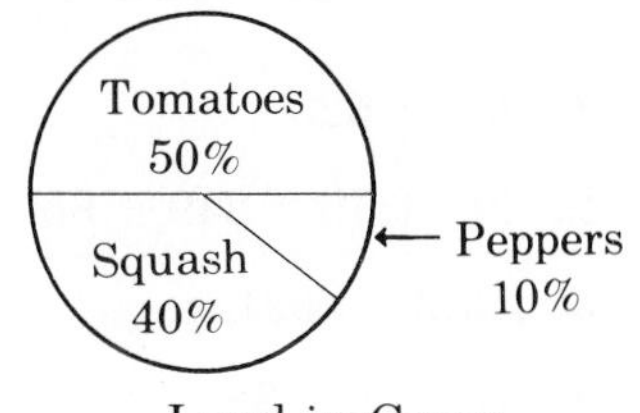

Land in Crops

Answers for Unit 5 test

1. $^-8, ^-6, 5, 7$ **2.** 3 **3.** $^-14$ **4.** 22 **5.** $^-7$ **6.** $^-24$ **7.** 9 **8.** $^-2$ **9.** 18 **10.** 4 **11.** $^-25$
12. 3.7 **13.** $^-15$ **14.** $^-6$ **15.** $^-5$ **16.** 3 **17.** (2, 3) **18.** $y = 2$ **19.** $(^-2, ^-3)$ **20.** $y = 1$
21. 28 points **22.** 2.19 m **23.** 30 meters per second **24.** 2 amps **25.** $^-6$

Answers for Unit 6 test

1. 22 cm **2.** 25.12 m **3.** 14 m^2 **4.** 4 m^2 **5.** 254.34 m^2 **6.** 108 cm^2 **7.** 150 cm^2 **8.** 62.8 cm^2
9. 131.88 cm^2 **10.** 27 m^3 **11.** 6280 m^3 **12.** 1570 m^3 **13.** 113.04 m^3 **14.** 81 **15.** 9801
16. 9.2 **17.** 13 m **18.** 5/12 **19.** .799 **20.** 8.48 cm **21.** Yes **22.** \$179.80 **23.** 4050 m^2
24. 14.4 m^3 **25.** 216 cm^3

Answers for End-of-book test, Part A

1. 641 **2.** 999 **3.** 428 **4.** 4444 **5.** 608 **6.** 3185 **7.** 14,592 **8.** 187,473 **9.** 235 **10.** 162
11. 390 **12.** 261 **13.** 8.581 **14.** 57.678 **15.** 13.539 **16.** .0868 **17.** 6.327 **18.** 19.02
19. 47.472 **20.** 12.848 **21.** .5976 **22.** 12.425 **23.** .06104 **24.** .00481 **25.** 2.13 **26.** 54.7
27. 36 **28.** .0326 **29.** 15 **30.** 45 **31.** 3 m **32.** 1 ℓ **33.** 200 g **34.** 100°C **35.** $\frac{11}{12}$
36. $12\frac{9}{10}$ **37.** $9\frac{1}{8}$ **38.** $\frac{1}{12}$ **39.** $2\frac{1}{3}$ **40.** $4\frac{3}{7}$ **41.** $5\frac{3}{10}$ **42.** $\frac{3}{14}$ **43.** $3\frac{3}{4}$ **44.** 6 **45.** $\frac{9}{14}$
46. $\frac{1}{15}$ **47.** $2\frac{7}{10}$ **48.** $1\frac{1}{3}$ **49.** $\frac{1}{2}$ **50.** 3

Answers for End-of-book test, Part B

1. 18 **2.** 6 **3.** 42 **4.** 90% **5.** .07 **6.** $\frac{3}{4}$ **7.** 30% **8.** 6 **9.** 34.2 **10.** 80% **11.** 75%
12. 22 **13.** 35 **14.** 9 **15.** 5 **16.** 10 **17.** 5 **18.** 80 million **19.** 1972 **20.** 3, 6, 7, 12
21. $^-10, ^-8, ^-5, ^-1$ **22.** $^-9, ^-4, 2, 11$ **23.** $^-12, ^-6, ^-3, 8$ **24.** $^-5$ **25.** $^-3$ **26.** 3 **27.** 10
28. $^-1$ **29.** $^-8$ **30.** 20 **31.** $^-16$ **32.** $^-18$ **33.** 3 **34.** $^-3$ **35.** $^-4$ **36.** 3 **37.** $^-22$ **38.** $^-24$
39. $^-5$ **40.** 5 **41.** $n = 8$ **42.** $r = 22$ **43.** $k = 14$ **44.** $w = 3$ **45.** $m = ^-7$ **46.** $a = 10$
47. $c = ^-6$ **48.** $x = 2$ **49.** $s = 1$ **50.** $r = 3$

Answers for End-of-book test, Part C

1. $(4, ^-3)$ **2.** $(^-4, 1)$ **3.** (2, 3) **4.** $(^-2, ^-3)$ **5.** (3, 2) **6.** $(^-3, ^-2)$ **7.** $(^-3, 2)$ **8.** $(3, ^-2)$
9. Point T **10.** Point J **11.** Point D **12.** Point W **13.** Point L **14.** Point F **15.** Point A
16. Point N **17.** $y = 2$ **18.** $y = 1$ **19.** $y = 0$ **20.** $y = 3$ **21.** 52 m **22.** 20 m **23.** 25.12 m
24. 10 m^2 **25.** 100 m^2 **26.** 12 m^2 **27.** 78.5 m^2 **28.** 236 m^2 **29.** 96 m^2 **30.** 301.44 m^2
31. 160 m^3 **32.** 1000 m^3 **33.** 471 m^3 **34.** 40 m^3 **35.** 37.68 m^3 **36.** $a = 3$ cm **37.** $m/5$
38. 4/5 **39.** $m/4$ **40.** 28.2 cm

test

Unit 1
Whole Numbers   pages 3-62

1. $238 + 523$
2. $301 + 75 + 249 + 68$
3. $5432 - 2391$
4. $69 + 15 - 32$
5. Find t. $36 + t = 94$
6. Find m. $m - 18 = 57$
7. 80×4000
8. 324×7
9. 14×76
10. $\begin{array}{r} 138 \\ \times \; 25 \\ \hline \end{array}$
11. $\begin{array}{r} 621 \\ \times 384 \\ \hline \end{array}$
12. $42 - 3(9)$
13. $4\overline{)249}$
14. $24\overline{)1272}$
15. $16\overline{)2631}$
16. $6\overline{)3021}$
17. $324\overline{)1946}$
18. $3(8) - \dfrac{15 + 3}{2}$
19. Find n. $5n = 75$
20. Find w. $\dfrac{w}{6} = 18$
21. Find the cost of this automobile trip.

Gasoline	\$110
Meals	\$72
Lodging	\$165

22. The meter on an oil truck read 2849 liters before an oil delivery and 1931 liters after the delivery. How many liters of oil were delivered?
23. One metric ton of corn yields 28 cases of processed corn. 215 metric tons of corn will yield how many cases of processed corn?
24. Mrs. Castaneda receives a yearly salary of \$11,820. How much is her average monthly salary?
25. 3 cans for 85¢

    Find the price if you buy just 1 can.

test

Unit 2
Decimals and the Metric System pages 67–126

1. Write an equal decimal for .4 in thousandths.
2. 14.6 + .32
3. 15.62 − 8.91
4. 25.3 × .14
5. .31 × .24
6. $7\overline{).252}$
7. 100 × 12.3
8. 4.23 ÷ 10
9. $.05\overline{)2.25}$
10. $.012\overline{)16.8}$
11. Round 12.37 to the nearest tenth.
12. Round the quotient to the nearest hundredth.

    $6\overline{)2.293}$
13. Estimate the length of this bar in millimeters. Then use a ruler to find the actual length to the nearest millimeter.
14. Choose the most sensible measure for the height of a house.

    10 millimeters (mm)
    10 centimeters (cm)
    10 meters (m)
    10 kilometers (km)
15. Count squares to find the area of this figure in square centimeters.

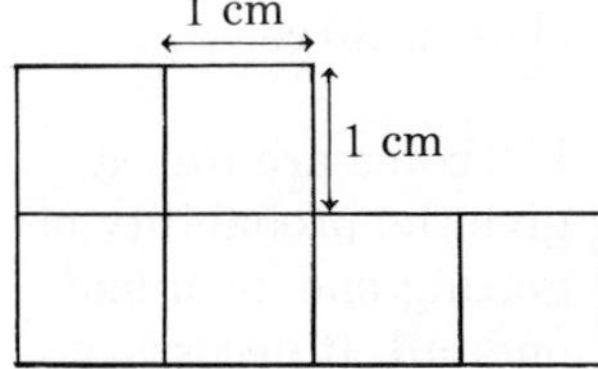

16. Count cubes to find the volume of this figure in cubic centimeters.

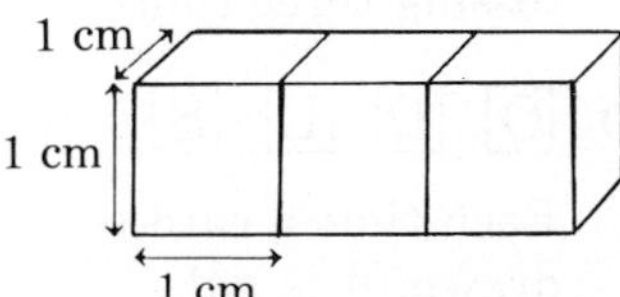

17. Choose the more sensible measure for the amount of cocoa in a cup.

    130 milliliters (ml)
    130 liters (ℓ)
18. Choose the most sensible measure for the mass of a man.

    80 milligrams (mg)
    80 grams (g)
    80 kilograms (kg)
19. Complete this statement.

    6 cm^3 of water is ▒ ml of water and has a mass of ▒ g.
20. Choose the more sensible temperature for a glass of cold water.

    6°C   48°C
21. Find the total amount of the deposit.

CASH	CURRENCY	15	43
	COIN	3	24
CHECKS		141	00
		70	10
		200	05
TOTAL			

22. What is the total cost of 1.6 kilograms of meat priced at $2.49 per kilogram?
23. Gloria Montes worked 32.5 hours at a rate of $4.75 an hour. How much did she earn?
24. The total amount of Ed's loan is $5229. If he pays back the loan in 36 equal payments, what will be the amount of each payment?
25. A recipe calls for 160 ml of milk. How much milk is needed for 3 recipes?

test Unit 3
Fractions, Mixed Numbers, and Probability pages 131–190

1. Write a fraction for point S.

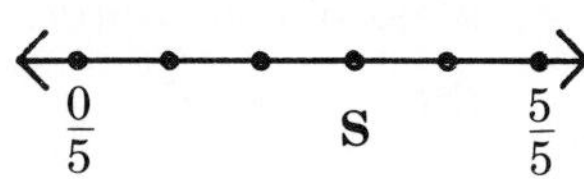

2. Reduce $\frac{18}{24}$ to lowest terms.

3. Write $6\frac{2}{3}$ as a fraction.

4. Write $\frac{3}{5}$ as a decimal.

5. $\frac{3}{8} \times \frac{8}{9}$

6. $\frac{4}{5} \times 3\frac{1}{3}$

7. $2\frac{1}{2} \times 1\frac{1}{4}$

8. $2\frac{1}{2} \div \frac{3}{8}$

9. $1\frac{1}{6} \div 2\frac{1}{2}$

10. Write $\frac{2}{3}$ and $\frac{4}{5}$ as fractions with a common denominator.

11. Compare $4\frac{2}{3}$ and $4\frac{5}{6}$. Use $>$, $<$, or $=$.

12. $\frac{1}{2} + \frac{3}{8} + \frac{1}{4}$

13. $\frac{5}{8} - \frac{1}{3}$

14. $\begin{array}{r} 4\frac{2}{3} \\ +\,3\frac{5}{6} \\ \hline \end{array}$

15. $\begin{array}{r} 7\frac{1}{8} \\ -\,3\frac{1}{4} \\ \hline \end{array}$

16. A die may land in any of 6 ways. Give the probability that the roll of a die will show a three.

17. If 2 coins are tossed, give the probability of getting one head and one tail. If necessary, make a tree diagram.

18. Multiply to find all possible outcomes for tossing three coins.

19. O D D S

Each time a card is drawn, it is *not* replaced before the next draw. Give the probability of making two draws that show *D*.

20. Use the results of this experiment to predict the probability that, on the next toss, the cup will land top up.

Outcome	Tally
Top up	𝍷
Top down	𝍸
Side	𝍸 𝍸 𝍸 𝍸 𝍷𝍷𝍷𝍷

21. Jake rides his bicycle at a speed of one lap every $1\frac{4}{5}$ minutes. How long will it take him to complete 10 laps?

22. How many sections that are $5\frac{1}{2}$ inches long can be cut from a 66-inch log?

23. How many seconds did Mary use to drill all three braces?

1st brace, $17\frac{2}{5}$ seconds
2nd brace, $16\frac{7}{10}$ seconds
3rd brace, $16\frac{1}{2}$ seconds

24. The low price of a stock is $35\frac{1}{4}$ and the high price is $37\frac{1}{2}$. How much can Dale save if she buys the stock at the low price?

25. If the probability that a customer will buy a cherry sno-cone is $\frac{50}{125}$ and a total of 500 sno-cones will be sold, about how many cherry sno-cones will be sold?

test Mid-book
Part A Chapters 1–5

1. 1348 + 7265
2. 84 + 203 + 91 + 570
3. 418 − 65
4. 9063 − 1725
5. Find k. $592 + k = 736$
6. Find s. $s - 48 = 17$
7. 40 × 100
8. 200 × 800
9. 3 × 621
10. 5 × 719
11. 80 × 43
12. 67 × 25
13. 93 × 841
14. 700 × 953
15. 624 × 831
16. 456 × 907
17. $6\overline{)314}$
18. $8\overline{)2072}$
19. $42\overline{)718}$
20. $14\overline{)1190}$
21. $15\overline{)3075}$
22. $31\overline{)8385}$
23. $216\overline{)1769}$
24. $408\overline{)22935}$
25. Find n. $6n = 42$
26. Find x. $\frac{x}{20} = 8$
27. Write an equal decimal for .8 in thousandths.
28. Write an equal decimal for .3700 in hundredths.
29. 15.49 + 8.36
30. 2.73 + .61 + 1.85
31. 7.098 − 3.465
32. 6.29 − 4.517
33. 8 × .192
34. .24 × 37.6
35. .31 × .056
36. .018 × .24
37. $34\overline{)88.74}$
38. $8\overline{).256}$
39. 100 × .9367
40. 1000 × .8
41. 1.8 ÷ 10
42. 4.52 ÷ 100
43. $.25\overline{).625}$
44. $.08\overline{)75.6}$
45. $.017\overline{)9.18}$
46. Round 78.36 to the nearest tenth.
47. Round 52.419 to the nearest tenth.
48. Round 8.627 to the nearest hundredth.
49. Round the quotient to the nearest hundredth.
    $8\overline{)2.513}$
50. Round the quotient to the nearest tenth.
    $.24\overline{)3.679}$

test Mid-book
Part B Chapters 6–9

Choose the more sensible measure for the

1. length of a desk.

   150 millimeters
   150 centimeters

2. height of a tree.

   5 meters
   5 kilometers

3. amount of water in a washing machine.

   40 milliliters
   40 liters

4. amount of milk in a thermos bottle.

   500 milliliters
   500 liters

5. mass of a straight pin.

   125 milligrams
   125 grams

6. mass of an egg.

   50 grams
   50 kilograms

7. temperature on a summer day.

   97 °C   40 °C

8. normal temperature of your body.

   37 °C   73 °C

9. Reduce $\frac{8}{20}$ to lowest terms.

10. Write $\frac{27}{5}$ as a mixed number.

11. Write $3\frac{2}{3}$ as a fraction.

12. $\frac{2}{3} \times \frac{4}{7}$

13. $\frac{4}{9} \times \frac{3}{10}$

14. $8 \times \frac{5}{6}$

15. $\frac{3}{4} \times 1\frac{1}{2}$

16. $2\frac{2}{5} \times 10$

17. $5\frac{1}{3} \times 1\frac{1}{8}$

18. $1\frac{1}{4} \times 2\frac{1}{5}$

19. $\frac{3}{5} \times \frac{1}{2} \times \frac{5}{6}$

20. $\frac{2}{3} \div \frac{3}{4}$

21. $\frac{4}{7} \div 14$

22. $\frac{1}{2} \div 1\frac{1}{3}$

23. $10 \div \frac{4}{5}$

24. $8 \div 1\frac{1}{2}$

25. $2\frac{2}{3} \div 12$

26. $1\frac{3}{4} \div \frac{5}{6}$

27. $1\frac{2}{5} \div 1\frac{3}{4}$

28. Write $\frac{5}{6}$ and $\frac{7}{8}$ as fractions with a common denominator.

29. $\frac{3}{7} + \frac{6}{7}$

30. $\frac{1}{2} + \frac{3}{8}$

31. $3\frac{11}{18} + 1\frac{4}{9}$

32. $4\frac{1}{4} + 2\frac{2}{3}$

33. $\frac{7}{8} - \frac{3}{8}$

34. $\frac{5}{6} - \frac{3}{4}$

35. $9 - 4\frac{6}{7}$

36. $7\frac{1}{2} - 2\frac{5}{6}$

37. A die may land in any of six ways. Give the probability that the roll of the die will show a five.

38. Give the expected number of rolls that will show a five if a die is rolled 12 times.

39. If 2 coins are tossed, give the probability of getting two heads. If necessary, make a tree diagram to help you.

40. Multiply to find all possible outcomes for rolling 2 die.

test

Unit 4
Ratio, Percent, and Statistics pages 195–254

1. Write a ratio for 6 sit-ups to 9 seconds.

2. Find m. $\frac{8}{m} = \frac{4}{5}$

3. Find t. $\frac{12}{18} = \frac{t}{3}$

4. The triangles are similar. Which side corresponds to side BC?

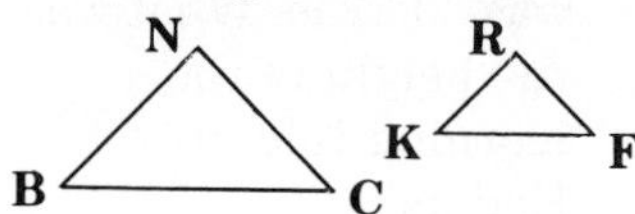

5. The triangles are similar. Use a proportion to find n.

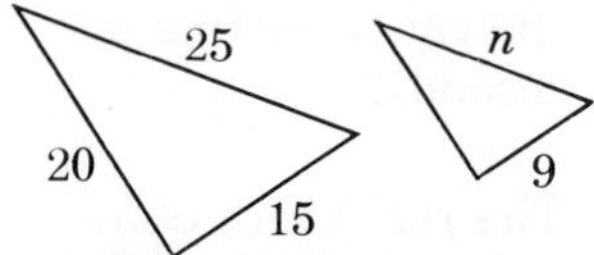

6. Write 86% as a decimal.

7. Write 35% as a fraction.

8. Write $\frac{2}{5}$ as a percent.

9. Find 16% of 70.

10. Find $33\frac{1}{3}$% of 6.

11. 9 is what percent of 15?

12. 42 is what percent of 50?

13. 10 is 25% of what number?

14. 37 is 10% of what number?

15. Find the mean of 70, 85, 74, 80, and 91.

16. Find the median of 8, 4, 9, 6, 2, 8, and 1.

17. In which year was the volume of mail more than 70 billion?

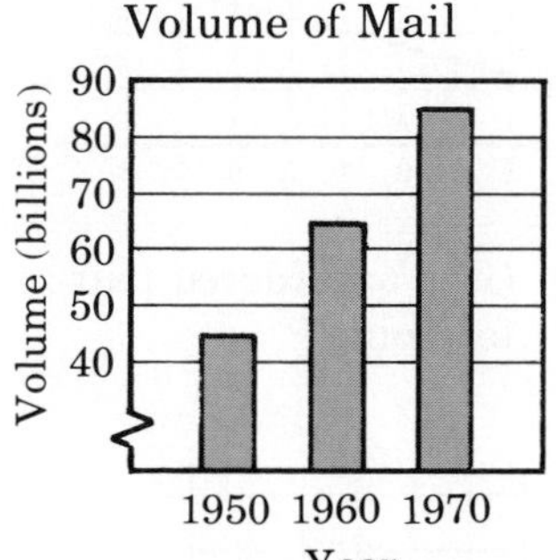

18. Buffalo receives less than 40 centimeters of snow in which month?

Average Snowfall for Buffalo, N.Y.

Snow (cm): 60, 50, 40, 30, 20

Dec. Jan. Feb. Mar.

Month

19. What percent of the concrete mix is gravel?

Dry Concrete Mix

Gravel 50%
Sand 30%
20% Cement

20. Construct a circle graph to show the percent of land Kate planted for each crop.

Crops planted	
Green peppers	10%
Squash	40%
Tomatoes	50%

21. The Wilsons spent \$54 for food in 3 days. At this rate, how much will they spend for food in 12 days?

22. If it takes 3 hours to drive 250 kilometers, how long will it take to drive 750 kilometers?

23. The regular price of a sweater was \$24. How much did Jake save if he bought it at a 25% discount?

24. Jackie wanted to buy a \$250 CB radio. She borrowed the money for 6 months at an interest rate of 2% per month. How much interest did she have to pay?
$i = p \times r \times t$

25. These are Stan's scores on four tests. What was his mean score?

88 94 85 97

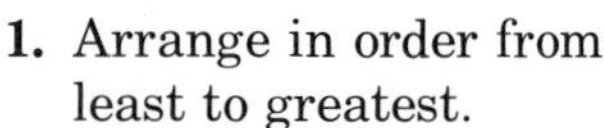

Unit 5 Algebra pages 259–318

1. Arrange in order from least to greatest.

   $5, {}^-6, {}^-8, 7$

2. $7 + {}^-4$
3. ${}^-5 + {}^-9$
4. $15 - {}^-7$
5. ${}^-6 - 1$
6. ${}^-8 \times 3$
7. ${}^-36 \div {}^-4$
8. $18 \div {}^-9$

Evaluate each expression when $a = 4$ and $b = {}^-2$.

9. $16 + a + b$
10. $3a + 4b$
11. $12b + a - 5$

Find each missing number.

12. $n - 1.2 = 2.5$
13. $15a = {}^-225$
14. $8b + 16 = {}^-32$
15. $4c - 10 = {}^-30$
16. $14m + 6 - 3m = 39$
17. Give an ordered pair for point A.

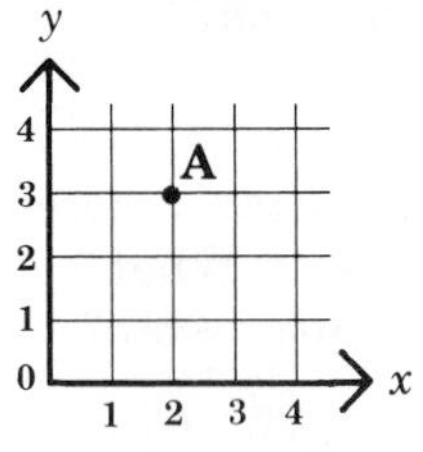

18. Read the graph below. to find the value of y in $(4, y)$.

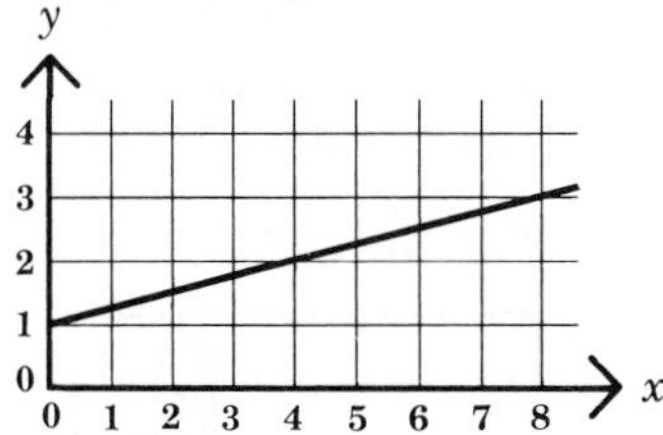

19. Give an ordered pair for point P.

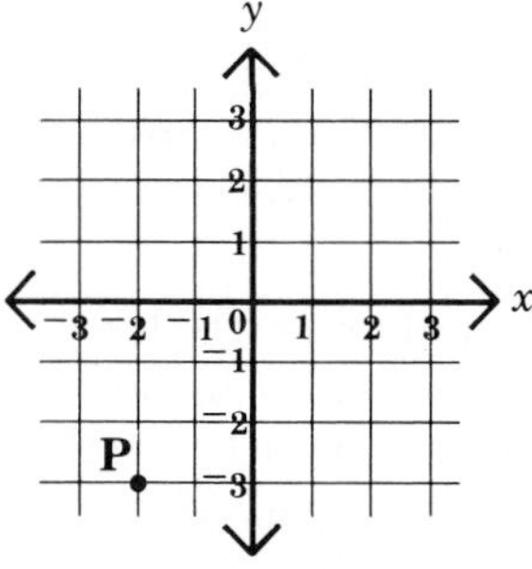

20. Read the graph below to find the value of y in $(3, y)$.

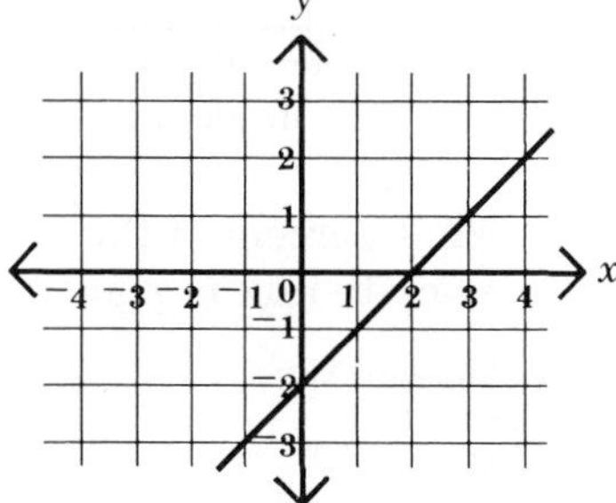

21. In a game of pinochle, Rita bid 19 points. She melded 15 points and made 13 points in the play of the hand. What was her score?
22. A morning tide height for Boston was 2.71 m. The height difference of the tide in Kodiak was ${}^-0.52$ m. What was the height of the morning tide in Kodiak?
23. A car traveled 360 meters in 12 seconds. What was the speed of the car in meters per seconds?
24. The resistance of a blender is 55 ohms (R) when the blender is using 110 volts (E). How many amps (I) is the blender using? ($E = I \times R$)
25. What is the freezing point for a solution that is 10% antifreeze?

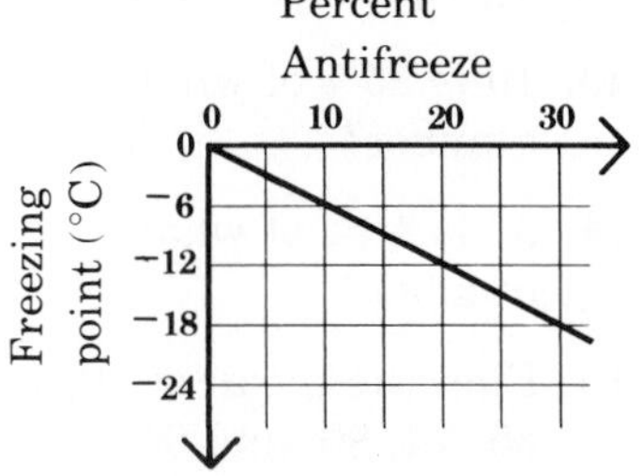

1. Rectangle. Length is 5 centimeters; width is 6 centimeters. Find the perimeter. $P = 2l + 2w$

2. Circle. Diameter is 8 millimeters. Find the circumference. $C = \pi d$

Find the area. Each dimension is in meters.

3. Parallelogram. Base is 7; height is 2. $A = bh$

4. Triangle. Height is 4; base is 2. $A = \frac{1}{2}bh$

5. Circle. Radius is 9. $A = \pi r^2$

Find the surface area. Each dimension is in centimeters.

6. Rectangular prism. Width is 3; height is 4; length is 6. $A = 2lw + 2lh + 2wh$

7. Cube. Length of each side is 5. $A = 6s^2$

8. Cylinder. Height is 3; radius is 2. $A = 2\pi rh + 2\pi r^2$

9. Cylinder. Height is 4; radius is 3.

Find the volume. Each dimension is in meters.

10. Cube. Length of each side is 3. $V = s^3$

11. Cylinder. Height is 20; radius is 10. $V = \pi r^2 h$

12. Cone. Radius is 10; height is 15. $V = \frac{1}{3}\pi r^2 h$

13. Sphere. Radius is 3. $V = \frac{4}{3}\pi r^3$

14. Compute 3^4.

Use the table on page 418 for items 15, 16, and 17.

15. Find 99^2.

16. Find $\sqrt{84}$ to the nearest tenth.

17. Use $a^2 + b^2 = c^2$. Find the length of side ST.

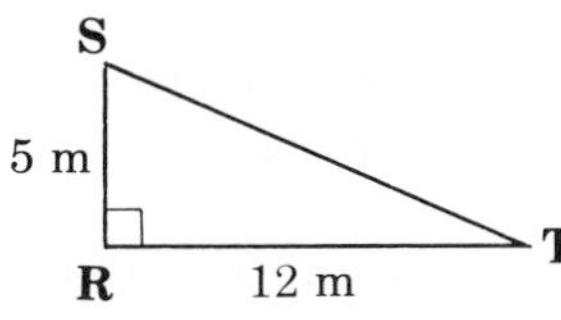

18. Use the triangle in item 17. Give the tangent of ∠ T as a ratio.

Use the table on page 419 for items 19, 20, and 21.

19. Give the sine of 53° as a decimal to the nearest thousandth.

20. Find b to the nearest tenth.

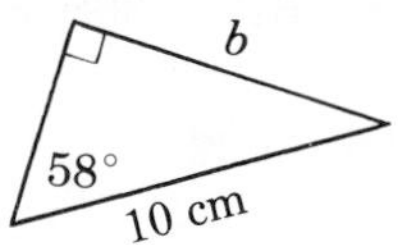

21. Would these lengths form a right triangle?

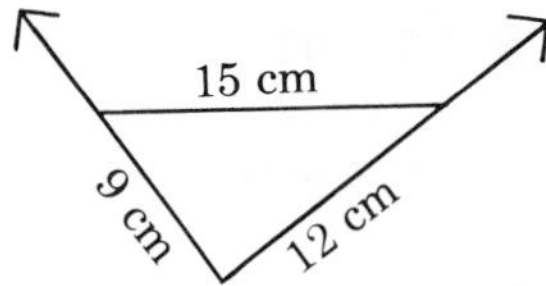

22. Carpeting costs $8.99 per square meter. Find the cost of carpeting a room that is 5 meters long and 4 meters wide.

23. Find the area of a lawn if the property is 75 meters by 60 meters and the house is 15 meters by 30 meters.

24. How many cubic meters of concrete are needed to pour a rectangular patio that measures 6 meters by 8 meters and is 0.3 meters deep?

25. A candle has the shape of a cube. Each side is 6 cm by 6 cm. How many cubic centimeters of wax were used for this candle?

test

End-of-book
Part A Chapters 1–9

1. $368 + 273$
2. $49 + 617 + 308 + 25$
3. $784 - 356$
4. $9152 - 4708$
5. 8×76
6. 35×91
7. 24×608
8. 741×253
9. $9\overline{)2115}$
10. $54\overline{)8748}$
11. $7\overline{)2730}$
12. $108\overline{)28188}$
13. $4.862 + 3.719$
14. $50.73 + 6.948$
15. $7.08 + .359 + 6.1$
16. $.8493 - .7625$
17. $15.407 - 9.08$
18. $26.3 - 7.28$
19. $.092 \times 516$
20. $16 \times .803$
21. $.72 \times .83$
22. $.25 \times 49.7$
23. $.56 \times .109$
24. $.37 \times .013$
25. $35\overline{)74.55}$
26. $.08\overline{)4.376}$
27. $.107\overline{)3.852}$
28. $19\overline{).6194}$
29. $.24\overline{)3.6}$
30. $.066\overline{)2.97}$

Choose the more sensible measure for the

31. width of a hallway.
    3 centimeters
    3 meters
32. amount of soup in a pan.
    1 milliliter
    1 liter
33. mass of a cupcake.
    200 grams
    200 kilograms
34. temperature of steam.
    100°C 212°C
35. $\frac{1}{3} + \frac{7}{12}$
36. $4\frac{1}{2} + 8\frac{2}{5}$
37. $6\frac{7}{8} + 2\frac{1}{4}$
38. $\frac{3}{4} - \frac{2}{3}$
39. $4\frac{5}{6} - 2\frac{1}{2}$
40. $8 - 3\frac{4}{7}$
41. $7\frac{1}{5} - 1\frac{9}{10}$
42. $\frac{3}{7} \times \frac{1}{2}$
43. $1\frac{2}{3} \times 2\frac{1}{4}$
44. $1\frac{4}{5} \times 3\frac{1}{3}$
45. $\frac{3}{7} \div \frac{2}{3}$
46. $\frac{4}{5} \div 12$
47. $2\frac{1}{4} \div \frac{5}{6}$
48. $1\frac{1}{2} \div 1\frac{1}{8}$
49. Give the probability that the toss of a coin will show a head.
50. Give the expected number of tosses that will show a head if a coin is tossed 6 times.

test

End-of-book
Part B Chapters 10–14

1. Find m. $\frac{3}{7} = \frac{m}{42}$

2. Find r. $\frac{5}{r} = \frac{25}{30}$

3. Write 42% as a decimal.

4. Write .9 as a percent.

5. Write 7% as a decimal.

6. Write 75% as a fraction.

7. Write $\frac{6}{20}$ as a percent.

8. Find 50% of 12.

9. Find 38% of 90.

10. 8 is what percent of 10?

11. 9 is what percent of 12?

12. 11 is 50% of what number?

13. 14 is 40% of what number?

14. Find the mean of 6, 9, 10, 13, and 7.

15. Find the mean of 4, 6, 4, 8, 2, and 6.

16. Find the median of 8, 11, 10, 14, and 7.

17. Find the median of 5, 12, 3, 3, 9, 6, and 1.

Use the graph below for items 18 and 19.

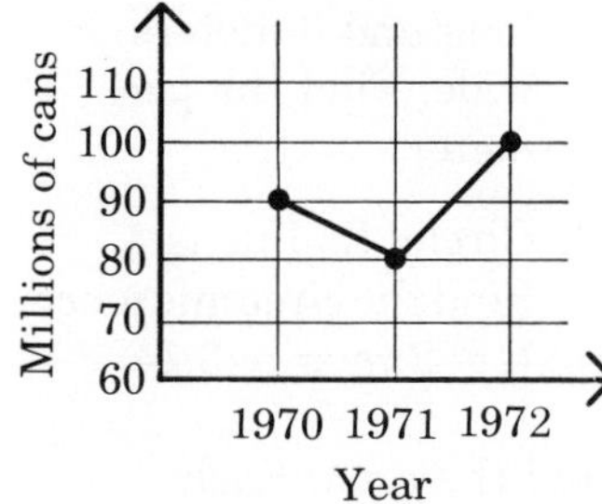

18. How many cans of apricots were produced in 1971?

19. Were more cans produced in 1970 or in 1972?

Arrange in order from least to greatest.

20. 7, 3, 12, 6

21. $^-8$, $^-10$, $^-5$, $^-1$

22. 11, $^-4$, $^-9$, 2

23. $^-6$, $^-3$, 8, $^-12$

Compute

24. $^-3 + {}^-2$

25. $^-8 + 5$

26. $7 + {}^-4$

27. $8 - {}^-2$

28. $5 - 6$

29. $^-9 - {}^-1$

30 $^-4 \times {}^-5$

31. $2 \times {}^-8$

32. $^-3 \times 6$

33. $^-15 \div {}^-5$

34. $21 \div {}^-7$

35. $^-36 \div 9$

Evaluate each expression when $k = 3$ and $m = {}^-6$.

36. $k + m + 6$

37. $5m + 8$

38. $3m - 2k$

39. $\frac{2m + {}^-3}{k}$

40. $4k - 1 + m$

Find each missing number.

41. $4 + n = 12$

42. $r + {}^-7 = 15$

43. $k - 6 = 8$

44. $9w = 27$

45. $2m = {}^-14$

46. $\frac{a}{^-5} = {}^-2$

47. $^-3c - 2 = 16$

48. $4x + 9 = 17$

49. $s - {}^-3 = 4$

50. $3r + 5r = 24$

End-of-book
Part C Chapters 15–18

Use the grid below for items 1–16.

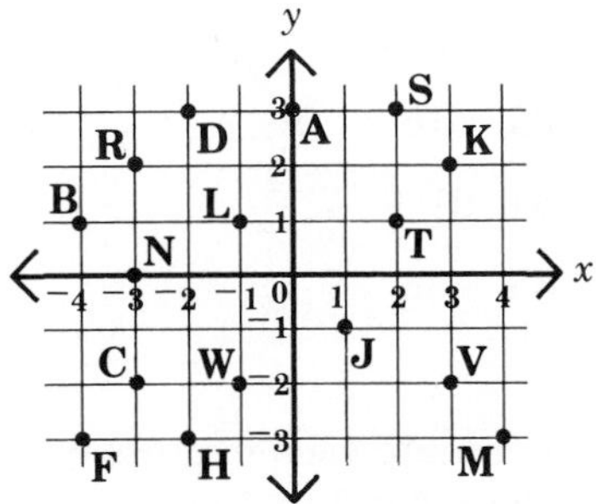

Give an ordered pair for

1. point M.
2. point B.
3. point S.
4. point H.
5. point K.
6. point C.
7. point R.
8. point V.

Name the point that is at

9. (2, 1)
10. (1, ⁻1)
11. (⁻2, 3)
12. (⁻1, ⁻2)
13. (⁻1, 1)
14. (⁻4, ⁻3)
15. (0, 3)
16. (⁻3, 0)

Read the graph below to find the value of y in

17. (4, y)
18. (2, y)
19. (0, y)
20. (6, y)

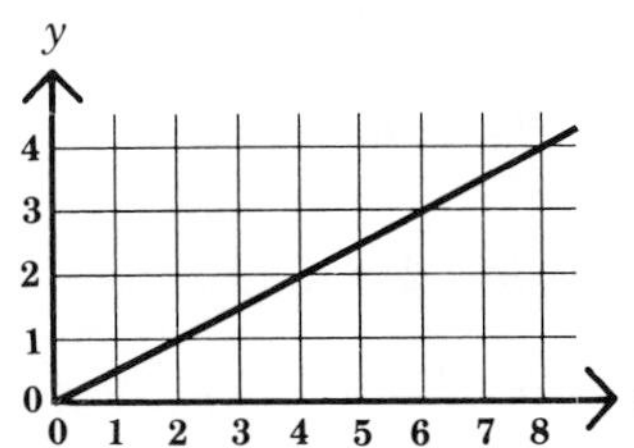

21. Each side of a square is 13 meters long. Find the perimeter.
22. A rectangle is 7 meters long and 3 meters wide. Find the perimeter.
23. Circle. Radius is 4. Find the circumference. $C = 2\pi r$. $\pi \approx 3.14$

Find the area. Each dimension is in meters.

24. Parallelogram. Base is 5; height is 2. $A = bh$
25. Square. Length of each side is 10. $A = s^2$
26. Triangle. Height is 6; base is 4. $A = \frac{1}{2}bh$
27. Circle. Radius is 5. $A = \pi r^2$

Find the surface area. Each dimension is in meters.

28. Rectangular prism. Width is 5; height is 6; length is 8. $A = 2lw + 2lh + 2wh$
29. Cube. Length of each side is 4. $A = 6s^2$
30. Cylinder. Height is 8; radius is 4. $A = 2\pi rh + 2\pi r^2$

Find the volume. Each dimension is in meters.

31. Rectangular prism. Length is 8; height is 5; width is 4. $V = lwh$
32. Cube. Length of each side is 10. $V = s^3$
33. Cylinder. Height is 6; radius is 5. $V = \pi r^2 h$
34. Pyramid. Length is 10; height is 2; width is 6. $V = \frac{1}{3}lwh$
35. Sphere. Radius is 3. $V = \frac{4}{3}\pi r^2$

Use the triangle below for items 36–39.

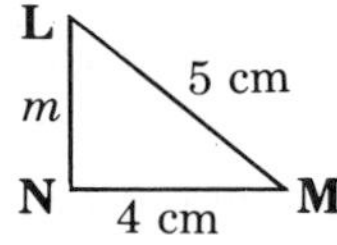

36. Use $a^2 + b^2 = c^2$. Find the length of side LN.
37. Give the sine of ∠ M as a ratio.
38. Give the cosine of ∠M as a ratio.
39. Give the tangent of ∠ M as a ratio.
40. Find w. The cosine of 20° is .940.

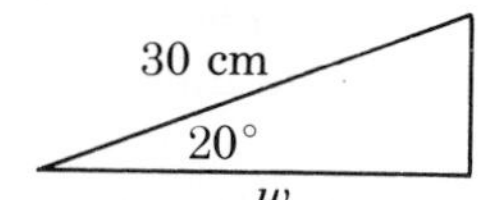

Page 239 Set E

1.

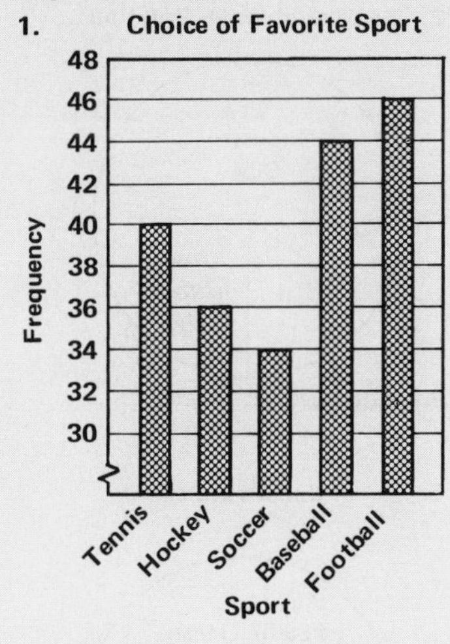

2.

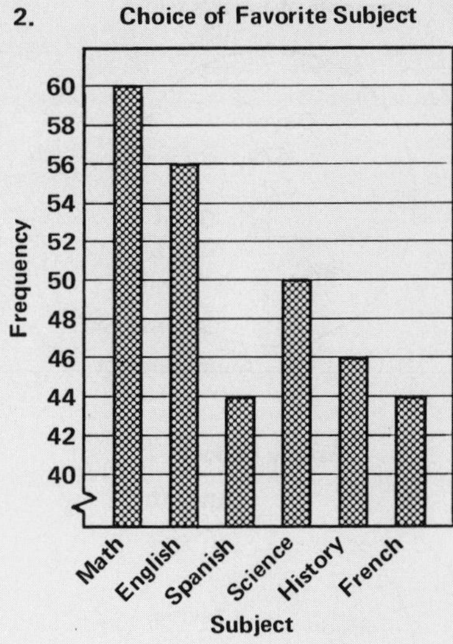

3.

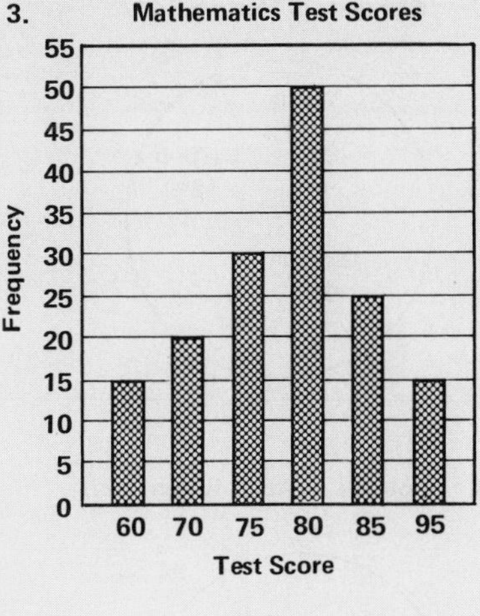

Page 245 Set J

1.

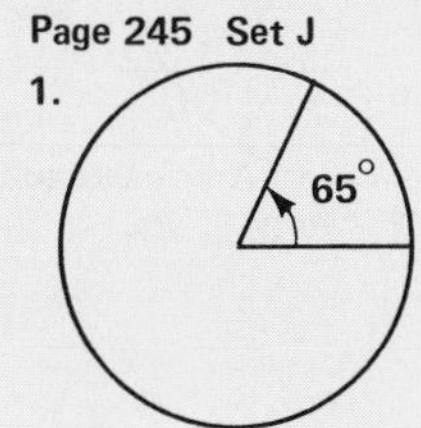

2.

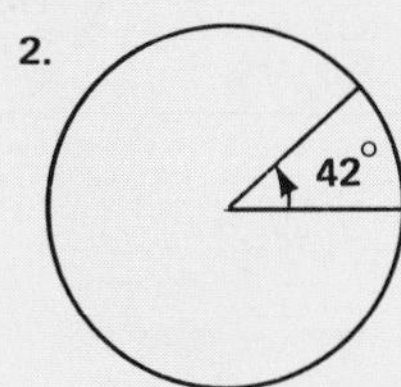

3.

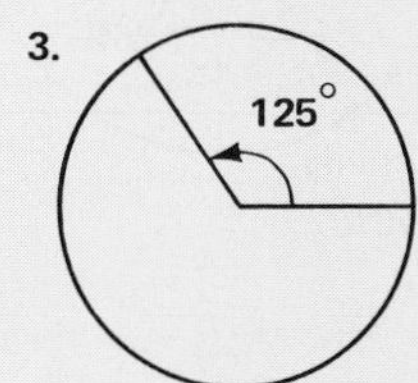

4.

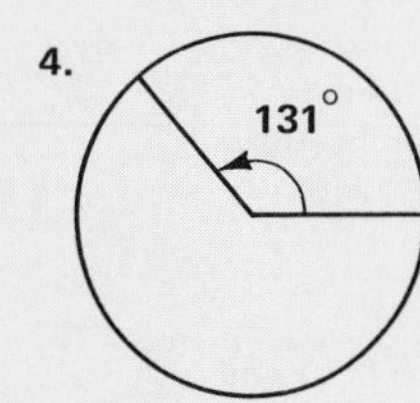

5.

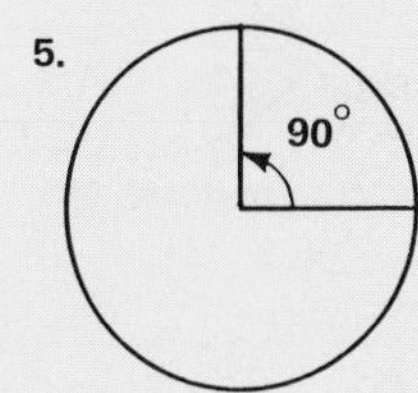

6.

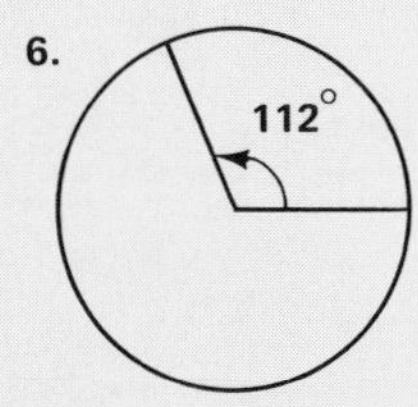

7.

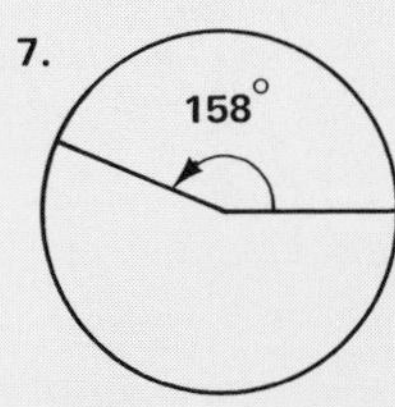

8.

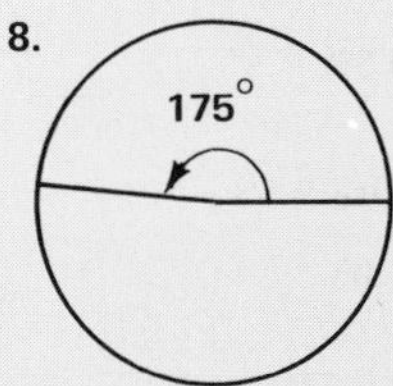

9.

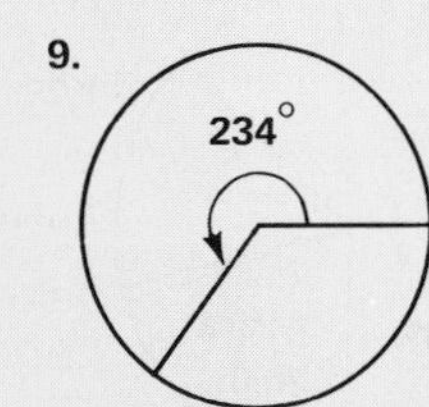

10.

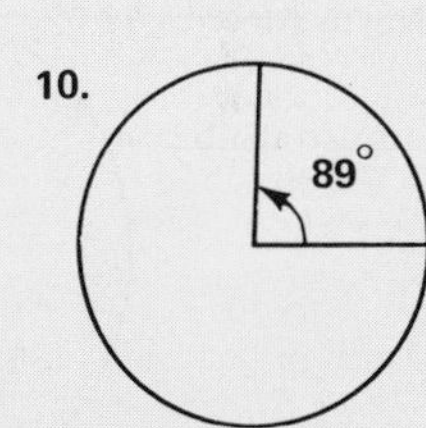

Page 245 Set K

1. Elements of Human Body

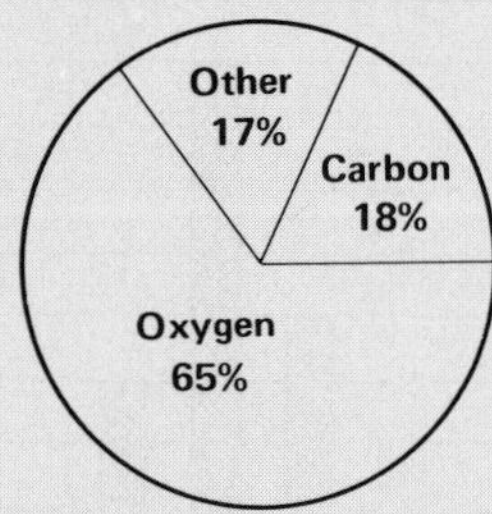

2. Elements of Earth's Crust

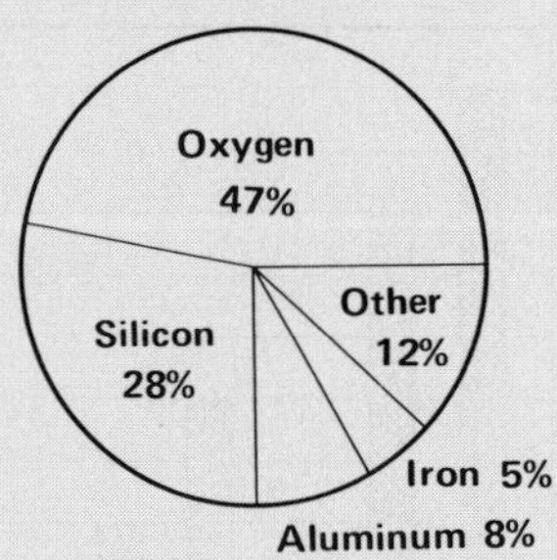

3. Sources of Water Polution

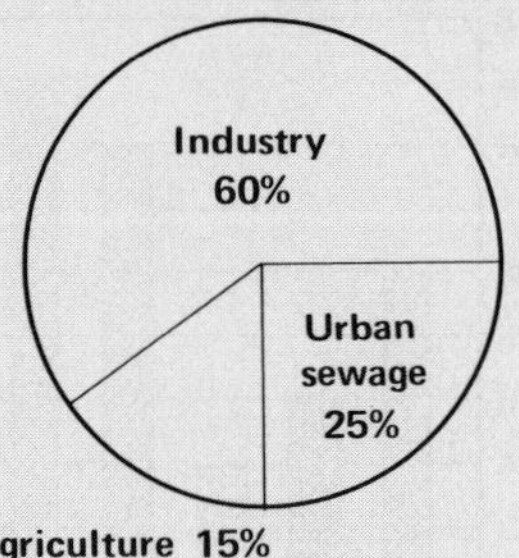

4. Sources of Air Polution

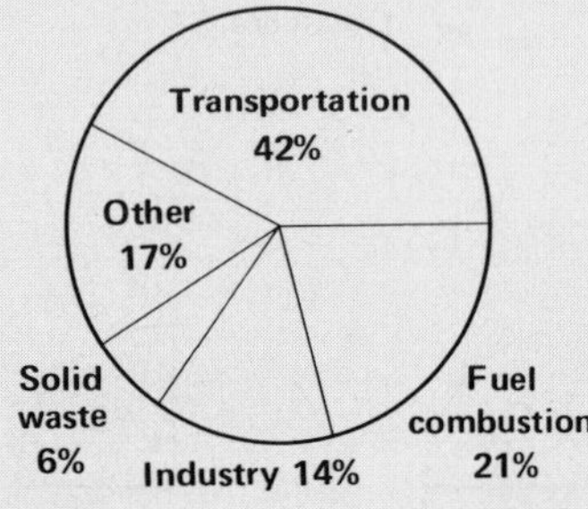

5. Family Budget

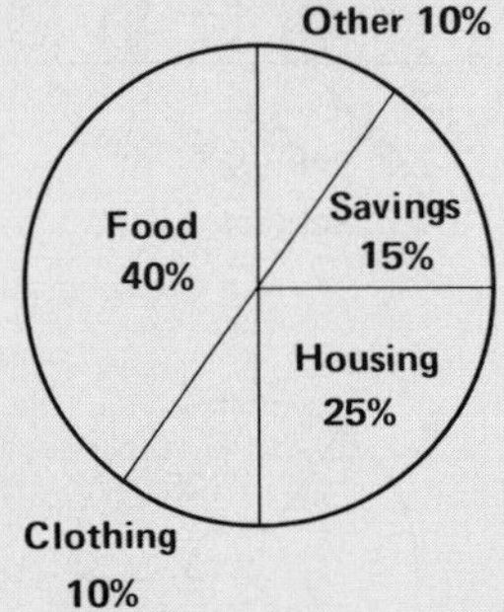

6. Earth's Water

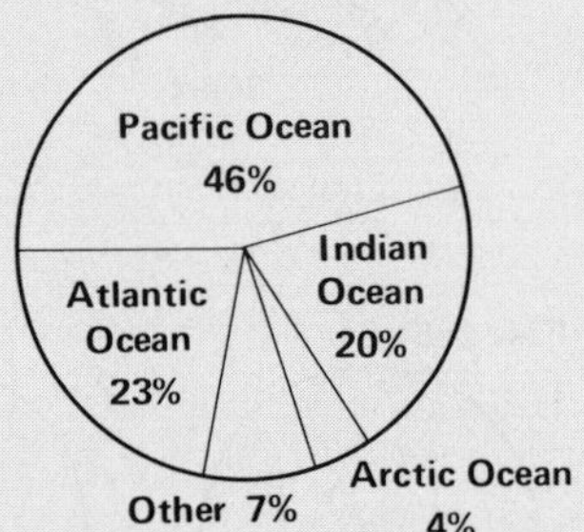

7. Earth's Land

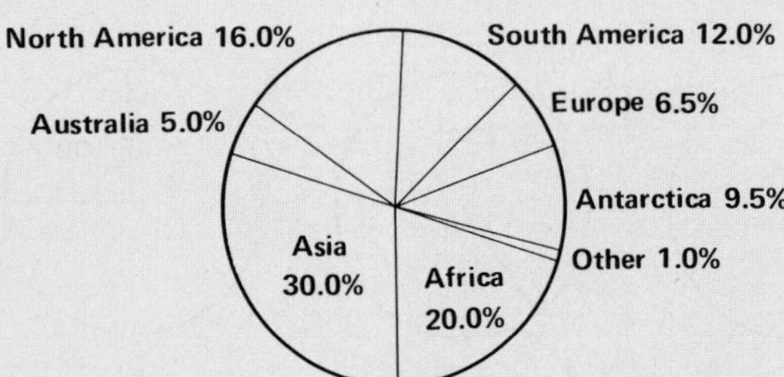

Page 250

2.

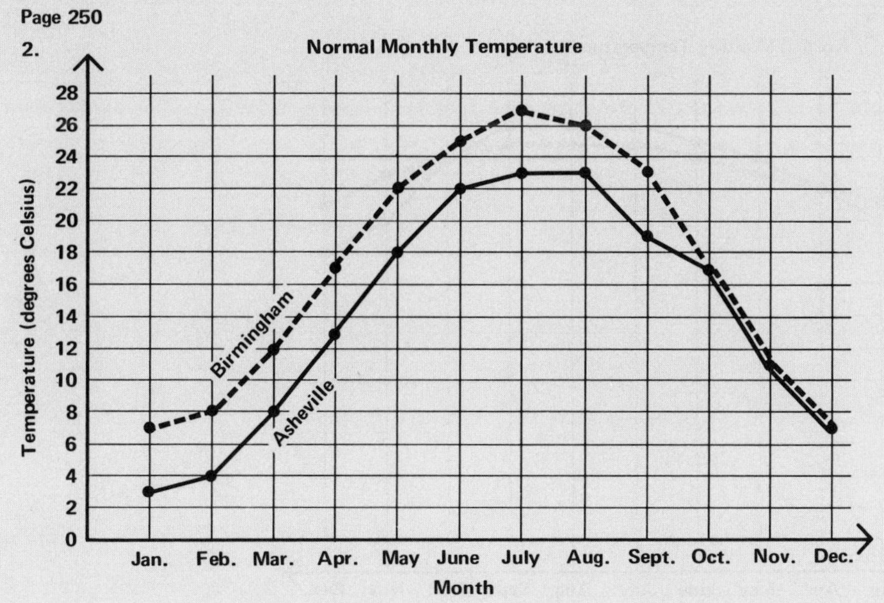

Normal Monthly Temperature
Temperature (degrees Celsius)
28
26
24
22
20
18
16
14
12
10
8
6
4
2
0
Birmingham
Asheville
Jan.
Feb.
Mar.
Apr.
May
June
July
Aug.
Sept.
Oct.
Nov.
Dec.
Month

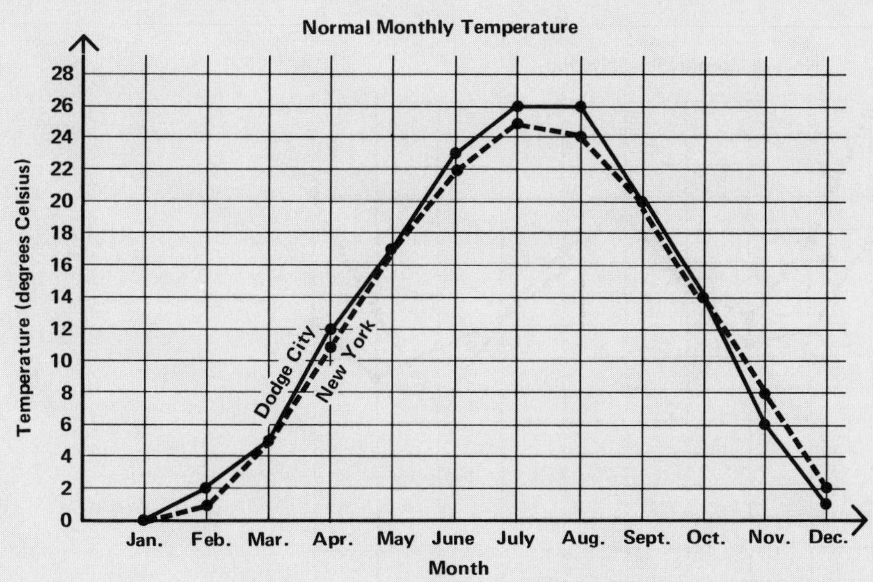

Normal Monthly Temperature
Temperature (degrees Celsius)
28
26
24
22
20
18
16
14
12
10
8
6
4
2
0
Dodge City
New York
Jan.
Feb.
Mar.
Apr.
May
June
July
Aug.
Sept.
Oct.
Nov.
Dec.
Month

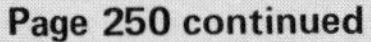

Page 250 continued

2.

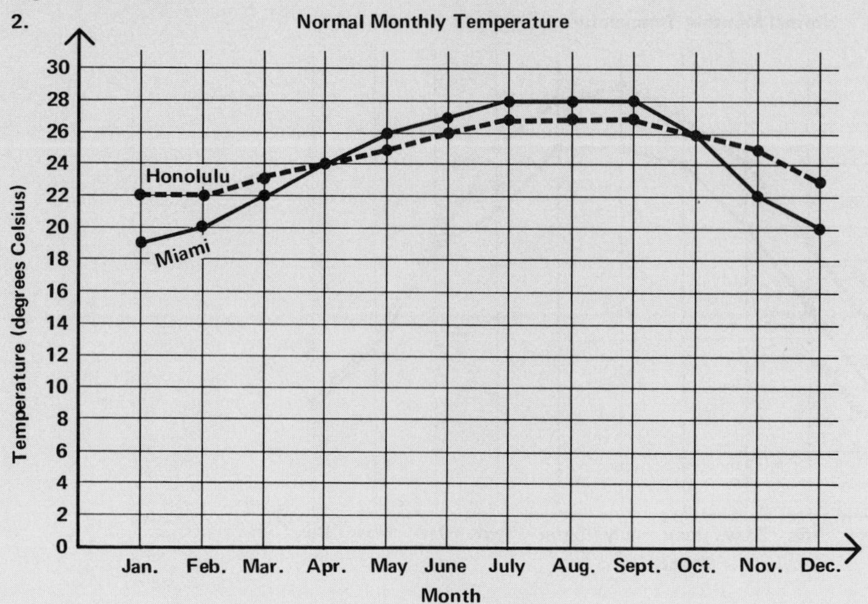

Page 251

4.

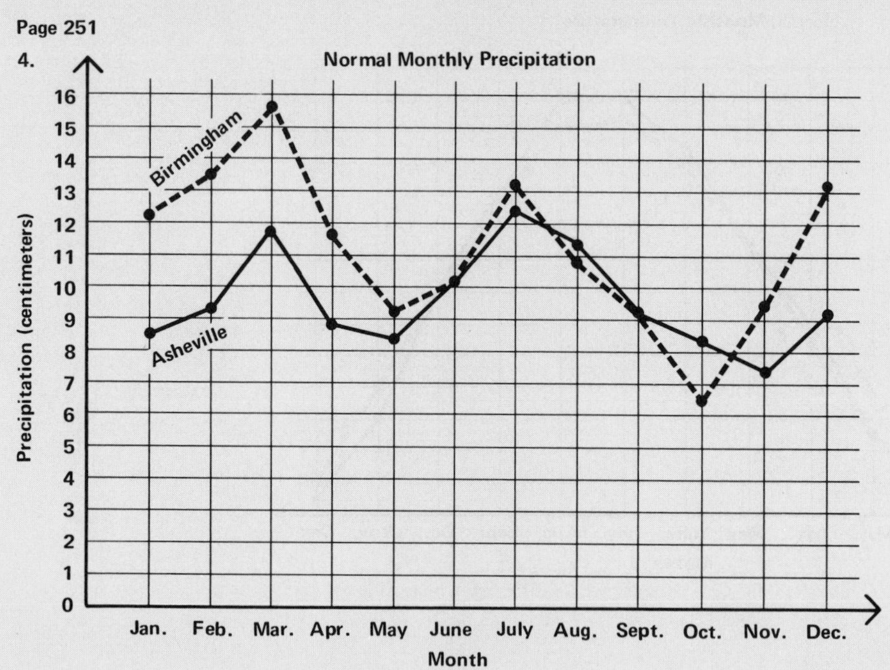

Page 251 continued

4.

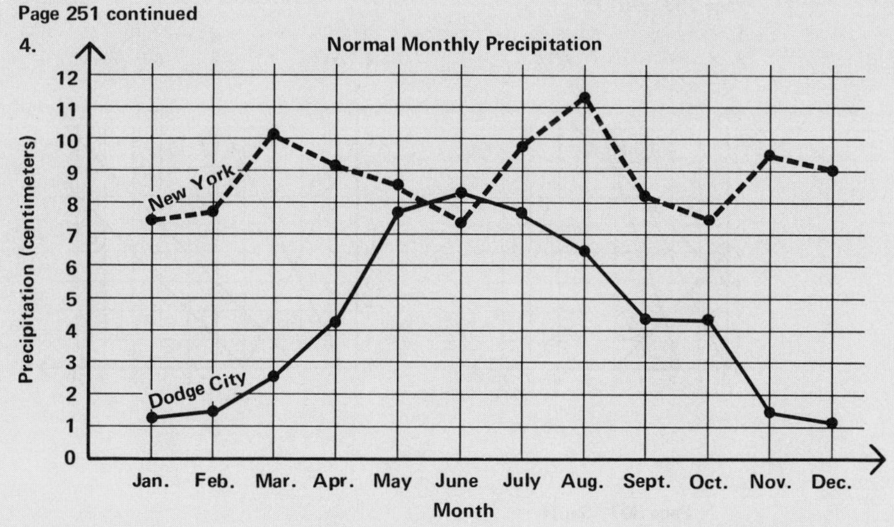

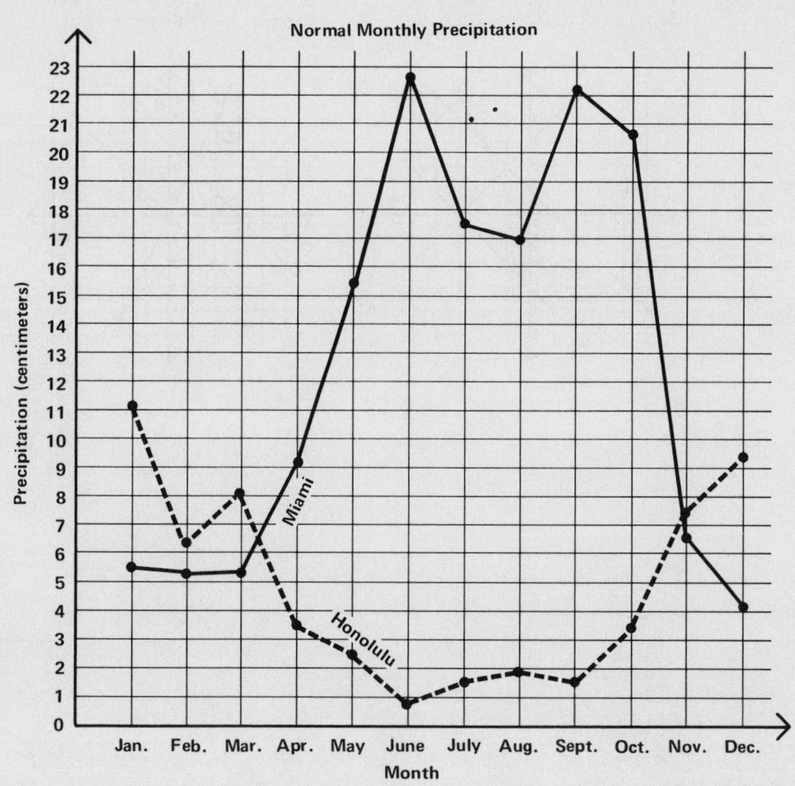

Page 254

7. **Production of Canned Asparagus**

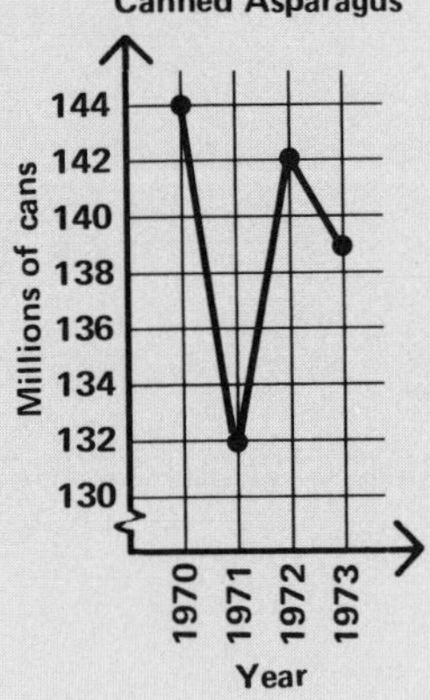

Page 303 Set D

1. $y = x + 3$ **5.** $y = 3x - 5$
3. $y = 2x$ **7.** $y = 4 - x$

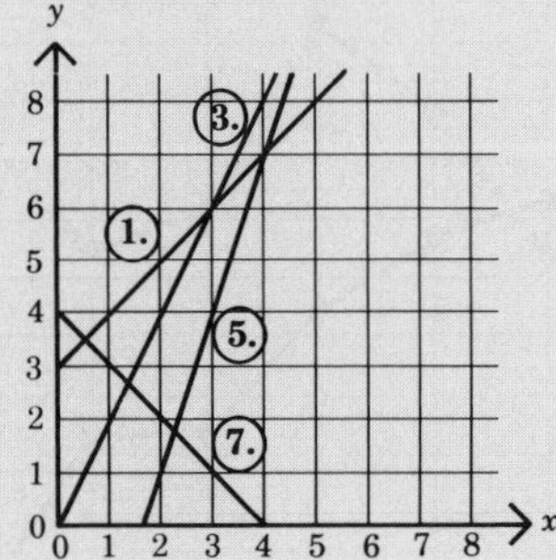

2. $y = x - 2$ **6.** $y = x - 4$
4. $y = 2x - 1$ **8.** $y = 8 - 2x$

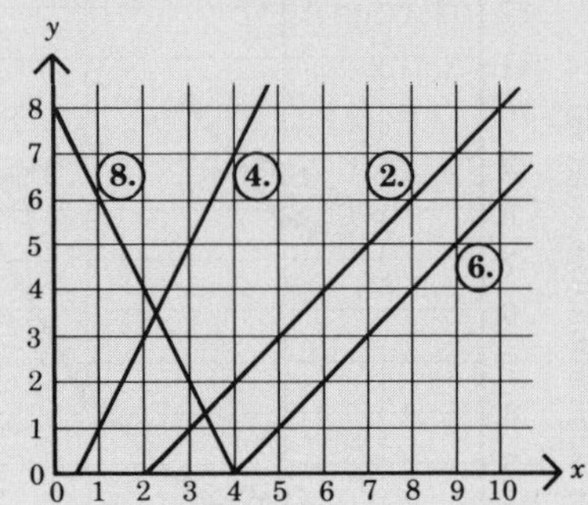

Page 305 Set F

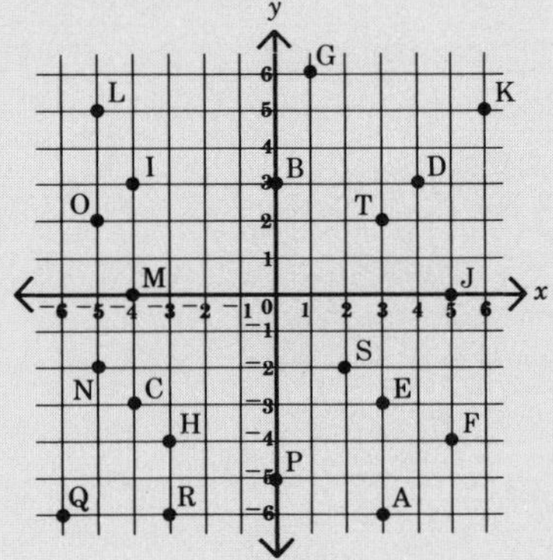

Page 307 Set H

1. $y = x + 1$ **5.** $y = 2x - 1$
3. $y = x - 3$ **7.** $y = 3 - x$

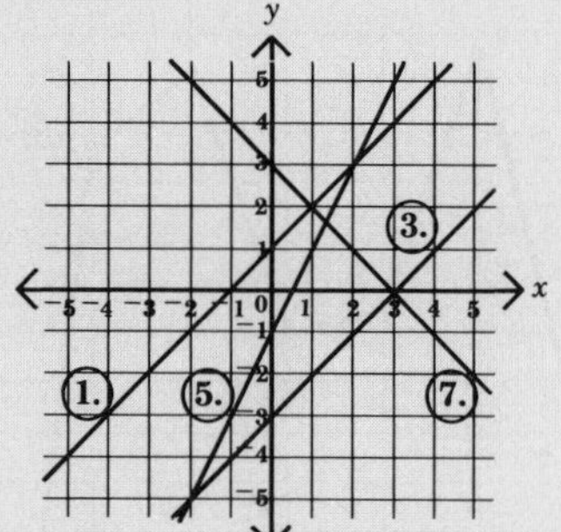

2. $y = {}^-2x$ **6.** $y = {}^-2 - x$
4. $y = x$ **8.** $y = x + 3$

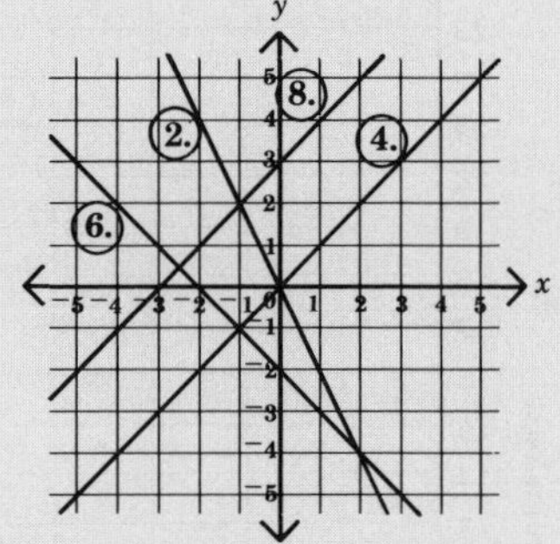

Mathematics in Life — Skills • Consumer and Career Applications

Please complete this questionnaire after you have finished teaching the Scott, Foresman MATHEMATICS IN LIFE textbook for the school year. Remove the questionnaire from the book. Fold and staple it so that the address label shows. No postage is required. The information we obtain from you will be useful to us in planning revisions and in developing new programs.

Name ______________________________ Date ______________

School ______________ City ______________ State ________ Zip code ________

Circle 1, 2, 3, or 4 to complete each statement.

1. I have used the book	**1** 1 year	**2** 2 years	**3** 3 years	**4** 4 years
2. My school is located in	**1** large city	**2** suburb	**3** small town	**4** rural area
3. Total school enrollment is	**1** up to 200	**2** 201–500	**3** 501–1000	**4** over 1000
4. Grade 9 general math enrollment is	**1** 0–50	**2** 51–100	**3** 101–200	**4** over 200
5. Grade 9 algebra enrollment is	**1** 0–50	**2** 51–100	**3** 101–200	**4** over 200

Indicate your reaction to each of the following for the MATHEMATICS IN LIFE textbook by circling 1, 2, 3, 4, or 5 on each scale. Add comments on the right if you wish.

	Poor	Fair	Satisfactory	Very Good	Excellent	Comments
6. Readability	1	2	3	4	5	________
7. Teaching examples	1	2	3	4	5	________
8. Number of practice exercises	1	2	3	4	5	________
9. Selection of content in skills lessons	1	2	3	4	5	________
10. Consumer lessons	1	2	3	4	5	________
11. Careers lessons	1	2	3	4	5	________
12. Keying test items to skills lessons	1	2	3	4	5	________
13. Testing	1	2	3	4	5	________
14. Student interest	1	2	3	4	5	________
15. Student success	1	2	3	4	5	________

Indicate your reaction to each of the following by circling 1, 2, 3, or 4 on each scale.

Student's Text

	Never used	Not useful	Somewhat useful	Very useful
16. Pretest	1	2	3	4
17. Posttest	1	2	3	4
18. Chapter Test	1	2	3	4
19. Break Time	1	2	3	4
20. Skills Tune-up	1	2	3	4
21. Calculator Exercises	1	2	3	4
22. To the Student (pages iii–vii)	1	2	3	4
23. The Metric System (pages xiv–xv)	1	2	3	4
24. Answers to Odd-numbered Exercises	1	2	3	4
25. Careers Chart	1	2	3	4
26. Glossary	1	2	3	4

Teacher's Edition

	Never used	Not useful	Somewhat useful	Very useful
27. Reference Charts (pages T10–T15)	1	2	3	4
28. Notes (pages T16–T27)	1	2	3	4
29. Tests (pages T28–T40)	1	2	3	4
30. Scoring tables on tests	1	2	3	4

Supplementary Materials

	Never used	Not useful	Somewhat useful	Very useful
31. Tests in duplicating masters	1	2	3	4
32. Criterion Referenced Individual Record Form	1	2	3	4
33. Class Test Record Form	1	2	3	4
34. Solution Key	1	2	3	4

35. With which grade did you use the book?

    7 8 9 10 11 12

36. How do you rate the level of difficulty?

    1 too easy **2** about right **3** too difficult

37. Would you be willing to complete a questionnaire after teaching the program another year? **Yes** **No**

FOLD FOL

FIRST CLASS
PERMIT No. 282
GLENVIEW, ILL.

POSTAGE WILL BE PAID BY

SCOTT, FORESMAN AND COMPANY
LEARNER VERIFICATION DEPT.
1900 EAST LAKE AVENUE
GLENVIEW, ILLINOIS 60025

Mathematics in Life

Skills, Consumer and Career Applications

L. Carey Bolster

H. Douglas Woodburn

Scott, Foresman and Company

Glenview, Illinois; Dallas, Texas;
Oakland, New Jersey; Tucker, Georgia;
Palo Alto, California

Authors

L. Carey Bolster
Supervisor of Mathematics
Baltimore County Public Schools
Towson, Maryland

H. Douglas Woodburn
Chairman of the Mathematics Department
Perry Hall Junior High School
Baltimore County, Maryland

Reader/Consultants

Thelma T. Daley
Career Education Specialist
Baltimore County
Towson, Maryland

Robert Y. Hamada
Mathematics Department Chairman
Curtiss Junior High School
Los Angeles, California

Sidney Sharron
Supervisor, Instructional Planning Division
Los Angeles City Unified School District
Los Angeles, California

Acknowledgments

For permission to reproduce the photographs on the pages indicated, acknowledgment is made to the following:

Dennis Brack/Black Star: 164; Superior Electric Company, Bristol, Connecticut: 312

Bottles on 58–59 courtesy of 7UP®. Seismograph on 314–315 courtesy of Soiltest, Inc., Evanston, Illinois

ISBN: 0-673-13100-9

2345678910-BWI-8584838281807978777 6

to the student

You might go over pages iii–vii with the students to familiarize them with the organization, lessons, tests, and special features of the book.

Study pages iii–vii to help you become acquainted with your book.

Organization

Units The text is divided into six units.

Chapters Each unit contains three chapters. There are 18 chapters in all.

Within chapters See the sample table of contents given below. Each chapter focuses first on skills *(pretest, skills lessons, posttest)* and then on consumer and career applications of those skills *(consumer lessons, career lessons)*. See pages iv–vii for samples of lessons, tests, and special features.

Chapter 3
Dividing Whole Numbers

Pretest on skills Each chapter begins with a pretest on the skills that are taught in the chapter. For each skill on the pretest, there is a page reference to a skills lesson. Each skill is then broken down into problem types which appear as lettered items on the pretest and also as lettered examples and exercise sets in the skills lessons.

Skills lesson Skills lessons follow the pretest and are tinted either green or orange. A skills lesson is either on one page or on two facing pages. The lesson title tells the skill that is being taught.

Examples Each example in a skills lesson is the same problem type as the pretest item with the same letter. Examples are lettered consecutively throughout a chapter.

Exercise sets Each exercise set contains exercises that are the same problem type as the example with the same letter.

page 83

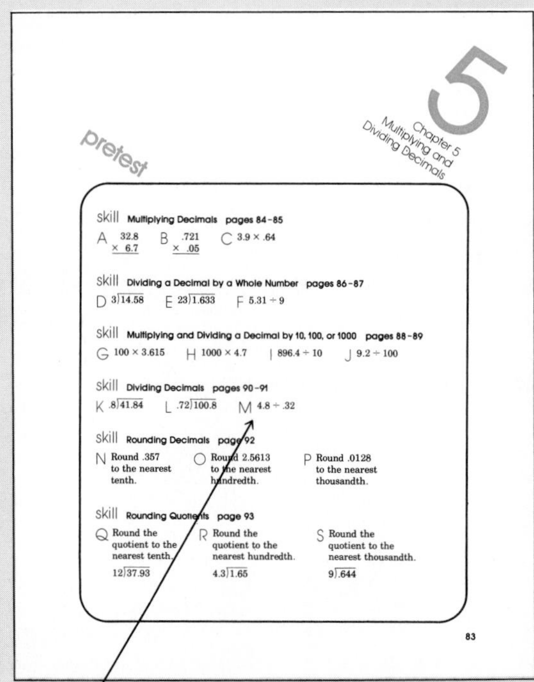

5 Chapter 5 Multiplying and Dividing Decimals

pretest

skill Multiplying Decimals pages 84-85

A 32.8 × 6.7 B .721 × .05 C 3.9 × .64

skill Dividing a Decimal by a Whole Number pages 86-87

D 3)14.58 E 23)1.633 F 5.31 ÷ 9

skill Multiplying and Dividing a Decimal by 10, 100, or 1000 pages 88-89

G 100 × 3.615 H 1000 × 4.7 I 896.4 ÷ 10 J 9.2 ÷ 100

skill Dividing Decimals pages 90-91

K .8)41.84 L .72)100.8 M 4.8 ÷ .32

skill Rounding Decimals page 92

N Round .357 to the nearest tenth. O Round 2.5613 to the nearest hundredth. P Round .0128 to the nearest thousandth.

skill Rounding Quotients page 93

Q Round the quotient to the nearest tenth. 12)37.93 R Round the quotient to the nearest hundredth. 4.3)1.65 S Round the quotient to the nearest thousandth. 9).644

83

Item M on a pretest is the same problem type as . . .

page 90

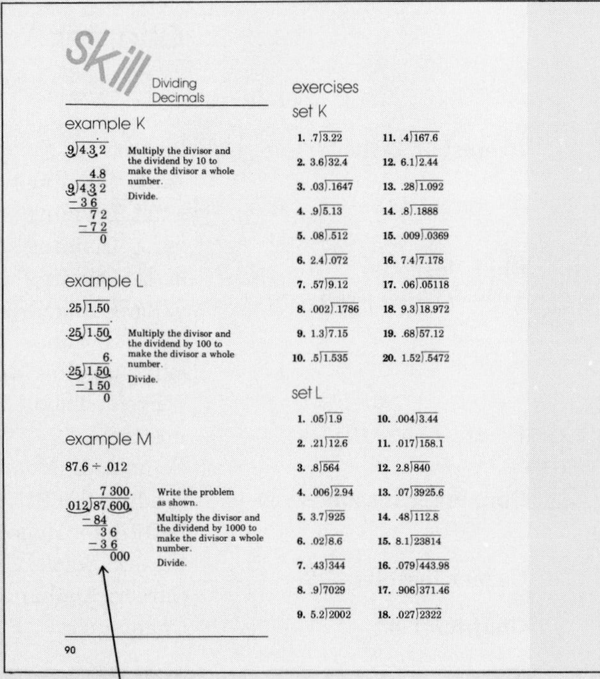

Skill Dividing Decimals

example K

.9)4.32 Multiply the divisor and the dividend by 10 to make the divisor a whole number.

Divide.

4.8
9)43.2
−36
72
−72
0

example L

.25)1.50

.25)1.50 Multiply the divisor and the dividend by 100 to make the divisor a whole number.

Divide.

6.
25)150.
−150
0

example M

87.6 ÷ .012

Write the problem as shown.

Multiply the divisor and the dividend by 1000 to make the divisor a whole number.

Divide.

7 300.
.012)87.600
−84
36
−36
000

exercises

set K

1.	.7)3.22	11.	.4)167.6
2.	3.6)32.4	12.	6.1)2.44
3.	.03).1647	13.	.28)1.092
4.	.9)5.13	14.	.8).1888
5.	.08).512	15.	.009).0369
6.	2.4).072	16.	7.4)7.178
7.	.57)9.12	17.	.06).05118
8.	.002).1786	18.	9.3)18.972
9.	1.3)7.15	19.	.68)57.12
10.	.5)1.535	20.	1.52).5472

set L

1.	.05)1.9	10.	.004)3.44
2.	.21)12.6	11.	.017)158.1
3.	.8)564	12.	2.8)840
4.	.006)2.94	13.	.07)3925.6
5.	3.7)925	14.	.48)112.8
6.	.02)8.6	15.	8.1)23814
7.	.43)344	16.	.079)443.98
8.	.9)7029	17.	.906)371.46
9.	5.2)2002	18.	.027)2322

90

example M in a skills lesson and as . . .

Break Time
A recreational puzzle or problem. There are 1, 2, or 3 Break Times within the skills lessons of each chapter.

Posttest on skills A posttest on skills follows the skills lessons in a chapter. The posttest is an alternate form of the pretest with the same page references to skills lessons and with similar lettered test items.

page 91

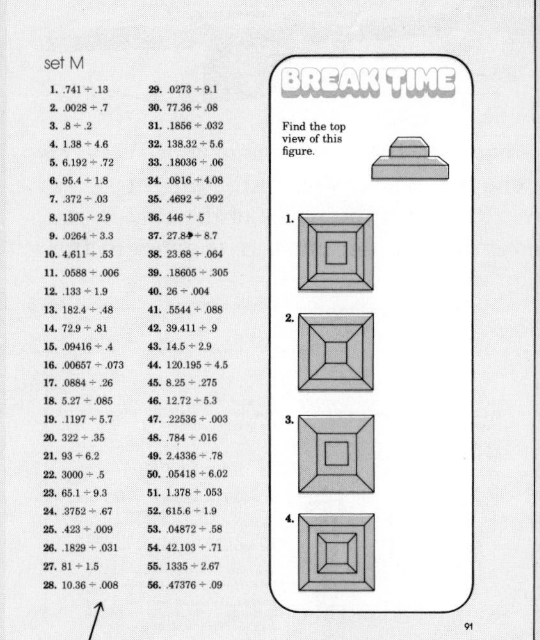

set M

1.	.741 ÷ .13	**29.**	.0273 ÷ 9.1
2.	.0028 ÷ .7	**30.**	77.36 ÷ .08
3.	.8 ÷ .2	**31.**	.1856 ÷ .032
4.	1.38 ÷ 4.6	**32.**	138.32 ÷ 5.6
5.	6.192 ÷ .72	**33.**	.18036 ÷ .06
6.	95.4 ÷ 1.8	**34.**	.0816 ÷ 4.08
7.	.372 ÷ .03	**35.**	.4692 ÷ .092
8.	1305 ÷ 2.9	**36.**	446 ÷ .5
9.	.0264 ÷ 3.3	**37.**	27.84 ÷ 8.7
10.	4.611 ÷ .53	**38.**	23.68 ÷ .064
11.	.0588 ÷ .006	**39.**	.18605 ÷ .305
12.	.133 ÷ 1.9	**40.**	26 ÷ .004
13.	182.4 ÷ .48	**41.**	.5544 ÷ .088
14.	72.9 ÷ .81	**42.**	39.411 ÷ .9
15.	.09416 ÷ .4	**43.**	14.5 ÷ 2.9
16.	.00657 ÷ .073	**44.**	120.195 ÷ 4.5
17.	.0884 ÷ .26	**45.**	8.25 ÷ .275
18.	5.27 ÷ .085	**46.**	12.72 ÷ 5.3
19.	.1197 ÷ 5.7	**47.**	.22536 ÷ .003
20.	322 ÷ .35	**48.**	.784 ÷ .016
21.	93 ÷ 6.2	**49.**	2.4336 ÷ .78
22.	3000 ÷ .5	**50.**	.05418 ÷ 6.02
23.	65.1 ÷ 9.3	**51.**	1.378 ÷ .053
24.	.3752 ÷ .67	**52.**	615.6 ÷ 1.9
25.	.423 ÷ .009	**53.**	.04872 ÷ .58
26.	.1829 ÷ .031	**54.**	42.103 ÷ .71
27.	81 ÷ 1.5	**55.**	1335 ÷ 2.67
28.	10.36 ÷ .008	**56.**	.47376 ÷ .09

BREAK TIME

Find the top view of this figure.

1. **2.** **3.** **4.**

91

the exercises in set M and as . . .

page 94

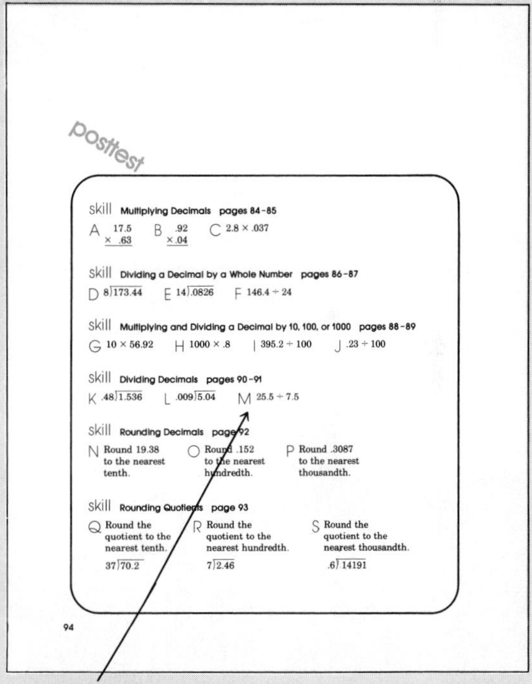

posttest

skill **Multiplying Decimals** pages 84–85

A 17.5 × .63 B .92 × .04 C 2.8 × .037

skill **Dividing a Decimal by a Whole Number** pages 86–87

D $8\overline{)173.44}$ E $14\overline{).0826}$ F 146.4 ÷ 24

skill **Multiplying and Dividing a Decimal by 10, 100, or 1000** pages 88–89

G 10 × 56.92 H 1000 × .8 I 395.2 ÷ 100 J .23 ÷ 100

skill **Dividing Decimals** pages 90–91

K $.48\overline{)1.536}$ L $.009\overline{)5.04}$ M 25.5 ÷ 7.5

skill **Rounding Decimals** page 92

N Round 19.38 to the nearest tenth. O Round .152 to the nearest hundredth. P Round .3087 to the nearest thousandth.

skill **Rounding Quotients** page 93

Q Round the quotient to the nearest tenth. $37\overline{)70.2}$ R Round the quotient to the nearest hundredth. $7\overline{)2.46}$ S Round the quotient to the nearest thousandth. $.6\overline{)14191}$

94

item M on the posttest.

Consumer lessons After the posttest on skills in each chapter, there are two or more consumer lessons. These lessons show how the skills in the chapter, along with skills taught previously, are used in everyday life. Each lesson is either on one page or on two facing pages.

pages 56–57

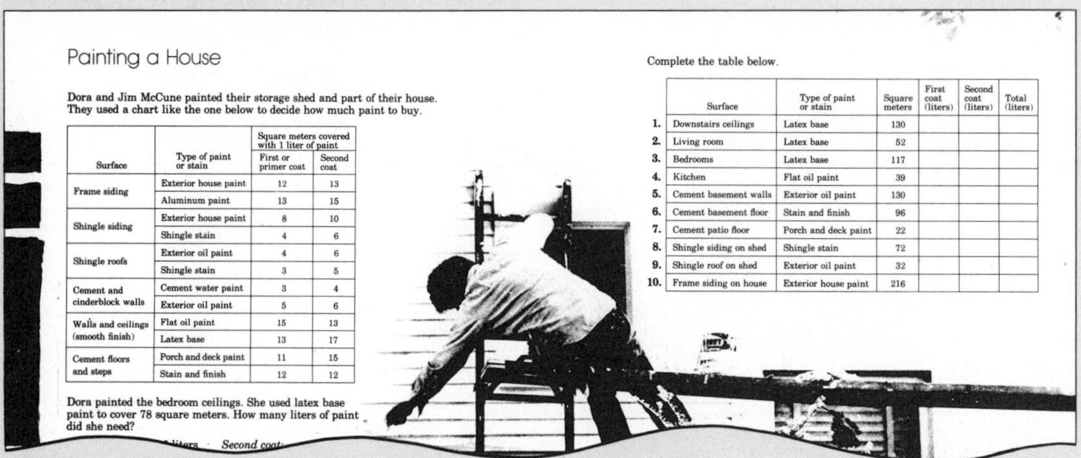

Painting a House

Dora and Jim McCune painted their storage shed and part of their house. They used a chart like the one below to decide how much paint to buy.

Surface	Type of paint or stain	Square meters covered with 1 liter of paint	
		First or primer coat	Second coat
Frame siding	Exterior house paint	12	13
	Aluminum paint	13	15
Shingle siding	Exterior house paint	8	10
	Shingle stain	4	6
Shingle roofs	Exterior oil paint	4	6
	Shingle stain	3	5
Cement and cinderblock walls	Cement water paint	3	4
	Exterior oil paint	5	6
Walls and ceilings (smooth finish)	Flat oil paint	15	13
	Latex base	13	17
Cement floors and steps	Porch and deck paint	11	15
	Stain and finish	12	12

Dora painted the bedroom ceilings. She used latex base paint to cover 78 square meters. How many liters of paint did she need?

Second coat:

Complete the table below.

	Surface	Type of paint or stain	Square meters	First coat (liters)	Second coat (liters)	Total (liters)
1.	Downstairs ceilings	Latex base	130			
2.	Living room	Latex base	52			
3.	Bedrooms	Latex base	117			
4.	Kitchen	Flat oil paint	39			
5.	Cement basement walls	Exterior oil paint	130			
6.	Cement basement floor	Stain and finish	96			
7.	Cement patio floor	Porch and deck paint	22			
8.	Shingle siding on shed	Shingle stain	72			
9.	Shingle roof on shed	Exterior oil paint	32			
10.	Frame siding on house	Exterior house paint	216			

Career lessons After the consumer lessons in a chapter, there are one or more career lessons. These lessons show how the skills in the chapter, along with skills taught previously, are used in various careers. The lesson title gives the name of the career and the career cluster. More information about jobs in various career clusters is given in the Careers Chart on pages 420–423.

pages 122–123

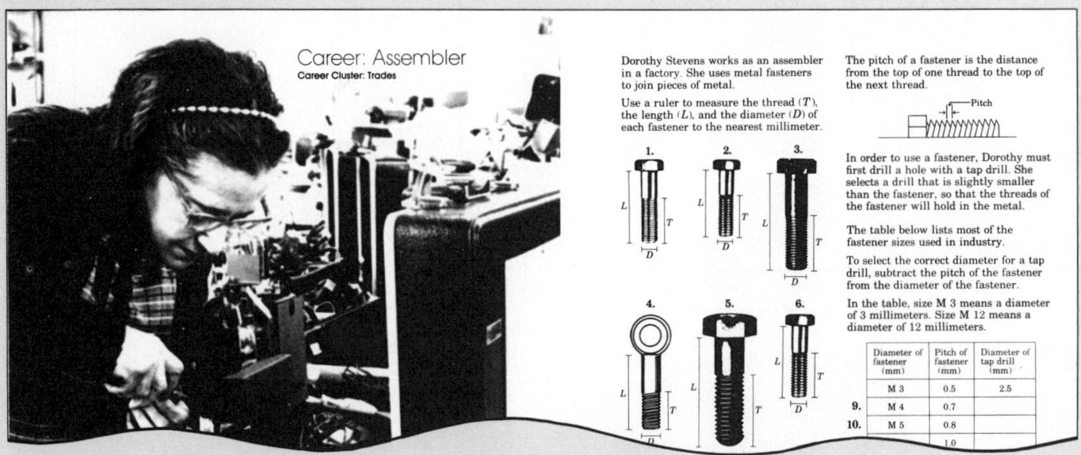

Career: Assembler

Career Cluster: Trades

Dorothy Stevens works as an assembler in a factory. She uses metal fasteners to join pieces of metal.

Use a ruler to measure the thread (T), the length (L), and the diameter (D) of each fastener to the nearest millimeter.

The pitch of a fastener is the distance from the top of one thread to the top of the next thread.

In order to use a fastener, Dorothy must first drill a hole with a tap drill. She selects a drill that is slightly smaller than the fastener, so that the threads of the fastener will hold in the metal.

The table below lists most of the fastener sizes used in industry.

To select the correct diameter for a tap drill, subtract the pitch of the fastener from the diameter of the fastener.

In the table, size M 3 means a diameter of 3 millimeters. Size M 12 means a diameter of 12 millimeters.

	Diameter of fastener (mm)	Pitch of fastener (mm)	Diameter of tap drill (mm)
	M 3	0.5	2.5
9.	M 4	0.7	
10.	M 5	0.8	
		1.0	

Chapter Test and End-of-unit Features

Chapter Test The test at the end of each chapter tests the skills as well as the consumer and career applications from the chapter.

page 82

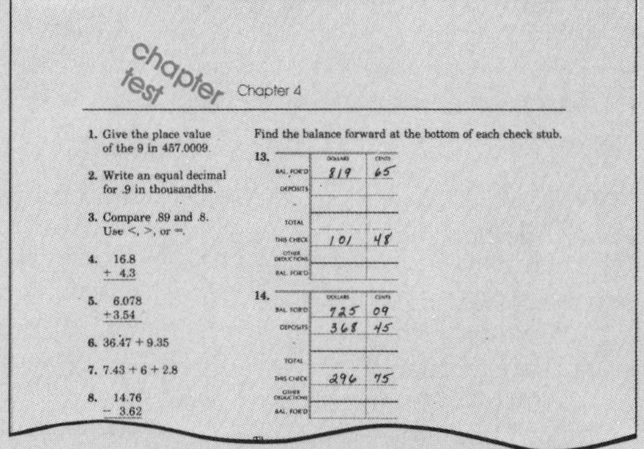

chapter test Chapter 4

1. Give the place value of the 9 in 457.0009.
2. Write an equal decimal for .9 in thousandths.
3. Compare .89 and .8. Use <, >, or =.
4. 16.8 + 4.3
5. 6.078 + 3.54
6. 36.47 + 9.35
7. 7.43 + 6 + 2.8
8. 14.76 − 3.62

Find the balance forward at the bottom of each check stub.

13.

	DOLLARS	CENTS
BAL. FOR'D	819	65
DEPOSITS		
TOTAL		
THIS CHECK	101	48
OTHER DEDUCTIONS		
BAL. FOR'D		

14.

	DOLLARS	CENTS
BAL. FOR'D	725	09
DEPOSITS	368	45
TOTAL		
THIS CHECK	296	75
OTHER DEDUCTIONS		
BAL. FOR'D		

Skills Tune-up Near the end of each unit, there is a page containing sets of exercises that maintain skills taught previously in the book. References at the beginning of each set indicate where the skill was taught.

page 127

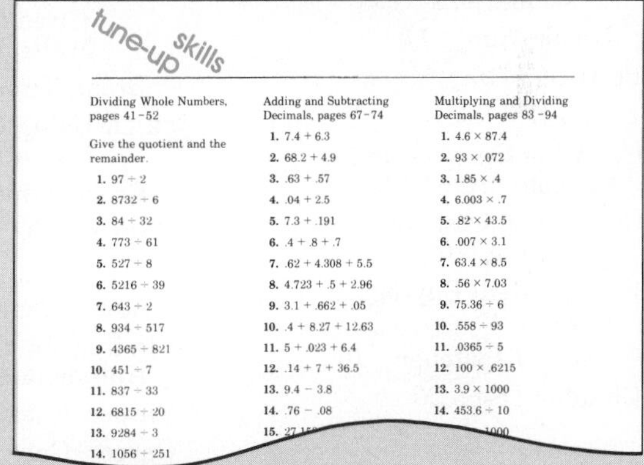

skills tune-up

Dividing Whole Numbers, pages 41–52

Give the quotient and the remainder.

1. 97 ÷ 2
2. 8732 ÷ 6
3. 84 ÷ 32
4. 773 ÷ 61
5. 527 ÷ 8
6. 5216 ÷ 39
7. 643 ÷ 2
8. 934 ÷ 517
9. 4365 ÷ 821
10. 451 ÷ 7
11. 837 ÷ 33
12. 6815 ÷ 20
13. 9284 ÷ 3
14. 1056 ÷ 251

Adding and Subtracting Decimals, pages 67–74

1. 7.4 + 6.3
2. 68.2 + 4.9
3. .63 + .57
4. .04 + 2.5
5. 7.3 + .191
6. .4 + .8 + .7
7. .62 + 4.308 + 5.5
8. 4.723 + .5 + 2.96
9. 3.1 + .662 + .05
10. .4 + 8.27 + 12.63
11. 5 + .023 + 6.4
12. .14 + 7 + 36.5
13. 9.4 − 3.8
14. .76 − .08

Multiplying and Dividing Decimals, pages 83–94

1. 4.6 × 87.4
2. 93 × .072
3. 1.85 × .4
4. 6.003 × .7
5. .82 × 43.5
6. .007 × 3.1
7. 63.4 × 8.5
8. .56 × 7.03
9. 75.36 ÷ 6
10. .558 ÷ 93
11. .0365 ÷ 5
12. 100 × .6215
13. 3.9 × 1000
14. 453.6 ÷ 10

Calculator Exercises At the end of each unit, there is a page of optional exercises to be done on a simple, four-function calculator. The exercises include skills that were taught in the unit as well as applications of those skills.

page 64

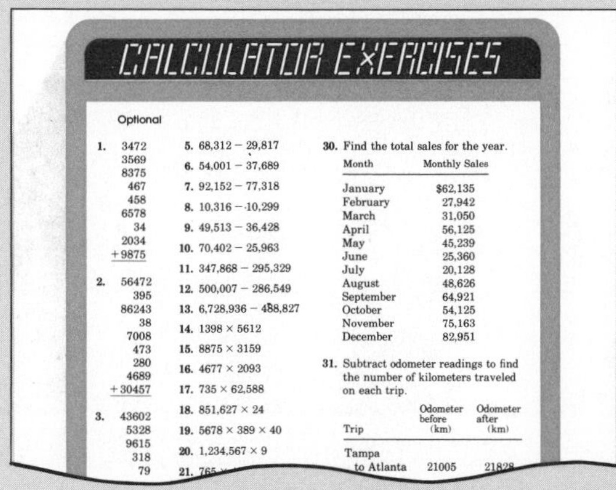

CALCULATOR EXERCISES

Optional

1. 3472 + 3569 + 8375 + 467 + 458 + 6578 + 34 + 2034 + 9875
2. 56472 + 395 + 86243 + 38 + 7008 + 473 + 280 + 4689 + 30457
3. 43602, 5328, 9615, 318, 79

5. 68,312 − 29,817
6. 54,001 − 37,689
7. 92,152 − 77,318
8. 10,316 − 10,299
9. 49,513 − 36,428
10. 70,402 − 25,963
11. 347,868 − 295,329
12. 500,007 − 286,549
13. 6,728,936 − 488,827
14. 1398 × 5612
15. 8875 × 3159
16. 4677 × 2093
17. 735 × 62,588
18. 851,627 × 24
19. 5678 × 389 × 40
20. 1,234,567 × 9

30. Find the total sales for the year.

Month	Monthly Sales
January	$62,135
February	27,942
March	31,050
April	56,125
May	45,239
June	25,360
July	20,128
August	48,626
September	64,921
October	54,125
November	75,163
December	82,951

31. Subtract odometer readings to find the number of kilometers traveled on each trip.

Trip	Odometer before (km)	Odometer after (km)
Tampa to Atlanta	21005	21828

Unit 1 Whole Numbers

Chapter 1
Adding and Subtracting Whole Numbers

Chapter 2
Multiplying Whole Numbers

Chapter 3
Dividing Whole Numbers

Unit 2 Decimals and the Metric System

Chapter 4
Adding and Subtracting Decimals

Chapter 5
Multiplying and Dividing Decimals

Chapter 6
The Metric System

Fractions, Mixed Numbers, and Probability

Chapter 7

Multiplying and Dividing Fractions and Mixed Numbers

Chapter 8

Adding and Subtracting Fractions and Mixed Numbers

Chapter 9

Probability

Ratio, Percent, and Statistics

Chapter 10
Ratio, Proportion, and Similarity

Chapter 11
Percent

Chapter 12
Statistics

Unit 5 Algebra

Chapter 13

Positive and Negative Numbers

Chapter 14

Expressions and Equations

Chapter 15

Graphing

Unit 6 Geometry and Right-Triangle Relations

Chapter 16

Perimeter and Area

Chapter 17

Surface Area and Volume

Chapter 18

The Pythagorean Rule and Trigonometry

End-of-book Materials

Students can use these two pages as a reference at any time.
Chapter 6 provides a complete development of the metric system.

The Metric System

Length

The base unit of length is the meter. The width of a door is about one meter.

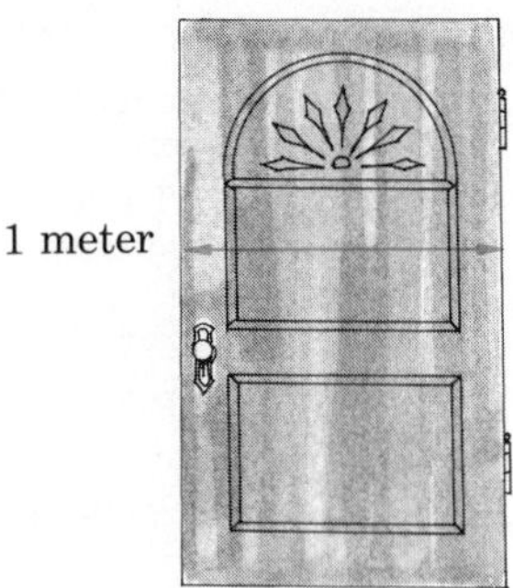

Millimeter, centimeter, and kilometer are other commonly used units of length.

The thickness of the wire in a paper clip is about one millimeter.

The diameter of an ordinary piece of chalk is almost one centimeter.

A distance of five city blocks is about one kilometer. It takes about ten minutes to walk one kilometer.

Time

The base unit of time is the second. Other units of time in the metric system are familiar units such as minutes and hours.

Mass

The base unit of mass is the kilogram.* The mass of this butter is about one kilogram.

Gram is another commonly used unit of mass. The mass of an aspirin is about one gram.

Temperature

The base unit of temperature is the kelvin. However, the Celsius scale is commonly used in countries employing the metric system.

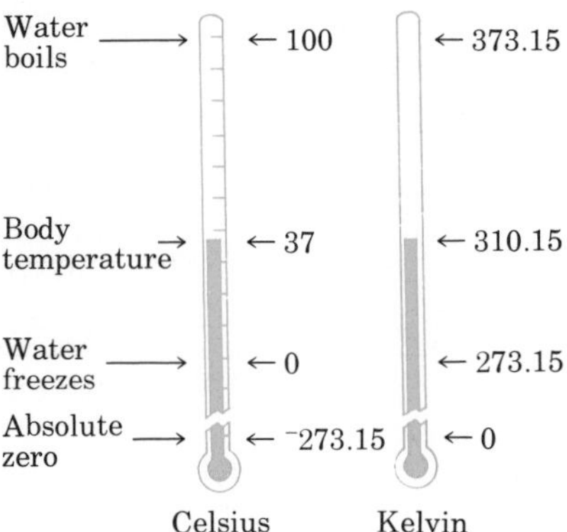

*The mass of an object is the same on the moon as it is on the earth. The gravitational force on an object is less on the moon than it is on the earth.

In common usage, units of mass are often referred to as units of weight. The term *weight* is also used to mean the gravitional force on an object.

Area

Square meter and square centimeter are commonly used units of area. The area of this thumbnail is about one square centimeter.

1 square centimeter

Volume

Cubic meter and cubic centimeter are commonly used units of volume. The amount of water in this eyedropper is one cubic centimeter, or one milliliter. The mass of the water is one gram.

1 cubic centimeter
1 milliliter
1 gram

Cubic decimeter is another unit of volume. This carton holds almost one cubic decimeter, or one liter. If it were filled with water, the mass of the water would be about one kilogram.

1 cubic decimeter
1 liter
1 kilogram

Prefixes and symbols

This table shows the most commonly used prefixes in the metric system.

Prefix	Symbol	Meaning
mega-	M	million
kilo-	k	thousand
hecto-	h	hundred
deka-	da	ten
deci-	d	tenth
centi-	c	hundredth
milli-	m	thousandth
micro-	μ	millionth

Here are symbols for some of the metric units of measure. Periods are not used after these symbols, and an *-s* is not added for the plural form.

Unit of measure	Symbol
meter*	m
kilometer	km
centimeter	cm
millimeter	mm
liter*	ℓ
milliliter	ml
kilogram	kg
gram	g
milligram	mg
square meter	m^2
square centimeter	cm^2
square millimeter	mm^2
cubic meter	m^3
cubic decimeter	dm^3
cubic centimeter	cm^3
cubic millimeter	mm^3

*The root words *meter* and *liter* may be spelled "metre" and "litre." The "-er" spelling appears in this book and is in common usage in the United States.

Whole Numbers

Chapter 1
Adding and Subtracting Whole Numbers

Chapter 2
Multiplying Whole Numbers

Chapter 3
Dividing Whole Numbers

On each Pretest, Posttest, and Chapter Test you will find a table such as this to help score the test. For scores of 50% correct or better, the percent correct is listed below the number of test items missed. The use of this table is optional. You may prefer to record particular items missed by each student, rather than finding percent scores.

Chapter 1 Adding and Subtracting Whole Numbers

Number of test items - 11

Number missed	1	2	3	4	5
Percent correct	91	82	73	64	55

skill Adding Whole Numbers pages 4-5

A $432 + 57$ 489

B $678 + 374$ 1052

C $218 + 47 + 862$ 1127

D $38 + 247 + 8563 + 2$ 8850

skill Subtracting Whole Numbers pages 6-7

E $3875 - 263$ 3612

F $2043 - 485$ 1558

G $2841 - 857$ 1984

skill Using Order of Operations pages 8-9

H $32 - 7 + 5$ 30

I $18 - (8 - 4)$ 14

skill Solving Addition and Subtraction Equations pages 10-11

J Find x.

$x + 26 = 94$ $x = 68$

K Find a.

$a - 87 = 114$ $a = 201$

The Pretest for each chapter assesses student understanding of the skills developed in that chapter. Each skill is broken down into problem types. These problem types appear on the Pretest, in the skills lessons, and on the Posttest. They are lettered A, B, C, and so on, consecutively throughout the chapter. Item A on the Pretest is the same problem type as example A in a skills lesson (page 4), and as the exercises in set A (page 4), and as item A on the Posttest (page 12). Notice that the skills for a chapter are tested again on the Chapter Test (page 20) along with applications.

You may choose to individualize assignments for your students according to the items missed on the Pretest. On the other hand, you may choose to use the Pretest simply as a preview of the skills to be taught in the chapter. If all students do well on the Pretest, you may choose to go directly to the applications (pages 13–19).

See page T16 for additional notes on Chapter 1.

Objective: Add whole numbers.

Adding Whole Numbers

See pages T10–T15 for a listing of all of the objectives in each chapter.

The lesson title names the mathematical skill being taught in this lesson.

example A Without renaming

```
  247
+  31
  278
```

Add ones.
Add tens.
Add hundreds.

Each skill is broken down into problem types. The problem type is explained here.

example B With renaming

```
  11
  395
+ 897
 1292
```

Add ones.
Carry 1 into tens column. Carry 1 into hundreds column.

example C Three or more addends

```
  12
  865
   39
+  78
  982
```

Add down columns.
Carry when necessary.

Remind students that they can check their work by adding "up" in each column.

example D Horizontal form

370 + 84 + 5458 + 3

```
  21
  370
   84
 5458
+   3
 5915
```

Write problem vertically, lining up columns correctly. Add. Carry when necessary.

The exercises in set A correspond to example A, set B corresponds to example B, and so on, throughout the chapter.

exercises

Answers to odd-numbered exercises are given at the end of the pupils' book on pages 385–416.

set A

1. 34 + 52 — 86
2. 423 + 532 — 955
3. 45 + 23 — 68
4. 206 + 721 — 927
5. 8743 + 152 — 8895
6. 370 + 28 — 398
7. 247 + 52 — 299
8. 7405 + 123 — 7528
9. 1064 + 913 — 1977
10. 2417 + 4561 — 6978

set B

1. 37 + 29 — 66
2. 847 + 58 — 905
3. 495 + 14 — 509
4. 528 + 73 — 601
5. 9274 + 683 — 9957
6. 57 + 45 — 102
7. 429 + 573 — 1002
8. 2984 + 374 — 3358
9. 65 + 435 — 500
10. 8347 + 198 — 8545
11. 999 + 99 — 1098
12. 86457 + 9842 — 96,299
13. 2073 + 159 — 2232
14. 258 + 7543 — 7801

set C

1. $\begin{array}{r} 35 \\ 48 \\ +79 \\ \hline 162 \end{array}$

2. $\begin{array}{r} 567 \\ 42 \\ +2311 \\ \hline 2920 \end{array}$

3. $\begin{array}{r} 147 \\ 2497 \\ +\quad 38 \\ \hline 2682 \end{array}$

4. $\begin{array}{r} 301 \\ 572 \\ +648 \\ \hline 1521 \end{array}$

5. $\begin{array}{r} 472 \\ 528 \\ +560 \\ \hline 1560 \end{array}$

6. $\begin{array}{r} 122 \\ 47 \\ +5604 \\ \hline 5773 \end{array}$

7. $\begin{array}{r} 18 \\ 57 \\ 96 \\ +44 \\ \hline 215 \end{array}$

8. $\begin{array}{r} 307 \\ 5 \\ 68 \\ +711 \\ \hline 1091 \end{array}$

9. $\begin{array}{r} 72 \\ 9 \\ 18 \\ 45 \\ 3 \\ +12 \\ \hline 159 \end{array}$

10. $\begin{array}{r} 6397 \\ 245 \\ +1062 \\ \hline 7704 \end{array}$

11. $\begin{array}{r} 8146 \\ 597 \\ +3002 \\ \hline 11{,}745 \end{array}$

12. $\begin{array}{r} 2671 \\ 453 \\ +8742 \\ \hline 11{,}866 \end{array}$

13. $\begin{array}{r} 43 \\ 620 \\ 78 \\ 5 \\ +3199 \\ \hline 3945 \end{array}$

14. $\begin{array}{r} 3684 \\ 15 \\ 278 \\ +54110 \\ \hline 58{,}087 \end{array}$

15. $\begin{array}{r} 578901 \\ 3459 \\ +396672 \\ \hline 979{,}032 \end{array}$

16. $\begin{array}{r} 82 \\ 67 \\ 425 \\ 13 \\ 1482 \\ +\quad 98 \\ \hline 2167 \end{array}$

17. $\begin{array}{r} 8175 \\ 24 \\ 63 \\ 807 \\ 33 \\ +\quad 248 \\ \hline 9350 \end{array}$

set D

1. 16 + 5 + 284 — 305

2. 67 + 869 + 21 — 957

3. 47 + 38 + 29 — 114

4. 663 + 9 + 4870 — 5542

5. 863 + 68 + 82 — 1013

6. 18 + 234 + 5420 — 5672

7. 27 + 495 — 522

8. 9 + 7 + 6 + 5 + 3 + 7 — 37

9. 3 + 8 + 6 + 4 + 5 + 1 — 27

10. 2847 + 63 — 2910

11. 510 + 6758 — 7268

12. 24 + 6 + 873 + 5 — 908

13. 18 + 24 + 865 — 907

14. 195 + 34 + 5764 — 5993

15. 12 + 345 + 6 + 7890 — 8253

16. 381 + 642 — 1023

17. 573 + 1007 — 1580

18. 21 + 63 + 95 + 72 — 251

19. 84 + 25 + 71 + 66 — 246

20. 34,795 + 6832 — 41,627

21. 28,007 + 6449 — 34,456

22. 7 + 68 + 112 + 4 + 19 — 210

23. 586 + 40 + 795 — 1421

24. 389 + 4054 + 2003 + 18 — 6464

25. 16 + 4721 + 8 + 754 — 5499

26. 5601 + 3599 + 2464 — 11,664

27. 3 + 17 + 98 + 5 + 256 — 379

28. 589 + 2309 + 9 + 876 — 3783

Objective: Subtract whole numbers.

Subtracting Whole Numbers

example E Without renaming

```
 4897
− 625
 4272
```

Subtract ones, tens, hundreds, and thousands.

Remind students to check their answers by adding.

example F With renaming

```
     1 12
  4 0 2̸ 2̸
−   8 3 7
        5
```

Rename to get 10 more ones. Subtract ones.

```
 3 10 1 12
  4̸ 0̸ 2̸ 2̸
−   8 3 7
        5
```

You need more tens. First rename to get 10 more hundreds.

```
    9 11
 3 1̸0̸ 1̸ 12
  4̸ 0̸ 2̸ 2̸
−   8 3 7
  3 1 8 5
```

Then rename to get 10 more tens. Subtract tens, hundreds, and thousands.

example G Horizontal form

43,541 − 1867 Point out that the first number is the minuend and goes on top when the problem is written vertically.

```
   2 14
    4̸ 13
     3̸ 11
  4 3̸ 5̸ 4̸ 1̸
−   1 8 6 7
  4 1 6 7 4
```

Write problem vertically, lining up columns correctly. Subtract. Rename as necessary.

exercises

set E

1. 847 − 235 = 612
2. 189 − 52 = 137
3. 2864 − 743 = 2121
4. 4783 − 251 = 4532
5. 28976 − 8006 = 20,970
6. 9427 − 8304 = 1123
7. 3974 − 1652 = 2322
8. 58206 − 17104 = 41,102
9. 4773 − 1022 = 3751
10. 6758 − 521 = 6237

set F

1. 1263 − 375 = 888
2. 481 − 57 = 424
3. 82 − 26 = 56
4. 7381 − 96 = 7285
5. 5192 − 304 = 4888
6. 871 − 85 = 786
7. 6253 − 470 = 5783
8. 924 − 38 = 886
9. 2613 − 893 = 1720
10. 94 − 75 = 19
11. 903 − 56 = 847
12. 260 − 172 = 88
13. 3105 − 921 = 2184
14. 1200 − 248 = 952

15. 836
− 798
38

16. 1824
− 957
867

17. 3204
− 597
2607

18. 5279
− 690
4589

19. 4182
− 495
3687

20. 273
− 195
78

21. 403
− 86
317

22. 3708
− 998
2710

23. 4700
− 89
4611

24. 2543
− 509
2034

25. 5768
− 4089
1679

26. 9101
− 472
8629

27. 28004
− 3608
24,396

28. 30112
− 9873
20,239

29. 4781
− 869
3912

30. 4000
− 2181
1819

31. 25712
− 6333
19,379

32. 8010
− 5478
2532

33. 47821
− 8939
38,882

34. 20510
− 7438
13,072

35. 34123
− 7777
26,346

36. 75490
− 682
74,808

37. 14352
− 6788
7564

38. 40702
− 957
39,745

39. 80004
− 4376
75,628

40. 21653
− 19407
2246

41. 60241
− 59946
295

42. 50982
− 23661
27,321

set G

1. 325 − 64 261

2. 95 − 37 58

3. 4215 − 87 4128

4. 531 − 46 485

5. 72 − 68 4

6. 127 − 35 92

7. 250 − 19 231

8. 698 − 59 639

9. 401 − 83 318

10. 100 − 70 30

11. 574 − 231 343

12. 8654 − 1333 7321

13. 5421 − 85 5336

14. 8524 − 372 8125

15. 4905 − 299 4606

16. 6471 − 583 5888

17. 8007 − 79 7928

18. 3508 − 752 2756

19. 86,054 − 54,681 31,373

20. 5300 − 61 5239

21. 18,406 − 9520 8886

22. 46,031 − 999 45,032

23. 73,020 − 24,561 48,459

24. 60,035 − 56,174 3861

25. 53,400 − 38,642 14,758

26. 60,000 − 9387 50,613

27. 45,011 − 21,539 23,472

28. 9201 − 8795 406

The applications on pages 13–19 may be used anytime after this lesson.

Objective: Compute following order of operations involving addition and subtraction.

Using Order of Operations

Without parentheses

example H

55 − 12 + 3

43 + 3

46

Add or subtract in order from left to right.

With parentheses

example I

15 − **(8 + 3)**

15 − **11**

4

First do operations inside parentheses. Then add or subtract.

Emphasize that operations inside parentheses should be performed first. You might give students exercises such as these:

Insert parentheses, if necessary, to make each statement true.

1. 25 - 16 - 8 = 17 [25 - (16 - 8)]
2. 31 - 10 - 9 = 12 [not necessary]
3. 42 + 6 - 3 = 45 [not necessary]
4. 17 - 12 + 3 = 2 [17 - (12 + 3)]
5. 70 - 30 + 5 = 35 [70 - (30 + 5)]
6. 61 - 57 - 18 = 22 [61 - (57 -18)]
7. 84 + 16 + 3 = 103 [not necessary]
8. 52 + 20 - 17 = 55 [not necessary]

exercises

set H

1. 32 − 7 − 18 7

2. 2 + 25 − 11 16

3. 13 − 10 + 22 25

4. 45 + 6 + 19 70

5. 60 − 3 − 17 40

6. 4 + 26 − 15 15

7. 37 − 10 + 5 32

8. 41 + 17 − 2 56

9. 75 − 35 − 16 24

10. 12 + 3 + 29 44

11. 63 − 27 + 4 40

12. 7 + 52 − 36 23

13. 81 + 13 − 9 85

14. 23 − 19 + 38 42

15. 64 − 35 − 12 17

16. 11 + 43 − 26 28

17. 6 + 55 − 9 52

18. 59 − 10 + 8 57

19. 16 + 53 − 60 9

20. 3 + 71 − 48 26

21. 85 − 23 − 51 11

22. 94 − 64 + 70 100

23. 19 + 380 − 84 315

24. 264 − 21 − 97 146

25. 79 + 126 − 35 170

Break Times are recreational puzzles or problems that occur in the skills lessons of each chapter. You can use them in a variety of ways—assign them to students who complete their regular work early; use them for class discussion; create a puzzle corner in your classroom; have puzzle-solving contests. The puzzles often do not require computational skills, so encourage students of all ability levels to try them.

set I

1. 25 − (17 − 4) 12

2. (28 − 16) + 5 17

3. (36 − 9) − 20 7

4. 24 − (7 + 6) 11

5. 51 + (10 − 8) 53

6. (35 − 20) − 9 6

7. (6 + 41) + 75 122

8. (83 − 64) + 5 24

9. 48 − (27 + 12) 9

10. (52 − 18) − 4 30

11. 9 + (18 + 140) 167

12. 39 − (51 − 48) 36

13. 66 − (23 + 15) 28

14. (12 + 71) − 46 37

15. 54 + (9 + 27) 90

16. (73 − 68) − 5 0

17. (35 + 14) + 62 111

18. 53 + (91 − 89) 55

19. (15 + 8) + 16 39

20. 50 − (97 − 68) 21

21. (131 + 25) + 6 162

22. 75 − (44 − 19) 50

23. 125 − (66 + 47) 12

24. (230 − 85) + 152 297

25. 99 + (780 − 371) 508

26. (602 − 98) + 75 579

27. 30 − (964 − 959) 25

28. 340 − (56 + 82) 202

BREAK TIME

What is the customer buying? House numbers

Objective: Solve addition and subtraction equations.

Solving Addition and Subtraction Equations

example J

Missing addend

Point out that the variable represents a number. Any letter could be used for the variable.

Find n.

$$n + 47 = 83$$

$$n + 47 - \mathbf{47} = 83 - \mathbf{47}$$

$$n = 36$$

47 is added to n. To undo the addition and get n by itself on one side of the equation, subtract 47 from $n + 47$. To keep the equation in balance, also subtract 47 from 83.

Check:
Does $36 + 47 = 83$? Yes

Check by substituting 36 for n in the original equation.

example K

Missing minuend

Find x.

$$x - 86 = 137$$

$$x - 86 + \mathbf{86} = 137 + \mathbf{86}$$

$$x = 223$$

86 is subtracted from x. To undo the subtraction, add 86 to $x - 86$. Also add 86 to 137.

Students should examine the problem before solving for x. Note that x has to be greater than 137.

Check:
Does $223 - 86 = 137$? Yes

Check by substituting 223 for x in the original equation.

Solving simple equations is introduced in this lesson and on pages 50–51 so that students will be able to work with variables when needed. Formulas, tables with variables, and equations are used in various chapters throughout the book.
A more complete study of solving equations is given in Chapter 14.

exercises set J

Find each missing number.

1. $x + 18 = 53$ $x = 35$
2. $245 + a = 565$ $a = 320$
3. $23 + n = 45$ $n = 22$
4. $54 = d + 29$ $d = 25$
5. $104 = 82 + b$ $b = 22$
6. $q + 35 = 96$ $q = 61$
7. $c + 19 = 40$ $c = 21$
8. $71 + t = 83$ $t = 12$
9. $g + 25 = 90$ $g = 65$
10. $18 + y = 72$ $y = 54$
11. $83 = h + 56$ $h = 27$
12. $41 = 28 + v$ $v = 13$
13. $k + 64 = 99$ $k = 35$
14. $17 + p = 45$ $p = 28$
15. $a + 38 = 56$ $a = 18$
16. $79 = z + 22$ $z = 57$
17. $w + 49 = 62$ $w = 13$
18. $53 + f = 100$ $f = 47$
19. $15 + x = 81$ $x = 66$
20. $120 + s = 400$ $s = 280$
21. $93 = r + 55$ $r = 38$
22. $42 + h = 257$ $h = 215$
23. $347 = b + 185$ $b = 162$
24. $817 = 753 + g$ $g = 64$
25. $k + 247 = 1258$ $k = 1011$

set K

Find each missing number.

1. $n - 52 = 87$ $n = 139$
2. $94 = g - 35$ $g = 129$
3. $k - 8 = 25$ $k = 33$
4. $d - 43 = 43$ $d = 86$
5. $68 = c - 15$ $c = 83$
6. $b - 25 = 13$ $b = 38$
7. $v - 37 = 7$ $v = 44$
8. $48 = w - 10$ $w = 58$
9. $31 = y - 59$ $y = 90$
10. $d - 66 = 24$ $d = 90$
11. $14 = f - 71$ $f = 85$
12. $z - 50 = 87$ $z = 137$
13. $r - 42 = 16$ $r = 58$
14. $n - 9 = 105$ $n = 114$
15. $38 = s - 23$ $s = 61$
16. $h - 75 = 48$ $h = 123$
17. $98 = j - 59$ $j = 157$
18. $p - 83 = 36$ $p = 119$
19. $100 = a - 3$ $a = 103$
20. $q - 55 = 74$ $q = 129$
21. $x - 864 = 21$ $x = 885$
22. $0 = y - 52$ $y = 52$
23. $185 = z - 56$ $z = 241$
24. $t - 347 = 899$ $t = 1246$
25. $283 = w - 62$ $w = 345$

BREAK TIME

Place the numbers 1 to 11 in the circles so that the sum of the three numbers in each line is 18.

Answers may vary.

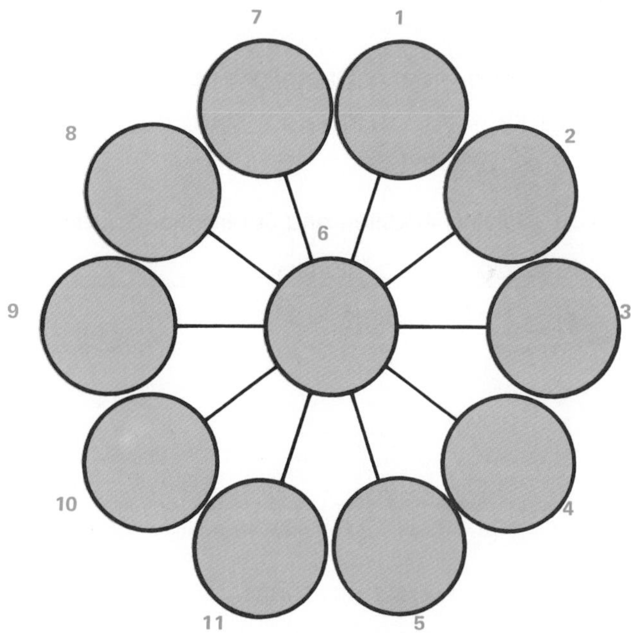

posttest

Number of test items - 11

Number missed	1	2	3	4	5
Percent correct	91	82	73	64	55

skill Adding Whole Numbers pages 4-5

A $\begin{array}{r} 125 \\ +304 \\ \hline \end{array}$ 429

B $\begin{array}{r} 596 \\ +217 \\ \hline \end{array}$ 813

C $\begin{array}{r} 93 \\ 454 \\ +186 \\ \hline \end{array}$ 733

D $237 + 82 + 569 + 98$ 986

skill Subtracting Whole Numbers pages 6-7

E $\begin{array}{r} 5368 \\ -\ 147 \\ \hline \end{array}$ 5221

F $\begin{array}{r} 3605 \\ -\ 927 \\ \hline \end{array}$ 2678

G $4312 - 523$ 3789

skill Using Order of Operations pages 8-9

H $8 + 53 - 6$ 55

I $27 - (9 + 5)$ 13

skill Solving Addition and Subtraction Equations pages 10-11

J Find x.

$x + 19 = 75$ $x = 56$

K Find y.

$y - 23 = 62$ $y = 85$

The Posttest parallels the Pretest, item for item. Students who miss problems on the Posttest can refer to the pages listed to find a worked-out example and a set of practice exercises.

Objective: Solve problems involving addition and subtraction of whole numbers.

In this lesson students compute the total number of calories and grams of carbohydrate for a given menu.

Counting Calories and Carbohydrates

Consumer and career applications occur in each chapter after the skills lessons. The applications use the skills from that chapter and from previous chapters.

Bob wants to lose some weight. His doctor told him to limit his food intake to about 1500 calories and 60 grams of carbohydrate daily.

1. Find the totals in each column for Monday and Tuesday.

Monday		
Food	Calories	Grams of carbohydrate
2 fried eggs	200	0
3 strips of bacon	240	0
1 glass of milk	160	12
1 buttered toast	110	11
1 hamburger patty	250	0
2 slices of cheese	220	2
1 glass of milk	160	12
2 pork chops	600	0
1 salad	150	3
1 serving of peas	60	9
1 ice cream bar	150	11
Totals	2300	60

Tuesday		
Food	Calories	Grams of carbohydrate
1 bowl of cereal	230	36
1 muffin	145	28
1 orange	77	19
1 jelly sandwich	220	50
1 glass of cola	73	18
1 bowl of soup	150	20
1 banana	80	21
1 macaroni dinner	201	34
1 lemonade	60	15
1 bowl of jello	80	19
1 candy bar	120	18
Totals	1436	278

2. On Monday, Bob was over his diet by how many calories? 800 calories

3. On Tuesday, he was over his diet by how many grams of carbohydrate? 218 grams

4. On Wednesday, Bob started to find the totals for his breakfast and lunch. For each day below, find how many calories and grams of carbohydrate Bob can have for supper.

Totals for breakfast and lunch

		Wednesday	Thursday	Friday	Saturday	Sunday
Calories		985	1075	850	1150	935
Grams		41	37	28	39	43
Supper	Calories	515	425	650	350	565
	Grams	19	23	32	21	17

Objective: Solve problems involving addition and subtraction of whole numbers.

In this lesson students find the difference in travel costs for various forms of transportation.

The method of travel chosen determines other expenses. These factors must be taken into consideration when planning an economical trip.

Comparing Costs of Traveling

Mr. and Mrs. Irwin are planning a trip from New York to Miami to visit friends. They want to find the most economical way to travel.

Approximate round-trip costs for two adults are listed below. Add to find the total cost for each form of transportation.

NEW YORK TO MIAMI

1. *Airplane*
   Tourist fare $283
   Meals No charge
   $283
2. *Train*
   Coach fare $252
   Meals $53
   $305
3. *Bus*
   Fare $196
   Meals $53
   $249
4. *Automobile*
   Gasoline and repairs $185
   Tolls $20
   Meals $66
   Lodging $40
   $311
5. Which form of travel is most economical? Bus

How much money would Mr. and Mrs. Irwin save traveling

6. by bus instead of by automobile? $62
7. by bus instead of by airplane? $34
8. by airplane instead of by train? $22
9. by train instead of by automobile? $6
10. It takes about 3 hours to travel from New York to Miami by airplane and about 48 hours by automobile. How much time would the Irwins save on a *round trip* by airplane instead of by automobile? 90 hours

Approximate round-trip costs for two adults are listed below. Find the total cost for each form of transportation.

WASHINGTON TO DENVER

11. *Airplane* (4 hours one way)
Tourist fare $385
Meals No charge
$385

12. *Train* (42 hours one way)
Coach fare $342
Meals $94
$436

13. *Bus* (44 hours one way)
Fare $307
Meals $64
$371

14. *Automobile* (72 hours one way)
Gasoline and repairs $234
Tolls $6
Meals $149
Lodging $80
$469

15. How much money could a couple save traveling by bus instead of by automobile? $98

16. How much time could a couple save on a round trip by bus instead of by automobile? 56 hours

Point out that on most vacations, time is a factor. Most people must balance time against expenses when planning a trip.

Approximate round-trip costs for two adults are listed below. Find the total cost for each form of transportation.

CHICAGO TO SAN FRANCISCO

17. *Airplane* (5 hours one way)
Tourist fare $443
Meals No charge
$443

18. *Train* (50 hours one way)
Coach fare $371
Meals $106
$477

19. *Bus* (53 hours one way)
Fare $350
Meals $119
$469

20. *Automobile* (120 hours one way)
Gasoline and repairs $299
Tolls $1
Meals $225
Lodging $160
$685

21. How much money could a couple save traveling by airplane instead of by automobile? $242

22. How much time could a couple save on a round trip by airplane instead of by automobile? 230 hours

Objective: Solve problems involving subtraction of whole numbers.

In this lesson students find the amount of real buying power for a certain income, when given the amounts of taxes and the decrease in buying power for one year.

Finding Real Buying Power

Each year your annual net income will buy about 10% less than it did the year before.

You may wish to discuss such terms as inflation and recession. Point out that during inflationary periods, the value of the dollar decreases.

"The motor is OPTIONAL. It's our way of keeping the price the same as last year."

Lee Parks had a gross income of $6000 last year. If her salary and taxes remain the same this year, you can find her **real buying power** by following these steps.

Gross income	$6000
Subtract federal tax	− 140
Income less federal tax	5860
Subtract social security tax	− 351
Net income	5509
Subtract 10% of net income for decrease in buying power	− 551
Real buying power	$4958

The federal income tax used in this lesson is based on 1975 tax rates for a joint return having $5000 in deductions and exemptions. The social security tax is figured with the 1975 rate and maximum income limit.

This year Lee's net income will be $5509. But $5509 this year will only buy goods and services worth $4958 last year.

Complete the table to find the real buying power for these incomes.

	Gross income	Federal tax	Income less federal tax	Social security tax	Net income	Decrease in buying power	Real buying power
	$6000	$140	$5860	$351	$5509	$551	$4958
1.	$7000	$290	$6710	$410	$6300	$630	$5670
2.	$8000	$450	$7550	$468	$7082	$708	$6374
3.	$9000	$620	$8380	$527	$7853	$785	$7068
4.	$10,000	$810	$9190	$585	$8605	$861	$7744
5.	$11,000	$1000	$10,000	$644	$9356	$936	$8420
6.	$12,000	$1190	$10,810	$702	$10,108	$1011	$9097
7.	$13,000	$1380	$11,620	$761	$10,859	$1086	$9773
8.	$14,000	$1600	$12,400	$820	$11,580	$1158	$10,422
9.	$15,000	$1820	$13,180	$820	$12,360	$1236	$11,124
10.	$16,000	$2040	$13,960	$820	$13,140	$1314	$11,826
11.	$17,000	$2260	$14,740	$820	$13,920	$1392	$12,528
12.	$18,000	$2510	$15,490	$820	$14,670	$1467	$13,203
13.	$19,000	$2760	$16,240	$820	$15,420	$1542	$13,878
14.	$20,000	$3010	$16,990	$820	$16,170	$1617	$14,553

Objective: Solve problems involving addition and subtraction of whole numbers.

In this lesson students solve problems involving degree days and deliveries of heating oil.

See the Careers Chart beginning on page 420 for more jobs and other information about this career cluster.

Career: Dispatcher

Career Cluster: Business Detail

Ms. Liester is a dispatcher for a fuel company. In order to determine when heating oil needs to be delivered, she uses a unit called a **degree day.**

If the average daily temperature is less than 18 degrees Celsius (18°C), the number of degree days is found by using this formula.

$$18 - \text{Average temperature} = \text{Number of degree days}$$

On October 5 the average temperature was 12°C.

$18 - 12 = 6$

Six degree days were counted for October 5.

You might want to use pages xiv and xv in the front of the pupil's book for a quick review of metric units of measure. A more complete development of the metric system occurs in Chapter 6.

Find the number of degree days for each date.

	Date	Average temperature	
1.	October 7	13°C	5 degree days
2.	October 8	17°C	1 degree day
3.	October 9	16°C	2 degree days
4.	October 10	11°C	7 degree days
5.	October 11	4°C	14 degree days
6.	October 12	9°C	9 degree days
7.	October 13	0°C	18 degree days

8. What was the total number of degree days for October 7–13? 56 degree days

Ms. Liester begins to record degree days on the day that a customer receives oil. After about 440 degree days, she dispatches a truck to deliver oil again.

9. Here are the number of degree days recorded from January 4 to January 31. Find the total.

Week of	Degree days
January 4–10	75
January 11–17	120
January 18–24	109
January 25–31	124
	428

10. The Taylor home received heating oil on January 4. After January 31, how many more degree days will be recorded before oil is delivered again? 12 degree days

11. The Garcias received oil January 18. After January 31, how many more degree days will be recorded before oil is delivered again? 207 degree days

Ms. Liester uses truck drivers' tickets to find the amount of heating oil that has been delivered.

Each truck has a meter that tells the number of liters of oil left in the truck. The driver reads the meter after each delivery.

This meter is called a Preset Quantrol meter. It works like an odometer on a car, but it counts backward from maximum quantity to minimum quantity.

Find the amount of oil delivered to each address and the total amount delivered by each truck.

The amounts of oil delivered are given in liters.

	Truck 31			
	Address	Meter before	Meter after	Amount delivered
12.	514 Locust St	9475	8417	1058
13.	268 Locust St.	8417	7605	812
14.	301 Holly. Ave	7605	6671	934
15.	915 Maple Ave	6671	5968	703
16.	362 Spruce Dr.	5968	4833	1135
17.	890 Pine St	4833	3481	1352
18.			Total	5994

	Truck 56			
	Address	Meter before	Meter after	Amount delivered
19.	2910 Ellis	8320	7348	972
20.	1415 Frolic	7348	6050	1298
21.	1508 Baldwin	6050	5067	983
22.	2802 Ellis	5067	3972	1095
23.	500 Grand	3972	3263	709
24.	652 Lewis	3263	2276	987
25.			Total	6044

Number of test items - 18

Number missed	1	2	3	4	5	6	7	8	9
Percent correct	94	89	83	78	72	67	61	56	50

Chapter 1

The letter in color next to a test item indicates the skills problem type that is being tested.

A **1.** 173 + 214 = 387

B **2.** 596 + 348 = 944

C **3.** 12 + 998 + 47 = 1057

D **4.** 3651 + 7 + 92 + 458 4208

E **5.** 5983 − 3842 = 2141

F **6.** 3017 − 1428 = 1589

G **7.** 35,162 − 26,704 8458

H **8.** 74 − 26 + 31 79

I **9.** 27 − (65 − 58) 20

Find each missing number.

J **10.** $37 + d = 72$ $d = 35$

K **11.** $t - 21 = 17$ $t = 38$

The Chapter Test covers both the skills lessons and the applications in a chapter. On this test, items 1-11 correspond to problem types A-K in Chapter 1. Test items 12-18 correspond to the consumer and career applications found on pages 13-19.

For each Chapter Test in the students' book, there is an alternate form of the test in the *Tests and Record Forms: Duplicating Masters.* The alternate form matches the Chapter Test, item for item. The alternate form of the Chapter 1 Test can be found on pages 1-2 of the masters.

12. Sadie recorded her calorie intake for one day. Find the total number of calories.

Food	Calories
1 doughnut	233
1 glass of milk	160
1 ham sandwich	216
1 apple	80
10 potato chips	114
1 glass of cola	73
1 hamburger	250
1 serving of corn	88
1 salad	150
3 cookies	120

1484 calories

13. Find the total cost of this automobile trip.

Gasoline	$195
Repairs	$48
Tolls	$8
Lodging	$75

$326

Fill in the missing numbers to find the real buying power for a gross income of $22,000.

Gross income	$22000
Federal tax	− 3540
14. Income less federal tax	$18,460
Social security tax	− 820
15. Net income	$17,640
Decrease in buying power	− 1764
16. Real buying power	$15,876

17. In March, 279 degree days were recorded. This is how many less than 440 degree days? 161 degree days

18. The meter on an oil truck read 2645 liters before an oil delivery and 1798 liters after the delivery. How many liters of oil were delivered? 847 liters

Chapter 2
Multiplying Whole Numbers

pretest

Number of test items - 15

Number missed	1	2	3	4	5	6	7
Percent correct	93	87	80	73	67	60	53

skill Multiplying by Multiples of 10, 100, and 1000 pages 22–23

A 30×1000 30,000

B 200×60 12,000

skill Multiplying with One-digit Multipliers pages 24–25

C 62×4 248

D 27×6 162

E 5034×8 40,272

F 6×472 2832

skill Multiplying with Two-digit Multipliers pages 26–27

G 38×40 1520

H 36×24 864

I 6084×27 164,268

J 32×156 4992

skill Multiplying with Three-digit Multipliers pages 28–29

K 847×600 508,200

L 282×109 30,738

M 653×274 178,922

skill Using Order of Operations pages 30–31

N $6(9) + 8(7)$ 110

O $25 - 6(1 + 2)$ 7

See page T16 for additional notes on Chapter 2.

Objective: Multiply multiples of powers of 10.

Multiplying by Multiples of 10, 100, and 1000

example A

Multiplying by a power of 10

70 × 1000

7 0 × 1 0 0 0 = 7 0, 0 0 0

1 zero — 3 zeros — 4 zeros

The number of zeros in the product equals the total number of zeros in the factors.

example B

Multiplying by multiples of powers of 10

6000 × 400

6 0 0 0 × 4 0 0 = 2, 4 0 0, 0 0 0

3 zeros — 2 zeros — 5 zeros

Multiply the nonzero digits. Then write as many zeros in the product as there are in all the factors.

exercises

Encourage students to do the exercises in sets A and B mentally without rewriting them in vertical form.

set A

1. 100 × 80
8000
2. 6 × 1000
6000
3. 100 × 10
1000
4. 10 × 5
50
5. 300 × 1000
300,000
6. 10 × 10
100
7. 100 × 9
900
8. 100 × 100
10,000
9. 60 × 100
6000
10. 1000 × 2
2000
11. 800 × 1000
800,000
12. 100 × 7000
700,000
13. 1000 × 10
10,000
14. 10 × 100
1000
15. 1000 × 4
4000
16. 80 × 10
800
17. 100 × 400
40,000
18. 1000 × 100
100,000
19. 10 × 8
80
20. 1000 × 1000
1,000,000
21. 100 × 6000
600,000
22. 3 × 100
300
23. 40 × 1000
40,000
24. 1000 × 500
500,000
25. 10 × 10,000
100,000
26. 10,000 × 10,000
10,000,000
27. 100 × 5
500
28. 700 × 100
70,000
29. 1000 × 25
25,000
30. 100 × 10,000
1,000,000
31. 10 × 2000
20,000
32. 300 × 10
3000
33. 100 × 30
3000
34. 56 × 100
5600
35. 100 × 25
2500
36. 1000 × 10,000
10,000,000
37. 10 × 4000
40,000
38. 68 × 10,000
680,000
39. 1000 × 50
50,000
40. 10,000 × 10
100,000
41. 100 × 74
7400
42. 90 × 100
9000
43. 10 × 200
2000
44. 10,000 × 100
1,000,000
45. 7000 × 1000
7,000,000
46. 9 × 10,000
90,000
47. 1000 × 300
300,000
48. 100 × 63
6300
49. 2000 × 1000
2,000,000
50. 10,000 × 32
320,000

set B

1. 700×50
35,000
2. 6000×4
24,000
3. 80×90
7200
4. 3×50
150
5. 40×800
32,000
6. 7000×30
210,000
7. 400×600
240,000
8. 900×4
3600
9. 600×70
42,000
10. 7×9000
63,000
11. 60×30
1800
12. 200×8
1600
13. 50×9000
450,000
14. 7×30
210
15. 300×700
210,000
16. 20×500
10,000
17. 40×20
800
18. 2000×60
120,000
19. 3000×8
24,000
20. $5 \times 30{,}000$
150,000
21. 800×900
720,000
22. 70×80
5600
23. 90×4000
360,000
24. 2×6000
12,000
25. 40×7
280
26. 800×80
64,000
27. 400×500
200,000
28. 60×60
3600

29. 700×800
560,000
30. 9000×3
27,000
31. 70×7000
490,000
32. 600×4
2400
33. 2000×7000
14,000,000
34. 90×500
45,000
35. 4×3000
12,000
36. 50×20
1000
37. 6000×30
180,000
38. $90 \times 40{,}000$
3,600,000
39. 8×200
1600
40. 2000×9000
18,000,000
41. 60×3
180
42. 20×4000
80,000
43. 8000×5
40,000
44. $9 \times 50{,}000$
450,000
45. 600×400
240,000
46. 700×50
35,000
47. 4000×200
800,000
48. 600×3
1800
49. 5000×7000
35,000,000
50. $700 \times 80{,}000$
56,000,000
51. 6000×400
2,400,000
52. $20 \times 50{,}000$
1,000,000
53. $700 \times 30{,}000$
21,000,000
54. $80{,}000 \times 40$
3,200,000
55. $300 \times 80{,}000$
24,000,000
56. $900 \times 20{,}000$
18,000,000

BREAK TIME

How can you connect these links to make a 15-link chain by opening and closing just 3 links? See below.

Break Time: Open the first 3 links and use them to connect the other sets of links.

Objective: Multiply whole numbers with a one-digit multiplier.

Multiplying with One-digit Multipliers

example C
Two-digit multiplicand, without renaming

$$\begin{array}{r} 62 \\ \times\ 3 \\ \hline 186 \end{array}$$

$3 \times 2 = 6$
$3 \times 6 = 18$

example D
Two-digit multiplicand, with renaming

$$\begin{array}{r} 56 \\ \times\ 8 \\ \hline 448 \end{array}$$

$8 \times 6 = 48$ Carry 4.
$8 \times 5 = 40$ $40 + 4 = 44$

example E
Three or more digits in multiplicand

$$\begin{array}{r} 5038 \\ \times\ \ \ 9 \\ \hline 45342 \end{array}$$

$9 \times 8 = 72$ Carry 7.
$9 \times 3 = 27$ $27 + 7 = 34$
Carry 3. $9 \times 0 = 0$ $0 + 3 = 3$
$9 \times 5 = 45$

You might demonstrate other problems involving zeros before students do sets E and F.

example F
Horizontal form

7×9512

$$\begin{array}{r} 9512 \\ \times\ \ \ 7 \\ \hline 66584 \end{array}$$

Write problem vertically.
Multiply.

Students who make a lot of errors or work very slowly might benefit from additional oral or written work on multiplication basic facts.

exercises

set C

1. 92×4 = 368
2. 73×3 = 219
3. 64×2 = 128
4. 31×5 = 155
5. 72×2 = 144
6. 83×2 = 166
7. 41×3 = 123
8. 24×2 = 48
9. 81×4 = 324
10. 13×3 = 39

set D

1. 25×7 = 175
2. 68×4 = 272
3. 55×6 = 330
4. 32×9 = 288
5. 47×7 = 329
6. 38×6 = 228
7. 99×4 = 396
8. 35×3 = 105
9. 64×9 = 576
10. 85×7 = 595
11. 29×2 = 58
12. 38×6 = 228
13. 23×7 = 161
14. 94×6 = 564
15. 29×5 = 145
16. 38×4 = 152

set E

1. 5714 × 8
45,712

2. 836 × 4
3344

3. 927 × 3
2781

4. 7519 × 7
52,633

5. 805 × 2
1610

6. 53907 × 9
485,163

7. 670 × 3
2010

8. 6024 × 5
30,120

9. 2896 × 7
20,272

10. 302 × 6
1812

11. 9703 × 4
38,812

12. 842 × 8
6736

13. 87714 × 9
789,426

14. 956 × 2
1912

15. 45362 × 4
181,448

16. 7056 × 5
35,280

17. 347 × 3
1041

18. 2009 × 6
12,054

19. 37827 × 9
340,443

20. 885 × 3
2655

21. 6513 × 7
45,591

22. 9006 × 5
45,030

23. 677 × 4
2708

24. 44328 × 2
88,656

25. 8893 × 5
44,465

26. 409 × 6
2454

27. 73524 × 8
588,192

28. 804067 × 9
7,236,603

set F

1. 6 × 4257
25,542
2. 98 × 3
294
3. 8 × 287
2296
4. 2043 × 7
14,301
5. 9 × 67
603
6. 8 × 355
2840
7. 3 × 82943
248,829
8. 53 × 5
265
9. 2 × 9507
19,014
10. 8 × 674
5392
11. 57621 × 4
230,484
12. 309 × 8
2472
13. 7 × 45
315
14. 34572 × 6
207,432
15. 926 × 6
5556
16. 3 × 8243
24,729
17. 62 × 2
124
18. 4 × 94880
379,520
19. 70409 × 8
563,272
20. 5 × 747
3735
21. 7 × 88
616
22. 4 × 5764
23,056
23. 263 × 2
526
24. 9 × 60028
540,252
25. 56 × 8
448
26. 6 × 9299
55,794
27. 64382 × 3
193,146
28. 5 × 71
355
29. 804 × 6
4824
30. 9 × 526
4734
31. 5 × 8003
40,015
32. 90407 × 4
361,628
33. 6 × 31107
186,642
34. 5 × 925
4625
35. 3 × 35
105
36. 6 × 7562
45,372
37. 881 × 5
4405
38. 4 × 28514
114,056
39. 4821 × 7
33,747
40. 5 × 42
210
41. 8765 × 9
78,885
42. 67 × 5
335
43. 603 × 4
2412
44. 7 × 9440
66,080
45. 9 × 64835
583,515
46. 289 × 3
867
47. 5 × 3175
15,875
48. 4 × 54
216
49. 19823 × 6
118,938
50. 7 × 480
3360
51. 6070 × 8
48,560
52. 52614 × 5
263,070
53. 6 × 3829
22,974
54. 687 × 8
5496
55. 4 × 69843
279,372
56. 5 × 71566
357,830

The applications on pages 33-35 may be used anytime after this lesson.

Multiplying with Two-digit Multipliers

example G

Two-digit multiplicand, zero in multiplier

```
  57
× 30
1710
```

Write 0 in the ones place. Then multiply 3 and 57.

example H

Two-digit multiplicand

Students need not write zero in the ones place if they are not used to doing so.

```
  36
× 28
 288   [8 × 36
 720   [20 × 36  Write 0 in the ones place. Then multiply 2 and 36.
1008   [Add 288 and 720.
```

example I

Three or more digits in multiplicand

```
  4705
×   97
 32935   [7 × 4705
423450   [90 × 4705  Write 0 in the ones place. Then multiply 9 and 4705.
456385   [Add 32935 and 423450.
```

example J

Horizontal form

45 × 629

```
  629
×  45
 3145
25160
28305
```

Write problem vertically. Multiply.

exercises

set G

1. 65 × 70 (4550)
2. 59 × 30 (1770)
3. 43 × 60 (2580)
4. 85 × 20 (1700)
5. 76 × 90 (6840)
6. 57 × 50 (2850)
7. 68 × 40 (2720)
8. 95 × 90 (8550)
9. 62 × 30 (1860)
10. 51 × 80 (4080)

set H

1. 84 × 29 (2436)
2. 54 × 39 (2106)
3. 45 × 18 (810)
4. 36 × 83 (2988)
5. 38 × 24 (912)
6. 28 × 75 (2100)
7. 45 × 62 (2790)
8. 61 × 18 (1098)
9. 49 × 22 (1078)
10. 95 × 37 (3515)
11. 53 × 94 (4982)
12. 32 × 47 (1504)
13. 64 × 53 (3392)
14. 25 × 48 (1200)
15. 77 × 42 (3234)
16. 94 × 29 (2726)

set I

1. 594 × 78
   46,332
2. 8465 × 27
   228,555
3. 21957 × 15
   329,355
4. 9070 × 64
   580,480
5. 673 × 29
   19,517
6. 3880 × 93
   360,840
7. 4563 × 52
   237,276
8. 958 × 37
   35,446
9. 6304 × 46
   289,984
10. 80006 × 68
    5,440,408
11. 407 × 36
    14,652
12. 3281 × 24
    78,744
13. 682 × 19
    12,958
14. 42763 × 75
    3,207,225
15. 4682 × 83
    388,606
16. 291 × 25
    7275
17. 89752 × 36
    3,231,072
18. 3504 × 38
    133,152
19. 603 × 87
    52,461
20. 7009 × 52
    364.468
21. 827 × 73
    60,371
22. 78623 × 65
    5,110,495
23. 564 × 28
    15,792
24. 6507 × 34
    221,238
25. 322144 × 56
    18,040,064
26. 677 × 48
    32,496
27. 91508 × 97
    8,876,276
28. 82463 × 39
    3,216,057

set J

1. 37 × 527
   19,499
2. 93 × 42
   3906
3. 58 × 6415
   372,070
4. 63 × 806
   50,778
5. 94 × 3080
   289,520
6. 87 × 58
   5046
7. 60 × 7624
   457,440
8. 23,061 × 51
   1,176,111
9. 29 × 9271
   268,859
10. 45 × 490
    22,050
11. 52 × 76
    3952
12. 83 × 5813
    482,479
13. 56,104 × 20
    1,122,080
14. 66 × 753
    49,698
15. 64 × 57
    3648
16. 30 × 8563
    256,890
17. 95 × 9218
    875,710
18. 68 × 30,009
    2,040,612
19. 700 × 54
    37,800
20. 88 × 70
    6160
21. 26 × 95,324
    2,478,424
22. 6007 × 83
    498,581
23. 90 × 80,711
    7,263,990
24. 46 × 56
    2576
25. 642 × 29
    18,618
26. 70,602 × 50
    3,530,100
27. 57 × 3456
    196,992
28. 95 × 65
    6080
29. 20 × 875
    17,500
30. 85 × 2014
    171,190
31. 21 × 563
    11,823
32. 88,007 × 45
    3,960,315
33. 76 × 3833
    291,308
34. 23 × 93
    2139
35. 906 × 60
    54,360
36. 38 × 30,082
    1,143,116
37. 43,152 × 62
    2,675.424
38. 19 × 14
    266
39. 80 × 757
    60,560
40. 70,900 × 35
    2,481,500
41. 67 × 2025
    135,675
42. 884 × 18
    15,912
43. 75 × 98,514
    7,388,550
44. 94 × 56
    5264
45. 2919 × 70
    204,330
46. 14 × 299
    4186
47. 83 × 600
    49,800
48. 73,620 × 11
    809,820
49. 30 × 563
    16,890
50. 97 × 2654
    257,438
51. 39 × 89
    3471
52. 16 × 5770
    92,320
53. 378 × 40
    15,120
54. 81 × 58,140
    4,709,340
55. 7843 × 66
    517,638
56. 90 × 52
    4680

The applications on pages 38-39
may be used anytime after this lesson.

Objective: Multiply whole numbers with a three-digit multiplier.

Multiplying with Three-digit Multipliers

example K

Three-digit multiplicand, two zeros in multiplier

$$\begin{array}{r} 629 \\ \times 400 \\ \hline 251600 \end{array}$$

Write 0 in the ones place and tens place. Multiply 4 and 629.

example L

Three-digit multiplicand, one zero in multiplier

$$\begin{array}{r} 852 \\ \times 706 \\ \hline 5112 \\ 596400 \\ \hline 601512 \end{array}$$

- 5112: 6 × 852
- 596400: 700 × 852 Write 0 in the ones place and tens place. Then multiply 7 and 852.
- 601512: Add.

example M

Three or more digits in multiplicand, no zeros in multiplier

$$\begin{array}{r} 421 \\ \times 698 \\ \hline 3368 \\ 37890 \\ 252600 \\ \hline 293858 \end{array}$$

- 3368: 8 × 421
- 37890: 90 × 421 Write 0 in the ones place. Then multiply 9 and 421.
- 252600: 600 × 421 Write 0 in the ones place and tens place. Then multiply 6 and 421.
- 293858: Add.

exercises

set K

1. 578 × 300 — 173,400
2. 643 × 700 — 450,100
3. 827 × 500 — 413,500
4. 905 × 400 — 362,000
5. 658 × 900 — 592,200
6. 760 × 800 — 608,000
7. 824 × 600 — 494,400
8. 993 × 300 — 297,900
9. 428 × 700 — 299,600
10. 706 × 900 — 635,400

set L

1. 673 × 304 — 204,592
2. 892 × 940 — 838,480
3. 470 × 805 — 378,350
4. 629 × 106 — 66,674
5. 804 × 301 — 242,004
6. 799 × 920 — 735,080
7. 523 × 607 — 317,461
8. 622 × 806 — 501,332
9. 714 × 290 — 207,060
10. 683 × 730 — 498,590
11. 408 × 170 — 69,360
12. 549 × 990 — 543,510
13. 278 × 603 — 167,634
14. 634 × 505 — 320,170
15. 857 × 720 — 617,040
16. 253 × 409 — 103,477

set M

1. 625 × 914
571,250

2. 4826 × 352
1,698,752

3. 957 × 674
645,018

4. 309 × 315
97,335

5. 675 × 938
633,150

6. 1824 × 742
1,353,408

7. 980 × 945
926,100

8. 652 × 386
251,672

9. 1095 × 417
456,615

10. 6803 × 824
5,605,672

11. 11221 × 399
4,477,179

12. 655 × 428
280,340

13. 472 × 826
389,872

14. 115 × 728
83,720

15. 10201 × 346
3,529,546

16. 222 × 376
83,472

17. 755 × 198
149,490

18. 815 × 926
754,690

19. 82631 × 997
82,383,107

20. 76120 × 325
24,739,000

21. 7010 × 226
1,584,260

22. 5629 × 374
2,105,246

23. 242 × 898
217,316

24. 6204 × 342
2,121,768

25. 7003 × 731
5,119,193

26. 209 × 465
97,185

27. 3815 × 723
2,758,245

28. 58614 × 978
57,324,492

BREAK TIME

Here are 17 straws.

Move 3 straws to make 5 squares that are the same size. Answers may vary. A sample answer is given below left.

Start over again. This time remove 5 straws so that exactly 3 squares remain.

Answers may vary. A sample answer is given below left.

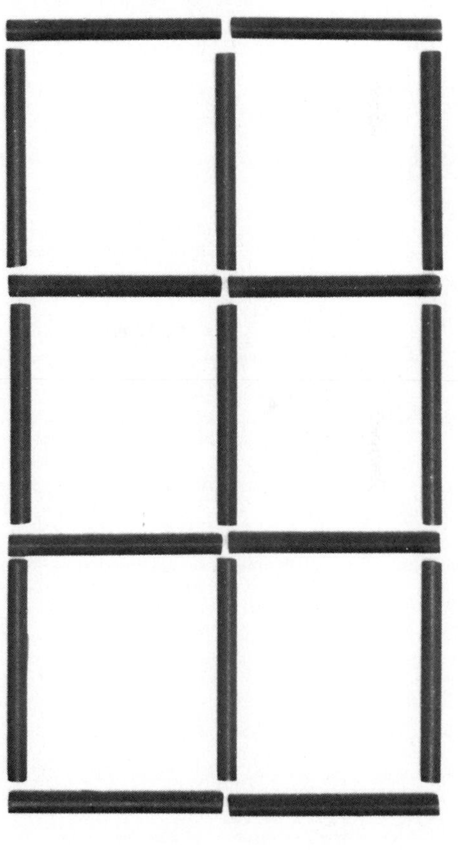

The applications on pages 36-37 may be used anytime after this lesson.

Objective: Compute following order of operations involving addition, subtraction, and multiplication.

Using Order of Operations

example N Without operations inside parentheses

$32 - 7(3)$

Follow these general rules.

First do all operations inside parentheses.
Then do remaining multiplications.
Then do remaining additions and subtractions.

$32 - 7(3)$	Do multiplication.
$32 - 21$	Do subtraction.
11	

Point out that if the subtraction was done first, the answer would be 75.

example O With operations inside parentheses

$6(5) + 4(9 - 2)$	Follow rules in example N. Do operations inside parentheses.
$6(5) + 4(7)$	Do multiplications.
$30 + 28$	Do addition.
58	

Order of operations involving addition and subtraction was introduced in Chapter 1, pages 8-9. Here multiplication is included. In Chapter 3, pages 48-49, division is included. More work on order of operations is provided in Chapters 13 and 14.

exercises set N

1. $12 + 7 - 3(2)$ 13
2. $4 + 9 + 6(5)$ 43
3. $50 - 2(3)(4)$ 26
4. $6(7) - 5(4)$ 22
5. $7(2)(4) - 9$ 47
6. $8 + 9(2) + 4$ 30
7. $8(5) - 6(3)$ 22
8. $5(4)(3) + 6$ 66
9. $2 + 3(5) + 1$ 18
10. $3 + 3(6)$ 21
11. $8(7) - 2$ 54
12. $28 + 15 - 3(7)$ 22
13. $6(9) - 2(7)$ 40
14. $9(2)(4) - 22$ 50
15. $10(4) - 13 + 6$ 33
16. $15 + 6(7) - 1$ 56
17. $14 + 7(6)(3)$ 140
18. $9(7) - 6(3)$ 45
19. $2 + 4(6) - 7$ 19
20. $14 + 2(30)$ 74
21. $20(4) - 3(2)(3)$ 62
22. $35 - 3(2)$ 29
23. $5(2)(7) + 4(3) - 6$ 76
24. $6(2) + 5(2) + 6$ 28
25. $9 + 3(2)(4) + 7(2)$ 47

set O

1. $30 - 4(8 - 2)$ 6
2. $25 - (2 + 4)3$ 7
3. $4(3 + 2) + 9$ 29
4. $5(7 + 6 + 8)$ 105
5. $(6 + 4)3$ 30
6. $2(8 + 5)$ 26
7. $24 - 2(6 + 3)$ 6
8. $(14 + 2)30$ 480
9. $2(7 - 3) + 6$ 14
10. $6(7 + 9)$ 96
11. $3(9 + 16 - 2)$ 69
12. $(42 - 9 - 8)6$ 150
13. $80 - 8(13 - 9)$ 48
14. $65 - 4(21 - 9)$ 17
15. $55 - (16 - 8)2$ 39
16. $18 + 7(32 - 6)$ 200
17. $5(18 - 9) - 42$ 3
18. $26 - 3(5 + 1)$ 8
19. $3(8 + 4) - 20$ 16
20. $5(14 + 7) - 12$ 93
21. $35 - 7(8 - 5)$ 14
22. $54 - 2(15 - 8)$ 40
23. $27 - 2(4 - 1)$ 21
24. $3(2) + 8(4 + 1)$ 46
25. $5(4) - (7 + 2)$ 11
26. $12 + (8 - 3)7 - 20$ 27
27. $(4 + 3)2 + (9 - 1)5$ 54
28. $2(6 + 3) - (7 + 1)$ 10

BREAK TIME

The line on the clock face below separates the numbers into 2 groups. The sum of the numbers in each group is not the same.

Copy the clock face. Draw a line across it so that the sum of the numbers in each group is the same. See below.

Copy the face again. This time draw 2 lines to form 3 groups so that the sum of the numbers in each group is the same. See below.

Each sum is 39. Each sum is 26.

$$\begin{array}{r} 9 \\ 10 \\ 11 \\ 12 \\ +\ 1 \\ \hline 43 \end{array} \qquad \begin{array}{r} 2 \\ 3 \\ 4 \\ 5 \\ 6 \\ 7 \\ +8 \\ \hline 35 \end{array}$$

Note that the sum of the numbers 1 through 12 is 78.
39 + 39 = 78 and 26 + 26 + 26 = 78.

posttest

Number of test items - 15

Number missed	1	2	3	4	5	6	7
Percent correct	93	87	80	73	67	60	53

skill Multiplying by Multiples of 10, 100, and 1000 pages 22-23

A 1000×60 60,000 B 300×400 120,000

skill Multiplying with One-digit Multipliers pages 24-25

C 82×3 246 D 38×4 152 E 7609×3 22,827 F 4×1829 7316

skill Multiplying with Two-digit Multipliers pages 26-27

G 63×50 3150 H 95×37 3515 I 7123×46 327,658 J 27×283 7641

skill Multiplying with Three-digit Multipliers pages 28-29

K 584×700 408,800 L 638×903 576,114 M 531×495 262,845

skill Using Order of Operations pages 30-31

N $45 - 3(6)$ 27 O $2(10) - 3(5 - 1)$ 8

Objective: Solve problems involving multiplication of whole numbers.

In this lesson students complete score cards for a game of Triple Yahtzee®.

Finding Game Scores

Dee and Barbara played Triple Yahtzee®. The object of the game is to get the highest score by rolling 5 dice and filling in various categories. Complete the score cards to find the winner.

By working down the columns and reading the directions at the left, students should be able to complete the score cards.

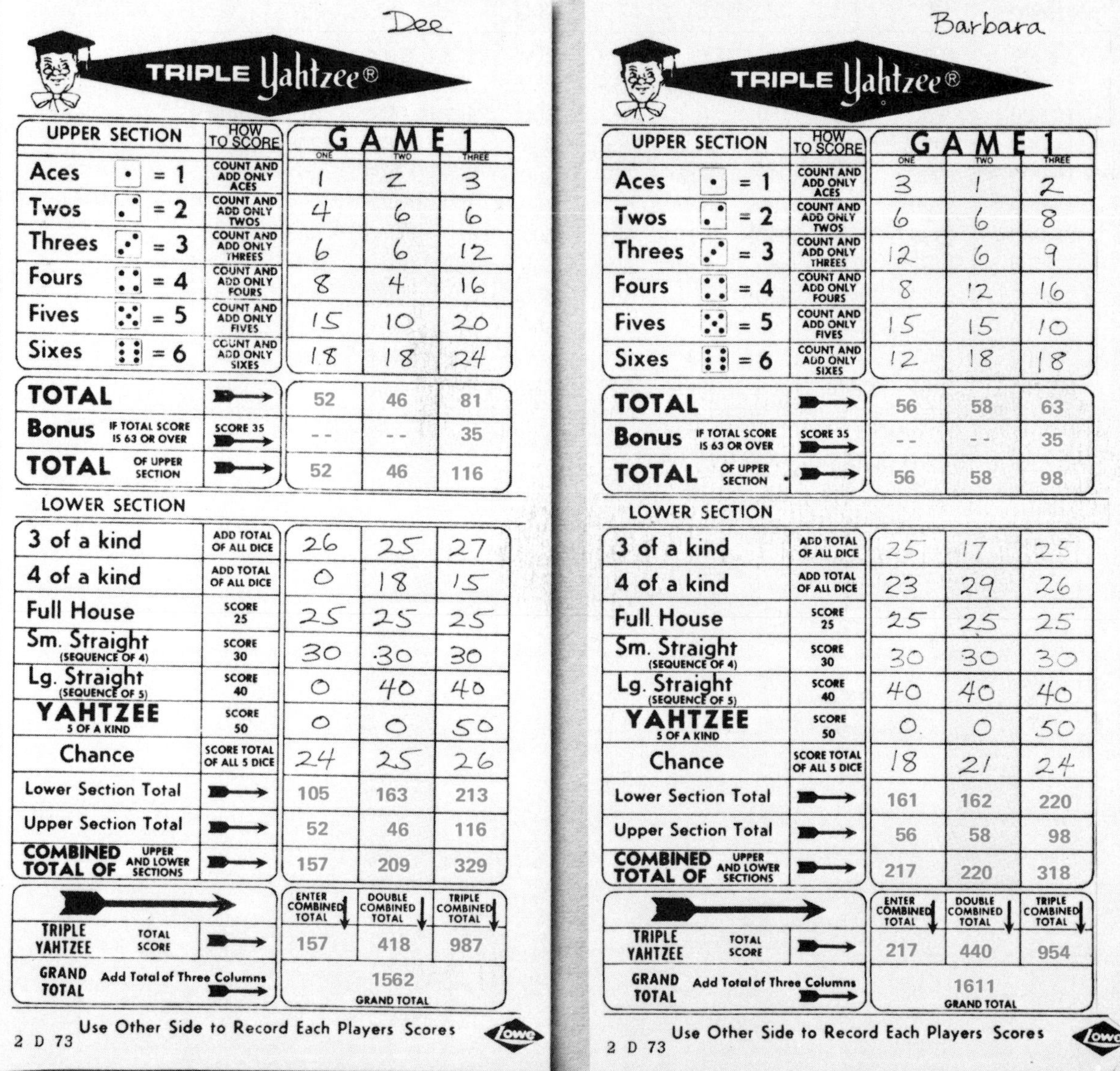

Dee

TRIPLE Yahtzee®

UPPER SECTION	HOW TO SCORE	GAME 1 ONE	TWO	THREE
Aces ⚀ = 1	COUNT AND ADD ONLY ACES	1	2	3
Twos ⚁ = 2	COUNT AND ADD ONLY TWOS	4	6	6
Threes ⚂ = 3	COUNT AND ADD ONLY THREES	6	6	12
Fours ⚃ = 4	COUNT AND ADD ONLY FOURS	8	4	16
Fives ⚄ = 5	COUNT AND ADD ONLY FIVES	15	10	20
Sixes ⚅ = 6	COUNT AND ADD ONLY SIXES	18	18	24
TOTAL	→	52	46	81
Bonus IF TOTAL SCORE IS 63 OR OVER	SCORE 35 →	--	--	35
TOTAL OF UPPER SECTION	→	52	46	116
LOWER SECTION				
3 of a kind	ADD TOTAL OF ALL DICE	26	25	27
4 of a kind	ADD TOTAL OF ALL DICE	0	18	15
Full House	SCORE 25	25	25	25
Sm. Straight (SEQUENCE OF 4)	SCORE 30	30	30	30
Lg. Straight (SEQUENCE OF 5)	SCORE 40	0	40	40
YAHTZEE 5 OF A KIND	SCORE 50	0	0	50
Chance	SCORE TOTAL OF ALL 5 DICE	24	25	26
Lower Section Total	→	105	163	213
Upper Section Total	→	52	46	116
COMBINED TOTAL OF UPPER AND LOWER SECTIONS	→	157	209	329
→		ENTER COMBINED TOTAL ↓	DOUBLE COMBINED TOTAL ↓	TRIPLE COMBINED TOTAL ↓
TRIPLE YAHTZEE TOTAL SCORE	→	157	418	987
GRAND TOTAL	Add Total of Three Columns →	1562 GRAND TOTAL		

2 D 73 Use Other Side to Record Each Players Scores Lowe

Barbara

TRIPLE Yahtzee®

UPPER SECTION	HOW TO SCORE	GAME 1 ONE	TWO	THREE
Aces ⚀ = 1	COUNT AND ADD ONLY ACES	3	1	2
Twos ⚁ = 2	COUNT AND ADD ONLY TWOS	6	6	8
Threes ⚂ = 3	COUNT AND ADD ONLY THREES	12	6	9
Fours ⚃ = 4	COUNT AND ADD ONLY FOURS	8	12	16
Fives ⚄ = 5	COUNT AND ADD ONLY FIVES	15	15	10
Sixes ⚅ = 6	COUNT AND ADD ONLY SIXES	12	18	18
TOTAL	→	56	58	63
Bonus IF TOTAL SCORE IS 63 OR OVER	SCORE 35 →	--	--	35
TOTAL OF UPPER SECTION	→	56	58	98
LOWER SECTION				
3 of a kind	ADD TOTAL OF ALL DICE	25	17	25
4 of a kind	ADD TOTAL OF ALL DICE	23	29	26
Full House	SCORE 25	25	25	25
Sm. Straight (SEQUENCE OF 4)	SCORE 30	30	30	30
Lg. Straight (SEQUENCE OF 5)	SCORE 40	40	40	40
YAHTZEE 5 OF A KIND	SCORE 50	0	0	50
Chance	SCORE TOTAL OF ALL 5 DICE	18	21	24
Lower Section Total	→	161	162	220
Upper Section Total	→	56	58	98
COMBINED TOTAL OF UPPER AND LOWER SECTIONS	→	217	220	318
→		ENTER COMBINED TOTAL ↓	DOUBLE COMBINED TOTAL ↓	TRIPLE COMBINED TOTAL ↓
TRIPLE YAHTZEE TOTAL SCORE	→	217	440	954
GRAND TOTAL	Add Total of Three Columns →	1611 GRAND TOTAL		

2 D 73 Use Other Side to Record Each Players Scores Lowe

Triple Yahtzee® is a game of the Milton Bradley Company.

Ask who won the game and by how many points. [Barbara; by 49 points]

Objective: Solve problems involving multiplication of whole numbers.

In this lesson students find the cost of automobile fuel by reading a table.

Finding the Cost of Automobile Fuel

You can use this chart to find approximate annual gasoline costs if the price of gasoline is 20¢ per liter.

Annual Gasoline Cost										
Kilometers traveled per year	Kilometers per liter									
	3	4	5	6	7	8	9	10	11	12
8000	$533	$400	$320	$267	$229	$200	$178	$160	$145	$133
10,000	667	500	400	333	286	250	222	200	182	167
12,000	800	600	480	400	343	300	267	240	218	200
14,000	933	700	560	467	400	350	311	280	255	233
16,000	1067	800	640	533	457	400	356	320	291	267
18,000	1200	900	720	600	514	450	400	360	327	300
20,000	1333	1000	800	667	571	500	444	400	364	333
22,000	1467	1100	880	733	629	550	489	440	400	367
24,000	1600	1200	960	800	686	600	533	480	436	400
26,000	1733	1300	1040	867	743	650	578	520	473	433
28,000	1867	1400	1120	933	800	700	622	560	509	467
30,000	2000	1500	1200	1000	857	750	667	600	545	500

Find the annual gasoline cost for each of these situations.

	Kilometers traveled per year	Kilometers per liter	
1.	8000	5	$320
2.	8000	9	$178
3.	22,000	5	$880
4.	10,000	11	$182
5.	16,000	3	$1067

Here are some data for eight cars.

Car	Description and number of cylinders	Kilometers per liter	Ex. 6
1	Subcompact, 4 cyl.	11	$ 364
2	Subcompact, 6 cyl.	9	$ 444
3	Compact, 6 cyl.	8	$ 500
4	Compact, 8 cyl.	6	$ 667
5	Intermediate, 6 cyl.	7	$ 571
6	Intermediate, 8 cyl.	6	$ 667
7	Full-sized, 8 cyl.	5	$ 800
8	Station wagon, 8 cyl.	4	$1000

6. The average car is driven about 20,000 kilometers per year. At this rate, what is the annual gasoline cost for *each* of cars 1–8? See above.

7. At 20,000 kilometers per year, how much would a driver spend on gasoline

a. for car 3 in 2 years? $1000

b. for car 3 in 5 years? $2500

c. for cars 2 and 7 in 1 year? $1244

d. for cars 2 and 7 in 5 years? $6220

e. for cars 4 and 8 in 3 years? $5001

8. At 26,000 kilometers per year, how much money would a driver save on gasoline if the driver owned

a. car 3 instead of car 4? $217

b. car 2 instead of car 5? $165

c. car 4 instead of car 7? $173

d. car 1 instead of car 8? $827

9. For each driver below, find the total cost of the car plus gasoline *for 5 years* at 24,000 kilometers per year.

Driver	Price of car	Kilometers per liter	
Mr. Diaz	$3750	6	$7750
Ms. Todd	5100	12	$7100
Ms. Wong	4630	5	$9430

10. Which driver's total cost for 5 years was greatest? Ms. Wong

Point out that the most expensive car (Ms. Todd's) did not have the highest total cost for 5 years.

Objective: Solve problems involving multiplication of whole numbers.

In this lesson students solve problems involving production and packaging of canned corn.

Career: Farm Manager

Career Cluster: Technical See the Careers Chart beginning on page 420 for more jobs and other information about this career cluster.

Wilbur Pearce is the farm manager at the Mitchell Parker Corn Packing Company. The corn is grown in fields which the company either owns or leases.

Field	Field location	Size in thousands of square meters
a	North Miller Pond	310
b	South Miller Pond	110
c	Curley Avenue	480
d	Tassel Street	580
e	Husk Hollow	130
f	Johnson property	250
g	Santos property	120
h	Old Homeplace	330
i	River Road	270
j	North Perryman	950
k	South Perryman	350
l	Little Care's Stable	960
m	Glenville South	560
n	Lower Chesapeake	210

	1.	2.	3.
a.	3720 ℓ	279,000 kg	279 metric tons
b.	1320 ℓ	99,000 kg	99 metric tons
c.	5760 ℓ	432,000 kg	432 metric tons
d.	6960 ℓ	522,000 kg	522 metric tons
e.	1560 ℓ	117,000 kg	117 metric tons
f.	3000 ℓ	225,000 kg	225 metric tons
g.	1440 ℓ	108,000 kg	108 metric tons
h.	3960 ℓ	297,000 kg	297 metric tons
i.	3240 ℓ	243,000 kg	243 metric tons
j.	11,400 ℓ	855,000 kg	855 metric tons
k.	4200 ℓ	315,000 kg	315 metric tons
l.	11,520 ℓ	864,000 kg	864 metric tons
m.	6720 ℓ	504,000 kg	504 metric tons
n.	2520 ℓ	189,000 kg	189 metric tons

Here are the steps involved in producing and packing the corn. Wilbur oversees each step until the corn reaches the packing house.

Plow, fertilize, and plant fields.

1. 12 liters of fertilizer per thousand square meters

   How many liters of fertilizer were sprayed on *each* field? See page 36.

Harvest crop.

2. 900 kilograms of corn produced per thousand square meters

   How many kilograms of corn were produced by *each* field? See page 36.

3. 1000 kilograms is 1 metric ton.
   156,000 kilograms is 156 metric tons.
   250,000 kilograms is 250 metric tons.

   How many metric tons of corn were produced by *each* field? See page 36.

4. How many metric tons of corn were produced in all? 5049 metric tons

Transport corn to packing house.

Transport trucks are weighed on large scales. Subtract the EVW from the LVW to find the weight of each load of corn.

	Empty vehicle weight (EVW) in kilograms	Loaded vehicle weight (LVW) in kilograms	
5.	5044	10,470	5426 kilograms
6.	5552	12,778	7226 kilograms
7.	6498	14,596	8098 kilograms
8.	7340	15,988	8648 kilograms
9.	6210	13,876	7666 kilograms
10.	5487	11,862	6375 kilograms

Husk corn, separate from cob, pack and seal in cans, cook in cans, label cans, pack in cases, ship cases.

11. 28 cases of processed corn yielded by each metric ton of corn

    How many cases of corn were yielded in all? (Use answer from exercise 4.) 141,372 cases

12. 24 cans per case

    How many cans were needed in all? 3,392,928 cans

13. Each case sold for $7. What was the total sales of the Mitchell Parker Company that season? $989,604

Objective: Solve problems involving multiplication of whole numbers.

In this lesson students solve problems involving preparation of food and ordering of supplies for a catering service.

Career: Caterer

Career Cluster: Social Service

See the Careers Chart beginning on page 420 for more jobs and other information about this career cluster.

Mr. and Mrs. Perez are caterers. They use special ovens which stack in order to prepare large amounts of food.

Notice that the number of pan changes per hour *(C)* depends on the cooking time.

Complete the chart below. $S \times P \times C = T$

	Dish	Cooking time in minutes	Servings on 1 pan (S)	Number of pans (P)	Pan changes per hour (C)	Total servings per hour: 1 oven (T)	2 ovens ($2T$)	3 ovens ($3T$)	4 ovens ($4T$)
1.	Hamburgers	15	8	6	4	192	384	576	768
2.	Steaks	8	6	6	7	252	504	756	1008
3.	Cutlets	12	6	6	5	180	360	540	720
4.	Sausages	9	6	6	6	216	432	648	864
5.	Liver	6	6	6	10	360	720	1080	1440
6.	Rolls	17	13	3	3	117	234	351	468
7.	Pastries	10	10	6	6	360	720	1080	1440

Mr. and Mrs. Perez order supplies every two weeks.
Complete this table to find what needs to be ordered.

	Item	Number used per day	Number needed for 2 weeks (14 days)	Reserve needed	Total needed for 2 weeks	Number on hand	Number to be ordered
8.	Napkins	500	7000 (14 × 500)	500	7500 (7000 + 500)	1000	6500 (7500 − 1000)
9.	Hotcups	150	2100	100	2200	300	1900
10.	Cold cups	100	1400	100	1500	200	1300
11.	Plates	300	4200	200	4400	600	3800
12.	Bowls	180	2520	150	2670	210	2460
13.	Forks	600	8400	400	8800	500	8300
14.	Coasters	280	3920	180	4100	240	3860
15.	Placemats	200	2800	80	2880	110	2770

Number of test items - 20

Number missed	1	2	3	4	5	6	7	8	9	10
Percent correct	95	90	85	80	75	70	65	60	55	50

Chapter 2

A **1.** 60×7000 420,000

B **2.** 400×300 120,000

C **3.** 42×3
126

D **4.** 58×7
406

E **5.** 8217×4
32,868

F **6.** 3×295 885

G **7.** 54×30
1620

H **8.** 29×18
522

I **9.** 6507×83
540,081

J **10.** 26×218 5668

K **11.** 492×800
393,600

L **12.** 653×704
459,712

M **13.** 215×747
160,605

N **14.** $3(6) - 2(4)$ 10

O **15.** $7(5) + 3(2 + 4)$ 53

16. Give the missing number.

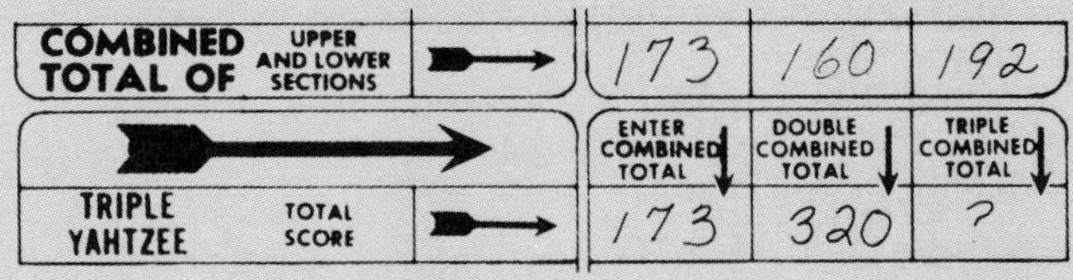

576

17. What is the total cost of gasoline for both cars for 3 years? $3846

Gasoline cost	
Car 1	$467 per year
Car 2	$815 per year

18. One metric ton of corn yields 28 cases of processed corn. 180 metric tons of corn will yield how many cases of processed corn? 5040 cases

19. Servings on 1 pan (S): 8
Number of pans (P): 6
Pan changes per hour (C): 5

Multiply $S \times P \times C$ to find the total servings per hour for the oven. 240 servings per hour

20. Find the total servings per hour for 4 ovens.
960 servings per hour

 See pages 3–4 of the *Tests and Record Forms: Duplicating Masters* for an alternate form of the Chapter 2 Test.

Chapter 3 Dividing Whole Numbers

Number of test items - 17

Number missed	1	2	3	4	5	6	7	8
Percent correct	94	88	82	76	71	65	59	53

skill Dividing with One-digit Divisors pages 42–43

A $8\overline{)61}$ 7 R5   B $3\overline{)84}$ 28   C $5\overline{)436}$ 87 R1   D $7\overline{)4825}$ 689 R2   E $473 \div 6$ 78 R5

skill Dividing with Two-digit Divisors pages 44–45

F $23\overline{)95}$ 4 R3   G $31\overline{)771}$ 24 R27   H $38\overline{)955}$ 25 R5   I $34\overline{)2314}$ 68 R2

skill Dividing with Zeros in the Quotient page 46

J $8\overline{)4831}$ 603 R7   K $53\overline{)3742}$ 70 R32

skill Dividing with Three-digit Divisors page 47

L $379\overline{)865}$ 2 R107   M $823\overline{)4762}$ 5 R647

skill Using Order of Operations pages 48–49

N $\frac{4(5)}{12-2} + \frac{16}{2}$ 18   O $\frac{2(5+1)}{3} + \frac{30}{5(2)}$ 7

skill Solving Multiplication and Division Equations pages 50–51

P Find n.

$4n = 340$

$n = 85$

Q Find x.

$\frac{x}{12} = 50$

$x = 600$

For items A–M and for exercise sets A–M, have students give answers as quotients with remainders. Remind them that the answers could also be written as mixed numbers.

See page T17 for additional notes on Chapter 3.

Dividing with One-digit Divisors

example A Two-digit dividend, basic facts

$$\begin{array}{r} 5 \\ 7\overline{)38} \\ -35 \\ \hline 3 \end{array}$$

How many 7's in 3? *None*
How many 7's in 38? *5*
Multiply 5 × 7. Subtract.

Answer: 5 R3

example B Two-digit dividend

$$\begin{array}{r} 2 \\ 4\overline{)95} \\ -8 \\ \hline 1 \end{array}$$

How many 4's in 9? *2*
Write 2 above the 9.
Multiply. Subtract.

$$\begin{array}{r} 23 \\ 4\overline{)95} \\ -8\downarrow \\ \hline 15 \\ -12 \\ \hline 3 \end{array}$$

Bring down the 5.
How many 4's in 15? *3*

Answer: 23 R3

example C Three-digit dividend

$$\begin{array}{r} 7 \\ 6\overline{)452} \\ -42 \\ \hline 3 \end{array}$$

How many 6's in 4? *None*
How many 6's in 45? *7*
Write 7 above the 5.

$$\begin{array}{r} 75 \\ 6\overline{)452} \\ -42 \\ \hline 32 \\ -30 \\ \hline 2 \end{array}$$

How many 6's in 32? *5*

Answer: 75 R2

example D Four or more digits in dividend

$$\begin{array}{r} 4 \\ 8\overline{)3492} \\ -32 \\ \hline 2 \end{array}$$

How many 8's in 3? *None*
How many 8's in 34? *4*

$$\begin{array}{r} 43 \\ 8\overline{)3492} \\ -32 \\ \hline 29 \\ -24 \\ \hline 5 \end{array}$$

How many 8's in 29? *3*

$$\begin{array}{r} 436 \\ 8\overline{)3492} \\ -32 \\ \hline 29 \\ -24 \\ \hline 52 \\ -48 \\ \hline 4 \end{array}$$

How many 8's in 52? *6*

Answer: 436 R4

example E Horizontal form

754 ÷ 3

$$\begin{array}{r} 251 \\ 3\overline{)754} \\ -6 \\ \hline 15 \\ -15 \\ \hline 4 \\ -3 \\ \hline 1 \end{array}$$

Write the problem
as shown.
Divide.

Answer: 251 R1

Remind students that they can multiply and add to check an answer. (4 x 23) + 3 = 95
For example, here are two ways to show a check for example B.

$$\begin{array}{r} 23 \\ \times\ 4 \\ \hline 92 \\ +\ 3 \\ \hline 95 \end{array}$$

exercises

set A

1. 9)65 7 R2
2. 7)46 6 R4
3. 5)39 7 R4
4. 6)33 5 R3
5. 3)22 7 R1
6. 5)42 8 R2
7. 8)27 3 R3
8. 7)41 5 R6
9. 4)25 6 R1
10. 3)29 9 R2

set B

1. 3)57 19
2. 6)90 15
3. 2)93 46 R1
4. 3)84 28
5. 2)43 21 R1
6. 4)73 18 R1
7. 5)88 17 R3
8. 7)94 13 R3
9. 8)97 12 R1
10. 4)56 14

set C

1. 8)235 29 R3
2. 4)953 238 R1
3. 7)581 83
4. 6)729 121 R3
5. 9)263 29 R2
6. 4)370 92 R2
7. 3)814 271 R1
8. 5)182 36 R2
9. 2)471 235 R1
10. 6)520 86 R4
11. 3)855 285
12. 7)406 58
13. 5)906 181 R1
14. 8)399 49 R7
15. 2)174 87
16. 4)758 189 R2

set D

1. 4)5316 1329
2. 6)91427 15,237 R5
3. 8)2529 316 R1
4. 7)9308 1329 R5
5. 8)924135 115,516 R7
6. 3)2917 972 R1
7. 2)15326 7663
8. 3)172630 57,543 R1
9. 6)7535 1255 R5
10. 8)4600 575
11. 2)6511 3255 R1
12. 5)83355 16,671
13. 4)186275 46,568 R3
14. 9)2652 294 R6
15. 5)927421 185,484 R1
16. 8)6614 826 R6
17. 3)28096 9365 R1
18. 6)1342761 223,793 R3
19. 7)26543 3791 R6
20. 3)5440 1813 R1

set E

1. 6234 ÷ 5 1246 R4
2. 976 ÷ 3 325 R1
3. 8095 ÷ 7 1156 R3
4. 772 ÷ 5 154 R2
5. 158 ÷ 6 26 R2
6. 76,431 ÷ 9 8492 R3
7. 214 ÷ 3 71 R1
8. 3288 ÷ 7 469 R5
9. 6843 ÷ 5 1368 R3
10. 47 ÷ 2 23 R1
11. 7402 ÷ 8 925 R2
12. 381 ÷ 4 95 R1
13. 91,357 ÷ 4 22,839 R1
14. 320 ÷ 5 64
15. 73 ÷ 9 8 R1
16. 389,952 ÷ 4 97,488
17. 825 ÷ 6 137 R3
18. 95,422 ÷ 7 13,631 R5
19. 156 ÷ 2 78
20. 85 ÷ 8 10 R5
21. 4372 ÷ 6 728 R4
22. 95,114 ÷ 4 23,778 R2
23. 201,764 ÷ 6 33,627 R2
24. 66,230 ÷ 9 7358 R8
25. 45,029 ÷ 8 5628 R5
26. 856,754 ÷ 2 428,377

The applications on pages 54–55 may be used anytime after this lesson.

Objective: Divide whole numbers with a two-digit divisor.

Dividing with Two-digit Divisors

example F

Two-digit dividend, first estimate works

$$\begin{array}{r} 2 \\ 31\overline{)85} \\ -\,62 \\ \hline 23 \end{array}$$

How many 31's in 8? *None*
How many 31's in 85?
Think: How many 3's in 8? *2*
Write 2 above the 5.

Answer: 2 R23

example G

Three-digit dividend, some estimates too large

$$\begin{array}{r} 2 \\ 32\overline{)861} \\ -\,64 \\ \hline 22 \end{array}$$

How many 32's in 8? *None*
In 86? Think: How many 3's in 8? *2* Write 2 above the 6.

$$\begin{array}{r} 27 \\ 32\overline{)861} \\ -\,64 \\ \hline 221 \\ -\,224 \\ \hline \end{array}$$

How many 32's in 221?
Think: How many 3's in 22? 7

But you cannot subtract 224 from 221. 7 is too large.
Try 6.

$$\begin{array}{r} 26 \\ 32\overline{)861} \\ -\,64 \\ \hline 221 \\ -\,192 \\ \hline 29 \end{array}$$

Answer: 26 R29

example H

Three-digit dividend, round divisor up, some estimates too small

$$\begin{array}{r} 2 \\ 28\overline{)817} \\ -\,56 \\ \hline 25 \end{array}$$

28 is close to 30.
How many 30's in 817?
Think: How many 3's in 8? *2*
Write 2 above the 1.

$$\begin{array}{r} 28 \\ 28\overline{)817} \\ -\,56 \\ \hline 257 \\ -\,224 \\ \hline 33 \end{array}$$

How many 30's in 257?
Think: How many 3's in 25? *8*

But 33 is greater than 28.
8 is too small. Try 9.

$$\begin{array}{r} 29 \\ 28\overline{)817} \\ -\,56 \\ \hline 257 \\ -\,252 \\ \hline 5 \end{array}$$

Answer: 29 R5

example I

Four or more digits in dividend

$$\begin{array}{r} 3 \\ 82\overline{)2991} \\ -\,246 \\ \hline 53 \end{array}$$

Think: How many 8's in 29? *3*

$$\begin{array}{r} 36 \\ 82\overline{)2991} \\ -\,246 \\ \hline 531 \\ -\,492 \\ \hline 39 \end{array}$$

Think: How many 8's in 53? *6*

Answer: 36 R39

exercises

set F

1. 34)75 — 2 R7
2. 53)60 — 1 R7
3. 81)92 — 1 R11
4. 21)58 — 2 R16
5. 32)74 — 2 R10
6. 41)88 — 2 R6
7. 80)95 — 1 R15
8. 52)77 — 1 R25
9. 24)96 — 4
10. 33)87 — 2 R21

set G

1. 21)704 — 33 R11
2. 53)238 — 4 R26
3. 62)927 — 14 R59
4. 74)356 — 4 R60
5. 33)534 — 16 R6
6. 81)422 — 5 R17
7. 90)535 — 5 R85
8. 24)492 — 20 R12
9. 13)604 — 46 R6
10. 62)687 — 11 R5
11. 95)251 — 2 R61
12. 80)745 — 9 R25
13. 71)463 — 6 R37
14. 12)817 — 68 R1
15. 64)215 — 3 R23
16. 32)736 — 23
17. 51)423 — 8 R15
18. 34)620 — 18 R8
19. 22)158 — 7 R4
20. 43)676 — 15 R31

set H

1. 39)743 — 19 R2
2. 57)256 — 4 R28
3. 28)624 — 22 R8
4. 65)314 — 4 R54
5. 46)821 — 17 R39
6. 79)260 — 3 R23
7. 19)620 — 32 R12
8. 25)114 — 4 R14
9. 47)253 — 5 R18
10. 17)507 — 29 R14
11. 76)915 — 12 R3
12. 28)226 — 8 R2
13. 79)627 — 7 R74
14. 26)842 — 32 R10
15. 48)773 — 16 R5
16. 35)180 — 5 R5
17. 99)614 — 6 R20
18. 48)904 — 18 R40
19. 27)131 — 4 R23
20. 18)355 — 19 R13

set I

1. 42)3147 — 74 R39
2. 36)82197 — 2283 R9
3. 17)2956 — 173 R15
4. 24)8734 — 363 R22
5. 68)32468 — 477 R32
6. 35)2653 — 75 R28
7. 46)136517 — 2967 R35
8. 97)3214 — 33 R13
9. 28)8160 — 291 R12
10. 51)17562 — 344 R18
11. 60)4329 — 72 R9
12. 42)93374 — 2223 R8
13. 85)201573 — 2371 R38
14. 38)5820 — 153 R6
15. 67)42601 — 635 R56
16. 21)7511 — 357 R14
17. 92)3102 — 33 R66
18. 46)733299 — 15,941 R13
19. 93)4753 — 51 R10
20. 15)6428 — 428 R8
21. 68)35192 — 517 R36
22. 84)9634 — 114 R58
23. 18)506724 — 28,151 R6
24. 77)3227 — 41 R70
25. 43)2956317 — 68,751 R24
26. 16)84763 — 5297 R11
27. 56)391044 — 6982 R52
28. 13)8262107 — 635,546 R9

Objective: Divide whole numbers with a zero in the quotient.

Dividing with Zeros in the Quotient

example J One-digit divisor

$$\begin{array}{r} 4 \\ 9\overline{)3658} \\ -36 \\ \hline 5 \end{array}$$

There are four 9's in 36.
How many 9's in 5? *None*

$$\begin{array}{r} 406 \\ 9\overline{)3658} \\ -36 \\ \hline 58 \\ -54 \\ \hline 4 \end{array}$$

Write 0 above the 5.
Continue dividing.

Answer: 406 R4

example K Two-digit divisor

$$\begin{array}{r} 3 \\ 24\overline{)739} \\ -72 \\ \hline 19 \end{array}$$

How many 24's in 19? *None*

$$\begin{array}{r} 30 \\ 24\overline{)739} \\ -72 \\ \hline 19 \end{array}$$

Write 0 above the 9.

Answer: 30 R19

exercises

set J

1. $7\overline{)2138}$ 305 R3
2. $8\overline{)485}$ 60 R5
3. $5\overline{)3527}$ 705 R2
4. $3\overline{)2884}$ 961 R1
5. $8\overline{)16334}$ 2041 R6
6. $3\overline{)122}$ 40 R2
7. $9\overline{)32422}$ 3602 R4
8. $4\overline{)28440}$ 7110
9. $7\overline{)432}$ 61 R5
10. $5\overline{)154}$ 30 R4
11. $3\overline{)1812}$ 604
12. $5\overline{)20018}$ 4003 R3
13. $9\overline{)4685}$ 520 R5
14. $3\overline{)6017}$ 2005 R2
15. $6\overline{)48121}$ 8020 R1
16. $7\overline{)5532}$ 790 R2
17. $9\overline{)36553}$ 4061 R4
18. $8\overline{)64077}$ 8009 R5

set K

1. $56\overline{)6000}$ 107 R8
2. $92\overline{)5541}$ 60 R21
3. $21\overline{)637}$ 30 R7
4. $78\overline{)795}$ 10 R15
5. $36\overline{)7418}$ 206 R2
6. $85\overline{)4250}$ 50
7. $24\overline{)7205}$ 300 R5
8. $43\overline{)30127}$ 700 R27
9. $23\overline{)9430}$ 410
10. $15\overline{)30071}$ 2004 R11
11. $72\overline{)7915}$ 109 R67
12. $63\overline{)8194}$ 130 R4
13. $38\overline{)212883}$ 5602 R7
14. $91\overline{)6392}$ 70 R22
15. $39\overline{)7891}$ 202 R13
16. $71\overline{)61085}$ 860 R25
17. $45\overline{)9307}$ 206 R37
18. $32\overline{)128652}$ 4020 R12
19. $62\overline{)18943}$ 305 R33
20. $42\overline{)126264}$ 3006 R12

The applications on pages 53, 56–59 may be used anytime after this lesson.

Objective: Divide whole numbers with a three-digit divisor.

Dividing with Three-digit Divisors

example L Three-digit dividend

```
       2
287)726
   - 574
     152
```

287 is close to 300.
How many 300's in 726?
Think: How many 3's in 7? *2*

Answer: 2 R152

example M Four or more digits in dividend

```
       5
714)37218
   - 3570
      151
```

How many 714's in 3? *None*
In 37? *None* In 372? *None*
In 3721? Think: How many 7's in 37? *5*

```
      52
714)37218
   - 3570
     1518
   - 1428
       90
```

Think: How many 7's in 15? *2*

Answer: 52 R90

exercises

set L

1. 315)927 — 2 R297

2. 695)731 — 1 R36

3. 107)875 — 8 R19

4. 534)743 — 1 R209

5. 278)820 — 2 R264

6. 186)825 — 4 R81

7. 920)976 — 1 R56

8. 212)715 — 3 R79

9. 576)682 — 1 R106

10. 342)904 — 2 R220

set M

1. 592)48763 — 82 R219

2. 437)2507 — 5 R322

3. 903)5005 — 5 R490

4. 812)69342 — 85 R322

5. 425)2697 — 6 R147

6. 384)23400 — 60 R360

7. 688)9215 — 13 R271

8. 412)6717 — 16 R125

9. 735)61394 — 83 R389

10. 574)7315 — 12 R427

11. 394)26530 — 67 R132

12. 641)4881 — 7 R394

13. 216)1195 — 5 R115

14. 827)62103 — 75 R78

15. 396)9247 — 23 R139

16. 402)15724 — 39 R46

17. 263)6553 — 24 R241

18. 924)30052 — 32 R484

19. 317)4145 — 13 R24

20. 860)7194 — 8 R314

21. 692)39820 — 57 R376

22. 357)5423 — 15 R68

23. 611)24713 — 40 R273

24. 352)635947 — 1806 R235

25. 822)3762 — 4 R474

26. 284)50438 — 177 R170

27. 443)243976 — 550 R326

28. 921)802114 — 870 R844

The applications on pages 60–61 may be used anytime after this lesson.

Objective: Compute following order of operations involving addition, subtraction, multiplication, and division.

Using Order of Operations

example N Without operations inside parentheses

$$\frac{8(5)}{10} - \frac{6+8}{9-2}$$

Follow these general rules.

First do all operations inside parentheses; also any operations above and below division bars.

Then do all remaining multiplications and divisions.

Then do all remaining additions and subtractions.

$\frac{8(5)}{10} - \frac{6+8}{9-2}$	Do all operations above and below division bars.
$\frac{40}{10} - \frac{14}{7}$	Do remaining divisions.
$4 - 2$	Do remaining subtraction.
2	

example O With operations inside parentheses

$\frac{6(7-3)}{8} + \frac{20}{9-5} - 3(2)$	Follow rules in example N. Do operation inside parentheses.
$\frac{6(4)}{8} + \frac{20}{9-5} - 3(2)$	Do operations above and below division bars.
$\frac{24}{8} + \frac{20}{4} - 3(2)$	Do remaining multiplication and divisions.
$3 + 5 - 6$	Do remaining addition and subtraction.
2	

exercises set N

1. $\frac{16-4}{3(2)} + 4(2)$ 10
2. $35 - \frac{5+3}{7-5}$ 31
3. $\frac{40}{2(4)} - 3$ 2
4. $\frac{27+9}{8+4}$ 3
5. $3(7) + \frac{15-3}{2}$ 27
6. $\frac{12+48}{5(4)}$ 3
7. $\frac{8(2)}{4} + \frac{7(4)}{2}$ 18
8. $4(5) + \frac{100}{25} - 7(2)$ 10
9. $\frac{28+5}{3(2)+5}$ 3
10. $\frac{2(8)-4}{3}$ 4
11. $\frac{10-4}{17-15} + \frac{18+42}{6(2)}$ 8
12. $\frac{72}{9} - \frac{21+3}{4}$ 2
13. $\frac{9(4)}{3(2)} - \frac{8(6)}{4(2)}$ 0
14. $\frac{20}{4} + \frac{6(3)}{2} + \frac{21}{5+2}$ 17

set O

1. $\frac{30}{5} + \frac{3(7-5)}{2}$ 9

2. $\frac{36}{3(7-3)}$ 3

3. $\frac{6(5)}{3} - (5+2)$ 3

4. $\frac{2(1+4)}{5} + \frac{20}{4}$ 7

5. $\frac{32}{8} - (11-9)$ 2

6. $\frac{2(8+4)}{3(9-7)}$ 4

7. $\frac{4(7+3)}{5} - \frac{24}{12}$ 6

8. $\frac{25}{5} - \frac{2(3+7)}{4}$ 0

9. $\frac{80}{4(5-3)}$ 10

10. $\frac{6(9+1)}{3} - 11$ 9

11. $17 - \frac{2(5+3)}{4}$ 13

12. $3(6) + \frac{35-25}{5-3}$ 23

13. $\frac{8(2)}{4} - \frac{6(3+2)}{10}$ 1

14. $\frac{4(7+2)}{3+9} + \frac{(19-5)6}{4+2}$ 17

BREAK TIME

Copy this figure. Show how to divide it into 2 equal parts. Each part must have the same size and shape. See below.

Copy the figure again. Show how to divide it into 3 equal parts. See below.

Copy the figure again. Show how to divide it into 4 equal parts. See below.

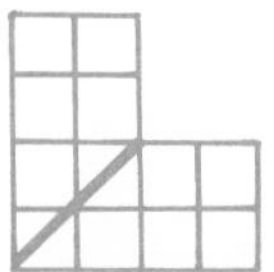

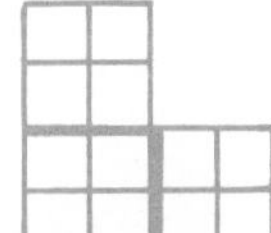

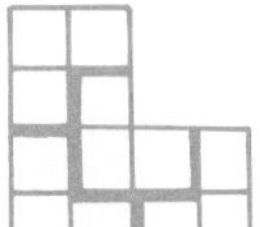

Objective: Solve multiplication and division equations.

Solving Multiplication and Division Equations

example P

Missing factor

Find n.

$$25n = 375$$

n is multiplied by 25. To undo the multiplication and get n by itself on one side of the equation, divide both sides of the equation by 25.

$$\frac{25n}{25} = \frac{375}{25}$$

$$n = 15$$

Check:
Does $25(15) = 375$? Yes

Check by substituting 15 for n in the original equation.

example Q

Missing dividend

Find x.

$$\frac{x}{35} = 20$$

x is divided by 35. To undo the division, multiply both sides of the equation by 35.

$$(35)\frac{x}{35} = (35)20$$

$$x = 700$$

Check:
Does $\frac{700}{35} = 20$? Yes

Addition and subtraction equations are found in Chapter 1 on pages 10–11. A more complete study of equations is given in Chapter 14.

exercises

set P

Find each missing number.

1. $35n = 140$ $n = 4$
2. $126 = 7t$ $t = 18$
3. $891 = 33r$ $r = 27$
4. $6z = 150$ $z = 25$
5. $108 = 4b$ $b = 27$
6. $12n = 132$ $n = 11$
7. $3c = 78$ $c = 26$
8. $126 = 3q$ $q = 42$
9. $385 = 11y$ $y = 35$
10. $207 = 23d$ $d = 9$
11. $12v = 192$ $v = 16$
12. $25e = 25$ $e = 1$
13. $0 = 71y$ $y = 0$
14. $51 = 17u$ $u = 3$
15. $160 = 32g$ $g = 5$
16. $752 = 8w$ $w = 94$
17. $57c = 342$ $c = 6$
18. $24t = 120$ $t = 5$
19. $9y = 126$ $y = 14$
20. $4x = 340$ $x = 85$
21. $15d = 120$ $d = 8$
22. $98 = 14h$ $h = 7$
23. $352 = 32m$ $m = 11$
24. $8a = 112$ $a = 14$
25. $6w = 102$ $w = 17$

set Q

Find each missing number.

1. $\frac{x}{21} = 14$

   $x = 294$

2. $\frac{n}{25} = 3$

   $n = 75$

3. $\frac{w}{13} = 13$

   $w = 169$

4. $9 = \frac{y}{200}$

   $y = 1800$

5. $\frac{k}{12} = 9$

   $k = 108$

6. $\frac{m}{8} = 160$

   $m = 1280$

7. $\frac{n}{15} = 5$

   $n = 75$

8. $42 = \frac{k}{7}$

   $k = 294$

9. $7 = \frac{t}{14}$

   $t = 98$

10. $\frac{n}{100} = 8$

    $n = 800$

11. $\frac{b}{31} = 7$

    $b = 217$

12. $\frac{v}{7} = 61$

    $v = 427$

13. $6 = \frac{n}{32}$

    $n = 192$

14. $95 = \frac{v}{5}$

    $v = 475$

15. $12 = \frac{g}{36}$

    $g = 432$

16. $\frac{e}{4} = 13$

    $e = 52$

17. $20 = \frac{s}{4}$

    $s = 80$

18. $\frac{t}{61} = 8$

    $t = 488$

19. $\frac{m}{45} = 2$

    $m = 90$

20. $\frac{v}{3} = 25$

    $v = 75$

21. $\frac{d}{7} = 90$

    $d = 630$

22. $9 = \frac{x}{35}$

    $x = 315$

23. $\frac{m}{4} = 23$

    $m = 92$

24. $\frac{n}{6} = 91$

    $n = 546$

25. $15 = \frac{t}{300}$

    $t = 4500$

26. $\frac{b}{6} = 260$

    $b = 1560$

27. $\frac{c}{15} = 55$

    $c = 825$

28. $62 = \frac{s}{24}$

    $s = 1488$

BREAK TIME

If it takes 12 minutes to cut a log into 3 pieces, how long would it take to cut the log into 4 pieces?

18 minutes

posttest

Number of test items - 17

Number missed	1	2	3	4	5	6	7	8
Percent correct	94	88	82	76	71	65	59	53

skill Dividing with One-digit Divisors pages 42–43

A $5\overline{)38}$ 7 R3 B $2\overline{)73}$ 36 R1 C $9\overline{)351}$ 39 D $3\overline{)2540}$ 846 R2 E $792 \div 6$ 132

skill Dividing with Two-digit Divisors pages 44–45

F $22\overline{)74}$ 3 R8 G $23\overline{)846}$ 36 R18 H $68\overline{)415}$ 6 R7 I $59\overline{)3265}$ 55 R20

skill Dividing with Zeros in the Quotient page 46

J $4\overline{)2429}$ 607 R1 K $31\overline{)17678}$ 570 R8

skill Dividing with Three-digit Divisors page 47

L $294\overline{)682}$ 2 R94 M $615\overline{)9274}$ 15 R49

skill Using Order of Operations pages 48–49

N $2(8) - \frac{4(9)}{10 - 7}$ 4 O $\frac{6(6-2)}{4(5-2)} + 7(2)$ 16

skill Solving Multiplication and Division Equations pages 50–51

P Find n.

$23n = 184$ $n = 8$

Q Find x.

$\frac{x}{12} = 6$ $x = 72$

Objective: Solve problems involving division of whole numbers.

In this lesson students use annual salaries to compute monthly and weekly salaries.

Computing Monthly and Weekly Salaries

Huang Choi arrived in the United States in 1975. To help plan his future, he looked up average annual salaries for various occupations.

Complete his chart below.

	Occupation	Salary		
		Annual	Monthly	Weekly
	Apprentice barber	$6240	$520 (6240 ÷ 12)	$120 (6240 ÷ 52)
1.	Automobile mechanic	$10,920	$910	$210
2.	Bricklayer (journeyman)*	$12,480	$1040	$240
3.	Bulldozer operator*	$10,920	$910	$210
4.	Carpenter*	$12,168	$1014	$234
5.	Cook	$7020	$585	$135
6.	Custodian	$6864	$572	$132
7.	Electrician	$13,416	$1118	$258
8.	Fabric worker	$8424	$702	$162
9.	Nurse	$9048	$754	$174
10.	Painter	$12,012	$1001	$231
11.	Photoengraver	$12,324	$1027	$237
12.	Police officer	$8580	$715	$165
13.	Sheet-metal worker	$13,884	$1157	$267
14.	Social worker	$7176	$598	$138
15.	Tilesetter	$11,700	$975	$225

*Seasonal outside work. Salary affected by weather conditions.

Objective: Solve problems involving division of whole numbers.

In this lesson students find the price for one item, when given the price for more than one item.

Finding the Price per Item

When Mr. and Mrs. Housum shop for groceries, they keep a running total of their purchases.

Applesauce: 3 cans for 85¢

They bought 1 can of applesauce.
How much will they pay for 1 can?

```
  28  →  29     There is a remainder.
3)85            Round up to the next cent.
 -6
  25
 -24
   1
```

One can of applesauce will cost 29¢.

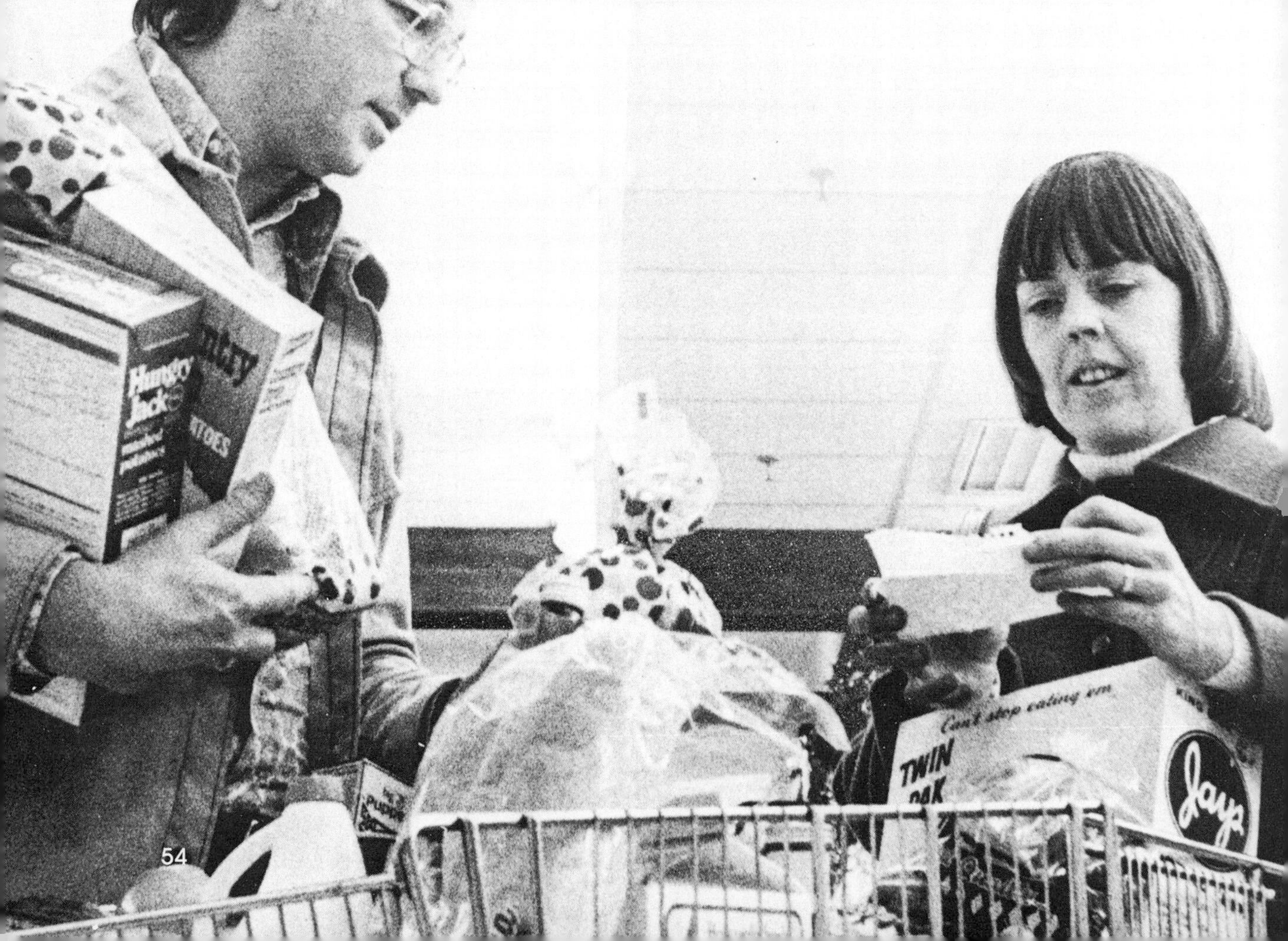

For each exercise, find the price if just 1 item is purchased.

	Item	Marked price	
1.	Bean soup	2 cans for 51¢	26¢
2.	Cat food	3 cans for 74¢	25¢
3.	Tomato sauce	5 cans for 84¢	17¢
4.	Gelatin	3 boxes for 76¢	26¢
5.	Cucumbers	5 for 89¢	18¢
6.	Peas	2 cans for 87¢	44¢
7.	Vegetable soup	4 cans for 75¢	19¢
8.	Salt	3 boxes for 52¢	18¢
9.	Soda	5 cans for 92¢	19¢
10.	Candy bars	6 for 69¢	12¢
11.	Tomatoes	3 cans for 98¢	33¢
12.	Beans	4 cans for 87¢	22¢
13.	Facial tissues	2 boxes for 89¢	45¢
14.	Hand soap	3 bars for 79¢	27¢
15.	Bread	2 loaves for 85¢	43¢

In each exercise, the prices are for the same size can. Tell which brand is a better buy if just 1 can is purchased.

	Brand X	Brand Y	
16.	4 for 78¢	5 for 94¢	Brand Y
17.	3 for 51¢	4 for 73¢	Brand X
18.	4 for 97¢	2 for 53¢	Brand X
19.	3 for 56¢	5 for 98¢	Brand X
20.	3 for 67¢	4 for 86¢	Brand Y
21.	4 for 93¢	2 for 46¢	Brand Y
22.	5 for 72¢	6 for 79¢	Brand Y
23.	2 for 31¢	5 for 84¢	Brand X
24.	4 for 89¢	3 for 72¢	Brand X
25.	3 for 39¢	5 for 58¢	Brand Y
26.	6 for 99¢	4 for 63¢	Brand Y
27.	2 for 59¢	3 for 82¢	Brand Y
28.	3 for 40¢	6 for 87¢	Brand X
29.	5 for 56¢	8 for 99¢	Brand X
30.	2 for 47¢	3 for 75¢	Brand X

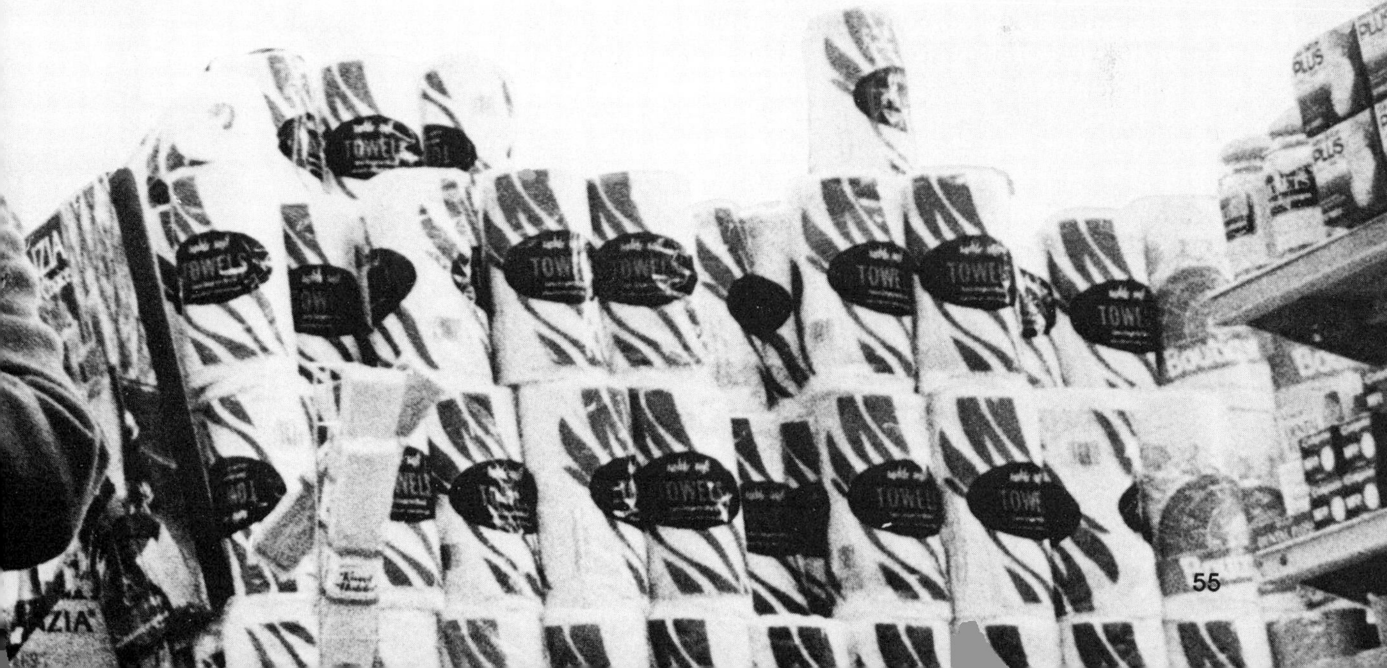

Objective: Solve problems involving division of whole numbers.

In this lesson students find the amount of paint or stain needed to cover a given area.

Painting a House

Dora and Jim McCune painted their storage shed and part of their house. They used a chart like the one below to decide how much paint to buy.

Surface	Type of paint or stain	Square meters covered with 1 liter of paint	
		First or primer coat	Second coat
Frame siding	Exterior house paint	12	13
	Aluminum paint	13	15
Shingle siding	Exterior house paint	8	10
	Shingle stain	4	6
Shingle roofs	Exterior oil paint	4	6
	Shingle stain	3	5
Cement and cinderblock walls	Cement water paint	3	4
	Exterior oil paint	5	6
Walls and ceilings (smooth finish)	Flat oil paint	15	13
	Latex base	13	17
Cement floors and steps	Porch and deck paint	11	15
	Stain and finish	12	12

Dora painted the bedroom ceilings. She used latex base paint to cover 78 square meters. How many liters of paint did she need?

First coat: 6 liters

$13\overline{)78}$

Square meters covered with 1 liter of paint (Read from chart.) ↗ 13

↑ Square meters (78)

Second coat: 4→5 liters

$$\begin{array}{r} 4 \\ 17\overline{)78} \\ -68 \\ \hline 10 \end{array}$$

There is a remainder. Round up to 5 liters.

Total number of liters: 6 + 5, or 11

Complete the table below. Remind students to find both the correct surface and the correct type of paint or stain in the chart on page 56.

	Surface	Type of paint or stain	Square meters	First coat (liters)	Second coat (liters)	Total (liters)
1.	Downstairs ceilings	Latex base	130	10	8	18
2.	Living room	Latex base	52	4	4	8
3.	Bedrooms	Latex base	117	9	7	16
4.	Kitchen	Flat oil paint	39	3	3	6
5.	Cement basement walls	Exterior oil paint	130	26	22	48
6.	Cement basement floor	Stain and finish	96	8	8	16
7.	Cement patio floor	Porch and deck paint	22	2	2	4
8.	Shingle siding on shed	Shingle stain	72	18	12	30
9.	Shingle roof on shed	Exterior oil paint	32	8	6	14
10.	Frame siding on house	Exterior house paint	216	18	17	35

Objective: Solve problems involving division of whole numbers.

In this lesson students solve problems involving production and deliveries in a bottling plant.

Career: Bottling-Plant Supervisor

Career Cluster: Trades See the Careers Chart beginning on page 420 for more jobs and other information about this career cluster.

Carla Johnson supervises assembly lines in a bottling plant.

Assembly line 1 fills returnable liter bottles.
Assembly line 2 fills returnable half-liter bottles.
Assembly line 3 fills one-way, two-liter bottles.

Complete the table.

		Line 1	Line 2	Line 3
	Bottles per minute	156	336	72
	Bottles per case	12	24	6
1.	Cases per minute	13 (156 ÷ 12)	14 (336 ÷ 24)	12
2.	Cases per hour (60 min.)	780 (60 × 13)	840 (60 × 14)	720
3.	Cases per day (8 hours)	6240 (8 × 780)	6720	5760
4.	Cases per week (5 days)	31,200 (5 × 6240)	33,600	28,800

How many cases can be filled

5. on line 1 in 3 minutes? (3×13) 39 cases
6. on line 1 in 5 minutes? (5×13) 65 cases
7. on line 1 in 2 hours? (2×780) 1560 cases
8. on line 2 in 10 minutes? 140 cases
9. on line 2 in 4 weeks? 134,400 cases
10. on line 3 in 5 hours? 3600 cases
11. on line 3 in 52 weeks? 1,497,600 cases

Carla received these orders. Divide by the number of cases per minute to find how many minutes it would take to fill each order.

12. 78 cases of returnable liter bottles. (Line 1; $78 \div 13$) 6 minutes
13. 360 cases of one-way, two-liter bottles (Line 3; $360 \div 12$) 30 minutes
14. 252 cases of returnable half-liter bottles 18 minutes
15. 650 cases of returnable liter bottles 50 minutes
16. 84 cases of one-way, two-liter bottles 7 minutes
17. 1170 cases of returnable liter bottles. 90 minutes
18. 630 cases of returnable half-liter bottles 45 minutes

Soft drinks are delivered these two ways.

Bulk delivery vans:
1200 cases per van

Conventional delivery trucks:
250 cases per truck

How many cases can be delivered by

19. 3 bulk delivery vans? 3600 cases
20. 20 bulk delivery vans? 24,000 cases
21. 8 conventional delivery trucks? 2000 cases
22. 5 bulk delivery vans and 12 conventional delivery trucks? 9000 cases
23. 40 bulk delivery vans and 100 conventional delivery trucks? 73,000 cases

Vans deliver to large supermarkets. Trucks deliver to small grocery stores and to coin-operated machines.

The photograph shows returnable liter bottles of 7UP®.

Objective: Solve problems involving division of whole numbers.

In this lesson students compute inventory turnover rates for appliance stores.

Career: Appliance Store Buyer

Career Cluster: Business Detail

John Blake is a buyer for Daley's Appliance Center.

He needs to know how fast merchandise is being sold.

First he finds the **total cost of goods sold** for six months.

Cost of goods sold	
January	$2470
February	1675
March	2572
April	2863
May	3347
June	4521
Total →	**$17448**

The total cost of goods sold is the total amount that the store paid for the goods. It is not the total amount that the customers paid for the goods.

Then he finds the **average inventory** for the store. Inventory was taken 3 times during the six months.

Inventory (cost of goods in stock)	
On February 28	$4127
On April 30	4698
On June 30	4261

To find the average, add and divide the total by 3.

$$\begin{array}{r} 4127 \\ 4598 \\ +\,4261 \\ \hline 13086 \end{array} \qquad 3\overline{)13086}\text{ } = 4362$$

The average inventory was **$4362.**

Then he computes the **inventory turnover rate** for the six months.

$$\frac{\text{Total cost of goods sold}}{\text{Average inventory}} = \begin{matrix}\text{Inventory} \\ \text{turnover} \\ \text{rate}\end{matrix}$$

$$\frac{\mathbf{17448}}{\mathbf{4362}} = 4$$

The inventory turnover rate for six months was 4. This means that the store turned over (sold) its inventory about 4 times during six months.

Here are some data for three other appliance stores.

	Cost of goods sold		
Month	Happ's Store	Greco's Store	Lee's Store
January	$3145	$2530	$2945
February	2976	1819	2383
March	4042	2240	3104
April	3416	2701	3062
May	2759	3142	3406
June	3617	4221	2312

	Inventory		
Date	Happ's Store	Greco's Store	Lee's Store
February 28	$3519	$2379	$3972
April 30	4766	2087	4530
June 30	3688	2671	4407

1. For *each* of the three stores, find

a. the total cost of goods sold.
Happ's: $19,955 Greco's: $16,653 Lee's: $17,212

b. the average inventory.
Happ's: $3991 Greco's: $2379 Lee's: $4303

c. the inventory turnover rate.
Happ's: 5 Greco's: 7 Lee's: 4

2. Which of the three stores had the greatest total cost of goods sold? Happ's

3. Which store had the greatest inventory turnover rate? Greco's
Happ's store sold more dollars worth of goods, but Greco's store sold its goods faster.

Number of test items - 22

Number missed	1	2	3	4	5	6	7	8	9	10	11
Percent correct	95	91	86	82	77	73	68	64	59	55	50

Chapter 3

A **1.** $6\overline{)45}$ 7 R3

B **2.** $3\overline{)77}$ 25 R2

C **3.** $6\overline{)295}$ 49 R1

D **4.** $8\overline{)3924}$ 490 R4

E **5.** $495 \div 3$ 165

F **6.** $22\overline{)75}$ 3 R9

G **7.** $23\overline{)851}$ 37

H **8.** $39\overline{)904}$ 23 R7

I **9.** $52\overline{)2615}$ 50 R15

J **10.** $7\overline{)4231}$ 604 R3

K **11.** $23\overline{)702}$ 30 R12

L **12.** $291\overline{)857}$ 2 R275

M **13.** $615\overline{)24730}$ 40 R130

N **14.** $\frac{9(4)}{6} + \frac{18+6}{5+3}$ 9

O **15.** $\frac{2(8)}{4} - \frac{5(7-4)}{3+2}$ 1

P **16.** Find x. $6x = 144$ $x = 24$

Q **17.** Find y. $\frac{y}{30} = 6$ $y = 180$

18. Annual salary: $12,324

Find the monthly salary. $1027

19. 3 cans for 82¢

Find the price if you buy just 1 can. 28¢

20.

Type of paint	Square meters covered with 1 liter of paint	
	First coat	Second coat
Latex base	13	17

Find how many liters of paint are needed to cover 78 square meters with 2 coats of latex base paint. 11 liters

21. An assembly line fills 14 cases of bottles per minute. How many minutes does it take to fill 588 cases? 42 minutes

22. Find the average inventory below. $1200

Date	Inventory
Feb. 28	$1250
Mar. 30	$1000
June 30	$1350

See pages 5–6 of the *Tests and Record Forms: Duplicating Masters* for an alternate form of the Chapter 3 Test.
For a test on Unit 1, see page T30 of this book and pages 7–8 of the duplicating masters.

tune-up skills

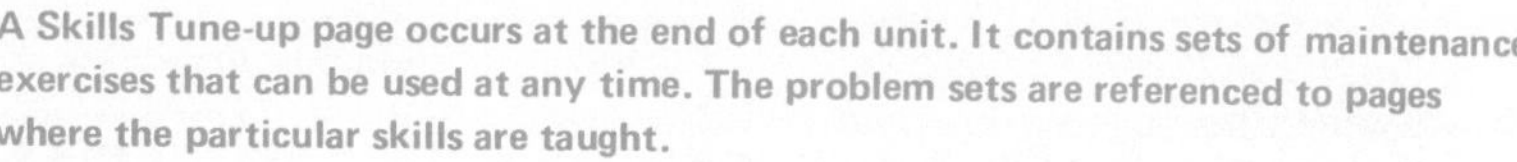

A Skills Tune-up page occurs at the end of each unit. It contains sets of maintenance exercises that can be used at any time. The problem sets are referenced to pages where the particular skills are taught.

Adding and Subtracting Whole Numbers, pages 3–12

Problem	Answer
1. 25 + 64	89
2. 17 + 81	98
3. 451 + 309	760
4. 84 + 37 + 129	250
5. 56 + 28 + 17	101
6. 478 + 295 + 86	859
7. 49 + 10 + 61	120
8. 39 + 94 + 87	220
9. 86 + 5432 + 518 + 16	6052
10. 51 + 4 + 18	73
11. 1754 + 2396	4150
12. 41,628 + 39,099	80,727
13. 2 + 18 + 138 + 97	255
14. 950 + 741 + 35 + 9	1735
15. 97 − 35	62
16. 2568 − 29	2539
17. 762 − 143	619
18. 8052 − 391	7661
19. 6834 − 289	6545
20. 5004 − 347	4657
21. 2936 − 888	2048
22. 47,869 − 29,543	18,326
23. 4502 − 733	3769
24. 2115 − 1357	758
25. 30,025 − 9868	20,157

Multiplying Whole Numbers, pages 21–32

Problem	Answer
1. 3 × 29	87
2. 37 × 48	1776
3. 50 × 310	15,500
4. 9 × 420	3780
5. 573 × 21	12,033
6. 18 × 407	7326
7. 125 × 652	81,500
8. 900 × 60	54,000
9. 68 × 29	1972
10. 315 × 66	20,790
11. 30 × 1000	30,000
12. 78 × 2351	183,378
13. 906 × 37	33,522
14. 88 × 526	46,288
15. 147 × 94	13,818
16. 8 × 1225	9800
17. 4000 × 300	1,200,000
18. 638 × 409	260,942
19. 3650 × 3	10,950
20. 7 × 652,198	4,565,386
21. 23 × 4626	106,398
22. 70,000 × 800	56,000,000
23. 2365 × 218	515,570
24. 34 × 8073	274,482
25. 798 × 5162	4,119,276

Dividing Whole Numbers, pages 41–52

Problem	Answer
1. 543 ÷ 3	181
2. 3000 ÷ 60	50
3. 9062 ÷ 5	1812 R2
4. 7634 ÷ 25	305 R9
5. 1395 ÷ 40	34 R35
6. 471 ÷ 52	9 R3
7. 54,000 ÷ 90	600
8. 793 ÷ 38	20 R33
9. 40,152 ÷ 2	20,076
10. 855 ÷ 19	45
11. 5040 ÷ 630	8
12. 7582 ÷ 800	9 R382
13. 3010 ÷ 86	35
14. 9638 ÷ 421	22 R376
15. 1284 ÷ 26	49 R10
16. 7496 ÷ 7	1070 R6
17. 27,000 ÷ 300	90
18. 1417 ÷ 35	40 R17
19. 9000 ÷ 15	600
20. 4859 ÷ 97	50 R9
21. 26,697 ÷ 33	809
22. 7839 ÷ 13	603
23. 25,128 ÷ 709	35 R313
24. 6001 ÷ 94	63 R79
25. 65,583 ÷ 347	189

CALCULATOR EXERCISES

Optional — Calculator Exercises occur on the last page of each unit. They are optional, but all students might be encouraged to do them if calculators are available. The exercises involve skills taught in the unit. All of the problems can be d one on a simple four-function calculator with an eight-digit display.

1.
3472
3569
8375
467
458
6578
34
2034
+9875
34,862

2.
56472
395
86243
38
7008
473
280
4689
+30457
186,055

3.
43602
5328
9615
318
79
50301
4587
7848
+29184
150,862

4.
61800
94321
7109
36502
41975
2388
+66079
310,174

5. 68,312 − 29,817 38,495

6. 54,001 − 37,689 16,312

7. 92,152 − 77,318 14,834

8. 10,316 − 10,299 17

9. 49,513 − 36,428 13,085

10. 70,402 − 25,963 44,439

11. 347,868 − 295,329 52,539

12. 500,007 − 286,549 213,458

13. 6,728,936 − 488,827 6,240,109

14. 1398 × 5612 7,845,576

15. 8875 × 3159 28,036,125

16. 4677 × 2093 9,788,961

17. 735 × 62,588 46,002,180

18. 851,627 × 24 20,439,048

19. 5678 × 389 × 40 88,349,680

20. 1,234,567 × 9 11,111,103

21. 765 × 482 × 39 14,380,470

22. 3 × 2986 × 8472 75,892,176

23. 57 × 362 × 895 18,467,430

24. 478 × 861 × 12 × 18 88,896,528

25. 15,924,816 ÷ 386 41,256

26. 16,472,324 ÷ 36,524 451

27. 3,418,805 ÷ 4589 745

28. 5,539,376 ÷ 922 6008

29. 4,782,968 ÷ 547 8744

30. Find the total sales for the year.

Month	Monthly Sales
January	$62,135
February	27,942
March	31,050
April	56,125
May	45,239
June	25,360
July	20,128
August	48,626
September	64,921
October	54,125
November	75,163
December	82,951
	$593,765

31. Subtract odometer readings to find the number of kilometers traveled on each trip.

Trip	Odometer before (km)	Odometer after (km)
Tampa to Atlanta	823 km 21005	21828
Fresno to Reno	512 km 64998	65510
Chicago to Dallas	1608 km 9875	11483

32. Find the daily salary for each employee.

Name	Annual salary	Days worked	
Ms. Dupre	$15,189	183	$83
Mr. Funk	11,544	156	$74
Ms. Chu	24,250	194	$125

Decimals and the Metric System

Chapter 4
Adding and Subtracting Decimals

Chapter 5
Multiplying and Dividing Decimals

Chapter 6
The Metric System

Chapter 4 Adding and Subtracting Decimals

Number of test items - 11

Number missed	1	2	3	4	5
Percent correct	91	82	73	64	55

skill Writing and Comparing Decimals pages 68-69

A Give the place value of the 4 in 336.0524.
ten thousandths

B Write an equal decimal for .6 in thousandths.
.600

C Compare .7 and .701. Use <, >, or =.
.7 < .701, or .701 > .7

skill Adding Decimals pages 70-71

D
$$\begin{array}{r} 5.4 \\ 24.7 \\ +\ 3.5 \\ \hline 33.6 \end{array}$$

E
$$\begin{array}{r} 3.002 \\ 45.73 \\ +12.8 \\ \hline 61.532 \end{array}$$

F 27.25 + .37 + 6.04 33.66

G 6.1 + 8.53 + 7 21.63

skill Subtracting Decimals pages 72-73

H
$$\begin{array}{r} 9.63 \\ -\ .42 \\ \hline 9.21 \end{array}$$

I
$$\begin{array}{r} 15.6 \\ -\ 9.37 \\ \hline 6.23 \end{array}$$

J 12.5 − 4.8 7.7

K 8.26 − 4.3 3.96

See page T18 for additional notes on Chapter 4.

Skill

Objective: Write and compare decimals.

Writing and Comparing Decimals

example A Place value

Give the place value of the 6 in each of these numbers.

435.6892
2.136
50.317926

thousands	hundreds	tens	ones	tenths	hundredths	thousandths	ten thousandths	hundred thousandths	millionths
	4	3	5	6	8	9	2		
			2	1	3	6			
		5	0	3	1	7	9	2	6

435.6892	6 tenths
2.136	6 thousandths
50.317926	6 millionths

example B Equal decimals

Write an equal decimal for .8 in hundredths and thousandths.

.8 = .80
.8 = .800

You can write zeros to show equal decimals.

Write an equal decimal for .4700 in hundredths and thousandths.

.4700 = .47
.4700 = .470

You can drop zeros to show equal decimals.

example C Comparing decimals

Compare these decimals.
Use <, >, or =.

.374 and .422
.374 < .422

374 thousandths is less than 422 thousandths.

.042 and .02
.042 and .020
.042 > .020
.042 > .02

Write an equal decimal for .02 in thousandths. 42 thousandths is greater than 20 thousandths.

.34 and .3400
.34 and .34
.34 = .34
.34 = .3400

Write an equal decimal for .3400 in hundredths. 34 hundredths is equal to 34 hundredths.

You might want to give the students these whole numbers to compare for a short review of the symbols < and >.

68 and 75 [<]	896 and 895 [>]
32 and 34 [<]	597 and 579 [>]
98 and 45 [>]	1079 and 1709 [<]
757 and 759 [<]	3845 and 3485 [>]

You could use number lines to show students that .8 = .80 = .800. Notice that number lines are calibrated in tenths, hundredths, and thousandths.

.800 .810 .820 .830 .840 .850 .860 .870 .880 .890 .900

exercises

set A

Give the place value of the 3 in each number.

1. 7.138
hundredths
2. 6.309
tenths
3. 1.2873
ten thousandths
4. 13.67
ones
5. 218.003
thousandths
6. 136.51
tens
7. 8.01673
hundred thousandths
8. 719.3
tenths
9. 310.6
hundreds
10. .019653
millionths
11. 216.03
hundredths
12. 75.013
thousandths
13. 21.38
tenths
14. 3016.2
thousands
15. .874093
millionths
16. .92315
thousandths
17. .71683
hundred thousandths
18. 6.0153
ten thousandths
19. 31,675.1
ten thousands
20. .01763
hundred thousandths

set B

Write an equal decimal in hundredths and in thousandths.

1. .6
.60, .600
2. .4200
.42, .420
3. .3800
.38, .380
4. .2600
.26, .260
5. .1
.10, .100
6. .2
.20, .200
7. .9100
.91, .910
8. .7
.70, .700
9. .6300
.63, .630
10. .5800
.58, .580
11. .9
.90, .900
12. .3
.30, .300
13. 1.6
1.60, 1.600
14. .8200
.82, .820
15. .3700
.37, .370
16. 7.6100
7.61, 7.610
17. .5
.50, .500
18. 2.9
2.90, 2.900
19. 3.2500
3.25, 3.250
20. .4
.40, .400

set C

Compare these decimals.
Replace ● with <, >, or =.

1. .29 ● .31 <
2. .782 ● .693 >
3. .218 ● .256 <
4. .05 ● .039 >
5. .168 ● .06 >
6. .27 ● .270 =
7. .638 ● .6 >
8. .065 ● .05 >
9. .390 ● .39 =
10. .489 ● .49 <
11. .061 ● .1 <
12. .901 ● .109 >
13. .9 ● .876 >
14. .009 ● .01 <
15. .38 ● .83 <
16. .890 ● .89 =
17. .760 ● .706 >
18. .003 ● .03 <
19. .006 ● .060 <
20. .29 ● .290 =
21. .038 ● .380 <
22. .68 ● .7 <
23. .010 ● .001 >
24. .080 ● .08 =
25. .056 ● .560 <

Objective: Add decimals.

Adding Decimals

example D Same number of decimal places

```
   7.6     Line up decimal points.
  12.8     Add tenths, ones, and tens.
+  9.2     Place decimal point in sum.
  29.6
```

example E Different number of decimal places

```
   4.3     Line up decimal points.
  12.75    Add.
+   .093
  17.143
```

example F Horizontal form, same number of decimal places

36.47 + 2.38 + .09

```
  36.47    Write problem vertically.
   2.38    Line up decimal points.
+   .09    Add.
  38.94
```

example G Horizontal form, different number of decimal places

.07 + 3.864 + 17.2

```
   .07     Write problem vertically.
  3.864    Line up decimal points.
+17.2      Add.
 21.134
```

You might want to give students these additional problems before assigning set G.
7.2 + 59.5 + .491 [67.191]
3.2 + .84 + 7.605 [11.645]
.09 + .8 + 7 + .46 [8.35]
.25 + 4.7 + 6 + .387 [11.337]

exercises

set D

1. 10.8 + 7.9 = 18.7
2. 67.3 + 89.4 = 156.7
3. 9.72 + 5.46 = 15.18
4. 8.59 + 14.32 = 22.91
5. .072 + .135 = .207
6. 2.934 + 5.708 = 8.642
7. 219.6 + .4 + 58.3 = 278.3
8. 10.34 + .96 + 25.41 = 36.71
9. 16.842 + .061 + 2.954 = 19.857

set E

1. .5 + .204 + .16 = .864
2. .386 + .01 + .5 = .896
3. .675 + .9 + .38 = 1.955
4. 6.943 + .2 + 3.57 = 10.713
5. 4.251 + 7.9 + .38 = 12.531
6. 31.6 + 1.892 + 7.05 = 40.542
7. 12.48 + .673 + 9.1 = 22.253
8. 25.6 + 3.841 + 9.02 = 38.461
9. 50.001 + 3.96 + 27.8 = 81.761
10. 29.387 + .8 + 1.62 = 31.807

Break Time: You need move only the second glass. Pick it up and pour the liquid into the fifth glass.

set F

1. 4.2 + 3.7 7.9
2. 5.9 + 2.4 8.3
3. 6.4 + 3.5 9.9
4. 13.8 + 9.1 22.9
5. .81 + .57 1.38
6. .34 + .07 .41
7. 2.06 + 7.29 9.35
8. 6.78 + .56 7.34
9. 1.96 + 3.75 5.71
10. 1.35 + 2.76 4.11
11. .062 + .814 .876
12. .395 + .627 1.022
13. 1.039 + 3.684 4.723
14. 5.487 + 4.396 9.883
15. 8.013 + 1.789 9.802
16. 5.348 + 9.215 14.563
17. .2 + .6 + .4 1.2
18. 1.8 + 13.6 + 2.9 18.3
19. .75 + .83 + .47 2.05
20. 16.89 + 3.21 + 12.05 32.15
21. .684 + .703 + .541 1.928
22. .013 + .208 + .009 .23
23. 1.098 + 8.635 + 2.174 11.907
24. .675 + 2 + 5.432 8.107
25. .8 + .6 + .3 + .9 2.6
26. .32 + .68 + .74 + .91 2.65

set G

1. .09 + 3.6 3.69
2. .16 + .014 .174
3. 2.8 + .139 2.939
4. 65.39 + 7.064 72.454
5. .437 + 2.59 3.027
6. .85 + .002 .852
7. 32.5 + .43 32.93
8. 78.1 + 5 83.1
9. 8.45 + .652 9.102
10. .085 + 5.32 5.405
11. .91 + .2 + .078 1.188
12. .62 + 2.5 + .3 3.42
13. .942 + .7 + .48 2.122
14. 17.5 + 2.46 + 8.3 28.26
15. 1.2 + 2.86 + .093 4.153
16. .39 + .017 + 1.6 2.007
17. 8.725 + .23 + 2.46 11.415
18. 4.9 + 6 + 3.25 14.15
19. 5.37 + 2.938 + .05 8.358
20. .098 + 1.7 + .6 2.398
21. .72 + 3.921 + 7.5 12.141
22. 7 + .096 + 1.8 8.896
23. 14.9 + .72 + 3.6 + .01 19.23
24. .963 + .68 + 1.7 + .15 3.493
25. 1.8 + 2.63 + .012 + 6 10.442
26. 13.04 + 8 + 2.1 + .79 23.93

BREAK TIME

Move *only one* glass so that the empty glasses alternate with the full glasses. See above.

The applications on pages 76–77 may be used anytime after this lesson.

Objective: Subtract decimals.

Subtracting Decimals

example H

Same number of decimal places

$$\begin{array}{r} 4.72 \\ -2.65 \\ \hline 2.07 \end{array}$$

Line up decimal points. Subtract hundredths, tenths, and ones. Place decimal point in difference.

example I

Different number of decimal places

$$\begin{array}{r} 7.6 \\ -4.362 \end{array}$$

Line up decimal points.

$$\begin{array}{r} 7.600 \\ -4.362 \\ \hline 3.238 \end{array}$$

Write zeros to show thousandths. Subtract.

Review the fact that annexing zeros does not change the value of the decimal. See example B.

example J

Horizontal form, same number of decimal places

14.25 − 8.59

$$\begin{array}{r} 14.25 \\ -\ 8.59 \\ \hline 5.66 \end{array}$$

Write problem vertically. Line up decimal points. Subtract.

example K

Horizontal form, different number of decimal places

18.76 − 5.9

$$\begin{array}{r} 18.76 \\ -\ 5.9 \\ \hline 12.86 \end{array}$$

Write problem vertically. Line up decimal points. Subtract.

You might want to give students these additional problems before assigning set K.
8.296 - 4.32 [3.976]
6.2 - 3.18 [3.02]
9 - 1.6 [7.4]
7.1 - 5.076 [2.024]

exercises

set H

1. 5.6 − 3.2 = 2.4
2. 7.8 − .9 = 6.9
3. .67 − .28 = .39
4. 9.75 − 4.67 = 5.08
5. 5.81 − 3.96 = 1.85
6. 12.03 − 8.15 = 3.88
7. .892 − .371 = .521
8. .943 − .217 = .726
9. .769 − .085 = .684
10. 9.138 − 2.079 = 7.059
11. 8.602 − 5.314 = 3.288
12. 7.001 − 6.358 = .643

set I

1. 5.9 − 1.86 = 4.04
2. 4.7 − 2.63 = 2.07
3. 7.1 − 3.45 = 3.65
4. 3.67 − 1.8 = 1.87
5. 4.3 − 2.68 = 1.62
6. 7.2 − 4.91 = 2.29
7. .59 − .372 = .218
8. .64 − .258 = .382
9. .581 − .39 = .191
10. 4.35 − 1.762 = 2.588
11. 7.251 − 2.37 = 4.881
12. 7.6 − 3.789 = 3.811

set J

1. 4.6 − 3.2 1.4
2. 8.1 − 6.7 1.4
3. 9.4 − 5.8 3.6
4. 7.6 − 3.9 3.7
5. .81 − .64 .17
6. .72 − .03 .69
7. 6.83 − 4.27 2.56
8. 9.35 − 7.48 1.87
9. 7.41 − 5.63 1.78
10. 8.03 − 2.16 5.87
11. 5.36 − 1.49 3.87
12. 9.25 − 4.36 4.89
13. 15.37 − 9.48 5.89
14. 27.58 − 16.79 10.79
15. 35.21 − 26.35 8.86
16. .875 − .396 .479
17. .312 − .045 .267
18. 1.826 − .739 1.087
19. 8.215 − 7.326 .889
20. 4.362 − 1.475 2.887
21. 5.106 − 3.724 1.382
22. 9.001 − 5.382 3.619
23. 7.284 − 2.395 4.889
24. 12.013 − 8.136 3.877
25. 38.154 − 17.237 20.917
26. 65.003 − 58.351 6.652
27. .7684 − .0369 .7315
28. .4092 − .3671 .0421

set K

1. 8.75 − 2.6 6.15
2. 5.36 − 1.8 3.56
3. 7.2 − 3 4.2
4. 8.1 − 5.23 2.87
5. 9.4 − 7.25 2.15
6. 8.37 − 6.4 1.97
7. 8.256 − 4.13 4.126
8. 9.137 − 5.29 3.847
9. 4.28 − 2.195 2.085
10. 6.35 − 3.182 3.168
11. 8.104 − 5 3.104
12. 7.18 − 5.091 2.089
13. 8.16 − 3.894 4.266
14. 9.13 − 5.062 4.068
15. 7.639 − 4.1 3.539
16. 5.381 − 2.6 2.781
17. 6.8 − 4.521 2.279
18. 9 − 6.7 2.3
19. 7.5 − 3.276 4.224
20. 18.1 − 3.105 14.995
21. 17.365 − 12.19 5.175
22. 18.21 − 18.096 .114
23. 39.32 − 24.732 14.588
24. 28 − 15.36 12.64
25. 49.2 − 36.895 12.305
26. 37.389 − 26 11.389
27. .9062 − .001 .9052
28. .01 − .009 .001

See page T16 for an explanation.

Donna is going to use candles for this experiment. She lights and burns each candle until $\frac{1}{3}$ of it remains. Then she makes a new candle by putting three candle stubs together.

Using this technique, how many candles in all will Donna be able to light if she starts with nine candles? 13 candles

posttest

Number of test items - 11

Number missed	1	2	3	4	5
Percent correct	91	82	73	64	55

skill Writing and Comparing Decimals pages 68-69

A Give the place value of the 5 in 782.0459.
thousandths

B Write an equal decimal for .2 in thousandths.
.200

C Compare .9 and .091. Use <, >, or =.
.9 > .091, or .091 < .9

skill Adding Decimals pages 70-71

D $\begin{array}{r} 12.7 \\ 3.5 \\ +\ 9.1 \\ \hline \end{array}$
25.3

E $\begin{array}{r} 21.9 \\ 3.067 \\ +16.39 \\ \hline \end{array}$
41.357

F $16.72 + .38 + 5.09$ 22.19

G $8.3 + 1.65 + 9$ 18.95

skill Subtracting Decimals pages 72-73

H $\begin{array}{r} 7.25 \\ -\ .14 \\ \hline \end{array}$
7.11

I $\begin{array}{r} 12.9 \\ -\ 6.35 \\ \hline \end{array}$
6.55

J $16.3 - 10.7$ 5.6

K $9.35 - 7.4$ 1.95

Objective: Solve problems involving subtraction of decimals.

In this lesson students read the code for a discount catalog and compute the savings between the list price and actual cost.

Buying From a Discount Catalog

Marie plans to buy a blender from this discount catalog.

14-SPEED BLENDER
Features easy access and positive push-button control. Hi-Lo switch doubles blending speed instantly. Large 44 oz. shatterproof container. Cord storage. Avocado. 110 V., AC

226 24E 1640 . . . . $28.95

↑ Stock number	↑ Discount price	↑ List price

She subtracted to find how much money she would save if she purchased this blender.

\$ 28.95	List price
− 16.40	Discount price
\$ 12.55	Savings

You might discuss reasons for the differences in prices of blenders, such as number of speeds, size, quality, and brand names.

Find the savings for each blender.

1. BLENDER A
Harvest Gold. 110V., AC
242 23E 1875 . . . . $29.95
$11.20

2. BLENDER B
Avocado. 110 V., AC
261 09E 1695 . . . . $31.95
$15.00

3. BLENDER C
Black and Chrome. 110 V., AC
242 22E 2740 . . . . $42.95
$15.55

4. BLENDER D
Avocado and Chrome. 110 V., AC
261 08E 2385 . . . . $42.95
$19.10

5. BLENDER E
Black and Chrome. 110 V., AC
242 21E 3490 . . . . $54.95
$20.05

6. BLENDER F
Black and Chrome. 115 V., AC
242 20E 4650 . . . . $74.95
$28.45

7. BLENDER G
110 V., AC
247 44E 5985 . . . . $89.95
$30.10

8. BLENDER H
110 V., AC
247 02E 6875 . . . . $99.50
$30.75

Objective: Solve problems involving addition of decimals.

In this lesson students compute the total amount of money that is recorded on a deposit slip.

Writing a Deposit Slip

When Jane opened a checking account at a bank, she made out a deposit slip for $61.74. She kept a copy of the deposit slip as proof that the deposit had been made.

The vertical line on the deposit slip serves in place of the decimal point to separate dollars and cents. The dollar sign is not used here, but it is understood that these are amounts of money.

Find the total amount of each of these deposits.

1.

CASH	CURRENCY	37	00
	COIN	16	38
CHECKS		25	71
		16	89
		5	14
TOTAL		101	12

2.

CASH	CURRENCY	25	00
	COIN	2	61
CHECKS		9	18
		67	34
		19	58
TOTAL		123	71

3.

CASH	CURRENCY	175	00
	COIN	39	47
CHECKS		82	51
		125	00
		396	28
TOTAL		818	26

4.

CASH	CURRENCY	92	00
	COIN	28	15
CHECKS		276	37
		65	42
		114	87
TOTAL		576	81

5.

CASH	CURRENCY	102	00
	COIN	28	76
CHECKS		275	49
		386	53
		92	18
TOTAL		884	96

6.

CASH	CURRENCY	136	00
	COIN	15	97
CHECKS		489	25
		16	34
		109	82
TOTAL		767	38

7.

CASH	CURRENCY	72	00
	COIN	45	79
CHECKS		106	91
		250	64
		718	12
TOTAL		1193	46

8.

CASH	CURRENCY	98	00
	COIN	12	36
CHECKS		509	62
		142	38
		12	73
TOTAL		775	09

9.

CASH	CURRENCY	124	00
	COIN	16	98
CHECKS		158	37
		27	16
		500	21
TOTAL		826	72

10.

CASH	CURRENCY	270	00
	COIN	86	17
CHECKS		439	58
		516	34
		28	75
TOTAL		1340	84

11.

CASH	CURRENCY	1025	00
	COIN	138	16
CHECKS		927	53
		4096	75
		6130	92
TOTAL		12,318	36

12.

CASH	CURRENCY	1725	00
	COIN	258	12
CHECKS		1064	98
		8536	51
		7102	49
TOTAL		18,687	10

Objective: Solve problems involving addition and subtraction of decimals.

In this lesson students write a check and complete check stubs.

Using a Checkbook

Jane pays each of her bills with a check.
She keeps each canceled check as proof that payment has been made.
She completes the check stub before she writes the check.
Then she knows how much money will be left in her account.

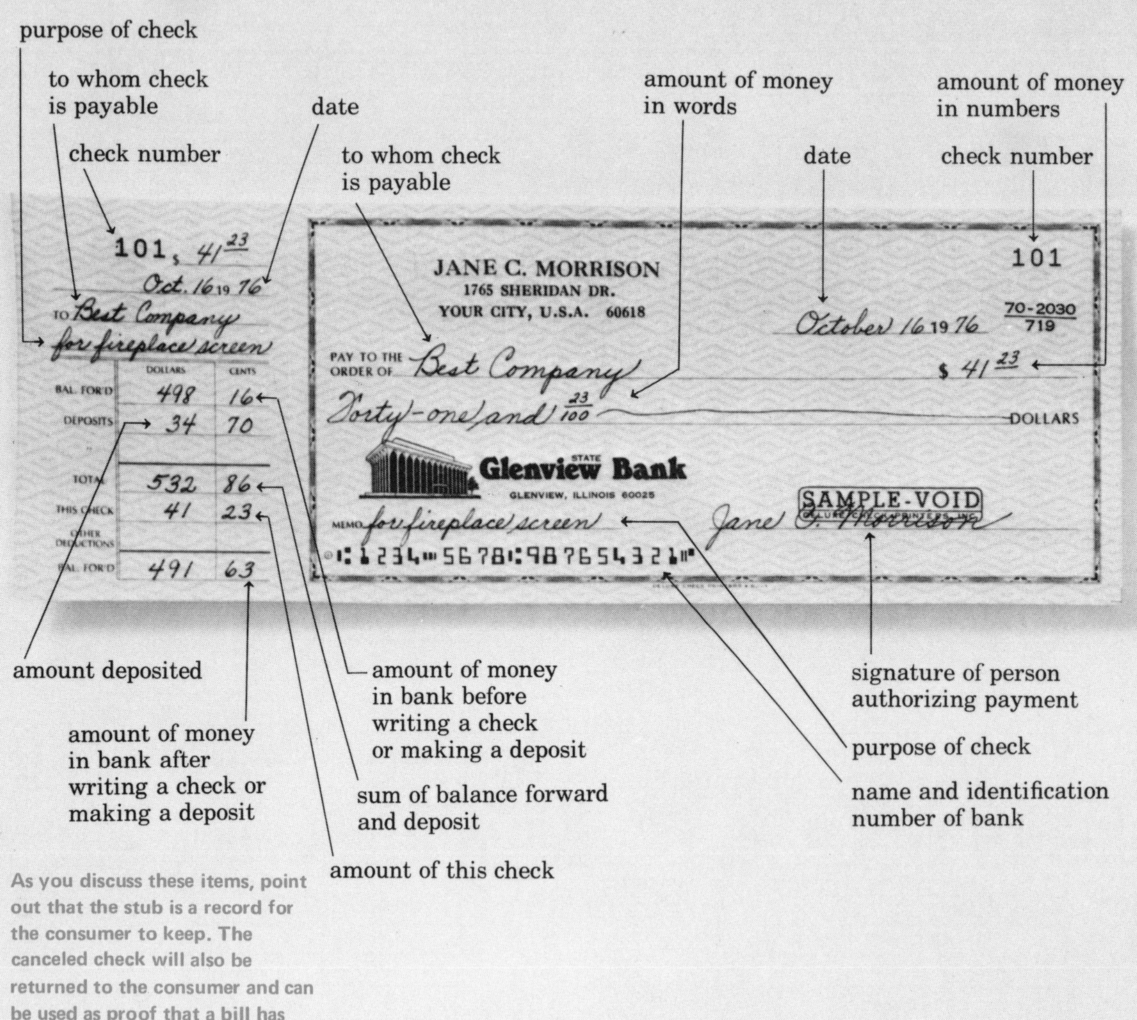

As you discuss these items, point out that the stub is a record for the consumer to keep. The canceled check will also be returned to the consumer and can be used as proof that a bill has been paid.

Use the data on the check stub to help you complete the data missing on the check.

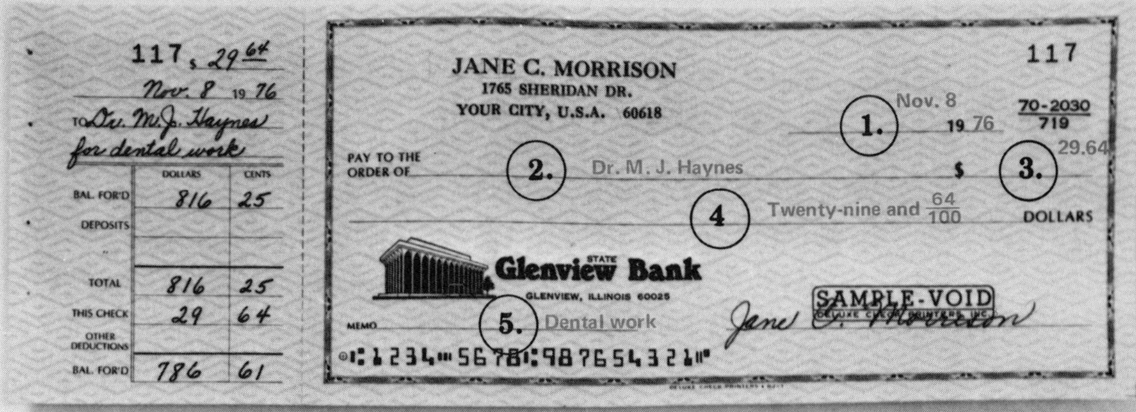

117 $ 29.64
Nov. 8 19 76
To Dr. M. J. Haynes
for dental work

	DOLLARS	CENTS
BAL. FOR'D	816	25
DEPOSITS		
"		
TOTAL	816	25
THIS CHECK	29	64
OTHER DEDUCTIONS		
BAL. FOR'D	786	61

JANE C. MORRISON
1765 SHERIDAN DR.
YOUR CITY, U.S.A. 60618

117

70-2030
719

1. Nov. 8 19 76

PAY TO THE ORDER OF 2. Dr. M. J. Haynes $ 3. 29.64

4 Twenty-nine and 64/100 DOLLARS

STATE Glenview Bank
GLENVIEW, ILLINOIS 60025

MEMO 5. Dental work

SAMPLE-VOID

Jane C. Morrison

⑆1234⑈5678⑆987654321⑈

Find the balance forward at the bottom of each check stub.

6.

	DOLLARS	CENTS
BAL. FOR'D	215	36
DEPOSITS		
"		
TOTAL		
THIS CHECK	38	61
OTHER DEDUCTIONS		
BAL. FOR'D	176	75

7.

	DOLLARS	CENTS
BAL. FOR'D	782	65
DEPOSITS		
"		
TOTAL		
THIS CHECK	349	76
OTHER DEDUCTIONS		
BAL. FOR'D	432	89

8.

	DOLLARS	CENTS
BAL. FOR'D	524	79
DEPOSITS	282	65
"		
TOTAL	807	44
THIS CHECK	116	75
OTHER DEDUCTIONS		
BAL. FOR'D	690	69

Find the balance forward at the bottom of each check stub.
This amount becomes the balance forward at the top of the next stub.

9.

	DOLLARS	CENTS
BAL. FOR'D	475	16
DEPOSITS	38	14
"		
TOTAL	513	30
THIS CHECK	243	98
OTHER DEDUCTIONS		
BAL. FOR'D	269	32

10.

	DOLLARS	CENTS
BAL. FOR'D	269	32
DEPOSITS		
"		
TOTAL		
THIS CHECK	114	68
OTHER DEDUCTIONS		
BAL. FOR'D	154	64

11.

	DOLLARS	CENTS
BAL. FOR'D	154	64
DEPOSITS	375	83
"		
TOTAL	530	47
THIS CHECK	112	96
OTHER DEDUCTIONS		
BAL. FOR'D	417	51

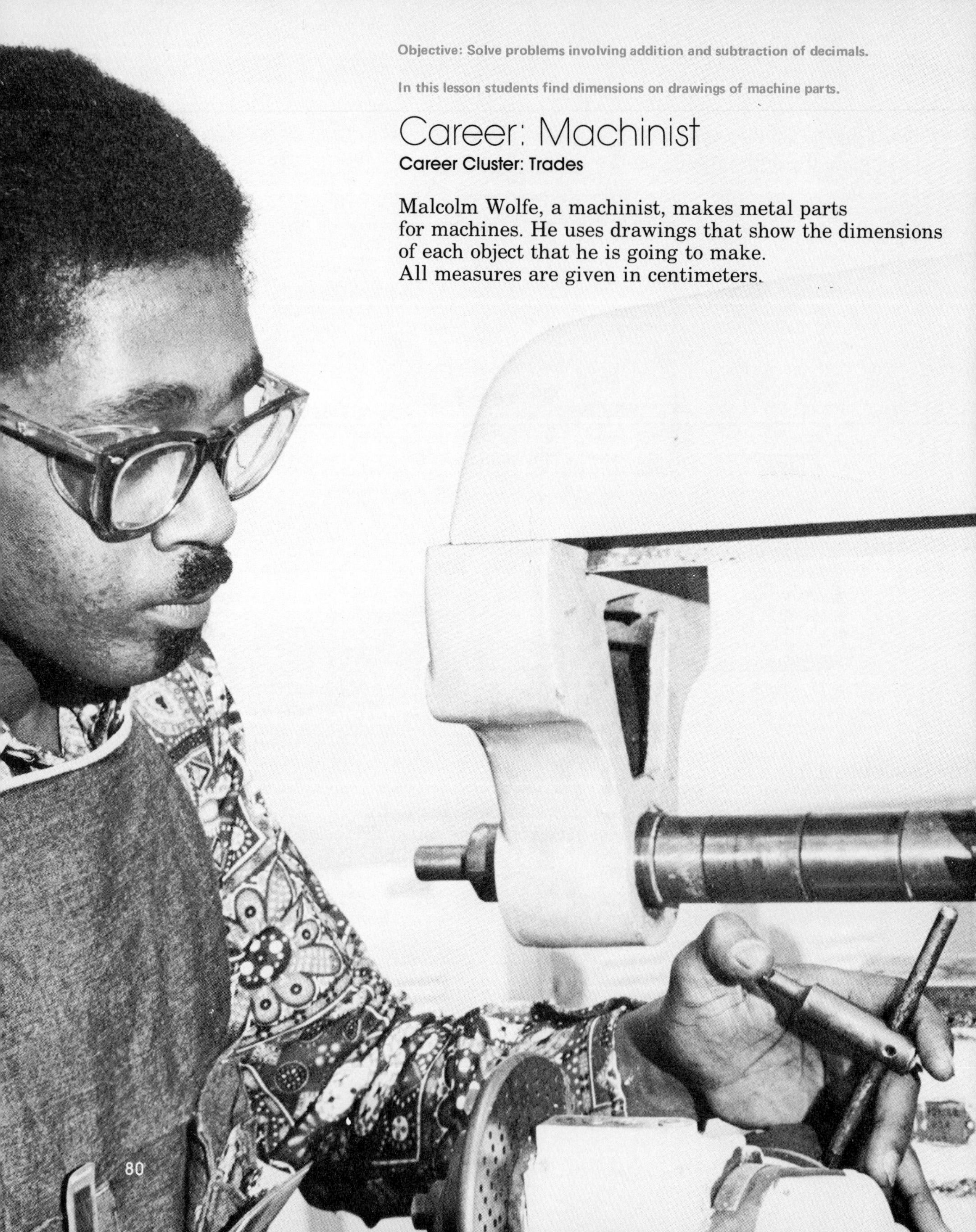

Objective: Solve problems involving addition and subtraction of decimals.

In this lesson students find dimensions on drawings of machine parts.

Career: Machinist

Career Cluster: Trades

Malcolm Wolfe, a machinist, makes metal parts for machines. He uses drawings that show the dimensions of each object that he is going to make. All measures are given in centimeters.

Before assigning these problems, you might wish to discuss with students which measures should be added or subtracted to find the missing dimensions.

1. Find the total length. 6.426 cm

2. Find the total width. 2.01 cm

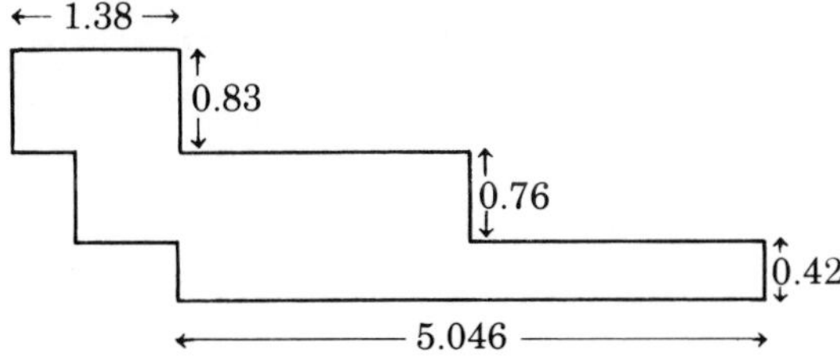

3. Find the total length. 6.992 cm

4. Find the total width. 2.272 cm

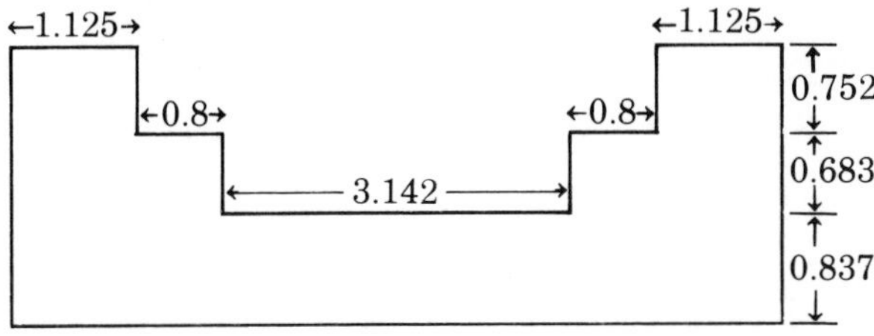

5. Find the total length. 3.25 cm

6. Find the total height. 1.7 cm

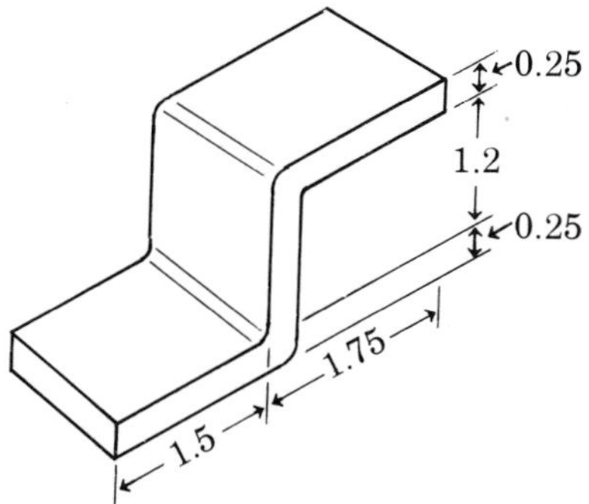

7. Find the distance between the centers of the holes. 7.25 cm

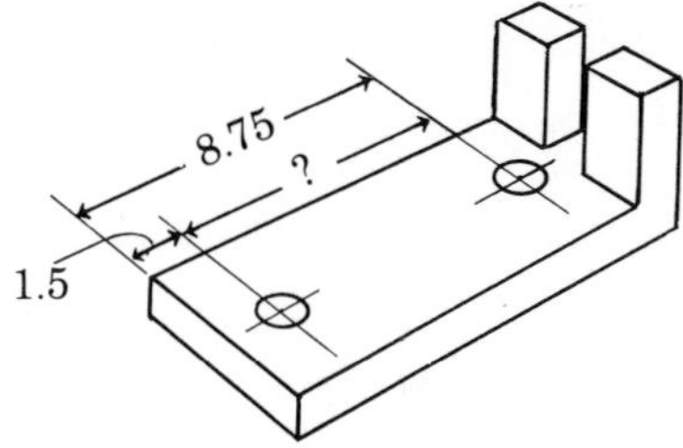

8. Find the distance between the centers of the holes. 18.2 cm

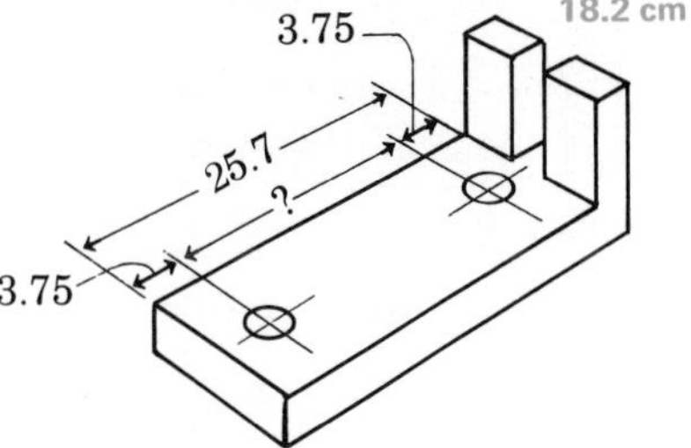

9. Find the inside diameter. 3.342 cm

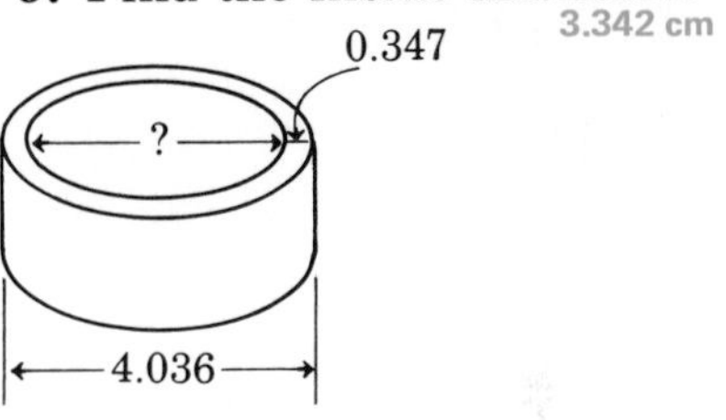

10. Find the outside diameter. 3.472 cm

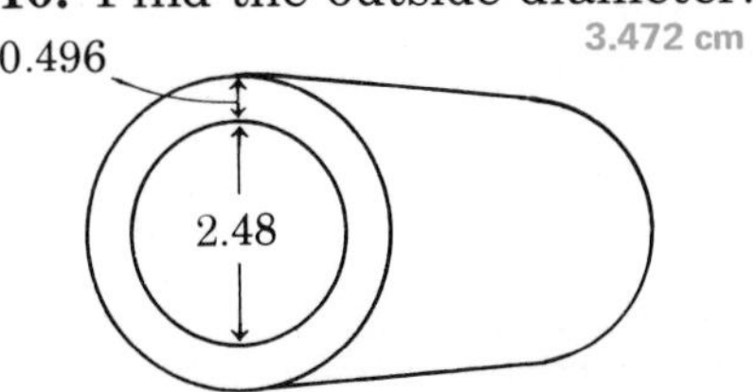

11. Find the inside diameter. 0.53 cm

1.46

0.465

Number of test items - 16

Number missed	1	2	3	4	5	6	7
Percent correct	94	88	81	75	69	63	56

Chapter 4

A **1.** Give the place value of the 9 in 457.0009.
ten thousandths

B **2.** Write an equal decimal for .9 in thousandths. .900

C **3.** Compare .89 and .8. Use <, >, or =.
.89 > .8, or .8 < .89

D **4.**
$$\begin{array}{r} 16.8 \\ +\ 4.3 \\ \hline 21.1 \end{array}$$

E **5.**
$$\begin{array}{r} 6.078 \\ +3.54 \\ \hline 9.618 \end{array}$$

F **6.** 36.47 + 9.35 45.82

G **7.** 7.43 + 6 + 2.8 16.23

H **8.**
$$\begin{array}{r} 14.76 \\ -\ 3.62 \\ \hline 11.14 \end{array}$$

I **9.**
$$\begin{array}{r} 4.12 \\ -1.865 \\ \hline 2.255 \end{array}$$

J **10.** 12.48 − 5.39 7.09

K **11.** 25.72 − 6.8 18.92

12. Find the total amount of the deposit.

CASH	CURRENCY	21	96
	COIN	6	34
CHECKS		548	25
		101	36
		5	47
TOTAL		683	38

Find the balance forward at the bottom of each check stub.

13.

	DOLLARS	CENTS
BAL. FOR'D	819	65
DEPOSITS		
"		
TOTAL		
THIS CHECK	101	48
OTHER DEDUCTIONS		
BAL. FOR'D	718	17

14.

	DOLLARS	CENTS
BAL. FOR'D	725	09
DEPOSITS	368	45
"		
TOTAL	1093	54
THIS CHECK	296	75
OTHER DEDUCTIONS		
BAL. FOR'D	796	79

The measures in each of the following drawings are given in centimeters.

15. Find the total length. 6.26 cm

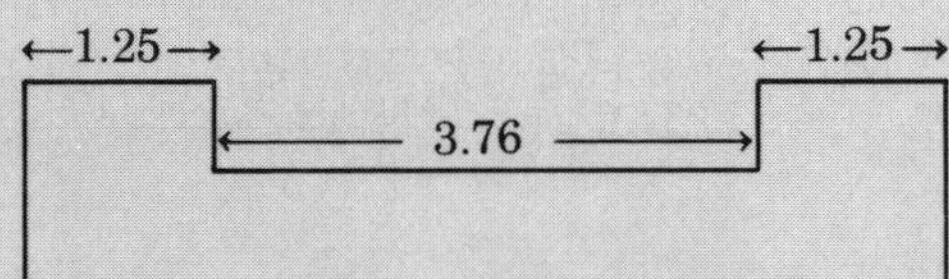

16. Find the distance between the center of the holes.
10.92 cm

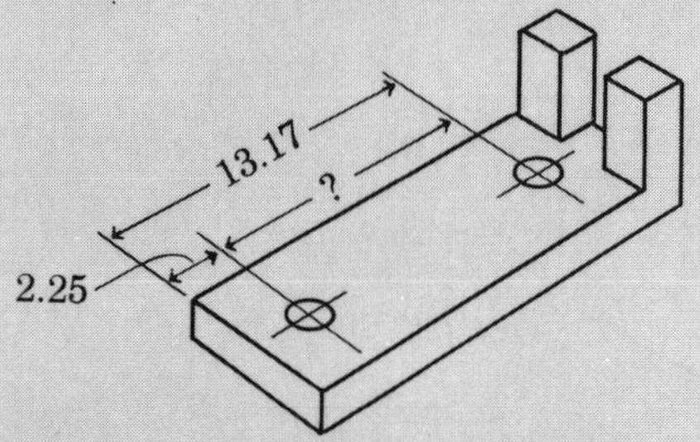

 See pages 9–10 of the *Tests and Record Forms: Duplicating Masters* for an alternate form of the Chapter 4 Test.

Chapter 5 Multiplying and Dividing Decimals

pretest

Number of test items - 19

Number missed	1	2	3	4	5	6	7	8	9
Percent correct	95	89	84	79	74	68	63	58	53

skill Multiplying Decimals pages 84-85

A 32.8×6.7 219.76

B $.721 \times .05$ .03605

C $3.9 \times .64$ 2.496

skill Dividing a Decimal by a Whole Number pages 86-87

D $3\overline{)14.58}$ 4.86

E $23\overline{)1.633}$ .071

F $5.31 \div 9$ .59

skill Multiplying and Dividing a Decimal by 10, 100, or 1000 pages 88-89

G 100×3.615 361.5

H 1000×4.7 4700

I $896.4 \div 10$ 89.64

J $9.2 \div 100$ .092

skill Dividing Decimals pages 90-91

K $.8\overline{)41.84}$ 52.3

L $.72\overline{)100.8}$ 140

M $4.8 \div .32$ 15

skill Rounding Decimals page 92

N Round .357 to the nearest tenth. .4

O Round 2.5613 to the nearest hundredth. 2.56

P Round .0128 to the nearest thousandth. .013

skill Rounding Quotients page 93

Q Round the quotient to the nearest tenth. $12\overline{)37.93}$ 3.2

R Round the quotient to the nearest hundredth. $4.3\overline{)1.65}$ .38

S Round the quotient to the nearest thousandth. $9\overline{).644}$ .072

See page T18 for additional notes on Chapter 5.

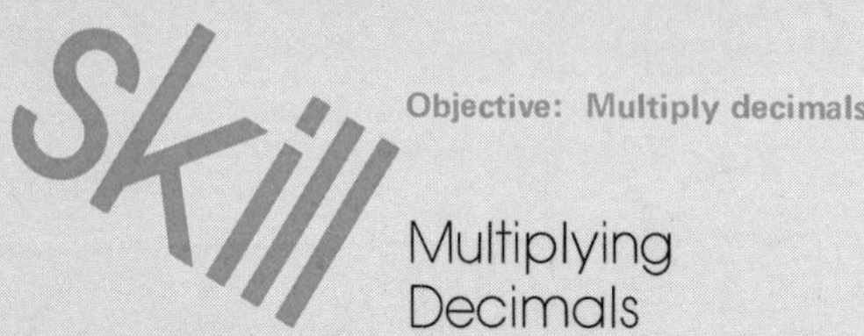

Objective: Multiply decimals.

Multiplying Decimals

example A Without writing zeros in the product

```
   8.67  ⟵ 2 decimal places
 ×  4.3  ⟵ 1 decimal place
  2 601
 34 680
 37.281  ⟵ 3 decimal places
```

To multiply decimals, multiply as with whole numbers. The number of decimal places in the product is the sum of the decimal places in the factors.

example B With writing zeros in the product

```
    .32  ⟵ 2 decimal places
 × .004  ⟵ 3 decimal places
 .00128  ⟵ 5 decimal places
```

When you multiply decimals, sometimes you need to write one or more zeros in the product.

example C Horizontal form

2.7 × 5.9

```
   2.7     Write problem vertically.
 × 5.9     Multiply.
  2 43
 13 50
 15.93
```

exercises

set A

1. 21.6 × 3.8 — 82.08
2. 40.7 × 9 — 366.3
3. 5.8 × 6.3 — 36.54
4. .42 × 1.9 — .798
5. 1.75 × 2.6 — 4.55
6. .91 × 33 — 30.03
7. 42.6 × 7 — 298.2
8. 5.4 × 9.6 — 51.84
9. 1.407 × 8 — 11.256
10. 3000 × 1.2 — 3600
11. 23.9 × 4.8 — 114.72
12. 6.2 × 8.8 — 54.56
13. 1.08 × 7 — 7.56
14. 56.7 × 3.2 — 181.44
15. 43.7 × .6 — 26.22
16. 900 × .28 — 252
17. 1.17 × 3.4 — 3.978
18. 2.08 × 7.5 — 15.6
19. 5362 × .08 — 428.96
20. 6.36 × 4.5 — 28.62
21. 14.28 × 9.3 — 132.804
22. 56.3 × 129 — 7262.7
23. 12.8 × 9.05 — 115.84
24. 4.79 × 32.6 — 156.154
25. 9.56 × 1.7 — 16.252
26. 1268 × .003 — 3.804
27. 8.33 × 2.56 — 21.3248
28. 6700 × .193 — 1293.1

set B

1. 6.7 × .009 = .0603
2. .42 × .12 = .0504
3. .316 × .07 = .02212
4. .0055 × .08 = .00044
5. 7.8 × .003 = .0234
6. .095 × .02 = .0019
7. .0321 × .008 = .0002568
8. .468 × .13 = .06084
9. .592 × .048 = .028416
10. 62.8 × .0009 = .05652
11. 2.31 × .002 = .00462
12. .0598 × .032 = .0019136
13. .2056 × .071 = .0145976
14. 3.05 × .009 = .02745
15. .9312 × .06 = .055872
16. .0082 × .29 = .002378
17. 1.09 × .062 = .06758
18. 4.333 × .006 = .025998
19. .0951 × .174 = .0165474
20. .0507 × .638 = .0323466
21. .634 × .0017 = .0010778
22. 7.081 × .0013 = .0092053
23. .1128 × .45 = .05076
24. 9.2175 × .007 = .0645225
25. .02715 × 1.34 = .036381
26. 1.098 × .0026 = .0028548
27. .17561 × .03 = .0052683
28. 8.9034 × .0076 = .0676658

set C

1. 3.7 × 62.1 — 229.77
2. .058 × 25 — 1.45
3. 1.36 × .8 — 1.088
4. 4.006 × .9 — 3.6054
5. .53 × 17.2 — 9.116
6. .004 × 9.6 — .0384
7. 25.7 × 1.2 — 30.84
8. .82 × 3.06 — 2.5092
9. 7.15 × .002 — .0143
10. 4.7 × .561 — 2.6367
11. 1.8 × .056 — .1008
12. 3.84 × 250 — 960
13. 54.1 × .06 — 3.246
14. 2000 × .75 — 1500
15. 1.73 × 2.8 — 4.844
16. .003 × .5691 — .0017073
17. 9.4 × .083 — .7802
18. .612 × 15 — 9.18
19. 7.26 × 400 — 2904
20. .19 × 5.367 — 1.01973
21. .09 × 2.36 — .2124
22. .51 × 3.9 — 1.989
23. .006 × 53.2 — .3192
24. 15.9 × 21 — 333.9
25. .6 × .043 — .0258
26. 91 × 2.5 — 227.5
27. 3.07 × 4 — 12.28
28. .4 × 2.5 — 1
29. 4.6 × .019 — .0874
30. 7.38 × 2.1 — 15.498
31. .507 × .02 — .01014
32. 351 × .066 — 23.166
33. 17.6 × .05 — .88
34. 3.1 × .91 — 2.821
35. .07 × 1.63 — .1141
36. .24 × 19 — 4.56
37. 2.3 × 8.2 — 18.86
38. 4.9 × .003 — .0147
39. 120 × .06 — 7.2
40. 1.5 × 32 — 48
41. .4 × 297 — 118.8
42. 3.8 × 2.6 — 9.88
43. 1.05 × 2.3 — 2.415
44. .66 × 1.8 — 1.188
45. .9 × 3.15 — 2.835
46. 62.04 × .9 — 55.836
47. 11 × 21.5 — 236.5
48. 3.03 × 28 — 84.84
49. 8 × 42.1 — 336.8
50. 23.5 × 4 — 94
51. 102.9 × .3 — 30.87
52. 35.7 × .5 — 17.85
53. 1.6 × 2.3 — 3.68
54. 8.01 × 6.4 — 51.264
55. 9.3 × 72 — 669.6
56. .1051 × .6 — .06306

Objective: Divide a decimal by a whole number.

Dividing a Decimal by a Whole Number

example D

Without writing zeros in the quotient

$$\begin{array}{r} . \\ 4\overline{)3.72} \end{array}$$

Place the decimal point for the quotient directly above the decimal point in the dividend.

$$\begin{array}{r} .93 \\ 4\overline{)3.72} \\ \underline{-3\,6} \\ 12 \\ \underline{-12} \\ 0 \end{array}$$

Divide as with whole numbers.

example E

With writing zeros in the quotient

$$\begin{array}{r} .0 \\ 5\overline{).145} \end{array}$$

How many 5's in 1? *None*
Write 0 above the 1.

$$\begin{array}{r} .029 \\ 5\overline{).145} \\ \underline{-10} \\ 45 \\ \underline{-45} \\ 0 \end{array}$$

Continue dividing.

example F

Horizontal form

$26.52 \div 68$

$$\begin{array}{r} .39 \\ 68\overline{)26.52} \\ \underline{-20\,4} \\ 6\,12 \\ \underline{-6\,12} \\ 0 \end{array}$$

Write the problem as shown.
Divide.

exercises

set D

1. $5\overline{)33.5}$ (6.7)
2. $8\overline{)45.6}$ (5.7)
3. $25\overline{)103.25}$ (4.13)
4. $18\overline{)16.92}$ (.94)
5. $7\overline{)18.2}$ (2.6)
6. $9\overline{)50.4}$ (5.6)
7. $38\overline{)198.36}$ (5.22)
8. $16\overline{)1.824}$ (.114)
9. $2\overline{)1.3174}$ (.6587)
10. $46\overline{)244.72}$ (5.32)
11. $4\overline{)8.64}$ (2.16)
12. $19\overline{)148.2}$ (7.8)
13. $27\overline{)99.9}$ (3.7)
14. $42\overline{)2826.6}$ (67.3)
15. $8\overline{)2.8376}$ (.3547)
16. $13\overline{)70.72}$ (5.44)
17. $6\overline{)75.36}$ (12.56)
18. $508\overline{)812.8}$ (1.6)
19. $211\overline{)4937.4}$ (23.4)
20. $71\overline{)6681.1}$ (94.1)

set E

1. $3\overline{).267}$ (.089)
2. $12\overline{).72}$ (.06)
3. $9\overline{).0432}$ (.0048)
4. $5\overline{).0365}$ (.0073)
5. $46\overline{)3.68}$ (.08)
6. $29\overline{).0203}$ (.0007)
7. $6\overline{).354}$ (.059)
8. $93\overline{).558}$ (.006)
9. $11\overline{).253}$ (.023)
10. $36\overline{).1944}$ (.0054)
11. $28\overline{).6384}$ (.0228)
12. $51\overline{)1.785}$ (.035)
13. $7\overline{).0574}$ (.0082)
14. $103\overline{).0412}$ (.0004)
15. $96\overline{)1.2864}$ (.0134)
16. $8\overline{).030352}$ (.003794)
17. $75\overline{)6.525}$ (.087)
18. $158\overline{).63042}$ (.00399)

set F

1. 21.56 ÷ 4 5.39
2. 53.6 ÷ 8 6.7
3. .665 ÷ 19 .035
4. 18.86 ÷ 23 .82
5. 198.36 ÷ 58 3.42
6. 132.93 ÷ 63 2.11
7. .376 ÷ 47 .008
8. 10.98 ÷ 9 1.22
9. 287.7 ÷ 3 95.9
10. 441.70 ÷ 70 6.31
11. 234.5 ÷ 5 46.9
12. .2414 ÷ 34 .0071
13. 494.64 ÷ 72 6.87
14. 3.5298 ÷ 6 .5883
15. .1581 ÷ 17 .0093
16. 201.69 ÷ 81 2.49
17. 29.304 ÷ 22 1.332
18. .0296 ÷ 37 .0008
19. 27.36 ÷ 9 3.04
20. 13.875 ÷ 25 .555
21. 3689.2 ÷ 92 40.1
22. 549.9 ÷ 13 42.3
23. .2886 ÷ 6 .0481
24. 148.5 ÷ 55 2.7
25. 3.451 ÷ 29 .119
26. 1119.72 ÷ 124 9.03
27. 201.02 ÷ 38 5.29
28. 23.192 ÷ 52 .446
29. 49.76 ÷ 8 6.22
30. 110.17 ÷ 23 4.79
31. 35.298 ÷ 53 .666
32. 88.274 ÷ 202 .437
33. 1868.1 ÷ 39 47.9
34. 342.6 ÷ 6 57.1
35. .1938 ÷ 57 .0034
36. 86.13 ÷ 33 2.61
37. 4.095 ÷ 7 .585
38. 82.98 ÷ 18 4.61
39. .035184 ÷ 4 .008796
40. 39.136 ÷ 16 2.446
41. 153.99 ÷ 531 .29
42. 78.54 ÷ 42 1.87
43. .225 ÷ 25 .009
44. 3.275 ÷ 5 .655
45. 1624.4 ÷ 31 52.4
46. 323.5 ÷ 5 64.7
47. 227.24 ÷ 92 2.47
48. 171.92 ÷ 28 6.14
49. 3801.4 ÷ 83 45.8
50. 12.09 ÷ 3 4.03
51. 304.2 ÷ 9 33.8
52. 57.642 ÷ 739 .078
53. 31.997 ÷ 49 .653
54. 393.12 ÷ 126 3.12
55. 761.9 ÷ 19 40.1
56. 2.492 ÷ 7 .356

BREAK TIME

All of these are Gleeps.

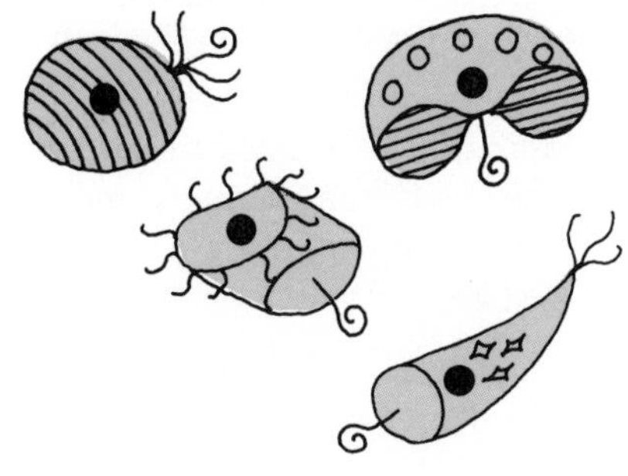

None of these are Gleeps.

Which of these are Gleeps?

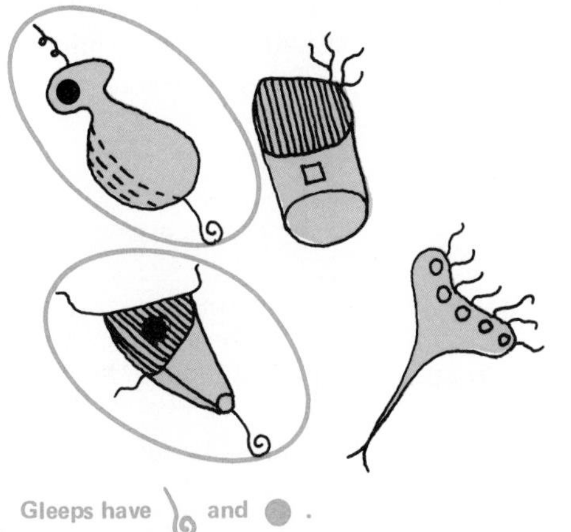

Gleeps have and .

Objective: Multiply or divide a decimal by 10, 100, or 1000.

Multiplying and Dividing a Decimal by 10, 100, or 1000

example G

Multiply without writing zeros in the product

$100 \times .6897$

$100 \times .6897 = 68.97$

100 has 2 zeros. Move the decimal point 2 places to the right.

When you multiply a decimal by 10, 100, or 1000, count the zeros in the multiplier, and move the decimal point that many places to the right.

For each problem type show other examples involving multiplication or division by 10, 100, and 1000.

example H

Multiply with writing zeros in the product

1000×15.6

$1000 \times 15.600 = 15{,}600$

1000 has 3 zeros. Write zeros after the 6 in order to move the decimal point 3 places to the right.

example I

Divide without writing zeros in the quotient

$116.7 \div 10$

$116.7 \div 10 = 11.67$

10 has 1 zero. Move the decimal point 1 place to the left.

When you divide a decimal by 10, 100, or 1000, count the zeros in the divisor, and move the decimal point that many places to the left.

example J

Divide with writing zeros in the quotient

$5.4 \div 100$

$05.4 \div 100 = .054$

100 has 2 zeros. Write a zero before the 5 in order to move the decimal point 2 places to the left.

exercises set G

1. 10×53.16 531.6

2. 100×1.08 108

3. $1000 \times .1685$ 168.5

4. 10×34.9 349

5. 25.1×10 251

6. 10×1.6 16

7. 3.0042×1000 3004.2

8. $1000 \times .791$ 791

9. 10×12.4 124

10. $100 \times .3895$ 38.95

11. 10×26.955 269.55

12. 351.7×10 3517

13. 100×64.201 6420.1

14. $1000 \times .93642$ 936.42

15. 1.387×1000 1387

16. 100×2.048 204.8

17. 53.92×100 5392

18. 10×6.072 60.72

19. 704.56×10 7045.6

20. 1000×12.8956 12895.6

21. 277.5×10 2775

22. 100×38.6108 3861.08

23. 9.533×10 95.33

24. $1000 \times .46511235$ 465.11235

25. 52.029612×1000 52029.612

set H

1. 100×5.6 560
2. 251.8×1000 251,800
3. 100×37.4 3740
4. 1005.4×100 100,540
5. 1000×68.1 68,100
6. $.3 \times 100$ 30
7. 100×215.9 21,590
8. $.7 \times 1000$ 700
9. 1000×73.51 73,510
10. 100×46.1 4610
11. $.08 \times 1000$ 80
12. 100×82.8 8280
13. 1.9×1000 1900
14. $1000 \times .06$ 60
15. 4.7×100 470
16. 100×1256.7 125,670
17. 1000×2.08 2080
18. $100 \times .9$ 90
19. 930.2×1000 930,200
20. 100×506.3 50,630
21. $.78 \times 1000$ 780
22. 100×9.8 980
23. 738.1×1000 738,100
24. 100×8.6 860
25. 20.7×100 2070
26. $1000 \times .9$ 900
27. 1.6×100 160
28. 589.03×1000 589,030

set I

1. $12.5 \div 10$ 1.25
2. $376.14 \div 100$ 3.7614
3. $194.3 \div 1000$ .1943
4. $24.8 \div 100$ .248
5. $801.6 \div 100$ 8.016
6. $2831.9 \div 1000$ 2.8319
7. $50.662 \div 10$ 5.0662
8. $9.33 \div 10$ .933
9. $61{,}521.5 \div 1000$ 61.5215
10. $480.45 \div 100$ 4.8045
11. $63.344 \div 10$ 6.3344
12. $797.15 \div 100$ 7.9715
13. $2640.91 \div 1000$ 2.64091
14. $118.7 \div 100$ 1.187
15. $56.027 \div 10$ 5.6027
16. $935.21 \div 100$ 9.3521
17. $3421.9 \div 1000$ 3.4219
18. $5602 \div 1000$ 5.602
19. $45 \div 100$ .45
20. $901.2 \div 100$ 9.012
21. $434.4 \div 10$ 43.44
22. $152 \div 10$ 15.2
23. $6300 \div 100$ 63
24. $4377.81 \div 1000$ 4.37781
25. $30{,}602 \div 100$ 306.02
26. $98.3478 \div 100$ .983478
27. $529.1 \div 10$ 52.91
28. $67{,}801.2 \div 100$ 678.012

set J

1. $34.6 \div 1000$ .0346
2. $.571 \div 10$ .0571
3. $1.7 \div 100$ .017
4. $.93 \div 100$ .0093
5. $.6 \div 10$ .06
6. $2.6 \div 1000$ .0026
7. $9.21 \div 100$ .0921
8. $.05 \div 10$ .005
9. $7.085 \div 1000$ .007085
10. $.306 \div 100$ .00306
11. $.02 \div 100$ .0002
12. $.32 \div 10$ .032
13. $.009 \div 10$ .0009
14. $.453 \div 1000$ .000453
15. $8.4 \div 100$ .084
16. $8 \div 100$ .08
17. $14.9 \div 1000$ .0149
18. $21 \div 1000$ .021
19. $.0019 \div 100$ .000019
20. $3.4651 \div 100$ .034651
21. $.4709 \div 10$ .04709
22. $.025 \div 1000$ .000025
23. $3 \div 100$ .03
24. $.0045 \div 10$ .00045
25. $6 \div 1000$ .006
26. $39.1 \div 1000$ .0391
27. $4.0897 \div 100$ .040897
28. $.06 \div 1000$ .00006

Objective: Divide decimals.

Dividing Decimals

example K

Without writing zeros in the dividend

$.9\overline{)4.32}$

Multiply the divisor and the dividend by 10 to make the divisor a whole number.

$$\begin{array}{r} 4.8 \\ 9\overline{)43.2} \\ -36 \\ \hline 7\,2 \\ -7\,2 \\ \hline 0 \end{array}$$

Divide.

You may wish to have students check their answers by multiplication.

example L

With writing zeros in the dividend

$.25\overline{)1.50}$

Multiply the divisor and the dividend by 100 to make the divisor a whole number.

$$\begin{array}{r} 6. \\ 25\overline{)150.} \\ -150 \\ \hline 0 \end{array}$$

Divide.

example M

Horizontal form

$87.6 \div .012$

$$\begin{array}{r} 7\,300. \\ 12\overline{)87\,600.} \\ -84 \\ \hline 3\,6 \\ -3\,6 \\ \hline 000. \end{array}$$

Write the problem as shown.

Multiply the divisor and the dividend by 1000 to make the divisor a whole number.

Divide.

exercises

set K

1. $.7\overline{)3.22}$ 4.6

2. $3.6\overline{)32.4}$ 9

3. $.03\overline{).1647}$ 5.49

4. $.9\overline{)5.13}$ 5.7

5. $.08\overline{).512}$ 6.4

6. $2.4\overline{).072}$ .03

7. $.57\overline{)9.12}$ 16

8. $.002\overline{).1786}$ 89.3

9. $1.3\overline{)7.15}$ 5.5

10. $.5\overline{)1.535}$ 3.07

11. $.4\overline{)167.6}$ 419

12. $6.1\overline{)2.44}$ .4

13. $.28\overline{)1.092}$ 3.9

14. $.8\overline{).1888}$ .236

15. $.009\overline{).0369}$ 4.1

16. $7.4\overline{)7.178}$ .97

17. $.06\overline{).05118}$ .853

18. $9.3\overline{)18.972}$ 2.04

19. $.68\overline{)57.12}$ 84

20. $1.52\overline{).5472}$ .36

set L

1. $.05\overline{)1.9}$ 38

2. $.21\overline{)12.6}$ 60

3. $.8\overline{)564}$ 705

4. $.006\overline{)2.94}$ 490

5. $3.7\overline{)925}$ 250

6. $.02\overline{)8.6}$ 430

7. $.43\overline{)344}$ 800

8. $.9\overline{)7029}$ 7810

9. $5.2\overline{)2002}$ 385

10. $.004\overline{)3.44}$ 860

11. $.017\overline{)158.1}$ 9300

12. $2.8\overline{)840}$ 300

13. $.07\overline{)3925.6}$ 56,080

14. $.48\overline{)112.8}$ 235

15. $8.1\overline{)23814}$ 2940

16. $.079\overline{)443.98}$ 5620

17. $.906\overline{)371.46}$ 410

18. $.027\overline{)2322}$ 86,000

set M

1. .741 ÷ .13 5.7
2. .0028 ÷ .7 .004
3. .8 ÷ .2 4
4. 1.38 ÷ 4.6 .3
5. 6.192 ÷ .72 8.6
6. 95.4 ÷ 1.8 53
7. .372 ÷ .03 12.4
8. 1305 ÷ 2.9 450
9. .0264 ÷ 3.3 .008
10. 4.611 ÷ .53 8.7
11. .0588 ÷ .006 9.8
12. .133 ÷ 1.9 .07
13. 182.4 ÷ .48 380
14. 72.9 ÷ .81 90
15. .09416 ÷ .4 .2354
16. .00657 ÷ .073 .09
17. .0884 ÷ .26 .34
18. 5.27 ÷ .085 62
19. .1197 ÷ 5.7 .021
20. 322 ÷ .35 920
21. 93 ÷ 6.2 15
22. 3000 ÷ .5 6000
23. 65.1 ÷ 9.3 7
24. .3752 ÷ .67 .56
25. .423 ÷ .009 47
26. .1829 ÷ .031 5.9
27. 81 ÷ 1.5 54
28. 10.36 ÷ .008 1295
29. .0273 ÷ 9.1 .003
30. 77.36 ÷ .08 967
31. .1856 ÷ .032 5.8
32. 138.32 ÷ 5.6 24.7
33. .18036 ÷ .06 3.006
34. .0816 ÷ 4.08 .02
35. .4692 ÷ .092 5.1
36. 446 ÷ .5 892
37. 27.84 ÷ 8.7 3.2
38. 23.68 ÷ .064 370
39. .18605 ÷ .305 .61
40. 26 ÷ .004 6500
41. .5544 ÷ .088 6.3
42. 39.411 ÷ .9 43.79
43. 14.5 ÷ 2.9 5
44. 120.195 ÷ 4.5 26.71
45. 8.25 ÷ .275 30
46. 12.72 ÷ 5.3 2.4
47. .22536 ÷ .003 75.12
48. .784 ÷ .016 49
49. 2.4336 ÷ .78 3.12
50. .05418 ÷ 6.02 .009
51. 1.378 ÷ .053 26
52. 615.6 ÷ 1.9 324
53. .04872 ÷ .58 .084
54. 42.103 ÷ .71 59.3
55. 1335 ÷ 2.67 500
56. .47376 ÷ .09 5.264

BREAK TIME

Find the top view of this figure. 4

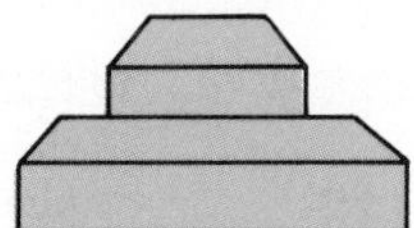

1.

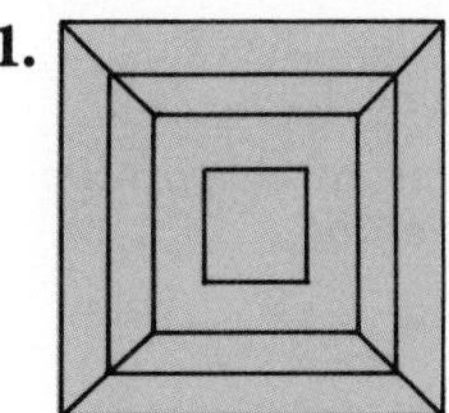

2.

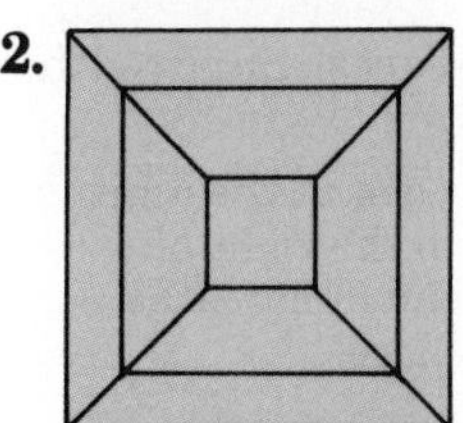

3.

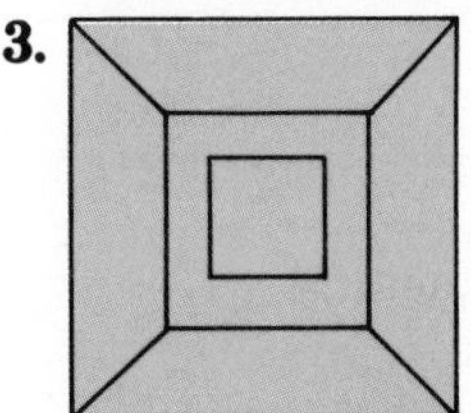

4.

Objective: Round decimals.

You may wish to have students refer to the place-value chart on page 68.

Rounding Decimals

example N To the nearest tenth

Round 3.413 to the nearest tenth.

tenths place
↓
3.**4**13

Look at the digit to the right of the tenths place. If it is 5 or more, round up. If it is less than 5, round down.

$3.413 \approx 3.4$

1 is less than 5. Round down.

≈ means *is approximately equal to.*

example O To the nearest hundredth

Round .7064 to the nearest hundredth.

hundredths place
↓
.70**6**4

Look at the digit to the right of the hundredths place.

$.7064 \approx .71$

6 is more than 5. Round up.

example P To the nearest thousandth

Round 2.9815 to the nearest thousandth.

thousandths place
↓
2.981**5**

Look at the digit to the right of the thousandths place.

$2.9815 \approx 2.982$

The digit is 5. Round up.

exercises

set N

Round each decimal to the nearest tenth.

1.	2.3094	2.3	**6.**	.3862	.4	**11.**	27.19	27.2
2.	1.56	1.6	**7.**	101.29	101.3	**12.**	9.3365	9.3
3.	.072	.1	**8.**	6.53	6.5	**13.**	.8801	.9
4.	.35	.4	**9.**	72.448	72.4	**14.**	2.451	2.5
5.	47.193	47.2	**10.**	.802	.8	**15.**	11.98	12.0

set O

Round each decimal to the nearest hundredth.

1.	5.327	5.33	**6.**	.3851	.39	**11.**	4.932	4.93
2.	.6194	.62	**7.**	24.054	24.05	**12.**	.39675	.40
3.	12.053	12.05	**8.**	3.162	3.16	**13.**	1.441	1.44
4.	6.11749	6.12	**9.**	41.977	42.98	**14.**	28.661	28.66
5.	95.1302	95.13	**10.**	.0082	.01	**15.**	7.5023	7.50

set P

Round each decimal to the nearest thousandth.

1.	.00367	.004	**6.**	9.0161	9.016	**11.**	7.2531	7.253
2.	5.1922	5.192	**7.**	.20453	.205	**12.**	.62588	.626
3.	.2847	.285	**8.**	1.9801	1.980	**13.**	.0079	.008
4.	6.1008	6.101	**9.**	8.3384	8.338	**14.**	71.1135	71.114
5.	.42831	.428	**10.**	.3796	.380	**15.**	2.4364	2.436

The applications on pages 95–97, 100–103 may be used anytime after this lesson.

Objective: Round quotients.

Rounding Quotients

example Q To the nearest tenth

Round the quotient to the nearest tenth.

$$3\overline{).79} = .26 \approx .3$$

```
   .26 ≈ .3
3).79
 - 6
   19
 - 18
    1
```

Divide until the quotient is in hundredths.
Round to the nearest tenth.

example R To the nearest hundredth

Round the quotient to the nearest hundredth.

$5.8\overline{).198}$

```
      .034 ≈ .03
5.8).1 980
   - 1 74
       240
     - 232
         8
```

Write one or more zeros in the dividend and divide until the quotient is in thousandths.
Round to the nearest hundredth.

example S To the nearest thousandth

Round the quotient to the nearest thousandth.

$24\overline{)1.7}$

```
    .0708 ≈ .071
24)1.7000
  - 1 68
      200
    - 192
        8
```

Write one or more zeros in the dividend and divide until the quotient is in ten thousandths.
Round to the nearest thousandth.

exercises

set Q

Round each quotient to the nearest tenth.

1. $.06\overline{)28.34}$ 472.3
2. $23\overline{)9.29}$ .4
3. $.7\overline{)38}$ 54.3
4. $15\overline{)53.1}$ 3.5
5. $4.9\overline{)30}$ 6.1
6. $.9\overline{)4.362}$ 4.8
7. $52\overline{)28.7}$ .6
8. $.05\overline{)3.976}$ 79.5
9. $6.4\overline{)9.348}$ 1.5
10. $.72\overline{).6555}$ .9

set R

Round each quotient to the nearest hundredth.

1. $.4\overline{)9.6351}$ 24.09
2. $6.7\overline{).82}$ .12
3. $.02\overline{).00735}$ .37
4. $36\overline{)1.52}$ .04
5. $5.1\overline{).961}$ .19
6. $2.8\overline{)3.03}$ 1.08
7. $.014\overline{).05937}$ 4.24
8. $.83\overline{)2.115}$ 2.55

set S

Round each quotient to the nearest thousandth.

1. $19\overline{)5.0162}$ .264
2. $.7\overline{).044336}$ .063
3. $5.2\overline{)7.32}$ 1.408
4. $3\overline{)1.79}$ .597
5. $.06\overline{).375162}$ 6.253
6. $73\overline{)4.08}$ .056
7. $1.4\overline{).6501}$ .464
8. $.28\overline{).092}$ .329

posttest

Number of test items - 19

Number missed	1	2	3	4	5	6	7	8	9
Percent correct	95	89	84	79	74	68	63	58	53

skill Multiplying Decimals pages 84-85

A $\begin{array}{r} 17.5 \\ \times\ .63 \\ \hline 11.025 \end{array}$

B $\begin{array}{r} .92 \\ \times .04 \\ \hline .0368 \end{array}$

C $2.8 \times .037$ .1036

skill Dividing a Decimal by a Whole Number pages 86-87

D $8\overline{)173.44}$ 21.68

E $14\overline{).0826}$ .0059

F $146.4 \div 24$ 6.1

skill Multiplying and Dividing a Decimal by 10, 100, or 1000 pages 88-89

G 10×56.92 569.2

H $1000 \times .8$ 800

I $395.2 \div 100$ 3.952

J $.23 \div 100$ .0023

skill Dividing Decimals pages 90-91

K $.48\overline{)1.536}$ 3.2

L $.009\overline{)5.04}$ 560

M $25.5 \div 7.5$ 3.4

skill Rounding Decimals page 92

N Round 19.38 to the nearest tenth. 19.4

O Round .152 to the nearest hundredth. .15

P Round .3087 to the nearest thousandth. .309

skill Rounding Quotients page 93

Q Round the quotient to the nearest tenth.
$37\overline{)70.2}$ 1.9

R Round the quotient to the nearest hundredth.
$7\overline{)2.46}$ .35

S Round the quotient to the nearest thousandth.
$.6\overline{).14191}$ .237

Objective: Solve problems involving multiplication of decimals.

Finding the Cost of Groceries

In this lesson students find the costs of various quantities of meat and fish.

Answers are rounded up as the actual prices in a grocery store would be.

Mr. Ozu and Mr. Tribaldos shopped at the same market. Each man bought a total of 8.4 kilograms of meat and fish.

In each exercise, use the prices shown to find the cost of the meat or fish purchased. Always round your answer up to the next whole cent.

Meat	Price per kilogram
Sirloin steak	$5.09
Beef rump roast	3.98
Ground beef	2.19
Stew meat	2.98
Beef liver	1.79
Beef kidney	1.69
Pork shoulder	2.89
Lamb chops	7.29
Veal roast	4.59
Sliced ham	6.19
Perch	2.59
Steak fish	.99

Stress the importance of wise shopping. The meat and fish purchased by each man has the same nutritional value, even though Mr. Ozu's purchases cost more.

Mr. Ozu

1. 1.3 kg sirloin steak $6.62
2. 1.9 kg beef rump roast $7.57
3. 2.0 kg lamb chops $14.58
4. 1.6 kg veal roast $7.35
5. 0.7 kg sliced ham $4.34
6. 0.9 kg perch $2.34

Mr. Tribaldos

7. 1.9 kg ground beef $4.17
8. 1.8 kg pork shoulder $5.21
9. 1.1 kg beef liver $1.97
10. 0.7 kg beef kidney $1.19
11. 1.5 kg stew meat $4.47
12. 1.4 kg steak fish $1.39
13. What was the total cost of the meat and fish purchased by Mr. Ozu? $42.80
14. What was the total cost of the meat and fish purchased by Mr. Tribaldos? $18.40
15. Mr. Ozu spent how much more than Mr. Tribaldos? $24.40

Objective: Solve problems involving multiplication of decimals.

In this lesson students find the total cost of a nutritious weekly diet for a family of two adults and two children.

Finding the Cost of a Nutritious Diet

These tables list foods in a typical balanced diet. The amounts purchased are for a family of two adults and two children for one week. The average price per unit and the amount purchased are based upon family income level.

Complete each table. Round your answers to the nearest cent.

Low Cost Nutritious Diet All answers are rounded up to the next whole cent.

	Food	Average price per unit	Amount purchased for one week	Cost	
1.	Milk	$.42 per liter	14.5 liters	(.42 × 14.5)	$6.09
2.	Meat, poultry	$2.39 per kilogram	7.3 kilograms	$17.45	
3.	Eggs	$.90 per dozen	1.5 dozen	$1.35	
4.	Dry beans, peas, nuts	$1.83 per kilogram	0.5 kilogram	$.92	
5.	Flour, cereal, baked goods	$1.01 per kilogram	2.6 kilograms	$2.63	
6.	Fresh fruit	$.51 per kilogram	0.9 kilogram	$.46	
7.	Green vegetables	$.62 per kilogram	4.5 kilograms	$2.79	
8.	Potatoes	$.28 per kilogram	4.7 kilograms	$1.32	
9.	Other vegetables, fruits	$.61 per kilogram	4.7 kilograms	$2.87	
10.	Fats, oil	$1.46 per kilogram	0.9 kilogram	$1.32	
11.	Sugars, sweets	$1.25 per kilogram	1.1 kilograms	$1.38	
12.			Total cost	$38.58	

The moderate cost diet includes larger quantities of meat and vegetables and fruit than the low cost diet, and allows for more frequent purchase of the higher priced cuts of meat and out-of-season foods. This plan also allows for meals with more variety, less home preparation, and greater discard of food.

Moderate Cost Nutritious Diet

	Food	Average price per unit	Amount purchased for one week	Cost
13.	Milk	$.42 per liter	17.2 liters	$7.23
14.	Meat, poultry	$2.77 per kilogram	9.5 kilograms	$26.32
15.	Eggs	$.90 per dozen	2 dozen	$1.80
16.	Dry beans, peas, nuts	$2.48 per kilogram	0.5 kilogram	$1.24
17.	Flour, cereal, baked goods	$1.16 per kilogram	4.1 kilograms	$4.76
18.	Fresh fruit	$.53 per kilogram	3.9 kilograms	$2.07
19.	Green vegetables	$.68 per kilogram	0.9 kilogram	$.62
20.	Potatoes	$.44 per kilogram	2.8 kilograms	$1.24
21.	Other vegetables, fruits	$.68 per kilogram	8.6 kilograms	$5.85
22.	Fats, oil	$1.61 per kilogram	0.9 kilogram	$1.45
23.	Sugars, sweets	$1.45 per kilogram	1.3 kilograms	$1.89
24.			Total cost	$54.47

25. The total amount spent for the moderate cost diet is how much more than the total amount spent for the low cost diet? $15.89

Point out that if a family saved $15.89 per week on food costs, then in one year they could save 52 X $15.89, or $826.28.

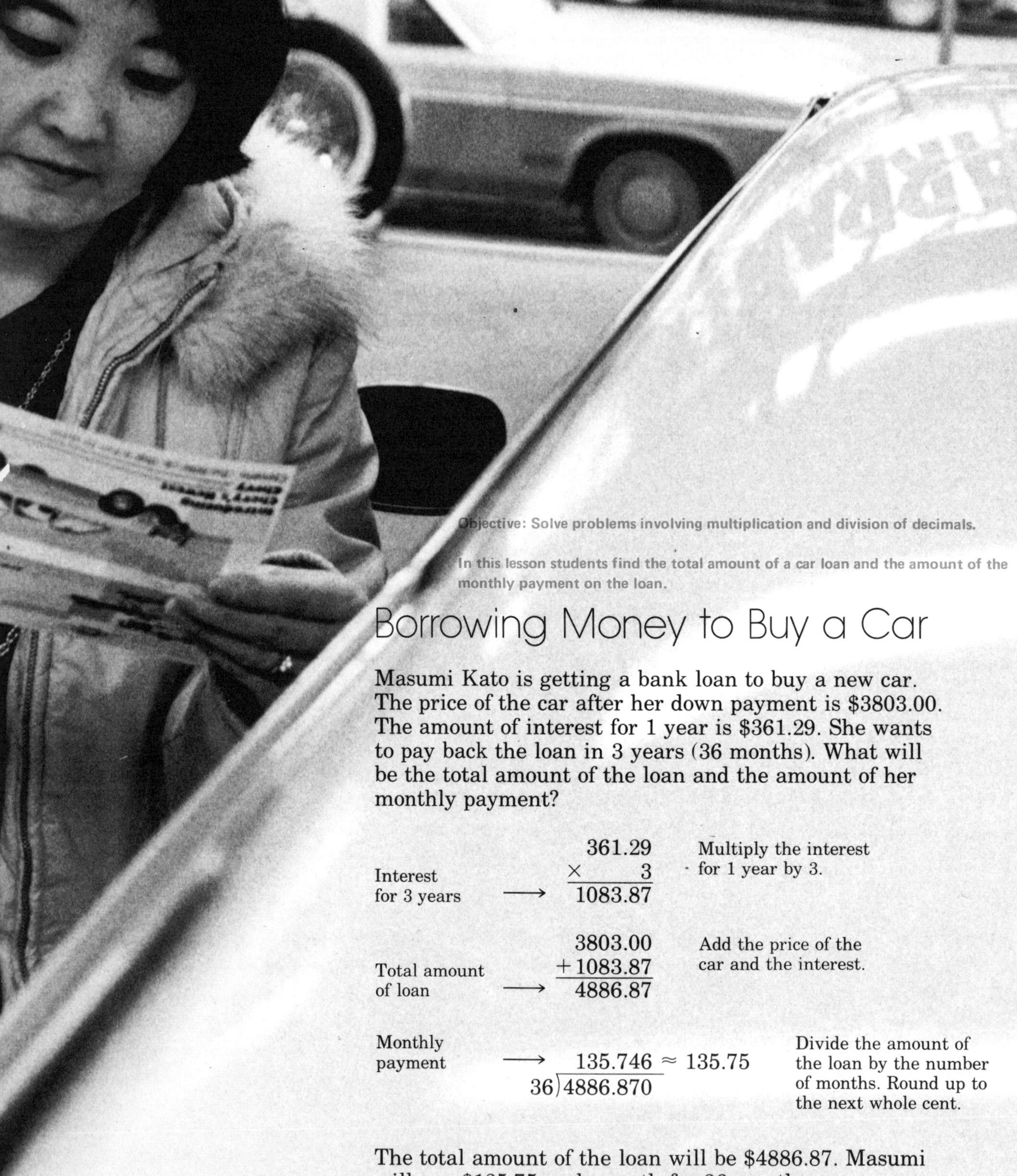

Objective: Solve problems involving multiplication and division of decimals.

In this lesson students find the total amount of a car loan and the amount of the monthly payment on the loan.

Borrowing Money to Buy a Car

Masumi Kato is getting a bank loan to buy a new car. The price of the car after her down payment is $3803.00. The amount of interest for 1 year is $361.29. She wants to pay back the loan in 3 years (36 months). What will be the total amount of the loan and the amount of her monthly payment?

Interest for 3 years ⟶

$$\begin{array}{r} 361.29 \\ \times \quad 3 \\ \hline 1083.87 \end{array}$$

Multiply the interest for 1 year by 3.

Total amount of loan ⟶

$$\begin{array}{r} 3803.00 \\ +1083.87 \\ \hline 4886.87 \end{array}$$

Add the price of the car and the interest.

Monthly payment ⟶

$$36\overline{)4886.870} = 135.746 \approx 135.75$$

Divide the amount of the loan by the number of months. Round up to the next whole cent.

The total amount of the loan will be $4886.87. Masumi will pay $135.75 each month for 36 months.

Warranty Available

Car	Price	Interest for 1 year
A	$4806.00	$456.57
B	5358.00	509.01
C	4290.00	407.61
D	3967.35	376.90
E	9356.50	888.87

Use the information above to complete each table. Round your answers up to the next whole cent.

	Car	Interest for 3 years	Total amount of loan	Amount of monthly payment (36 payments)
1.	A	$1369.71	$ 6175.71	$171.55
2.	B	1527.03	6885.03	191.26
3.	C	1222.83	5512.83	153.14
4.	D	1130.70	5098.05	141.62
5.	E	2666.61	12,023.11	333.98

	Car	Interest for 2.5 years	Total amount of loan	Amount of monthly payment (30 payments)
6.	A	$ 1141.43	$ 5947.43	$ 198.25
7.	B	1272.53	6630.53	221.02
8.	C	1019.03	5309.03	176.97
9.	D	942.25	4909.60	163.66
10.	E	2222.18	11,578.68	385.96

	Car	Interest for 2 years	Total amount of loan	Amount of monthly payment (24 payments)
11.	A	$ 913.14	$ 5719.14	$ 238.30
12.	B	1018.02	6376.02	265.67
13.	C	815.22	5105.22	212.72
14.	D	753.80	4721.15	196.72
15.	E	1777.74	11,134.24	463.93

After students have completed the tables, have them compare the cost of financing each car for different periods of time. That is, have them compare their answers to exercises 1, 6, and 11; exercises 2, 7, and 12; and so on.

Objective: Solve problems involving multiplication and division of decimals.

In this lesson students compute the cost of using certain electrical appliances for one month.

Finding the Cost of Electricity

The cost of electricity is based upon the number of kilowatt-hours used.

One **kilowatt** is 1000 watts.

One **kilowatt-hour** is the amount of electricity used in one hour by a 1000-watt appliance.

In a certain city, the amount charged for electricity is $.04 per kilowatt-hour. Find the cost of using a 950-watt power sander for 2 hours.

First use this formula to find the number of kilowatt-hours used.

Kilowatt-hours = Hours × Watts ÷ 1000

$K = H \times W \div 1000$

$K = 2 \times 950 \div 1000$

$K = 1900 \div 1000$

$K = 1.9$

Then use this formula to find the cost. Round the cost up to the next whole cent.

Cost = Rate × Kilowatt-hours

$C = .04 \times K$

$C = .04 \times 1.9$

$C = .076$

$C \approx .08$

The cost of using the power sander for 2 hours is about $.08.

Complete the table to find the cost of using each appliance for a month. Round the cost up to the next whole cent.

	Appliance	Hours used per month (H)	Watts (W)	Kilowatt-hours ($K = H \times W \div 1000$)	Cost ($C = .04 \times K$)
	Television	150	210	31.5	$1.26
1.	Light bulb	90	150	13.5	$.54
2.	Iron	8.5	1350	11.475	$.46
3.	Coffeepot	24	500	12	$.48
4.	Sound amplifier	35	180	6.3	$.26
5.	Power saw	5.5	1700	9.35	$.38
6.	Hair setter	7.5	400	3	$.12
7.	Vacuum cleaner	10.5	1500	15.75	$.63
8.	Toaster	22	1325	29.15	$1.17
9.	Air conditioner	220	1275	280.5	$11.22
10.	Power drill	3.25	420	1.365	$.06
11.	Blender	7	875	6.125	$.25
12.	Trash compactor	2.75	280	.77	$.04
13.	Floodlight	250	500	125	$5.00
14.	Clothes washer	26	8100	210.6	$8.43
15.	Clothes dryer	19	5650	107.35	$4.30

Objective: Solve problems involving multiplication of decimals.

In this lesson students find the weekly gross income for employees paid by the hour or by a piece-work rate.

Career: Payroll Clerk

Career Cluster: Business Detail

You may wish to use the classified section of the newspaper for examples of jobs that pay by hourly rates or by piece-work rates.

Cathy Freis is a payroll clerk at a clothing factory. She computes an employee's gross income each week by multiplying the hourly rate by the number of hours worked.

Hours worked × Hourly rate = Gross income

Gross income is total income without deductions.

Complete the table. Give the gross income for each employee to the nearest cent.

	Name	Hours worked						Hourly rate	Gross income
		M	T	W	Th	F	Total		
	Braniff, James	8	7	4	10	6	35	$4.75	$166.25
1.	Diaz, Ana	7	8	7	7	7	36	3.25	117.00
2.	Elliot, Hugh	8	5	9	8	8	38	2.50	95.00
3.	Herman, Sam	7	7	6	8	5	33	3.23	106.59
4.	Hoover, Jo Anne	9	4.5	12	3	8	36.5	4.50	164.25
5.	Madlem, Naomi	6.5	5	8	7	8	34.5	4.75	163.88
6.	Reinhardt, Fred	8	8	8	8	8	40	3.94	157.60
7.	Saterlie, Mary Ellen	7	6.5	9	6.5	8	37	4.62	170.94
8.	Snyder, Lex	5.5	12	8	8	3	36.5	2.78	101.47
9.	Tanaka, Iyo	8	8	8	8	8	40	3.76	150.40
10.	Turner, Charles	4.5	7.5	3.5	8	6	29.5	3.25	95.88

Some employees at the factory are paid by the number of pieces of clothing they work on. This is called piece work. Each week, Cathy finds the gross income for these employees by multiplying the rate per piece by the total number of pieces worked on by the employee.

Pieces worked on × Rate per piece = Gross income

Complete the table to find the gross income for each employee.

	Name	Pieces worked on: M	T	W	Th	F	Total	Rate per piece	Gross income
	Beagle, Grace	105	84	98	110	91	488	$ .34	$165.92
11.	Cheek, Audrey	97	113	102	120	71	503	.34	171.02
12.	Jedlicka, John	43	59	68	32	80	282	.65	183.30
13.	Klein, Ann	94	115	101	82	75	467	.34	158.78
14.	Lopez, Rita	35	42	64	51	58	250	.57	142.50
15.	Peters, John	110	105	64	101	98	478	.32	152.96
16.	Raimondi, Maria	85	91	73	95	67	411	.36	147.96
17.	Refo, Harvey	90	74	85	92	81	422	.43	181.46
18.	Sanchez, Cardo	62	71	53	41	70	297	.75	222.75
19.	Wagstaff, Virginia	112	95	103	115	99	524	.32	167.68
20.	Wilson, David	25	36	32	32	32	157	.98	153.86

The gross income is determined by the rate per piece and the number of pieces produced. Often the number of pieces worked on does not vary greatly. However, the rate per piece can be changed. You might have students compute the increase in each weekly gross income if the rate per piece were increased by $.05.

Number of test items - 25

Number missed	1	2	3	4	5	6	7	8	9	10	11	12
Percent correct	96	92	88	84	80	76	72	68	64	60	56	52

Chapter 5

A **1.** $\begin{array}{r} 4.9 \\ \times 3.6 \\ \hline \end{array}$ 17.64

B **2.** $\begin{array}{r} .539 \\ \times\ .07 \\ \hline \end{array}$ .03773

C **3.** $21.2 \times .37$ 7.844

D **4.** $6\overline{)14.82}$ 2.47

E **5.** $8\overline{).536}$ .067

F **6.** $110.2 \div 38$ 2.9

G **7.** 10×5.623 56.23

H **8.** 100×12.9 1290

I **9.** $460.32 \div 10$ 46.032

J **10.** $.29 \div 1000$ .00029

K **11.** $.7\overline{)6.58}$ 9.4

L **12.** $.09\overline{)28.8}$ 320

M **13.** $1.003 \div 1.7$ .59

N **14.** Round 14.68 to the nearest tenth. 14.7

O **15.** Round .0739 to the nearest hundredth. .07

P **16.** Round 2.34158 to the nearest thousandth. 2.342

Q **17.** Round the quotient to the nearest tenth.
$2.6\overline{)3.581}$ 1.4

R **18.** Round the quotient to the nearest hundredth.
$5\overline{)2.401}$ .48

S **19.** Round the quotient to the nearest thousandth.
$34\overline{).87528}$ .026

20. What is the total cost of 1.4 kilograms of chicken priced at $1.25 per kilogram? $1.75

21. What is the total cost of 9 kilograms of potatoes priced at $1.65 per kilogram? $14.85

22. Grace Royer is borrowing money to buy a new car priced at $4734.51. Interest on the loan is $449.83 per year for three years. If Grace pays back the loan in 36 equal payments, what will be the amount of each payment? $169

23. The rate charged for electricity in a certain city is $.07 per kilowatt-hour. What is the cost of using 1025 kilowatt-hours? $71.75

24. Harry Klein worked 32.5 hours at a rate of $4.50 per hour. What was his gross income? $146.25

25. In one week Luisa Valdes worked on 512 shirts. She was paid $.31 per shirt. What was her gross income for the week? $158.72

 See pages 11-12 of the *Tests and Record Forms: Duplicating Masters* for an alternate form of the Chapter 5 Test.

pretest

Materials: A ruler marked in centimeters and millimeters for items A and B.

Number of test items - 16

Number missed	1	2	3	4	5	6	7
Percent correct	94	88	81	75	69	63	56

skill Estimating and Measuring Length page 107

A Estimate the length of this bar in centimeters. Then use a ruler to find the actual length to the nearest centimeter. 5 centimeters

B Estimate the length of this bar in millimeters. Then use a ruler to find the actual length to the nearest millimeter. 24 millimeters
Accept answers close to this.

skill Using Units of Length pages 108–109

C Choose the most sensible measure for the length of a pencil.

18 mm (18 cm) 18 m 18 km

D 3.9 m = ▒ cm
390

skill Using Units of Area page 110

E Count squares to find the area of this figure in square centimeters.
4.5 square centimeters, or 4.5 cm^2

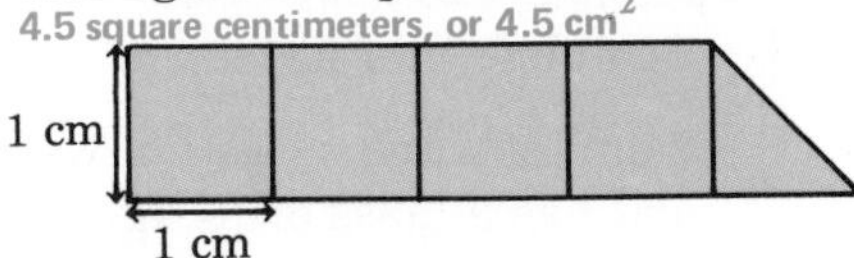

F Give the area of the figure in item E in square millimeters.
450 square millimeters, or 450 mm^2

skill Using Units of Volume page 111

G Count cubes to find the volume of this figure in cubic centimeters.
5 cubic centimeters, or 5 cm^3

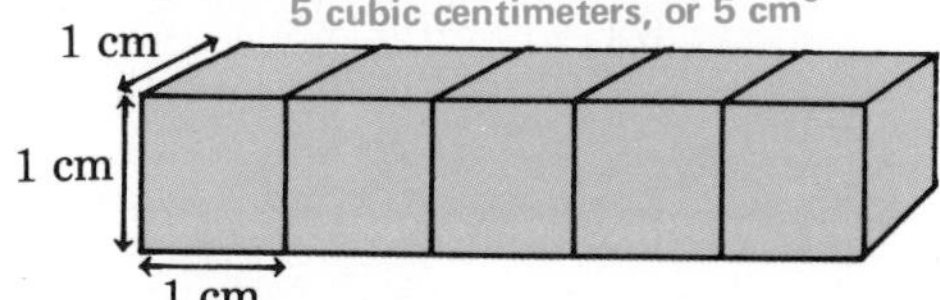

H Give the volume of the figure in item G in cubic millimeters.
5000 cubic millimeters, or 5000 mm^3

Pretest continued on page 106.

Pretest continued from page 105.

Skill Using Units of Capacity page 112

I Choose the more sensible measure for the amount of orange juice in a glass.

(180 ml) 180 ℓ

J 9.2 ℓ = ▒ ml 9200

Skill Using Units of Mass page 113

K Choose the most sensible measure for the mass of a loaf of bread.

454 mg (454 g) 454 kg

L 36 kg = ▒ g 36,000

Skill Relating Units of Volume, Capacity, and Mass page 114

M Complete this statement.

23 cm^3 of water is ▒ (23) ml of water and has a mass of ▒ (23) g.

N Complete this statement.

5 dm^3 of water is ▒ (5) ℓ of water and has a mass of ▒ (5) kg.

Skill Using Units of Temperature page 115

O Tell whether the temperature should be labeled kelvins or degrees Celsius. degrees Celsius

Warm summer day: 33

P Choose the more sensible temperature for ice skating.

($^-3$°C) 20°C

Materials: A ruler marked in centimeters and millimeters for sets A and B.

Objective: Estimate and measure the length of a segment to the nearest centimeter or millimeter.

Estimating and Measuring Length

example A Centimeters

Estimate the length of this bar in centimeters. Then use a ruler to find the actual length to the nearest centimeter.

Estimate: About 5 centimeters

Measure: 4 centimeters, to the nearest centimeter

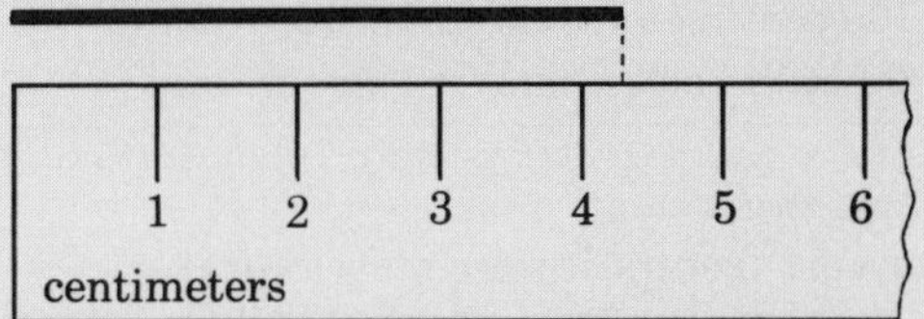

example B Millimeters

Estimate the length of this bar in millimeters. Then use a ruler to find the actual length to the nearest millimeter.

Estimate: About 55 millimeters

Measure: 58 millimeters, to the nearest millimeter

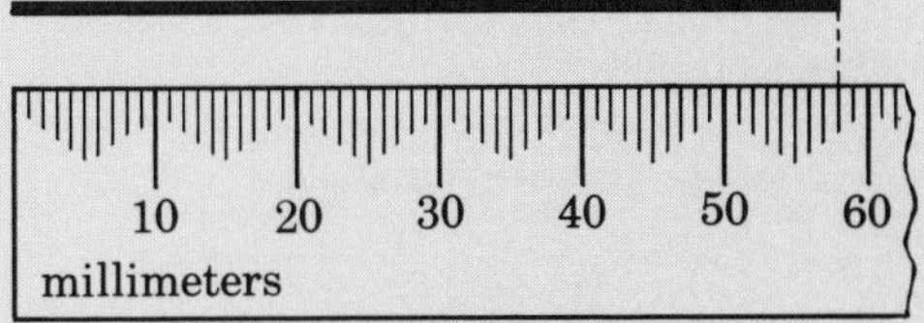

exercises

set A

Estimate the length of each bar in centimeters. Then use a ruler to find the actual length to the nearest centimeter.

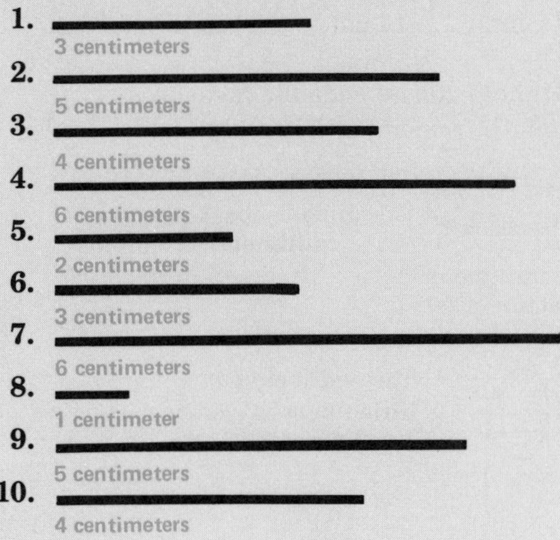

1. 3 centimeters
2. 5 centimeters
3. 4 centimeters
4. 6 centimeters
5. 2 centimeters
6. 3 centimeters
7. 6 centimeters
8. 1 centimeter
9. 5 centimeters
10. 4 centimeters

set B

Estimate the length of each bar in millimeters. Then use a ruler to find the actual length to the nearest millimeter.

Accept answers close to those given.

1. 36 millimeters
2. 52 millimeters
3. 7 millimeters
4. 24 millimeters
5. 46 millimeters
6. 61 millimeters
7. 17 millimeters
8. 29 millimeters
9. 56 millimeters
10. 39 millimeters

Have students estimate and then measure the lengths of small objects in the room.

The applications on pages 122-123 may be used anytime after this lesson.

Objective: Choose sensible measures and do conversions involving metric units of length.

Using Units of Length

example C Choosing sensible measures of length

Choose the most sensible measure for the height of a coffee can.

14 mm 14 cm 14 m 14 km

To help choose sensible measures of length, remember these objects.

1 millimeter (actual size)

The thickness of a dime is about 1 **millimeter** (1 mm).

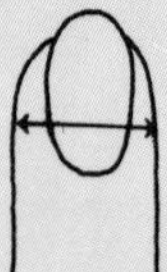

1 centimeter (actual size)

The width of your little finger is about 1 **centimeter** (1 cm).

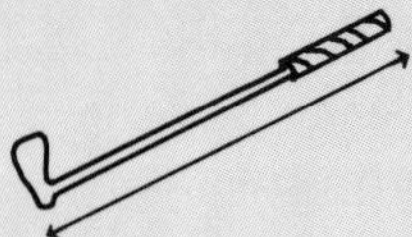

1 meter (not actual size)

The length of a golf club is about 1 **meter** (1 m).

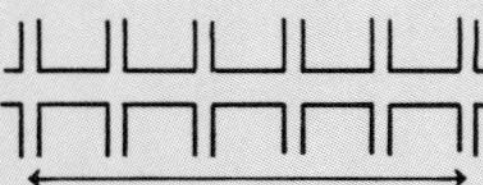

1 kilometer (not actual size)

A distance of 5 city blocks is about 1 **kilometer** (1 km).

A coffee can is about 14 cm tall.

example D Converting units of length

9.82 m = ▦ mm

Use the table below.

Equal metric units of length
1 kilometer (km) = 1000 meters (m)
1 hectometer (hm) = 100 meters (m)
1 dekameter (dam) = 10 meters (m)
10 decimeters (dm) = 1 meter (m)
100 centimeters (cm) = 1 meter (m)
1000 millimeters (mm) = 1 meter (m)

Emphasize that each unit of measure is 10 times as large as the next smaller unit.

To convert from a larger metric unit of measure to a smaller one, *multiply* by a number such as 10, 100, or 1000.

To convert from a smaller metric unit of measure to a larger one, *divide* by a number such as 10, 100, or 1000.

Remember, to multiply by 10, 100, or 1000, move the decimal point to the right. To divide by 10, 100, or 1000, move the decimal point to the left.

9.82 m = ▦ mm — Multiply 9.82 by 1000.

9.82 m = 9820 mm

You might also demonstrate conversion from a smaller unit to a larger one.

54 mm = ▦ m — Divide 54 by 1000.

54 mm = 0.054 m — Move the decimal point 3 places to the left.

exercises

set C

Choose the most sensible measure.

1. Length of a small paper clip

   (31 mm) 31 cm 31 m 31 km

2. Length of a tennis racket

   68 mm (68 cm) 68 m 68 km

3. Distance around a racetrack

   2 mm 2 cm 2 m (2 km)

4. Length of a canoe

   4 mm 4 cm (4 m) 4 km

5. Length of a key

   (54 mm) 54 cm 54 m 54 km

6. Height of a woman

   160 mm (160 cm) 160 m 160 km

7. Width of a room

   8 mm 8 cm (8 m) 8 km

8. Distance from New York to Boston

   348 mm 348 cm 348 m (348 km)

9. Length of a bowling alley

   18 mm 18 cm (18 m) 18 km

10. Height of a giant redwood tree

    76 mm 76 cm (76 m) 76 km

11. Length of a safety pin

    (26 mm) 26 cm 26 m 26 km

12. Width of a desk

    75 mm (75 cm) 75 m 75 km

13. Long-distance run

    10,000 cm (10,000 m) 10,000 km

Notice that these exercises stress only the most commonly used units of length: kilometer, meter, centimeter, and millimeter.

set D

1. 38 km = ▦ m 38,000
2. 0.4 m = ▦ cm 40
3. 758 mm = ▦ m 0.758
4. 24.3 dm = ▦ m 2.43
5. 8.5 m = ▦ mm 8500
6. 7 km = ▦ m 7000
7. 155 cm = ▦ m 1.55
8. 9.21 m = ▦ dm 92.1
9. 1245 m = ▦ km 1.245
10. 247 cm = ▦ m 2.47
11. 16.5 m = ▦ cm 1650
12. 1475 mm = ▦ m 1.475

BREAK TIME

Bonnie has coins totaling more than one dollar, but she cannot make change for a dollar.

What is the greatest amount of money in coins that she could have? $1.19

3 quarters (or a fifty-cent piece and a quarter), 4 dimes, and 4 pennies

The applications on pages 120–121 may be used anytime after this lesson.

Objective: Find areas of figures and do conversions involving metric units of area.

Using Units of Area

example E Counting square centimeters

Count squares to find the area in square centimeters.

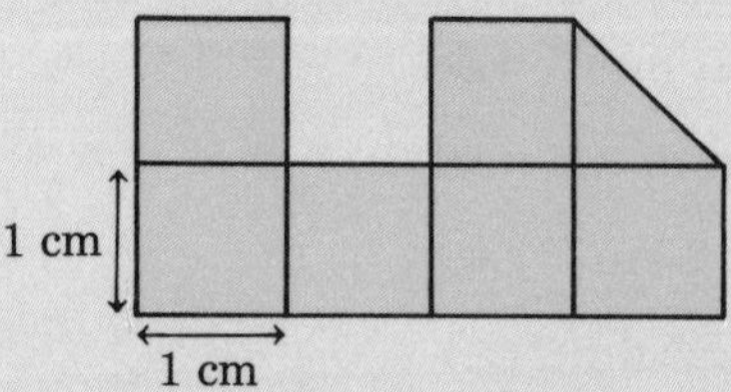

Here are some metric units of area.

Square kilometer (km^2)
Square meter (m^2)
Square centimeter (cm^2)
Square millimeter (mm^2)

The area of the figure is 6.5 square centimeters (6.5 cm^2).

example F Converting units of area

Give the area of the figure in example E in square millimeters.

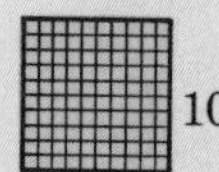

$1 \text{ cm}^2 = 100 \text{ mm}^2$

To convert from square centimeters to square millimeters, multiply by 100.

$6.5 \text{ cm}^2 = \text{▒} \text{ mm}^2$ Multiply 6.5 by 100.

$6.5 \text{ cm}^2 = 650 \text{ mm}^2$

The area of the figure in example E is 650 square millimeters (650 mm^2).

exercises

set E

Count to find the area in square centimeters.

1. 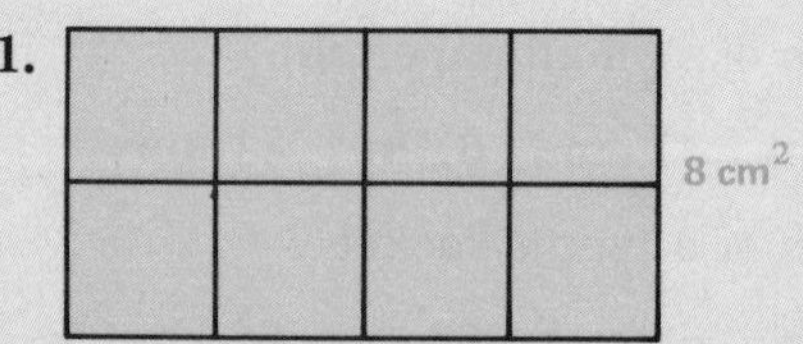
8 cm^2

2. 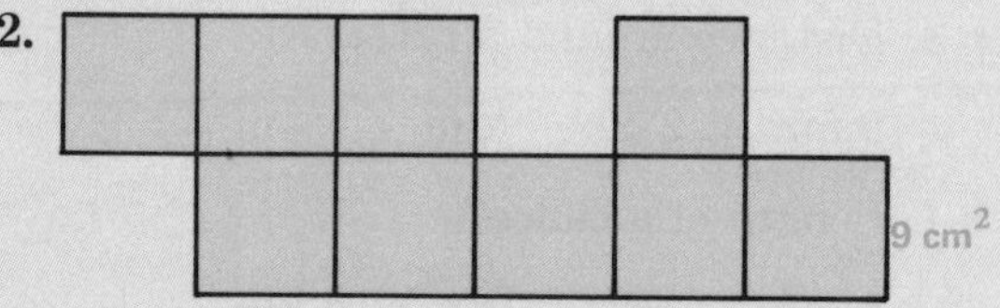
9 cm^2

3. 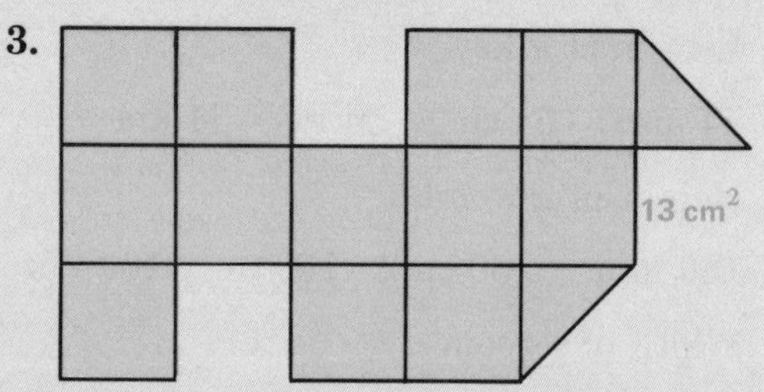
13 cm^2

4. 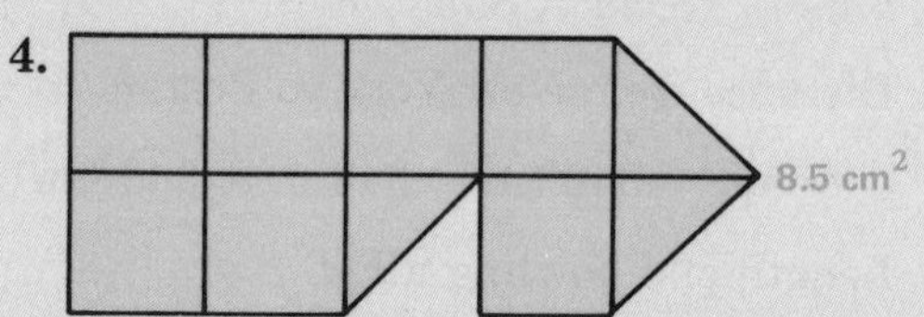
8.5 cm^2

5. 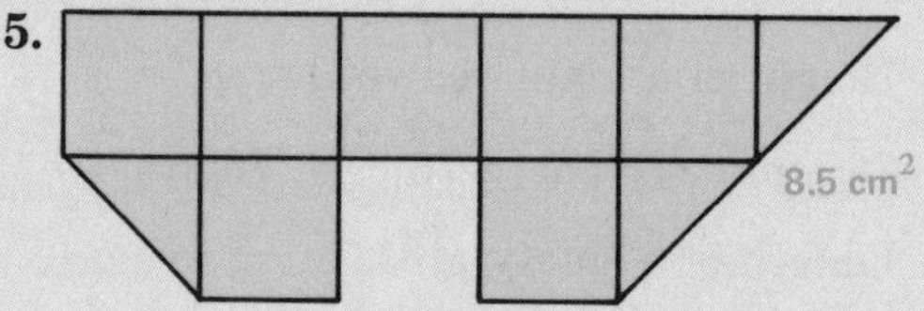
8.5 cm^2

set F

You might have students estimate and measure the area of the chalkboard in square meters and the area of tracings of their hands in square centimeters.

1–5. Give the area of each figure in set E in square millimeters.

1. 800 mm^2 4. 850 mm^2
2. 900 mm^2 5. 850 mm^2
3. 1300 mm^2

Objective: Find volumes of figures and do conversions involving metric units of volume.

Using Units of Volume

example G Counting cubic centimeters

Count cubes to find the volume in cubic centimeters.

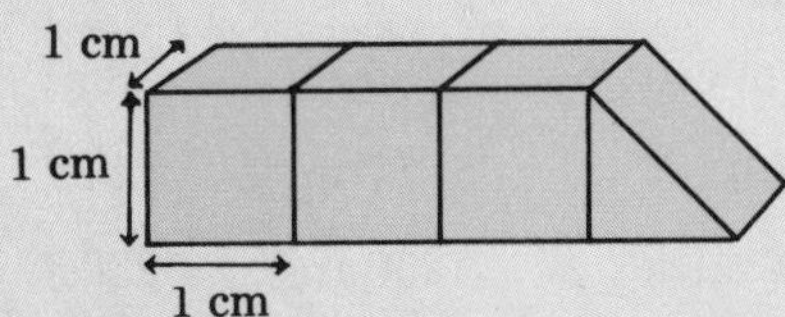

Here are some metric units of volume.

Cubic meter (m^3)
Cubic decimeter (dm^3)
Cubic centimeter (cm^3)
Cubic millimeter (mm^3)

The volume of the figure is 4.5 cubic centimeters (4.5 cm^3).

example H Converting units of volume

Give the volume of the figure in example G in cubic millimeters.

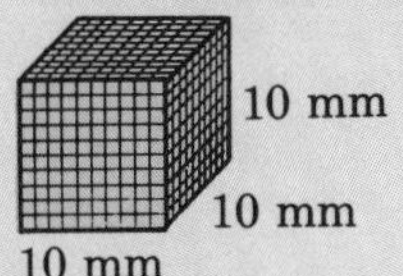

$1 \text{ cm}^3 = 1000 \text{ mm}^3$

To convert from cubic centimeters to cubic millimeters, multiply by 1000.

$4.5 \text{ cm}^3 = \blacksquare \text{ mm}^3$ Multiply 4.5 by 1000.

$4.5 \text{ cm}^3 = 4500 \text{ mm}^3$

The volume of the figure in example G is 4500 cubic millimeters (4500 mm^3).

exercises

set G

Count to find the volume in cubic centimeters.

1. 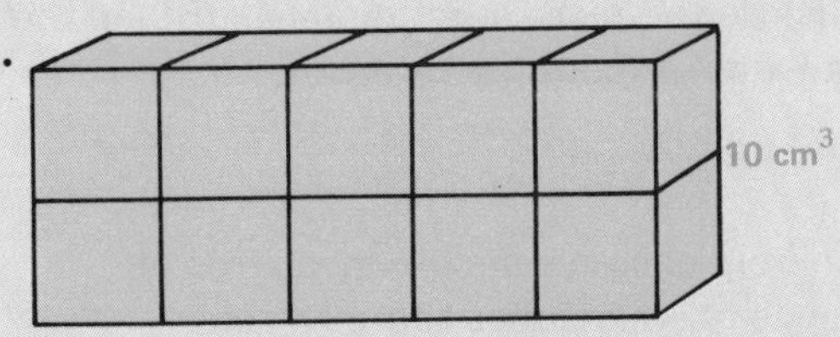

2. 

3. 

4. 

5. 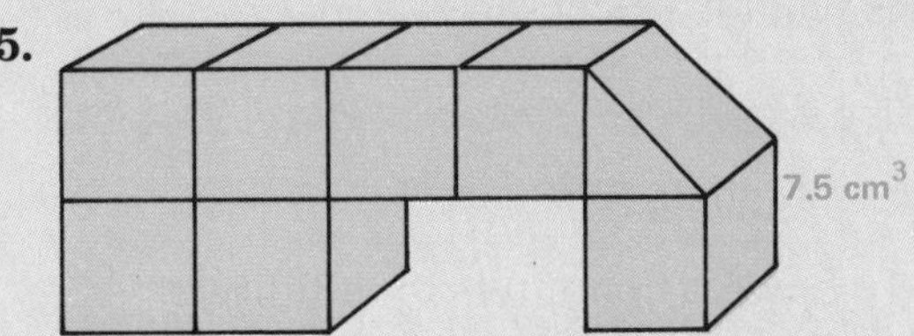

set H

1–5. Give the volume of each figure in set G in cubic millimeters.

1. 10,000 mm^3 4. 6000 mm^3
2. 8000 mm^3 5. 7500 mm^3
3. 11,000 mm^3

Using Units of Capacity

example I

Choosing sensible measures of capacity

Choose the more sensible measure for the amount of root beer in a can.

360 ml   360 ℓ

To help choose sensible measures of capacity, remember these objects.

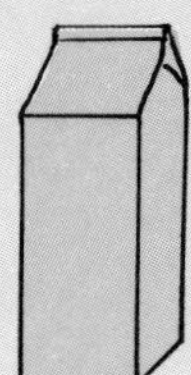

The amount of milk in this type of carton is about 1 **liter** (1 ℓ).

1 liter

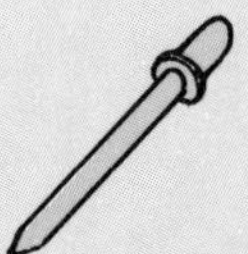

The amount of liquid in an eyedropper is about 1 **milliliter** (1 ml).

1 milliliter

The amount of root beer in a can is about 360 ml.

example J

Converting units of capacity

7.4 ℓ = ▦ ml

1 ℓ = 1000 ml

To convert from liters to milliliters, multiply by 1000.

To convert from milliliters to liters, divide by 1000.

7.4 ℓ = 7400 ml   Multiply 7.4 by 1000.

exercises

set I

Choose the more sensible measure.

1.	Coffeepot	2 ml	(2 ℓ)
2.	Can of juice	(165 ml)	165 ℓ
3.	Carton of cream	(235 ml)	235 ℓ
4.	Fish tank	17 ml	(17 ℓ)
5.	Glass of milk	(250 ml)	250 ℓ
6.	Bathtub	400 ml	(400 ℓ)
7.	Teakettle	(700 ml)	700 ℓ
8.	Test tube	(75 ml)	75 ℓ
9.	Bucket	8 ml	(8 ℓ)
10.	Bottle of cola	(500 ml)	500 ℓ
11.	Kitchen sink	50 ml	(50 ℓ)
12.	Cup of coffee	(200 ml)	200 ℓ

set J

1. 25 ℓ = ▦ ml 25,000

2. 435 ml = ▦ ℓ 0.435

3. 82.7 ml = ▦ ℓ 0.0827

4. 0.8 ℓ = ▦ ml 800

5. 375 ℓ = ▦ ml 375,000

6. 85 ml = ▦ ℓ 0.085

7. 5 ℓ = ▦ ml 5000

8. 28.2 ml = ▦ ℓ 0.0282

9. 4370 ml = ▦ ℓ 4.370 or 4.37

10. 3.2 ℓ = ▦ ml 3200

11. 83.4 ml = ▦ ℓ 0.0834

12. 0.25 ℓ = ▦ ml 250

Objective: Choose sensible measures and do conversions involving metric units of mass.

Using Units of Mass

example K
Choosing sensible measures of mass

Choose the most sensible measure for the mass of an egg.

54 mg 54 g 54 kg

To help choose sensible measures of mass, remember these objects.

The mass of an adult's pair of shoes is about 1 **kilogram** (1 kg).

1 kilogram

The mass of a raisin is about 1 **gram** (1 g).

1 gram

The mass of a straight pin is 125 **milligrams** (125 mg). 1000 mg = 1 g

125 milligrams

The mass of an egg is about 54 g.

See page T19 for information about the terms "weight" and "mass."

example L
Converting units of mass

9.5 kg = ▒ g

1 kg = 1000 g

To convert from kilograms to grams, multiply by 1000.

To convert from grams to kilograms, divide by 1000.

9.5 kg = 9500 g   Multiply 9.5 by 1000.

exercises

set K

Choose the most sensible measure.

1.	Dog	8 mg	8 g	8 kg
2.	Can of beans	453 mg	453 g	453 kg
3.	Pencil	5 mg	5 g	5 kg
4.	Paper clip	515 mg	515 g	515 kg
5.	TV set	19 mg	19 g	19 kg
6.	Woman	50 mg	50 g	50 kg
7.	Can of soup	305 mg	305 g	305 kg
8.	Lion	170 mg	170 g	170 kg
9.	Nickel	5 mg	5 g	5 kg
10.	Basketball	566 mg	566 g	566 kg
11.	Sewing needle	380 mg	380 g	380 kg
12.	Bowling ball	7 mg	7 g	7 kg

Notice that these exercises stress only the most commonly used units of mass: kilogram and gram.

set L

1. 38 kg = ▒ g 38,000

2. 715 g = ▒ kg 0.715

3. 0.4 kg = ▒ g 400

4. 67.2 g = ▒ kg 0.0672

5. 31 g = ▒ kg 0.031

6. 283 kg = ▒ g 283,000

7. 7 kg = ▒ g 7000

8. 45.8 g = ▒ kg 0.0458

9. 6420 g = ▒ kg 6.420 or 6.42

10. 9.3 kg = ▒ g 9300

11. 850 g = ▒ kg 0.850 or 0.85

12. 0.36 kg = ▒ g 360

The applications on pages 124–125 may be used anytime after this lesson.

Objective: Write measures for given amounts of water using related units of volume, capacity, and mass.

Relating Units of Volume, Capacity, and Mass

example M Relating cm^3, ml, and g

Complete this statement.

7 cm^3 of water is ▒ ml of water and has a mass of ▒ g.

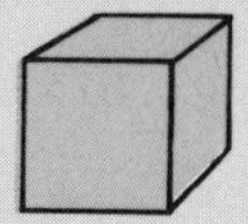

A container with a volume of 1 cubic centimeter holds 1 milliliter of water. The mass of the water is 1 gram.

1 cm^3

Technically this relationship holds when the water is at 4°C.

1 ml

1 g

7 cm^3 of water is 7 ml of water and has a mass of 7 g.

example N Relating dm^3, ℓ, and kg

Complete this statement.

16 dm^3 of water is ▒ ℓ of water and has a mass of ▒ kg.

1 dm^3

1 ℓ

1 kg

A container with a volume of 1 cubic decimeter holds 1 liter of water. The mass of the water is 1 kilogram.

16 dm^3 of water is 16 ℓ of water and has a mass of 16 kg.

You might demonstrate this relationship by using an approximation of a cubic decimeter in the form of a half-gallon milk carton which has been cut off 1 decimeter above the base. The cut-off carton will hold about 1 liter.

exercises

set M

Complete each description of an amount of water.

1. 30 cm^3 30 ▒ ml 30 ▒ g

2. 8.2 ml 8.2 ▒ cm^3 8.2 ▒ g

3. 950 g 950 ▒ ml 950 ▒ cm^3

4. 7 cm^3 7 ▒ g 7 ▒ ml

5. 63 g 63 ▒ ml 63 ▒ cm^3

6. 0.4 ml 0.4 ▒ cm^3 0.4 ▒ g

7. 16.3 ml 16.3 ▒ g 16.3 ▒ cm^3

8. 12 cm^3 12 ▒ ml 12 ▒ g

9. 8.9 g 8.9 ▒ cm^3 8.9 ▒ ml

10. 250 cm^3 250 ▒ ml 250 ▒ g

set N

Complete each description of an amount of water.

1. 8 dm^3 8 ▒ ℓ 8 ▒ kg

2. 5.6 ℓ 5.6 ▒ kg 5.6 ▒ dm^3

3. 0.3 kg 0.3 ▒ dm^3 0.3 ▒ ℓ

4. 2.45 ℓ 2.45 ▒ dm^3 2.45 ▒ kg

5. 12.3 kg 12.3 ▒ ℓ 12.3 ▒ dm^3

6. 30 dm^3 30 ▒ kg 30 ▒ ℓ

7. 85 ℓ 85 ▒ dm^3 85 ▒ kg

8. 16 dm^3 16 ▒ ℓ 16 ▒ kg

9. 0.7 kg 0.7 ▒ dm^3 0.7 ▒ ℓ

10. 280 ℓ 280 ▒ dm^3 280 ▒ kg

Objective: Choose sensible measures involving metric units of temperature.

Using Units of Temperature

example O Choosing kelvins or degrees Celsius

Tell whether the temperature should be labeled kelvins or degrees Celsius.

Air in a classroom: 22

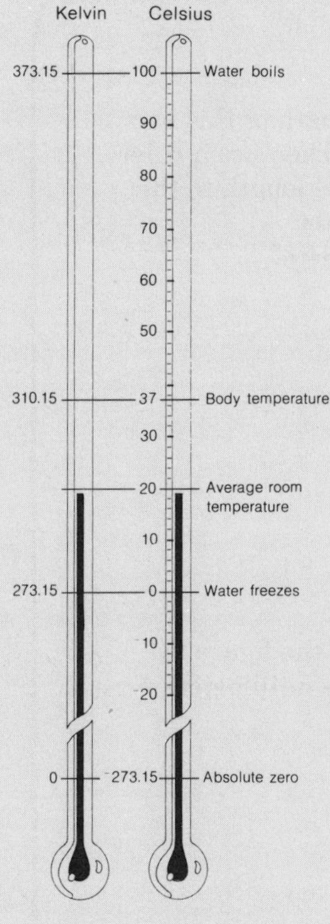

Thermometers in most countries measure temperature in **degrees Celsius** (°C). Scientists use thermometers that measure temperature in **kelvins** (K).

The air in a classroom is about 22°C.

example P Choosing sensible measures in degrees Celsius

Choose the more sensible temperature for the water in a bathtub.

27°C 80°C

Water in a bathtub is about 27°C.

exercises set O

Notice that the word *kelvins* is not capitalized and that the degree symbol is not used with the symbol K.

Tell whether the temperature should be labeled kelvins or degrees Celsius.

1. Cold glass of milk: 5 °C
2. Summer day: 300 K
3. Hot oven: 220 °C
4. Water in river: 11 °C
5. Boiling water: 373.15 K
6. Snowball: $^{-}2$ °C
7. Melted butter: 43 °C
8. Cold winter day: $^{-}15$ °C
9. Warm bread: 32 °C
10. Desert air: 313 K

set P

Choose the more sensible temperature.

1.	Hot soup	25°C	(58°C)
2.	Spring day	(20°C)	65°C
3.	Boiling water	(100°C)	50°C
4.	Winter day	45°C	($^{-}7$°C)
5.	Drinking water	(10°C)	70°C
6.	Fall day	(13°C)	60°C
7.	Ice cream	30°C	(4°C)
8.	Hot fudge	130°C	(40°C)
9.	Ice cube	(0°C)	32°C
10.	Rain water	60°C	(18°C)
11.	Warm milk	(15°C)	55°C
12.	Cold pudding	(8°C)	40°C

The applications on pages 118-119 may be used anytime after this lesson.

Materials: A ruler marked in centimeters and millimeters for items A and B.

Number of test items - 16

posttest

Number missed	1	2	3	4	5	6	7
Percent correct	94	88	81	75	69	63	56

skill Estimating and Measuring Length page 107

A Estimate the length of this bar in centimeters. Then use a ruler to find the actual length to the nearest centimeter. 6 centimeters

B Estimate the length of this bar in millimeters. Then use a ruler to find the actual length to the nearest millimeter.
32 millimeters Accept answers close to this.

skill Using Units of Length pages 108–109

C Choose the most sensible measure for the length of a room.

9 mm 9 cm (9 m) 9 km

D 6.53 m = ▒ cm
653

skill Using Units of Area page 110

E Count squares to find the area of this figure in square centimeters. $3.5\ cm^2$

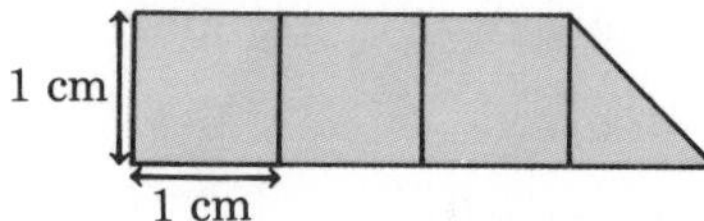

F Give the area of the figure in item E in square millimeters. $350\ mm^2$

skill Using Units of Volume page 111

G Count cubes to find the volume of this figure in cubic centimeters. $4.5\ cm^3$

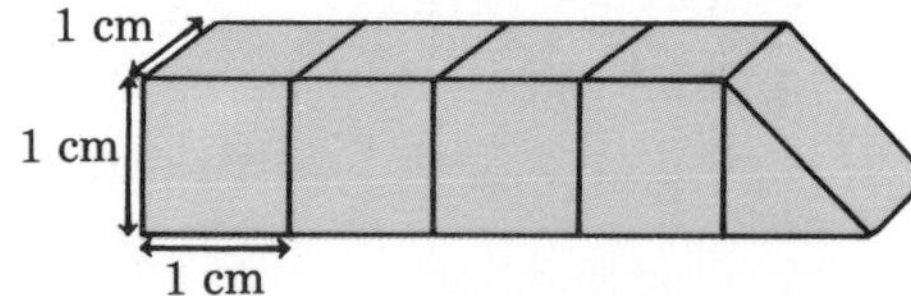

H Give the volume of the figure in item G in cubic millimeters. $4500\ mm^3$

Posttest continued on page 117.

Posttest continued from page 116.

Skill Using Units of Capacity page 112

I Choose the more sensible measure for the capacity of an automobile gas tank.

80 ml (80 ℓ)

J 7.35ℓ = ▒ ml 7350

Skill Using Units of Mass page 113

K Choose the most sensible measure for the mass of a shoe.

500 mg (500 g) 500 kg

L 4.6 kg = ▒ g 4600

Skill Relating Units of Volume, Capacity, and Mass page 114

M Complete this statement.

9.1 cm^3 of water is ▒ (9.1) ml of water and has a mass of ▒ (9.1) g.

N Complete this statement.

35 dm^3 of water is ▒ (35) ℓ of water and has a mass of ▒ (35) kg.

Skill Using Units of Temperature page 115

O Tell whether the temperature should be labeled kelvins or degrees Celsius.

Warm apple pie: 42 °C

P Choose the more sensible temperature for a mild winter day.

(9°C) 45°C

Objective: Solve problems involving metric units of measure.

In this lesson students increase and decrease recipes that use metric measures.

Using Metric Measures in Cooking

GRAHAM MUFFINS

Makes 12 muffins

165 g graham cracker crumbs	1. 495 g
7 g baking powder	21 g
1 egg	3
125 ml milk	375 ml
75 ml corn oil	225 ml
50 ml corn syrup	150 ml
55 g chopped pecans	165 g

Grease 12 muffin cups. Combine cracker crumbs and baking powder. Beat egg. Add milk, oil, and syrup. Add to crumbs. Stir. Add nuts. Cook at 190°C for 20 minutes.

LAZY DAY LASAGNE

Serves 4 people

170 g lasagne noodles	3. 340 g
1 ml dried, crushed oregano	2 ml
500 g spaghetti sauce with meat	1000 g
250 ml cream-style cottage cheese	500 ml
180 g sliced mozzarella cheese	360 g

Cook noodles. Add oregano to spaghetti sauce. In baking dish, make layers of noodles, cottage cheese, cheese slices and sauce. Repeat layers. Bake at 185°C for 30 minutes.

1. Tom wants to triple the recipe for graham muffins. How much of each ingredient should he use? See recipe above.

Discuss and/or demonstrate ways to measure dry ingredients in grams [spring scale or pan balance] and ways to measure liquid or dry ingredients in milliliters [glass containers, metal containers, or measuring spoons].

2. The Smiths want to serve lasagne to 8 people. They need to multiply each ingredient by ▒. 2

3. How much of each ingredient should they use? See recipe above.

4. Mr. Williams wants to make lasagne for himself and his wife. How much of each ingredient should he use?

85 g lasagne noodles
0.5 ml dried, crushed oregano
250 g spaghetti sauce with meat
125 ml cream-style cottage cheese
90 g sliced mozzarella cheese

Point out the oven temperatures given in degrees Celsius. Here are some other oven temperatures. Warm: 150°C
Moderate: 180°C Hot: 210°C Very hot: 240°C Broil: 270°C

CEREAL COOKIES

Makes 24 cookies

Ingredient	6.
100 g shortening	600 g
140 g sugar	840 g
2 eggs	12
5 ml vanilla extract	30 ml
3 g salt	18 g
2 g baking powder	12 g
150 g flour	900 g
80 g high-protein cereal	480 g

Blend shortening, sugar, vanilla. Add eggs and beat. Add dry ingredients and 20 g of cereal. Make into balls. Roll in remaining cereal. Flatten. Bake at 190°C for 11 minutes.

SPECIAL HAMBURGERS

Serves 6 people

Ingredient	7.
0.5 kg ground beef	0.25 kg
30 ml finely chopped green pepper	15 ml
60 ml chopped onion	30 ml
80 ml catsup	40 ml
15 ml horseradish	7.5 ml
7 ml dry mustard	3.5 ml
2 ml salt	1 ml

Combine ingredients. Form patties. Bake at 190°C for 30 minutes.

5. Chris wants to make 144 cereal cookies. Each ingredient should be multiplied by ▒. 6

6. How much of each ingredient should Chris use? See recipe above.

7. Harvey Bruder plans to make special hamburgers for 3 people. How much of each ingredient should he use? See recipe above.

Mr. and Mrs. Kelch plan to make special hamburgers and cereal cookies for 12 people.

8. How much of each cookie ingredient should they use? See below.

9. How much of each hamburger ingredient should they use? See below.

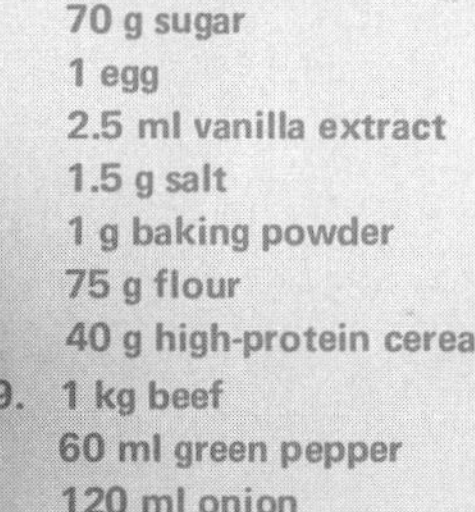

8. 50 g shortening
70 g sugar
1 egg
2.5 ml vanilla extract
1.5 g salt
1 g baking powder
75 g flour
40 g high-protein cereal

9. 1 kg beef
60 ml green pepper
120 ml onion
160 ml catsup
30 ml horseradish
14 ml mustard
4 ml salt

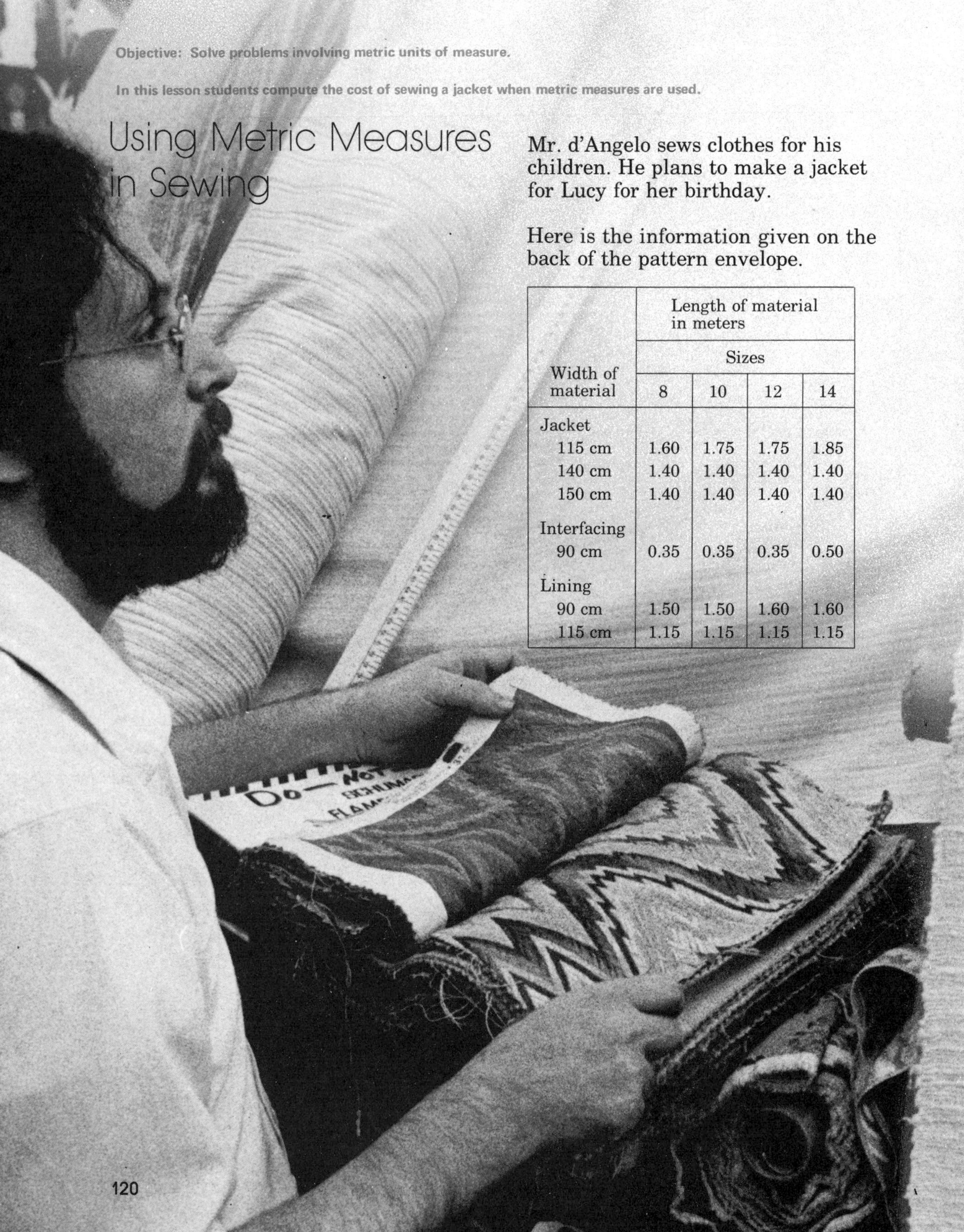

Objective: Solve problems involving metric units of measure.

In this lesson students compute the cost of sewing a jacket when metric measures are used.

Using Metric Measures in Sewing

Mr. d'Angelo sews clothes for his children. He plans to make a jacket for Lucy for her birthday.

Here is the information given on the back of the pattern envelope.

Width of material	Length of material in meters			
	Sizes			
	8	10	12	14
Jacket				
115 cm	1.60	1.75	1.75	1.85
140 cm	1.40	1.40	1.40	1.40
150 cm	1.40	1.40	1.40	1.40
Interfacing				
90 cm	0.35	0.35	0.35	0.50
Lining				
90 cm	1.50	1.50	1.60	1.60
115 cm	1.15	1.15	1.15	1.15

Interfacing is stiff material used to hold shape.

Lucy is size 8. Complete this table to find the cost of her jacket.

	Item	Width	Length needed in meters	Price per meter	Cost rounded up to next whole cent
	Material	115 cm	1.60	$3.25	$5.20
1.	Interfacing	90 cm	0.35	$1.75	$.62
2.	Lining	90 cm	1.50	$2.15	$3.23
	Zipper				$1.55
3.				Total cost of all items	$10.60

At a second store, similar material in a different width was on sale. Find the costs at that store.

	Item	Width	Length needed in meters	Price per meter	Cost rounded up to next whole cent
4.	Material	150 cm	1.40	$3.30	$4.62
5.	Interfacing	90 cm	0.35	$1.70	$.60
6.	Lining	115 cm	1.15	$2.30	$2.65
	Zipper				$1.49
7.				Total cost of all items	$9.36

8. The total cost is how much less at the second store? $1.24

Find the cost of making a size 14 jacket for Lucy's mother using different material.

	Item	Width	Length needed in meters	Price per meter	Cost rounded up to next whole cent
9.	Material	115 cm	1.85	$3.49	$6.46
10.	Interfacing	90 cm	0.50	$1.75	$.88
11.	Lining	90 cm	1.60	$2.29	$3.67
	Zipper				$2.15
12.				Total cost of all items	$13.16

You might have students bring in patterns which show both metric and U.S. customary measures.

Career: Assembler

Career Cluster: Trades

Materials: A ruler marked in millimeters for exercises 1–8.

Objective: Solve problems involving metric units of measure.

In this lesson students measure parts of metal fasteners to the nearest millimeter and compute diameters of tap drills used with metal fasteners.

Dorothy Stevens works as an assembler in a factory. She uses metal fasteners to join pieces of metal.

Use a ruler to measure the thread (T), the length (L), and the diameter (D) of each fastener to the nearest millimeter.

Accept answers close to those given.

1.

T = 16 mm
L = 25 mm
D = 6 mm

2.

T = 15 mm
L = 23 mm
D = 5 mm

3.

4.

5.

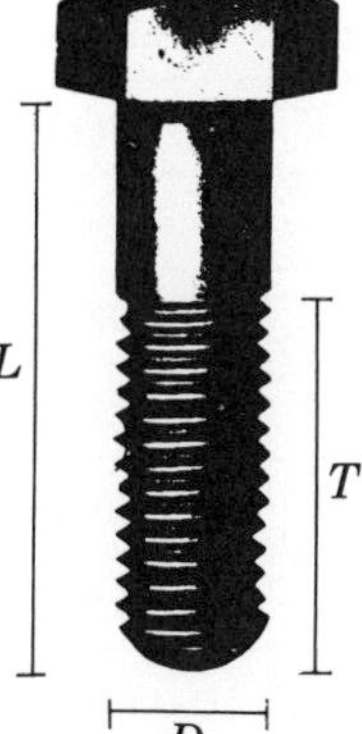

6.

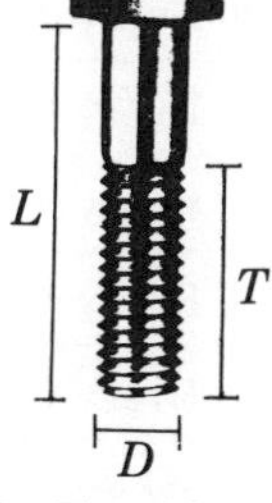

7.

8.

3. T = 19 mm
L = 34 mm
D = 8 mm
4. T = 13 mm
L = 26 mm
D = 7 mm
5. T = 25 mm
L = 38 mm
D = 11 mm
6. T = 15 mm
L = 25 mm
D = 6 mm
7. T = 15 mm
L = 23 mm
D = 5 mm
8. T = 13 mm
L = 23 mm
D = 5 mm

A transparent metric ruler and some bolts can be used to demonstrate which measures are to be taken.

The pitch of a fastener is the distance from the top of one thread to the top of the next thread.

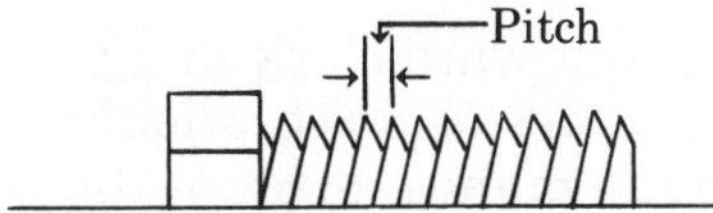

In order to use a fastener, Dorothy must first drill a hole with a tap drill. She selects a drill that is slightly smaller than the fastener, so that the threads of the fastener will hold in the metal.

The table below lists most of the fastener sizes used in industry.

To select the correct diameter for a tap drill, subtract the pitch of the fastener from the diameter of the fastener.

In the table, size M 3 means a diameter of 3 millimeters. Size M 12 means a diameter of 12 millimeters.

	Diameter of fastener (mm)	Pitch of fastener (mm)	Diameter of tap drill (mm)
	M 3	0.5	2.5
9.	M 4	0.7	3.3
10.	M 5	0.8	4.2
11.	M 6	1.0	5.0
12.	M 8	1.25	6.75
13.	M 10	1.5	8.5
14.	M 12	1.75	10.25
15.	M 16	2.0	14.0
16.	M 20	2.5	17.5
17.	M 24	3.0	21.0
18.	M 30	3.5	26.5
19.	M 36	4.0	32.0

Objective: Solve problems involving metric units of measure.

In this lesson students work with dosages of medicines and dispensed units of medicine involving metric measures.

Career: Hospital-Ward Clerk

Career Cluster: Health See the Careers Chart beginning on page 420 for more jobs and other information about this career cluster.

Yin Lim is a ward clerk in a big-city hospital. He prepares medical records, serves as a receptionist, and handles most of the clerical work involved in management of the third floor.

Yin received the request form shown below. He must compute the supply of each medication that will be needed for that day. Here is an example.

Dosage: 1.5 g Rate: Every 4 hours. Find the total daily dosage.
First divide 24 hours by the rate to find the number of dosages per day. $24 \div 4 = 6$
Then multiply to find the total daily dosage. $6 \times 1.5 = 9.0$ Total daily dosage: 9.0 g

Complete the request form. The illnesses for which the drugs are prescribed are given below.

Floor: 3rd — Pharmaceutical Request Form — Date: November 15

	Patient	Medication	Dosage	Rate	Total daily dosage
1.	Braniff, Sheila	Digoxin	0.125 mg	Every 6 hours	0.5 mg
2.	Heart attack	Morphine sulfate	10 mg	Every 4 hours	60 mg
3.		Valium	5 mg	Every 6 hours	20 mg
4.	Zaniello, Al	Meprobamate	500 mg	Every 4 hours	3000 mg
5.	Stomach spasms	Maalox	30 cm^3	Every 4 hours	180 cm^3
6.		Donnatol elixer	5 cm^3	Every 6 hours	20 cm^3
7.	Ramirez, Linda	Librium	10 mg	Every 4 hours	60 mg
8.	High blood pressure with convulsions	Dilantin	0.1 g	Every 8 hours	0.3 g
9.		Aldomet	250 mg	Every 12 hours	500 mg
10.	Turner, Francis	Gantanol	1 g	Every 8 hours	3 g
11.	Urinary tract infection	Darvon plain	65 mg	Every 6 hours	260 mg
12.		Chloral hydrate	500 mg	Every 4 hours	3000 mg
13.	Valdes, Rosalia	Ampicillin	500 mg	Every 24 hours	500 mg
14.	Appendicitis	Meperidine	75 mg	Every 6 hours	300 mg

Yin receives medicines from the pharmacy in bulk quantities. He dispenses the medicines to the nurses in smaller quantities called units.

The bulk quantity for staphene is 5 liters. It is dispensed in 250-milliliter units. How many units are dispensed from 5 liters?

First convert 5 liters to milliliters.
$5\ell \times 1000$ ml per $\ell = 5000$ ml

Then divide to find the number of units.
5000 ml ÷ 250 ml per unit = 20 units

Find the number of units for each item listed below.

	Item	Bulk amount	Size of dispensed unit	Number of units
15.	Alcohol	5 ℓ	100 ml	50
16.	Penicillin	1 ℓ	20 ml	50
17.	Quinine	1 ℓ	5 ml	200
18.	Iodine	2 kg	2 g	1000
19.	Sodium Bicarbonate	5 kg	10 g	500
20.	Saparated Creosol	1 ℓ	4 ml	250

Number of test items - 20

Number missed	1	2	3	4	5	6	7	8	9	10
Percent correct	95	90	85	80	75	70	65	60	55	50

Chapter 6 **Materials:** A ruler marked in centimeters and millimeters for items 1, 2, and 19.

A **1.** Estimate the length of this bar in centimeters. Then use a ruler to find the actual length to the nearest centimeter. 3 centimeters

B **2.** Estimate the length of this bar in millimeters. Then use a ruler to find the actual length to the nearest millimeter. 17 millimeters
Accept answers close to this.

C **3.** Choose the most sensible measure for the height of a school building.

12 mm   12 cm

(12 m)   12 km

D **4.** 6.52 m = ▒ mm 6520

E **5.** Count squares to find the area of this figure in square centimeters. 5 cm^2

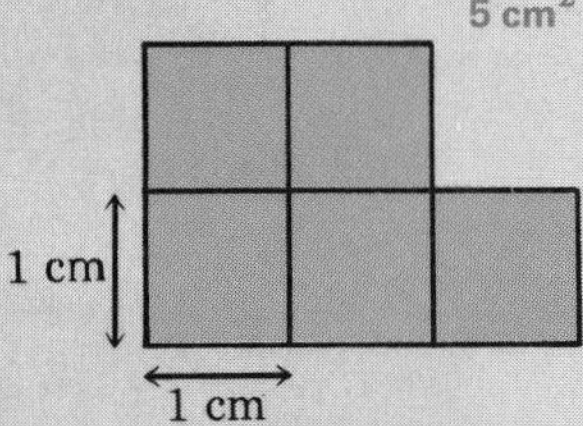

F **6.** Give the area of the figure in item 5 in square millimeters. 500 mm^2

G **7.** Count cubes to find the volume of this figure in cubic centimeters. 2 cm^3

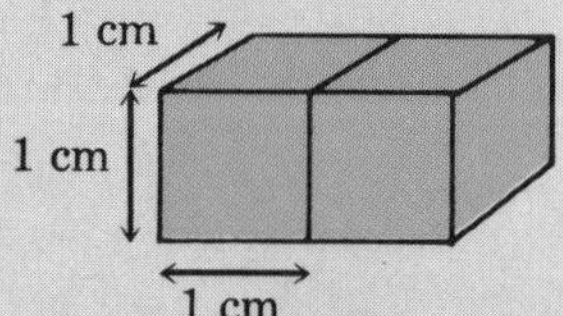

H **8.** Give the volume of the figure in item 7 in cubic millimeters. 2000 mm^3

I **9.** Choose the more sensible measure for the amount of water in a pail.

6 ml   (6 ℓ)

J **10.** 8.25 ℓ = ▒ ml 8250

K **11.** Choose the most sensible measure for the mass of a small child.

15 mg   15 g   (15 kg)

L **12.** 4.5 kg = ▒ g 4500

M **13.** Complete this statement.

4 cm^3 of water is ▒ ml (4) of water and has a mass of ▒ g. (4)

N **14.** Complete this statement.

9 dm^3 of water is ▒ ℓ (9) of water and has a mass of ▒ kg. (9)

O **15.** Tell whether the temperature should be labeled kelvins or degrees Celsius.

Hot toast: 50° C

P **16.** Choose the more sensible temperature for a cold drink.

47°C

17. A recipe calls for 150 ml of milk. How much milk is needed for a triple recipe? 450 ml

18. What is the cost of 1.5 meters of material at \$3.50 per meter? \$5.25

19. Measure the thread (T), the length (L), and the diameter (D) of this fastener to the nearest millimeter. Accept answers close to those given.

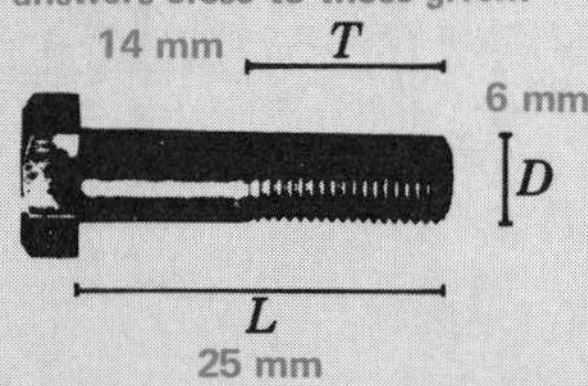

20. Dosage: 25 g
Rate: Every 4 hours

Find the total daily dosage. 150 g

See pages 13–14 of the *Tests and Record Forms: Duplicating Masters* for an alternate form of the Chapter 6 Test. For a test on Unit 2, see page T31 of this book and pages 15–16 of the duplicating masters.

tune-up skills

Dividing Whole Numbers, pages 41–52

Give the quotient and the remainder.

1. 97 ÷ 2 48 R1
2. 8732 ÷ 6 1455 R2
3. 84 ÷ 32 2 R20
4. 773 ÷ 61 12 R41
5. 527 ÷ 8 65 R7
6. 5216 ÷ 39 133 R29
7. 643 ÷ 2 321 R1
8. 934 ÷ 517 1 R417
9. 4365 ÷ 821 5 R260
10. 451 ÷ 7 64 R3
11. 837 ÷ 33 25 R12
12. 6815 ÷ 20 340 R15
13. 9284 ÷ 3 3094 R2
14. 1056 ÷ 251 4 R52
15. 652 ÷ 5 130 R2
16. 5106 ÷ 28 182 R10
17. 7692 ÷ 183 42 R6
18. 11,823 ÷ 48 246 R15
19. 95,624 ÷ 3 31,874 R2
20. 7422 ÷ 64 115 R62
21. 4861 ÷ 709 6 R607
22. 872,417 ÷ 9 96,935 R2
23. 3391 ÷ 52 65 R11
24. 75,614 ÷ 326 231 R308

Adding and Subtracting Decimals, pages 67–74

1. 7.4 + 6.3 13.7
2. 68.2 + 4.9 73.1
3. .63 + .57 1.20
4. .04 + 2.5 2.54
5. 7.3 + .191 7.491
6. .4 + .8 + .7 1.9
7. .62 + 4.308 + 5.5 10.428
8. 4.723 + .5 + 2.96 8.183
9. 3.1 + .662 + .05 3.812
10. .4 + 8.27 + 12.63 21.3
11. 5 + .023 + 6.4 11.423
12. .14 + 7 + 36.5 43.64
13. 9.4 − 3.8 5.6
14. .76 − .08 .68
15. 27.153 − 6.284 20.869
16. 6.104 − 2 4.104
17. 5.18 − 2.099 3.081
18. 14 − .263 13.737
19. .825 − .327 .498
20. 45.006 − 28.397 16.609
21. 38.41 − 8.047 30.363
22. 17.6 − 12.205 5.395
23. 36.44 − 15 21.44
24. .425 − .057 .368
25. 68.72 − 6.923 61.797

Multiplying and Dividing Decimals, pages 83–94

1. 4.6 × 87.4 402.04
2. 93 × .072 6.696
3. 1.85 × .4 .74
4. 6.003 × .7 4.2021
5. .82 × 43.5 35.67
6. .007 × 3.1 .0217
7. 63.4 × 8.5 538.9
8. .56 × 7.03 3.9368
9. 75.36 ÷ 6 12.56
10. .558 ÷ 93 .006
11. .0365 ÷ 5 .0073
12. 100 × .6215 62.15
13. 3.9 × 1000 3900
14. 453.6 ÷ 10 45.36
15. 2.7 ÷ 1000 .0027
16. 7.15 ÷ 1.3 5.5
17. 112.8 ÷ 48 2.35
18. 65.1 ÷ 9.3 7

Round each quotient to the nearest hundredth.

19. 3.257 ÷ .6 5.43
20. .95 ÷ 4.2 .23
21. .00521 ÷ .09 .06
22. 2.74 ÷ 58 .05
23. .422 ÷ 6.8 .06
24. .05724 ÷ .023 2.49

CALCULATOR EXERCISES

Optional

1. 2471.75, 835.67, 1492.94, 863.38, 1452.55, 229.23, 70.59, 4143.42, + 698.66 — 12,258.19

2. 8.0427, 9.6315, 27.4266, 9.507, 2.633, 18.238, 67.597, +42.618 — 185.6938

3. 7847.6, 395.73, 1426.5, 891.47, 5263.90, 7.04, 61.25, 943.68, + 0.75 — 16,837.92

4. 924.816, 43.95, 182.674, 23.931, 521.298, 35.74, 637.6, +815.008 — 3185.017

5. 347.6 − 285.7 61.9

6. 82.409 − 73.6 8.809

7. 95.3 − 8.247 87.053

8. 167.35 − 14.82 152.53

9. 62.6 − .0417 62.5583

10. 45.73 − 16.95 28.78

11. 7884.3 − 28.9 7855.4

12. 594.2 − 3.64 590.56

13. 2.74 × 6.858 18.79092

14. 9576.2 × .075 718.215

15. 81.64 × 49.18 4015.0552

16. 99.47 × .0632 6.286504

17. 2.8 × 63 × .77 135.828

18. 16.753 × 8.14 136.36942

19. 6.42 × 5 × 8.9 285.69

20. 1.4 × 6.8 × 7 66.64

Round each quotient to the nearest thousandth.

21. 14.295 ÷ 6.8 2.102

22. 57 ÷ 9.24 6.169

23. 8.7 ÷ 46.5 .187

24. 695 ÷ 82.7 .404

25. 4.698 ÷ 2.4 1.958

26. 8.12 ÷ 19.47 .417

27. Find the total of these expenses.

Rent	$215.00
Car payment	114.65
Gasoline	35.78
Car maintenance	17.52
Electricity	28.14
Phone	19.65
Insurance	28.42
Food	123.84
Medical	12.63
Miscellaneous	65.38
	$661.01

In each exercise, find the price per unit rounded up to the next hundredth cent. Tell which brand has a lower unit price.

	Brand X		Brand Y	
28.	(450 g for 85¢) (85 ÷ 450)	.19 ¢	475 g for 96¢ (96 ÷ 475)	.21 ¢
29.	320 g for 79¢	.25 ¢	(350 g for 84¢)	.24 ¢
30.	250 ml for 87¢	.35 ¢	(225 ml for 74¢)	.33 ¢
31.	(500 ml for 39¢)	.08 ¢	700 ml for 65¢	.10 ¢

Give the total distance each car can travel on a tank of gas to the nearest kilometer.

	Liters of gas	Kilometers per liter	
32.	36.2	9.8	355 kilometers
33.	85.2	5.6	477 kilometers
34.	45.3	8.5	385 kilometers
35.	50.7	6.7	340 kilometers
36.	95.3	3.2	305 kilometers

Fractions, Mixed Numbers, and Probability

7

Chapter 7
Multiplying and Dividing Fractions and Mixed Numbers

8

Chapter 8
Adding and Subtracting Fractions and Mixed Numbers

9

Chapter 9
Probability

Chapter 7
Multiplying and Dividing Fractions and Mixed Numbers

Number of test items - 19

Number missed	1	2	3	4	5	6	7	8	9
Percent correct	95	89	84	79	74	68	63	58	53

skill Writing Fractions and Mixed Numbers pages 132–133

A Write a fraction for the gray part. $\frac{3}{5}$

B Write a mixed number for point Z. $7\frac{2}{3}$

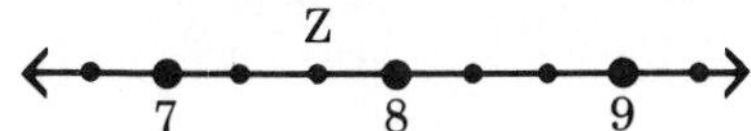

skill Renaming Fractions and Mixed Numbers page 134

C Reduce $\frac{8}{20}$ to lowest terms. $\frac{2}{5}$

D Write $\frac{17}{2}$ as a mixed number or as a whole number. $8\frac{1}{2}$

E Write $6\frac{3}{4}$ as a fraction. $\frac{27}{4}$

skill Writing a Fraction as a Decimal page 135

F Write $\frac{2}{5}$ as a decimal. .4

G Write $\frac{7}{15}$ as a decimal. Round your answer to the nearest thousandth. .467

skill Multiplying Fractions pages 136–137

H $\frac{2}{3} \times \frac{5}{7}$ $\frac{10}{21}$ I $\frac{3}{4} \times \frac{8}{9}$ $\frac{2}{3}$ J $\frac{3}{4} \times \frac{2}{5} \times \frac{5}{6}$ $\frac{1}{4}$ K $\frac{5}{8} \times 16$ 10

skill Multiplying Mixed Numbers pages 138–139

L $4\frac{1}{2} \times \frac{2}{5}$ $1\frac{4}{5}$ M $2\frac{2}{3} \times 15$ 40 N $1\frac{1}{4} \times 5\frac{1}{10}$ $6\frac{3}{8}$ O $10 \times \frac{3}{5} \times 1\frac{1}{2}$ 9

skill Dividing Fractions and Mixed Numbers pages 140–141

P Write the reciprocal of $\frac{2}{9}$. $\frac{9}{2}$

Q $\frac{3}{4} \div \frac{5}{8}$ $1\frac{1}{5}$ R $\frac{7}{10} \div 6$ $\frac{7}{60}$ S $3\frac{1}{2} \div 2\frac{3}{4}$ $1\frac{3}{11}$

See page T20 for additional notes on Chapter 7.

Objective: Write fractions and mixed numbers

Writing Fractions and Mixed Numbers

example A Writing fractions

Write a fraction for the gray part.

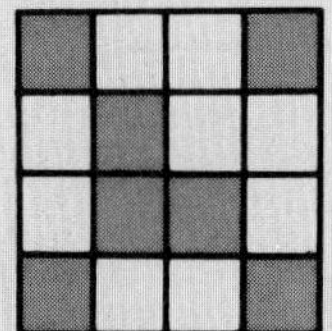

Denominator: ⟶ total number of parts

$\frac{7}{16}$

⟵ **Numerator:** number of gray parts

$\frac{7}{16}$ is also shown on this number line at point W.

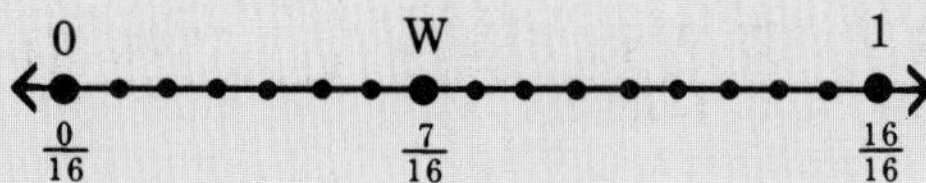

example B Writing mixed numbers

Write a mixed number for point Y.

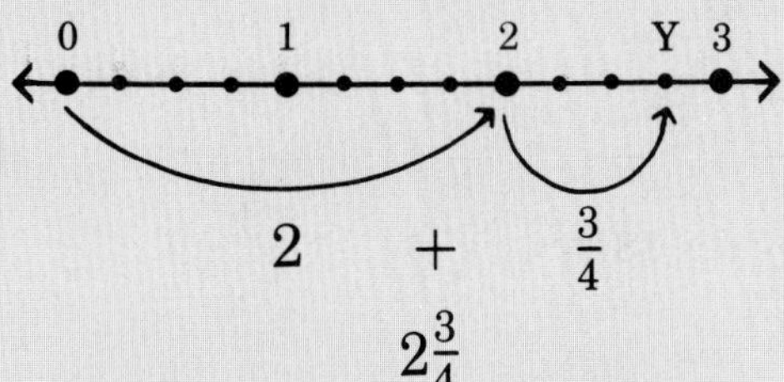

$2\frac{3}{4}$ is also shown as the gray part in this picture.

exercises

set A

Write a fraction for the gray part.

1. $\frac{2}{5}$

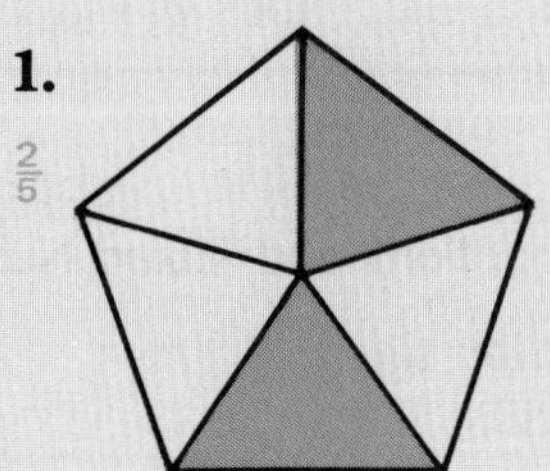

2. $\frac{3}{8}$

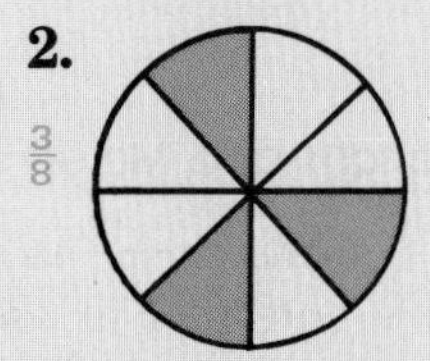

3. $\frac{7}{12}$

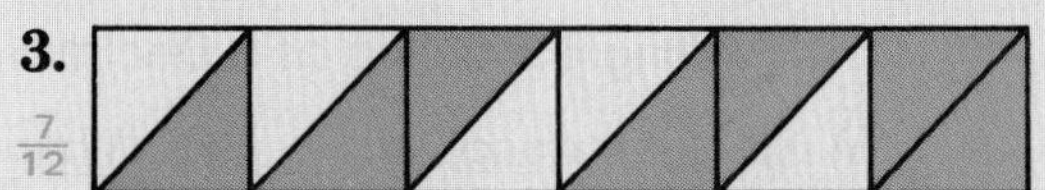

4. $\frac{8}{16}$

5. $\frac{5}{10}$

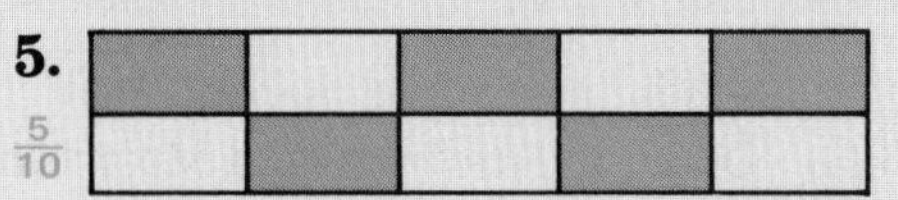

Write a fraction for each point labeled with a letter.

6. 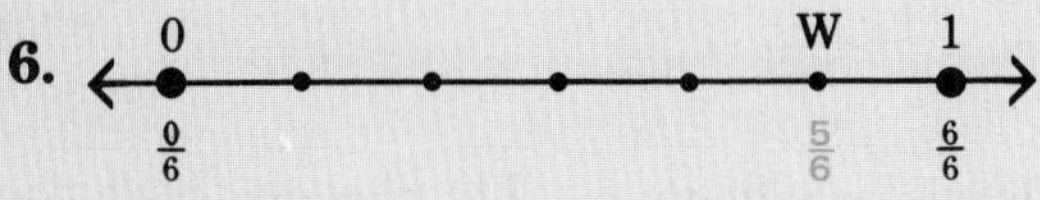

7. 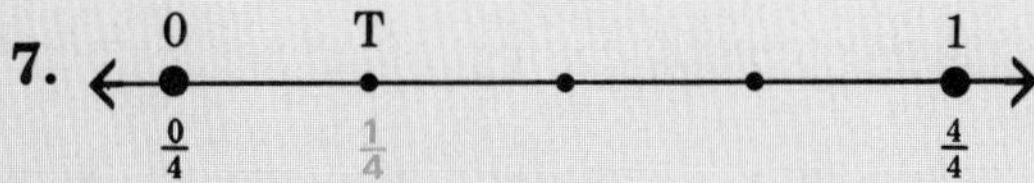

8. 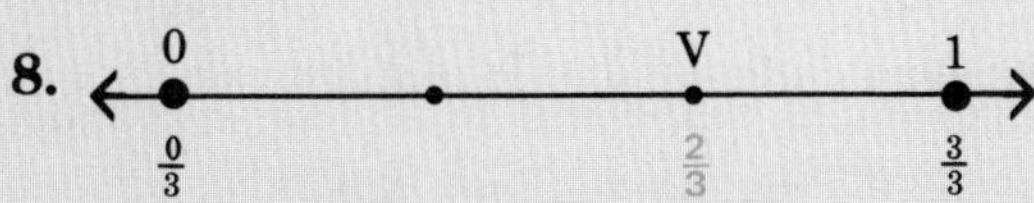

9. 0 L 1

$\frac{0}{8}$ $\frac{5}{8}$ $\frac{8}{8}$

10. 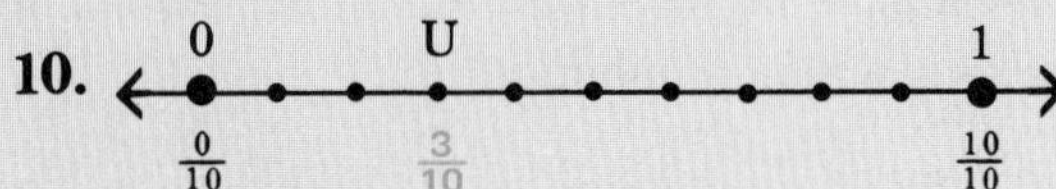

set B

Write a mixed number for each point labeled with a letter.

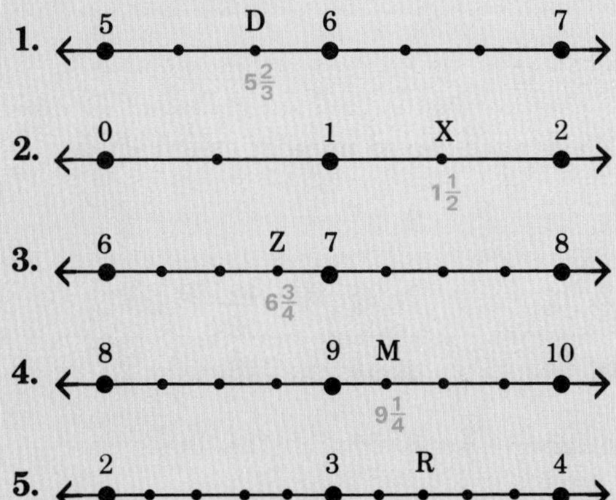

Write a mixed number for the gray part.

6. $2\frac{2}{3}$

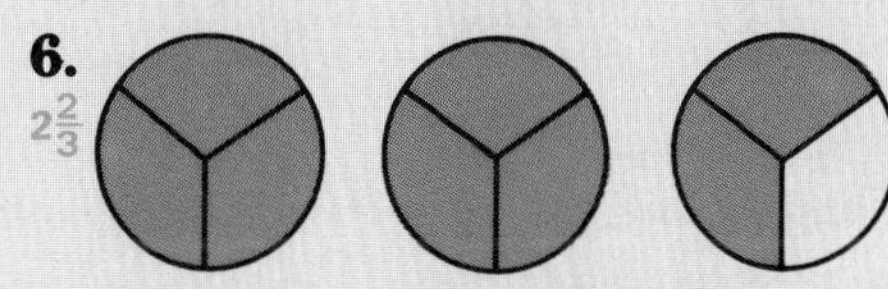

7. $2\frac{1}{4}$

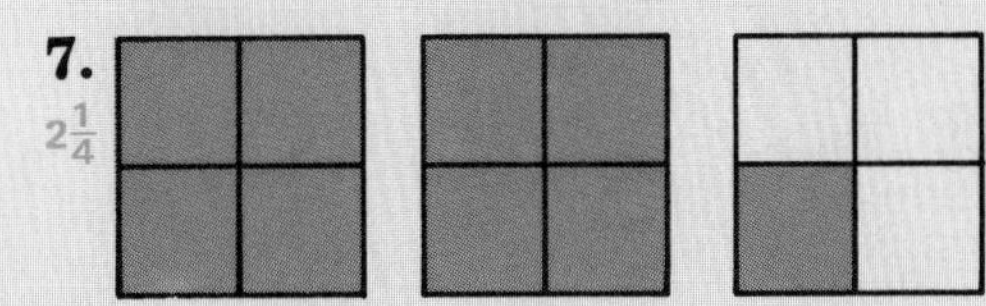

8. $6\frac{2}{5}$

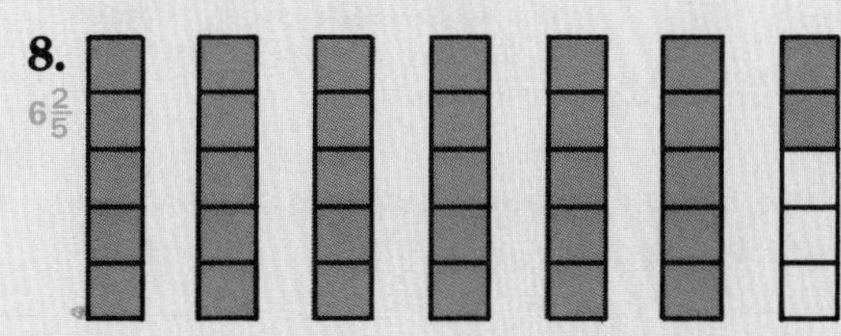

9. $4\frac{1}{2}$

10. $1\frac{5}{6}$

Objective: Rename fractions and mixed numbers.

Renaming Fractions and Mixed Numbers

example C Reducing fractions

Reduce $\frac{28}{42}$ to lowest terms.

$$\frac{28}{42} = \frac{4}{6} = \frac{2}{3}$$

($28 \div 7$, $42 \div 7$; $4 \div 2$, $6 \div 2$)

$$\frac{28}{42} = \frac{2}{3}$$

To reduce a fraction, divide the numerator and the denominator by a common factor greater than 1.

A fraction is in lowest terms when it cannot be reduced.

example D Writing improper fractions as mixed numbers or as whole numbers

Write $\frac{63}{5}$ as a mixed number or as a whole number.

$$\frac{63}{5} = 63 \div 5$$

$$\begin{array}{r} 12\frac{3}{5} \\ 5\overline{)63} \\ -5 \\ \hline 13 \\ -10 \\ \hline 3 \end{array}$$

Divide the numerator by the denominator.

If the remainder is not zero, write the remainder as a fraction.

example E Writing mixed numbers as fractions

Write $7\frac{1}{2}$ as a fraction.

$$7\frac{1}{2} = \frac{15}{2}$$

Multiply 2 and 7 to find how many halves in 7. Then add 1.

exercises

set C

Reduce each fraction to lowest terms.

1. $\frac{8}{12}$ $\frac{2}{3}$	**6.** $\frac{4}{32}$ $\frac{1}{8}$	**11.** $\frac{15}{80}$ $\frac{3}{16}$
2. $\frac{6}{24}$ $\frac{1}{4}$	**7.** $\frac{33}{55}$ $\frac{3}{5}$	**12.** $\frac{48}{54}$ $\frac{8}{9}$
3. $\frac{10}{20}$ $\frac{1}{2}$	**8.** $\frac{21}{35}$ $\frac{3}{5}$	**13.** $\frac{75}{100}$ $\frac{3}{4}$
4. $\frac{9}{27}$ $\frac{1}{3}$	**9.** $\frac{30}{36}$ $\frac{5}{6}$	**14.** $\frac{18}{63}$ $\frac{2}{7}$
5. $\frac{12}{16}$ $\frac{3}{4}$	**10.** $\frac{24}{40}$ $\frac{3}{5}$	**15.** $\frac{24}{72}$ $\frac{1}{3}$

set D

Write each fraction as a mixed number or as a whole number.

1. $\frac{109}{5}$ $21\frac{4}{5}$	**5.** $\frac{35}{7}$ 5	**9.** $\frac{44}{3}$ $14\frac{2}{3}$
2. $\frac{23}{4}$ $5\frac{3}{4}$	**6.** $\frac{52}{8}$ $6\frac{1}{2}$	**10.** $\frac{197}{6}$ $32\frac{5}{6}$
3. $\frac{38}{6}$ $6\frac{1}{3}$	**7.** $\frac{48}{2}$ 24	**11.** $\frac{283}{10}$ $28\frac{3}{10}$
4. $\frac{73}{9}$ $8\frac{1}{9}$	**8.** $\frac{59}{6}$ $9\frac{5}{6}$	**12.** $\frac{130}{10}$ 13

set E

Write each mixed number as a fraction.

1. $14\frac{1}{3}$ $\frac{43}{3}$	**6.** $3\frac{7}{8}$ $\frac{31}{8}$	**11.** $10\frac{5}{8}$ $\frac{85}{8}$
2. $1\frac{2}{5}$ $\frac{7}{5}$	**7.** $2\frac{5}{9}$ $\frac{23}{9}$	**12.** $21\frac{2}{3}$ $\frac{65}{3}$
3. $7\frac{3}{4}$ $\frac{31}{4}$	**8.** $9\frac{5}{6}$ $\frac{59}{6}$	**13.** $5\frac{5}{16}$ $\frac{85}{16}$
4. $25\frac{9}{10}$ $\frac{259}{10}$	**9.** $8\frac{4}{5}$ $\frac{44}{5}$	**14.** $36\frac{1}{2}$ $\frac{73}{2}$
5. $6\frac{1}{16}$ $\frac{97}{16}$	**10.** $12\frac{1}{2}$ $\frac{25}{2}$	**15.** $85\frac{3}{4}$ $\frac{343}{4}$

Objective: Write a fraction as a decimal.

Writing a Fraction as a Decimal

example F Terminating decimals

Write $\frac{7}{8}$ as a decimal.

$\frac{7}{8} = 7 \div 8$

```
    .875
 8)7.000
 - 6 4
     60
   - 56
     40
   - 40
      0
```

Divide the numerator by the denominator.

Write zeros in the dividend and continue dividing until the remainder is zero.

example G Nonterminating decimals

Write $\frac{1}{6}$ as a decimal. Round your answer to the nearest thousandth.

$\frac{1}{6} = 1 \div 6$

```
   .1666 ≈ .167
 6)1.0000
  - 6
    40
  - 36
    40
   - 36
     40
    - 36
       4
```

Divide the numerator by the denominator.

Write zeros in the dividend and divide until the quotient is in ten thousandths. Round to the nearest thousandth.

exercises

set F

Write each fraction as a decimal. Divide until the remainder is zero.

1. $\frac{1}{4}$ .25	**9.** $\frac{1}{2}$ .5	**17.** $\frac{1}{80}$ .0125
2. $\frac{5}{16}$ .3125	**10.** $\frac{1}{32}$ .03125	**18.** $\frac{13}{1000}$ .013
3. $\frac{3}{4}$ .75	**11.** $\frac{4}{5}$ .8	**19.** $\frac{7}{16}$ .4375
4. $\frac{3}{5}$ .6	**12.** $\frac{3}{8}$ .375	**20.** $\frac{19}{40}$ .475
5. $\frac{7}{10}$ .7	**13.** $\frac{9}{10}$ .9	**21.** $\frac{11}{20}$ .55
6. $\frac{1}{5}$ .2	**14.** $\frac{3}{20}$ .15	**22.** $\frac{8}{25}$ .32
7. $\frac{1}{20}$ .05	**15.** $\frac{17}{100}$ .17	**23.** $\frac{9}{50}$ .18
8. $\frac{5}{8}$ .625	**16.** $\frac{3}{16}$ .1875	**24.** $\frac{9}{16}$ .5625

set G

Write each fraction as a decimal. Round each answer to the nearest thousandth.

1. $\frac{1}{3}$ .333	**9.** $\frac{5}{6}$ .833	**17.** $\frac{5}{9}$ .556
2. $\frac{2}{7}$ .286	**10.** $\frac{5}{12}$ .417	**18.** $\frac{11}{12}$ .917
3. $\frac{1}{9}$ .111	**11.** $\frac{3}{7}$ .429	**19.** $\frac{6}{7}$ .857
4. $\frac{7}{12}$ .583	**12.** $\frac{4}{15}$ .267	**20.** $\frac{8}{9}$ .889
5. $\frac{2}{3}$ .667	**13.** $\frac{9}{11}$ .818	**21.** $\frac{17}{18}$ .944
6. $\frac{4}{11}$ .364	**14.** $\frac{1}{12}$ .083	**22.** $\frac{5}{21}$ .238
7. $\frac{1}{15}$ .067	**15.** $\frac{1}{18}$ .056	**23.** $\frac{3}{17}$ .176
8. $\frac{2}{9}$ .222	**16.** $\frac{4}{7}$ .571	**24.** $\frac{13}{19}$ .684

Objective: Multiply fractions.

Multiplying Fractions

example H Two fractions, without reducing

$\frac{3}{4} \times \frac{1}{5} = \frac{3}{20}$

Multiply the numerators.
Multiply the denominators.

example I Two fractions, with reducing

$\frac{5}{8} \times \frac{7}{10} = \frac{35}{80} = \frac{7}{16}$

Multiply.
Reduce $\frac{35}{80}$ to lowest terms.

Sometimes you can use a shortcut when you multiply.

$\frac{\overset{1}{\cancel{5}}}{8} \times \frac{7}{\underset{2}{\cancel{10}}} = \frac{7}{16}$

If possible, divide a denominator and a numerator by the same number. Then multiply.

example J Three fractions

$\frac{1}{6} \times \frac{9}{10} \times \frac{5}{7}$

$\frac{1}{\underset{2}{\cancel{6}}} \times \frac{\overset{3}{\cancel{9}}}{\underset{2}{\cancel{10}}} \times \frac{\overset{1}{\cancel{5}}}{7} = \frac{3}{28}$

Use the shortcut.
Divide a denominator, 6, and a numerator, 9, by 3.
Divide a denominator, 10, and a numerator, 5, by 5.
Multiply.

example K A fraction and a whole number

$\frac{7}{8} \times 36$

$\frac{7}{\underset{2}{\cancel{8}}} \times \frac{\overset{9}{\cancel{36}}}{1} = \frac{63}{2} = 31\frac{1}{2}$

Write 36 as $\frac{36}{1}$.
Use the shortcut.
Multiply.
Write $\frac{63}{2}$ as a mixed number.

exercises

set H

1. $\frac{2}{3} \times \frac{4}{5}$ $\frac{8}{15}$
2. $\frac{1}{8} \times \frac{3}{4}$ $\frac{3}{32}$
3. $\frac{5}{6} \times \frac{1}{3}$ $\frac{5}{18}$
4. $\frac{3}{4} \times \frac{5}{8}$ $\frac{15}{32}$
5. $\frac{1}{7} \times \frac{2}{5}$ $\frac{2}{35}$
6. $\frac{1}{2} \times \frac{3}{8}$ $\frac{3}{16}$
7. $\frac{7}{16} \times \frac{1}{3}$ $\frac{7}{48}$
8. $\frac{3}{5} \times \frac{7}{8}$ $\frac{21}{40}$
9. $\frac{1}{4} \times \frac{11}{12}$ $\frac{11}{48}$
10. $\frac{9}{10} \times \frac{3}{7}$ $\frac{27}{70}$

set I

1. $\frac{3}{8} \times \frac{4}{5}$ $\frac{3}{10}$
2. $\frac{2}{7} \times \frac{14}{15}$ $\frac{4}{15}$
3. $\frac{5}{8} \times \frac{4}{7}$ $\frac{5}{14}$
4. $\frac{6}{11} \times \frac{5}{12}$ $\frac{5}{22}$
5. $\frac{8}{9} \times \frac{5}{16}$ $\frac{5}{18}$
6. $\frac{9}{10} \times \frac{1}{6}$ $\frac{3}{20}$
7. $\frac{6}{7} \times \frac{7}{8}$ $\frac{3}{4}$
8. $\frac{4}{9} \times \frac{3}{16}$ $\frac{1}{12}$
9. $\frac{3}{10} \times \frac{5}{6}$ $\frac{1}{4}$
10. $\frac{7}{12} \times \frac{3}{4}$ $\frac{7}{16}$
11. $\frac{2}{3} \times \frac{9}{16}$ $\frac{3}{8}$
12. $\frac{4}{5} \times \frac{7}{8}$ $\frac{7}{10}$
13. $\frac{5}{8} \times \frac{9}{10}$ $\frac{9}{16}$
14. $\frac{3}{4} \times \frac{8}{9}$ $\frac{2}{3}$
15. $\frac{7}{10} \times \frac{2}{3}$ $\frac{7}{15}$
16. $\frac{2}{5} \times \frac{15}{16}$ $\frac{3}{8}$
17. $\frac{7}{18} \times \frac{6}{7}$ $\frac{1}{3}$
18. $\frac{11}{12} \times \frac{4}{11}$ $\frac{1}{3}$
19. $\frac{5}{6} \times \frac{18}{25}$ $\frac{3}{5}$
20. $\frac{7}{32} \times \frac{8}{21}$ $\frac{1}{12}$
21. $\frac{9}{16} \times \frac{8}{15}$ $\frac{3}{10}$
22. $\frac{5}{12} \times \frac{3}{20}$ $\frac{1}{16}$
23. $\frac{9}{100} \times \frac{25}{27}$ $\frac{1}{12}$
24. $\frac{3}{16} \times \frac{16}{3}$ 1

set J

1. $\frac{2}{3} \times \frac{6}{7} \times \frac{14}{15}$ $\frac{8}{15}$

2. $\frac{10}{21} \times \frac{3}{5} \times \frac{7}{8}$ $\frac{1}{4}$

3. $\frac{8}{9} \times \frac{3}{5} \times \frac{1}{4}$ $\frac{2}{15}$

4. $\frac{3}{4} \times \frac{1}{2} \times \frac{5}{9}$ $\frac{5}{24}$

5. $\frac{9}{16} \times \frac{5}{6} \times \frac{12}{25}$ $\frac{9}{40}$

6. $\frac{3}{8} \times \frac{4}{5} \times \frac{1}{2}$ $\frac{3}{20}$

7. $\frac{16}{25} \times \frac{10}{27} \times \frac{9}{8}$ $\frac{4}{15}$

8. $\frac{5}{6} \times \frac{2}{3} \times \frac{9}{16}$ $\frac{5}{16}$

9. $\frac{2}{3} \times \frac{1}{2} \times \frac{3}{4}$ $\frac{1}{4}$

10. $\frac{5}{8} \times \frac{3}{16} \times \frac{7}{10}$ $\frac{21}{256}$

11. $\frac{5}{6} \times \frac{12}{21} \times \frac{7}{20}$ $\frac{1}{6}$

12. $\frac{3}{8} \times \frac{7}{9} \times \frac{4}{5}$ $\frac{7}{30}$

13. $\frac{3}{10} \times \frac{4}{7} \times \frac{5}{9}$ $\frac{2}{21}$

14. $\frac{10}{27} \times \frac{3}{8} \times \frac{9}{20}$ $\frac{1}{16}$

15. $\frac{4}{9} \times \frac{3}{16} \times \frac{2}{5}$ $\frac{1}{30}$

16. $\frac{2}{9} \times \frac{21}{22} \times \frac{9}{14}$ $\frac{3}{22}$

17. $\frac{6}{7} \times \frac{14}{27} \times \frac{15}{28}$ $\frac{5}{21}$

18. $\frac{7}{8} \times \frac{8}{7} \times \frac{3}{5}$ $\frac{3}{5}$

19. $\frac{5}{7} \times \frac{2}{3} \times \frac{1}{7}$ $\frac{10}{147}$

20. $\frac{1}{2} \times \frac{3}{4} \times \frac{5}{8}$ $\frac{15}{64}$

set K

1. $\frac{2}{3} \times 18$ 12

2. $\frac{1}{2} \times 8$ 4

3. $9 \times \frac{1}{6}$ $1\frac{1}{2}$

4. $\frac{5}{8} \times 16$ 10

5. $\frac{3}{8} \times 20$ $7\frac{1}{2}$

6. $\frac{2}{3} \times 32$ $21\frac{1}{3}$

7. $\frac{4}{5} \times 30$ 24

8. $\frac{6}{7} \times 5$ $4\frac{2}{7}$

9. $\frac{7}{10} \times 50$ 35

10. $12 \times \frac{3}{7}$ $5\frac{1}{7}$

11. $\frac{1}{2} \times 20$ 10

12. $60 \times \frac{3}{4}$ 45

13. $\frac{3}{5} \times 100$ 60

14. $4 \times \frac{5}{6}$ $3\frac{1}{3}$

15. $\frac{3}{10} \times 11$ $3\frac{3}{10}$

16. $\frac{3}{4} \times 28$ 21

17. $7 \times \frac{2}{5}$ $2\frac{4}{5}$

18. $\frac{1}{6} \times 16$ $2\frac{2}{3}$

19. $40 \times \frac{7}{8}$ 35

20. $\frac{4}{9} \times 54$ 24

21. $\frac{3}{10} \times 19$ $5\frac{7}{10}$

22. $\frac{1}{12} \times 48$ 4

23. $27 \times \frac{3}{4}$ $20\frac{1}{4}$

24. $\frac{2}{5} \times 21$ $8\frac{2}{5}$

25. $\frac{3}{16} \times 32$ 6

26. $11 \times \frac{9}{10}$ $9\frac{9}{10}$

27. $\frac{7}{9} \times 36$ 28

28. $148 \times \frac{1}{4}$ 37

29. $10 \times \frac{7}{16}$ $4\frac{3}{8}$

30. $\frac{1}{5} \times 235$ 47

31. $\frac{1}{3} \times 300$ 100

32. $\frac{7}{12} \times 72$ 42

33. $\frac{5}{16} \times 800$ 250

34. $100 \times \frac{7}{8}$ $87\frac{1}{2}$

35. $75 \times \frac{2}{3}$ 50

36. $90 \times \frac{1}{4}$ $22\frac{1}{2}$

37. $\frac{1}{10} \times 150$ 15

38. $\frac{2}{3} \times 9000$ 6000

39. $\frac{4}{5} \times 6000$ 4800

40. $2400 \times \frac{3}{8}$ 900

Objective: Multiply mixed numbers.

Multiplying Mixed Numbers

example L

A mixed number and a fraction

$2\frac{3}{4} \times \frac{1}{6}$

$\frac{11}{4} \times \frac{1}{6} = \frac{11}{24}$

Write $2\frac{3}{4}$ as a fraction.
Multiply.

example M

A mixed number and a whole number

$3\frac{1}{4} \times 5$

$\frac{13}{4} \times \frac{5}{1} = \frac{65}{4} = 16\frac{1}{4}$

Write $3\frac{1}{4}$ and 5 as fractions.
Multiply.
Write $\frac{65}{4}$ as a mixed number.

example N

Two mixed numbers

$2\frac{1}{3} \times 5\frac{1}{6}$

$\frac{7}{3} \times \frac{31}{6} = \frac{217}{18} = 12\frac{1}{18}$

Write $2\frac{1}{3}$ and $5\frac{1}{6}$ as fractions.
Multiply.
Write $\frac{217}{18}$ as a mixed number.

example O

Three factors

$4\frac{1}{5} \times \frac{5}{7} \times 9$

$\frac{\overset{3}{\cancel{21}}}{\underset{1}{\cancel{5}}} \times \frac{\overset{1}{\cancel{5}}}{\underset{1}{\cancel{7}}} \times \frac{9}{1} = \frac{27}{1} = 27$

Write $4\frac{1}{5}$ and 9 as fractions.
Use the shortcut.
Multiply.
Write $\frac{27}{1}$ as a whole number.

exercises

set L

1. $1\frac{2}{5} \times \frac{5}{8}$ $\frac{7}{8}$	**10.** $\frac{2}{3} \times 8\frac{2}{5}$ $5\frac{3}{5}$
2. $3\frac{1}{7} \times \frac{3}{4}$ $2\frac{5}{14}$	**11.** $\frac{1}{2} \times 5\frac{3}{4}$ $2\frac{7}{8}$
3. $\frac{1}{6} \times 3\frac{2}{5}$ $\frac{17}{30}$	**12.** $7\frac{1}{2} \times \frac{1}{3}$ $2\frac{1}{2}$
4. $5\frac{1}{2} \times \frac{1}{3}$ $1\frac{5}{6}$	**13.** $6\frac{3}{10} \times \frac{5}{7}$ $4\frac{1}{2}$
5. $2\frac{2}{3} \times \frac{3}{8}$ 1	**14.** $\frac{8}{9} \times 1\frac{11}{16}$ $1\frac{1}{2}$
6. $\frac{9}{10} \times 1\frac{1}{9}$ 1	**15.** $\frac{1}{2} \times 15\frac{3}{10}$ $7\frac{13}{20}$
7. $\frac{5}{8} \times 1\frac{7}{9}$ $1\frac{1}{9}$	**16.** $21\frac{1}{3} \times \frac{3}{8}$ 8
8. $6\frac{1}{4} \times \frac{4}{5}$ 5	**17.** $\frac{2}{9} \times 4\frac{1}{2}$ 1
9. $9\frac{1}{2} \times \frac{4}{7}$ $5\frac{3}{7}$	**18.** $10\frac{3}{5} \times 25$ 265

set M

1. $3\frac{2}{3} \times 9$ 33	**11.** $6\frac{5}{6} \times 2$ $13\frac{2}{3}$
2. $2\frac{1}{2} \times 3$ $7\frac{1}{2}$	**12.** $3 \times 4\frac{3}{5}$ $13\frac{4}{5}$
3. $5\frac{1}{3} \times 4$ $21\frac{1}{3}$	**13.** $10\frac{3}{7} \times 14$ 146
4. $7 \times 5\frac{1}{2}$ $38\frac{1}{2}$	**14.** $6 \times 3\frac{9}{10}$ $23\frac{2}{5}$
5. $6 \times 4\frac{1}{2}$ 27	**15.** $30 \times 12\frac{1}{3}$ 370
6. $1\frac{7}{8} \times 16$ 30	**16.** $2\frac{7}{8} \times 32$ 92
7. $8\frac{1}{4} \times 12$ 99	**17.** $12 \times 1\frac{1}{2}$ 18
8. $7\frac{1}{5} \times 10$ 72	**18.** $2\frac{3}{8} \times 40$ 95
9. $1\frac{3}{4} \times 13$ $22\frac{3}{4}$	**19.** $2 \times 16\frac{1}{2}$ 33
10. $8 \times 9\frac{3}{8}$ 75	**20.** $100 \times 3\frac{1}{5}$ 320

set N

1. $1\frac{1}{2} \times 3\frac{1}{4}$ $4\frac{7}{8}$
2. $2\frac{1}{2} \times 2\frac{2}{3}$ $6\frac{2}{3}$
3. $5\frac{1}{4} \times 2\frac{2}{7}$ 12
4. $1\frac{7}{10} \times 3\frac{1}{3}$ $5\frac{2}{3}$
5. $3\frac{3}{5} \times 1\frac{1}{6}$ $4\frac{1}{5}$
6. $1\frac{4}{5} \times 2\frac{7}{9}$ 5
7. $7\frac{5}{8} \times 3\frac{1}{5}$ $24\frac{2}{5}$
8. $9\frac{1}{3} \times 1\frac{3}{7}$ $13\frac{1}{3}$
9. $4\frac{2}{5} \times 1\frac{4}{11}$ 6
10. $6\frac{2}{3} \times 2\frac{1}{4}$ 15
11. $1\frac{7}{8} \times 1\frac{1}{3}$ $2\frac{1}{2}$
12. $3\frac{3}{4} \times 9\frac{1}{3}$ 35
13. $12\frac{1}{2} \times 1\frac{1}{10}$ $13\frac{3}{4}$
14. $2\frac{1}{7} \times 2\frac{1}{3}$ 5
15. $8\frac{3}{4} \times 2\frac{1}{7}$ $18\frac{3}{4}$
16. $10\frac{2}{3} \times 1\frac{3}{8}$ $14\frac{2}{3}$
17. $5\frac{1}{2} \times 1\frac{1}{4}$ $6\frac{7}{8}$
18. $3\frac{3}{7} \times 2\frac{5}{8}$ 9
19. $2\frac{4}{5} \times 3\frac{4}{7}$ 10
20. $15\frac{5}{6} \times 1\frac{1}{2}$ $23\frac{3}{4}$

set O

1. $\frac{2}{3} \times 2\frac{1}{2} \times 5\frac{1}{4}$ $8\frac{3}{4}$
2. $6\frac{1}{4} \times 5\frac{1}{2} \times 8$ 275
3. $\frac{1}{3} \times \frac{6}{7} \times 2\frac{1}{8}$ $\frac{17}{28}$
4. $1\frac{3}{4} \times 12 \times \frac{2}{3}$ 14
5. $3\frac{1}{3} \times 6 \times \frac{4}{5}$ 16
6. $\frac{4}{7} \times 2\frac{1}{3} \times 5$ $6\frac{2}{3}$
7. $15 \times 2 \times \frac{5}{6}$ 25
8. $4\frac{1}{2} \times 1\frac{1}{7} \times \frac{7}{9}$ 4
9. $7\frac{2}{5} \times \frac{5}{6} \times \frac{1}{2}$ $3\frac{1}{12}$
10. $24 \times \frac{1}{8} \times 9\frac{1}{2}$ $28\frac{1}{2}$

BREAK TIME

Anita had a collection of posters. She decided to throw away $\frac{1}{3}$ of them because they were faded. Then she gave $\frac{2}{3}$ of the remaining posters to her friends. She had 12 posters left. How many did she have to begin with? 54 posters

See page T20 for an explanation.

The applications on pages 146–147 may be used anytime after this lesson.

Objective: Divide fractions and mixed numbers.

Dividing Fractions and Mixed Numbers

example P Writing reciprocals

Give the reciprocals of $\frac{2}{5}$, 7, and $3\frac{1}{4}$.

Two numbers whose product is 1 are **reciprocals.**

The reciprocal of $\frac{2}{5}$ is $\frac{5}{2}$. $\quad \frac{2}{5} \times \frac{5}{2} = 1$

The reciprocal of 7 is $\frac{1}{7}$. $\quad 7 = \frac{7}{1} \longrightarrow \frac{7}{1} \times \frac{1}{7} = 1$

The reciprocal of $3\frac{1}{4}$ is $\frac{4}{13}$. $\quad 3\frac{1}{4} = \frac{13}{4} \longrightarrow \frac{13}{4} \times \frac{4}{13} = 1$

example Q A fraction divisor

$$\frac{3}{4} \div \frac{2}{7}$$

$$\frac{3}{4} \times \frac{7}{2} = \frac{21}{8} = 2\frac{5}{8}$$

To divide fractions, multiply by the reciprocal of the divisor. The reciprocal of $\frac{2}{7}$ is $\frac{7}{2}$.

example R A whole-number divisor

$$\frac{4}{5} \div 8$$

$$\frac{4}{5} \div \frac{8}{1} = \frac{\overset{1}{\cancel{4}}}{5} \times \frac{1}{\underset{2}{\cancel{8}}} = \frac{1}{10}$$

Multiply by the reciprocal of 8.

example S A mixed-number divisor

$$6\frac{2}{3} \div 1\frac{1}{9}$$

$$\frac{20}{3} \div \frac{10}{9} = \frac{\overset{2}{\cancel{20}}}{\underset{1}{\cancel{3}}} \times \frac{\overset{3}{\cancel{9}}}{\underset{1}{\cancel{10}}} = \frac{6}{1} = 6$$

Multiply by the reciprocal of $1\frac{1}{9}$.

exercises

set P

Give the reciprocal of each number.

1. $\frac{3}{4}$ $\frac{4}{3}$		**11.** $7\frac{1}{4}$ $\frac{4}{29}$
2. 12 $\frac{1}{12}$		**12.** $\frac{9}{10}$ $\frac{10}{9}$
3. $\frac{1}{9}$ $\frac{9}{1}$		**13.** $4\frac{6}{7}$ $\frac{7}{34}$
4. $2\frac{1}{2}$ $\frac{2}{5}$		**14.** $10\frac{1}{3}$ $\frac{3}{31}$
5. 6 $\frac{1}{6}$		**15.** $\frac{7}{16}$ $\frac{16}{7}$
6. $3\frac{5}{8}$ $\frac{8}{29}$		**16.** $1\frac{2}{9}$ $\frac{9}{11}$
7. $\frac{4}{5}$ $\frac{5}{4}$		**17.** $3\frac{5}{8}$ $\frac{8}{29}$
8. 52 $\frac{1}{52}$		**18.** $\frac{11}{12}$ $\frac{12}{11}$
9. $\frac{7}{100}$ $\frac{100}{7}$		**19.** $15\frac{3}{4}$ $\frac{4}{63}$
10. $4\frac{2}{3}$ $\frac{3}{14}$		**20.** 99 $\frac{1}{99}$

set Q

1. $\frac{3}{5} \div \frac{6}{7}$ $\frac{7}{10}$

2. $9 \div \frac{3}{4}$ 12

3. $\frac{2}{3} \div \frac{4}{9}$ $1\frac{1}{2}$

4. $\frac{5}{6} \div \frac{9}{16}$ $1\frac{13}{27}$

5. $\frac{3}{4} \div \frac{1}{2}$ $1\frac{1}{2}$

6. $\frac{9}{16} \div \frac{1}{2}$ $1\frac{1}{8}$

7. $\frac{5}{6} \div \frac{2}{3}$ $1\frac{1}{4}$

8. $7 \div \frac{1}{2}$ 14

9. $10 \div \frac{7}{10}$ $14\frac{2}{7}$

10. $\frac{2}{5} \div \frac{2}{3}$ $\frac{3}{5}$

11. $1 \div \frac{4}{5}$ $1\frac{1}{4}$

12. $\frac{6}{7} \div \frac{3}{8}$ $2\frac{2}{7}$

13. $\frac{5}{8} \div \frac{10}{11}$ $\frac{11}{16}$

14. $\frac{5}{16} \div \frac{5}{7}$ $\frac{7}{16}$

15. $8 \div \frac{1}{4}$ 32

16. $10 \div \frac{3}{4}$ $13\frac{1}{3}$

17. $10 \div \frac{1}{100}$ 1000

18. $\frac{3}{16} \div \frac{6}{7}$ $\frac{7}{32}$

19. $\frac{3}{8} \div \frac{5}{9}$ $\frac{27}{40}$

20. $5\frac{2}{5} \div \frac{3}{10}$ 18

21. $4\frac{1}{4} \div \frac{3}{8}$ $11\frac{1}{3}$

22. $10 \div \frac{1}{2}$ 20

23. $\frac{7}{12} \div \frac{5}{6}$ $\frac{7}{10}$

24. $4\frac{1}{3} \div \frac{1}{2}$ $8\frac{2}{3}$

25. $\frac{7}{8} \div \frac{7}{8}$ 1

26. $\frac{1}{6} \div \frac{7}{9}$ $\frac{3}{14}$

27. $12 \div \frac{1}{5}$ 60

28. $\frac{1}{4} \div \frac{11}{12}$ $\frac{3}{11}$

29. $5\frac{1}{2} \div \frac{3}{4}$ $7\frac{1}{3}$

30. $9 \div \frac{5}{16}$ $28\frac{4}{5}$

set R

1. $\frac{3}{8} \div 2$ $\frac{3}{16}$

2. $\frac{6}{7} \div 10$ $\frac{3}{35}$

3. $\frac{8}{15} \div 4$ $\frac{2}{15}$

4. $1\frac{1}{2} \div 12$ $\frac{1}{8}$

5. $\frac{9}{16} \div 3$ $\frac{3}{16}$

6. $\frac{1}{2} \div 2$ $\frac{1}{4}$

7. $\frac{3}{4} \div 15$ $\frac{1}{20}$

8. $\frac{5}{6} \div 2$ $\frac{5}{12}$

9. $\frac{2}{3} \div 7$ $\frac{2}{21}$

10. $\frac{1}{4} \div 5$ $\frac{1}{20}$

11. $\frac{2}{5} \div 4$ $\frac{1}{10}$

12. $2\frac{1}{3} \div 14$ $\frac{1}{6}$

13. $4\frac{1}{6} \div 5$ $\frac{5}{6}$

14. $\frac{4}{7} \div 3$ $\frac{4}{21}$

15. $\frac{9}{10} \div 6$ $\frac{3}{20}$

16. $\frac{2}{3} \div 20$ $\frac{1}{30}$

17. $\frac{1}{5} \div 9$ $\frac{1}{45}$

18. $7\frac{1}{2} \div 3$ $2\frac{1}{2}$

19. $\frac{23}{100} \div 23$ $\frac{1}{100}$

20. $\frac{3}{16} \div 6$ $\frac{1}{32}$

21. $\frac{7}{8} \div 2$ $\frac{7}{16}$

22. $3\frac{1}{5} \div 8$ $\frac{2}{5}$

23. $\frac{1}{2} \div 50$ $\frac{1}{100}$

24. $1\frac{2}{3} \div 35$ $\frac{1}{21}$

25. $\frac{7}{10} \div 3$ $\frac{7}{30}$

26. $\frac{5}{16} \div 15$ $\frac{1}{48}$

27. $5\frac{1}{4} \div 7$ $\frac{3}{4}$

28. $\frac{11}{12} \div 22$ $\frac{1}{24}$

29. $\frac{5}{8} \div 2$ $\frac{5}{16}$

30. $1\frac{3}{4} \div 3$ $\frac{7}{12}$

set S

1. $6\frac{1}{2} \div 9\frac{1}{3}$ $\frac{39}{56}$

2. $\frac{3}{5} \div 1\frac{1}{5}$ $\frac{1}{2}$

3. $6\frac{2}{3} \div 7\frac{1}{2}$ $\frac{8}{9}$

4. $3\frac{7}{8} \div 1\frac{1}{4}$ $3\frac{1}{10}$

5. $1\frac{1}{4} \div 7\frac{1}{2}$ $\frac{1}{6}$

6. $2\frac{3}{4} \div 2\frac{3}{8}$ $1\frac{3}{19}$

7. $\frac{3}{4} \div 6\frac{1}{2}$ $\frac{3}{26}$

8. $10\frac{1}{2} \div 1\frac{3}{4}$ 6

9. $\frac{1}{10} \div 1\frac{2}{5}$ $\frac{1}{14}$

10. $3\frac{2}{3} \div 2\frac{1}{3}$ $1\frac{4}{7}$

11. $7 \div 4\frac{9}{10}$ $1\frac{3}{7}$

12. $3\frac{1}{3} \div 2\frac{1}{2}$ $1\frac{1}{3}$

13. $\frac{5}{6} \div 2\frac{1}{12}$ $\frac{2}{5}$

14. $4\frac{1}{6} \div 7\frac{1}{2}$ $\frac{5}{9}$

15. $2\frac{4}{5} \div 1\frac{3}{4}$ $1\frac{3}{5}$

16. $1 \div 8\frac{3}{4}$ $\frac{4}{35}$

17. $4\frac{1}{5} \div 4\frac{1}{5}$ 1

18. $13\frac{3}{4} \div 1\frac{2}{3}$ $8\frac{1}{4}$

19. $\frac{1}{2} \div 1\frac{1}{3}$ $\frac{3}{8}$

20. $4 \div 1\frac{2}{3}$ $2\frac{2}{5}$

21. $6\frac{1}{4} \div 2\frac{1}{2}$ $2\frac{1}{2}$

22. $2\frac{2}{7} \div 5\frac{1}{3}$ $\frac{3}{7}$

23. $5 \div 3\frac{1}{3}$ $1\frac{1}{2}$

24. $1\frac{3}{4} \div 2\frac{1}{2}$ $\frac{7}{10}$

25. $3\frac{1}{4} \div 1\frac{1}{6}$ $2\frac{11}{14}$

26. $8\frac{1}{4} \div 1\frac{1}{2}$ $5\frac{1}{2}$

27. $10 \div 4\frac{3}{8}$ $2\frac{2}{7}$

28. $1\frac{7}{8} \div 1\frac{2}{3}$ $1\frac{1}{8}$

29. $\frac{5}{8} \div 3\frac{1}{2}$ $\frac{5}{28}$

30. $15 \div 2\frac{1}{7}$ 7

posttest

Number of test items - 19

Number missed	1	2	3	4	5	6	7	8	9
Percent correct	95	89	84	79	74	68	63	58	53

skill Writing Fractions and Mixed Numbers pages 132–133

A Write a fraction for the gray part. $\frac{5}{9}$

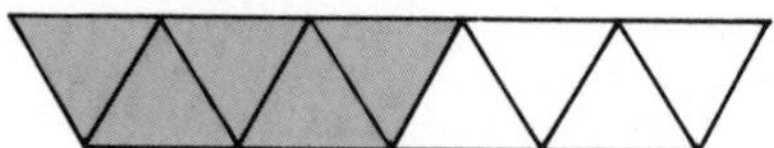

B Write a mixed number for point X.

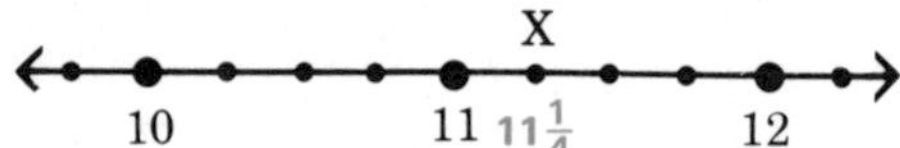

skill Renaming Fractions and Mixed Numbers page 134

C Reduce $\frac{12}{24}$ to lowest terms. $\frac{1}{2}$

D Write $\frac{35}{8}$ as a mixed number or as a whole number. $4\frac{3}{8}$

E Write $2\frac{3}{5}$ as a fraction. $\frac{13}{5}$

skill Writing a Fraction as a Decimal page 135

F Write $\frac{1}{8}$ as a decimal. .125

G Write $\frac{1}{7}$ as a decimal. Round your answer to the nearest thousandth. .143

skill Multiplying Fractions pages 136–137

H $\frac{1}{2} \times \frac{3}{5}$ $\frac{3}{10}$ I $\frac{3}{10} \times \frac{5}{9}$ $\frac{1}{6}$ J $\frac{3}{4} \times \frac{1}{6} \times \frac{8}{9}$ $\frac{1}{9}$ K $\frac{2}{3} \times 24$ 16

skill Multiplying Mixed Numbers pages 138–139

L $2\frac{1}{3} \times \frac{3}{8}$ $\frac{7}{8}$ M $4\frac{2}{5} \times 10$ 44 N $3\frac{3}{8} \times 1\frac{7}{9}$ 6 O $8 \times 7\frac{5}{6} \times \frac{1}{4}$ $15\frac{2}{3}$

skill Dividing Fractions and Mixed Numbers pages 140–141

P Write the reciprocal of $1\frac{1}{2}$. $\frac{2}{3}$

Q $\frac{4}{5} \div \frac{1}{3}$ $2\frac{2}{5}$ R $3\frac{5}{6} \div 4$ $\frac{23}{24}$ S $11 \div 5\frac{1}{2}$ 2

Objective: Solve problems involving multiplication and division of fractions and mixed numbers.

In this lesson students solve problems involving times and distances for riding a bicycle and jogging.

Finding Exercise Times and Distances

Eva and Luis Ortiz exercise regularly at a nearby track. Luis rides a bicycle and Eva jogs. There are small posts in the ground to mark the fractional parts of one lap of the track.

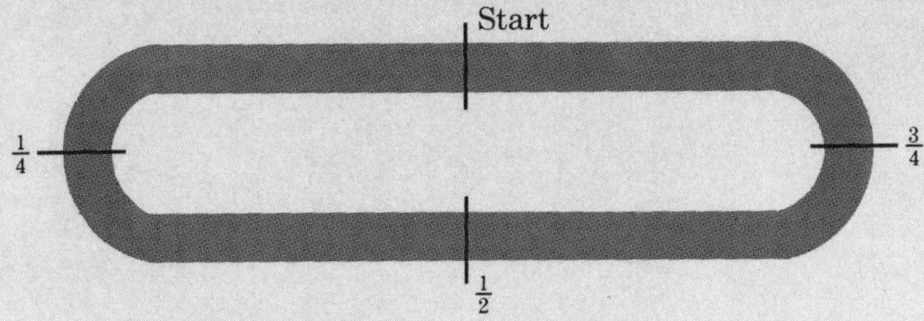

Luis rides at a speed of one lap every $1\frac{1}{2}$ minutes. How long will it take him to complete

1. 3 laps? $(3 \times 1\frac{1}{2})$ $4\frac{1}{2}$ minutes
2. 7 laps? $10\frac{1}{2}$ minutes
3. 12 laps? 18 minutes
4. $1\frac{1}{2}$ laps? $2\frac{1}{4}$ minutes
5. $5\frac{3}{4}$ laps? $8\frac{5}{8}$ minutes

How many laps can Luis complete in

6. 3 minutes? $(3 \div 1\frac{1}{2})$ 2 laps
7. 6 minutes? 4 laps
8. $10\frac{1}{2}$ minutes? 7 laps
9. $12\frac{3}{4}$ minutes? $8\frac{1}{2}$ laps
10. 15 minutes? 10 laps

Eva jogs at a speed of one lap every $4\frac{1}{4}$ minutes. How long will it take her to complete

11. 2 laps? $8\frac{1}{2}$ minutes
12. 5 laps? $21\frac{1}{4}$ minutes
13. $2\frac{1}{2}$ laps? $10\frac{5}{8}$ minutes
14. $4\frac{1}{2}$ laps? $19\frac{1}{8}$ minutes
15. $\frac{1}{2}$ lap? $2\frac{1}{8}$ minutes

How many laps can Eva complete in

16. 17 minutes? 4 laps
17. $21\frac{1}{4}$ minutes? 5 laps
18. $8\frac{1}{2}$ minutes? 2 laps
19. $12\frac{3}{4}$ minutes? 3 laps
20. $38\frac{1}{4}$ minutes? 9 laps

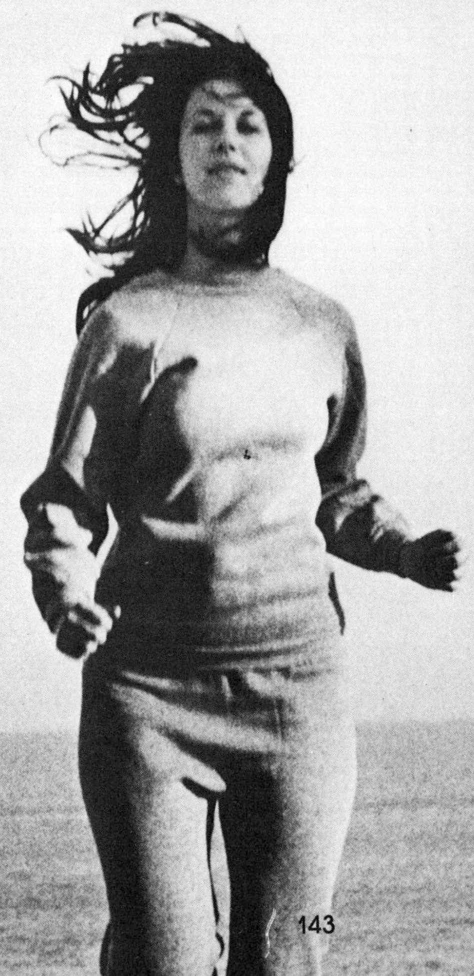

Objective: Solve problems involving multiplication and division of fractions and mixed numbers.

In this lesson students solve problems involving measuring with a "C" clamp.

Using a "C" Clamp for Measuring

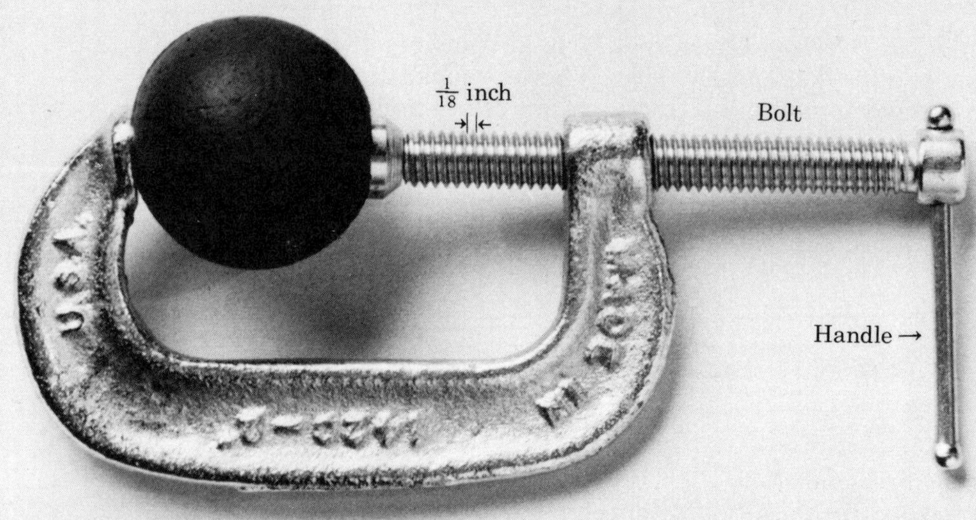

A "C" clamp is used in workshops to hold materials in place. It could also be used to measure the width of an object, such as the rubber ball shown in the picture.

On the bolt of the "C" clamp, the distance from the top of one thread to the top of another is $\frac{1}{18}$ inch. If the handle is turned completely around once, the bolt moves $\frac{1}{18}$ inch.

When the ball is removed from the clamp, it takes $22\frac{1}{2}$ turns of the handle to close the clamp. You can multiply to find the diameter of the ball.

Turns of handle		Amount bolt moves for each turn (inches)				Width of object (inches)
$22\frac{1}{2}$	×	$\frac{1}{18}$				
$\frac{\overset{5}{\cancel{45}}}{2}$	×	$\frac{1}{\underset{2}{\cancel{18}}}$	=	$\frac{5}{4}$	=	$1\frac{1}{4}$

The diameter of the ball is about $1\frac{1}{4}$ inches.

You might obtain a "C" clamp from the Industrial Arts Department and have students use it to measure objects. Find the distance from the top of one thread to the top of another by counting the number of grooves in 1 inch of the bolt. For example, if there are 20 grooves in 1 inch, then the distance between threads is $\frac{1}{20}$ inch.

Each exercise gives the number of turns of the handle needed to close the "C" clamp when an object is removed. Multiply by $\frac{1}{18}$ inch to find the width of each object.

	Object	Turns of handle	
1.	Bolt	9	$\frac{1}{2}$ inch
2.	Pencil	5	$\frac{5}{18}$ inch
3.	Bottle	18	1 inch
4.	Nail	$2\frac{1}{4}$	$\frac{1}{8}$ inch
5.	Chalk	6	$\frac{1}{3}$ inch
6.	Golf ball	30	$1\frac{2}{3}$ inches
7.	Thumb	$10\frac{1}{2}$	$\frac{7}{12}$ inch
8.	Wrist	24	$1\frac{1}{3}$ inches
9.	Spool	14	$\frac{7}{9}$ inch
10.	Magazine	$4\frac{1}{2}$	$\frac{1}{4}$ inch

Each exercise gives the width of an object. Divide by $\frac{1}{18}$ inch to find the number of turns needed to close the "C" clamp when the object is removed.

	Object	Width (inches)	
11.	Candle	$1\frac{1}{2}$	27 turns
12.	Drill bit	$\frac{3}{8}$	$6\frac{3}{4}$ turns
13.	Gumball	$\frac{3}{4}$	$13\frac{1}{2}$ turns
14.	Lipstick	$\frac{5}{8}$	$11\frac{1}{4}$ turns
15.	Grape	$\frac{5}{6}$	15 turns

This design is to be made on a wood lathe. Divide each width by $\frac{1}{18}$ to find how many turns of the "C" clamp are needed to check that width.

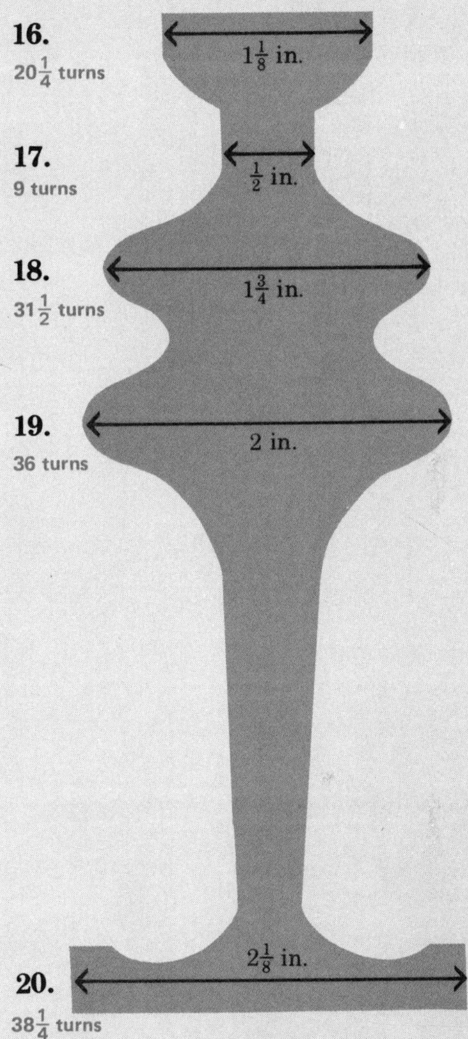

16. $20\frac{1}{4}$ turns

17. 9 turns

18. $31\frac{1}{2}$ turns

19. 36 turns

20. $38\frac{1}{4}$ turns

Objective: Solve problems involving multiplication of fractions and mixed numbers.

In this lesson students find measures to be used in scale drawings.

Career: Mechanical Designer

Career Cluster: Technical

Marlene Vance is a mechanical designer at the Diecraft Precision Instrument Company. She makes scale drawings of parts that are used for instruments.

The pictures show machine parts actual size. They are not scale drawings.

Marlene plans to make a drawing of this part. In her drawing, each length will be $\frac{1}{2}$ as long as the actual length. Multiply to find each measure for the scale drawing.

1. AB ($\frac{1}{2} \times 2\frac{3}{8}$) $1\frac{3}{16}$ in.
2. BC $\frac{1}{8}$ in.
3. CD $\frac{7}{8}$ in.
4. DE $\frac{7}{16}$ in.
5. EF $\frac{11}{16}$ in.
6. FG $\frac{3}{16}$ in.
7. GH $1\frac{3}{8}$ in.
8. HA $\frac{3}{4}$ in.
9. JK $\frac{1}{2}$ in.
10. KL $\frac{5}{16}$ in.

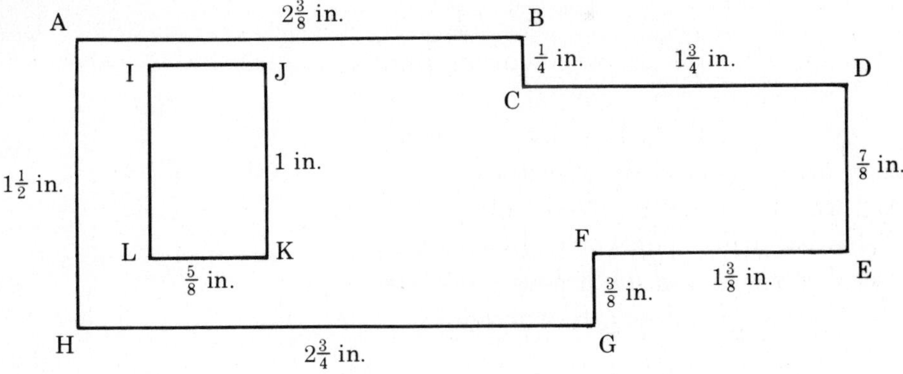

In the scale drawing for this part, each length will be $\frac{3}{4}$ as long as the actual length. Multiply to find each measure for the scale drawing.

11. AB $1\frac{1}{8}$ in.
12. BC $\frac{9}{16}$ in.
13. CD $\frac{3}{4}$ in.
14. DE $\frac{15}{16}$ in.
15. EF $1\frac{7}{8}$ in.
16. FA $\frac{3}{8}$ in.

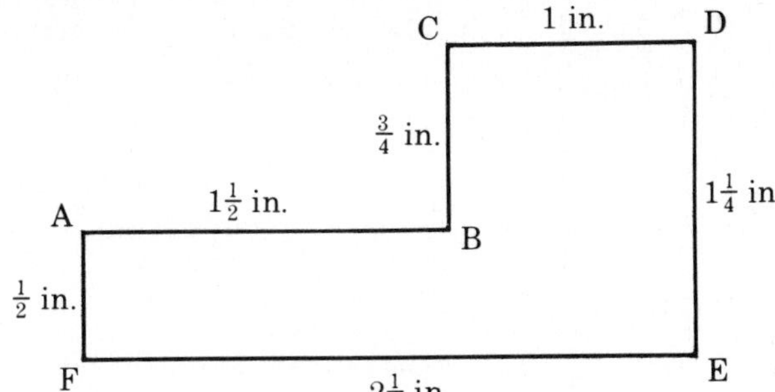

In the scale drawing for this part, each length will be $\frac{5}{8}$ as long as the actual length. In each exercise, measure the length of the side to the nearest $\frac{1}{8}$ inch. Then multiply to find each measure for the scale drawing.

	Side	Actual length	Length in scale drawing
17.	AB	$1\frac{1}{2}$ in.	$\frac{15}{16}$ in.
18.	BC	1 in.	$\frac{5}{8}$ in.
19.	GH	$\frac{3}{4}$ in.	$\frac{15}{32}$ in.
20.	HI	$\frac{1}{2}$ in.	$\frac{5}{16}$ in.

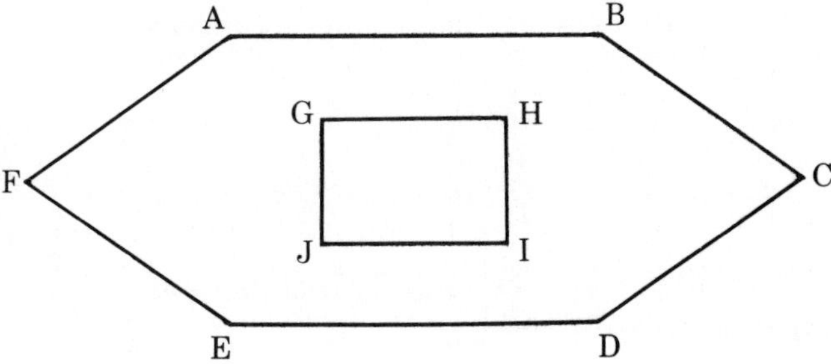

Objective: Solve problems involving multiplication and division of fractions and mixed numbers.

In this lesson students find the number of decoys that can be made from a log of a given length.

Career: Wood Carver

Career Cluster: Arts

See the Careers Chart beginning on page 420 for more jobs and other information about this career cluster.

Madison Mitchell is a wood carver who makes duck decoys. Years ago his decoys were used by hunters, but today they are purchased by collectors.

Mr. Mitchell uses the wood from discarded utility poles or well-seasoned timbers. He carves the decoys $\frac{3}{4}$ or $\frac{3}{8}$ as long as the actual length of the duck.

If the actual length of a mallard duck is 20 inches, what will be the length of a section of log needed for a $\frac{3}{8}$-scale decoy?

Scale	Actual length (inches)	Length of section for decoy (inches)
$\frac{3}{8}$	$\times$ 20	

$$\frac{3}{\cancel{8}_{2}} \times \frac{\cancel{20}^{5}}{1} = \frac{15}{2} = 7\frac{1}{2}$$

The length of the section will be $7\frac{1}{2}$ inches.

How many of these $7\frac{1}{2}$-inch sections can be cut from a 16-foot (192-inch) log?

Length of log (inches)	Length of section for decoy (inches)	Sections per log
192 $\div$	$7\frac{1}{2}$	

$$\frac{192}{1} \div \frac{15}{2} = \frac{\cancel{192}^{64}}{1} \times \frac{2}{\cancel{15}_{5}} = \frac{128}{5} = 25\frac{3}{5}$$

25 sections that are each $7\frac{1}{2}$ inches long can be cut from the log.

Mr. Mitchell can carve 2 decoys from each section. How many decoys can he make from the 16-foot log?

Sections per log		Decoys per section		Decoys per log
25	$\times$	2	=	50

Mr. Mitchell can make 50 mallard duck decoys from a 16-foot log.

Complete the table.

	Type of bird	Scale	Actual length (inches)	Length of section for decoy (inches)	Length of log (inches)	Sections per log	Decoys per section	Decoys per log
	Mallard	$\frac{3}{8}$	20	$7\frac{1}{2}$	192	25	2	50
1.	Black duck	$\frac{3}{8}$	20	$7\frac{1}{2}$	216	28	3	84
2.	Baldpate duck	$\frac{3}{4}$	18	$13\frac{1}{2}$	60	4	2	8
3.	Pintail duck	$\frac{3}{8}$	28	$10\frac{1}{2}$	72	6	2	12
4.	Blue-winged teal	$\frac{3}{4}$	15	$11\frac{1}{4}$	216	19	3	57
5.	Greater snow goose	$\frac{3}{8}$	30	$11\frac{1}{4}$	120	10	1	10
6.	Canada goose	$\frac{3}{8}$	36	$13\frac{1}{2}$	240	17	1	17
7.	Canvas-back duck	$\frac{3}{4}$	21	$15\frac{3}{4}$	192	12	2	24
8.	Whistling swan	$\frac{3}{8}$	48	18	192	10	1	10

9. Mr. Mitchell carves a mallard duck decoy in about $1\frac{1}{4}$ hours. How long will it take him to carve 50 decoys? $62\frac{1}{2}$ hours

10. A collector bought a pintail duck decoy from Mr. Mitchell for $12. The collector sold the decoy in his shop for $2\frac{1}{2}$ times that price. What was the selling price? $30

Number of test items - 24

Number missed	1	2	3	4	5	6	7	8	9	10	11	12
Percent correct	96	92	88	83	79	75	71	67	63	58	54	50

Chapter 7

A **1.** Write a fraction for point R.

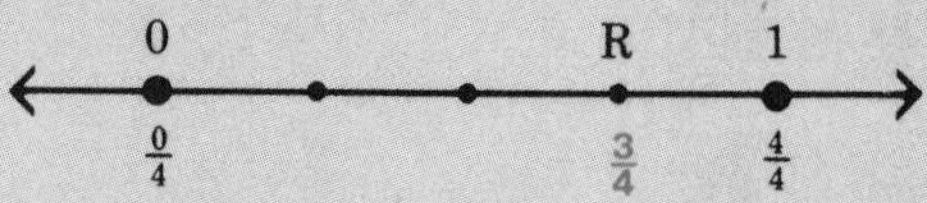

B **2.** Write a mixed number for the dark gray part. $3\frac{1}{2}$

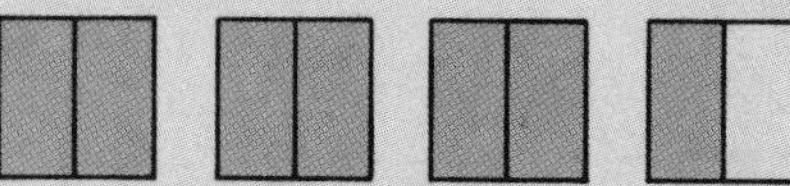

C **3.** Reduce $\frac{16}{28}$ to lowest terms. $\frac{4}{7}$

D **4.** Write $\frac{24}{5}$ as a mixed number or as a whole number. $4\frac{4}{5}$

E **5.** Write $4\frac{3}{8}$ as a fraction. $\frac{35}{8}$

F **6.** Write $\frac{3}{4}$ as a decimal. .75

G **7.** Write $\frac{5}{7}$ as a decimal. Round your answer to the nearest thousandth. .714

H **8.** $\frac{3}{4} \times \frac{1}{8}$ $\frac{3}{32}$

I **9.** $\frac{2}{3} \times \frac{9}{10}$ $\frac{3}{5}$

J **10.** $\frac{7}{8} \times \frac{4}{5} \times \frac{2}{7}$ $\frac{1}{5}$

K **11.** $\frac{1}{2} \times 19$ $9\frac{1}{2}$

L **12.** $3\frac{1}{3} \times \frac{4}{5}$ $2\frac{2}{3}$

M **13.** $2\frac{5}{6} \times 12$ 34

N **14.** $5\frac{5}{8} \times 1\frac{1}{3}$ $7\frac{1}{2}$

O **15.** $\frac{3}{4} \times 12 \times \frac{5}{6}$ $7\frac{1}{2}$

P **16.** Write the reciprocal of 9. $\frac{1}{9}$

Q **17.** $\frac{7}{10} \div \frac{4}{5}$ $\frac{7}{8}$

R **18.** $4\frac{1}{3} \div 2$ $2\frac{1}{6}$

S **19.** $\frac{7}{8} \div 3\frac{1}{2}$ $\frac{1}{4}$

20. Debbie rides her bicycle at a speed of one lap every $1\frac{3}{4}$ minutes. How long will it take her to complete 8 laps? 14 minutes

21. Phil jogs at a speed of one lap every $5\frac{1}{2}$ minutes. How many laps can he complete in 22 minutes? 4 laps

22. The bolt of a "C" clamp moves $\frac{1}{20}$ inch in one turn. How far will it move in $7\frac{1}{2}$ turns? $\frac{3}{8}$ inch

23. In the scale drawing for this part, each length will be $\frac{1}{2}$ as long as the actual length. Find the measure of side AB for the scale drawing. $\frac{15}{16}$ inch

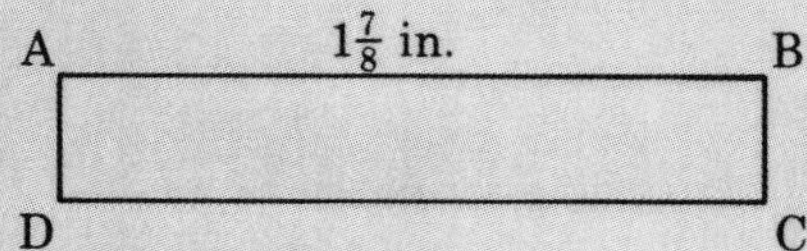

24. How many sections that are each $8\frac{1}{4}$ inches long can be cut from a 192-inch log? 23 sections

 See pages 17–18 of the *Tests and Record Forms: Duplicating Masters* for an alternate form of the Chapter 7 test.

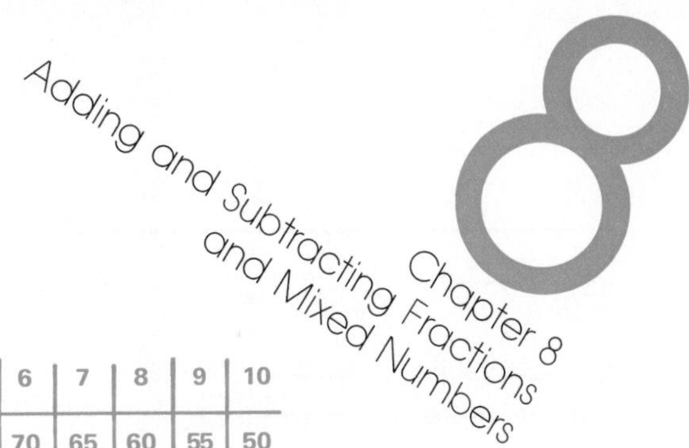

Number of test items - 20

Number missed	1	2	3	4	5	6	7	8	9	10
Percent correct	95	90	85	80	75	70	65	60	55	50

skill Finding Common Denominators page 152

A Write $\frac{1}{3}$ and $\frac{2}{5}$ as fractions with a common denominator. $\frac{5}{15}, \frac{6}{15}$

B Write $\frac{1}{2}$, $\frac{1}{3}$, and $\frac{1}{4}$ as fractions with a common denominator. $\frac{6}{12}, \frac{4}{12}, \frac{3}{12}$

skill Comparing Fractions and Mixed Numbers page 153

C Compare $\frac{7}{8}$ and $\frac{5}{8}$. Use <, >, or =. $\frac{7}{8} > \frac{5}{8}$, or $\frac{5}{8} < \frac{7}{8}$

D Compare $\frac{5}{8}$ and $\frac{3}{4}$. Use <, >, or =. $\frac{5}{8} < \frac{3}{4}$, or $\frac{3}{4} > \frac{5}{8}$

E Compare $2\frac{8}{16}$ and $2\frac{1}{2}$. Use <, >, or =. $2\frac{8}{16} = 2\frac{1}{2}$

skill Adding Fractions pages 154–155

F $\frac{2}{5} + \frac{4}{5}$ $1\frac{1}{5}$

G $\frac{5}{8} + \frac{3}{4}$ $1\frac{3}{8}$

H $\frac{1}{2} + \frac{2}{3} + \frac{1}{6}$ $1\frac{1}{3}$

skill Subtracting Fractions pages 156–157

I $\frac{4}{5} - \frac{1}{5}$ $\frac{3}{5}$

J $\frac{7}{16} - \frac{1}{8}$ $\frac{5}{16}$

K $\frac{3}{4} - \frac{2}{3}$ $\frac{1}{12}$

skill Adding Mixed Numbers pages 158–159

L $6\frac{2}{5} + 2\frac{3}{10}$ $8\frac{7}{10}$

M Rename $4\frac{9}{8}$. $4\frac{9}{8} = 5\frac{\square}{8}$ 1

N $3\frac{1}{2} + 9\frac{4}{5}$ $13\frac{3}{10}$

O $7\frac{2}{3} + 4\frac{1}{3}$ 12

skill Subtracting Mixed Numbers pages 160–161

P $5\frac{3}{4} - 1\frac{1}{2}$ $4\frac{1}{4}$

Q Rename $7\frac{1}{3}$. $7\frac{1}{3} = 6\frac{\square}{3}$ 4

R $9\frac{5}{8} - 4\frac{7}{8}$ $4\frac{3}{4}$

S $7\frac{1}{5} - 2\frac{3}{4}$ $4\frac{9}{20}$

T $8 - 4\frac{1}{2}$ $3\frac{1}{2}$

See page T20 for additional notes on Chapter 8.

Objective: Find common denominators.

Finding Common Denominators

example A Two fractions

Write $\frac{2}{3}$ and $\frac{1}{4}$ as fractions with a common denominator.

A **common denominator** of $\frac{2}{3}$ and $\frac{1}{4}$ is a common multiple of 3 and 4.

List the multiples of 4 until you have a common multiple of 3 and 4.

4 8 **12** 12 is a common denominator of $\frac{2}{3}$ and $\frac{1}{4}$.

Now find the fractions equal to $\frac{2}{3}$ and $\frac{1}{4}$ that have a denominator of 12.

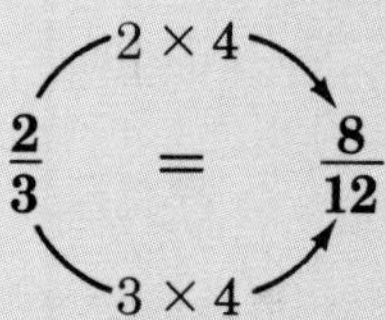

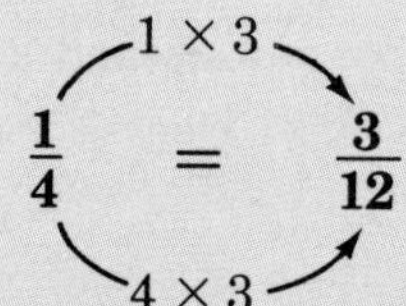

$\frac{2}{3} = \frac{8}{12}$ $\frac{1}{4} = \frac{3}{12}$

Point out that students can first divide 3 into 12 to get 4, and then multiply 2 and 4 to get 8.

example B Three fractions

Write $\frac{1}{2}$, $\frac{1}{3}$, and $\frac{5}{8}$ as fractions with a common denominator.

List the multiples of 8 until you have a common multiple of 2, 3, and 8.

8 16 **24** 24 is a common denominator for $\frac{1}{2}$, $\frac{1}{3}$, and $\frac{5}{8}$.

Now find the fractions equal to $\frac{1}{2}$, $\frac{1}{3}$, and $\frac{5}{8}$ that have a denominator of 24.

$\frac{1}{2} = \frac{12}{24}$ $\frac{1}{3} = \frac{8}{24}$ $\frac{5}{8} = \frac{15}{24}$

exercises

set A

Write these fractions with a common denominator.

1. $\frac{3}{4}$ $\frac{9}{12}$ $\frac{1}{3}$ $\frac{4}{12}$
2. $\frac{1}{3}$ $\frac{2}{6}$ $\frac{5}{6}$ $\frac{5}{6}$
3. $\frac{5}{8}$ $\frac{5}{8}$ $\frac{1}{4}$ $\frac{2}{8}$
4. $\frac{1}{6}$ $\frac{2}{12}$ $\frac{7}{12}$ $\frac{7}{12}$
5. $\frac{1}{2}$ $\frac{3}{6}$ $\frac{1}{3}$ $\frac{2}{6}$
6. $\frac{4}{5}$ $\frac{8}{10}$ $\frac{1}{2}$ $\frac{5}{10}$
7. $\frac{2}{3}$ $\frac{10}{15}$ $\frac{3}{5}$ $\frac{9}{15}$
8. $\frac{1}{6}$ $\frac{4}{24}$ $\frac{3}{8}$ $\frac{9}{24}$
9. $\frac{3}{4}$ $\frac{15}{20}$ $\frac{2}{5}$ $\frac{8}{20}$
10. $\frac{7}{8}$ $\frac{21}{24}$ $\frac{1}{3}$ $\frac{8}{24}$
11. $\frac{4}{5}$ $\frac{12}{15}$ $\frac{1}{3}$ $\frac{5}{15}$
12. $\frac{3}{8}$ $\frac{9}{24}$ $\frac{7}{12}$ $\frac{14}{24}$
13. $\frac{5}{8}$ $\frac{10}{16}$ $\frac{3}{16}$ $\frac{3}{16}$
14. $\frac{2}{3}$ $\frac{16}{24}$ $\frac{1}{8}$ $\frac{3}{24}$
15. $\frac{3}{4}$ $\frac{9}{12}$ $\frac{1}{6}$ $\frac{2}{12}$
16. $\frac{5}{6}$ $\frac{15}{18}$ $\frac{7}{9}$ $\frac{14}{18}$
17. $\frac{3}{8}$ $\frac{9}{24}$ $\frac{7}{12}$ $\frac{14}{24}$
18. $\frac{5}{6}$ $\frac{20}{24}$ $\frac{5}{8}$ $\frac{15}{24}$
19. $\frac{2}{3}$ $\frac{20}{30}$ $\frac{7}{10}$ $\frac{21}{30}$
20. $\frac{4}{5}$ $\frac{32}{40}$ $\frac{5}{8}$ $\frac{25}{40}$

set B

Write these fractions with a common denominator.

1. $\frac{2}{3}$ $\frac{4}{6}$ $\frac{5}{6}$ $\frac{5}{6}$ $\frac{1}{2}$ $\frac{3}{6}$
2. $\frac{7}{8}$ $\frac{7}{8}$ $\frac{1}{2}$ $\frac{4}{8}$ $\frac{3}{4}$ $\frac{6}{8}$
3. $\frac{1}{2}$ $\frac{5}{10}$ $\frac{3}{5}$ $\frac{6}{10}$ $\frac{9}{10}$ $\frac{9}{10}$
4. $\frac{5}{6}$ $\frac{10}{12}$ $\frac{1}{3}$ $\frac{4}{12}$ $\frac{7}{12}$ $\frac{7}{12}$
5. $\frac{3}{5}$ $\frac{6}{10}$ $\frac{1}{2}$ $\frac{5}{10}$ $\frac{9}{10}$ $\frac{9}{10}$
6. $\frac{2}{3}$ $\frac{8}{12}$ $\frac{3}{4}$ $\frac{9}{12}$ $\frac{1}{2}$ $\frac{6}{12}$
7. $\frac{5}{8}$ $\frac{15}{24}$ $\frac{1}{4}$ $\frac{6}{24}$ $\frac{2}{3}$ $\frac{16}{24}$
8. $\frac{1}{2}$ $\frac{6}{12}$ $\frac{5}{6}$ $\frac{10}{12}$ $\frac{3}{4}$ $\frac{9}{12}$
9. $\frac{3}{4}$ $\frac{9}{12}$ $\frac{2}{3}$ $\frac{8}{12}$ $\frac{1}{6}$ $\frac{2}{12}$
10. $\frac{3}{8}$ $\frac{9}{24}$ $\frac{5}{6}$ $\frac{20}{24}$ $\frac{1}{3}$ $\frac{8}{24}$
11. $\frac{4}{5}$ $\frac{24}{30}$ $\frac{2}{3}$ $\frac{20}{30}$ $\frac{7}{10}$ $\frac{21}{30}$
12. $\frac{7}{8}$ $\frac{35}{40}$ $\frac{3}{5}$ $\frac{24}{40}$ $\frac{1}{10}$ $\frac{4}{40}$

Objective: Compare fractions and mixed numbers.

Comparing Fractions and Mixed Numbers

example C

Fractions with common denominators

You may wish to use a number line to illustrate this example.

Compare $\frac{4}{7}$ and $\frac{5}{7}$.

$\frac{4}{7}$ and $\frac{5}{7}$

To compare fractions with a common denominator, compare the numerators. $4 < 5$, so $\frac{4}{7} < \frac{5}{7}$.

$\frac{4}{7} < \frac{5}{7}$

example D

Fractions with different denominators

Compare $\frac{5}{6}$ and $\frac{2}{3}$.

$\frac{5}{6}$ and $\frac{2}{3}$

$\frac{5}{6}$ and $\frac{4}{6}$ — Write $\frac{5}{6}$ and $\frac{2}{3}$ as fractions with a common denominator.

$\frac{5}{6} > \frac{4}{6}$ — Compare the numerators. $5 > 4$, so $\frac{5}{6} > \frac{4}{6}$.

$\downarrow \qquad \downarrow$

$\frac{5}{6} > \frac{2}{3}$

example E

Mixed numbers

Compare $2\frac{1}{2}$ and $2\frac{4}{8}$.

$2\frac{1}{2}$ and $2\frac{4}{8}$

$2\frac{4}{8}$ and $2\frac{4}{8}$

The whole numbers are the same. Compare the fractions. Write $\frac{1}{2}$ and $\frac{4}{8}$ as fractions with a common denominator.

$2\frac{4}{8} = 2\frac{4}{8}$ — Compare the numerators. $4 = 4$, so $\frac{4}{8} = \frac{4}{8}$, and $2\frac{4}{8} = 2\frac{4}{8}$.

$\downarrow \qquad \downarrow$

$2\frac{1}{2} = 2\frac{4}{8}$

exercises

set C

Compare the numbers. Use <, >, or =.

1. $\frac{3}{4}$ ● $\frac{1}{4}$ >
2. $\frac{1}{3}$ ● $\frac{2}{3}$ <
3. $\frac{4}{5}$ ● $\frac{3}{5}$ >
4. $\frac{7}{8}$ ● $\frac{6}{8}$ >
5. $\frac{3}{6}$ ● $\frac{5}{6}$ <
6. $\frac{3}{7}$ ● $\frac{5}{7}$ <
7. $\frac{5}{9}$ ● $\frac{4}{9}$ >
8. $\frac{7}{12}$ ● $\frac{11}{12}$ <
9. $\frac{3}{10}$ ● $\frac{9}{10}$ <
10. $\frac{5}{16}$ ● $\frac{3}{16}$ >

set D

Compare the numbers. Use <, > , or =.

1. $\frac{3}{8}$ ● $\frac{1}{4}$ >
2. $\frac{2}{3}$ ● $\frac{5}{12}$ >
3. $\frac{2}{5}$ ● $\frac{7}{10}$ <
4. $\frac{1}{2}$ ● $\frac{4}{8}$ =
5. $\frac{3}{4}$ ● $\frac{2}{3}$ >
6. $\frac{1}{2}$ ● $\frac{3}{5}$ <
7. $\frac{1}{3}$ ● $\frac{1}{2}$ <
8. $\frac{3}{5}$ ● $\frac{2}{3}$ <
9. $\frac{3}{4}$ ● $\frac{5}{6}$ <
10. $\frac{1}{3}$ ● $\frac{3}{5}$ <

set E

Compare the numbers. Use <, >, or =.

1. $3\frac{2}{3}$ ● $3\frac{5}{6}$ <
2. $6\frac{1}{2}$ ● $6\frac{2}{3}$ <
3. $5\frac{3}{5}$ ● $5\frac{1}{2}$ >
4. $7\frac{1}{8}$ ● $7\frac{3}{16}$ <
5. $8\frac{2}{3}$ ● $8\frac{6}{9}$ =
6. $9\frac{1}{3}$ ● $9\frac{1}{4}$ >
7. $2\frac{3}{4}$ ● $2\frac{5}{6}$ <
8. $1\frac{4}{5}$ ● $1\frac{2}{3}$ >
9. $6\frac{2}{3}$ ● $6\frac{5}{8}$ >
10. $4\frac{3}{8}$ ● $4\frac{5}{6}$ <

Objective: Add fractions.

Adding Fractions

example F Common denominators

$$\begin{array}{r} \frac{7}{8} \\ +\ \frac{5}{8} \\ \hline \frac{12}{8} = 1\frac{4}{8} = 1\frac{1}{2} \end{array}$$

To add fractions that have a common denominator, add the numerators.
Write $\frac{12}{8}$ as a mixed number.
Reduce answer to lowest terms.

example G Different denominators

$$\begin{array}{r} \frac{5}{6} = \frac{5}{6} \\ +\ \frac{1}{3} = \frac{2}{6} \\ \hline \frac{7}{6} = 1\frac{1}{6} \end{array}$$

To add fractions with different denominators, first write $\frac{5}{6}$ and $\frac{1}{3}$ as fractions with a common denominator.
Then add the numerators.
Write $\frac{7}{6}$ as a mixed number.

example H Horizontal form, two or three addends

$\frac{3}{4} + \frac{2}{3} + \frac{1}{2}$

$$\begin{array}{r} \frac{3}{4} = \frac{9}{12} \\ \frac{2}{3} = \frac{8}{12} \\ +\ \frac{1}{2} = \frac{6}{12} \\ \hline \frac{23}{12} = 1\frac{11}{12} \end{array}$$

Write problem vertically.
Write $\frac{3}{4}$, $\frac{2}{3}$, and $\frac{1}{2}$ as fractions with a common denominator.
Add the numerators.
Write $\frac{23}{12}$ as a mixed number.

exercises

set F

1. $\frac{4}{5} + \frac{3}{5}$ $1\frac{2}{5}$
2. $\frac{3}{8} + \frac{7}{8}$ $1\frac{1}{4}$
3. $\frac{5}{6} + \frac{1}{6}$ 1
4. $\frac{2}{3} + \frac{2}{3}$ $1\frac{1}{3}$
5. $\frac{5}{6} + \frac{5}{6}$ $1\frac{2}{3}$
6. $\frac{7}{10} + \frac{9}{10}$ $1\frac{3}{5}$
7. $\frac{3}{4} + \frac{3}{4}$ $1\frac{1}{2}$
8. $\frac{7}{9} + \frac{8}{9}$ $1\frac{2}{3}$
9. $\frac{5}{12} + \frac{11}{12}$ $1\frac{1}{3}$
10. $\frac{5}{16} + \frac{13}{16}$ $1\frac{1}{8}$

set G

1. $\frac{3}{4} + \frac{3}{8}$ $1\frac{1}{8}$
2. $\frac{5}{6} + \frac{1}{3}$ $1\frac{1}{6}$
3. $\frac{1}{2} + \frac{3}{4}$ $1\frac{1}{4}$
4. $\frac{7}{9} + \frac{1}{3}$ $1\frac{1}{9}$
5. $\frac{7}{8} + \frac{5}{16}$ $1\frac{3}{16}$
6. $\frac{9}{14} + \frac{5}{7}$ $1\frac{5}{14}$
7. $\frac{1}{2} + \frac{5}{6}$ $1\frac{1}{3}$
8. $\frac{3}{4} + \frac{7}{12}$ $1\frac{1}{3}$
9. $\frac{3}{10} + \frac{4}{5}$ $1\frac{1}{10}$
10. $\frac{3}{4} + \frac{5}{16}$ $1\frac{1}{16}$
11. $\frac{7}{10} + \frac{1}{2}$ $1\frac{1}{5}$
12. $\frac{2}{3} + \frac{5}{12}$ $1\frac{1}{12}$
13. $\frac{11}{12} + \frac{1}{6}$ $1\frac{1}{12}$
14. $\frac{11}{18} + \frac{5}{6}$ $1\frac{4}{9}$

15. $\frac{3}{4} + \frac{1}{3}$ $1\frac{1}{12}$

16. $\frac{2}{3} + \frac{1}{2}$ $1\frac{1}{6}$

17. $\frac{4}{5} + \frac{1}{2}$ $1\frac{3}{10}$

18. $\frac{5}{6} + \frac{3}{8}$ $1\frac{5}{24}$

19. $\frac{2}{3} + \frac{4}{5}$ $1\frac{7}{15}$

20. $\frac{7}{8} + \frac{2}{3}$ $1\frac{13}{24}$

21. $\frac{3}{4} + \frac{3}{5}$ $1\frac{7}{20}$

22. $\frac{1}{4} + \frac{5}{6}$ $1\frac{1}{12}$

23. $\frac{5}{8} + \frac{7}{12}$ $1\frac{5}{24}$

24. $\frac{1}{6} + \frac{7}{8}$ $1\frac{1}{24}$

25. $\frac{1}{6} + \frac{8}{9}$ $1\frac{1}{18}$

26. $\frac{2}{3} + \frac{3}{4}$ $1\frac{5}{12}$

27. $\frac{1}{2} + \frac{6}{7}$ $1\frac{5}{14}$

28. $\frac{5}{6} + \frac{2}{9}$ $1\frac{1}{18}$

29. $\frac{4}{5} + \frac{3}{8}$ $1\frac{7}{40}$

30. $\frac{2}{3} + \frac{5}{8}$ $1\frac{7}{24}$

31. $\frac{7}{10} + \frac{1}{3}$ $1\frac{1}{30}$

32. $\frac{3}{8} + \frac{11}{12}$ $1\frac{7}{24}$

33. $\frac{1}{2} + \frac{3}{5}$ $1\frac{1}{10}$

34. $\frac{5}{8} + \frac{3}{5}$ $1\frac{9}{40}$

35. $\frac{3}{4} + \frac{3}{10}$ $1\frac{1}{20}$

36. $\frac{5}{6} + \frac{5}{8}$ $1\frac{11}{24}$

37. $\frac{3}{4} + \frac{5}{6}$ $1\frac{7}{12}$

38. $\frac{1}{2} + \frac{4}{7}$ $1\frac{1}{14}$

39. $\frac{8}{9} + \frac{1}{2}$ $1\frac{7}{18}$

40. $\frac{3}{8} + \frac{2}{3}$ $1\frac{1}{24}$

41. $\frac{5}{6} + \frac{4}{9}$ $1\frac{5}{18}$

42. $\frac{2}{3} + \frac{7}{10}$ $1\frac{11}{30}$

set H

1. $\frac{3}{7} + \frac{6}{7}$ $1\frac{2}{7}$
2. $\frac{1}{6} + \frac{2}{3}$ $\frac{5}{6}$
3. $\frac{2}{3} + \frac{7}{12}$ $1\frac{1}{4}$
4. $\frac{4}{5} + \frac{3}{10}$ $1\frac{1}{10}$
5. $\frac{2}{3} + \frac{1}{2}$ $1\frac{1}{6}$
6. $\frac{3}{4} + \frac{1}{3}$ $1\frac{1}{12}$
7. $\frac{1}{2} + \frac{4}{5}$ $1\frac{3}{10}$
8. $\frac{5}{6} + \frac{1}{4}$ $1\frac{1}{12}$
9. $\frac{7}{8} + \frac{1}{3}$ $1\frac{5}{24}$
10. $\frac{5}{8} + \frac{3}{8} + \frac{1}{8}$ $1\frac{1}{8}$
11. $\frac{2}{5} + \frac{1}{2} + \frac{3}{10}$ $1\frac{1}{5}$
12. $\frac{1}{3} + \frac{3}{4} + \frac{1}{12}$ $1\frac{1}{6}$
13. $\frac{1}{4} + \frac{3}{8} + \frac{7}{16}$ $1\frac{1}{16}$
14. $\frac{1}{3} + \frac{1}{2} + \frac{3}{4}$ $1\frac{7}{12}$
15. $\frac{3}{4} + \frac{1}{6} + \frac{1}{3}$ $1\frac{1}{4}$
16. $\frac{1}{8} + \frac{1}{3} + \frac{3}{4}$ $1\frac{5}{24}$
17. $\frac{2}{5} + \frac{1}{4} + \frac{1}{2}$ $1\frac{3}{20}$
18. $\frac{1}{2} + \frac{2}{5} + \frac{1}{3}$ $1\frac{7}{30}$

BREAK TIME

Mr. and Mrs. Motsinger have six daughters. Each daughter has two brothers.
How many children are there in the Motsinger family? 8 children

Objective: Subtract fractions.

Subtracting Fractions

example I Common denominators

$$\begin{array}{r} \frac{5}{6} \\ -\frac{1}{6} \\ \hline \frac{4}{6} = \frac{2}{3} \end{array}$$

To subtract fractions that have a common denominator, subtract the numerators. Reduce $\frac{4}{6}$ to lowest terms.

example J Different denominators

$$\begin{array}{r} \frac{7}{8} = \frac{14}{16} \\ -\frac{3}{16} = \frac{3}{16} \\ \hline \frac{11}{16} \end{array}$$

To subtract fractions with different denominators, first write $\frac{7}{8}$ and $\frac{3}{16}$ as fractions with a common denominator. Then subtract the numerators.

example K Horizontal form

$\frac{2}{3} - \frac{1}{4}$

Write problem vertically. Write $\frac{2}{3}$ and $\frac{1}{4}$ as fractions with a common denominator. Subtract the numerators.

$$\begin{array}{r} \frac{2}{3} = \frac{8}{12} \\ -\frac{1}{4} = \frac{3}{12} \\ \hline \frac{5}{12} \end{array}$$

exercises

set I

1. $\frac{2}{3} - \frac{1}{3}$ $\frac{1}{3}$
2. $\frac{4}{5} - \frac{2}{5}$ $\frac{2}{5}$
3. $\frac{5}{7} - \frac{2}{7}$ $\frac{3}{7}$
4. $\frac{5}{8} - \frac{3}{8}$ $\frac{1}{4}$
5. $\frac{3}{4} - \frac{1}{4}$ $\frac{1}{2}$
6. $\frac{8}{9} - \frac{2}{9}$ $\frac{2}{3}$
7. $\frac{9}{10} - \frac{3}{10}$ $\frac{3}{5}$
8. $\frac{1}{2} - \frac{2}{5}$ $\frac{1}{2}$

set J

1. $\frac{5}{6} - \frac{2}{3}$ $\frac{1}{6}$
2. $\frac{7}{8} - \frac{1}{2}$ $\frac{3}{8}$
3. $\frac{1}{2} - \frac{1}{4}$ $\frac{1}{4}$
4. $\frac{3}{5} - \frac{1}{10}$ $\frac{1}{2}$
5. $\frac{7}{12} - \frac{1}{3}$ $\frac{1}{4}$
6. $\frac{2}{3} - \frac{1}{2}$ $\frac{1}{6}$
7. $\frac{3}{4} - \frac{1}{3}$ $\frac{5}{12}$
8. $\frac{1}{2} - \frac{2}{5}$ $\frac{1}{10}$
9. $\frac{3}{4} - \frac{1}{6}$ $\frac{7}{12}$
10. $\frac{5}{6} - \frac{3}{8}$ $\frac{11}{24}$

set K

1. $\frac{4}{5} - \frac{3}{5}$ $\frac{1}{5}$
2. $\frac{6}{7} - \frac{1}{7}$ $\frac{5}{7}$
3. $\frac{2}{3} - \frac{1}{3}$ $\frac{1}{3}$
4. $\frac{7}{8} - \frac{5}{8}$ $\frac{1}{4}$
5. $\frac{3}{4} - \frac{1}{4}$ $\frac{1}{2}$
6. $\frac{8}{9} - \frac{5}{9}$ $\frac{1}{3}$
7. $\frac{5}{6} - \frac{1}{6}$ $\frac{2}{3}$
8. $\frac{9}{10} - \frac{3}{10}$ $\frac{3}{5}$
9. $\frac{11}{16} - \frac{3}{16}$ $\frac{1}{2}$
10. $\frac{11}{12} - \frac{7}{12}$ $\frac{1}{3}$
11. $\frac{1}{2} - \frac{1}{4}$ $\frac{1}{4}$
12. $\frac{5}{6} - \frac{1}{3}$ $\frac{1}{2}$
13. $\frac{1}{4} - \frac{1}{8}$ $\frac{1}{8}$
14. $\frac{5}{8} - \frac{1}{2}$ $\frac{1}{8}$
15. $\frac{2}{3} - \frac{4}{9}$ $\frac{2}{9}$
16. $\frac{5}{6} - \frac{1}{2}$ $\frac{1}{3}$
17. $\frac{11}{12} - \frac{1}{6}$ $\frac{3}{4}$
18. $\frac{3}{5} - \frac{1}{10}$ $\frac{1}{2}$
19. $\frac{3}{4} - \frac{7}{12}$ $\frac{1}{6}$
20. $\frac{11}{12} - \frac{2}{3}$ $\frac{1}{4}$
21. $\frac{3}{4} - \frac{1}{3}$ $\frac{5}{12}$
22. $\frac{2}{3} - \frac{1}{5}$ $\frac{7}{15}$
23. $\frac{1}{2} - \frac{2}{5}$ $\frac{1}{10}$
24. $\frac{2}{3} - \frac{1}{2}$ $\frac{1}{6}$
25. $\frac{4}{5} - \frac{1}{3}$ $\frac{7}{15}$
26. $\frac{5}{6} - \frac{3}{4}$ $\frac{1}{12}$
27. $\frac{7}{8} - \frac{5}{6}$ $\frac{1}{24}$
28. $\frac{2}{3} - \frac{3}{8}$ $\frac{7}{24}$
29. $\frac{3}{4} - \frac{1}{5}$ $\frac{11}{20}$
30. $\frac{7}{9} - \frac{1}{6}$ $\frac{11}{18}$
31. $\frac{4}{5} - \frac{3}{8}$ $\frac{17}{40}$
32. $\frac{6}{7} - \frac{1}{2}$ $\frac{5}{14}$
33. $\frac{5}{6} - \frac{2}{5}$ $\frac{13}{30}$
34. $\frac{5}{8} - \frac{1}{3}$ $\frac{7}{24}$
35. $\frac{3}{4} - \frac{1}{6}$ $\frac{7}{12}$
36. $\frac{5}{6} - \frac{3}{8}$ $\frac{11}{24}$
37. $\frac{2}{3} - \frac{3}{10}$ $\frac{11}{30}$
38. $\frac{9}{10} - \frac{3}{4}$ $\frac{3}{20}$
39. $\frac{11}{12} - \frac{5}{8}$ $\frac{7}{24}$
40. $\frac{5}{6} - \frac{7}{10}$ $\frac{2}{15}$

BREAK TIME

The faces on each cube are identical. Tell which symbol is opposite the circle. Arrow
Opposite the triangle. Star
Opposite the square. Diamond

Objective: Add mixed numbers.

Adding Mixed Numbers

example L No sums with improper fractions

$$\begin{array}{r} 7\frac{1}{3} = 7\frac{2}{6} \\ + 2\frac{1}{6} = 2\frac{1}{6} \\ \hline 9\frac{3}{6} = 9\frac{1}{2} \end{array}$$

Write $\frac{1}{3}$ and $\frac{1}{6}$ as fractions with a common denominator.
Add the fractions.
Add the whole numbers.
Reduce answer to lowest terms.

example M Renaming mixed numbers having improper fractions

Rename $8\frac{7}{5}$.

$8\frac{7}{5} = 8 + \frac{7}{5}$ Rename $\frac{7}{5}$ as $1\frac{2}{5}$.

$8\frac{7}{5} = 8 + 1\frac{2}{5}$ Add 8 to get $9\frac{2}{5}$.

$8\frac{7}{5} = 9\frac{2}{5}$

example N Renaming sums having improper fractions

$$\begin{array}{r} 6\frac{2}{3} = 6\frac{8}{12} \\ + 1\frac{3}{4} = 1\frac{9}{12} \\ \hline 7\frac{17}{12} = 8\frac{5}{12} \end{array}$$

Write $\frac{2}{3}$ and $\frac{3}{4}$ as fractions with a common denominator.
Add the fractions.
Add the whole numbers.
Rename the sum.

example O Horizontal form

$6\frac{3}{4} + 2\frac{1}{4}$

$$\begin{array}{r} 6\frac{3}{4} \\ + 2\frac{1}{4} \\ \hline 8\frac{4}{4} = 9 \end{array}$$

Write problem vertically.
Add the fractions.
Add the whole numbers.
Rename the sum.

exercises

set L

1. $3\frac{1}{5} + 4\frac{2}{5}$ $7\frac{3}{5}$
2. $6\frac{3}{7} + 1\frac{2}{7}$ $7\frac{5}{7}$
3. $5\frac{1}{2} + 6\frac{1}{4}$ $11\frac{3}{4}$
4. $2\frac{3}{8} + 9\frac{1}{4}$ $11\frac{5}{8}$
5. $8\frac{1}{6} + 7\frac{2}{3}$ $15\frac{5}{6}$
6. $7\frac{1}{2} + 1\frac{1}{3}$ $8\frac{5}{6}$
7. $8\frac{1}{4} + 6\frac{2}{3}$ $14\frac{11}{12}$
8. $7\frac{1}{4} + 3\frac{1}{6}$ $10\frac{5}{12}$
9. $4\frac{1}{2} + 3\frac{2}{5}$ $7\frac{9}{10}$
10. $5\frac{3}{8} + 6\frac{1}{3}$ $11\frac{17}{24}$

set M

Rename these mixed numbers.

1. $4\frac{3}{2}$ $5\frac{1}{2}$
2. $5\frac{11}{6}$ $6\frac{5}{6}$
3. $8\frac{7}{5}$ $9\frac{2}{5}$
4. $9\frac{5}{3}$ $10\frac{2}{3}$
5. $3\frac{11}{8}$ $4\frac{3}{8}$
6. $2\frac{5}{5}$ 3
7. $9\frac{5}{4}$ $10\frac{1}{4}$
8. $4\frac{11}{7}$ $5\frac{4}{7}$
9. $7\frac{4}{3}$ $8\frac{1}{3}$
10. $2\frac{7}{4}$ $3\frac{3}{4}$
11. $9\frac{13}{8}$ $10\frac{5}{8}$
12. $3\frac{9}{9}$ 4
13. $5\frac{10}{7}$ $6\frac{3}{7}$
14. $6\frac{11}{10}$ $7\frac{1}{10}$
15. $4\frac{17}{9}$ $5\frac{8}{9}$
16. $6\frac{17}{12}$ $7\frac{5}{12}$
17. $1\frac{6}{4}$ $2\frac{1}{2}$
18. $8\frac{14}{10}$ $9\frac{2}{5}$
19. $9\frac{14}{12}$ $10\frac{1}{6}$
20. $3\frac{10}{8}$ $4\frac{1}{4}$
21. $4\frac{22}{12}$ $5\frac{5}{6}$
22. $7\frac{10}{6}$ $8\frac{2}{3}$
23. $2\frac{18}{10}$ $3\frac{4}{5}$
24. $5\frac{12}{8}$ $6\frac{1}{2}$

set N

1. $1\frac{1}{2} + 3\frac{5}{8}$ $5\frac{1}{8}$
2. $7\frac{5}{6} + 2\frac{1}{3}$ $10\frac{1}{6}$
3. $6\frac{7}{10} + 9\frac{3}{5}$ $16\frac{3}{10}$
4. $5\frac{3}{4} + 8\frac{11}{12}$ $14\frac{2}{3}$
5. $4\frac{1}{2} + 1\frac{2}{3}$ $6\frac{1}{6}$
6. $9\frac{2}{3} + 2\frac{3}{4}$ $12\frac{5}{12}$
7. $8\frac{1}{4} + 6\frac{4}{5}$ $15\frac{1}{20}$
8. $2\frac{1}{3} + 7\frac{4}{5}$ $10\frac{2}{15}$
9. $3\frac{5}{6} + 1\frac{1}{4}$ $5\frac{1}{12}$
10. $7\frac{1}{2} + 6\frac{3}{5}$ $14\frac{1}{10}$
11. $5\frac{1}{2} + 3\frac{4}{7}$ $9\frac{1}{14}$
12. $4\frac{3}{5} + 8\frac{5}{6}$ $13\frac{13}{30}$
13. $7\frac{5}{6} + 5\frac{3}{8}$ $13\frac{5}{24}$
14. $6\frac{2}{3} + 7\frac{5}{8}$ $14\frac{7}{24}$
15. $9\frac{7}{10} + 2\frac{3}{4}$ $12\frac{9}{20}$
16. $7\frac{3}{8} + 6\frac{4}{5}$ $14\frac{7}{40}$
17. $1\frac{7}{10} + 5\frac{2}{3}$ $7\frac{11}{30}$
18. $3\frac{7}{8} + 4\frac{3}{10}$ $8\frac{7}{40}$
19. $7\frac{11}{12} + 1\frac{5}{8}$ $9\frac{13}{24}$
20. $3\frac{5}{6} + 1\frac{7}{12}$ $5\frac{5}{12}$

set O

1. $6\frac{1}{2} + 3\frac{1}{2}$ 10
2. $8\frac{2}{3} + 6\frac{2}{3}$ $15\frac{1}{3}$
3. $9\frac{4}{7} + 5\frac{3}{7}$ 15
4. $2\frac{3}{5} + 1\frac{4}{5}$ $4\frac{2}{5}$
5. $8\frac{3}{4} + 2\frac{3}{4}$ $11\frac{1}{2}$
6. $5\frac{3}{8} + 7\frac{5}{8}$ 13
7. $3\frac{11}{12} + 9\frac{7}{12}$ $13\frac{1}{2}$
8. $5\frac{7}{10} + 4\frac{9}{10}$ $10\frac{3}{5}$
9. $2\frac{5}{6} + 8\frac{5}{6}$ $11\frac{2}{3}$
10. $9\frac{3}{10} + 5\frac{7}{10}$ 15
11. $7\frac{1}{2} + 5\frac{3}{4}$ $13\frac{1}{4}$
12. $4\frac{3}{5} + 6\frac{7}{10}$ $11\frac{3}{10}$
13. $3\frac{5}{8} + 4\frac{1}{2}$ $8\frac{1}{8}$
14. $2\frac{5}{6} + 7\frac{1}{3}$ $10\frac{1}{6}$
15. $6\frac{3}{4} + 5\frac{3}{8}$ $12\frac{1}{8}$
16. $8\frac{1}{2} + 1\frac{9}{10}$ $10\frac{2}{5}$
17. $7\frac{5}{6} + 2\frac{1}{2}$ $10\frac{1}{3}$
18. $4\frac{11}{12} + 3\frac{1}{4}$ $8\frac{1}{6}$
19. $8\frac{1}{3} + 9\frac{11}{12}$ $18\frac{1}{4}$
20. $2\frac{5}{12} + 4\frac{5}{6}$ $7\frac{1}{4}$
21. $4\frac{2}{3} + 6\frac{1}{2}$ $11\frac{1}{6}$
22. $3\frac{4}{5} + 2\frac{1}{2}$ $6\frac{3}{10}$
23. $8\frac{1}{3} + 6\frac{3}{4}$ $15\frac{1}{12}$
24. $9\frac{4}{5} + 5\frac{1}{3}$ $15\frac{2}{15}$
25. $7\frac{1}{6} + 3\frac{5}{6}$ 11
26. $1\frac{3}{4} + 4\frac{5}{6}$ $6\frac{7}{12}$
27. $2\frac{7}{8} + 5\frac{2}{3}$ $8\frac{13}{24}$
28. $3\frac{3}{4} + 1\frac{2}{5}$ $5\frac{3}{20}$
29. $6\frac{1}{2} + 9\frac{5}{7}$ $16\frac{3}{14}$
30. $9\frac{2}{3} + 5\frac{7}{10}$ $15\frac{11}{30}$
31. $5\frac{3}{8} + 2\frac{5}{6}$ $8\frac{5}{24}$
32. $6\frac{7}{12} + 8\frac{5}{12}$ 15
33. $3\frac{5}{6} + 4\frac{2}{5}$ $8\frac{7}{30}$
34. $9\frac{3}{4} + 6\frac{3}{10}$ $16\frac{1}{20}$
35. $5\frac{7}{8} + 2\frac{3}{5}$ $8\frac{19}{40}$
36. $6\frac{1}{3} + 8\frac{7}{8}$ $15\frac{5}{24}$
37. $2\frac{5}{8} + 6\frac{7}{10}$ $9\frac{13}{40}$
38. $9\frac{3}{8} + 7\frac{11}{12}$ $17\frac{7}{24}$
39. $5\frac{1}{6} + 4\frac{7}{8}$ $10\frac{1}{24}$
40. $8\frac{7}{10} + 5\frac{5}{6}$ $14\frac{8}{15}$

The applications on page 163 may be used anytime after this lesson.

Objective: Subtract mixed numbers.

Subtracting Mixed Numbers

example P

Fractions with different denominators, no renaming the minuend

$$7\frac{5}{8} = 7\frac{5}{8}$$
$$-3\frac{1}{4} = 3\frac{2}{8}$$
$$4\frac{3}{8}$$

Write $\frac{5}{8}$ and $\frac{1}{4}$ as fractions with a common denominator.
Subtract the fractions.
Subtract the whole numbers.

example Q

Renaming a mixed number to show a greater fraction

Rename $9\frac{1}{5}$ to show more fifths.

$$9\frac{1}{5} = 8\frac{\square}{5}$$

$$9\frac{1}{5} = 9 + \frac{1}{5}$$ Rename 9 as $8\frac{5}{5}$.

$$9\frac{1}{5} = 8\frac{5}{5} + \frac{1}{5}$$ Add $\frac{1}{5}$ to get $8\frac{6}{5}$.

$$9\frac{1}{5} = 8\frac{6}{5}$$

example R

Fractions with common denominators, renaming the minuend

$$8\frac{1}{4} = 7\frac{5}{4}$$
$$-5\frac{3}{4} = 5\frac{3}{4}$$
$$2\frac{2}{4} = 2\frac{1}{2}$$

Rename $8\frac{1}{4}$ to show more fourths.
Subtract the fractions.
Subtract the whole numbers.
Reduce answer to lowest terms.

example S

Fractions with different denominators, renaming the minuend

$$6\frac{1}{3} = 6\frac{2}{6} = 5\frac{8}{6}$$
$$-4\frac{1}{2} = 4\frac{3}{6} = 4\frac{3}{6}$$
$$1\frac{5}{6}$$

Write $\frac{1}{3}$ and $\frac{1}{2}$ as fractions with a common denominator.
Rename $6\frac{2}{6}$ to show more sixths.
Subtract the fractions.
Subtract the whole numbers.

example T

Horizontal form

$$9 - 2\frac{1}{5}$$

$$9 = 8\frac{5}{5}$$
$$-2\frac{1}{5} = 2\frac{1}{5}$$
$$6\frac{4}{5}$$

Write problem vertically.
Rename 9 to show fifths.
Subtract the fractions.
Subtract the whole numbers.

exercises

set P

1. $6\frac{3}{4} - 1\frac{1}{2}$ $5\frac{1}{4}$ **4.** $9\frac{2}{3} - 3\frac{1}{4}$ $6\frac{5}{12}$

2. $5\frac{6}{7} - 3\frac{2}{7}$ $2\frac{4}{7}$ **5.** $7\frac{1}{2} - 2\frac{3}{10}$ $5\frac{1}{5}$

3. $8\frac{2}{3} - 4\frac{1}{6}$ $4\frac{1}{2}$ **6.** $3\frac{5}{6} - 2\frac{3}{4}$ $1\frac{1}{12}$

set Q

Find each missing number.

1. $3\frac{1}{4} = 2\frac{\square}{4}$ 5 **4.** $2\frac{1}{2} = 1\frac{\square}{2}$ 3

2. $4\frac{2}{5} = 3\frac{\square}{5}$ 7 **5.** $7\frac{5}{8} = 6\frac{\square}{8}$ 13

3. $6\frac{1}{3} = 5\frac{\square}{3}$ 4 **6.** $9\frac{1}{6} = 8\frac{\square}{6}$ 7

set R

1. $6\frac{2}{5} - 3\frac{4}{5}$ $2\frac{3}{5}$ **5.** $7\frac{1}{4} - 5\frac{3}{4}$ $1\frac{1}{2}$

2. $7\frac{5}{8} - 4\frac{7}{8}$ $2\frac{3}{4}$ **6.** $3\frac{4}{7} - 1\frac{6}{7}$ $1\frac{5}{7}$

3. $8\frac{1}{6} - 2\frac{5}{6}$ $5\frac{1}{3}$ **7.** $5\frac{3}{10} - 2\frac{7}{10}$ $2\frac{3}{5}$

4. $9\frac{1}{3} - 7\frac{2}{3}$ $1\frac{2}{3}$ **8.** $8\frac{5}{12} - 6\frac{7}{12}$ $1\frac{5}{6}$

set S

1. $5\frac{1}{4} - 1\frac{2}{3}$ $3\frac{7}{12}$ **5.** $8\frac{1}{6} - 5\frac{3}{4}$ $2\frac{5}{12}$

2. $9\frac{1}{2} - 7\frac{4}{5}$ $1\frac{7}{10}$ **6.** $12\frac{1}{3} - 7\frac{5}{8}$ $4\frac{17}{24}$

3. $7\frac{1}{2} - 4\frac{2}{3}$ $2\frac{5}{6}$ **7.** $10\frac{5}{8} - 2\frac{5}{6}$ $7\frac{19}{24}$

4. $6\frac{3}{5} - 4\frac{2}{3}$ $1\frac{14}{15}$ **8.** $15\frac{7}{12} - 9\frac{5}{8}$ $5\frac{23}{24}$

set T

1. $8\frac{4}{5} - 6\frac{1}{5}$ $2\frac{3}{5}$ **13.** $9 - 4\frac{7}{8}$ $4\frac{1}{8}$

2. $9\frac{5}{6} - 7\frac{1}{6}$ $2\frac{2}{3}$ **14.** $6\frac{4}{7} - 2\frac{6}{7}$ $3\frac{5}{7}$

3. $5\frac{3}{4} - 2\frac{1}{2}$ $3\frac{1}{4}$ **15.** $5\frac{1}{2} - 3\frac{2}{3}$ $1\frac{5}{6}$

4. $7 - 3\frac{1}{8}$ $3\frac{7}{8}$ **16.** $7 - 4\frac{1}{5}$ $2\frac{4}{5}$

5. $4\frac{1}{2} - 1\frac{1}{3}$ $3\frac{1}{6}$ **17.** $8\frac{1}{4} - 2\frac{5}{6}$ $5\frac{5}{12}$

6. $8\frac{2}{3} - 2\frac{5}{8}$ $6\frac{1}{24}$ **18.** $7\frac{1}{2} - 3\frac{4}{5}$ $3\frac{7}{10}$

7. $5\frac{3}{10} - 2\frac{9}{10}$ $2\frac{2}{5}$ **19.** $9\frac{1}{4} - 6\frac{2}{3}$ $2\frac{7}{12}$

8. $6\frac{3}{5} - 2\frac{4}{5}$ $3\frac{4}{5}$ **20.** $7\frac{1}{6} - 2\frac{3}{4}$ $4\frac{5}{12}$

9. $8 - 7\frac{2}{3}$ $\frac{1}{3}$ **21.** $6\frac{5}{8} - 4\frac{2}{3}$ $1\frac{23}{24}$

10. $4\frac{5}{12} - 2\frac{7}{12}$ $1\frac{5}{6}$ **22.** $4\frac{1}{6} - 1\frac{5}{8}$ $2\frac{13}{24}$

11. $7 - 3\frac{5}{6}$ $3\frac{1}{6}$ **23.** $8 - 6\frac{7}{10}$ $1\frac{3}{10}$

12. $2\frac{1}{4} - 1\frac{3}{4}$ $\frac{1}{2}$ **24.** $5\frac{3}{8} - 1\frac{7}{12}$ $3\frac{19}{24}$

posttest

Number of test items - 20										
Number missed	1	2	3	4	5	6	7	8	9	10
Percent correct	95	90	85	80	75	70	65	60	55	50

skill Finding Common Denominators page 152

A Write $\frac{2}{3}$ and $\frac{3}{4}$ as fractions with a common denominator. $\frac{8}{12}, \frac{9}{12}$

B Write $\frac{2}{3}$, $\frac{5}{6}$, and $\frac{1}{4}$ as fractions with a common denominator. $\frac{8}{12}, \frac{10}{12}, \frac{3}{12}$

skill Comparing Fractions and Mixed Numbers page 153

C Compare $\frac{2}{5}$ and $\frac{4}{5}$. Use <, >, or =. $\frac{2}{5} < \frac{4}{5}$, or $\frac{4}{5} > \frac{2}{5}$

D Compare $\frac{4}{6}$ and $\frac{2}{3}$. Use <, >, or =. $\frac{4}{6} = \frac{2}{3}$

E Compare $5\frac{7}{8}$ and $5\frac{3}{4}$. Use <, >, or =. $5\frac{7}{8} > 5\frac{3}{4}$, or $5\frac{3}{4} < 5\frac{7}{8}$

skill Adding Fractions pages 154–155

F $\frac{4}{7} + \frac{5}{7}$ $1\frac{2}{7}$

G $\frac{7}{12} + \frac{3}{4}$ $1\frac{1}{3}$

H $\frac{5}{8} + \frac{1}{2} + \frac{3}{4}$ $1\frac{7}{8}$

skill Subtracting Fractions pages 156–157

I $\frac{2}{3} - \frac{1}{3}$ $\frac{1}{3}$

J $\frac{1}{2} - \frac{1}{4}$ $\frac{1}{4}$

K $\frac{7}{8} - \frac{1}{3}$ $\frac{13}{24}$

skill Adding Mixed Numbers pages 158–159

L $7\frac{1}{4} + 2\frac{5}{8}$ $9\frac{7}{8}$

M Rename $7\frac{8}{5}$. $7\frac{8}{5} = 8\frac{\square}{5}$ 3

N $2\frac{1}{4} + 8\frac{5}{6}$ $11\frac{1}{12}$

O $7\frac{3}{5} + 4\frac{2}{5}$ 12

skill Subtracting Mixed Numbers pages 160–161

P $8\frac{5}{6} - 4\frac{2}{3}$ $4\frac{1}{6}$

Q Rename $5\frac{3}{8}$. $5\frac{3}{8} = 4\frac{\square}{8}$ 11

R $7\frac{1}{6} - 3\frac{5}{6}$ $3\frac{1}{3}$

S $6\frac{1}{3} - 2\frac{3}{4}$ $3\frac{7}{12}$

T $3 - 1\frac{3}{5}$ $1\frac{2}{5}$

Objective: Solve problems involving addition and subtraction of fractions and mixed numbers.

In this lesson students find number of hours worked and compute total wages received for a week.

Computing Weekly Wages

You might want to have students answer questions that are extensions of the exercises on the page, such as these.
1. How many hours did the housekeeper work during this six-week period? [208 hours]
2. How much did the housekeeper earn in this six-week period? [$624]
3. Did the housekeeper work more hours in the third or fourth week? [Third] How many more? [3 hours]
4. Did the housekeeper earn more money in the first or second week? [Second] How much more? [$24]

The Torochios' housekeeper kept an accurate record of the hours worked each day.

For each week, find the total number of hours the housekeeper worked. Then compute the total amount of money earned that week at a rate of $3 per hour.

1.

Day	Hours worked
Monday	$7\frac{1}{2}$
Tuesday	$4\frac{1}{4}$
Wednesday	5
Thursday	$3\frac{1}{2}$
Friday	$6\frac{3}{4}$ 27 hours $81

2.

Day	Hours worked
Monday	$6\frac{1}{2}$
Tuesday	$7\frac{1}{4}$
Wednesday	$4\frac{1}{4}$
Thursday	$6\frac{1}{2}$
Friday	$5\frac{1}{2}$ 30 hours $90

3.

Day	Hours worked
Monday	$8\frac{1}{6}$
Tuesday	$5\frac{1}{2}$
Wednesday	$5\frac{1}{2}$
Thursday	$4\frac{2}{3}$
Friday	6
Saturday	$9\frac{1}{6}$ 39 hours $117

4.

Day	Hours worked
Monday	$4\frac{5}{6}$
Tuesday	$7\frac{3}{4}$
Wednesday	$6\frac{3}{4}$
Thursday	$8\frac{1}{2}$
Friday	$8\frac{1}{6}$ 36 hours $108

5.

Day	Hours worked
Monday	$3\frac{1}{6}$
Tuesday	$7\frac{5}{6}$
Wednesday	$6\frac{3}{4}$
Thursday	$7\frac{1}{2}$
Friday	$7\frac{3}{4}$ 33 hours $99

6.

Day	Hours worked
Monday	$8\frac{2}{5}$
Tuesday	$6\frac{3}{4}$
Wednesday	$5\frac{1}{2}$
Thursday	$7\frac{3}{5}$
Friday	$6\frac{1}{4}$
Saturday	$3\frac{1}{2}$ 38 hours $114

Reading a Stock Market Report

Objective: Solve problems involving addition and subtraction of fractions and mixed numbers.

In this lesson students read a stock report and compute the difference between the closing price and the highest price for the day, the high and the low for the day, and the high and the low for the year.

Investing money in the stock market is sometimes a way of saving or earning money. Janet Littlebird owns stock in Abbott Laboratories. Because the price of a stock may change daily, she reads the stock report each day.

She looks first for AbbLab, the abbreviated name of the company. Then she looks at the columns to the right of AbbLab.

The *highest price* paid per share that day is $74\frac{1}{4}$ ($74\frac{1}{4}$ dollars). The *lowest price* paid per share that day is $71\frac{1}{2}$ ($71\frac{1}{2}$ dollars). The *closing price* paid per share that day is $73\frac{7}{8}$ ($73\frac{7}{8}$ dollars). The *net change* is $+2\frac{3}{8}$. This indicates that the last price paid per share today was $2\frac{3}{8}$ dollars higher than the last price paid yesterday.

Finally, she looks at the first two columns to find the highest price ($74\frac{3}{8}$ dollars) and the lowest price ($46\frac{1}{2}$ dollars) paid for one share of stock since the first of the year.

Be sure students understand new terms before assigning the exercises.

NEW YORK STOCK EXCHANGE
MONDAY

1975 High	1975 Low		High	Low	Close	Net Chg.
High	Low		High	Low	Last	Chg.
74 3/8	46 1/2	AbbLab	74 1/4	71 1/2	73 7/8	+ 2 3/8
45 3/4	33 1/4	ACF In	45 3/4	42 1/8	45 1/8	+ 3 1/8
10 3/8	7	AcmeClv	9 1/4	9	9 1/4	+ 1/8
3 7/8	1 3/4	AdmDg	3 3/4	3 1/2	3 1/2	− 1/4
10 1/4	7 3/4	AdmEx	9 7/8	9 1/8	9 7/8	+ 1/2
3 5/8	2 1/8	Adms Millis	3 1/8	3	3 1/8	+ 1/8
9 3/8	3 1/4	Addressog	9 1/8	8 5/8	8 7/8	....
10	7 1/4	Advinv	8 7/8	8 5/8	8 3/4	− 1/8
26 1/2	20	AetnaLf	24 3/4	24 1/4	24 5/8	....
39 3/4	31	AetnaLf	38 1/2	38 1/8	38 1/2	+ 3/4
7	4 3/8	Aguirre Co	6	5 3/4	5 3/4	....
11 7/8	6 7/8	Ahmans	11 7/8	11 5/8	11 3/4	+ 1/8
3 3/4	1 5/8	Aileen Inc	3 3/8	3	3 1/8	− 1/8
78 3/8	44 3/4	AirPrd	74 1/4	72 1/4	72 1/2	− 5/8
21 1/4	10 1/2	AircoInc	18 7/8	17 3/8	18 7/8	+ 5/8
2	1	AJ Industris	1 7/8	1 5/8	1 7/8	+ 1/8
17 1/4	10 1/2	Akzona	16 1/8	15	15 1/4	− 7/8
13	7 7/8	AlaGas	11 7/8	11 1/8	11 7/8	+ 1/2
94 1/2	78	AlaP	87	84	85 1/2	+ 3/8
84 1/2	69 1/2	AlaP	77	77	77	+ 1
81	70	AlaP	80	80	80	+ 2
17 1/8	9	Alaska Intrs	17 1/8	14 7/8	16 7/8	+ 1 1/2
19 5/8	13 7/8	AlbanyIn	17 1/8	16 5/8	16 3/4	− 1/4
7 3/8	4 5/8	AlbertoC	6 5/8	6 1/4	6 1/2	− 1/8
18 3/4	12 1/4	Albertsn	18 1/2	17 3/4	18 3/8	+ 3/8
24 3/8	18 7/8	AlcanAlu	23 1/8	22 1/4	22 3/4	− 1/8
11 7/8	7 1/2	AlcoStd	11 7/8	11	11 3/4	+ 3/8
27 1/4	15 1/4	AlconLb	26 3/4	25 5/8	26 1/8	+ 1/4
5 5/8	2 1/2	Alexdrs	5 3/8	4 3/4	5 1/4	+ 3/8
6 3/8	3	Alison Mtg	4	3 5/8	4	+ 1/8
11 3/8	6 7/8	AllegCp	10 3/8	9 3/4	10	− 1/8
26 7/8	20 3/8	AllgLud	24 5/8	23 1/2	24 1/8	....
36 7/8	31 5/8	AllgLud	35 3/8	35 1/4	35 3/8	....
18 1/4	12 7/8	AllgPw	18 1/4	17 3/4	18	+ 1/4
7	4 1/8	AllenGrp	7	6 1/4	7	+ 3/4
42	27	AlldCh	37 1/4	35 1/2	37	− 1/8
15 3/8	8 5/8	AlldMnt	14	13 3/8	14	+ 5/8
15 3/8	12 1/2	AlldProd	13 1/2	13 1/4	13 3/8	− 1/8
33	15 7/8	AlldStr	33	30 5/8	32 1/8	+ 1 3/4
4	2 1/8	Alld Supmkt	2 7/8	2 1/2	2 5/8	− 1/8
11 3/8	6 5/8	AllisChal	11 3/8	10 7/8	11 3/8	+ 1/8
8	5 1/8	AllrtAut	7 1/2	7 1/8	7 1/2	+ 3/8
10 7/8	7 3/8	AlphaPi	10 5/8	10 3/8	10 1/2	− 3/8
50 1/4	27 1/8	Alcoa	47 7/8	44 3/4	46	− 2
46 7/8	26 3/4	AmalgSug	37	35 5/8	37	+ 1 1/8
50	28 3/4	Amax	48 3/8	45	45 7/8	− 1 7/8

What could Janet save per share if she bought each stock at Monday's lowest price instead of Monday's highest price?

1. AbbLab ($74\frac{1}{4}-71\frac{1}{2}$) $2\frac{3}{4}$ dollars
2. Addressog $\frac{4}{8}$, or $\frac{1}{2}$ dollar
3. AlcanAlu $\frac{7}{8}$ dollar
4. AlconLb $1\frac{1}{8}$ dollars
5. Alexdrs $\frac{5}{8}$ dollar
6. AllegCp $\frac{5}{8}$ dollar
7. AlldStr $2\frac{3}{8}$ dollars

What could Janet save per share if she bought each stock at Monday's closing price instead of Monday's highest price?

8. AbbLab ($74\frac{1}{4}-73\frac{7}{8}$) $\frac{3}{8}$ dollar
9. Ahmans $\frac{1}{8}$ dollar
10. AirPrd $1\frac{3}{4}$ dollars
11. Akzona $\frac{7}{8}$ dollar
12. AlbanyIn $\frac{3}{8}$ dollar
13. AlldStr $\frac{7}{8}$ dollar
14. Alcoa $1\frac{7}{8}$ dollars

For each stock, find the difference between the highest and lowest prices paid per share since the first of the year.

15. AbbLab ($74\frac{3}{8}-46\frac{1}{2}$) $27\frac{7}{8}$ dollars
16. AcmeClv $3\frac{3}{8}$ dollars
17. AdmDg $2\frac{1}{8}$ dollars
18. Akzona $6\frac{3}{4}$ dollars
19. AlbanyIn $5\frac{6}{8}$, or $5\frac{3}{4}$ dollars
20. AlconLb 12 dollars
21. AllisChal $4\frac{6}{8}$, or $4\frac{3}{4}$ dollars

Objective: Solve problems involving addition and subtraction of fractions and mixed numbers.

In this lesson students find the cost of producing toys and compute the gross profit.

Career: Toy Manufacturer

Career Cluster: Trades

Mr. Richard Metti owns a toy factory. He supervises the purchasing of parts to make the toys and sees that they are assembled.

1. Find the total cost of the parts purchased to make each Quick McDraw Water Pistol. 8 ¢

Part	Cost in cents
Plastic gun	$3\frac{5}{8}$
Stopper	$\frac{5}{8}$
Barrel	$1\frac{1}{4}$
Trigger	$2\frac{1}{2}$

2. Craftwood Corporation sells the water pistol for 29 cents. Find the gross profit for each pistol. 21 ¢ (Sales price − cost)

3. Find the total cost of the parts purchased to make each Playtime Paddle Ball. $11\frac{3}{8}$ ¢

Part	Cost in cents
Paddle	$8\frac{1}{2}$
Ball	$2\frac{1}{4}$
Rubber band	$\frac{1}{2}$
Staple	$\frac{1}{8}$

4. Craftwood Corporation sells the paddle ball for 79 cents. Find the gross profit for each paddle ball. $67\frac{5}{8}$ ¢

5. Find the total cost of all the items in each Happy Homemaker Tool Set. $18\frac{5}{8}$ ¢

Item	Cost in cents
Saw	$3\frac{1}{4}$
Wrench	$2\frac{1}{2}$
Screwdriver	$3\frac{3}{8}$
Pliers	$5\frac{1}{2}$
Hammer	$2\frac{1}{4}$
File	$1\frac{3}{4}$

6. Craftwood Corporation sells the tool set for 77 cents. Find the gross profit for each tool set. $58\frac{3}{8}$ ¢

Several suppliers submitted prices to Mr. Metti for the component parts that make up the Mighty Motor Truck.

Part	Price in cents		
	Toyparts Company	Playthings, Inc.	Knickknacks, Ltd.
4 wheels with hubcaps	$4\frac{1}{4}$	4	$4\frac{1}{2}$
2 metal axles	5	$4\frac{1}{2}$	$4\frac{3}{4}$
Plastic windows and windshield	$2\frac{1}{8}$	$2\frac{1}{4}$	$2\frac{1}{8}$
Metal cab	$7\frac{1}{2}$	8	$7\frac{3}{4}$
Seats and steering wheel	$2\frac{1}{4}$	$2\frac{1}{4}$	$2\frac{1}{4}$
Metal truck bed	$12\frac{3}{4}$	$11\frac{7}{8}$	$11\frac{1}{2}$
Plastic cement mixer	$4\frac{1}{2}$	$4\frac{3}{4}$	$4\frac{5}{8}$

Find the total price for the component parts submitted by

7. Toyparts Company. $38\frac{3}{8}$ ¢

8. Playthings, Inc. $37\frac{5}{8}$ ¢

9. Knickknacks, Ltd. $37\frac{4}{8}$, or $37\frac{1}{2}$ ¢

Which company submitted the

10. lowest price? Knickknacks, Ltd.

11. highest price? Toyparts Company

12. How much cheaper was the lowest price submitted than the highest price? $\frac{7}{8}$ ¢

13. Find the total price of the component parts if Mr. Metti could select each individual part at the lowest price. $36\frac{3}{8}$ ¢

Mighty Motor Truck sells for 99 cents. Find the gross profit for each truck if Mr. Metti purchases parts from

14. Toyparts Company.

15. Playthings, Inc.

16. Knickknacks, Ltd.

14. $60\frac{5}{8}$ ¢

15. $61\frac{3}{8}$ ¢

16. $61\frac{1}{2}$ ¢

Objective: Solve problems involving addition and subtraction of fractions and mixed numbers.

In this lesson students find the total time for performing tasks and compute the time saved by making task modifications.

Career: Efficiency Expert

Career Cluster: Trades

John Mayahara is an efficiency expert. He keeps an accurate record of the time it takes an employee to perform a certain task. He then makes changes that allow the employee to perform the task more quickly.

1. Find the total time needed to assemble a nut and bolt. 20 seconds

Task	Time in seconds
Obtains bolt from bin.	$4\frac{3}{10}$
Obtains washer from bin.	$5\frac{1}{2}$
Positions washer on bolt.	$2\frac{3}{10}$
Obtains nut from bin.	$3\frac{2}{5}$
Assembles nut on bolt.	$4\frac{1}{2}$

2. Find the total time needed to assemble a nut and bolt after Mr. Mayahara moved the bins closer together. $10\frac{7}{10}$ seconds

Task	Time in seconds
Obtains bolt from bin.	$1\frac{1}{5}$
Obtains washer from bin.	$1\frac{1}{5}$
Positions washer on bolt.	$2\frac{3}{10}$
Obtains nut from bin.	$1\frac{1}{2}$
Assembles nut on bolt.	$4\frac{1}{2}$

After Mr. Mayahara moved the bins closer together, how many seconds were saved in assembling

3. a nut and bolt? $9\frac{3}{10}$ seconds

4. 10 nuts and bolts? 93 seconds

5. 100 nuts and bolts? 930 seconds

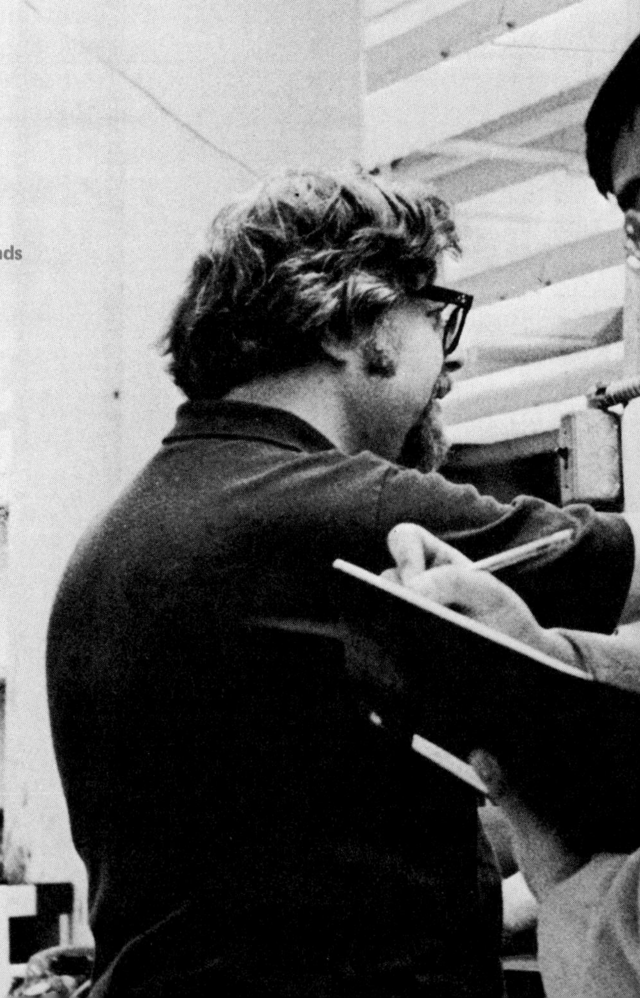

You might ask students to change 930 seconds to minutes. [$15\frac{1}{2}$ minutes]

Mr. Mayahara recorded how many seconds it took Mr. Woodfield to drill each of the four metal braces.

Task	Time in seconds			
	First brace	Second brace	Third brace	Fourth brace
Pick up piece and place it in drill.	$3\frac{1}{2}$	$3\frac{1}{5}$	$3\frac{4}{5}$	$3\frac{7}{10}$
Tighten set screw.	$1\frac{1}{2}$	$1\frac{3}{4}$	$1\frac{1}{2}$	$1\frac{3}{10}$
Advance drill to work.	$2\frac{1}{5}$	$3\frac{1}{2}$	$3\frac{1}{4}$	$2\frac{4}{5}$
Drill holes.	$5\frac{1}{5}$	$5\frac{1}{2}$	$5\frac{1}{2}$	$5\frac{3}{4}$
Loosen set screw.	$1\frac{1}{5}$	$1\frac{1}{2}$	1	$1\frac{4}{5}$
Remove piece.	$2\frac{1}{10}$	3	$2\frac{1}{10}$	$3\frac{1}{4}$
Blow out chips.	$\frac{1}{2}$	$\frac{1}{2}$	$\frac{3}{4}$	$\frac{3}{4}$

How many seconds were used to drill the

6. first brace? $16\frac{2}{10}$, or $16\frac{1}{5}$ seconds

7. second brace? $18\frac{19}{20}$ seconds

8. third brace? $17\frac{3}{20}$ seconds

9. fourth brace? $19\frac{7}{20}$ seconds

10. How many seconds were used to drill all four braces? $71\frac{13}{20}$ seconds

11. Divide the total time by 4 to find the average number of seconds used to drill each metal brace. $17\frac{73}{80}$ seconds

12. Mr. Mayahara made changes that allowed Mr. Woodfield to decrease his average time to $13\frac{1}{2}$ seconds. By how many seconds did his average time decrease? $4\frac{33}{80}$ seconds

You may wish to check answers to exercises 6-9 before having students work exercises 10-12.

Efficiency experts are used throughout all phases of industry. They analyze tasks and then make recommendations that help employees do the job more efficiently with less fatigue. This results in increased productivity per employee, and the company saves money.

Number of test items - 25

Number missed	1	2	3	4	5	6	7	8	9	10	11	12
Percent correct	96	92	88	84	80	76	72	68	64	60	56	52

Chapter 8

Write these fractions with a common denominator.

A **1.** $\frac{1}{2}$ $\frac{3}{6}$ $\frac{2}{3}$ $\frac{4}{6}$

B **2.** $\frac{3}{4}$ $\frac{9}{12}$ $\frac{5}{6}$ $\frac{10}{12}$ $\frac{1}{2}$ $\frac{6}{12}$

Compare the numbers. Use >, <, or =.

C **3.** $\frac{4}{7}$ ● $\frac{3}{7}$ >

D **4.** $\frac{6}{10}$ ● $\frac{3}{5}$ =

E **5.** $6\frac{5}{16}$ ● $6\frac{3}{8}$ <

F **6.** $\frac{3}{4} + \frac{3}{4}$ $1\frac{1}{2}$

G **7.** $\frac{3}{5} + \frac{7}{10}$ $1\frac{3}{10}$

H **8.** $\frac{2}{3} + \frac{5}{12} + \frac{1}{4}$ $1\frac{1}{3}$

I **9.** $\frac{5}{8} - \frac{3}{8}$ $\frac{1}{4}$

J **10.** $\frac{1}{2} - \frac{2}{5}$ $\frac{1}{10}$

K **11.** $\frac{3}{4} - \frac{1}{3}$ $\frac{5}{12}$

L **12.** $3\frac{1}{2} + 6\frac{3}{8}$ $9\frac{7}{8}$

M **13.** Rename $4\frac{10}{7}$.
$4\frac{10}{7} = 5\frac{▒}{7}$ 3

N **14.** $2\frac{1}{3} + 6\frac{7}{8}$ $9\frac{5}{24}$

O **15.** $5\frac{4}{7} + 8\frac{3}{7}$ 14

P **16.** $7\frac{3}{4} - 4\frac{2}{3}$ $3\frac{1}{12}$

Q **17.** Rename $8\frac{3}{5}$.
$8\frac{3}{5} = 7\frac{▒}{5}$ 8

R **18.** $5\frac{3}{8} - 2\frac{7}{8}$ $2\frac{1}{2}$

S **19.** $9\frac{3}{8} - 4\frac{5}{6}$ $4\frac{13}{24}$

T **20.** $10 - 3\frac{5}{8}$ $6\frac{3}{8}$

21. Find the total number of hours Tom worked last week. $16\frac{3}{20}$ hours

Day	Hours worked
Monday	$3\frac{4}{5}$
Tuesday	$2\frac{9}{10}$
Wednesday	$4\frac{1}{2}$
Thursday	$1\frac{3}{4}$
Friday	$3\frac{1}{5}$

22. How much money could Sue save if she bought AllenGrp at the day's lowest price per share instead of the day's highest price?

1975 High	1975 Low		High	Low	Close	Net Chg.
High	Low		High	Low	Last	Chg.
36 7/8	31 5/8	AllgLud	35 3/8	35 1/4	35 3/8	....
18 1/4	12 7/8	AllgPw	18 1/4	17 3/4	18	+ 1/4
7	4 1/8	AllenGrp	7	6 1/4	7	+ 3/4
42	27	AlldCh	37 1/4	35 1/2	37	− 1/8
15 3/8	8 5/8	AlldMnt	14	13 3/8	14	+ 5/8

$\frac{3}{4}$ dollars per share

23. Find the total cost of all the items in each toy tool set. $14\frac{3}{8}$ ¢

Item	Cost in cents
Hammer	$2\frac{1}{4}$
Saw	$3\frac{1}{4}$
Pliers	$5\frac{1}{2}$
Screwdriver	$3\frac{3}{8}$

24. The toy manufacturer sells the tool set for 49 cents. Find the gross profit for each toy tool set. $34\frac{5}{8}$ ¢

25. How many seconds did Jenny use to drill all three braces? $56\frac{3}{5}$ seconds

1st brace, $19\frac{1}{5}$ seconds
2nd brace, $18\frac{9}{10}$ seconds
3rd brace, $18\frac{1}{2}$ seconds

 See pages 19-20 of the *Tests and Record Forms: Duplicating Masters* for an alternate form of the Chapter 8 Test.

D	First coin	Second coin	Possible outcomes
	head	head	head, head
		tail	head, tail
	tail	head	tail, head
		tail	tail, tail

pretest

Number of test items - 10

Number missed	1	2	3	4	5
Percent correct	90	80	70	60	50

Chapter 9 Probability

skill Finding Probabilities and Predicting Outcomes pages 172-173

A Give the probability that the roll of a die will show two. $\frac{1}{6}$

B Give the probability that the roll of a die will show two or four. $\frac{2}{6}$, or $\frac{1}{3}$

C Give the expected number of rolls that will result in two if a die were rolled 30 times. 5

skill Finding Probabilities Using Tree Diagrams pages 174-175

D Make a tree diagram to find the number of outcomes for tossing two coins. 4
See above.

E Give the probability of getting two heads if two coins were tossed. $\frac{1}{4}$

skill Finding Probabilities Using Multiplication pages 176-177

F Multiply to find the number of possible outcomes for choosing a four-digit code number if each digit is chosen at random. 10,000

G Give the probability that a four-digit code number chosen at random will be 0495 or 7326. $\frac{2}{10{,}000}$, or $\frac{1}{5000}$

skill Finding Probabilities Involving Dependent Events pages 178-179

H Give the probability of drawing two cards at random that show *L* if the first card is *not* replaced before making the second draw.

T A L L Y $\frac{2}{20}$, or $\frac{1}{10}$

skill Using Experiments to Make Predictions pages 180-181

I Using the results of the experiment at the right, predict the probability that, on the next toss, the tack would land point up. $\frac{18}{24}$, or $\frac{3}{4}$

Outcome	Tally
Point up	卌 卌 卌 III
Point down	卌 I

J Give the expected number of tosses that will land point up if the tack used in the experiment were tossed 60 times. 45

See page T21 for additional notes on Chapter 9.

Skill

Objective: Find probabilities and make predictions.

Finding Probabilities and Predicting Outcomes

example A
Finding probability, one favorable outcome

Give the probability that the roll of a die will show four.

Use this formula to find the probability of a given outcome when all outcomes are equally likely.

$$\textbf{Probability} = \frac{\textbf{number of favorable outcomes}}{\textbf{number of possible outcomes}}$$

The die may land in any of 6 ways.
All are equally likely to occur.
There are 6 possible outcomes.
Four is 1 of the 6 possible outcomes.

$\frac{1}{6}$ ⟵ Number of favorable outcomes (numerator); Number of possible outcomes (denominator)

The probability that the die will show four is $\frac{1}{6}$.

example B
Finding probability, more than one favorable outcome

Use the formula to give the probability that the roll of a die will show four or six.

There are 6 possible outcomes.
All are equally likely to occur.
Four is 1 of the possible outcomes.
Six is another. Therefore, there are 2 favorable outcomes.

$\frac{2}{6}$ ⟵ Number of favorable outcomes (numerator); Number of possible outcomes (denominator)

The probability that the die will show four or six is $\frac{2}{6}$, or $\frac{1}{3}$.

example C
Predicting outcomes

Give the expected number of rolls that will result in four if a die were rolled 18 times.

First, find the probability.

$\frac{1}{6}$ ⟵ Number of favorable outcomes (numerator); Number of possible outcomes (denominator)

Then multiply to find the expected number of favorable outcomes.

Probability of rolling a four		Number of rolls		Expected number of favorable outcomes
$\frac{1}{6}$	$\times$	18	=	3

One could expect about 3 out of 18 rolls to result in four.

exercises

set A

Give the probability that the roll of a die will show

1. two. $\frac{1}{6}$
2. six. $\frac{1}{6}$
3. five. $\frac{1}{6}$
4. one. $\frac{1}{6}$
5. three. $\frac{1}{6}$

set B

Give the probability that the roll of a die will show

1. two or four. $\frac{2}{6}$, or $\frac{1}{3}$
2. one, two, or six. $\frac{3}{6}$, or $\frac{1}{2}$
3. five. $\frac{1}{6}$
4. two, three, or five. $\frac{3}{6}$, or $\frac{1}{2}$
5. five or six. $\frac{2}{6}$, or $\frac{1}{3}$
6. a number less than five. $\frac{4}{6}$, or $\frac{2}{3}$
7. a number greater than one. $\frac{5}{6}$
8. an even number. $\frac{3}{6}$, or $\frac{1}{2}$

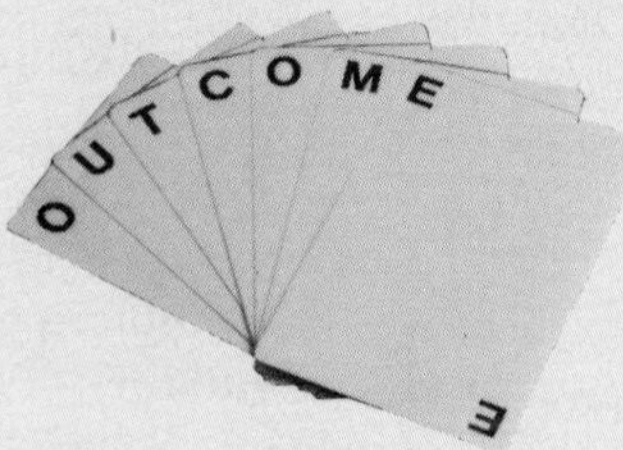

Give the probability of drawing a card that shows

9. T. $\frac{1}{7}$
10. U. $\frac{1}{7}$
11. O. $\frac{2}{7}$
12. T or U. $\frac{2}{7}$
13. T or O. $\frac{3}{7}$
14. T, U, or O. $\frac{4}{7}$

Give the probability of drawing a card that shows

15. P. $\frac{1}{11}$
16. R. $\frac{1}{11}$
17. B. $\frac{2}{11}$
18. I. $\frac{2}{11}$
19. P or B. $\frac{3}{11}$
20. B or I. $\frac{4}{11}$

set C

Give the expected number of rolls that will result in two if a die were rolled

1. 6 times. 1
2. 12 times. 2
3. 24 times. 4
4. 60 times. 10
5. 90 times. 15
6. 120 times. 20

Give the expected number of rolls that will result in five or six if a die were rolled

7. 12 times. 4
8. 15 times. 5
9. 21 times. 7
10. 27 times. 9
11. 42 times. 14
12. 90 times. 30

Give the expected number of rolls that will result in a number less than five if a die were rolled

13. 9 times. 6
14. 18 times. 12
15. 24 times. 16
16. 30 times. 20
17. 42 times. 28
18. 60 times. 40

Objective: Find probabilities using tree diagrams.

Finding Probabilities Using Tree Diagrams

example D Finding possible outcomes

Make a tree diagram to find the number of possible outcomes for choosing one marble from each jar.

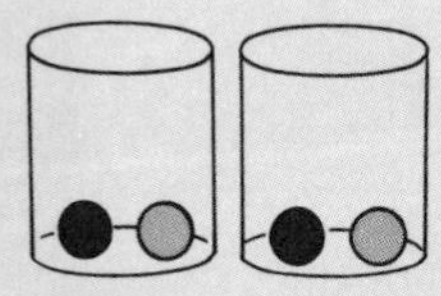

First jar	Second jar	Possible outcomes
black	black	black, black
	gray	black, gray
gray	black	gray, black
	gray	gray, gray

A tree diagram shows that there are 4 possible outcomes.

example E Finding probability, independent events

If a marble were chosen from each jar, give the probability of choosing one black and one gray marble.

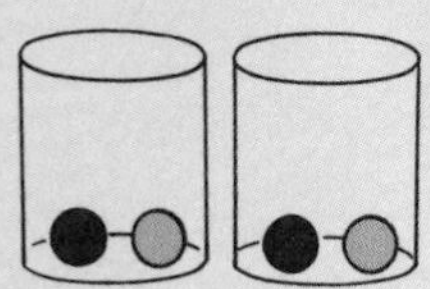

There are 4 possible outcomes.
There are 2 favorable outcomes.
Black, *gray* is one; *gray*, *black* is the other.

$2 \leftarrow$ Number of favorable outcomes
$4 \leftarrow$ Number of possible outcomes

The probability of choosing one black and one gray marble is $\frac{2}{4}$, or $\frac{1}{2}$.

exercises

set D

Complete each tree diagram to find the number of possible outcomes for

1. choosing a sweater and a skirt from the ones listed. 6

Sweater—yellow, orange
Skirt—gray, green, brown

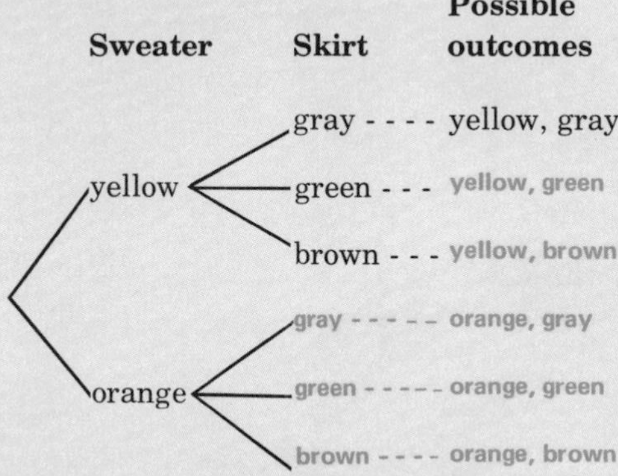

2. choosing a catcher and a pitcher from the athletes listed. 8

Catcher—Joan, Mona

Pitcher—Donna, Karen, Beth, Paula

Catcher	Pitcher	Possible outcomes
Joan	Donna	Joan, Donna
	Karen	Joan, Karen
	Beth	Joan, Beth
	Paula	Joan, Paula
Mona	Donna	Mona, Donna
	Karen	Mona, Karen
	Beth	Mona, Beth
	Paula	Mona, Paula

3. tossing two coins. 4

First coin	Second coin	Possible outcomes
head	head	head, head
	tail	head, tail
tail	head	tail, head
	tail	tail, tail

4. tossing three coins. 8

First coin	Second coin	Third coin	Possible outcomes
head	head	head	head, head, head
		tail	head, head, tail
	tail	head	head, tail, head
		tail	head, tail, tail
tail	head	head	tail, head, head
		tail	tail, head, tail
	tail	head	tail, tail, head
		tail	tail, tail, tail

5. choosing the answers in a true-false test with three questions. 8

First question	Second question	Third question	Possible outcomes
true	true	true	true, true, true
		false	true, true, false
	false	true	true, false, true
		false	true, false, false
false	true	true	false, true, true
		false	false, true, false
	false	true	false, false, true
		false	false, false, false

set E

If two coins were tossed, give the probability of getting

1. two heads. $\frac{1}{4}$
2. two tails. $\frac{1}{4}$
3. one head and one tail. $\frac{2}{4}$, or $\frac{1}{2}$
4. one or more heads. $\frac{3}{4}$
5. one or more tails. $\frac{3}{4}$

If three coins were tossed, give the probability of getting

6. three heads. $\frac{1}{8}$
7. two heads and one tail. $\frac{3}{8}$
8. one or more heads. $\frac{7}{8}$
9. three tails. $\frac{1}{8}$
10. one or more tails. $\frac{7}{8}$
11. two or more heads. $\frac{4}{8}$, or $\frac{1}{2}$
12. two or more tails. $\frac{4}{8}$, or $\frac{1}{2}$

If a student answered three questions in a true-false test only by guessing, give the probability of writing

13. *true* once and *false* twice. $\frac{3}{8}$
14. *true* at least twice. $\frac{4}{8}$, or $\frac{1}{2}$
15. the correct set of answers for the test. $\frac{1}{8}$

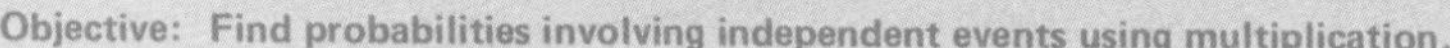

Objective: Find probabilities involving independent events using multiplication.

Finding Probabilities Using Multiplication

example F Finding possible outcomes

Multiply to find the number of possible outcomes for choosing a three-digit code number if each digit is chosen at random.

Ways to choose first digit		Ways to choose second digit		Ways to choose third digit		Possible outcomes
10	×	10	×	10	=	1000

example G Finding probability, independent events

Give the probability that a three-digit code number chosen at random will be 684 or 092.

There are 1000 possible outcomes.
There are 2 favorable outcomes (684 and 092).

$\frac{2}{1000}$ ← Number of favorable outcomes / Number of possible outcomes

The probability of choosing 684 or 092 at random is $\frac{2}{1000}$, or $\frac{1}{500}$.

exercises set F

Multiply to find the number of possible outcomes for choosing at random a

1. two-digit code number. 100
2. four-digit code number. 10,000
3. five-digit code number. 100,000
4. six-digit code number. 1,000,000

Multiply to find the number of possible outcomes for tossing

5. two coins. ($2 \times 2 = ▩$) 4
6. three coins. ($2 \times 2 \times 2 = ▩$) 8
7. four coins. 16
8. five coins. 32
9. six coins. 64
10. seven coins. 128
11. two dice. ($6 \times 6 = ▩$) 36
12. three dice. ($6 \times 6 \times 6 = ▩$) 216
13. two coins and one die. ($2 \times 2 \times 6 = ▩$) 24
14. two coins and two dice. 144
15. three coins and three dice. 1728

See page T21 for more information concerning these answers.

set G

Give the probability that a two-digit code number chosen at random will be

1. 26. $\frac{1}{100}$
2. 30 or 08. $\frac{2}{100}$, or $\frac{1}{50}$
3. 17, 93, or 46. $\frac{3}{100}$
4. a number whose last digit is 5. $\frac{10}{100}$, or $\frac{1}{10}$
5. a number greater than 90. $\frac{9}{100}$
6. a multiple of 10. $\frac{9}{100}$

Give the probability that a three-digit code number chosen at random will be

7. 368 or 792. $\frac{2}{1000}$, or $\frac{1}{500}$
8. 431. $\frac{1}{1000}$
9. a number whose first digit is 7. $\frac{100}{1000}$, or $\frac{1}{10}$
10. a multiple of 100. $\frac{9}{1000}$

Give the probability that a four-digit code number chosen at random will be

11. 7864. $\frac{1}{10,000}$
12. 6392 or 0819. $\frac{2}{10,000}$, or $\frac{1}{5000}$
13. a multiple of 100. $\frac{99}{10,000}$

Give the probability that a five-digit code number chosen at random will be

14. 13,496. $\frac{1}{100,000}$
15. 25,147 or 94,777. See below.
16. a multiple of 1000. $\frac{99}{100,000}$

The applications on page 183 may be used anytime after this lesson.

BREAK TIME

Clyde made four straight cuts to divide the pizza into eleven pieces. There was exactly one piece of pepperoni in each serving of pizza. Trace the figure and show four cuts that Clyde could have made.

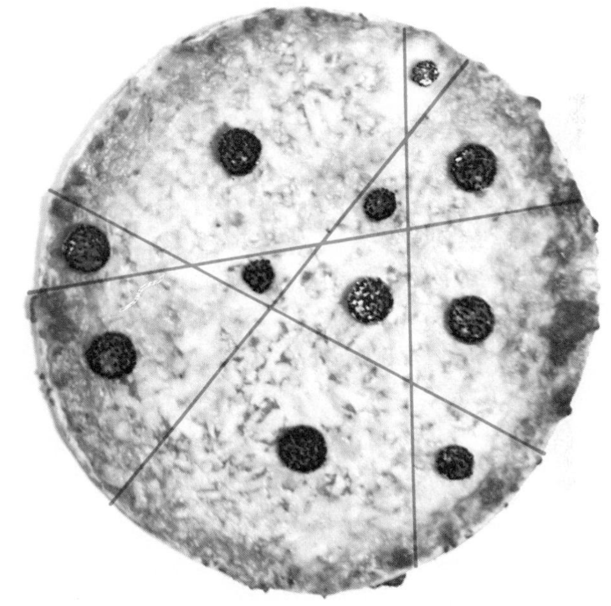

15. $\frac{2}{100,000}$, or $\frac{1}{50,000}$

Objective: Find probabilities involving dependent events using multiplication.

Finding Probabilities Involving Dependent Events

example H Finding probability, dependent events

Give the probability of drawing two cards at random that show *I* if the first card is *not* replaced before making the second draw.

Multiply to find the number of possible outcomes.

Ways to choose first card		Ways to choose second card		Possible outcomes
13	×	12	=	156

Next, multiply to find the number of favorable outcomes.

Ways to choose *I* for the first card		Ways to choose *I* for the second card		Favorable outcomes
3	×	2	=	6

Then give the probability of making two draws that show *I*.

$\frac{6}{156}$ ← Number of favorable outcomes / Number of possible outcomes

The probability of making two draws that show *I* is $\frac{6}{156}$, or $\frac{1}{26}$.

For exercises 11-20, the number of possible outcomes is 13 X 12 X 11, or 1716.

11. $\frac{6}{1716}$, or $\frac{1}{286}$
12. $\frac{2}{1716}$, or $\frac{1}{858}$
13. $\frac{6}{1716}$, or $\frac{1}{286}$
14. $\frac{2}{1716}$, or $\frac{1}{858}$
15. $\frac{12}{1716}$, or $\frac{1}{143}$
16. $\frac{1}{1716}$
17. $\frac{2}{1716}$, or $\frac{1}{858}$
18. $\frac{3}{1716}$, or $\frac{1}{572}$
19. $\frac{6}{1716}$, or $\frac{1}{286}$
20. $\frac{3}{1716}$, or $\frac{1}{572}$

exercises set H

Use the cards in example H for exercises 1-20. In each exercise, when a card is drawn, it is *not* replaced before the next draw.

Give the probability of making two draws that show

1. *B*. $\frac{2}{156}$, or $\frac{1}{78}$
2. *B*, then *R*. $\frac{2}{156}$, or $\frac{1}{78}$
3. *P*, then *S*. $\frac{1}{156}$
4. *T*, then *I*. $\frac{3}{156}$, or $\frac{1}{52}$
5. *L*, then *B*. $\frac{2}{156}$, or $\frac{1}{78}$
6. *I*, then *E*. $\frac{3}{156}$, or $\frac{1}{52}$
7. *A*, then *T*. $\frac{1}{156}$
8. *B*, then *I*. $\frac{6}{156}$, or $\frac{1}{26}$
9. *R*, then *E*. $\frac{1}{156}$
10. *S*, then *I*. $\frac{3}{156}$, or $\frac{1}{52}$

Give the probability of making three draws in order that show

11. *I*.
12. *P*, then *B*, then *B*.
13. *I*, then *A*, then *I*.
14. *L*, then *B*, then *B*.
15. *B*, then *I*, then *I*.
16. *P*, then *R*, then *O*.
17. *B*, then *A*, then *E*.
18. *S*, then *I*, then *R*.
19. *B*, then *I*, then *S*.
20. *L*, then *I*, then *T*.

Use these cards for exercises 21–40. Each time a card is drawn, it is *not* replaced before the next draw.

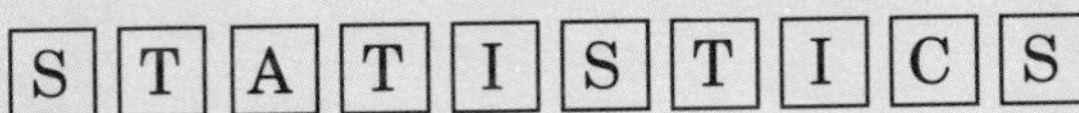

The number of possible outcomes is 10 X 9, or 90.

Give the probability of making two draws that show

21. *S*. $\frac{6}{90}$, or $\frac{1}{15}$
22. *I*. $\frac{2}{90}$, or $\frac{1}{45}$
23. *T*. $\frac{6}{90}$, or $\frac{1}{15}$
24. *A*, then *C*. $\frac{1}{90}$
25. *A*, then *S*. $\frac{3}{90}$, or $\frac{1}{30}$
26. *T*, then *S*. $\frac{9}{90}$, or $\frac{1}{10}$
27. *I*, then *C*. $\frac{2}{90}$, or $\frac{1}{45}$
28. *T*, then *I*. $\frac{6}{90}$, or $\frac{1}{15}$
29. *S*, then *C*. $\frac{3}{90}$, or $\frac{1}{30}$
30. *A*, then *I*. $\frac{2}{90}$, or $\frac{1}{45}$

The number of possible outcomes is 10 X 9 X 8, or 720.

Give the probability of making three draws that show

31. *T*. $\frac{6}{720}$, or $\frac{1}{120}$
32. *S*. $\frac{6}{720}$, or $\frac{1}{120}$
33. *T*, then *C*, then *T*. $\frac{6}{720}$, or $\frac{1}{120}$
34. *S*, then *I*, then *S*. $\frac{12}{720}$, or $\frac{1}{60}$
35. *S*, then *A*, then *S*. $\frac{6}{720}$, or $\frac{1}{120}$
36. *T*, then *S*, then *C*. $\frac{9}{720}$, or $\frac{1}{80}$
37. *S*, then *T*, then *A*. $\frac{9}{720}$, or $\frac{1}{80}$
38. *S*, then *T*, then *I*. $\frac{18}{720}$, or $\frac{1}{40}$
39. *A*, then *C*, then *T*. $\frac{3}{720}$, or $\frac{1}{240}$
40. *I*, then *A*, then *S*. $\frac{6}{720}$, or $\frac{1}{120}$

Trace these figures without taking your pencil from the paper and without crossing any lines.

Answers may vary.

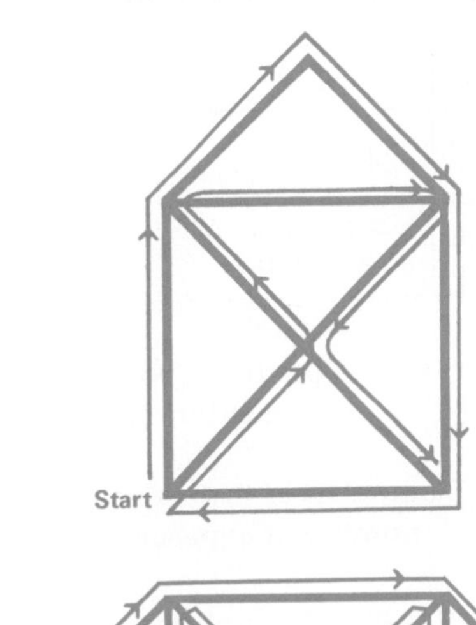

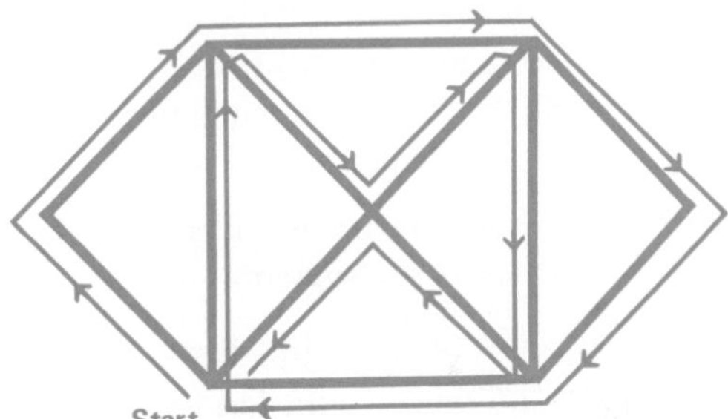

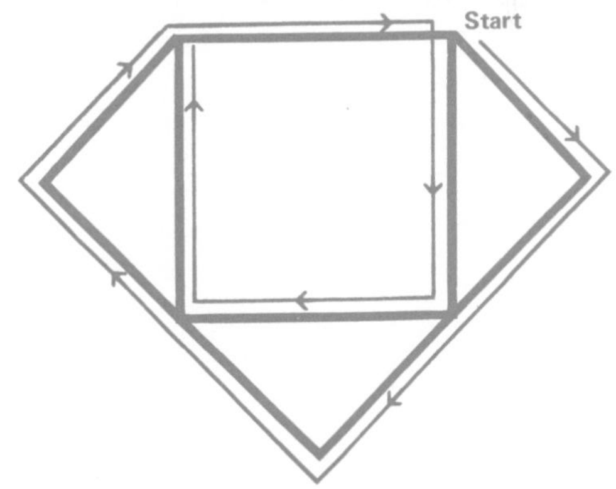

Skill

Objective: Use experiments to make predictions.

Using Experiments to Make Predictions

example I Predicting probability

Using the results of the experiment below, predict the probability that, on the next toss, the tack would land point up.

Outcome	Tally
Point up	𝍸 III
Point down	𝍸 𝍸 II 𝍸 𝍸

Use this formula to predict probability that is based on experimentation.

$$\textbf{Probability} = \frac{\textbf{number of favorable outcomes}}{\textbf{number of experimental tosses}}$$

There are 30 experimental tosses.
There are 8 favorable outcomes because eight tosses landed point up.

$\frac{8}{30}$ ← Number of favorable outcomes / ← Number of experimental tosses

Thus, one could predict that the probability the tack would land point up on the next toss would be $\frac{8}{30}$, or $\frac{4}{15}$.

Because tacks vary in size, shape, and construction, the outcomes for this experiment can vary greatly. Point out that a better prediction could be made by tossing the tack more times.

example J Predicting outcomes based on predicted probability

Using the results of the experiment in example I, give the expected number of tosses that will land point up if the tack is tossed 60 times.

Multiply to find the expected number of favorable outcomes.

Predicted probability		Number of tosses		Expected number of favorable outcomes
$\frac{4}{15}$	$\times$	60	=	16

One could expect about 16 out of 60 tosses to land point up.

exercises

set I

For each experiment, predict the probability that, on the next toss, the tack would land point up.

	Number of times tack was tossed	Number of times tack landed point up	
1.	16	4	$\frac{4}{16}$, or $\frac{1}{4}$
2.	25	5	$\frac{5}{25}$, or $\frac{1}{5}$
3.	36	9	$\frac{9}{36}$, or $\frac{1}{4}$
4.	14	4	$\frac{4}{14}$, or $\frac{2}{7}$
5.	28	18	$\frac{18}{28}$, or $\frac{9}{14}$
6.	13	10	$\frac{10}{13}$
7.	60	18	$\frac{18}{60}$, or $\frac{3}{10}$
8.	42	10	$\frac{10}{42}$, or $\frac{5}{21}$
9.	34	8	$\frac{8}{34}$, or $\frac{4}{17}$
10.	17	5	$\frac{5}{17}$
11.	90	33	$\frac{33}{90}$, or $\frac{11}{30}$
12.	58	16	$\frac{16}{58}$, or $\frac{8}{29}$
13.	81	21	$\frac{21}{81}$, or $\frac{7}{27}$
14.	72	30	$\frac{30}{72}$, or $\frac{5}{12}$
15.	68	26	$\frac{26}{68}$, or $\frac{13}{34}$
16.	75	25	$\frac{25}{75}$, or $\frac{1}{3}$
17.	150	75	$\frac{75}{150}$, or $\frac{1}{2}$
18.	92	36	$\frac{36}{92}$, or $\frac{9}{23}$
19.	125	45	$\frac{45}{125}$, or $\frac{9}{25}$
20.	500	200	$\frac{200}{300}$, or $\frac{2}{5}$
21.	83	16	$\frac{16}{83}$
22.	102	34	$\frac{34}{102}$, or $\frac{1}{3}$

set J

Give the expected number of tosses that will land point up.

	Predicted probability tack will land point up	Number of times tack will be tossed			Predicted probability tack will land point up	Number of times tack will be tossed	
1.	$\frac{1}{4}$	28	7	**20.**	$\frac{7}{15}$	75	35
2.	$\frac{1}{5}$	60	12	**21.**	$\frac{7}{20}$	80	28
3.	$\frac{1}{4}$	72	18	**22.**	$\frac{5}{18}$	36	10
4.	$\frac{3}{8}$	24	9	**23.**	$\frac{7}{12}$	108	63
5.	$\frac{1}{4}$	60	15	**24.**	$\frac{4}{11}$	99	36
6.	$\frac{3}{10}$	40	12	**25.**	$\frac{3}{7}$	35	15
7.	$\frac{4}{15}$	30	8	**26.**	$\frac{5}{9}$	90	50
8.	$\frac{4}{7}$	14	8	**27.**	$\frac{5}{16}$	80	25
9.	$\frac{2}{5}$	35	14	**28.**	$\frac{3}{10}$	170	51
10.	$\frac{5}{12}$	84	35	**29.**	$\frac{2}{5}$	125	50
11.	$\frac{5}{16}$	112	35	**30.**	$\frac{1}{4}$	280	70
12.	$\frac{1}{3}$	90	30	**31.**	$\frac{5}{11}$	110	50
13.	$\frac{2}{5}$	100	40	**32.**	$\frac{7}{18}$	180	70
14.	$\frac{3}{8}$	72	27	**33.**	$\frac{6}{25}$	300	72
15.	$\frac{7}{12}$	144	84	**34.**	$\frac{11}{50}$	200	44
16.	$\frac{4}{9}$	45	20	**35.**	$\frac{26}{75}$	150	52
17.	$\frac{4}{15}$	90	24	**36.**	$\frac{15}{38}$	380	150
18.	$\frac{3}{10}$	150	45	**37.**	$\frac{51}{200}$	400	102
19.	$\frac{3}{8}$	48	18	**38.**	$\frac{29}{100}$	500	145

For set I, have students also predict the probability that, on the next toss, the tack would land point down. For set J, have students also give the expected number of tosses that will land point down.

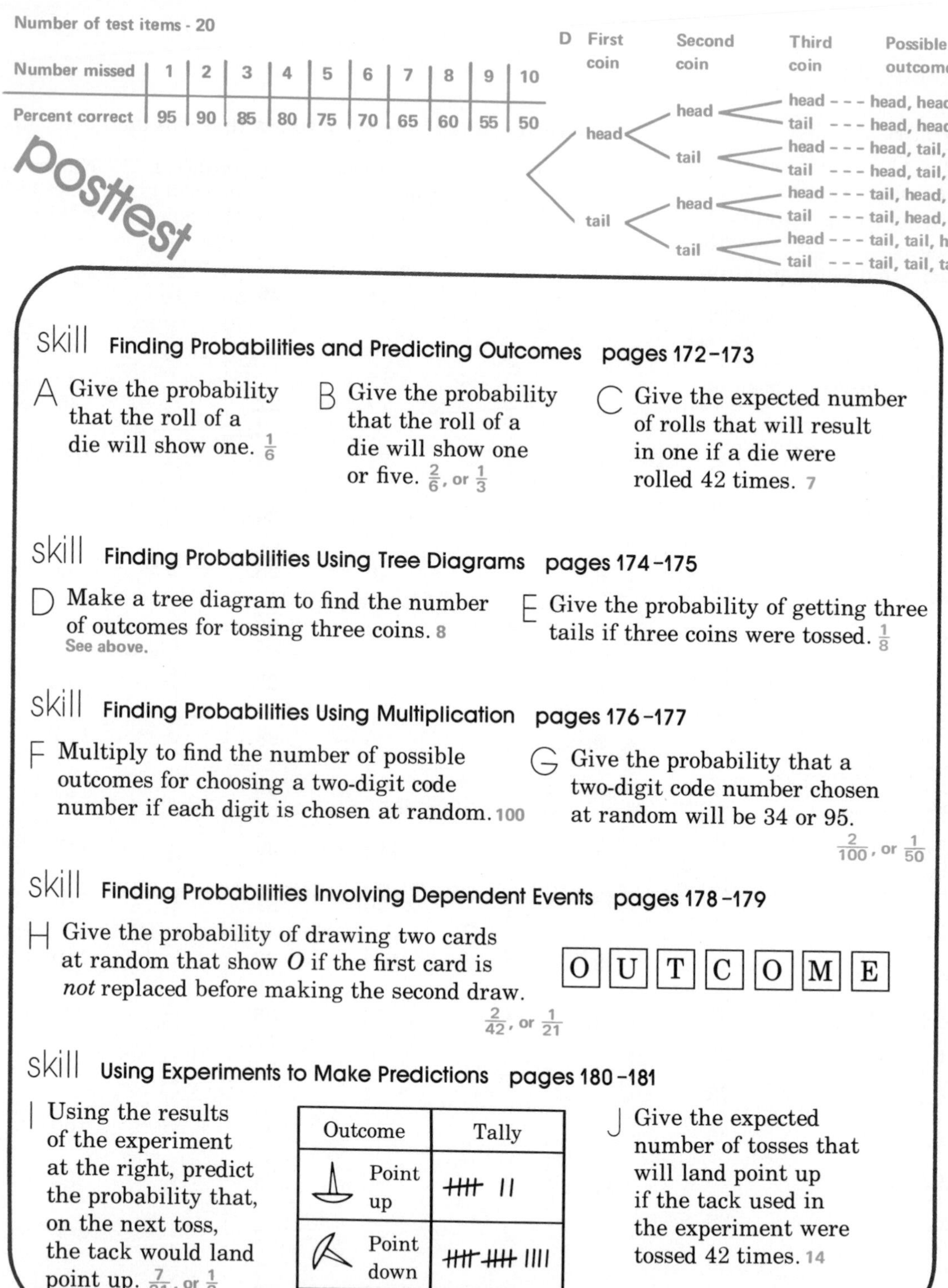

Number of test items - 20

Number missed	1	2	3	4	5	6	7	8	9	10
Percent correct	95	90	85	80	75	70	65	60	55	50

posttest

D

First coin	Second coin	Third coin	Possible outcomes
head	head	head	head, head, head
		tail	head, head, tail
	tail	head	head, tail, head
		tail	head, tail, tail
tail	head	head	tail, head, head
		tail	tail, head, tail
	tail	head	tail, tail, head
		tail	tail, tail, tail

skill Finding Probabilities and Predicting Outcomes pages 172–173

A Give the probability that the roll of a die will show one. $\frac{1}{6}$

B Give the probability that the roll of a die will show one or five. $\frac{2}{6}$, or $\frac{1}{3}$

C Give the expected number of rolls that will result in one if a die were rolled 42 times. 7

skill Finding Probabilities Using Tree Diagrams pages 174–175

D Make a tree diagram to find the number of outcomes for tossing three coins. 8
See above.

E Give the probability of getting three tails if three coins were tossed. $\frac{1}{8}$

skill Finding Probabilities Using Multiplication pages 176–177

F Multiply to find the number of possible outcomes for choosing a two-digit code number if each digit is chosen at random. 100

G Give the probability that a two-digit code number chosen at random will be 34 or 95. $\frac{2}{100}$, or $\frac{1}{50}$

skill Finding Probabilities Involving Dependent Events pages 178–179

H Give the probability of drawing two cards at random that show *O* if the first card is *not* replaced before making the second draw. $\frac{2}{42}$, or $\frac{1}{21}$

O	U	T	C	O	M	E

skill Using Experiments to Make Predictions pages 180–181

I Using the results of the experiment at the right, predict the probability that, on the next toss, the tack would land point up. $\frac{7}{21}$, or $\frac{1}{3}$

Outcome	Tally
Point up	𝍸 II
Point down	𝍸 𝍸 IIII

J Give the expected number of tosses that will land point up if the tack used in the experiment were tossed 42 times. 14

Objective: Solve problems involving probability.

In this lesson students find the probability of getting a certain license plate.

Finding Probabilities for License Plates

Gloria Simpson ordered her license plates. In her area, license plates show two letters followed by four digits.

GS 3591

1. How many license plates are possible? (Complete row 1 in the chart below to find the number of possible outcomes.) 6, 760, 000

What is the probability that Gloria will get

2. GS 3591? (1 favorable outcome) $\frac{1}{6,760,000}$

3. GS 3591 or GS 1978? (2 favorable outcomes) $\frac{2}{6,760,000}$, or $\frac{1}{3,380,000}$

4. GS followed by any digits? (Complete row 2 to find favorable outcomes.) $\frac{10,000}{6,760,000}$, or $\frac{1}{676}$

5. any letters followed by 1234 in order? (Complete row 3.) $\frac{676}{6,760,000}$, or $\frac{1}{1000}$

6. all letters alike and all digits alike, as in DD 2222? (Complete row 4.) $\frac{260}{6,760,000}$, or $\frac{1}{26,000}$

7. any letters followed by a number ending in 3? (Complete row 5.) $\frac{676,000}{6,760,000}$, or $\frac{1}{10}$

8. all letters alike followed by a number greater than 4999? (Complete row 6.) $\frac{130,000}{6,760,000}$, or $\frac{1}{52}$

9. HI followed by a number greater than 2999? $\frac{7000}{6,760,000}$, or $\frac{7}{6760}$

10. GO followed by all digits alike? $\frac{10}{6,760,000}$, or $\frac{1}{676,000}$

	Number of choices for first letter		Number of choices for second letter		Number of choices for first digit		Number of choices for second digit		Number of choices for third digit		Number of choices for fourth digit		Number of outcomes
Row 1	26	×	26	×	10	×	10	×	10	×	10	=	6,760,000
Row 2	1	×	1	×	10	×	10	×	10	×	10	=	10,000
Row 3	26	×	26	×	1	×	1	×	1	×	1	=	676
Row 4	26	×	1	×	10	×	1	×	1	×	1	=	260
Row 5	26	×	26	×	10	×	10	×	10	×	1	=	676,000
Row 6	26	×	1	×	5	×	10	×	10	×	10	=	130,000

Objective: Solve problems involving probability.

In this lesson students find the probabilities for various outcomes on a Big Six carnival wheel.

Finding Probabilities for a Carnival Wheel

This wheel is similar to a Big 6 Wheel which is used at carnivals, barbecues, and other fund raising events.

A player places money or chips on a board that shows the numbers 1–6. Then the operator spins the wheel.

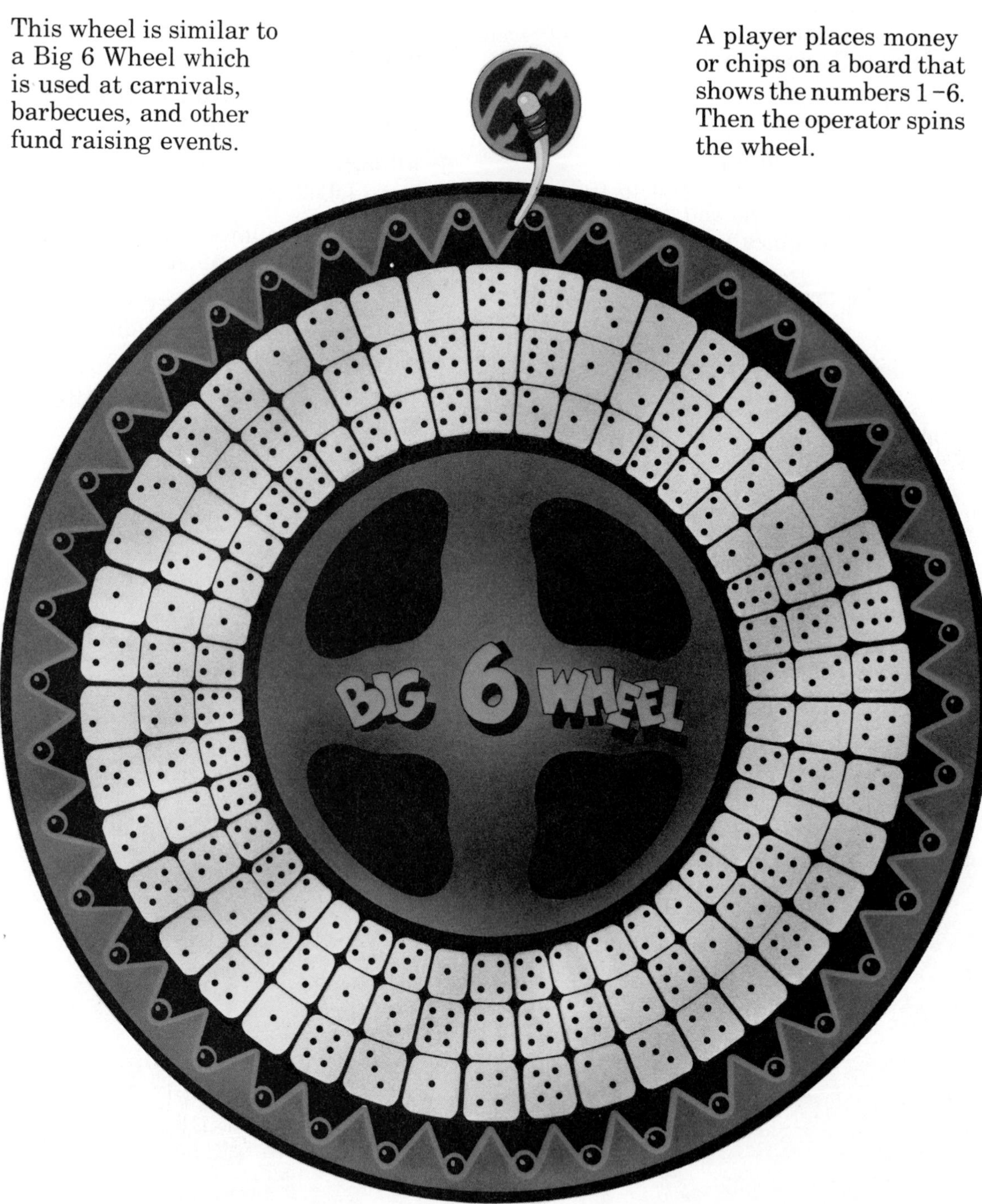

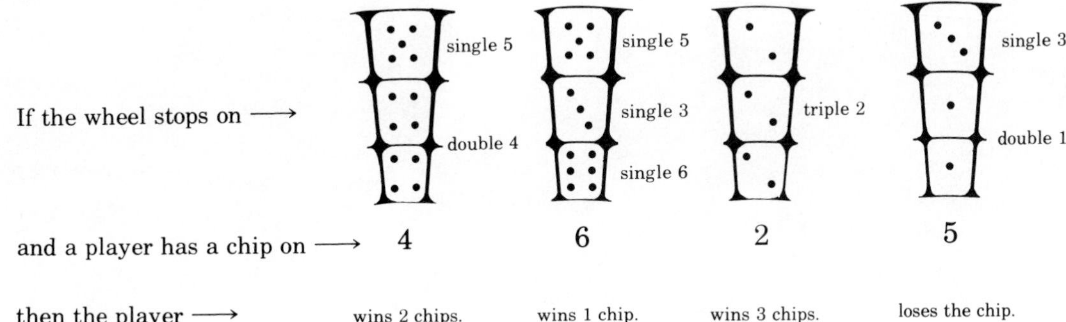

Use the wheel to help you complete the chart below.

	Number	Number of sections showing each type			Total number of sections showing the number
		Single	Double	Triple	
1.	1	//	卌	///	10
2.	2	卌 //	////	//	13
3.	3	卌 ///	卌	/	14
4.	4	卌 /	///	///	12
5.	5	卌 卌 /	//	//	15
6.	6	卌 卌 //	///	/	16

You might check students' answers to exercises 1–6, before they do exercises 7–26.

There are 42 sections in all. Find the probability that the wheel will stop on a section that shows a "double 4."

$$\frac{\text{Favorable outcomes}}{\text{Possible outcomes}} = \frac{\text{Number of sections with a double 4}}{\text{Total number of sections}} = \frac{3}{42}$$

Give the probability that the wheel will stop on a section that shows

7. a triple 4. See below.

8. a single 4. See below.

9. any 4. $\frac{12}{42}$, or $\frac{2}{7}$

10. a double 3. $\frac{5}{42}$

11. any 3. $\frac{14}{42}$, or $\frac{1}{3}$

12. a triple 5. $\frac{2}{42}$, or $\frac{1}{21}$

13. any 5. $\frac{15}{42}$, or $\frac{5}{14}$

14. a triple 6. $\frac{1}{42}$

15. a double 6. $\frac{3}{42}$, or $\frac{1}{14}$

16. any six. $\frac{16}{42}$, or $\frac{8}{21}$

7. $\frac{3}{42}$, or $\frac{1}{14}$ 8. $\frac{6}{42}$, or $\frac{1}{7}$

On the average, the wheel will stop on each section every 42 spins. Suppose the wheel is spun 42 times and stops once on each section. If Leslie puts a chip on the number 1 each time,

17. on how many sections will she win? 10 sections

18. how many chips will she win? 21 chips

19. on how many sections will she lose? 32 sections

20. how many chips will she lose? 32 chips

21. what will be her net gain or loss? A net loss of 11 chips

What would be her net gain or loss if, instead, she put a chip each time

A net loss of. . .

22. on 2? 8 chips

23. on 3? 7 chips

24. on 4? 9 chips

25. on 5? 6 chips

26. on 6? 5 chips

On the average, Leslie will have a net loss, but she will have the smallest net loss if she always puts a chip on 6.

Objective: Solve problems involving probability.

In this lesson students use sales records to predict the probability of selling a certain flavor of sno-cone and then use that probability to find expected sales.

Career: Route Salesperson

Career Cluster: Business Contact

See the Careers Chart beginning on page 420 for more jobs and other information about this career cluster.

Andrew Scholl leased a Frostee Freeze truck during the summer. He traveled the same route almost every day selling sno-cones made of flavored crushed ice.

1. Andrew kept his record of daily sales at different temperatures. Find the total for each temperature.

	Number of sno-cones sold				
Flavor	15°C Cool	20°C Mild	25°C Warm	30°C Hot	35°C Very hot
Lime	5	8	12	15	20
Blueberry	7	10	18	20	28
Raspberry	12	13	14	15	23
Chocolate	15	20	30	35	50
Vanilla	8	13	16	20	26
Almond	6	11	14	16	19
Strawberry	9	16	20	22	29
Totals	62	91	124	143	195

Use Andrew's chart to predict the probability that a customer will buy a lime sno-cone when it is 20°C.

$$\frac{\text{Favorable outcomes}}{\text{Possible outcomes}} = \frac{\text{Number of lime sno-cones for } 20°\text{C}}{\text{Total number of sno-cones for } 20°\text{C}} = \frac{8}{91}$$

Predict the probability that a customer will buy

2. a lime sno-cone when it is 30°C. $\frac{15}{143}$

3. a raspberry sno-cone when it is 25°C. See below.

4. a strawberry sno-cone when it is 15°C. $\frac{9}{62}$

5. a chocolate sno-cone when it is 20°C. $\frac{20}{91}$

Andrew has permission to sell sno-cones at a carnival. The temperature will be 35°C. What is the probability that a customer will buy

6. lime? $\frac{20}{195}$, or $\frac{4}{39}$

7. blueberry? $\frac{28}{195}$

8. raspberry? $\frac{23}{195}$

9. chocolate? $\frac{50}{195}$, or $\frac{10}{39}$

10. vanilla? $\frac{26}{195}$, or $\frac{2}{15}$

11. almond? $\frac{19}{195}$

12. strawberry? $\frac{29}{195}$

3. $\frac{14}{124}$, or $\frac{7}{62}$

Andrew expects to sell 500 sno-cones at the carnival. How many of these can he expect to be lime? Round the answer up to the next whole number.

Probability of lime		Total number		Expected number of lime sno-cones		
$\frac{20}{195}$	×	500	=	$51\frac{55}{195}$	≈	52

How many of the 500 sno-cones can he expect to be

13. blueberry? 72

14. raspberry? 59

15. chocolate? 129

16. vanilla? 67

17. almond? 49

18. strawberry? 75

It takes 1 liter of syrup to make 10 sno-cones. How many liters of lime syrup will Andrew need for the carnival? Round up to the next whole liter.

Expected number of lime sno-cones		Sno-cones per liter of syrup		Liters of lime syrup needed		
52	÷	10	=	5.2	≈	6

How many liters of each of these flavors will Andrew need for the carnival?

19. Blueberry 8 liters

20. Raspberry 6 liters

21. Chocolate 13 liters

22. Vanilla 7 liters

23. Almond 5 liters

24. Strawberry 8 liters

Objective: Solve problems involving probability.

In this lesson students use a mortality table to predict the probability of dying at a given age and to predict the probability, in decimal form, that a person of a given age will live to another age.

The table on page 189 is a simplified version of the Table of Mortality, Commissioners 1958 Standard Ordinary which is still in use today.

Career: Insurance Actuary

Career Cluster: Business Contact

Jo Boyd, an actuary, uses mortality tables to determine life insurance rates.

Use the table on page 189 to find the probability of dying at age 10.

$$\frac{\text{Number of deaths at age 10}}{\text{Number living at age 10}} = \frac{12}{9806}$$

Give the probability of dying at

See top of page 189.

1. age 2. **4.** age 35. **7.** age 75.

2. age 11. **5.** age 42. **8.** age 80.

3. age 20. **6.** age 65. **9.** age 90.

Probabilities are expressed in the table as deaths per 1000. For example, at age 10:

$\frac{12}{9806} \approx \frac{1.2}{1000}$ or 1.2 deaths per 1000

Use the table to tell at what age or ages

10. the number of deaths per 1000 is highest. age 99

11. the number of deaths per 1000 is lowest. ages 7–12

12. the number of deaths is highest. ages 75 and 76

13. the number of deaths is lowest. age 99

What is the probability that a 16-year old person will live to age 80?

$$\frac{\text{Number living at age 80}}{\text{Number living at age 16}} = \frac{2626}{9729}$$

This fraction can be written as a decimal to the nearest hundredth.

$\frac{2626}{9729} \approx .27 \qquad 9729\overline{)2626.000}$ quotient $.269 \approx .27$

The probability that a 16-year old will live to age 80 is about .27.

Use a fraction and a decimal to the nearest hundredth to give the probability that

14. a 20-year old will live to age 30.

15. a 60-year old will live to age 80.

16. a 4-year old will live to age 50.

17. a 15-year old will live to age 30.

18. a 40-year old will live to age 42.

See bottom of page 189.

19. an 80-year old will live to age 85.

20. a 10-year old will live to age 75.

14. $\frac{9480}{9665} \approx .98$ 16. $\frac{8762}{9982} \approx .88$

15. $\frac{2626}{7699} \approx .34$ 17. $\frac{9480}{9743} \approx .97$

1. $\frac{15}{9912}$, or $\frac{5}{3304}$ 3. $\frac{17}{9665}$ 5. $\frac{38}{9173}$ 7. $\frac{303}{4130}$ 9. $\frac{107}{468}$

2. $\frac{12}{9794}$, or $\frac{6}{4897}$ 4. $\frac{23}{9373}$ 6. $\frac{216}{6801}$, or $\frac{72}{2267}$ 8. $\frac{288}{2626}$, or $\frac{144}{1313}$

Table of Mortality

Age	Number living	Deaths each year	Deaths per 1000	Age	Number living	Deaths each year	Deaths per 1000	Age	Number living	Deaths each year	Deaths per 1000
0	10,000	71	7.1	34	9396	23	2.4	67	6356	242	38.1
1	9929	17	1.7	35	9373	23	2.5	68	6114	255	41.7
2	9912	15	1.5	36	9350	24	2.6	69	5859	267	45.6
3	9897	15	1.5	37	9326	27	2.9	70	5592	278	49.7
4	9982	14	1.4	38	9299	28	3.0	71	5314	288	54.2
5	9868	13	1.3	39	9271	30	3.2	72	5026	295	58.7
6	9855	13	1.3	40	9241	33	3.6	73	4731	299	63.2
7	9842	12	1.2	41	9208	35	3.8	74	4432	302	68.1
8	9830	12	1.2	42	9173	38	4.1	75	4130	303	73.4
9	9818	12	1.2	43	9135	41	4.5	76	3827	303	79.2
10	9806	12	1.2	44	9094	45	4.9	77	3524	302	85.7
11	9794	12	1.2	45	9049	48	5.3	78	3222	300	93.1
12	9782	12	1.2	46	9001	53	5.9	79	2922	296	101.3
13	9770	13	1.3	47	8948	57	6.4	80	2626	288	109.7
14	9757	14	1.4	48	8891	62	7.0	81	2338	279	119.3
15	9743	14	1.4	49	8829	67	7.6	82	2059	266	129.2
16	9729	15	1.5	50	8762	73	8.3	83	1793	250	139.4
17	9714	16	1.6	51	8689	79	9.1	84	1543	232	150.4
18	9698	16	1.6	52	8610	86	10.0	85	1311	211	158.5
19	9682	17	1.8	53	8524	93	10.9	86	1100	190	172.7
20	9665	17	1.8	54	8431	100	11.9	87	910	169	185.7
21	9648	18	1.9	55	8331	108	13.0	88	741	147	198.4
22	9630	18	1.9	56	8223	117	14.2	89	594	126	212.1
23	9612	18	1.9	57	8106	126	15.5	90	468	107	228.6
24	9594	18	1.9	58	7980	135	16.9	91	361	89	246.5
25	9576	19	2.0	59	7845	146	18.6	92	272	72	264.7
26	9557	19	2.0	60	7699	157	20.4	93	200	58	290.0
27	9538	19	2.0	61	7542	168	22.2	94	142	45	316.9
28	9519	19	2.0	62	7374	179	24.3	95	97	34	350.5
29	9500	20	2.1	63	7195	191	26.5	96	63	25	396.8
30	9480	20	2.1	64	7004	203	29.0	97	38	19	500.0
31	9460	21	2.2	65	6801	216	31.8	98	19	13	684.2
32	9439	21	2.2	66	6585	229	34.8	99	6	6	1000.0
33	9418	22	2.3								

18. $\frac{9173}{9241} \approx .99$ 19. $\frac{1311}{2626} \approx .50$ 20. $\frac{4130}{9806} \approx .42$

Number of test items - 15

Number missed	1	2	3	4	5	6	7
Percent correct	93	87	80	73	67	60	53

Chapter 9

A **1.** Give the probability that the roll of a die will show five. $\frac{1}{6}$

B **2.** Give the probability that the roll of a die will show two or six. $\frac{2}{6}$, or $\frac{1}{3}$

C **3.** Give the expected number of rolls that will result in six if a die were rolled 24 times. 4

D **4.** Make a tree diagram to find the number of possible outcomes for tossing a coin and a die. 12
See below.

E **5.** If a coin and a die are tossed, give the probability that the coin will show heads and the die will show five. $\frac{1}{12}$

F **6.** Multiply to find the number of possible outcomes for choosing a five-digit code number if each digit is chosen at random. 100,000

G **7.** Give the probability that a five-digit code number chosen at random will be 09644 or 21735.

$\frac{2}{100,000}$, or $\frac{1}{50,000}$

H **8.** Give the probability of drawing two of these cards at random that show *S* if the first card is *not* replaced before making the second draw.

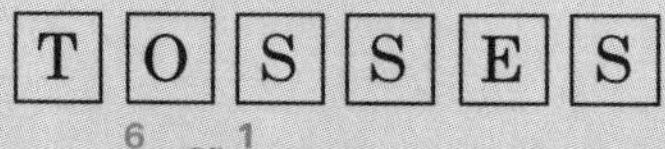

$\frac{6}{30}$, or $\frac{1}{5}$

I **9.** Use the results of this experiment to predict the probability that, on the next toss, the paper cup will land top down. $\frac{5}{30}$, or $\frac{1}{6}$

Outcome	Tally
Top up	|
Top down	𝍸
Side	𝍸 𝍸 𝍸 𝍸 ||||

J **10.** Give the expected number of tosses that will land top down if the cup used in the experiment above were tossed 60 times. 10

4. Coin Die Outcomes

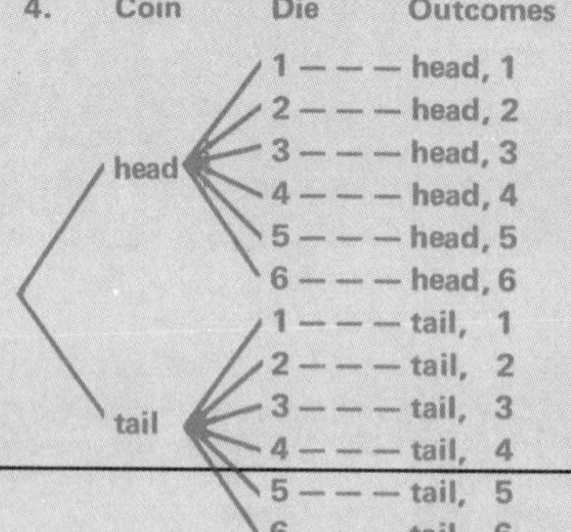

11. How many license plates are possible that show 2 letters followed by 3 digits? 676,000 license plates

12. There are 42 sections on a Big 6 Wheel. If there are 7 sections that show a single 2, what is the probability that the wheel will stop on a single 2? $\frac{7}{42}$, or $\frac{1}{6}$

13. If the probability that a customer will buy a lime sno-cone is $\frac{18}{150}$ and a total of 300 sno-cones will be sold, about how many lime sno-cones will be sold?
36 lime sno-cones

14. If there are 278 deaths at age 70 out of 5592 people living at age 70, give the probability as a fraction that a person will die at age 70.
$\frac{278}{5592}$, or $\frac{139}{2796}$

15. If there are 7699 people living at age 60 and 9049 people living at age 45, give the probability as a decimal to the nearest hundredth that a 45-year-old person will live to age 60. .85

See pages 21–22 of the *Tests and Record Forms: Duplicating Masters* for an alternate form of the Chapter 9 Test. For a test on Unit 1, see page T31 of this book and pages 23–24 of the duplicating masters. A mid-book test is found in the masters on pages 25–28.

tune-up skills

Multiplying Whole Numbers, pages 21–32

1. 8×76 608
2. 700×30 21,000
3. 25×78 1950
4. 768×32 24,576
5. 12×607 7284
6. 37×92 3404
7. 9×1362 12,258
8. 215×88 18,920
9. 4×7000 28,000
10. 52×3478 180,856
11. 127×326 41,402
12. 709×85 60,265
13. 40×1000 40,000
14. 66×395 26,070
15. 178×98 17,444
16. 34×1274 43,316
17. 752×4 3008
18. 921×605 557,205
19. $800 \times 20{,}000$ 16,000,000
20. $5 \times 382{,}145$ 1,910,725
21. 2188×176 385,088
22. 29×8073 234,117
23. 17×36 612
24. 90×470 42,300
25. 634×9276 5,880,984

Multiplying and Dividing Decimals, pages 83–94

1. 5.8×21.7 125.86
2. $.39 \times 800$ 312
3. $4.6 \times .017$ .0782
4. $.0017 \times .925$ .0015725
5. $.07 \times .003$ .00021
6. $.12 \times .41$ .0492
7. 1.8×3000 5400
8. $.0075 \times 1.3051$ .0097882
9. $.01 \times .01$ .0001
10. $.105 \div .07$ 1.5
11. $16.5 \div 5$ 3.3
12. $23.32 \div 53$ .44
13. $.002 \div .025$ .08
14. $1.05 \div 7$ .15
15. $1.065 \div 21.3$ .05
16. $737.2 \div 388$ 1.9
17. $105.57 \div 1.7$ 62.1
18. $.00735 \div .525$ .014

Round each quotient to the nearest hundredth.

19. $4.083 \div 8.7$ .47
20. $.48 \div .033$ 14.55
21. $.733 \div .051$ 14.37
22. $68.79 \div 2.56$ 26.87
23. $.894 \div .013$ 68.77
24. $7.28 \div .0036$ 2022.22

Multiplying and Dividing Fractions and Mixed Numbers, pages 131–142

1. $\frac{1}{4} \times \frac{8}{9}$ $\frac{2}{9}$
2. $3\frac{1}{3} \times 2$ $6\frac{2}{3}$
3. $\frac{5}{8} \times 40$ 25
4. $2\frac{1}{2} \times \frac{1}{10}$ $\frac{1}{4}$
5. $\frac{7}{10} \times \frac{5}{6}$ $\frac{7}{12}$
6. $\frac{5}{8} \times \frac{3}{4}$ $\frac{15}{32}$
7. $3\frac{1}{2} \times 2\frac{1}{3}$ $8\frac{1}{6}$
8. $\frac{7}{12} \times 5$ $2\frac{11}{12}$
9. $2\frac{1}{3} \times 12$ 28
10. $\frac{5}{7} \div \frac{4}{5}$ $\frac{25}{28}$
11. $5\frac{1}{3} \div 8$ $\frac{2}{3}$
12. $\frac{9}{10} \div 1\frac{1}{2}$ $\frac{3}{5}$
13. $12 \div 1\frac{1}{2}$ 8
14. $1\frac{3}{4} \div 2\frac{1}{2}$ $\frac{7}{10}$
15. $1\frac{1}{4} \div 7\frac{1}{2}$ $\frac{1}{6}$
16. $3\frac{2}{3} \div 2\frac{1}{3}$ $1\frac{4}{7}$
17. $1 \div 3\frac{4}{5}$ $\frac{5}{19}$
18. $\frac{7}{8} \div 5$ $\frac{7}{40}$

CALCULATOR EXERCISES

Optional

Divide to write each fraction as a decimal rounded to the nearest ten-thousandth.

1. $\frac{5}{7}$ .7143
2. $\frac{11}{15}$ .7333
3. $\frac{7}{12}$ .5833
4. $\frac{184}{7}$ 26.2875
5. $\frac{17}{64}$ .2656
6. $\frac{382}{9}$ 42.4444
7. $\frac{14}{265}$ .0528
8. $\frac{473}{12}$ 39.4167
9. $\frac{953}{16}$ 59.5625
10. $\frac{61}{144}$ .4236

Write these fractions as decimals. Show just the first six decimal places.

11. $\frac{1}{11}$ .090909
12. $\frac{2}{11}$ .181818
13. $\frac{3}{11}$ .272727
14. $\frac{4}{11}$ .363636
15. $\frac{5}{11}$ .454545
16. $\frac{6}{11}$ .545454

Look for a pattern. Predict the decimals for these fractions. Check your predictions with the calculator.

17. $\frac{7}{11}$ .636363
18. $\frac{8}{11}$ .727272
19. $\frac{9}{11}$ .818181
20. $\frac{10}{11}$ .909090

Use a calculator to write $\frac{441}{16}$ as a mixed number. You want the answer in this form:

$▒\frac{▒}{16}$

First divide 441 by 16. The display is 27.5625. Now you know that:

$\frac{441}{16} = 27\frac{▒}{16}$

To find the missing numerator, follow these steps.

Multiply 16 × 27. Write it down. (16 × 27 = 432)

Subtract that from 441. (441 − 432 = 9)

$\frac{441}{16} = 27\frac{9}{16}$

Follow the same steps to give a mixed number for each of these fractions.

21. $\frac{563}{8}$ $70\frac{3}{8}$
22. $\frac{281}{9}$ $31\frac{2}{9}$
23. $\frac{709}{16}$ $44\frac{5}{16}$
24. $\frac{255}{7}$ $36\frac{3}{7}$
25. $\frac{719}{56}$ $12\frac{47}{56}$
26. $\frac{605}{24}$ $25\frac{5}{24}$

34. $\frac{4 \times 3 \times 2}{52 \times 51 \times 50}$

35. $\frac{13 \times 13 \times 12}{52 \times 51 \times 50}$

36. $\frac{26 \times 25 \times 24}{52 \times 51 \times 50}$

Find these products. Give each answer as a mixed number. Use the calculator to help you with the computing.

27. $58\frac{2}{3} \times 6\frac{7}{8}$ $403\frac{1}{3}$
28. $7\frac{11}{16} \times 23\frac{1}{4}$ $178\frac{47}{64}$
29. $8\frac{4}{9} \times 6\frac{3}{5}$ $55\frac{11}{15}$
30. $7\frac{5}{6} \times 14\frac{1}{2} \times \frac{3}{4}$ $85\frac{3}{16}$
31. $8\frac{3}{4} \times 37\frac{4}{5}$ $330\frac{3}{4}$
32. $43\frac{5}{7} \times 12\frac{3}{8}$ $540\frac{27}{28}$

Joyce is going to deal herself 3 cards from a standard 52-card deck. Give as a decimal to the nearest ten-thousandth the probability that she will get

33. three hearts. .0129

$$\left(\frac{13 \times 12 \times 11}{52 \times 51 \times 50}\right)$$

34. three 5's. .0002 See below left.
35. a spade and then two hearts. .0153
36. three red cards. .1176

Ratio, Percent, and Statistics

Chapter 10
Ratio, Proportion, and Similarity

Chapter 11
Percent

Chapter 12
Statistics

Chapter 10 Ratio, Proportion, and Similarity

Number of test items - 8

Number missed	1	2	3	4
Percent correct	88	75	63	50

skill Writing Ratios pages 196–197

A Write the ratio of records to dollars.

3 records for \$14 $\frac{3}{14}$

B Give the next ratio in this list.

$\frac{5}{7} = \frac{10}{14} = \frac{15}{21}$ $\frac{20}{28}$

skill Solving Proportions pages 198–199

C Write cross-products. Then tell whether these ratios are equal. $\frac{8}{15}$ $\frac{12}{21}$

8 X 21 15 X 12
not equal

D Find the missing number in this proportion. $\frac{4}{10} = \frac{22}{n}$

$n = 55$

skill Identifying Similar Figures pages 200–201

E Give the letter of the figure that is similar to the figure on the left. a

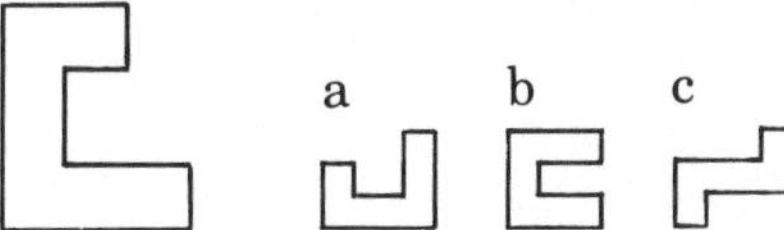

F The triangles are similar. Give 3 pairs of corresponding angles and 3 pairs of corresponding sides.

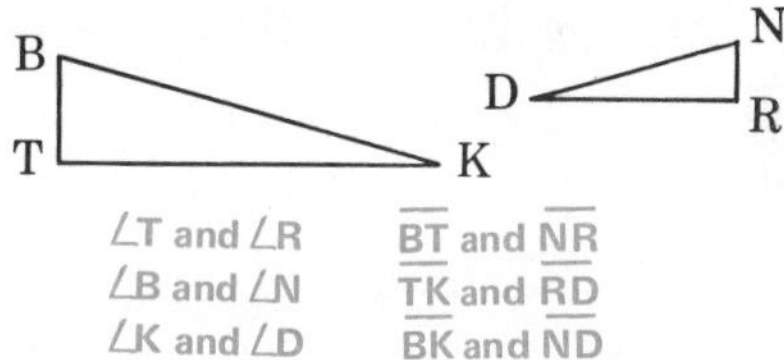

∠T and ∠R $\overline{BT}$ and $\overline{NR}$
∠B and ∠N $\overline{TK}$ and $\overline{RD}$
∠K and ∠D $\overline{BK}$ and $\overline{ND}$

skill Finding Missing Sides in Similar Triangles pages 202–203

G The triangles are similar. Complete these ratios of the lengths of corresponding sides.

$\frac{16}{24} = \frac{20}{30}$

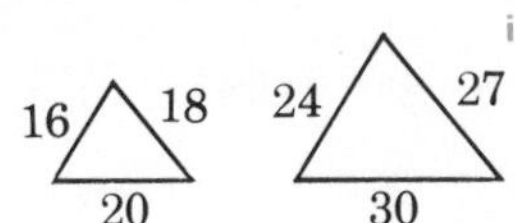

H The triangles are similar. Write a proportion and find n.

Proportions may vary. A sample is given. $\frac{60}{48} = \frac{110}{n}$ $n = 88$

60 m 110 m 130 m
48 m n

See page T22 for additional notes on Chapter 10.

Objective: Write ratios and lists of equal ratios.

Writing Ratios

example A **Writing ratios**

Write the ratio of pages to hours.

250 pages in 4 hours

$\frac{250}{4}$ ⟵ Pages / ⟵ Hours

The ratio $\frac{250}{4}$ is read "250 to 4."

example B **Equal ratios**

Give the next ratio in this list.

$$\frac{3}{10} = \frac{6}{20} = \frac{9}{30}$$

These equal ratios all describe the same rate.

You can multiply to find equal ratios.

$$\frac{3}{10} = \frac{6}{20} = \frac{9}{30} = \frac{12}{40}$$

(numerators: 2×3, 3×3, 4×3; denominators: 2×10, 3×10, 4×10)

$\frac{12}{40}$ is the next ratio in the list.

Point out that students need not always use lists to generate equal ratios. An equal ratio can be found by multiplying or dividing both numbers of a ratio by the same number. For example:

$$\frac{3}{5} = \frac{60}{100} \quad \left(\frac{20 \times 3}{20 \times 5}\right) \qquad \frac{18}{24} = \frac{3}{4} \quad \left(\frac{18 \div 6}{24 \div 6}\right)$$

exercises

set A

Write each ratio.

1. 100 kilometers on 12 liters of gasoline

$\frac{100}{12}$ ▒ ⟵ Kilometers / ▒ ⟵ Liters of gasoline

2. 18 girls and 16 boys in the class

$\frac{16}{18}$ ▒ ⟵ Boys / ▒ ⟵ Girls

3. 100 centimeters in 1 meter

$\frac{100}{1}$ ▒ ⟵ Centimeters / ▒ ⟵ Meters

4. 300 milliliters of ginger ale and 250 milliliters of orange juice

$\frac{250}{300}$ ▒ ⟵ Milliliters of orange juice / ▒ ⟵ Milliliters of ginger ale

5. 60 centimeters high and 21 centimeters wide

$\frac{21}{60}$ ▒ ⟵ Width in centimeters / ▒ ⟵ Height in centimeters

6. 7 completed passes out of 15 attempts

$\frac{7}{15}$ ▒ ⟵ Completed passes / ▒ ⟵ Attempts

7. 7 nickels for 4 dimes

$\frac{4}{7}$ ▒ ⟵ Dimes / ▒ ⟵ Nickels

8. 240 calories in 5 crackers

$\frac{240}{5}$ ▒ ⟵ Calories / ▒ ⟵ Crackers

9. 340 kilometers in 5 hours

$\frac{340}{5}$ $\frac{\square}{\square}$ $\begin{array}{l}\longleftarrow \text{Kilometers}\\ \longleftarrow \text{Hours}\end{array}$

10. 6 pencils for 29¢

$\frac{6}{29}$ $\frac{\square}{\square}$ $\begin{array}{l}\longleftarrow \text{Pencils}\\ \longleftarrow \text{Cents}\end{array}$

11. A 35-centimeter post that weighs 15 kilograms

$\frac{35}{15}$ $\frac{\square}{\square}$ $\begin{array}{l}\longleftarrow \text{Length in centimeters}\\ \longleftarrow \text{Weight in kilograms}\end{array}$

12. 8 heartbeats in 6 seconds

$\frac{8}{6}$ $\frac{\square}{\square}$ $\begin{array}{l}\longleftarrow \text{Heartbeats}\\ \longleftarrow \text{Seconds}\end{array}$

13. 2 centimeters on a map for an actual distance of 75 meters

$\frac{2}{75}$ $\frac{\square}{\square}$ $\begin{array}{l}\longleftarrow \text{Centimeters on map}\\ \longleftarrow \text{Actual meters}\end{array}$

14. 6 batteries for \$2.10

$\frac{6}{2.10}$ $\frac{\square}{\square}$ $\begin{array}{l}\longleftarrow \text{Batteries}\\ \longleftarrow \text{Dollars}\end{array}$

15. 9 turns of a bicycle pedal for 14 turns of the rear wheel

$\frac{9}{14}$ $\frac{\square}{\square}$ $\begin{array}{l}\longleftarrow \text{Pedal turns}\\ \longleftarrow \text{Rear wheel turns}\end{array}$

16. 1 centimeter on a model airplane for 32 centimeters on the actual airplane

$\frac{32}{1}$ $\frac{\square}{\square}$ $\begin{array}{l}\longleftarrow \text{Centimeters on actual plane}\\ \longleftarrow \text{Centimeters on model}\end{array}$

17. 3 drops of red for 4 drops of blue

$\frac{3}{7}$ $\frac{\square}{\square}$ $\begin{array}{l}\longleftarrow \text{Number of red drops}\\ \longleftarrow \text{Total number of drops}\end{array}$

set B

Give the next ratio in each list.

1. $\frac{2}{15} = \frac{4}{30} = \frac{6}{45}$ $\frac{8}{60}$

2. $\frac{4}{5} = \frac{8}{10} = \frac{12}{15} = \frac{16}{20}$ $\frac{20}{25}$

3. $\frac{7}{19} = \frac{14}{38} = \frac{21}{57}$ $\frac{28}{76}$

4. $\frac{12}{11} = \frac{24}{22} = \frac{36}{33} = \frac{48}{44}$ $\frac{60}{55}$

5. $\frac{4}{3} = \frac{8}{6} = \frac{12}{9} = \frac{16}{12}$ $\frac{20}{15}$

6. $\frac{8}{190} = \frac{16}{380} = \frac{24}{570}$ $\frac{32}{760}$

7. $\frac{8}{5} = \frac{16}{10} = \frac{24}{15}$ $\frac{32}{20}$

8. $\frac{12}{7} = \frac{24}{14} = \frac{36}{21} = \frac{48}{28}$ $\frac{60}{35}$

9. $\frac{25}{16} = \frac{50}{32} = \frac{75}{48}$ $\frac{100}{64}$

10. $\frac{4}{9} = \frac{8}{18} = \frac{12}{27} = \frac{16}{36}$ $\frac{20}{45}$

11. $\frac{2}{3} = \frac{4}{6} = \frac{6}{9} = \frac{8}{12} = \frac{10}{15}$ $\frac{12}{18}$

12. $\frac{6}{140} = \frac{12}{280} = \frac{18}{420}$ $\frac{24}{560}$

13. $\frac{15}{13} = \frac{30}{26} = \frac{45}{39} = \frac{60}{52}$ $\frac{75}{65}$

14. $\frac{21}{62} = \frac{42}{124} = \frac{63}{186}$ $\frac{84}{248}$

Objective: Find a missing number in a proportion by using cross-products.

Solving Proportions

example C Cross-products

Write cross-products. Then tell whether these ratios are equal.

$$\frac{4}{10} \quad \frac{14}{35}$$

Point out that these ratios can be found in a list of equal ratios.

$\frac{2}{5} = \frac{4}{10} = \frac{6}{15} = \frac{8}{20} = \frac{10}{25} = \frac{12}{30} = \frac{14}{35} = \frac{16}{40}$

$4 \times 35 \quad 10 \times 14$ — 4×35 and 10×14 are **cross-products.**

$140 = 140$ — The cross-products are equal.

$\frac{4}{10} = \frac{14}{35}$ — So the ratios are equal.

If the cross-products were not equal, the ratios would not be equal.

example D Solving proportions

Find the missing number in this proportion.

$\frac{12}{28} = \frac{k}{42}$ — Equal ratios form a **proportion.**

$12 \times 42 = 28 \times k$ — Write the cross-products.

$504 = 28 \times k$

$\frac{504}{28} = \frac{28 \times k}{28}$ — Divide both sides by 28.

$18 = k$

exercises set C

In each exercise, write cross-products. Then tell whether the ratios are equal.

1. $\frac{30}{9} \quad \frac{40}{12}$ equal — 30 X 12 9 X 40
2. $\frac{2}{3} \quad \frac{7}{16}$ not equal — 2 X 16 3 X 7
3. $\frac{.6}{.8} \quad \frac{1.5}{2.0}$ equal — .6 X 2.0 .8 X 1.5
4. $\frac{3}{6} \quad \frac{2}{5}$ not equal — 3 X 5 6 X 2
5. $\frac{15}{10} \quad \frac{20}{16}$ not equal — 15 X 16 10 X 20
6. $\frac{30}{36} \quad \frac{20}{24}$ equal — 30 X 24 36 X 20
7. $\frac{4}{7} \quad \frac{32}{56}$ equal — 4 X 56 7 X 32
8. $\frac{6.5}{1.3} \quad \frac{.5}{.1}$ equal — 6.5 X .1 1.3 X .5
9. $\frac{3}{8} \quad \frac{10}{27}$ not equal — 3 X 27 8 X 10
10. $\frac{18}{63} \quad \frac{4}{14}$ equal — 18 X 14 63 X 4
11. $\frac{40}{160} \quad \frac{8}{30}$ not equal — 40 X 30 160 X 8
12. $\frac{.16}{.36} \quad \frac{.4}{.9}$ equal — .16 X .9 .36 X .4
13. $\frac{8}{30} \quad \frac{12}{45}$ equal — 8 X 45 30 X 12
14. $\frac{9}{12} \quad \frac{12}{16}$ equal — 9 X 16 12 X 12
15. $\frac{1.1}{.3} \quad \frac{44}{12}$ equal — 1.1 X 12 .3 X 44
16. $\frac{28}{24} \quad \frac{7}{6}$ equal — 28 X 6 24 X 7
17. $\frac{9}{15} \quad \frac{81}{130}$ not equal — 9 X 130 15 X 81
18. $\frac{6}{11} \quad \frac{40}{77}$ not equal — 6 X 77 11 X 40
19. $\frac{2.8}{4.5} \quad \frac{2.1}{3.5}$ not equal — 2.8 X 3.5 4.5 X 2.1
20. $\frac{24}{42} \quad \frac{36}{60}$ not equal — 24 X 60 42 X 36
21. $\frac{.3}{.5} \quad \frac{3.0}{4.5}$ not equal — .3 X 4.5 .5 X 3.0
22. $\frac{14}{22} \quad \frac{21}{33}$ equal — 14 X 33 22 X 21
23. $\frac{12}{21} \quad \frac{10}{15}$ not equal — 12 X 15 21 X 10
24. $\frac{.08}{.18} \quad \frac{.24}{.52}$ not equal — .08 X .52 .18 X .24
25. $\frac{18}{14} \quad \frac{54}{42}$ equal — 18 X 42 14 X 54
26. $\frac{4.2}{9} \quad \frac{25.2}{50}$ not equal — 4.2 X 50 9 X 25.2

set D

Find each missing number.

1. $\frac{4}{18} = \frac{10}{n}$
   $n = 45$

2. $\frac{20}{25} = \frac{d}{45}$
   $d = 36$

3. $\frac{10}{t} = \frac{8}{28}$
   $t = 35$

4. $\frac{2}{3} = \frac{b}{42}$
   $b = 28$

5. $\frac{c}{18} = \frac{10}{4}$
   $c = 45$

6. $\frac{2.4}{2.8} = \frac{18}{a}$
   $a = 21$

7. $\frac{4}{1} = \frac{52}{s}$
   $s = 13$

8. $\frac{15}{g} = \frac{6}{10}$
   $g = 25$

9. $\frac{h}{12} = \frac{25}{20}$
   $h = 15$

10. $\frac{.7}{.9} = \frac{k}{36}$
    $k = 28$

11. $\frac{6}{21} = \frac{a}{70}$
    $a = 20$

12. $\frac{.4}{.9} = \frac{4.8}{e}$
    $e = 10.8$

13. $\frac{12}{40} = \frac{f}{9}$
    $f = 2.7$

14. $\frac{13}{26} = \frac{5}{r}$
    $r = 10$

15. $\frac{.12}{.28} = \frac{s}{42}$
    $s = 18$

16. $\frac{8}{50} = \frac{20}{x}$
    $x = 125$

17. $\frac{1}{6} = \frac{t}{78}$
    $t = 13$

18. $\frac{y}{27} = \frac{1.6}{2.4}$
    $y = 18$

19. $\frac{8}{12} = \frac{z}{54}$
    $z = 36$

20. $\frac{9}{b} = \frac{57}{19}$
    $b = 3$

21. $\frac{1}{17} = \frac{c}{51}$
    $c = 3$

22. $\frac{75}{100} = \frac{30}{x}$
    $x = 40$

23. $\frac{102}{17} = \frac{36}{d}$
    $d = 6$

24. $\frac{18}{a} = \frac{4.8}{5.6}$
    $a = 21$

25. $\frac{4}{g} = \frac{92}{23}$
    $g = 1$

26. $\frac{k}{40} = \frac{14}{16}$
    $k = 35$

27. $\frac{12}{20} = \frac{n}{25}$
    $n = 15$

28. $\frac{w}{.16} = \frac{.15}{.40}$
    $w = .06$

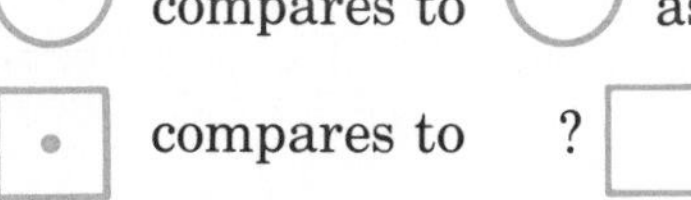

1. compares to as compares to ?

2. compares to as compares to ?

3. compares to as compares to ?

4. compares to as compares to ?

5. compares to as compares to ?

The applications on pages 205 and 208–209 may be used anytime after this lesson.

Identifying Similar Figures

example E Identifying similar figures

Give the letter of the figure that is similar to the figure on the left.

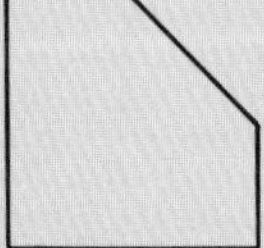

a

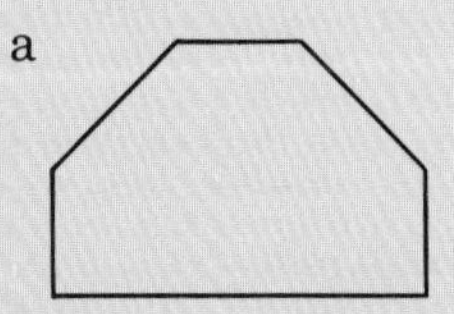

b

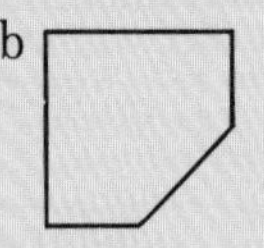

c

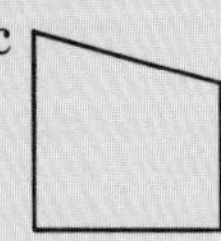

Similar figures have the same shape but not necessarily the same size.

Figure b is similar to the figure on the left.

example F Naming corresponding parts of similar triangles

The triangles are similar. Give 3 pairs of corresponding angles and 3 pairs of corresponding sides.

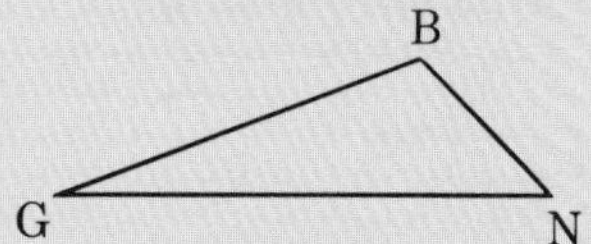

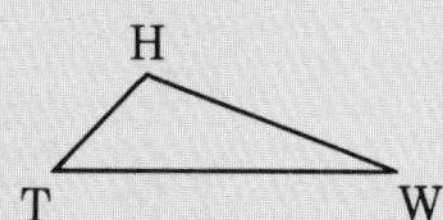

Corresponding angles	Corresponding sides
∠G and ∠W	$\overline{GB}$ and $\overline{WH}$
∠B and ∠H	$\overline{BN}$ and $\overline{HT}$
∠N and ∠T	$\overline{GN}$ and $\overline{TW}$

$\overline{GB}$ means "segment GB."

exercises

set E

In each exercise, give the letter of the figure that is similar to the figure on the left.

1. b

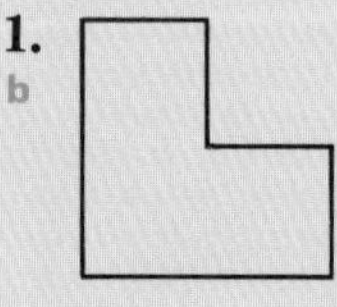

a c b

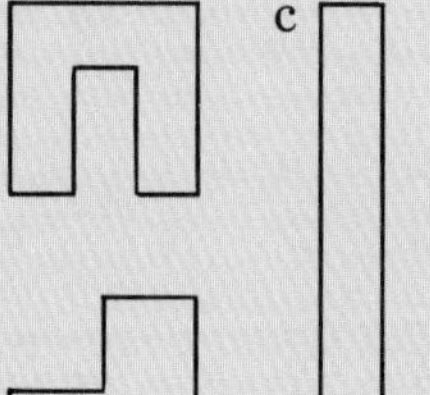

2. c

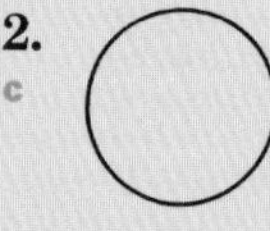

a b c

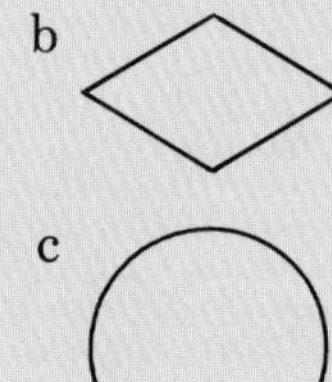

3. c

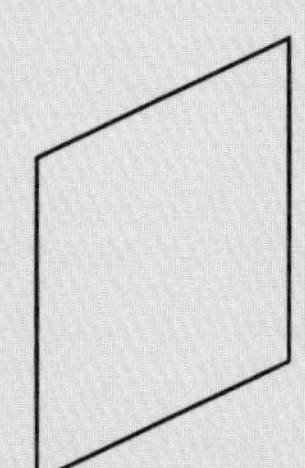

a b c

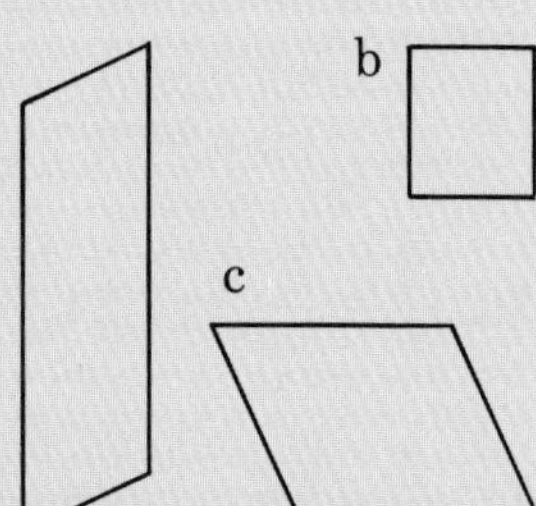

4. a

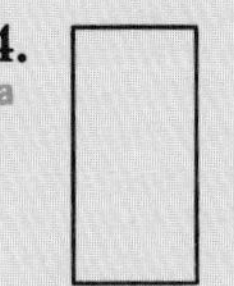

a

b c

5. b

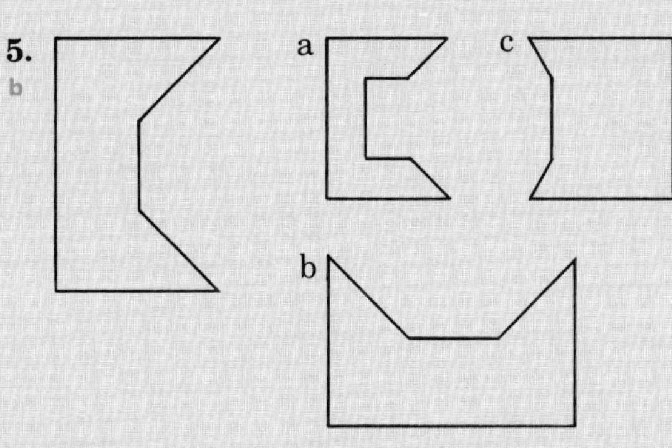

6. b

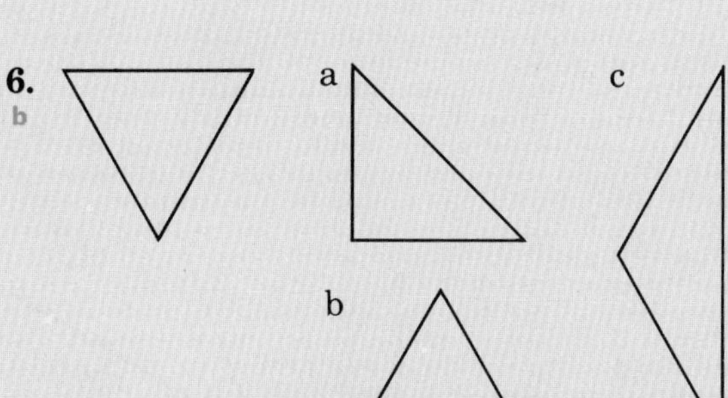

7. a

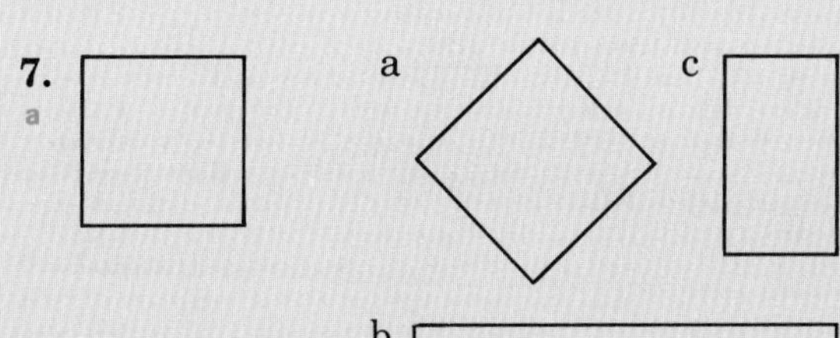

8. c

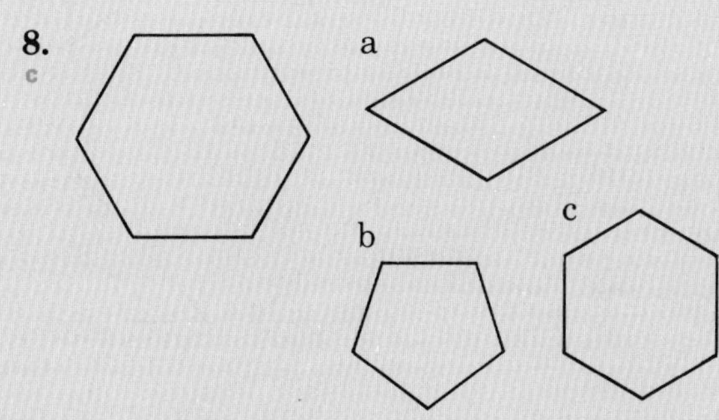

It may help some students to think of corresponding sides as sides opposite corresponding angles.

set F

In each exercise, the triangles are similar. For each exercise, give 3 pairs of corresponding angles and 3 pairs of corresponding sides.

1.

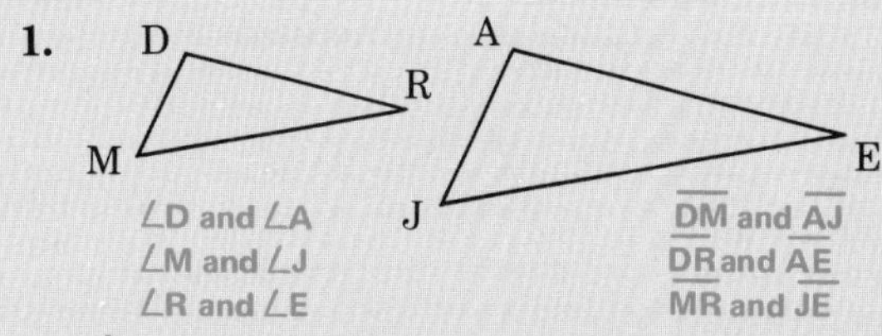

∠D and ∠A
∠M and ∠J
∠R and ∠E

$\overline{DM}$ and $\overline{AJ}$
$\overline{DR}$ and $\overline{AE}$
$\overline{MR}$ and $\overline{JE}$

2.

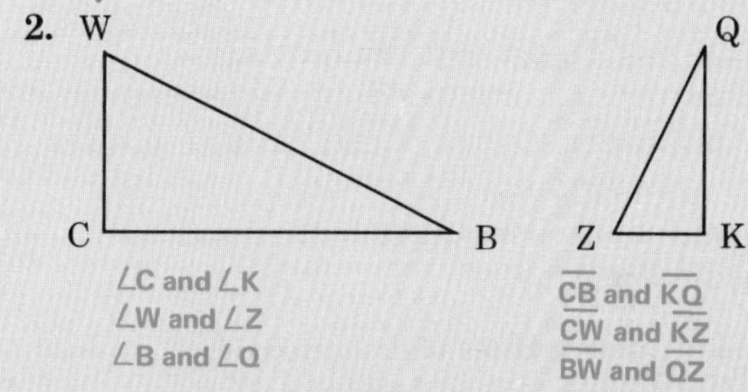

∠C and ∠K
∠W and ∠Z
∠B and ∠Q

$\overline{CB}$ and $\overline{KQ}$
$\overline{CW}$ and $\overline{KZ}$
$\overline{BW}$ and $\overline{QZ}$

3.

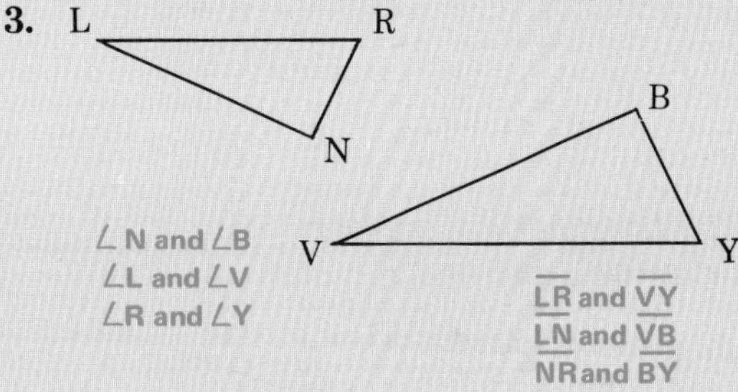

∠N and ∠B
∠L and ∠V
∠R and ∠Y

$\overline{LR}$ and $\overline{VY}$
$\overline{LN}$ and $\overline{VB}$
$\overline{NR}$ and $\overline{BY}$

4.

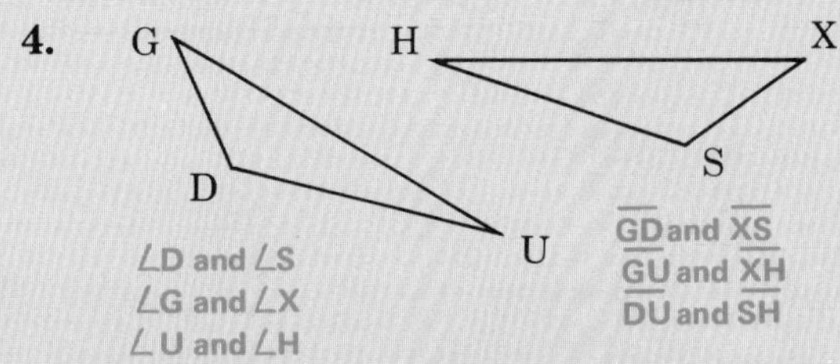

∠D and ∠S
∠G and ∠X
∠U and ∠H

$\overline{GD}$ and $\overline{XS}$
$\overline{GU}$ and $\overline{XH}$
$\overline{DU}$ and $\overline{SH}$

5.

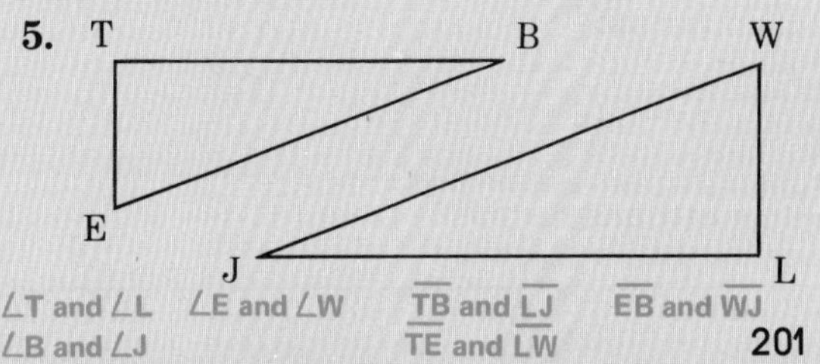

∠T and ∠L ∠E and ∠W $\overline{TB}$ and $\overline{LJ}$ $\overline{EB}$ and $\overline{WJ}$
∠B and ∠J $\overline{TE}$ and $\overline{LW}$

Skill

Objective: Find missing dimensions in similar triangles by using proportions.

Finding Missing Sides in Similar Triangles

example G Writing ratios of lengths of corresponding sides

The triangles are similar. Complete these ratios of the lengths of corresponding sides. All lengths are in meters.

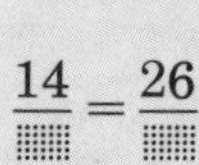

$\frac{14}{\square} = \frac{26}{\square}$

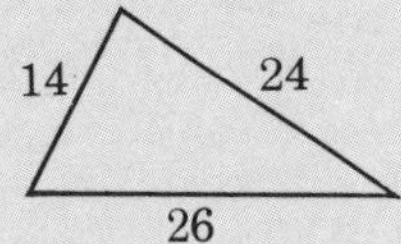

7 12

13

If two triangles are similar, the measures of corresponding angles are equal. Also, the measures of corresponding sides are proportional. This means that the ratios of the lengths of corresponding sides are equal.

$\frac{14}{7} = \frac{26}{13}$ ⟵ Sides of first triangle / ⟵ Sides of second triangle

example H Find missing dimensions

The triangles are similar. Write a proportion and find n.

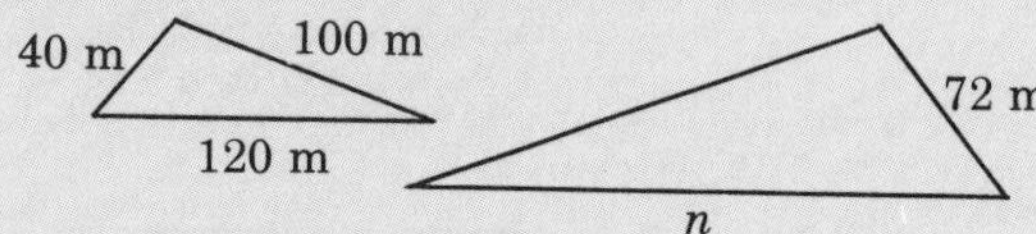

$$\frac{40}{72} = \frac{120}{n}$$

$40 \times n = 72 \times 120$

$40 \times n = 8640$

$n = 216$

n is 216 meters.

exercises set G

There are two exercises for each pair of similar triangles. Complete the ratios of the lengths of corresponding sides. All lengths are in meters.

1. $\frac{25}{\square} = \frac{20}{\square}$

15 12

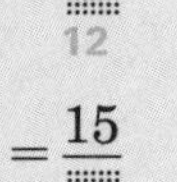

2. $\frac{25}{\square} = \frac{15}{\square}$

15 9

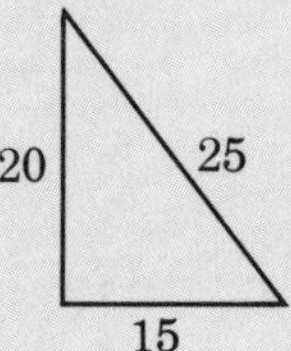

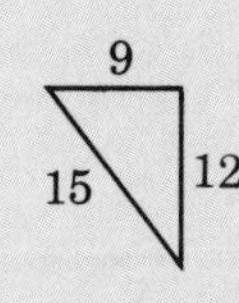

3. $\frac{60}{\square} = \frac{36}{\square}$

150 90

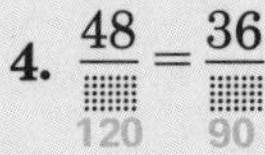

4. $\frac{48}{\square} = \frac{36}{\square}$

120 90

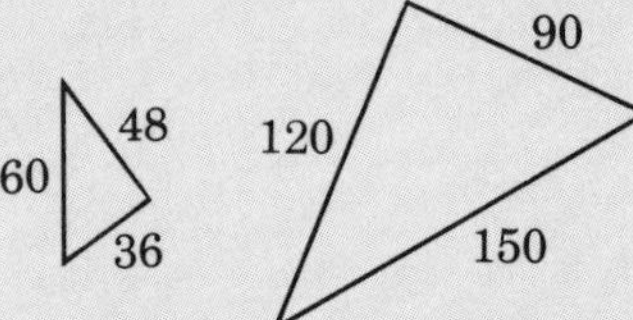

5. $\frac{240}{\square} = \frac{200}{\square}$

216 180

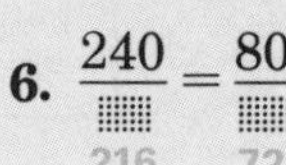

6. $\frac{240}{\square} = \frac{80}{\square}$

216 72

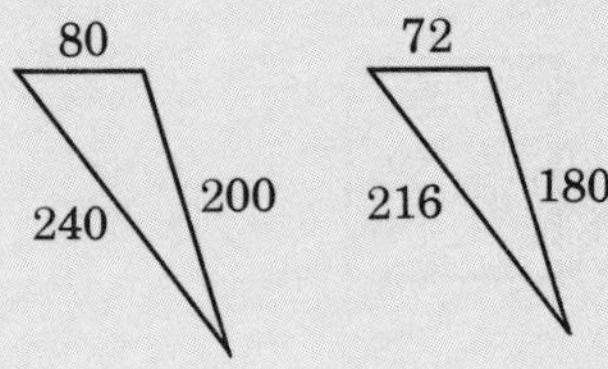

7. $\frac{6.0}{\square} = \frac{3.6}{\square}$

9.0 5.4

8. $\frac{4.8}{\square} = \frac{3.6}{\square}$

7.2 5.4

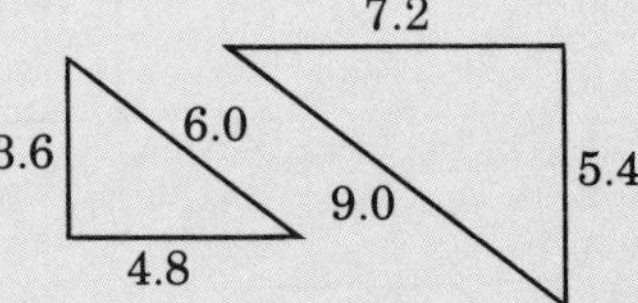

9. $\frac{104}{\square} = \frac{40}{\square}$

130 50

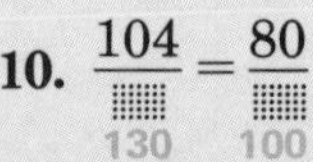

10. $\frac{104}{\square} = \frac{80}{\square}$

130 100

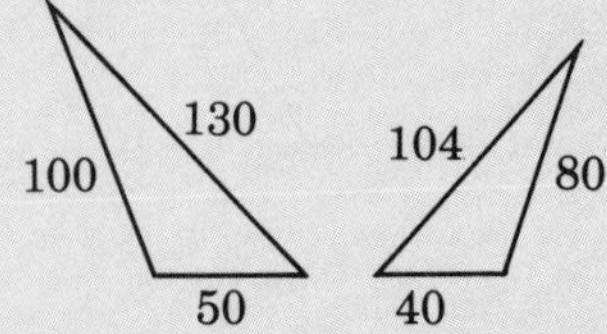

Proportions may vary. Sample proportions are given.

set H

In each exercise, the triangles are similar. Write a proportion and find n. All lengths are in meters.

1.

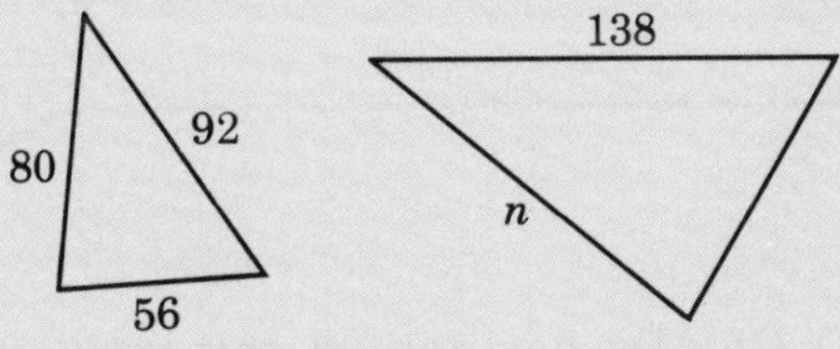

$\frac{92}{138} = \frac{80}{n}$ n is 120 meters

2.

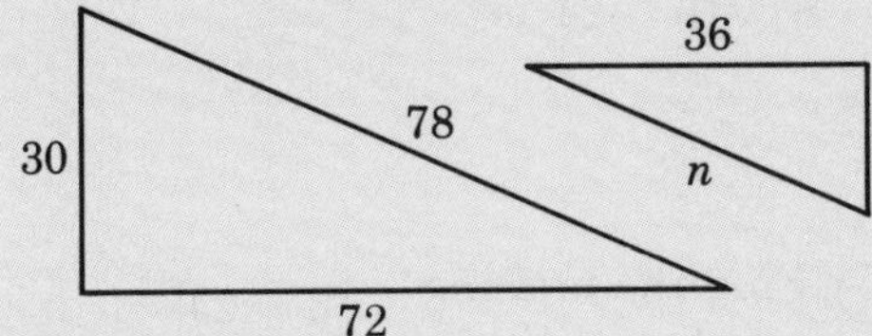

$\frac{72}{36} = \frac{78}{n}$ n is 39 meters

3.

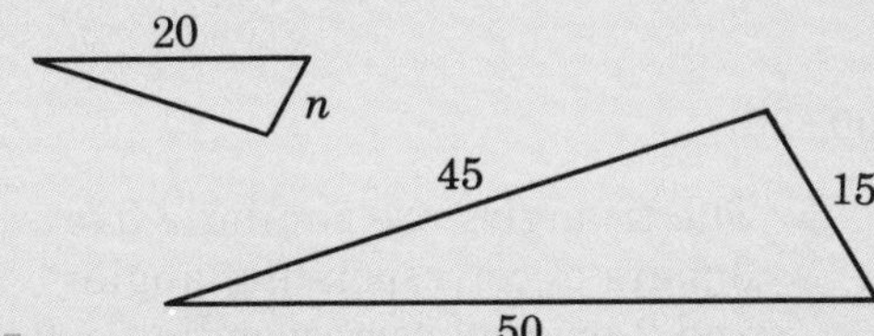

$\frac{50}{20} = \frac{15}{n}$ n is 6 meters.

4.

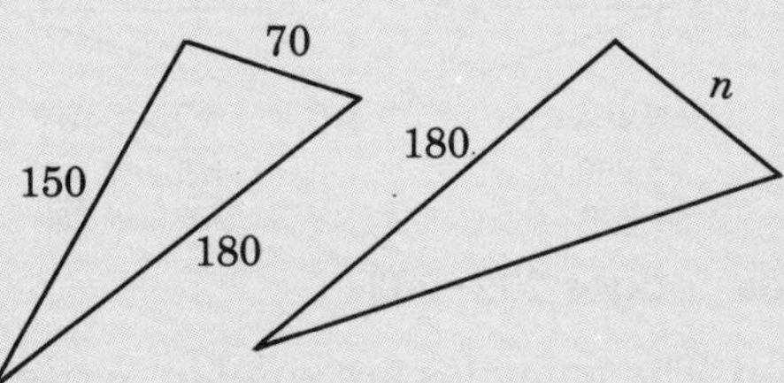

$\frac{150}{180} = \frac{70}{n}$ n is 84 meters.

5.

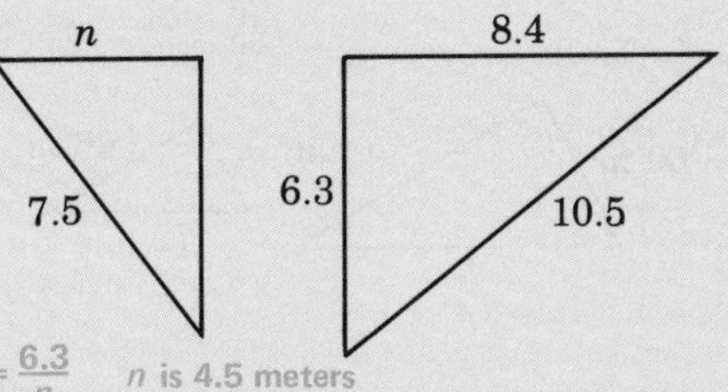

$\frac{10.5}{7.5} = \frac{6.3}{n}$ n is 4.5 meters

6.

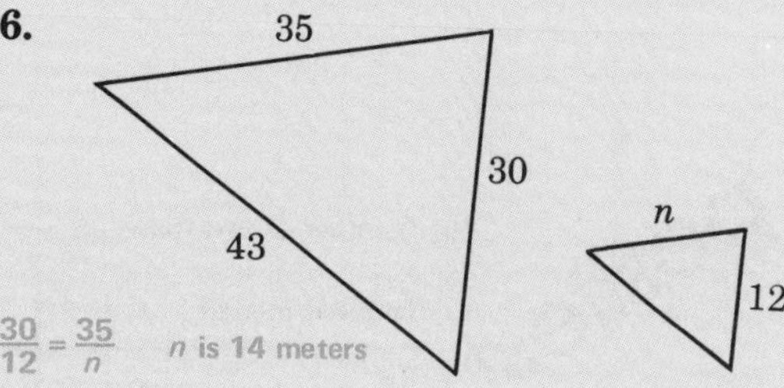

$\frac{30}{12} = \frac{35}{n}$ n is 14 meters

7.

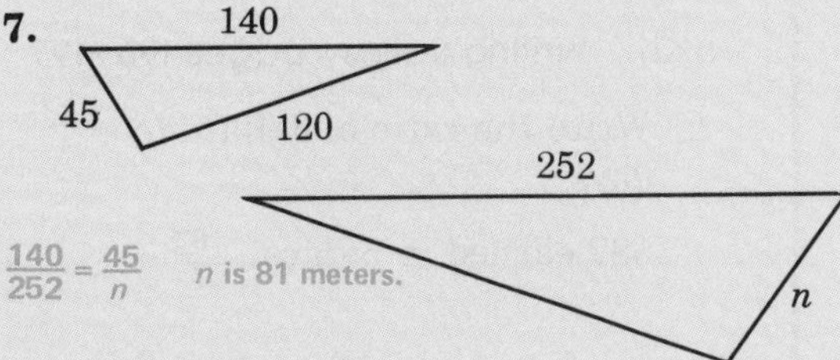

$\frac{140}{252} = \frac{45}{n}$ n is 81 meters.

8.

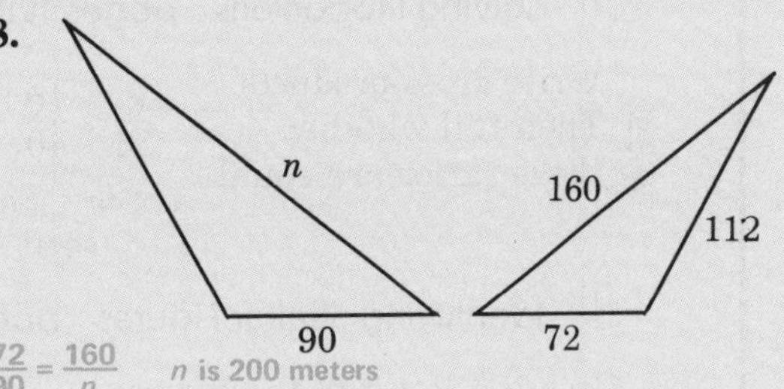

$\frac{72}{90} = \frac{160}{n}$ n is 200 meters

9.

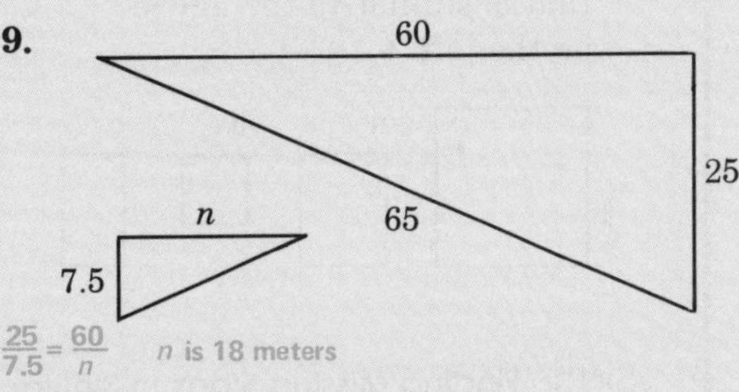

$\frac{25}{7.5} = \frac{60}{n}$ n is 18 meters

10.

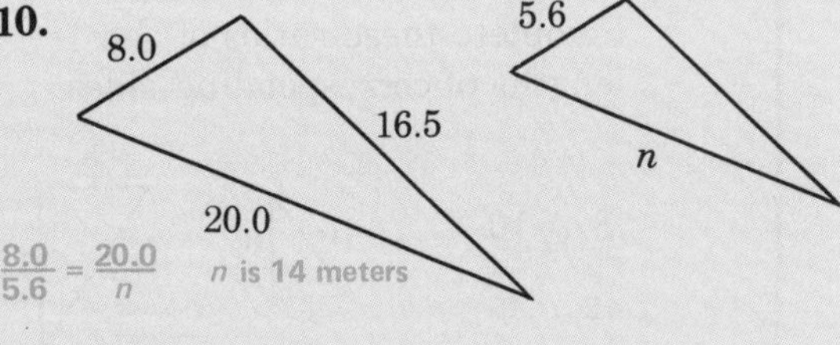

$\frac{8.0}{5.6} = \frac{20.0}{n}$ n is 14 meters

posttest

Number of test items - 8

Number missed	1	2	3	4
Percent correct	88	75	63	50

skill Writing Ratios pages 196–197

A Write the ratio of dollars to days.

$82 earned in 5 days $\frac{82}{5}$

B Give the next ratio in this list.

$\frac{9}{8} = \frac{18}{16} = \frac{27}{24}$ $\frac{36}{32}$

skill Solving Proportions pages 198–199

C Write cross-products. Then tell whether these ratios are equal.

$\frac{6}{16}$ $\frac{15}{40}$

6 X 40 16 X 15
equal

D Find the missing number in this proportion.

$\frac{18}{x} = \frac{24}{28}$

$x = 21$

skill Identifying Similar Figures pages 200–201

E Give the letter of the figure that is similar to the figure on the left. b

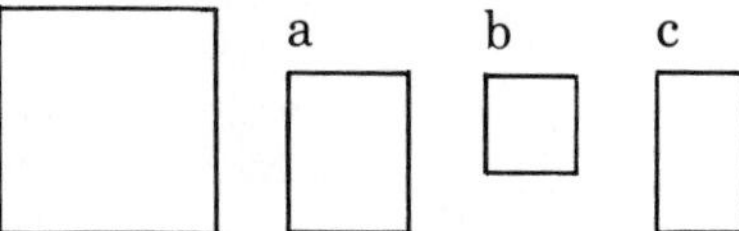

F The triangles are similar. Give 3 pairs of corresponding angles and 3 pairs of corresponding sides.

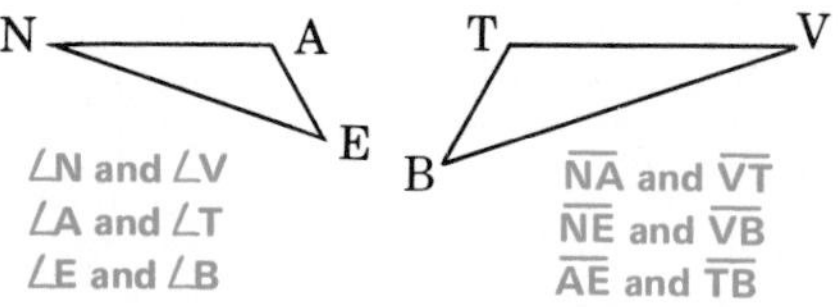

∠N and ∠V
∠A and ∠T
∠E and ∠B

$\overline{NA}$ and $\overline{VT}$
$\overline{NE}$ and $\overline{VB}$
$\overline{AE}$ and $\overline{TB}$

skill Finding Missing Sides in Similar Triangles pages 202–203

G The triangles are similar. Complete these ratios of the lengths of corresponding sides.

$\frac{8}{12} = \frac{10}{15}$

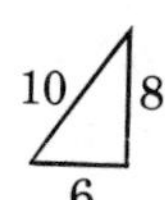

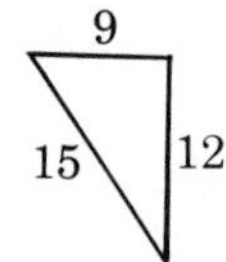

H The triangles are similar. Write a proportion and find n.

Proportions may vary. A sample is given.

$\frac{36}{60} = \frac{72}{n}$ $n = 120$

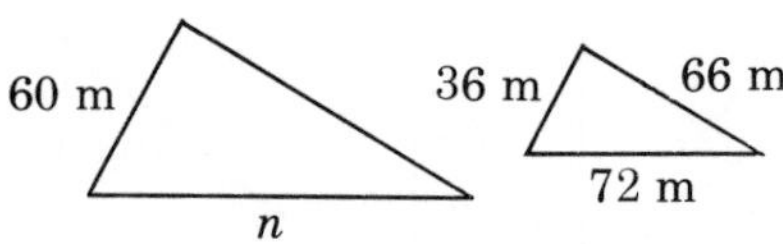

Objective: Solve problems involving ratio, proportion, and similarity.

In this lesson students solve problems involving driving rates, gasoline consumption, and expenses for a vacation trip.

Planning a Vacation

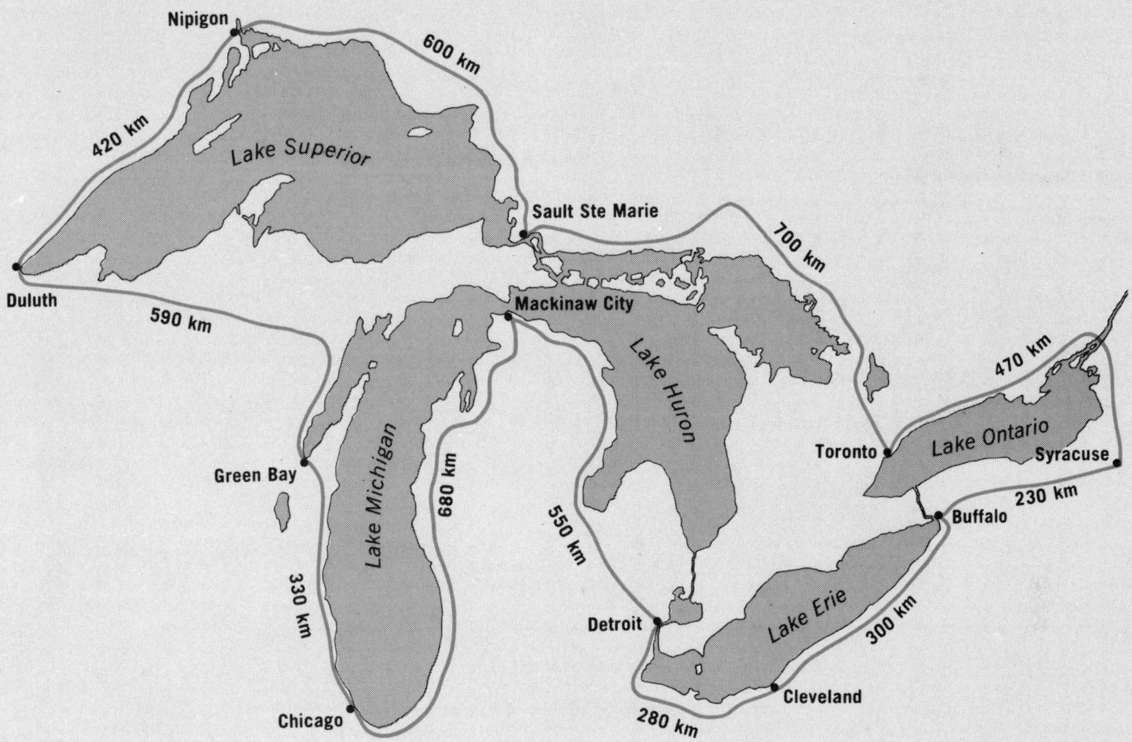

The Orozcos live in Detroit. They are driving around the Great Lakes on their vacation.

Their driving time from Detroit to Mackinaw City was 7 hours. At this rate, what will be their driving time between the following cities? Give each answer to the nearest tenth hour.

1. Mackinaw City to Chicago 8.7 hours

$$\frac{550}{7} = \frac{680}{n} \begin{array}{l} \leftarrow \text{Kilometers} \\ \leftarrow \text{Hours} \end{array}$$

2. Chicago to Green Bay 4.2 hours

$$\frac{550}{7} = \frac{330}{n} \begin{array}{l} \leftarrow \text{Kilometers} \\ \leftarrow \text{Hours} \end{array}$$

3. Green Bay to Duluth 7.5 hours

4. Duluth to Nipigon 5.3 hours

5. Nipigon to Sault Ste Marie 7.6 hours

6. Sault Ste Marie to Toronto 8.9 hours

7. Toronto to Syracuse 6.0 hours

8. Syracuse to Buffalo 2.9 hours

9. Buffalo to Cleveland 3.8 hours

10. Cleveland to Detroit 3.6 hours

11. Find the total distance for the trip. 5150 kilometers

12. If the Orozcos use 4 liters of gasoline every 25 kilometers, how much gasoline will they use for the entire trip? 824 liters

The Orozcos spent \$230 for food and motels the first 4 days. At this rate, how much will they spend for food and motels

13. in 10 days? \$575

14. in 14 days? \$805

Objective: Solve problems involving ratio, proportion, and similarity.

In this lesson students find heights and distances through indirect measurement by using similar triangles.

Finding Heights and Distances Using Similarity

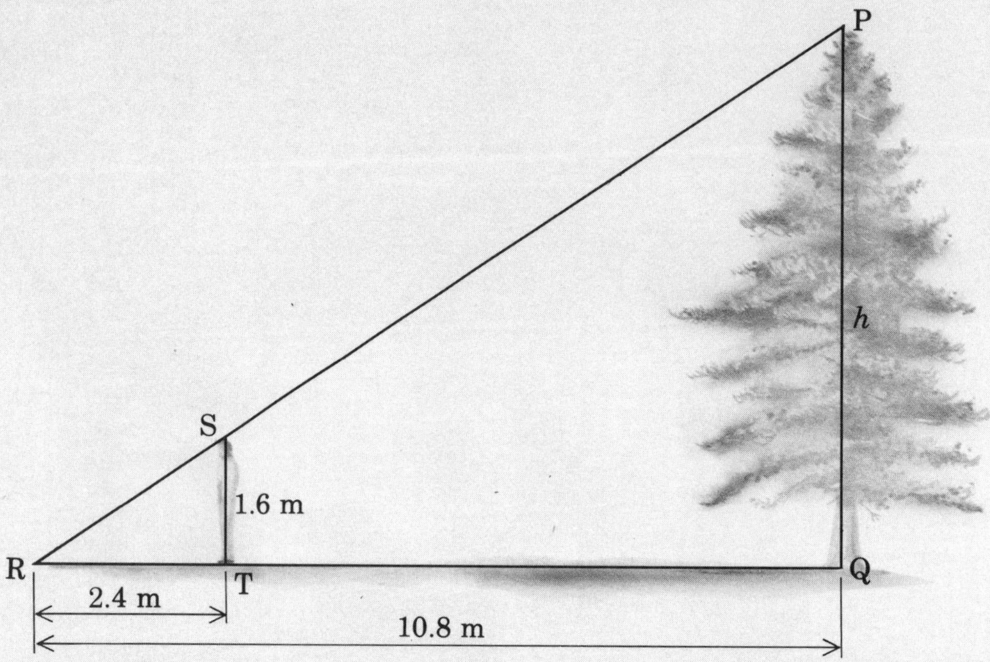

The Conrads visited a state park. Mr. Conrad used the following technique to estimate the height of a pine tree.

He stood so that his shadow extended as far as the shadow of the tree.

He recorded the measure of the tree's shadow, QR, his shadow, TR, and his height, ST.

Triangles PQR and STR are similar. So the measures of corresponding sides are proportional.

$$\frac{PQ}{ST} = \frac{QR}{TR}$$

$$\frac{h}{1.6} = \frac{10.8}{2.4}$$

$$h \times 2.4 = 1.6 \times 10.8$$

$$h \times 2.4 = 17.28$$

$$h = 7.2$$

The height of the tree is 7.2 meters.

Find the height of the tree if these were the values for QR, TR, and ST.

	QR (m)	TR (m)	ST (m)	
1.	22.4	2.8	1.6	12.8 m
2.	28.8	7.2	1.6	6.4 m
3.	12.8	0.8	1.7	27.2 m
4.	57.6	6.4	1.8	16.2 m
5.	8.4	1.2	1.5	10.5 m
6.	55.5	3.7	1.5	22.5 m
7.	25.2	1.2	1.8	37.8 m
8.	10.4	1.3	1.7	13.6 m

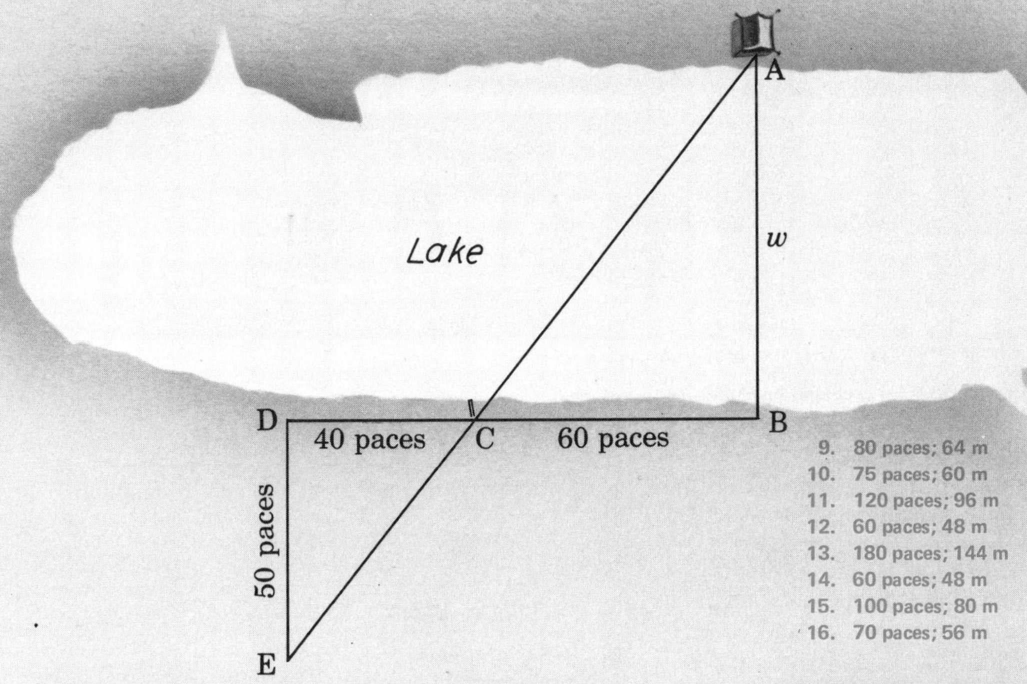

9. 80 paces; 64 m
10. 75 paces; 60 m
11. 120 paces; 96 m
12. 60 paces; 48 m
13. 180 paces; 144 m
14. 60 paces; 48 m
15. 100 paces; 80 m
16. 70 paces; 56 m

Mrs. Conrad planned to swim across the lake. First she used this technique to estimate the width of the lake.

She stood at B directly across from the tent at A. She turned left, walked 60 paces and put a stake into the ground. She continued for 40 paces. At D, she turned left and walked until she could line up C and A. This was 50 paces from D.

Triangles ABC and EDC are similar.

$$\frac{AB}{ED} = \frac{BC}{DC}$$

$$\frac{w}{50} = \frac{60}{40}$$

$$w \times 40 = 50 \times 60$$

$$w \times 40 = 3000$$

$$w = 75$$

The lake is 75 paces wide.

Each of Mrs. Conrad's paces is about 0.8 meters. The lake is about 75×0.8, or 60 meters wide.

Find the width of the lake in paces and in meters, if these were the values of BC, DC, and ED.

	BC (paces)	DC (paces)	ED (paces)
9.	16	10	50
10.	15	4	20
11.	42	14	40
12.	36	15	25
13.	40	12	54
14.	25	10	24
15.	60	9	15
16.	14	8	40

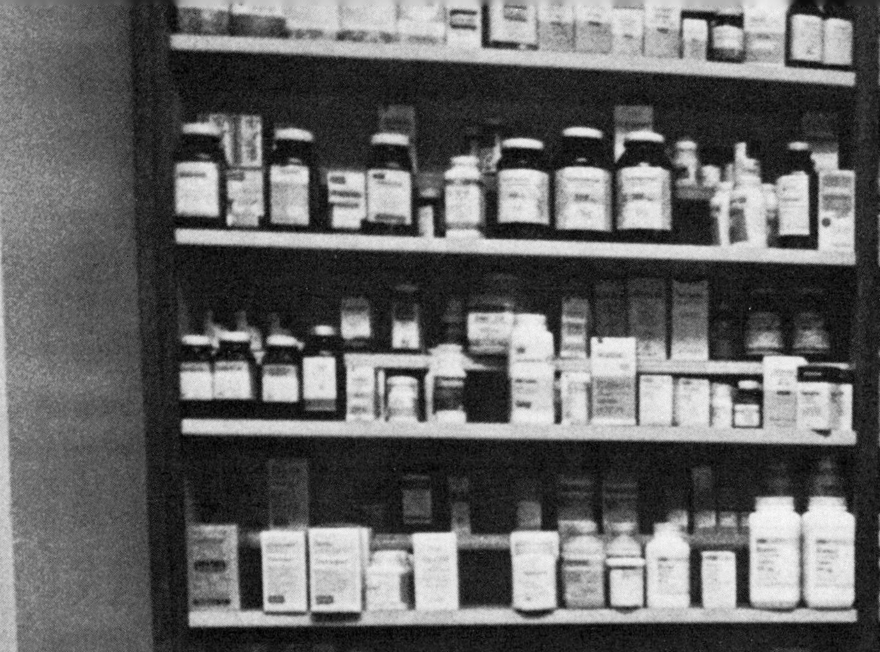

Career: Pharmacist

Career Cluster: Health

Objective: Solve problems involving ratio, proportion, and similarity.

In this lesson students solve problems involving amount of medication in solution and prices of tablets at a pharmacy.

Peggy Williams is a pharmacist. She uses proportions when filling prescriptions.

Aminophylline is a medication used to ease breathing for people with asthma. It comes in a solution.

The label says there is 250 mg of medication in 10 cm³ of solution. The prescription calls for 40 mg of medication. How much solution is needed?

$$\frac{250}{10} = \frac{40}{n} \begin{array}{l} \longleftarrow \text{Medication (mg)} \\ \longleftarrow \text{Solution (cm}^3\text{)} \end{array}$$

$n = 1.6$

1.6 cm³ of solution is needed.

Complete this table.

	Label on bottle	Amount of medication needed	Amount of solution or number of tablets needed
1.	350 mg in 10 cm³	105 mg	3 cm³
2.	0.5 g in 5 cm³	6 g	60 cm³
3.	84 mg in 3 tablets	476 mg	17 tablets
4.	1.5 g in 3 ml	0.4 g	0.8 ml
5.	160 mg in 5 cm³	800 mg	25 cm³
6.	0.15 mg in 1 tablet	3.6 mg	24 tablets
7.	3.5 mg in 5 tablets	8.4 mg	12 tablets
8.	250 mg in 10 ml	350 mg	14 ml
9.	0.4 g in 5 ml	3.4 g	42.5 ml
10.	2.4 g in 10 cm³	8.4 g	35 cm³
11.	0.6 mg in 4 tablets	4.5 mg	30 tablets
12.	1.8 g in 5 ml	9 g	25 ml

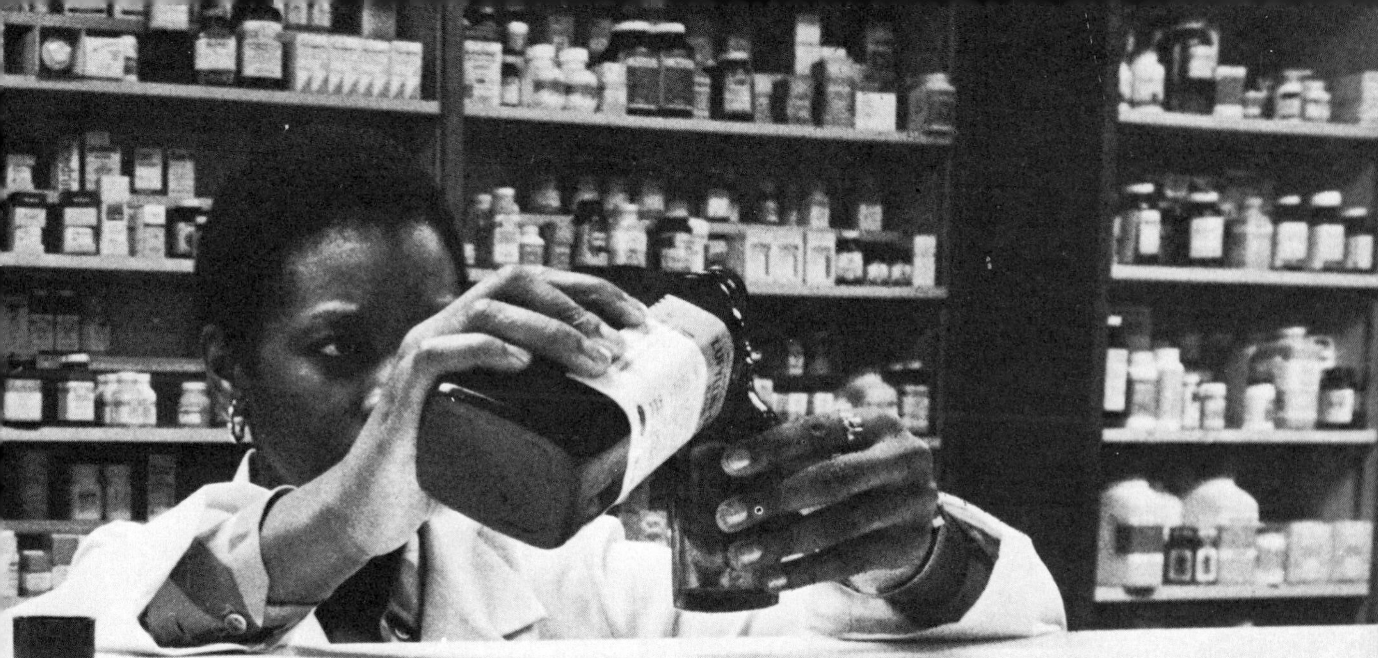

Peggy uses proportions to find the cost of prescriptions.

The pharmacy pays \$9.10 for 65 tablets of a certain medicine. A prescription calls for 24 tablets. What is the pharmacy's cost for 24 tablets?

$$\frac{9.10}{65} = \frac{n}{24} \begin{array}{l} \leftarrow \text{Dollars} \\ \leftarrow \text{Tablets} \end{array}$$

$$n = 3.36$$

The pharmacy's cost for 24 tablets is \$3.36.

Peggy will then add a fee to this cost to determine the price paid by the customer.

Complete this table. Give each answer rounded up to the next whole cent.

	Number of tablets in bottle	Pharmacy's cost for bottle	Number of tablets for prescription	Pharmacy's cost for prescription
13.	65	\$10.15	24	\$3.75
14.	50	9.02	36	\$6.50
15.	100	20.50	20	\$4.10
16.	56	13.90	28	\$6.95
17.	75	12.50	35	\$5.84
18.	100	18.00	12	\$2.16
19.	50	7.15	24	\$3.44
20.	100	21.30	30	\$6.39
21.	100	42.50	45	\$19.13
22.	50	7.18	60	\$8.62
23.	85	12.35	100	\$14.53
24.	60	14.70	15	\$3.68

Career: Photographer

Career Cluster: Arts

Objective: Solve problems involving ratio, proportion, and similarity.

In this lesson students find the ground distance shown in an aerial photograph, given the focal length of the camera lens, the altitude of the airplane, and the width of the photograph.

David Meyer does aerial photography. A photograph taken from an airplane can be used to find distances on the ground.

In the diagram below, light enters the camera through the lens and strikes the film.

f is the focal length of the lens.

a is the altitude of the airplane.

w is the width of the picture.

d is the ground distance shown in the photograph.

The triangle inside the camera is similar to the triangle outside the camera. Ratios of the lengths of corresponding sides are equal to the ratio of the focal length to the altitude.

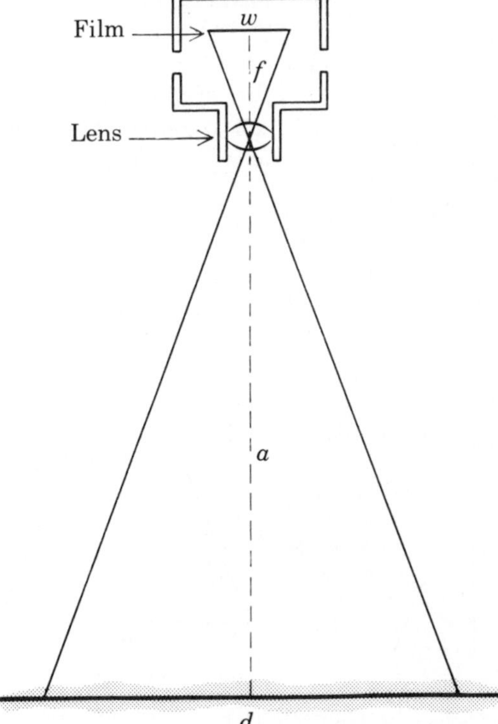

David uses this proportion to find d. Assume f is 30 centimeters, a is 10,000 meters, and w is 24 centimeters.

$$\frac{f}{a} = \frac{w}{d} \quad \begin{array}{l} \leftarrow \text{Centimeters inside camera} \\ \leftarrow \text{Meters outside camera} \end{array}$$

$$\frac{30}{10{,}000} = \frac{24}{d}$$

$$d = 8000$$

The ground distance shown in the photograph is 8000 meters.

Find the ground distance (d) in meters for these values of f, a, and w.

	f	a	w	
1.	50 cm	18,000 m	24 cm	8640 m
2.	50 cm	15,000 m	24 cm	7200 m
3.	50 cm	12,000 m	24 cm	5760 m
4.	50 cm	10,000 m	24 cm	4800 m
5.	50 cm	6000 m	24 cm	2880 m
6.	30 cm	18,000 m	24 cm	14,400 m
7.	30 cm	15,000 m	24 cm	12,000 m
8.	30 cm	12,000 m	24 cm	9600 m
9.	30 cm	10,000 m	24 cm	8000 m
10.	30 cm	6000 m	24 cm	4800 m
11.	24 cm	18,000 m	24 cm	18,000 m
12.	24 cm	15,000 m	24 cm	15,000 m
13.	24 cm	12,000 m	24 cm	12,000 m
14.	24 cm	10,000 m	24 cm	10,000 m
15.	24 cm	6000 m	24 cm	6000 m

You might ask questions like these: For a given focal length, as the altitude decreases, what happens to the ground distance? [It decreases.] For a given altitude, as the focal length decreases, what happens to the ground distance? [It increases.]

Number of test items - 12

Number missed	1	2	3	4	5	6
Percent correct	92	83	75	67	58	50

Chapter 10

A **1.** Write the ratio of knee bends to seconds.

11 knee bends in 15 seconds $\frac{11}{15}$

B **2.** Give the next ratio in this list.

$\frac{7}{15} = \frac{14}{30} = \frac{21}{45}$ $\frac{28}{60}$

C **3.** Write cross-products. Then tell whether these ratios are equal.

$\frac{15}{90}$ $\frac{12}{75}$ 15 X 75 90 X 12 not equal

D **4.** Find the missing number in this proportion.

$\frac{15}{9} = \frac{t}{21}$ $t = 35$

E **5.** Give the letter of the figure that is similar to the figure on the left. c

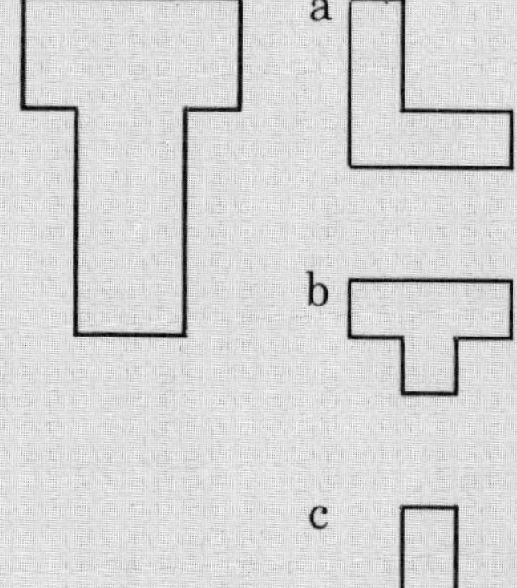

F **6.** The triangles are similar. Give 3 pairs of corresponding angles and 3 pairs of corresponding sides. ∠D and ∠H ∠B and ∠W ∠R and ∠C

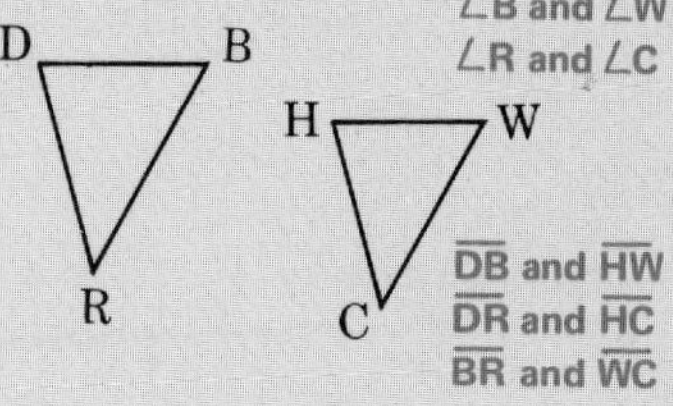

$\overline{DB}$ and $\overline{HW}$ $\overline{DR}$ and $\overline{HC}$ $\overline{BR}$ and $\overline{WC}$

G **7.** The triangles are similar. Complete these ratios of the lengths of corresponding sides. All lengths are in meters.

$\frac{56}{\square} = \frac{98}{\square}$ 40 70

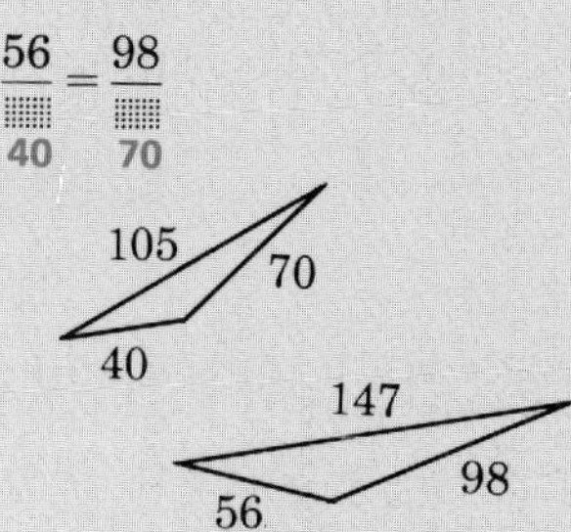

H **8.** The triangles are similar. Write a proportion and find n. All lengths are in meters. $\frac{26}{52} = \frac{24}{n}$ $n = 48$

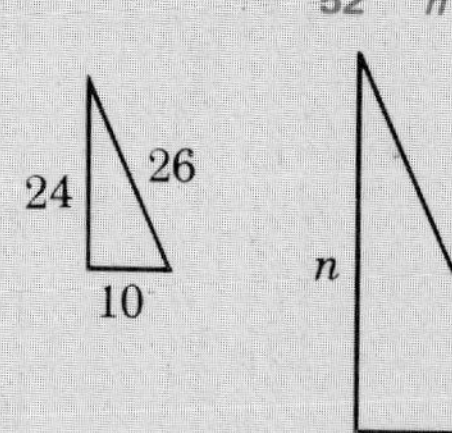

Proportions may vary. A sample is given.

9. If it takes 4 hours to drive 314 kilometers, how long does it take to drive 785 kilometers? 10 hours

10. Find h in meters. 3.2 meters

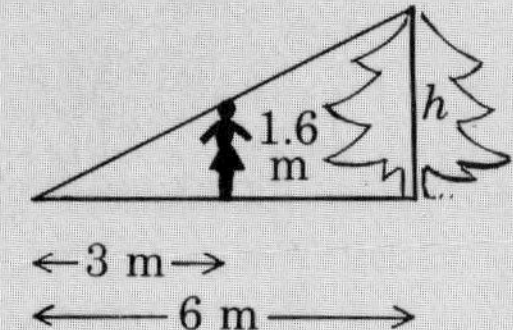

11. There are 250 mg of a medication in 10 cm^3 of solution. How much solution is needed to obtain 600 mg of the medication? 24 cm^3

12. Find d in meters if f is 30 centimeters, a is 14,000 meters, and w is 24 centimeters. 11,200 meters

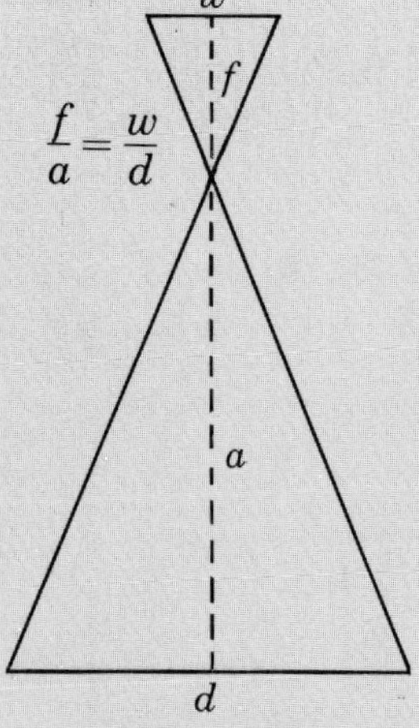

 See pages 29–30 of the *Tests and Record Forms: Duplicating Masters* for an alternate form of the Chapter 10 Test.

pretest

Number of test items - 11

Number missed	1	2	3	4	5
Percent correct	91	82	73	64	55

skill **Writing Percents and Decimals** pages 214-215

A Write 4.6% as a decimal. .046

B Write .08 as a percent. 8%

skill **Writing Percents and Fractions** pages 216-217

C Write 20% as a fraction in lowest terms. $\frac{1}{5}$

D Write $\frac{3}{4}$ as a percent. 75%

skill **Finding a Percent of a Number** pages 218-219

E Find 15% of 93. 13.95

F Find $33\frac{1}{3}$% of 27. 9

G Find .4% of 37. Round your answer to the nearest hundredth. .15

skill **Finding a Percent** pages 220-221

H 15 is what percent of 25? 60%

I 3 is what percent of 40? 7.5%

skill **Finding a Number When a Percent is Known** pages 222-223

J 6 is 30% of what number? 20

K 8 is $66\frac{2}{3}$% of what number? 12

See page T22 for additional notes on Chapter 11.

Objective: Write percents as decimals and decimals as percents.

Writing Percents and Decimals

example A Writing decimals

Write each percent as a decimal.

$49\% = .49$

$3\% = .03$

$100\% = 1.00$, or 1

$5.7\% = .057$

$.16\% = .0016$

$4\frac{1}{2}\% = 4.5\% = .045$

Percent means hundredths.

First write the numeral without the percent sign. Then move the decimal point two places to the left.

Encourage students to change a percent like $4\frac{1}{2}\%$ to a decimal without a fraction in order to make computation with the percent easier.

example B Writing percents

Write each decimal as a percent.

$.13 = 13\%$

$.04 = 4\%$

$2.9 = 290\%$

$.508 = 50.8\%$

$.001 = .1\%$

$.33\frac{1}{3} = 33\frac{1}{3}\%$

First move the decimal point two places to the right. Then write the numeral with a percent sign.

Point out that a decimal point is not placed between the whole number and the fraction.

exercises

set A

Students should know the decimal equivalents of $\frac{1}{2}$, $\frac{1}{4}$, and $\frac{3}{4}$.

Write each percent as a dcimal.

1. 9.6% .096
2. 53% .53
3. 2% .02
4. 350% 3.5
5. 270% 2.7
6. 215% 2.15
7. 32% .32
8. $6\frac{1}{2}\%$ .065
9. 1% .01
10. 605% 6.05
11. 95% .95
12. 700% 7.00, or 7
13. 8.5% .085
14. 9% .09
15. 12.7% .127
16. 99% .99
17. 80.4% .804
18. 13% .13
19. 800% 8.00, or 8
20. 6.23% .0623
21. 41% .41
22. .15% .0015
23. 5.13% .0513
24. .01% .0001
25. 147% 1.47
26. 4% .04
27. 100.5% 1.005
28. $3\frac{1}{2}\%$ .035
29. 80% .8
30. 150% 1.5
31. $1\frac{1}{4}\%$ .0125
32. 1.2% .012
33. 14% .14
34. 64% .64
35. $2\frac{1}{2}\%$ .025
36. 125% 1.25
37. .92% .0092
38. 561% 5.61
39. .9% .009
40. 35% .35
41. $7\frac{1}{4}\%$ .0725
42. 8% .08
43. 300% 3.00, or 3
44. .1% .001
45. 91.9% .919
46. 620% 6.2
47. $9\frac{1}{2}\%$ .095
48. 7% .07
49. .21% .0021
50. 4.09% .0409
51. $5\frac{1}{4}\%$ .0525
52. .3% .003
53. $6\frac{1}{4}\%$ .0625
54. 130% 1.3
55. 82% .82
56. $11\frac{1}{2}\%$ .115
57. 8.1% .081
58. .52% .0052
59. 5% .05
60. 91% .91
61. .8% .008
62. 13.2% .132
63. $1\frac{1}{2}\%$ .015
64. 79% .79
65. $\frac{1}{2}\%$ .005
66. 110% 1.1
67. 7.2% .072
68. 6% .06
69. .35% .0035
70. 56% .56
71. $8\frac{3}{4}\%$ .0875
72. 175% 1.75
73. .6% .006
74. 52.8% .528
75. 900% 9.00, or 9

set B

Write each decimal as a percent.

1.	.62	62%	**26.**	.05	5%	**51.**	.551	55.1%
2.	.06	6%	**27.**	.73	73%	**52.**	.4	40%
3.	.8	80%	**28.**	$.04\frac{1}{3}$	$4\frac{1}{3}\%$	**53.**	6.5	650%
4.	1.4	140%	**29.**	.5	50%	**54.**	.85	85%
5.	.17	17%	**30.**	8.25	825%	**55.**	.99	99%
6.	.201	20.1%	**31.**	.51	51%	**56.**	.131	13.1%
7.	.005	.5%	**32.**	.004	.4%	**57.**	.07	7%
8.	9.5	950%	**33.**	.08	8%	**58.**	$.12\frac{1}{2}$	$12\frac{1}{2}\%$
9.	.37	37%	**34.**	.411	41.1%	**59.**	.88	88%
10.	.318	31.8%	**35.**	.84	84%	**60.**	.39	39%
11.	5.01	501%	**36.**	$.66\frac{2}{3}$	$66\frac{2}{3}\%$	**61.**	.999	99.9%
12.	$.16\frac{2}{3}$	$16\frac{2}{3}\%$	**37.**	.03	3%	**62.**	.02	2%
13.	.28	28%	**38.**	.894	89.4%	**63.**	.007	.7%
14.	.04	4%	**39.**	.91	91%	**64.**	.23	23%
15.	.79	79%	**40.**	.0061	.61%	**65.**	.18	18%
16.	.923	92.3%	**41.**	4.92	492%	**66.**	3.7	370%
17.	.082	8.2%	**42.**	.29	29%	**67.**	.464	46.4%
18.	.45	45%	**43.**	.41	41%	**68.**	.56	56%
19.	.731	73.1%	**44.**	$.62\frac{1}{2}$	$62\frac{1}{2}\%$	**69.**	.626	62.6%
20.	.3	30%	**45.**	.09	9%	**70.**	.002	.2%
21.	$.37\frac{1}{2}$	$37\frac{1}{2}\%$	**46.**	7.2	720%	**71.**	.4	40%
22.	.68	68%	**47.**	.77	77%	**72.**	.11	11%
23.	.009	.9%	**48.**	.6	60%	**73.**	.01	1%
24.	.44	44%	**49.**	$.55\frac{5}{9}$	$55\frac{5}{9}\%$	**74.**	2.36	236%
25.	.008	.8%	**50.**	.0035	.35%	**75.**	1.5	150%

BREAK TIME

The people at a party are forming equal teams to play a game. When the people form groups of 2, 3, 4, 5, or 6, there is always exactly one person left.

What is the smallest number of people that could be at the party? 61 people

(The answer is the least common multiple of 2, 3, 4, 5, and 6; plus 1.)

Skill

Objective: Write percents as fractions and fractions as percents.

Writing Percents and Fractions

example C Writing fractions

Write each percent as a fraction in lowest terms.

$61\% = \frac{61}{100}$

Percent means hundredths.

$40\% = \frac{40}{100} = \frac{2}{5}$

$130\% = \frac{130}{100} = \frac{13}{10}$, or $1\frac{3}{10}$

Write the numeral as the numerator. Write 100 as the denominator. Reduce the fraction to lowest terms.

$$\frac{1}{4}\% = \frac{\frac{1}{4}}{100} = \frac{1}{4} \div 100 = \frac{1}{4} \times \frac{1}{100} = \frac{1}{400}$$

$$16\frac{2}{3}\% = \frac{16\frac{2}{3}}{100} = 16\frac{2}{3} \div 100 = \frac{50}{3} \div 100 = \frac{\overset{1}{\cancel{50}}}{3} \times \frac{1}{\underset{2}{\cancel{100}}} = \frac{1}{6}$$

example D Writing percents

Write each fraction as a percent.

$\frac{3}{5}$

$$\begin{array}{r} .60 = 60\% \\ 5\overline{)3.00} \\ -3\,0 \\ \hline 00 \end{array}$$

Divide the numerator by the denominator. Divide until the quotient is in hundredths. Write the quotient as a percent.

$\frac{3}{5} = 60\%$

$\frac{2}{3}$

$$\begin{array}{r} .66\frac{2}{3} = 66\frac{2}{3}\% \\ 3\overline{)2.00} \\ -1\,8 \\ \hline 20 \\ -18 \\ \hline 2 \end{array}$$

Divide until the quotient is in hundredths. If the remainder is not zero, write the remainder over the divisor to form a fraction.

Percents that contain a fraction such as $\frac{1}{3}$ or $\frac{2}{3}$ are usually written with a fraction rather than with a decimal.

$\frac{2}{3} = 66\frac{2}{3}\%$

exercises

set C

Write each percent as a fraction in lowest terms.

1. 7%	$\frac{7}{100}$	**26.** 75%	$\frac{3}{4}$
2. 53%	$\frac{53}{100}$	**27.** 43%	$\frac{43}{100}$
3. 10%	$\frac{1}{10}$	**28.** 103%	
4. 30%	$\frac{3}{10}$	**29.** 19%	$\frac{19}{100}$
5. 70%	$\frac{7}{10}$	**30.** $66\frac{2}{3}\%$	$\frac{2}{3}$
6. 90%	$\frac{9}{10}$	**31.** 300%	$\frac{3}{1}$, or 3
7. 67%	$\frac{67}{100}$	**32.** $12\frac{1}{2}\%$	$\frac{1}{8}$
8. 25%	$\frac{1}{4}$	**33.** 27%	$\frac{27}{100}$
9. 13%	$\frac{13}{100}$	**34.** 5%	$\frac{1}{20}$
10. 50%	$\frac{1}{2}$	**35.** 110%	$\frac{11}{10}$, or $1\frac{1}{10}$
11. 71%	$\frac{71}{100}$	**36.** 20%	$\frac{1}{5}$
12. 15%	$\frac{3}{20}$	**37.** 60%	$\frac{3}{5}$
13. $\frac{1}{2}\%$	$\frac{1}{200}$	**38.** 80%	$\frac{4}{5}$
14. 121%		**39.** 35%	$\frac{7}{20}$
15. $33\frac{1}{3}\%$	$\frac{1}{3}$	**40.** 93%	$\frac{93}{100}$
16. 89%	$\frac{89}{100}$	**41.** 81%	$\frac{81}{100}$
17. 8%	$\frac{2}{25}$	**42.** 59%	$\frac{59}{100}$
18. 14%	$\frac{7}{50}$	**43.** $11\frac{1}{9}\%$	$\frac{1}{9}$
19. 31%	$\frac{31}{100}$	**44.** 250%	$\frac{5}{2}$, or $2\frac{1}{2}$
20. 12%	$\frac{3}{25}$	**45.** $9\frac{1}{11}\%$	$\frac{1}{11}$
21. 150%		**46.** 91%	$\frac{91}{100}$
22. 2%	$\frac{1}{50}$	**47.** $83\frac{1}{3}\%$	$\frac{5}{6}$
23. $37\frac{1}{2}\%$	$\frac{3}{8}$	**48.** 107%	
24. 125%		**49.** $\frac{3}{4}\%$	$\frac{3}{400}$
25. 1%	$\frac{1}{100}$	**50.** 45%	$\frac{9}{20}$

14. $\frac{121}{100}$, or $1\frac{21}{100}$ 28. $\frac{103}{100}$, or $1\frac{3}{100}$

21. $\frac{3}{2}$, or $1\frac{1}{2}$ 48. $\frac{107}{100}$, or $1\frac{7}{100}$

24. $\frac{5}{4}$, or $1\frac{1}{4}$

set D

Write each fraction as a percent.

1. $\frac{1}{2}$	50%	**21.** $\frac{7}{8}$	$87\frac{1}{2}\%$
2. $\frac{1}{5}$	20%	**22.** $\frac{1}{4}$	25%
3. $\frac{2}{5}$	40%	**23.** $\frac{3}{4}$	75%
4. $\frac{3}{5}$	60%	**24.** $\frac{5}{6}$	$83\frac{1}{3}\%$
5. $\frac{1}{7}$	$14\frac{2}{7}\%$	**25.** $\frac{5}{4}$	125%
6. $\frac{4}{9}$	$44\frac{4}{9}\%$	**26.** $\frac{3}{7}$	$42\frac{6}{7}\%$
7. $\frac{8}{9}$	$88\frac{8}{9}\%$	**27.** $\frac{2}{3}$	$66\frac{2}{3}\%$
8. $\frac{1}{8}$	$12\frac{1}{2}\%$	**28.** $\frac{1}{15}$	$6\frac{2}{3}\%$
9. $\frac{7}{13}$	$53\frac{11}{13}\%$	**29.** $\frac{4}{5}$	80%
10. $\frac{3}{2}$	150%	**30.** $\frac{7}{12}$	$58\frac{1}{3}\%$
11. $\frac{19}{20}$	95%	**31.** $\frac{9}{16}$	$56\frac{1}{4}\%$
12. $\frac{1}{3}$	$33\frac{1}{3}\%$	**32.** $\frac{2}{7}$	$28\frac{4}{7}\%$
13. $\frac{5}{8}$	$62\frac{1}{2}\%$	**33.** $\frac{23}{100}$	23%
14. $\frac{4}{7}$	$57\frac{1}{7}\%$	**34.** $\frac{16}{15}$	$106\frac{2}{3}\%$
15. $\frac{57}{100}$	57%	**35.** $\frac{31}{90}$	$34\frac{4}{9}\%$
16. $\frac{1}{6}$	$16\frac{2}{3}\%$	**36.** $\frac{6}{19}$	$31\frac{11}{19}\%$
17. $\frac{9}{10}$	90%	**37.** $\frac{17}{30}$	$56\frac{2}{3}\%$
18. $\frac{11}{12}$	$91\frac{2}{3}\%$	**38.** $\frac{23}{45}$	$51\frac{1}{9}\%$
19. $\frac{7}{60}$	$11\frac{2}{3}\%$	**39.** $\frac{1}{200}$	$\frac{1}{2}\%$
20. $\frac{9}{40}$	$22\frac{1}{2}\%$	**40.** $\frac{3}{11}$	$27\frac{3}{11}\%$

BREAK TIME

A farmer has $2\frac{1}{2}$ stacks of hay in one field and $3\frac{1}{2}$ stacks of hay in another field.

If the farmer puts all the hay together, how many stacks will there be? 1 stack

Objective: Find a percent of a number.

Finding a Percent of a Number

example E Using a decimal

Find 7% of 4.1.

$7\% = .07$ Write the percent as a decimal.

$$\begin{array}{r} 4.1 \\ \times .07 \\ \hline .287 \end{array}$$

Multiply.

See page T22 for an alternate approach.

example F Using a fraction

Find $66\frac{2}{3}\%$ of 18.

Sometimes it is easier to write the percent as a fraction and multiply.

$66\frac{2}{3}\% = \frac{2}{3}$

$\frac{2}{3} \times 18$

$\frac{2}{\cancel{3}_1} \times \frac{\cancel{18}^6}{1} = \frac{12}{1} = 12$

example G Rounding the answer

Find $6\frac{1}{2}\%$ of 249. Round your answer to the nearest hundredth.

$6\frac{1}{2}\% = 6.5\% = .065$ Write $6\frac{1}{2}\%$ as a decimal.

Multiply.

$$\begin{array}{r} 249 \\ \times .065 \\ \hline 1\,245 \\ 14\,940 \\ \hline 16.185 \end{array}$$

Round to the nearest hundredth.

$16.185 \approx 16.19$

exercises set E

Find each number.

1. 15% of 36 5.4
2. 20% of 7 1.4
3. 6% of 29 1.74
4. 71% of 8 5.68
5. 30% of .26 .078
6. 16% of 90 14.4
7. 4.2% of 30 1.26
8. 9% of 651 58.59
9. 183% of 11 20.13
10. 4% of 65 2.6
11. 7.9% of 100 7.9
12. 25% of 36 9
13. 11% of 62 6.82
14. 80% of 28 22.4
15. 17% of 9 1.53
16. .5% of 37 .185
17. 78% of 40 31.2
18. 23% of 56 12.88
19. 12% of 71 8.52
20. 54% of 60 32.4
21. 62% of 15 9.3
22. 8% of 84 6.72
23. 4.5% of 90 4.05
24. 50% of 17 8.5
25. 1% of 235 2.35
26. $3\frac{1}{2}\%$ of 15 .525

27. 150% of 8 12

28. .7% of 91 .637

29. 13% of 84 10.92

30. 73% of 10 7.3

31. 94% of 50 47

32. 2% of 735 14.7

33. 24% of 46 11.04

34. .5% of 128 .64

35. 28% of 412 115.36

36. 88% of 50 44

37. 19% of 320 60.8

38. 75% of 400 300

39. 6.2% of 64 3.968

40. 3.5% of 54 1.89

41. 92% of 39 35.88

42. 32% of 362 115.84

43. 64% of 70 44.8

44. 80% of 55 44

45. 250% of 9 22.5

46. 9.2% of 20 1.84

47. 58% of 19 11.02

48. 77% of 13 10.01

49. 51% of 60 30.6

50. 125% of 40 50

51. 45% of 3.8 1.71

52. 6.25% of 75 4.6875

53. 48% of 1205 578.4

54. 300% of 6.75 20.25

55. 61% of .93 .5673

56. 96% of 13.8 13.248

set F

Find each number.

1. $66\frac{2}{3}$% of 30 20
2. $66\frac{2}{3}$% of 123 82
3. $33\frac{1}{3}$% of 90 30
4. $33\frac{1}{3}$% of 75 25
5. $33\frac{1}{3}$% of 27 9
6. $16\frac{2}{3}$% of 12 2
7. $16\frac{2}{3}$% of 600 100
8. $16\frac{2}{3}$% of 24 4
9. $83\frac{1}{3}$% of 72 60
10. $83\frac{1}{3}$% of 60 50
11. $83\frac{1}{3}$% of 48 40
12. $33\frac{1}{3}$% of 9000 3000
13. $66\frac{2}{3}$% of 282 188
14. 25% of 4 1
15. 25% of 16 4
16. 25% of 4000 1000
17. 25% of 36 9
18. $12\frac{1}{2}$% of 8 1
19. $12\frac{1}{2}$% of 48 6
20. $12\frac{1}{2}$% of 1600 200

set G

Find each number.
Round each answer to the nearest hundredth.

1. .3% of 126 .38
2. .05% of 24 .01
3. 29% of 5.8 1.68
4. 5.7% of 9 .51
5. 2.5% of 3.17 .08
6. 12% of 6.3 .76
7. 2.5% of 7 .18
8. 12% of 5.4 .65
9. .4% of 61 .24
10. 3.5% of 9 .32
11. 6% of 3.1 .19
12. 10% of .92 .09
13. 8% of .6 .05
14. 53% of 7.2 3.82
15. 49% of .08 .04
16. 5% of 48.7 2.44
17. 21% of 1.2 .25
18. 4.6% of 2.5 .12
19. 13% of .72 .09
20. 67% of 3.6 2.41
21. .9% of 17 .15
22. 84% of .28 .24
23. 73% of 1.52 1.11
24. 9.8% of .3 .03
25. 7% of 1.06 .07

The applications on pages 225, 228-231 may be used anytime after this lesson.

Objective: Find what percent one number is of another.

Finding a Percent

example H Whole-number percents

7 is what percent of 35?

$7 = n \times 35$ Write an equation.

$\frac{7}{35} = \frac{n \times 35}{35}$ Divide both sides by 35.

$\frac{7}{35} = n$

$$\begin{array}{r} .20 \\ 35\overline{)7.00} \\ -7\,0 \\ \hline 00 \end{array}$$

Divide until the quotient is in hundredths.

$n = .20$, or 20% Write the answer as a percent.

7 is 20% of 35. To check, substitute 20% for n in the original equation.

example I Fraction and mixed-number percents

2 is what percent of 24?

$2 = t \times 24$ Write an equation.

$\frac{2}{24} = \frac{t \times 24}{24}$ Divide both sides by 24.

$\frac{2}{24} = t$

$$\begin{array}{r} .08\frac{8}{24} = .08\frac{1}{3} \\ 24\overline{)2.00} \\ -1\,92 \\ \hline 8 \end{array}$$

Divide until the quotient is in hundredths.

$t = .08\frac{1}{3}$, or $8\frac{1}{3}\%$ Write the answer as a percent.

2 is $8\frac{1}{3}\%$ of 24.

Discuss how to write an equation for the problem: "What percent of 35 is 7?" [$n \times 35 = 7$] See exercises 38-42 in sets H and I.

exercises

set H

1. 4 is what percent of 16? 25%
2. 3 is what percent of 10? 30%
3. 18 is what percent of 24? 75%
4. 42 is what percent of 35? 120%
5. 6 is what percent of 15? 40%
6. 13 is what percent of 25? 52%
7. 15 is what percent of 5? 300%
8. 11 is what percent of 20? 55%
9. 47 is what percent of 50? 94%
10. 68 is what percent of 100? 68%
11. 10 is what percent of 8? 125%
12. 7 is what percent of 35? 20%
13. 64 is what percent of 200? 32%
14. 9 is what percent of 90? 10%
15. 46 is what percent of 92? 50%
16. 27 is what percent of 45? 60%
17. 2.4 is what percent of 30? 8%
18. 86 is what percent of 200? 43%
19. 13.3 is what percent of 19? 70%
20. 360 is what percent of 400? 90%
21. 17.5 is what percent of 7? 250%
22. 2.2 is what percent of 55? 4%
23. 27 is what percent of 20? 135%
24. 36.3 is what percent of 66? 55%
25. 12 is what percent of 80? 15%
26. 18.4 is what percent of 23? 80%
27. 3.6 is what percent of 7.2? 50%

28. 8 is what percent of 32? 25%

29. .91 is what percent of 91? 1%

30. 90 is what percent of 45? 200%

31. 72 is what percent of 96? 75%

32. 23 is what percent of 115? 20%

33. 4 is what percent of 25? 16%

34. 68 is what percent of 85? 80%

35. 57 is what percent of 57? 100%

36. 364 is what percent of 520? 70%

37. .7 is what percent of 35? 2%

38. What percent of 70 is 7? 10%

39. What percent of 18 is 9? 50%

40. What percent of 4 is 8? 200%

41. What percent of 64 is 16? 25%

42. What percent of 11 is 5.5? 50%

set I

1. 3 is what percent of 24? $12\frac{1}{2}$%

2. 15 is what percent of 18? $83\frac{1}{3}$%

3. 5 is what percent of 12? $41\frac{2}{3}$%

4. 4 is what percent of 7? $57\frac{1}{7}$%

5. 32 is what percent of 36? $88\frac{8}{9}$%

6. 4 is what percent of 3? $133\frac{1}{3}$%

7. 20 is what percent of 28? $71\frac{3}{7}$%

8. .5 is what percent of 1.1? $45\frac{5}{11}$%

9. 18 is what percent of 48? $37\frac{1}{2}$%

10. 6 is what percent of 13? $46\frac{2}{13}$%

11. 49 is what percent of 42? $116\frac{2}{3}$%

12. 100 is what percent of 300? $33\frac{1}{3}$%

13. 10 is what percent of 45? $22\frac{2}{9}$%

14. 35 is what percent of 56? $62\frac{1}{2}$%

15. 12 is what percent of 14? $85\frac{5}{7}$%

16. 5 is what percent of 400? $1\frac{1}{4}$%

17. 39 is what percent of 45? $86\frac{2}{3}$%

18. 2 is what percent of 28? $7\frac{1}{7}$%

19. 10 is what percent of 75? $13\frac{1}{3}$%

20. 5 is what percent of 16? $31\frac{1}{4}$%

21. 33 is what percent of 32? $103\frac{1}{8}$%

22. 16 is what percent of 26? $61\frac{7}{13}$%

23. 56 is what percent of 128? $43\frac{3}{4}$%

24. 2 is what percent of 32? $6\frac{1}{4}$%

25. 18 is what percent of 21? $85\frac{5}{7}$%

26. 70 is what percent of 80? $87\frac{1}{2}$%

27. 60 is what percent of 72? $83\frac{1}{3}$%

28. 17 is what percent of 51? $33\frac{1}{3}$%

29. 30 is what percent of 35? $85\frac{5}{7}$%

30. 7 is what percent of 22? $31\frac{9}{11}$%

31. 3.3 is what percent of 60? $5\frac{1}{2}$%

32. 7 is what percent of 84? $8\frac{1}{3}$%

33. 43 is what percent of 258? $16\frac{2}{3}$%

34. 14 is what percent of 21? $66\frac{2}{3}$%

35. 27 is what percent of 24? $112\frac{1}{2}$%

36. 48 is what percent of 108? $44\frac{4}{9}$%

37. 22 is what percent of 132? $16\frac{2}{3}$%

38. What percent of 15 is 10? $66\frac{2}{3}$%

39. What percent of 90 is 50? $55\frac{5}{9}$%

40. What percent of 16 is 6? $37\frac{1}{2}$%

41. What percent of 63 is 9? $14\frac{2}{7}$%

42. What percent of 57 is 19? $33\frac{1}{3}$%

The applications on pages 226-227
may be used anytime after this lesson.

Objective: Find a number when a percent of it is known.

Finding a Number When a Percent Is Known

example J

Using a decimal

22 is 40% of what number?

$22 = .4 \times n$ — Write an equation. Express the percent as a decimal.

$\frac{22}{.4} = \frac{.4 \times n}{.4}$ — Divide both sides by .4.

$\frac{22}{.4} = n$

$$\begin{array}{r} 55 \\ .4\overline{)22.0} \\ -20 \\ \hline 2\,0 \\ -2\,0 \\ \hline 0 \end{array}$$

Divide 22 by .4.

Discuss how to write an equation for the same problem stated this way: "40% of what number is 22?" [$.4 \times n = 22$] See exercises 36-40 in set J, and exercises 30-34 in set K.

$55 = n$

22 is 40% of 55.

example K

Using a fraction

17 is $33\frac{1}{3}$% of what number?

$17 = \frac{1}{3} \times w$ — Write an equation. Express the percent as a fraction.

$\frac{3}{1} \times 17 = \frac{3}{1} \times \frac{1}{3} \times w$ — Multiply both sides by the reciprocal of the fraction.

$\frac{3}{1} \times \frac{17}{1} = w$

$51 = w$

17 is $33\frac{1}{3}$% of 51.

exercises

set J

1. 9 is 20% of what number? 45
2. 24 is 32% of what number? 75
3. 19 is 95% of what number? 20
4. 90 is 4.5% of what number? 2000
5. 42 is 84% of what number? 50
6. 59 is 100% of what number? 59
7. 4 is 8% of what number? 50
8. 73 is 10% of what number? 730
9. 66 is 75% of what number? 88
10. 48 is 150% of what number? 32
11. 29 is 25% of what number? 116
12. 57 is 60% of what number? 95
13. 12 is $1\frac{1}{2}$% of what number? 800
14. 2 is .4% of what number? 500
15. 49 is 35% of what number? 140
16. 10.2 is 51% of what number? 20
17. 72 is 300% of what number? 24
18. 86 is 40% of what number? 215
19. 15 is 2.5% of what number? 600
20. 108 is 45% of what number? 240
21. 3 is $7\frac{1}{2}$% of what number? 40
22. 207 is 50% of what number? 414
23. 99 is 30% of what number? 330
24. 72 is .9% of what number? 8000
25. 39 is 25% of what number? 156
26. 91 is 65% of what number? 140
27. 63 is 12% of what number? 525

28. 13 is 4% of what number? 325

29. 45 is 250% of what number? 18

30. 14 is 70% of what number? 20

31. 6 is 6% of what number? 100

32. 58 is 200% of what number? 29

33. 108 is 3.6% of what number? 3000

34. 73.8 is 82% of what number? 90

35. 27 is 90% of what number? 30

36. 12% of what number is 96? 800

37. .25% of what number is 8? 3200

38. 2.1% of what number is 105? 5000

39. 98% of what number is 147? 150

40. .1% of what number is 13? 13,000

set K

1. 6 is $33\frac{1}{3}$% of what number? 18

2. 15 is $33\frac{1}{3}$% of what number? 45

3. 94 is $33\frac{1}{3}$% of what number? 282

4. 10 is $66\frac{2}{3}$% of what number? 15

5. 24 is $66\frac{2}{3}$% of what number? 36

6. 58 is $66\frac{2}{3}$% of what number? 87

7. 4 is $16\frac{2}{3}$% of what number? 24

8. 29 is $16\frac{2}{3}$% of what number? 174

9. 100 is $16\frac{2}{3}$% of what number? 600

10. 25 is $12\frac{1}{2}$% of what number? 200

11. 6 is $12\frac{1}{2}$% of what number? 48

12. 19 is $12\frac{1}{2}$% of what number? 152

13. 45 is $12\frac{1}{2}$% of what number? 360

14. 203 is $12\frac{1}{2}$% of what number? 1624

15. 9 is $37\frac{1}{2}$% of what number? 24

16. 21 is $37\frac{1}{2}$% of what number? 56

17. 45 is $37\frac{1}{2}$% of what number? 120

18. 2 is 25% of what number? 8

19. 31 is 25% of what number? 124

20. 28 is 25% of what number? 112

21. 115 is 25% of what number? 460

22. 72 is $33\frac{1}{3}$% of what number? 216

23. 81 is $16\frac{2}{3}$% of what number? 486

24. 65 is 25% of what number? 260

25. 14 is $12\frac{1}{2}$% of what number? 112

26. 30 is $11\frac{1}{9}$% of what number? 270

27. 16 is $133\frac{1}{3}$% of what number? 12

28. 63 is $37\frac{1}{2}$% of what number? 168

29. 56 is 50% of what number? 112

30. 50% of what number is 12? 24

31. $33\frac{1}{3}$% of what number is 37? 111

32. $66\frac{2}{3}$% of what number is 86? 129

33. $12\frac{1}{2}$% of what number is 91? 728

34. 50% of what number is 651? 1302

posttest

Number of test items - 11

Number missed	1	2	3	4	5
Percent correct	91	82	73	64	55

skill Writing Percents and Decimals pages 214-215

A Write 2.5% as a decimal. .025

B Write .326 as a percent. 32.6%

skill Writing Percents and Fractions pages 216-217

C Write 35% as a fraction in lowest terms. $\frac{7}{20}$

D Write $\frac{7}{10}$ as a percent. 70%

skill Finding a Percent of a Number pages 218-219

E Find 16% of 34. 5.44

F Find $33\frac{1}{3}$% of 21. 7

G Find 5.25% of 9. Round your answer to the nearest hundredth. .47

skill Finding a Percent pages 220-221

H 11 is what percent of 20? 55%

I 4 is what percent of 19? $21\frac{1}{19}$%

skill Finding a Number When a Percent is Known pages 222-223

J 23 is 50% of what number? 46

K 14 is $12\frac{1}{2}$% of what number? 112

Objective: Solve problems involving percent.

In this lesson students compute the amount of discount and the sale price for certain sports-equipment items.

Finding Amount of Discount and Sale Price

Phil Whitewing shopped at a sale and bought a toboggan at a 25% discount. The regular price of the toboggan was $37. How much did he save?

$37	Regular price
× .25	Percent of discount (25% = .25)
1 85	
7 40	
$9.25	Amount Phil saved

What was the sale price of the toboggan?

$37.00	Regular price
− $9.25	Amount saved
$27.75	Sale price

The amounts of the discounts are rounded to the nearest cent, rather than always being rounded *up* to the next whole cent. Stores commonly do not round amounts of money in favor of the customer.

For each item, find the amount saved. Round your answers to the nearest whole cent. Then find the sale price.

	Item	Regular price	Discount	Amount saved	Sale price
1.	Figure skates	$21.50	20%	$4.30	$17.20
2.	Hockey skates	$39.00	20%	$7.80	$31.20
3.	Hockey stick	$7.99	15%	$1.20	$6.79
4.	Skis	$159.00	10%	$15.90	$143.10
5.	Ski jacket	$44.95	20%	$8.99	$35.96
6.	Ski gloves	$22.50	30%	$6.75	$15.75
7.	Ski goggles	$18.98	30%	$5.69	$13.29
8.	Sled	$17.50	10%	$1.75	$15.75
9.	Insulated boots	$29.95	25%	$7.49	$22.46
10.	Snowmobile suit	$56.95	25%	$14.24	$42.71

Objective: Solve problems involving percent.

In this lesson students compute amounts of simple interest, total cost, and monthly interest rates for certain loans.

Finding Simple Interest

Mr. Stumfel wanted to buy a $300 stereo. He borrowed the money for 2 months at an interest rate of 2% per month. How much interest did he pay?

Use the **simple-interest** formula:

i	=	p	×	r	×	t
Interest		Principal (Amount borrowed)		Rate (Percent)		Time

$i = p \times r \times t$

$i = 300 \times 2\% \times 2$

$i = 300 \times .02 \times 2$ Write the percent as a decimal.

$i = 12.00$ Multiply.

Mr. Stumfel paid $12 interest.

If he paid back the loan in one payment, how much did Mr. Stumfel pay at the end of 2 months?

$300	Principal
+ 12	Interest
$312	Total amount paid

Mr. Stumfel paid a total amount of $312.

	Interest	Total paid
1.	$25.80	$240.80
2.	$15.75	$190.75
3.	$3.57	$122.57
4.	$22.58	$237.58
5.	$74.88	$386.88
6.	$6.25	$131.25
7.	$5.25	$180.25
8.	$21.36	$110.36
9.	$25.83	$312.83
10.	$220.05	$709.05

Monthly interest rates are given. Find the amount of interest charged on a loan to buy each item. Then find the total amount to be paid for each item.

See below.

1. Dresser: $215 at 3% for 4 months
2. Curtains: $175 at 1.5% for 6 months
3. Chair: $119 at 1% for 3 months
4. China: $215 at $1\frac{1}{2}$% for 7 months
5. Dinette set: $312 at 2% for 12 months
6. Desk: $125 at $1\frac{1}{4}$% for 4 months
7. Tiffany lamp: $175 at 1% for 3 months
8. End table: $89 at 2% for 12 months
9. Bed: $287 at 1.8% for 5 months
10. Television: $489 at 2.5% for 18 months

5%

1.5

9 ⅓

3 %

Mr. Stumfel borrowed money to buy a sofa priced at \$420. The interest for 3 months was \$31.50. What was the rate of interest?

Use this formula:

$$r = \frac{i}{p \times t} \quad \begin{array}{l} \text{— Interest} \\ \text{— Principal} \times \text{Time} \end{array}$$

Rate

$$r = \frac{i}{p \times t}$$

$$r = \frac{31.50}{420 \times 3}$$

$$r = \frac{31.50}{1260}$$ Multiply 420 and 3.

$$\begin{array}{r} .025 \\ 1260\overline{)31.500} \\ -25\ 20 \\ \hline 6\ 300 \\ -6\ 300 \\ \hline 0 \end{array}$$ Divide 31.50 by 1260.

$r = .025$, or 2.5% Write the rate as a percent.

The rate of interest was 2.5% per month.

Find the monthly interest rate charged by each company on a loan of \$1800.

11. Company A: \$81 interest for 3 months 1.5%

12. Company B: \$216 interest for 6 months 2%

13. Company C: \$90 interest for 4 months 1.25%

14. Company D: \$225 interest for 5 months 2.5%

15. Company E: \$40.50 interest for 1 month 2.25%

16. Company F: \$189 interest for 7 months 1.5%

17. Company G: \$63 interest for 2 months 1.75%

18. Company H: \$108 interest for 6 months 1%

19. Company I: \$72 interest for 2 months 2%

20. Company J: \$648 interest for 12 months 3%

Objective: Solve problems involving percent.

In this lesson students find the cost of a lawn tractor purchased on credit.

Buying on Credit

Mr. and Mrs. Rogers used their credit card to buy a $1500 lawn tractor. They paid for the tractor in monthly payments of $150 each. They also paid a monthly finance charge of 1% per month on the unpaid balance.

Stores have various plans for buying on installment and with revolving charge accounts. You may wish to have students gather information and discuss the advantages and disadvantages of this type of buying.

What was the balance on Mr. and Mrs. Rogers' account after the first monthly payment in April?

Beginning balance	$1500
Subtract April payment	− 150
New amount	$1350
Find 1% of new amount	× .01
Finance charge	$13.50
Add finance charge and new amount	+ 1350.00
Balance	$1363.50

After the April payment the balance was $1363.50.

Complete this table to find the balance on the Rogers' account after each monthly payment. In computing the finance charge, always round your answers up to the next whole cent.

	Month	Balance	Payment	New amount	1% finance charge	Balance
	April	$1500	$150	$1350	$13.50	$1363.50
1.	May	$1363.50	$150	($1363.50 − $150)	$12.14	$1225.64
2.	June	$1225.64	$150	$1213.50 $1075.64	$10.76	$1086.40
3.	July	$1086.40	$150	$936.40	$9.37	$945.77
4.	August	$945.77	$150	$795.77	$7.96	$803.73
5.	September	$803.73	$150	$653.73	$6.54	$660.27
6.	October	$660.27	$150	$510.27	$5.11	$515.38
7.	November	$515.38	$150	$365.38	$3.66	$369.04
8.	December	$369.04	$150	$219.04	$2.20	$221.24
9.	January	$221.24	$150	$71.24	$.72	$71.96
10.	February	$71.96	$71.96	$0.00	$0.00	$0.00

11. What was the total amount that Mr. and Mrs. Rogers paid in finance charges? $71.96

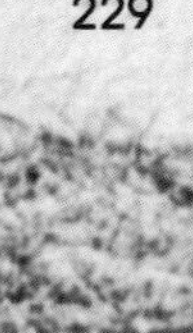

Objective: Solve problems involving percent.

In this lesson students find ohm ratings and acceptable ranges for resistors.

Career: Television Repair Person

Career Cluster: Trades

Kathy Krajenke is a television repair person. Part of her job is to test resistors in television sets to see if they have acceptable ohm ratings.

Resistors control the flow of electricity. The greater the ohm rating of a resistor, the slower the flow of electrical current through the resistor. Each resistor has colored bands that show its ohm rating. The code for the colored bands is in these tables.

Digit bands	
Brown (BR)	1
Red (R)	2
Orange (O)	3
Yellow (Y)	4
Green (G)	5
Blue (B)	6
Violet (V)	7
Gray (GY)	8
White (W)	9
Black (BK)	0

Factor band	
Gray (GY)	÷ 100
Gold (GD)	÷ 10
Black (BK)	÷ 1
Brown (BR)	× 10
Red (R)	× 100
Orange (O)	× 1000
Yellow (Y)	× 10,000
Green (G)	× 100,000
Blue (B)	× 1,000,000

Tolerance band	
No band	± 20%
Silver (S)	± 10%
Gold (GD)	± 5%
Red (R)	± 2%

Some resistors have a fifth band that gives the reliability rating. For the purposes of this lesson, the fifth band can be ignored.

The first two bands form a two-digit number.

The factor band tells you to multiply or to divide by a certain multiple of 10.

The tolerance band gives the possible percent of variation in the ohm rating.

The ohm rating of this resistor is 5.2 ohms, ± 10%.

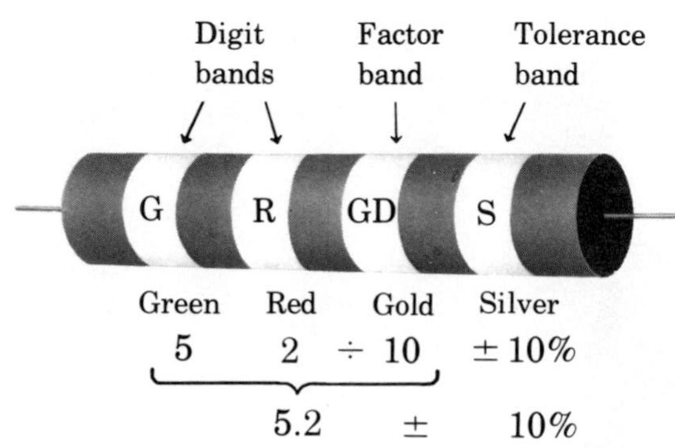

To find the acceptable range for this resistor, first find 10% of 5.2. Add 10% to 5.2. Then subtract 10% from 5.2.

10% of 5.2 is .52.

$$\begin{array}{r} 5.2 \\ +\ .52 \\ \hline 5.72 \end{array} \qquad \begin{array}{r} 5.20 \\ -\ .52 \\ \hline 4.68 \end{array}$$

The acceptable ohm rating for the resistor is between 4.68 ohms and 5.72 ohms.

Give the ohm rating and the acceptable range for each resistor.

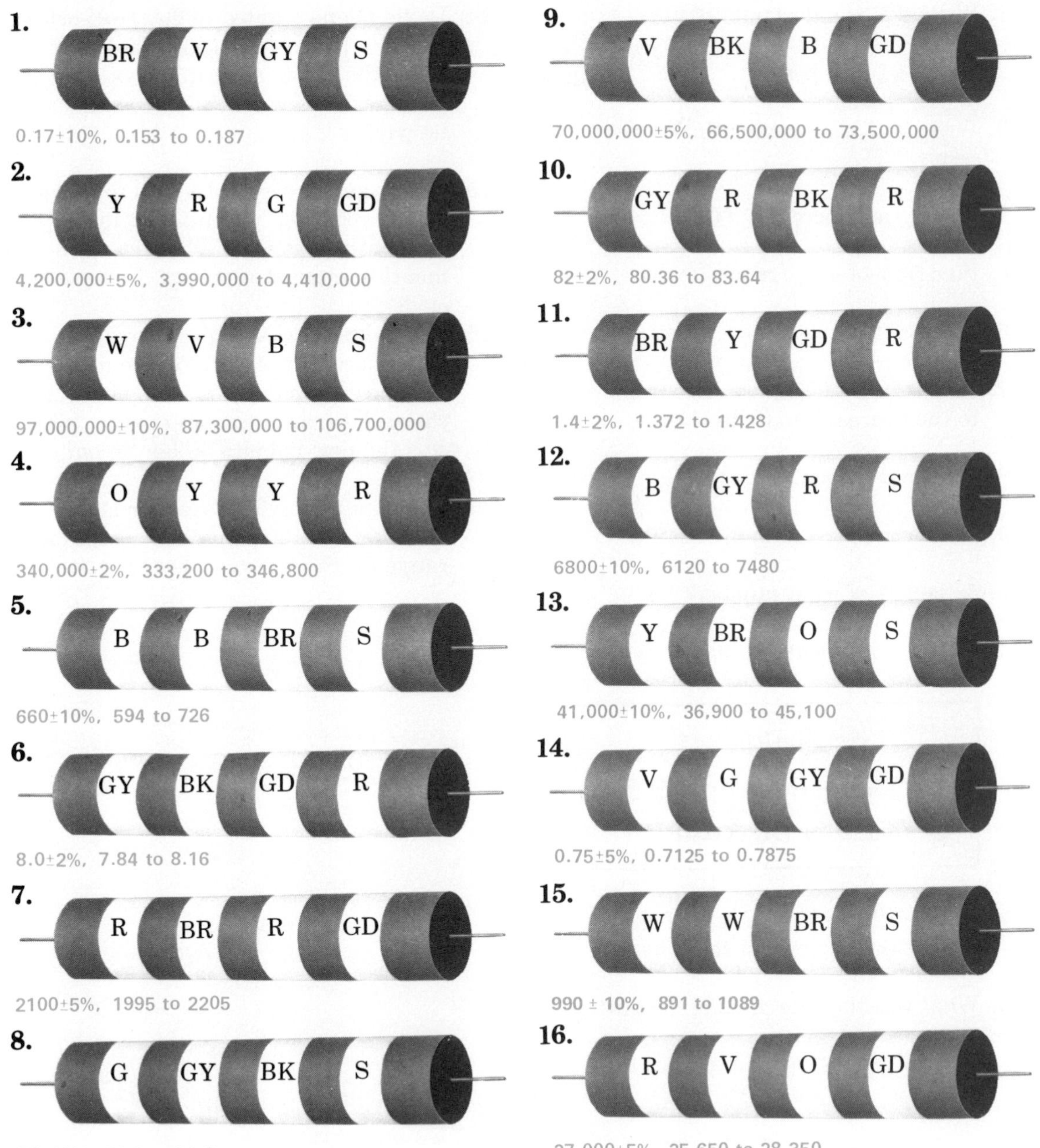

Number of test items - 17

Number missed	1	2	3	4	5	6	7	8
Percent correct	94	88	82	76	71	65	59	53

Chapter 11

A **1.** Write 2% as a decimal. .02

B **2.** Write .91 as a percent. 91%

C **3.** Write 75% as a fraction in lowest terms. $\frac{3}{4}$

D **4.** Write $\frac{1}{7}$ as a percent. $14\frac{2}{7}\%$

E **5.** Find 58% of 42. 24.36

F **6.** Find $66\frac{2}{3}\%$ of 90. 60

G **7.** Find 3.2% of 1.71. Round your answer to the nearest hundredth. .05

H **8.** 6 is what percent of 24? 25%

I **9.** 26 is what percent of 30? $86\frac{2}{3}\%$

J **10.** 52 is 65% of what number? 80

K **11.** 45 is $33\frac{1}{3}\%$ of what number? 135

> Sale
> Mittens – Regular $9.50
> 25% Discount

12. How much did Emma save if she bought the mittens on sale? $2.38

13. What was the sale price of the mittens? $7.12

14. David Glenn wanted to buy tires priced at $250. He borrowed the money for 6 months at an interest rate of 1.5% per month. How much interest did he pay? $22.50

15. Mr. Rugeles borrowed $1200 to buy a dining room set. The interest for 12 months was $288. What was the monthly interest rate? 2%

16. The balance on Ms. Blackhorse's charge account was $135. She made a $20 monthly payment. Then she was charged 1% for a finance charge. What was the new balance on her account? $116.15

17. The ohm rating for a resistor is 16.3 ohms, ±10%. Give the acceptable range for the resistor. 14.67 to 17.93

 See pages 31–32 of the *Tests and Record Forms: Duplicating Masters* for an alternate form of the Chapter 11 Test.

pretest

Number of test items - 11

Number missed	1	2	3	4	5
Percent correct	91	82	73	64	55

skill Finding the Mean page 235

A Find the mean height in centimeters for these students. Round the answer to the nearest tenth. 168.3 cm

172 168 163 180 172 178
160 154 167 172 165

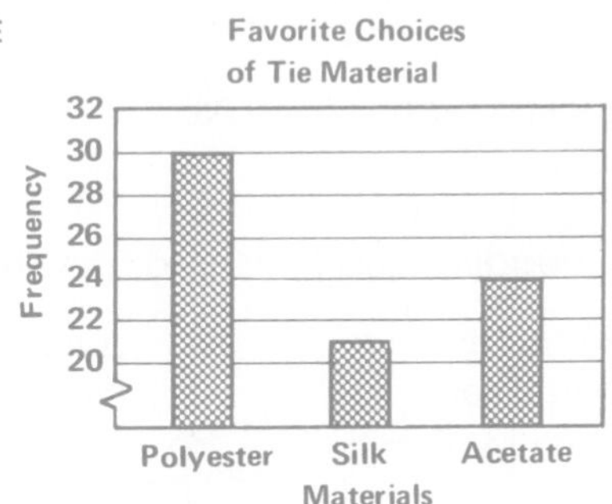

skill Finding the Median and the Mode pages 236–237

B Find the median height in centimeters for the set of data in item A. 168 cm

C Find the mode height in centimeters for the set of data in item A. 172 cm

skill Reading and Making a Bar Graph pages 238–239

D On which days were more than 24 ties sold?

Tie Sales

Number of ties sold: 28, 27, 26, 25, 24, 23, 22

Day: Mon., Tues., Wed.

Monday, Wednesday

E Make a bar graph using this frequency table.
See above.

Favorite Choices
of Tie Materials

Material	Frequency (Number of times chosen)
Polyester	30
Silk	21
Acetate	24

Pretest continued on page 234.

See page T23 for additional notes on Chapter 12.

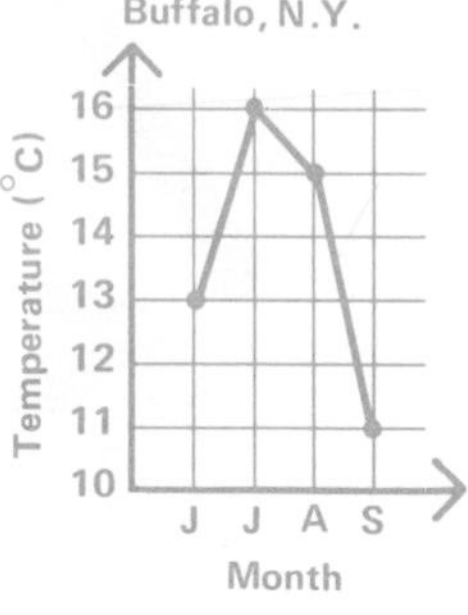

J

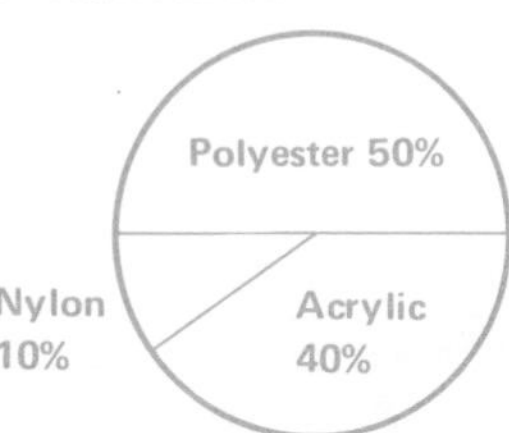

Pretest continued from page 233.

skill Reading and Making a Line Graph pages 240-241

F Find the average snowfall for Buffalo in March. 30 cm

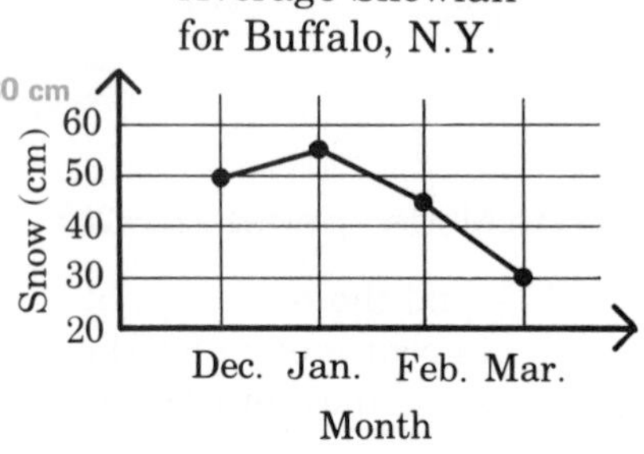

G Make a line graph to show the average monthly temperature for Buffalo from June to September.

June 13°C
July 16°C
August 15°C
September 11°C

See above.

skill Reading a Circle Graph pages 242-243

H Which ingredient would be used in greater quantity than the others to make dry concrete mix? Gravel

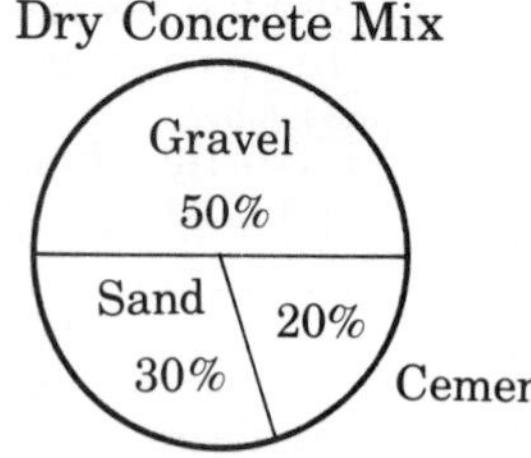

I Use the circle graph in item H to find how much gravel is needed to make 120 kilograms of dry concrete mix. 60 kg

skill Making a Circle Graph pages 244-245

J Draw a circle and construct a central angle of 105°. See above.

K Construct a circle graph to show the percent of each fiber that makes up this fabric blend. See above.

Fabric Blend		Central angle
Polyester	50%	180°
Acrylic	40%	144°
Nylon	10%	36°

Objective: Find the mean for a set of statistics.

Finding the Mean

example A Finding mean

Find the mean weight in kilograms for these students.

40 52 60 96 39 83

The average of a set of data is called the **mean.** To find the mean, first add the items.

$$\begin{array}{r} 40 \\ 52 \\ 60 \\ 96 \\ 39 \\ +83 \\ \hline 370 \end{array} \longleftarrow \text{Sum of items}$$

Then divide the sum by the number of items. Round the answer to the nearest tenth.

Number of items → 6; Sum of items → 370.00; Mean → 61.7

$$6\overline{)370.00} = 61.66 \approx 61.7$$

The mean weight is 61.7 kilograms.

exercises

set A

Find the mean for each set of data.
Round each answer to the nearest tenth.

1. 10 3 12 7 — 8
2. 24 28 16 17 — 21.3
3. 284 267 225 213 — 247.3
4. 387 963 435 172 — 489.3
5. 9 16 12 7 4 2 — 8.3
6. 13 23 25 16 18 20 — 19.2
7. 24 86 71 82 92 71 — 71
8. 16 38 92 75 43 67 — 55.2
9. 7 8 21 32 17 9 — 15.7
10. 46 45 32 37 39 51 — 41.7
11. 87 81 75 76 92 88 — 83.2
12. 95 43 67 88 76 79 — 74.7
13. 135 97 98 101 156 123 — 118.3
14. 109 132 145 168 173 198 — 154.2
15. 256 259 213 298 251 207 — 247.3
16. 916 102 168 521 798 812 — 552.8
17. 17 16 19 28 12 11 15 19 — 17.1
18. 28 25 23 17 34 27 26 25 — 25.6
19. 105 196 173 98 117 95 128 189 — 137.6
20. 207 123 58 396 148 275 312 251 — 221.3

Additional exercises may be given by assigning several rows as one exercise.

Objective: Find the median and the mode for a set of statistics.

Finding the Median and the Mode

example B Finding median

Find the median length in millimeters for these pieces of chalk.

25 40 68 75 32 90 59
85 16 79 88 28 46

Arrange the data in order. The **median** is the middle number. It has as many numbers above it as below it.

90
88
85
79
75
68
59 ⟵ 59 is the median.
46
40
32
28
25
16

The median length is 59 millimeters.

In this set of data, there are two middle numbers. The median is halfway between these two numbers.

90
85
⟵ 84 is the median.
83
76

example C Finding mode

Find the mode of these test scores.

76 39 45 76 98 27 19
98 76 18 93 52 76 21

Arrange the data in order. The **mode** is the number appearing most often.

98
98
93
76
76
76 ⟵ 76 is the mode.
76
52
45
39
27
21
19
18

The mode test score is 76.

For a particular set of data, there may be no mode, as well as two or more modes.

1. 1, 7
2. 2, 8
3. 3
4. 5
5. 16
6. 93
7. 359
8. 768
9. 12
10. 35
11. 178
12. 984
13. 9
14. 16
15. 76
16. 201
17. 3213
18. 8762, 8769
19. 12
20. 75
21. 19
22. 58, 76
23. 29
24. 375
25. 8791

exercises

set B

You might have students also find the mean for each set of data. Have them round their answers to the nearest tenth if necessary. The mean for each set is shown below in parentheses.

Find the median for each set of data.

1. 8 7 6 1 1 3 7 6 (4.7)

2. 9 8 1 2 2 5 8 5 (5)

3. 7 8 4 3 2 9 3 6 5 (5.3)

4. 8 4 7 9 5 5 5 7 6 (6.3)

5. 12 16 16 19 30 16 25 16 (19.1)

6. 75 93 93 16 89 93 72 89 (75.9)

7. 359 357 351 358 359 359 350 358 (356.1)

8. 769 768 793 772 768 791 768 769 (775.6)

9. 12 39 46 49 25 23 12 12 24 (27.3)

10. 35 37 37 35 32 35 39 38 36 (36)

11. 178 177 175 178
178 174 171 175 176 (175.8)

12. 986 981 986 984
988 984 987 984 985 (985)

13. 9 3 6 12 15 4 9 9 2 9 (7.7)

14. 16 28 15 16 15 28 27 16 12 16 (19.2)

15. 98 76 59 76 98 76 79 78 77 77 (79.7)

16. 210 216 215 201 200
209 201 206 208 208 (207.3)

17. 3167 3109 3213 3217 3213
3189 3192 3068 3105 3189 (3163.7)

18. 8762 8763 8761 8762 8769
8760 8772 8769 8705 8762 (8758.1)

19. 16 19 18 14 12 10 16
12 16 12 11 19 12 18 15 (14.6)

20. 58 75 63 72 54 75 67
74 63 72 79 75 75 78 73 (70)

21. 19 17 16 21 28 19 25 19
16 23 21 19 16 20 21 19 (20)

22. 12 36 92 95 47 58 76 58 58
76 20 76 62 91 87 62 (62.9)

23. 36 29 38 32 25 23 39 45 31
37 29 20 31 36 29 38 40 43
28 32 (33.1)

24. 368 374 379 362 375 371 376
375 368 371 369 375 375 368
365 371 379 371 (371.8)

25. 8719 8907 8019 8791 8279 8709
8018 8792 8297 8719 8710 8017
8791 8931 8139 8791 8718
8718 (8549.8)

set C

1–25. Find the mode for each set of data in set B. See above

Fill in the missing digits.

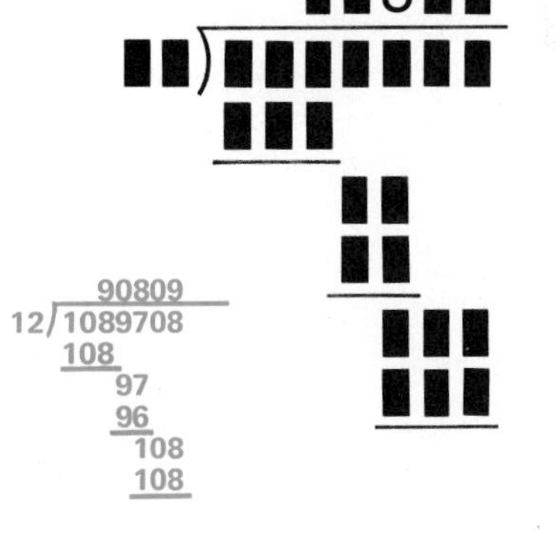

Skill

Objective: Read and make a bar graph.

Reading and Making a Bar Graph

example D Reading a bar graph

Which kinds of television shows were chosen as a favorite by 50 or more students?

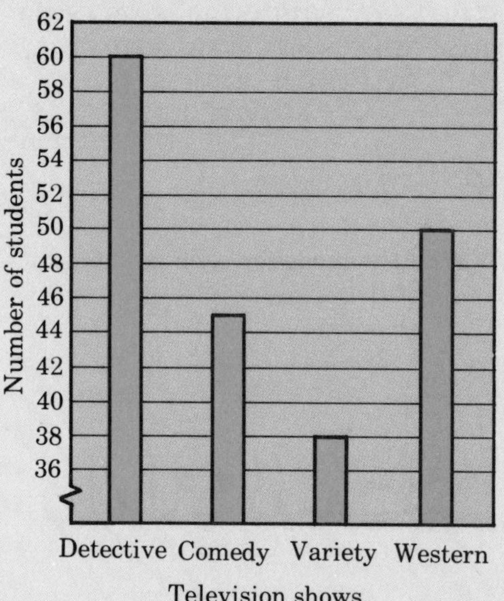

Detective and western shows were chosen as favorites by 50 or more students.

Discuss with students how the choice of scale can make differences in heights of bars more or less dramatic.

example E Making a bar graph

Make a **bar graph** for this frequency table.

Choice of Favorite Color
by 250 Students

Color	Frequency (Number of times chosen)
Blue	50
Pink	45
Red	54
Orange	49
Yellow	52

First draw and label a vertical scale to show frequencies. The break in the vertical scale shows that the frequencies between 0 and 44 have been omitted. Next draw and label a horizontal scale to show colors.

Then draw bars to show the number of times each color was chosen, and write a title for the graph.

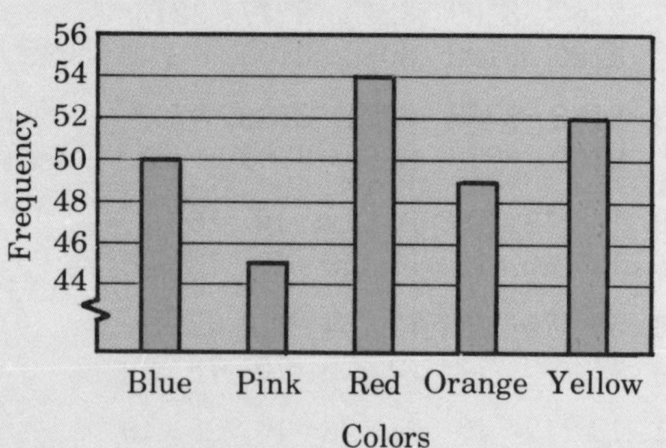

exercises

set D

Use this bar graph for exercises 1–14.

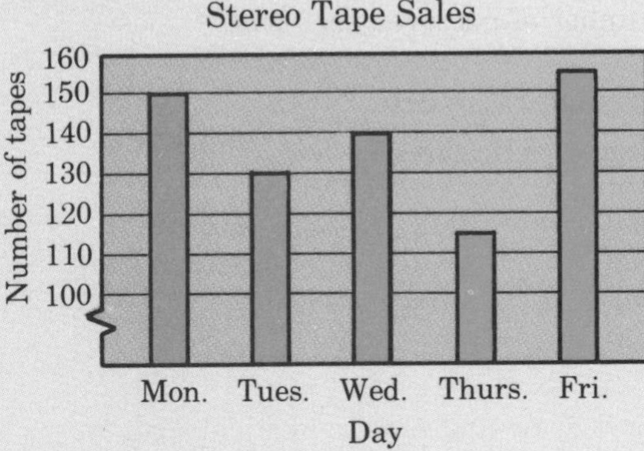

How many stereo tapes were sold on

1. Monday? 150 tapes
2. Tuesday? 130 tapes
3. Wednesday? 140 tapes
4. Thursday? 115 tapes
5. Friday? 155 tapes

On which days were

6. more than 130 stereo tapes sold? Mon., Wed., Fri.
7. 120 or more stereo tapes sold? Mon., Tues., Wed., Fri.
8. 140 or more stereo tapes sold? Mon., Wed., Fri.
9. fewer than 130 stereo tapes sold? Thurs.
10. 150 or fewer stereo tapes sold? Mon., Tues., Wed., Thurs.
11. 130 or fewer stereo tapes sold? Tues., Thurs.

Were more stereo tapes sold on

12. Monday or Wednesday? Monday
13. Tuesday or Thursday? Tuesday
14. Wednesday or Friday? Friday

set E

Make a bar graph for each frequency table.

See additional answers beginning on page T41.

1. Choice of Favorite Sport

Sport	Frequency
Tennis	40
Hockey	36
Soccer	34
Baseball	44
Football	46

2. Choice of Favorite Subject

Subject	Frequency
Math	60
English	56
Spanish	44
Science	50
History	46
French	44

3. Mathematics Test Scores

Test scores	Frequency
95	15
85	25
80	50
75	30
70	20
60	15

You may wish to include some questions that require computation, such as: "How many more stereo tapes were sold on Monday than on Tuesday?" [20 more tapes]

Skill

Objective: Read and make a line graph.

Reading and Making a Line Graph

example F Reading a line graph

How many millions of farms were there in 1960?

Number of Farms

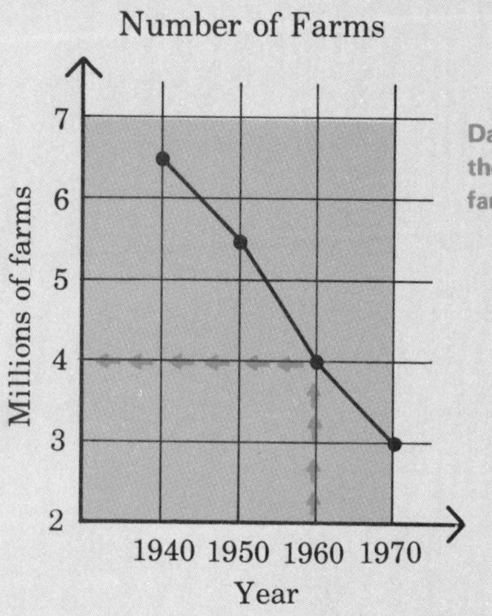

Data is rounded to the nearest 500,000 farms.

Locate 1960 on the horizontal scale. Move up to the point on the graph. Then move left to the number on the vertical scale.

The vertical scale shows that there were 4 million farms in 1960.

A line graph such as this is sometimes called a "broken line graph." It is similar to a bar graph and is not a linear function.

Note that here, too, the choice of scale can make the same data appear to be a whopping increase or simply a moderate increase.

example G Making a line graph

Make a **line graph** to show the average number of hectares per farm.

Average Farm Size

Year	Hectares
1940	70
1950	90
1960	120
1970	150

First draw and label a vertical scale to show the number of hectares. Notice that the vertical scale does not have to start at zero. Next draw and label a horizontal scale to show years.

Find a line for 1940 and one for 70. Locate a point where they meet. Then locate the points for the other years. Connect the points with a line.

Write a title for the graph.

Average Farm Size

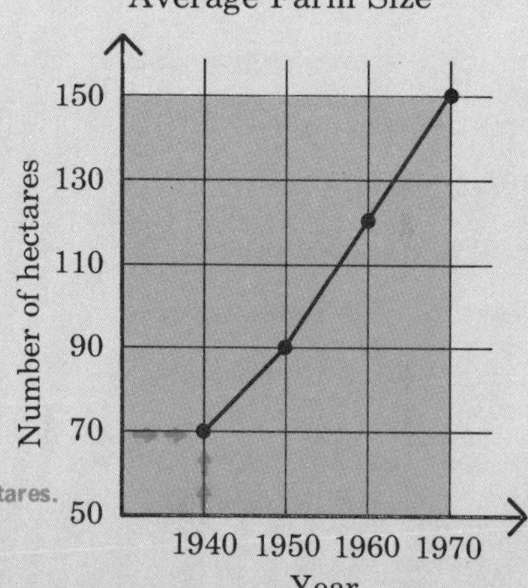

Data is rounded to the nearest 10 hectares.

1 hectare = 10,000 m^2

One hectare is about the area of two football fields.

exercises

set F

Exercises 1, 2, 3 may be done on one graph as an additional problem.

Use this line graph for exercises 1–13.

Data is rounded to the nearest 25 minutes.

Length of First Day Each Month

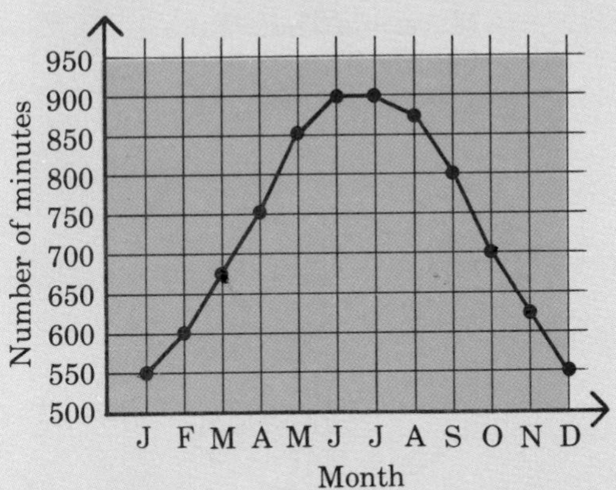

During which months does the graph show the first day to be

1. longer than 750 minutes?
   May, June, July, Aug., Sept.
2. shorter than 700 minutes?
   Jan., Feb., Mar., Nov., Dec.
3. 800 or more minutes?
   May, June, July, Aug., Sept.
4. 750 or fewer minutes?
   Jan., Feb., Mar., Apr., Oct., Nov., Dec.
5. shorter than 600 minutes?
   Jan., Dec.
6. longer than 850 minutes?
   June, July, Aug.
7. 700 or more minutes?
   Apr., May, June, July, Aug., Sept., Oct.

Was the first day longer in

8. March or October?
   October
9. May or September?
   May
10. April or October?
    April
11. June or August?
    June
12. February or November?
    November
13. How long was the first day of each month?

13. J-550, F-600, M-675, A-750, M-850, J-900, J-900, A-875, S-800, O-700, N-625, D-550

The answers in minutes are given above. You might also have students give the answers in hours.

set G

Make a line graph for each set of data.

1. Graduates in Law

Data is rounded to nearest 1000 graduates.

Year	Number of graduates
1955	8000
1960	9000
1965	12,000
1970	15,000

2. Graduates in Medicine

Data is rounded to nearest 500 graduates.

Year	Number of graduates
1950	5500
1955	7000
1960	7000
1965	7500
1970	8500

3. Graduates in Engineering

Data is rounded to nearest 5000 graduates.

Year	Number of graduates
1950	60,000
1955	30,000
1960	45,000
1965	50,000
1970	65,000

4. School Expenditures

Data is rounded to nearest 5 billion dollars.

Year	Billions of dollars
1970	70
1971	75
1972	85
1973	90
1974	95

1.

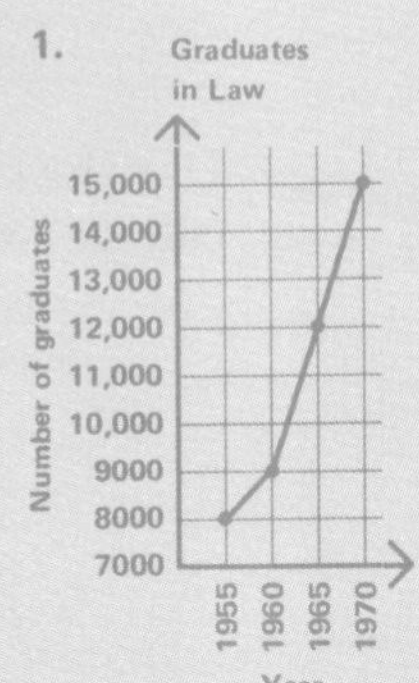

2.

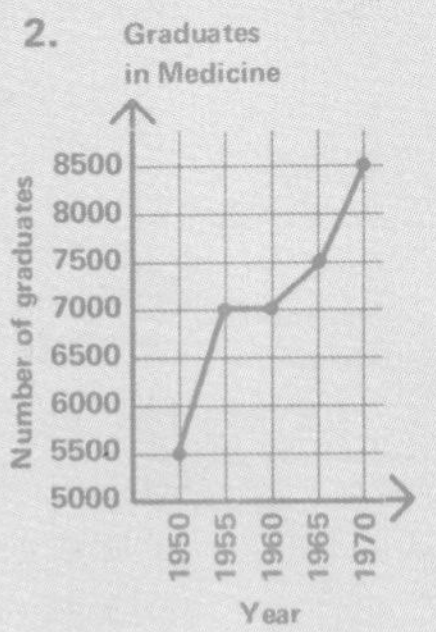

3.

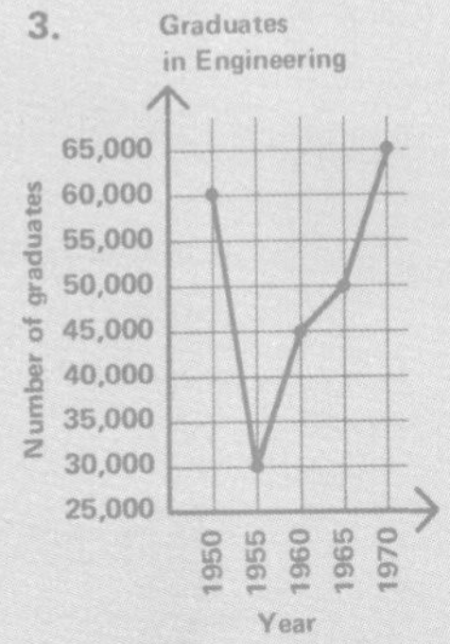

4.

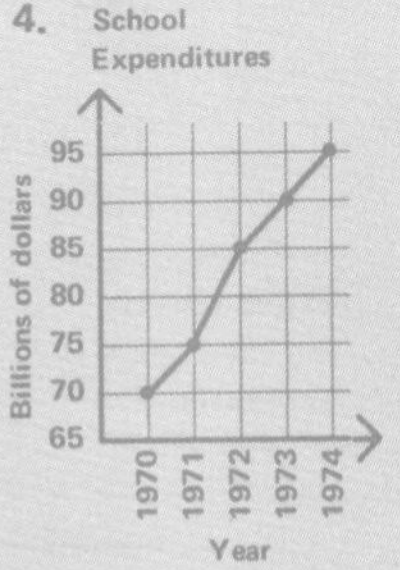

The applications on pages 248–253 may be used anytime after this lesson.

Objective: Read a circle graph.

Reading a Circle Graph

example H Reading and comparing percents

Use the **circle graph** to tell which college expense is the greatest.

Community College Expense

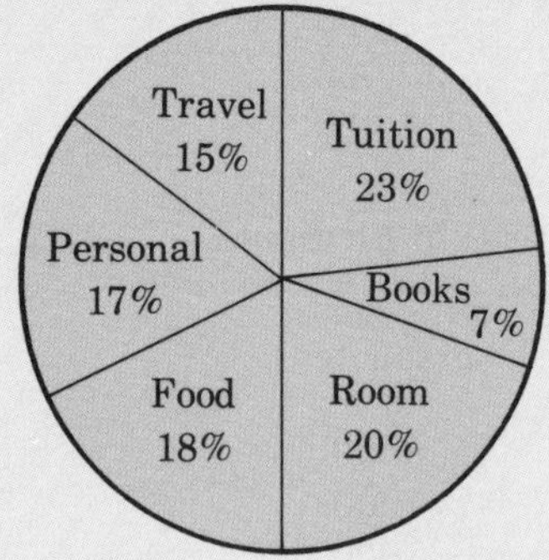

The section of the circle graph showing tuition is largest; therefore, tuition is the greatest expense at a community college.

example I Reading and finding a percent of a given total

Use the circle graph in example H to find how much money is spent on tuition if the total college expenses are $2400 for a year.

Find 23% of $2400.

$.23 \times 2400 = 552$ Write 23% as a decimal and multiply.

Tuition at a community college is $552 per year.

exercises

set H

Use this graph for exercises 1–11.

Materials That Make Up the Human Body

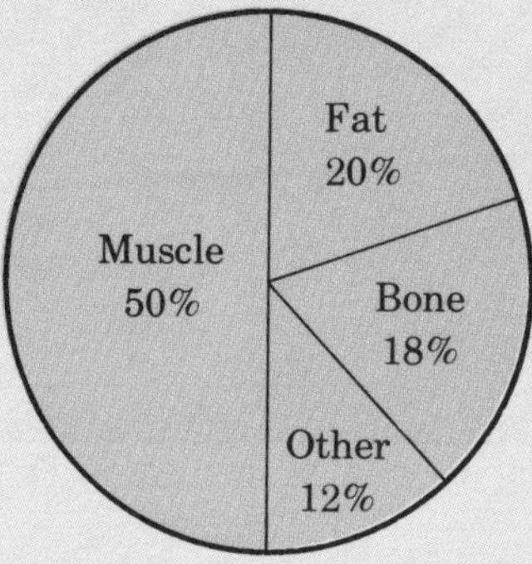

Which material makes up

1. the greatest part of the human body? Muscle
2. 50% of the human body? Muscle
3. 18% of the human body? Bone
4. 20% of the human body? Fat

Which materials make up

5. 10% or more of the human body? Muscle, Fat, Bone, Other
6. less than 50% of the human body? Fat, Bone, Other
7. more than 35% of the human body? Muscle
8. 20% or less of the human body? Fat, Bone, Other

Which of these materials make up the greater part of the human body?

9. Muscle or fat Muscle
10. Bone or muscle Muscle
11. Fat or bone Fat

In exercise 5, "Other" is listed because it is shown as more than 10% on the graph. However, each of the items comprising the other materials may be less than 10% of the human body.

set I

Use the circle graph in set H for exercises 1–4.

1. If a student weighed 90 kg, about how much of the body weight is

a. fat? 18 kg

b. bone? 16.2 kg

c. muscle? 45 kg

d. other? 10.8 kg

2. If a student weighed 55 kg, about how much of the body weight is

a. fat? 11 kg

b. bone? 9.9 kg

c. muscle? 27.5 kg

d. other? 6.6 kg

3. If a student weighed 82 kg, about how much of the body weight is

a. fat? 16.4 kg

b. bone? 14.76 kg

c. muscle? 41 kg

d. other? 9.84 kg

4. If a student weighed 64 kg, about how much of the body weight is

a. fat? 12.8 kg

b. bone? 11.52 kg

c. muscle? 32 kg

d. other? 7.68 kg

Use the circle graph in example H for exercises 5–7.

5. If the total community college expenses are \$2400 per year, about how much money is spent on

a. books? \$168

b. room? \$480

c. food? \$432

d. travel? \$360

6. If the total community college expenses are \$3000 per year, about how much money is spent on

a. tuition? \$690

b. books? \$210

c. room? \$600

d. food? \$540

e. travel? \$450

7. If the total community college expenses are \$2700 per year, about how much money is spent on

a. tuition? \$621

b. books? \$189

c. room? \$540

d. food? \$486

e. travel? \$405

BREAK TIME

Five of these eight purses contain a ten-dollar bill. Three contain a five-dollar bill. Two contain both.

How many contain neither? 2

Objective: Make a circle graph.

Making a Circle Graph

example J Constructing a central angle

Draw a circle and construct a central angle of 75°.

Draw segment AB.

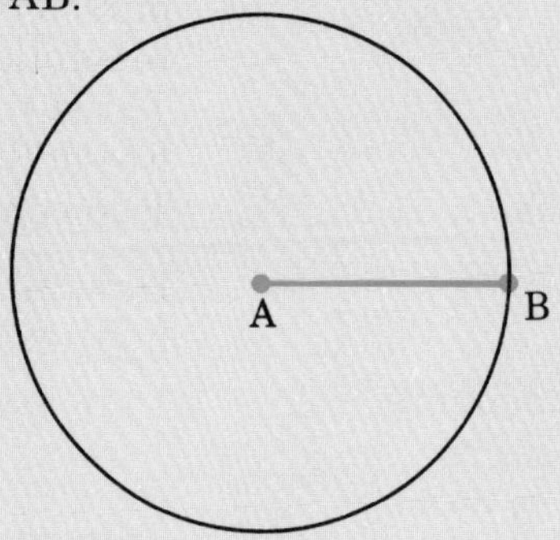

Mark point C at 75°.

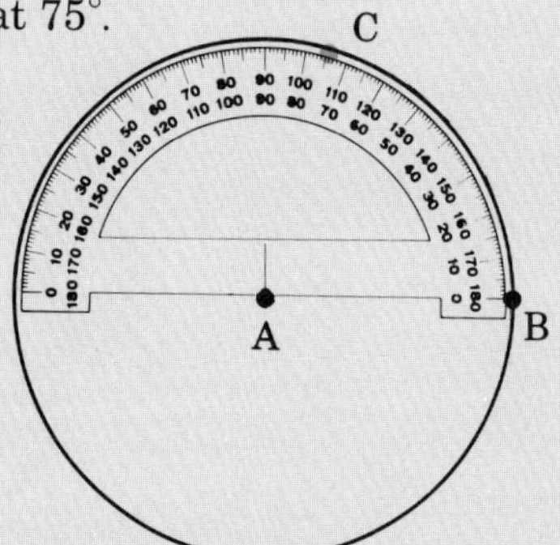

Draw segment AC.

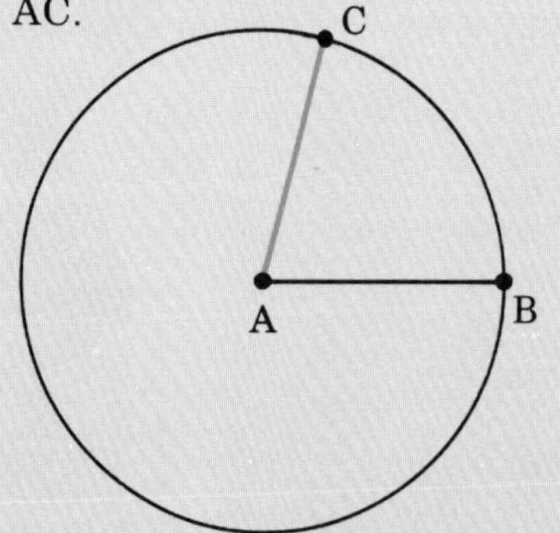

The measure of $\angle CAB$ is 75°.

example K Making a circle graph for a set of data

Construct a circle graph to show what percent of a student's budget is designated for each expense at a private school.

Travel	5%
Personal	16%
Food	14%
Room	10%
Books	3%
Tuition	52%

Write each percent as a decimal and multiply by 360° to find the size of each central angle. Round the answers to the nearest degree.

Travel	$.05 \times 360° = 18°$
Personal	$.16 \times 360° = 57.6° \approx 58°$
Food	$.14 \times 360° = 50.4° \approx 50°$
Room	$.10 \times 360° = 36°$
Books	$.03 \times 360° = 10.8° \approx 11°$
Tuition	$.52 \times 360° = 187.2 \approx 187°$

Draw a circle and construct each central angle. Label each section. Write a title for the graph.

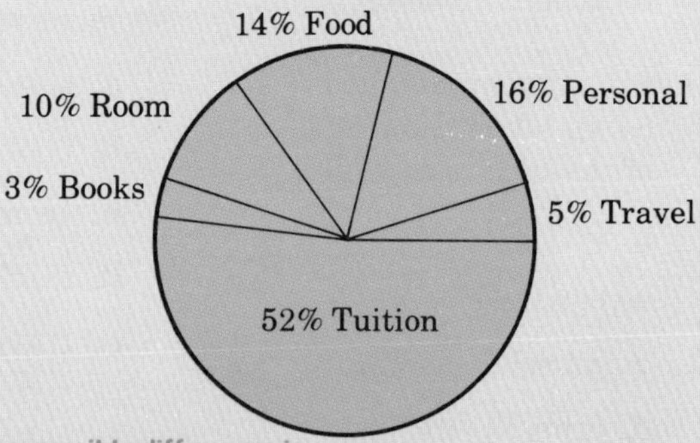

You might wish to discuss possible differences in expenses at other colleges. See page 242, example H.

exercises

set J

For each exercise, draw a circle and construct a central angle.

See additional answers beginning on page T41.

1. 65°
2. 42°
3. 125°
4. 131°
5. 90°
6. 112°
7. 158°
8. 175°
9. 234°
10. 89°

set K

Construct a circle graph to show each set of data.

1. Elements of Human Body

Oxygen	65%	234°
Carbon	18%	65°
Other	17%	61°

2. Elements of Earth's Crust

Oxygen	47%	169°
Silicon	28%	101°
Aluminum	8%	29°
Iron	5%	18°
Other	12%	43°

3. Sources of Water Pollution

Industry	60%	216°
Urban sewage	25%	90°
Agriculture	15%	54°

4. Sources of Air Pollution

Transportation	42%	151°
Fuel combustion	21%	76°
Industry	14%	50°
Solid waste	6%	22°
Other	17%	61°

5. Family Budget

Savings	15%	54°
Housing	25%	90°
Clothing	10%	36°
Food	40%	144°
Other	10%	36°

6. Earth's Water

Atlantic Ocean	23%	83°
Pacific Ocean	46%	166°
Indian Ocean	20%	72°
Arctic Ocean	4%	14°
Other	7%	25°

7. Earth's Land

Africa	20.0%	72°
Asia	30.0%	108°
Australia	5.0%	18°
North America	16.0%	58°
South America	12.0%	43°
Europe	6.5%	23°
Antarctica	9.5%	34°
Other	1.0%	4°

For set K, the measure of each central angle is given to the nearest degree. For graphs, see the additional answers beginning on page T41.

BREAK TIME

S	X	T	Y
I	U	R	E
F	O	E	O
I	V	T	N

Find as many spelled-out numbers as you can.

Start in any square and move in any direction. Do not enter the same square twice while spelling one word.

The sum of the numbers is 156.

ONE, FOUR, FIVE, SIX, TEN, FOURTEEN, SIXTEEN, FORTY, SIXTY

posttest

Number of test items - 11

Number missed	1	2	3	4	5
Percent correct	91	82	73	64	55

skill Finding the Mean page 235

A Find the mean test score for these students. Round the answer to the nearest tenth. 84.1

76 90 87 76 85 87
98 96 68 87 75

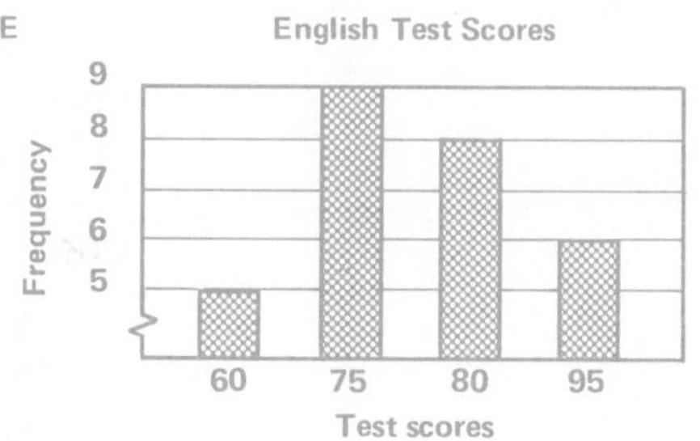

skill Finding the Median and the Mode pages 236–237

B Find the median test score for the set of data in item A. 87

C Find the mode test score for the set of data in item A. 87

skill Reading and Making a Bar Graph pages 238–239

D Which of these clubs have 18 or fewer members? Latin Club, French Club

Club Membership

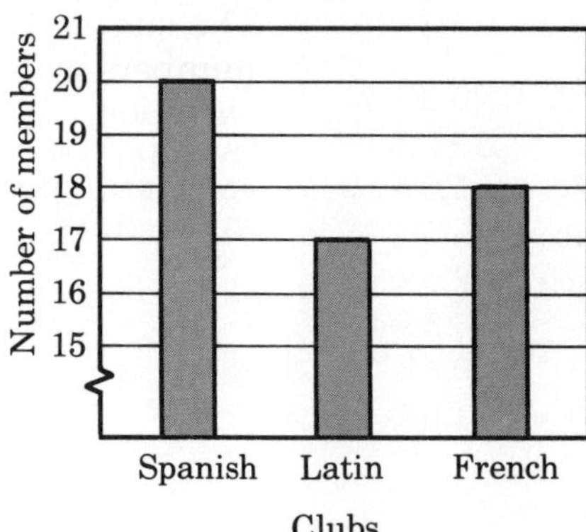

E Make a bar graph using this frequency table. See above.

English Test Scores

Test scores	Frequency
95	6
80	8
75	9
60	5

Posttest continued on page 247.

G

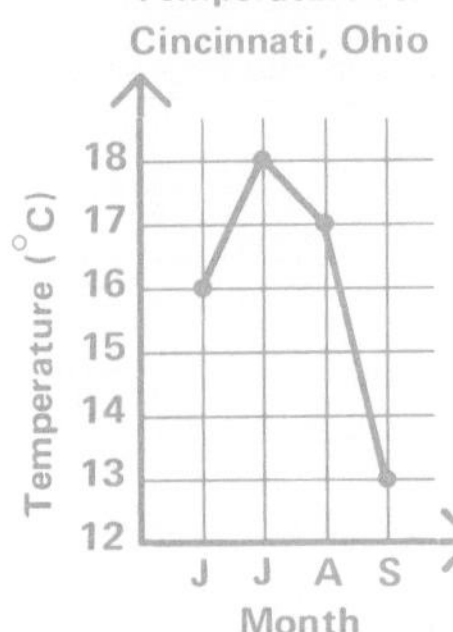

J

50°

K

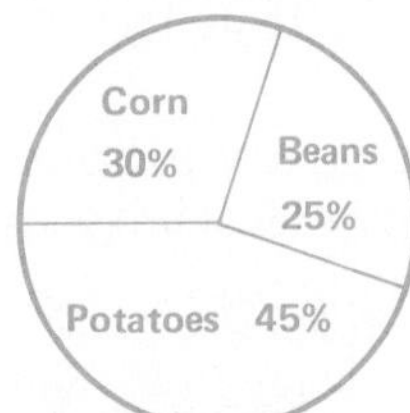

Posttest continued from page 246.

Skill Reading and Making a Line Graph pages 240-241

F Find the average snowfall for Cincinnati in January. 13 cm

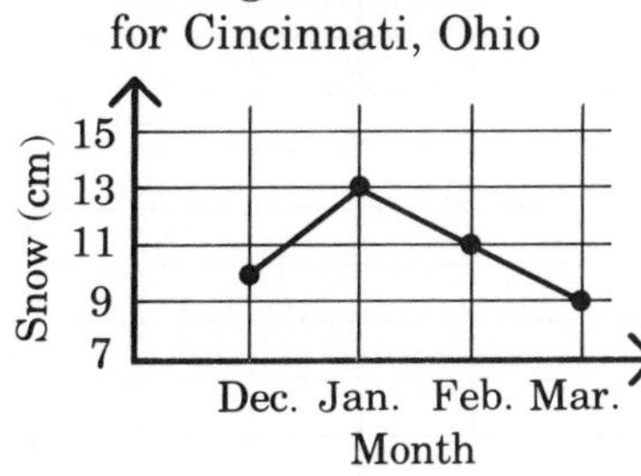

G Make a line graph to show the average monthly temperature for Cincinnati from June to September.

June 16°C
July 18°C
August 17°C
September 13°C

See above.

Skill Reading a Circle Graph pages 242-243

H Which type of book is favored by the greatest number of these students? Novel

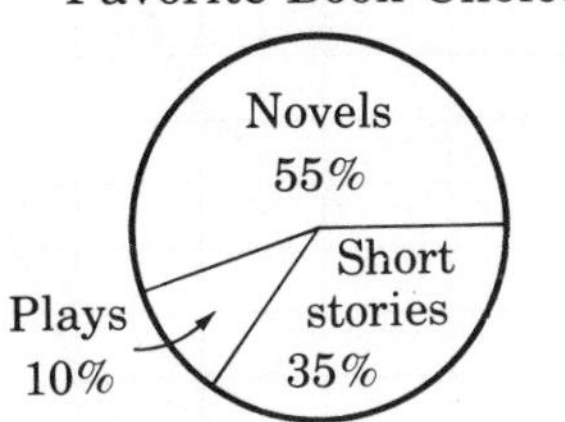

I Use the circle graph in item H to find how many of the 2500 students favored short stories. 875 Students

Skill Making a Circle Graph pages 244-245

J Draw a circle and construct a central angle of 50°. See above

K Construct a circle graph to show the percent of land this gardener planted for each crop. See above.

Crops Planted		Central angle
Corn	30%	108°
Beans	25%	90°
Potatoes	45%	162°

Objective: Solve problems involving statistics.

In this lesson students read a bar graph to compare electric expenses for 1968, 1969, and 1975; and also find amounts of equal monthly payments.

Using Graphs: Electric Bills

Maureen DeCourcey graphed the amount of money she paid each month for electricity in 1968, 1969, and 1975.

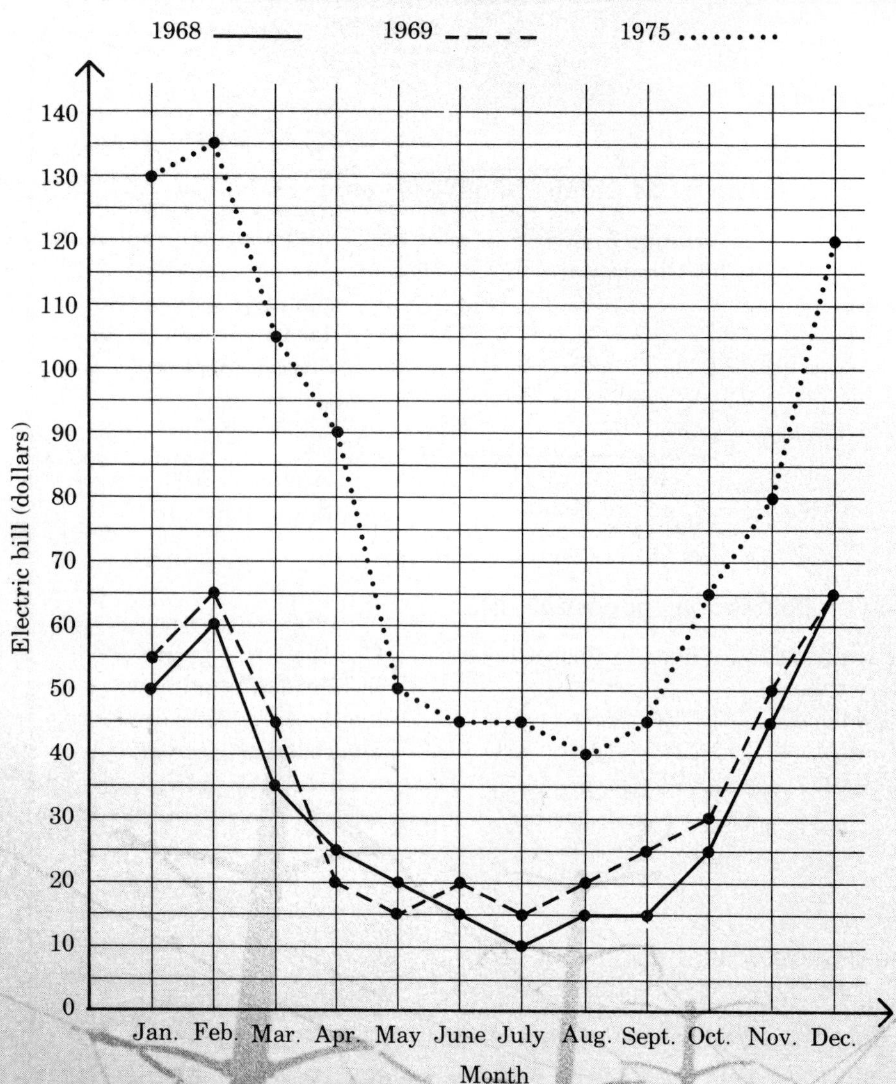

		Jan.	Feb.	Mar.	Apr.	May	June	July	Aug.	Sept.	Oct.	Nov.	Dec.
13.	1968	50	60	35	25	20	15	10	15	15	25	45	65
14.	1969	55	65	45	20	15	20	15	20	25	30	50	65
15.	1975	130	135	105	90	50	45	45	40	45	65	80	120

During which months in 1968 was the electric bill

1. less than $40?
Mar. through Oct.

2. $50 or less?
Jan., Mar. through Nov.

3. $25 or more?
Jan., Feb., Mar., Apr., Oct., Nov., Dec.

4. more than $15?
Jan. through May, Oct., Nov., Dec.

During which months in 1969 was the electric bill

5. more than $20?
Jan., Feb., Mar., Sept., Oct., Nov., Dec.

6. less than $40?
Apr. through Oct.

7. $30 or less?
Apr. through Oct.

8. $45 or more?
Jan., Feb., Mar., Nov., Dec.

During which months in 1975 was the electric bill

9. less than $80?
May through Oct.

10. $80 or more?
Jan., Feb., Mar., Apr., Nov., Dec.

11. $65 or less?
May through Oct.

12. more than $100?
Jan., Feb., Mar., Dec.

Find the amount of the electric bill for each month in See above.

13. 1968.

14. 1969.

15. 1975.

Electricity consumers can make equal monthly payments. Each payment is the average of last year's bills. Find the equal monthly payment for each of these years. Round answers to the nearest cent. (For 1969, find the average of the 1968 bills.)

16. 1969 $31.67
(To find the average of the electric bills for 1968, add the monthly bills and divide by 12.)

17. 1970 $35.42 (The 1969 average)

18. 1976 $79.17 (The 1975 average)

Equal monthly payments are adjusted each year as prices change.

For each of these months, give the year and the amount of the highest electric bill. The lowest electric bill. Then find the difference.

19. January

20. February

21. April

22. May

23. August

24. December

19. High: 1975, $130
Low: 1968, $50
Difference: $80

20. High: 1975, $135
Low: 1968, $60
Difference: $75

21. High: 1975, $90
Low: 1969, $20
Difference: $70

22. High: 1975, $50
Low: 1969, $15
Difference: $35

23. High: 1975, $40
Low: 1968, $15
Difference: $25

24. High: 1975, $120
Low: 1968, 1969, $65
Difference: $55

Objective: Solve problems involving statistics.

In this lesson students find annual mean temperature and precipitation, and make line graphs to show monthly temperatures and precipitation for certain cities.

Career: Meteorologist

Career Cluster: Science

See the Careers Chart beginning on page 420 for more jobs and other information about this career cluster.

Dail Currier is a meteorologist.
She uses this table to compare temperatures.

Normal Monthly Temperature (degrees Celsius)

	Jan.	Feb.	Mar.	Apr.	May	June	July	Aug.	Sept.	Oct.	Nov.	Dec.
Asheville, North Carolina	3	4	8	13	18	22	23	23	19	17	11	7
Birmingham, Alabama	7	8	12	17	22	25	27	26	23	17	11	7
Dodge City, Kansas	0	2	5	12	17	23	26	26	20	14	6	1
New York, New York	0	1	5	11	17	22	25	24	20	14	8	2
Miami, Florida	19	20	22	24	26	27	28	28	28	26	22	20
Honolulu, Hawaii	22	22	23	24	25	26	27	27	27	26	25	23

1. Find the annual mean temperature for each city.
Round answers to the nearest degree.

Asheville, 14°C; Birmingham, 17°C; Dodge City, 13°C; New York, 12°C; Miami, 24°C; Honolulu, 25°C

2. For each city, make a line graph that shows the monthly temperature.

See additional answers beginning on page T41.

For exercises 2 and 4, you might have students draw two graphs per grid, pairing Asheville and Birmingham, Dodge City and New York, and Miami and Honolulu. The temperature for each pair of cities are similar, but the precipitation varies.

She uses this table to compare amounts of precipitation.

Normal Monthly Precipitation (centimeters)

	Jan.	Feb.	Mar.	Apr.	May	June	July	Aug.	Sept.	Oct.	Nov.	Dec.
Asheville, North Carolina	8.6	9.1	11.9	8.9	8.4	10.2	12.4	11.4	9.1	8.4	7.4	9.1
Birmingham, Alabama	12.2	13.5	15.7	11.7	9.1	10.2	13.2	10.9	9.1	6.6	9.4	13.2
Dodge City, Kansas	1.3	1.5	2.8	4.3	7.9	8.4	7.9	6.6	4.3	4.3	1.5	1.3
New York, New York	7.4	7.9	10.2	9.1	8.6	7.4	9.9	11.4	8.1	7.6	9.7	9.1
Miami, Florida	5.6	5.1	5.3	9.1	15.5	22.9	17.5	17.0	22.1	20.8	6.9	4.1
Honolulu, Hawaii	11.1	6.4	8.1	3.6	2.5	0.8	1.5	2.0	1.8	3.8	7.6	9.4

3. Find the annual mean precipitation for each city.
Round answers to the nearest tenth of a centimeter.

Asheville, 9.6 cm; Birmingham, 11.2 cm; Dodge City, 4.3 cm; New York, 8.9 cm; Miami, 12.7 cm; Honolulu, 4.9 cm

4. For each city, make a line graph that shows the monthly precipitation.

See additional answers beginning on page T41.

In exercise 4, you might have students label each unit on the vertical scale in intervals of .5 degrees. The graphs in the teacher's edition are shown in intervals of 1 degree because of limited space.

Objective: Solve problems involving statistics.

In this lesson students make and analyze line graphs showing data on wind velocity, hydrocarbon, carbon monoxide, and ozone.

Career: Ecologist

Career Cluster: Science

Mike Goldstein is an ecologist. He studies air pollution and how it affects life. As part of his job, he interpreted and analyzed the data in this table.

		Sunday	Monday	Tuesday	Wednesday	Thursday	Friday	Saturday
Wind velocity (km/h)	Low	5.0	4.8	3.2	9.5	8.7	3.2	3.2
	Average	8.4	11.3	8.4	29.1	14.6	21.3	14.2
	High	13.2	27.3	11.3	53.2	20.9	36.7	20.9
Hydrocarbon*	Low	1.8	1.9	1.7	1.8	1.8	1.7	1.8
	Average	2.3	3.3	3.7	2.6	3.6	2.3	5.3
	High	3.2	8.0	8.0	5.4	6.6	3.8	9.4
Carbon monoxide*	Low	0.5	1.0	0.5	1.0	1.5	1.0	0.5
	Average	2.9	7.4	9.9	4.8	9.5	3.0	3.6
	High	6.0	23.0	31.5	20.0	21.0	10.0	14.0
Ozone*	Low	.005	.005	.005	.010	.005	.005	.010
	Average	.026	.017	.011	.028	.011	.022	.029
	High	.045	.045	.025	.045	.030	.035	.040

*Parts per million

He used the data in the table to make a graph that shows wind velocity. He shaded in the danger zone, which is any velocity less than 5 kilometers per hour.

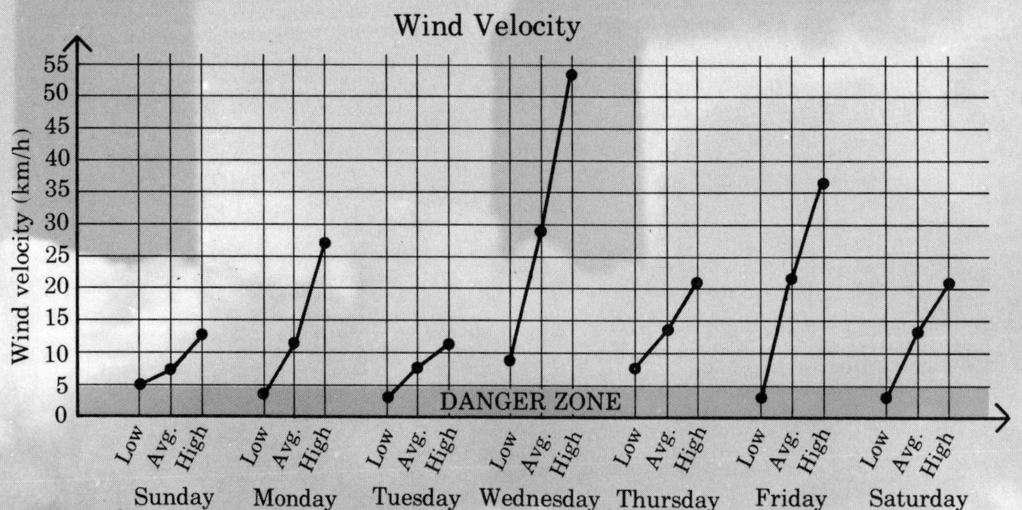

For each exercise, make a graph to show the condition listed. Use the same horizontal scale that was used to show wind velocity. Shade in the danger zone on each graph. See below.

Condition	Danger zone
1. Hydrocarbon	Any reading greater than 6.5
2. Carbon monoxide	Any reading greater than 36
3. Ozone	Any reading greater than .030

Mike uses graphs to help him report any of these special conditions. In considering B, tell students to look at three consecutive readings to find two increases.

A Danger zone

B Any high reading (except wind) that has increased for two consecutive days

C Any significant increase in the high from the previous day, except wind: hydrocarbon, an increase of 5; carbon monoxide, an increase of 7; ozone, an increase of .020

D Any two consecutive days' average wind velocity less than 12 kilometers per hour

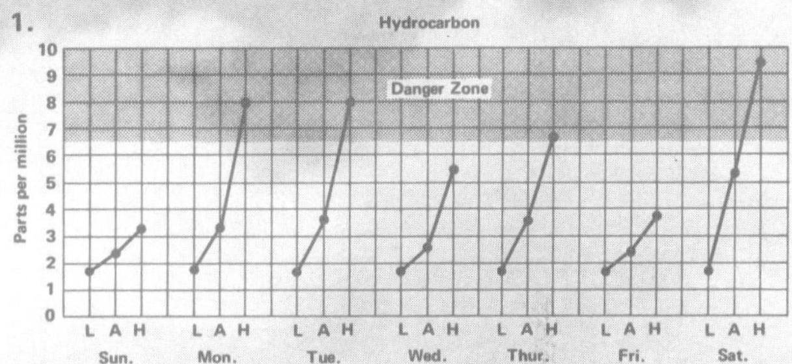

Complete the table. Use the letters to indicate the special conditions that Mike must report. Wind velocity has already been completed.

Point out that B is not a possibility for Sunday or Monday, but must be considered on Tuesday, or any day thereafter. Neither C nor D is a possibility for Sunday.

	Sunday	Monday	Tuesday	Wednesday	Thursday	Friday	Saturday
Wind velocity		**A, D**	**A, D**			**A**	**A**
4. Hydrocarbon		A	A		A		A, C
5. Carbon monoxide		C	B, C				
6. Ozone	A	A		A, C	A	A	A, B

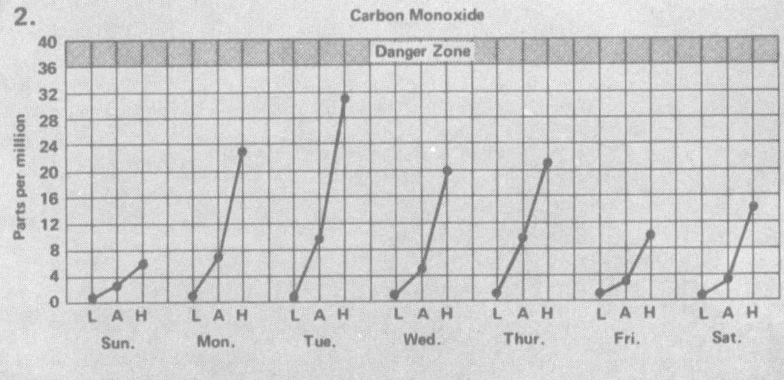

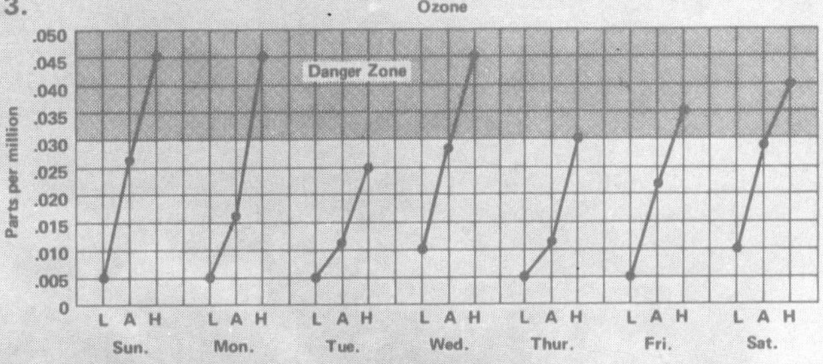

Chapter test

Number of test items - 13

Number missed	1	2	3	4	5	6
Percent correct	92	85	77	69	62	54

Chapter 12

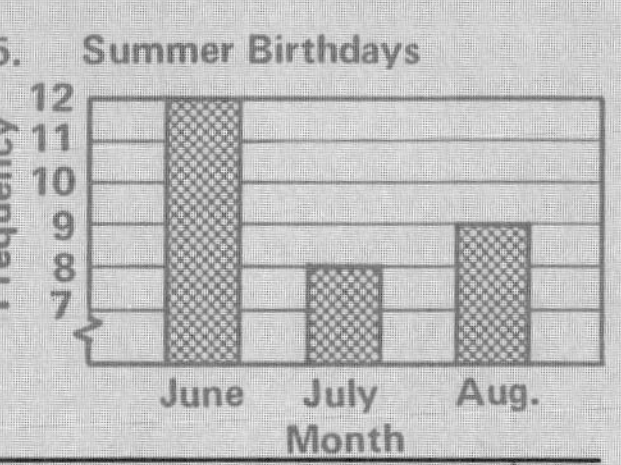

A **1.** Find the mean length in millimeters of these pencils. 11 mm

15	17	7
12	10	8
10	11	9

B **2.** Find the median length in millimeters for the set of data in item 1. 10 mm

C **3.** Find the mode length in millimeters for the set of data in item 1. 10 mm

D **4.** In which year was the volume of mail less than 50 billion? 1950

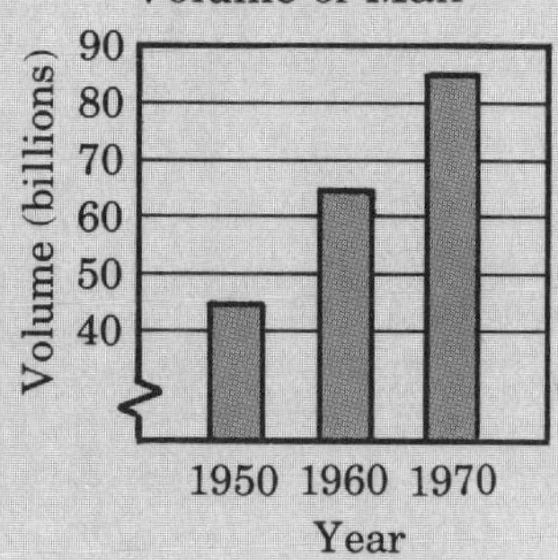

E **5.** Make a bar graph using this frequency table. See above.

Summer Birthdays

Month	Frequency
June	12
July	8
August	9

F **6.** Were more cans of apricots produced in 1971 or 1972? 1972

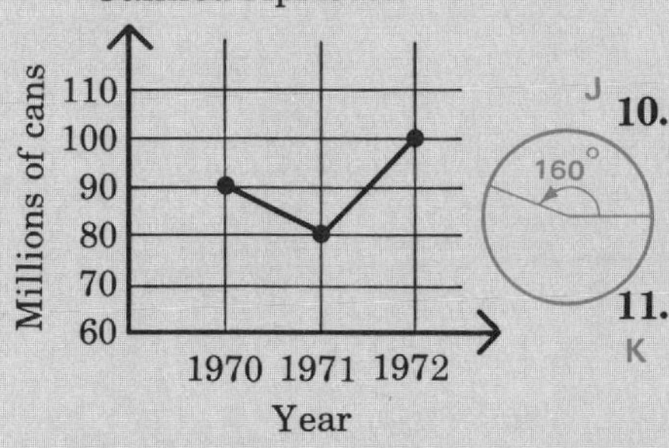

G **7.** Make a line graph to show this set of data.
See additional answers beginning on page T41.

Production of Canned Asparagus

1970	144 million cans
1971	132 million cans
1972	142 million cans
1973	139 million cans

H **8.** Which expense makes up less than 30% of this budget? Tuition

Student Budget

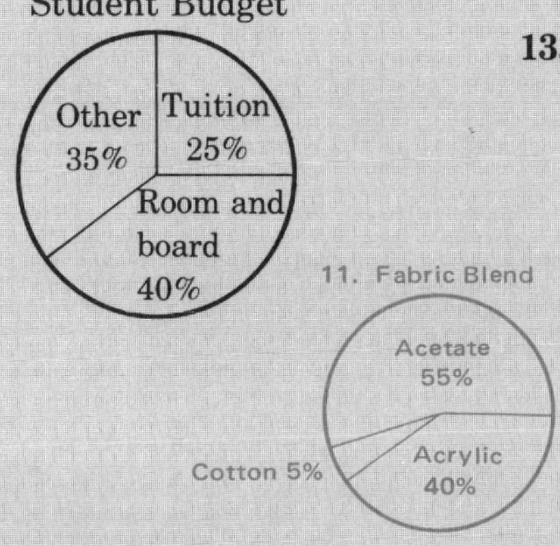

I **9.** Use the circle graph in item 8 to find how much money is spent on tuition if the student's total expenses are \$3200 per year. \$800

J **10.** Draw a circle and construct a central angle of 160°.

160°

K **11.** Construct a circle graph to show the percent of each fiber in this fabric blend. See below.

		Central angles
Acetate	55%	198°
Acrylic	40%	144°
Cotton	5%	18°

12. Find the average of these monthly electric bills for 1975 to get the equal monthly payment for 1976. \$93

\$152	\$95	\$59
\$160	\$71	\$65
\$127	\$68	\$63
\$110	\$60	\$86

13. The normal monthly temperatures for Oklahoma City are given in degrees Celsius. Find the mean annual temperature. Round to the nearest degree. 15.6°

2.6	20.1	22.8
5.2	24.9	16.9
9.0	27.5	9.6
15.8	28.3	4.4

 See pages 33-34 of the *Tests and Record Forms: Duplicating Masters* for an alternate form of the Chapter 12 Test. For a test on Unit 4, see page T35 of this book and pages 35-36 of the duplicating masters.

tune-up skills

Adding and Subtracting Whole Numbers, pages 3–12

1. 46 + 51 97
2. 34 + 16 50
3. 279 + 105 384
4. 1876 + 3924 5800
5. 82,097 + 16,123 98,220
6. 86 + 92 + 15 193
7. 14 + 109 + 37 160
8. 205 + 42 + 374 621
9. 68 + 71 + 102 241
10. 14 + 6235 + 719 6968
11. 29 + 16 + 9 + 102 156
12. 7 + 25 + 936 + 8 976
13. 63 − 41 22
14. 76 − 59 17
15. 318 − 209 109
16. 783 − 256 527
17. 813 − 725 88
18. 2638 − 119 2519
19. 9165 − 304 8861
20. 4002 − 137 3865
21. 2914 − 666 2248
22. 4501 − 873 3628
23. 6112 − 1274 4838
24. 52,576 − 48,241 4335
25. 70,015 − 24,627 45,388

Adding and Subtracting Decimals, pages 67–74

1. 3.8 + 9.1 12.9
2. 17.6 + 12.8 30.4
3. .75 + .34 1.09
4. .09 + 4.5 4.59
5. 8.7 + .261 8.961
6. .8 + .6 + .3 1.7
7. .35 + .541 + .7 1.591
8. 2.394 + .85 + 1.6 4.844
9. .58 + 3.75 + 1.362 5.692
10. 4.5 + 2.78 + .009 7.289
11. .013 + 4 + 6.2 10.213
12. .092 + .001 + 2.038 2.131
13. .37 + 14.8 + 9 24.17
14. 7.3 − 2.1 5.2
15. .68 − .09 .59
16. 7.035 − 4 3.035
17. 3.24 − 1.059 2.181
18. 8 − .172 7.828
19. .932 − .456 .476
20. 15.006 − 12.137 2.869
21. 56.41 − 28 28.41
22. 12.8 − 7.054 5.746
23. 15.32 − 7.059 8.261
24. .487 − .098 .389
25. 12.3 − 6.901 5.399

Adding and Subtracting Fractions and Mixed Numbers, pages 151–162

1. $\frac{4}{5} + \frac{3}{10}$ $1\frac{1}{10}$
2. $6\frac{1}{2} + 3\frac{5}{12}$ $9\frac{11}{12}$
3. $\frac{3}{4} + \frac{3}{4}$ $1\frac{1}{2}$
4. $\frac{1}{2} + \frac{5}{6} + \frac{1}{3}$ $1\frac{2}{3}$
5. $7\frac{3}{4} + 2\frac{5}{6}$ $10\frac{7}{12}$
6. $\frac{3}{8} + \frac{3}{4}$ $1\frac{1}{8}$
7. $4\frac{5}{6} + 2\frac{1}{2}$ $7\frac{1}{3}$
8. $5\frac{2}{3} + 7\frac{3}{8}$ $13\frac{1}{24}$
9. $1\frac{3}{4} + 2\frac{1}{2} + 1\frac{2}{3}$ $5\frac{11}{12}$
10. $\frac{4}{5} - \frac{1}{10}$ $\frac{7}{10}$
11. $6\frac{5}{8} - 2\frac{1}{8}$ $4\frac{1}{2}$
12. $\frac{5}{6} - \frac{1}{6}$ $\frac{2}{3}$
13. $5\frac{1}{4} - 1\frac{2}{3}$ $3\frac{7}{12}$
14. $\frac{1}{3} - \frac{1}{4}$ $\frac{1}{12}$
15. $6\frac{1}{3} - 2\frac{5}{8}$ $3\frac{17}{24}$
16. $\frac{3}{8} - \frac{1}{6}$ $\frac{5}{24}$
17. $3\frac{4}{7} - 1\frac{6}{7}$ $1\frac{5}{7}$
18. $7\frac{3}{5} - 4\frac{2}{3}$ $2\frac{14}{15}$

CALCULATOR EXERCISES

Optional

Find each missing number. Round answers to the nearest tenth.

1. $\frac{217}{586} = \frac{397}{n}$ n = 1072.1

2. $\frac{687}{n} = \frac{983}{215}$ n = 150.3

3. $\frac{n}{1096} = \frac{378}{563}$ n = 735.9

4. $\frac{7096}{1358} = \frac{n}{896}$ n = 4681.9

5. $\frac{8016}{n} = \frac{7532}{9617}$ n = 10235.0

Find each number.

6. 78% of 3619 2822.82
7. 7.6% of 10,982 834.632
8. .3% of 11,927 35.781
9. 13.7% of 8754 1199.298
10. 120% of 7698 9237.6

Find the mean salary. Round answer to the nearest cent. $21,037.78

11. $16,432.56
    57,962.14
    12,758.29
    9473.28
    8562.64

A person who sells property through a real estate agency must pay a brokerage fee. For each exercise, multiply to find the brokerage fee.

	Property value	Brokerage rate	Brokerage fee
12.	$65,500	4.5%	(.045 × 65,500) $2947.50
13.	$38,500	6.25%	$2406.25
14.	$78,000	5.5%	$4290.00
15.	$43,000	4.75%	$2042.50
16.	$98,000	5.25%	$5145.00
17.	$108,000	6.75%	$7290.00
18.	$256,400	6.5%	$16,666.00

Find the regular price for each purchase of steel bars. Round answers to the nearest cent.

	Number of steel bars	Weight of each bar in kilograms	Price per kilogram	Regular price
19.	60	19.9	$.236	$281.78 (60 × 19.9 × .236)
20.	90	21.6	$.297	$577.37
21.	100	15.34	$.368	$564.51
22.	50	13.7	$.349	$239.07
23.	98	20.5	$.256	$514.30
24.	165	17.38	$.315	$903.33

25. Find the discount for each purchase in exercises 19–24 if a 5% discount is given. Round answers to the nearest cent. Then subtract to find the sale price.

19. $14.09, $267.69
20. $28.87, $548.50
21. $28.23, $536.28
22. $11.95, $227.12
23. $25.72, $488.58
24. $45.17, $858.16

Algebra

13

Chapter 13
Positive and Negative Numbers

14

Chapter 14
Expressions and Equations

15

Chapter 15
Graphing

Chapter 13
Positive and Negative Numbers

pretest

Number of test items - 21

Number missed	1	2	3	4	5	6	7	8	9	10
Percent correct	95	90	86	81	76	71	67	62	57	52

skill Writing and Ordering Positive and Negative Numbers pages 260-261

A Write a number for point N on the number line.

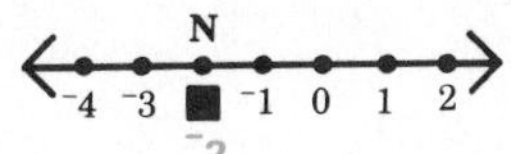

B Use the number line in item A to compare 2 and $^-1$. Use < or >. $2 > {}^-1$, or $^-1 < 2$

C Arrange these numbers in order from least to greatest. 3, 6, $^-1$, 0 $^-1$, 0, 3, 6

skill Adding Positive and Negative Numbers pages 262-263

D $5 + 2$ 7 E $^-3 + {}^-2$ $^-5$ F $2 + {}^-6$ $^-4$ G $^-6 + 2 + {}^-5 + 1$ $^-8$

skill Subtracting Positive and Negative Numbers pages 264-265

H Name the opposite of $^-6$. 6 I $4 - 6$ $^-2$ J $^-3 - {}^-4$ 1 K $^-4 - 3$ $^-7$

L $5 - {}^-1$ 6 M $12 - (6 - {}^-3)$ 3

skill Multiplying Positive and Negative Numbers pages 266-267

N 9×3 27 O $^-2 \times {}^-6$ 12 P $4 \times {}^-5$ $^-20$ Q $5(3) - 6({}^-2)$ 27

skill Dividing Positive and Negative Numbers pages 268-269

R $18 \div 2$ 9 S $^-21 \div {}^-3$ 7 T $^-15 \div 3$ $^-5$ U $\frac{7 - 12}{^-5}$ 1

See page T24 for additional notes on Chapter 13.

Objective: Write, compare, and order positive and negative numbers.

Writing and Ordering Positive and Negative Numbers

example A Writing integers

Write a positive or a negative number for each point labeled by a letter.

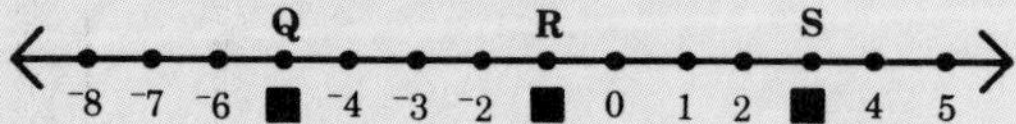

The numbers on this number line are called **integers.** The integers to the left of zero are negative. The integers to the right of zero are positive. Zero is neither positive nor negative.

Point Q $^{-}5$ negative 5
Point R $^{-}1$ negative 1
Point S 3 positive 3

example B Comparing integers

Use this number line to compare each pair of integers given below. Use $<$ or $>$.

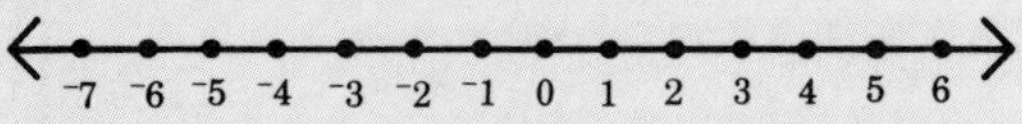

6 and 4	$6 > 4$	The number farther to the right is greater.
3 and $^{-}3$	$3 > {}^{-}3$	
$^{-}2$ and $^{-}7$	${}^{-}2 > {}^{-}7$	
4 and 0	$4 > 0$	
2 and 6	$2 < 6$	The number farther to the left is less.
$^{-}5$ and $^{-}1$	${}^{-}5 < {}^{-}1$	
$^{-}3$ and 0	${}^{-}3 < 0$	
0 and 2	$0 < 2$	

example C Ordering integers

Arrange these integers in order from least to greatest.

$^{-}5$ 0 $^{-}3$ 1

Write them from left to right in the order that they would appear on a number line.

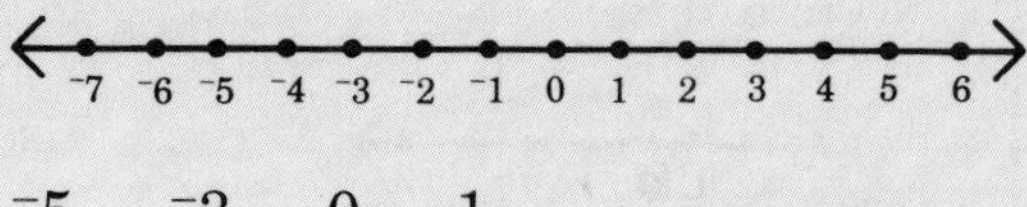

$^{-}5$ $^{-}3$ 0 1

exercises

set A

Write a positive or negative number for each point labeled by a letter.

1. 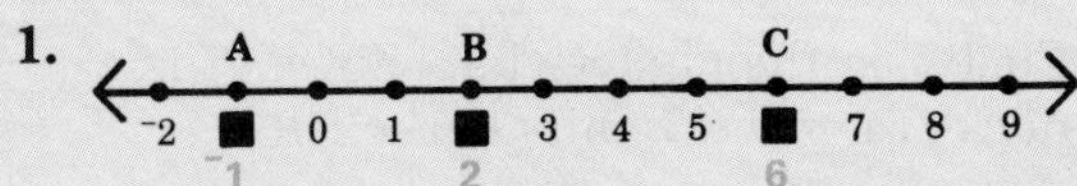

2. 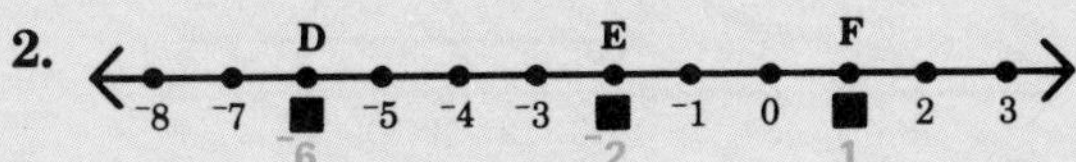

3. 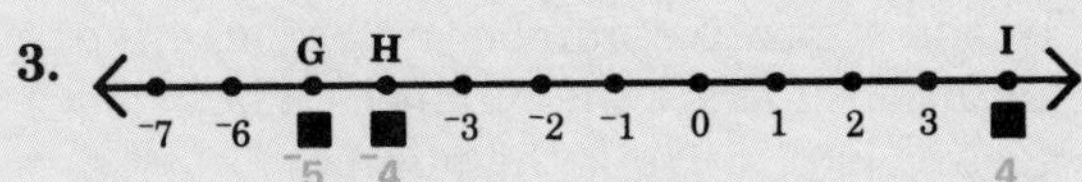

4. 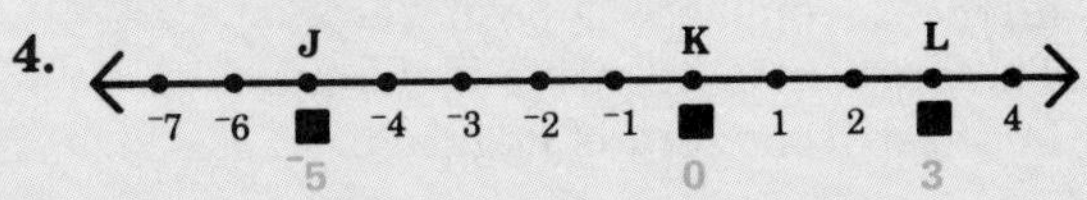

5. 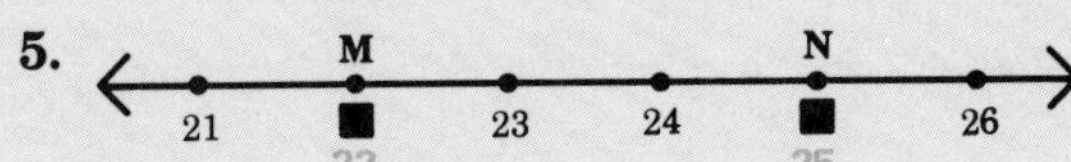

6. 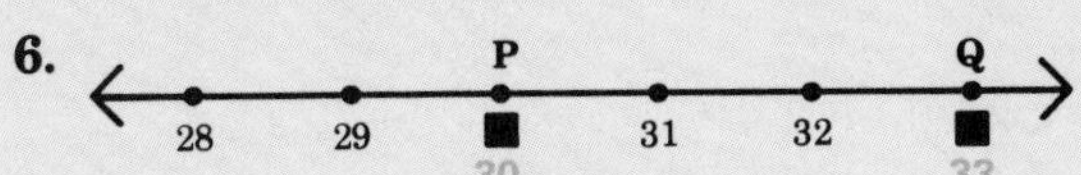

7. 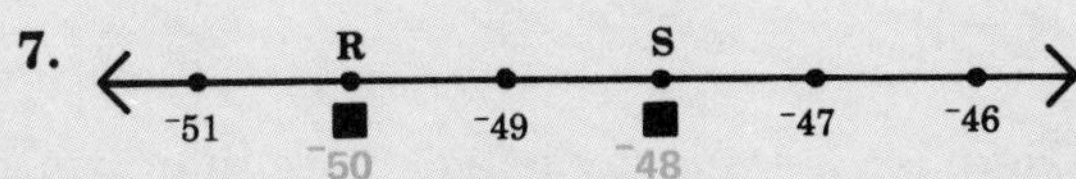

8. 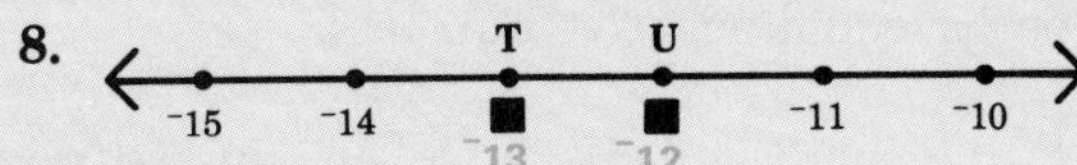

set B

Compare these numbers.
Replace ● with $>$ or $<$.

1. $^-8$ ● 0 $<$
2. 4 ● 2 $>$
3. 1 ● $^-9$ $>$
4. $^-7$ ● 7 $<$
5. $^-4$ ● $^-6$ $>$
6. $^-8$ ● $^-3$ $<$
7. 0 ● 8 $<$
8. $^-16$ ● 3 $<$
9. 6 ● 10 $<$
10. $^-17$ ● $^-13$ $<$
11. $^-19$ ● $^-13$ $<$
12. 78 ● 74 $>$
13. $^-38$ ● $^-62$ $>$
14. $^-14$ ● 10 $<$
15. $^-72$ ● $^-64$ $<$
16. $^-35$ ● $^-51$ $>$
17. 12 ● 3 $>$
18. $^-49$ ● 15 $<$
19. $^-31$ ● $^-42$ $>$
20. 37 ● $^-98$ $>$

set C

For each exercise, arrange the numbers in order from least to greatest.

1. 6, $^-4$, 3, $^-1$ — $^-4$, $^-1$, 3, 6
2. 1, $^-1$, 2, $^-2$ — $^-2$, $^-1$, 1, 2
3. 7, $^-3$, $^-5$, 9 — $^-5$, $^-3$, 7, 9
4. $^-13$, $^-15$, $^-19$, 14 — $^-19$, $^-15$, $^-13$, 14
5. 25, $^-10$, $^-30$, 40 — $^-30$, $^-10$, 25, 40
6. 5, $^-7$, 8, 3, $^-4$ — $^-7$, $^-4$, 3, 5, 8
7. $^-7$, 8, 0, $^-8$, $^-9$ — $^-9$, $^-8$, $^-7$, 0, 8
8. $^-6$, 7, $^-8$, 9, $^-10$ — $^-10$, $^-8$, $^-6$, 7, 9
9. 8, 0, $^-9$, 9, 7 — $^-9$, 0, 7, 8, 9
10. 5, $^-4$, 0, 6, $^-2$ — $^-4$, $^-2$, 0, 5, 6
11. $^-16$, 13, $^-14$, 0, 8 — $^-16$, $^-14$, 0, 8, 13
12. 35, 25, $^-18$, 10, $^-10$ — $^-18$, $^-10$, 10, 25, 35
13. 1, 5, 7, $^-1$, $^-5$, $^-7$ — $^-7$, $^-5$, $^-1$, 1, 5, 7
14. 8, $^-1$, 16, $^-12$, $^-8$ — $^-12$, $^-8$, $^-1$, 8, 16
15. $^-2$, 10, $^-7$, $^-10$, 6 — $^-10$, $^-7$, $^-2$, 6, 10
16. $^-15$, 15, $^-16$, 16, $^-17$, 17 — $^-17$, $^-16$, $^-15$, 15, 16, 17
17. $^-21$, $^-28$, 14, 16, $^-9$, $^-5$ — $^-28$, $^-21$, $^-9$, $^-5$, 14, 16
18. $^-6$, 3, $^-8$, 6, $^-7$, $^-9$, 10 — $^-9$, $^-8$, $^-7$, $^-6$, 3, 6, 10
19. $^-4$, $^-2$, $^-9$, 4, 9, 6, $^-5$ — $^-9$, $^-5$, $^-4$, $^-2$, 4, 6, 9
20. 78, $^-39$, $^-92$, 46, 52, $^-14$ — $^-92$, $^-39$, $^-14$, 46, 52, 78

Objective: Add positive and negative numbers.

Adding Positive and Negative Numbers

example D Two positive numbers

$1 + 4$

Find 1 on the number line. Since 4 is positive, move 4 units to the right.

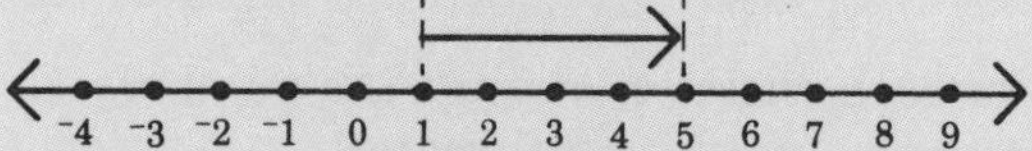

To add two positive numbers, find the sum of the two numbers. The answer is positive.

$1 + 4 = 5$

example E Two negative numbers

$^{-}2 + {}^{-}4$

Find $^{-}2$ on the number line. Since $^{-}4$ is negative, move 4 units to the left.

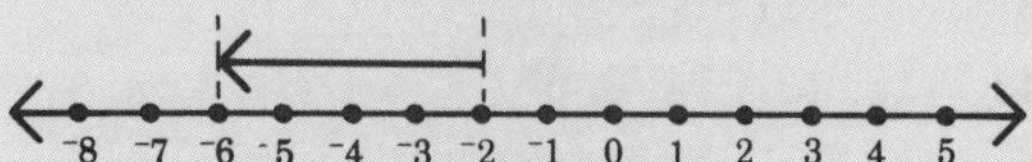

To add two negative numbers, find the sum of the two numbers. The answer is negative.

$^{-}2 + {}^{-}4 = {}^{-}6$

example F One positive and one negative number

$3 + {}^{-}7$

Find 3 on the number line. Since $^{-}7$ is negative, move 7 units to the left.

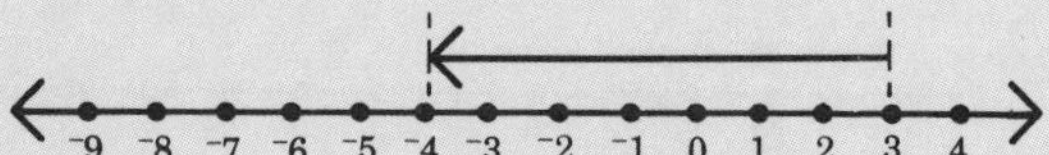

To add a positive number and a negative number, subtract the numbers. The answer is positive if the number farthest from zero is positive.
The answer is negative if the number farthest from zero is negative.

$3 + {}^{-}7 = {}^{-}4$

example G Three or more addends

$8 + 2 + {}^{-}3 + 1 + {}^{-}9$

Here is an easy way to add more than two positive and negative numbers.

$8 + 2 + {}^{-}3 + 1 + {}^{-}9$ — Add the positive numbers.

$11 + {}^{-}3 + {}^{-}9$ — Add the negative numbers.

$11 + {}^{-}12$ — Find the sum of the two answers.

$^{-}1$

$8 + 2 + {}^{-}3 + 1 + {}^{-}9 = {}^{-}1$

Throughout this chapter, you may wish to have students work with negative numbers on the calculator. If so, you might have students use calculators to check their answers to each set of exercises.

exercises

set D

1. $3 + 6$ 9
2. $92 + 48$ 140
3. $1.8 + 2.6$ 4.4
4. $813 + 295$ 1108
5. $1.56 + 9.75$ 11.31
6. $12.9 + 7.6$ 20.5
7. $295 + 167$ 462
8. $9.3 + .8$ 10.1
9. $36 + 45$ 81
10. $8.37 + 4.96$ 13.33

set E

1. ${}^{-}5 + {}^{-}6$ ${}^{-}11$
2. ${}^{-}12 + {}^{-}8$ ${}^{-}20$
3. ${}^{-}9.4 + {}^{-}2.9$ ${}^{-}12.3$
4. ${}^{-}876 + {}^{-}135$ ${}^{-}1011$
5. ${}^{-}3.5 + {}^{-}4.7$ ${}^{-}8.2$
6. ${}^{-}1.14 + {}^{-}1.27$ ${}^{-}2.41$
7. ${}^{-}28 + {}^{-}165$ ${}^{-}193$
8. ${}^{-}6.4 + {}^{-}1.8$ ${}^{-}8.2$
9. ${}^{-}3.9 + {}^{-}5.6$ ${}^{-}9.5$
10. ${}^{-}108 + {}^{-}792$ ${}^{-}900$
11. ${}^{-}49 + {}^{-}62$ ${}^{-}111$
12. ${}^{-}8.17 + {}^{-}9.54$ ${}^{-}17.71$
13. ${}^{-}1.5 + {}^{-}3.7$ ${}^{-}5.2$
14. ${}^{-}75 + {}^{-}16$ ${}^{-}91$
15. ${}^{-}748 + {}^{-}976$ ${}^{-}1724$

set F

1. $4 + {}^{-}8$ ${}^{-}4$
2. $9 + {}^{-}7$ 2
3. ${}^{-}16 + 4$ ${}^{-}12$
4. ${}^{-}12 + 10$ ${}^{-}2$
5. ${}^{-}8 + 23$ 15
6. $25 + {}^{-}76$ ${}^{-}51$
7. $1.9 + {}^{-}2.4$ ${}^{-}.5$
8. $84 + {}^{-}61$ 23
9. ${}^{-}9.2 + 6.9$ ${}^{-}2.3$
10. $.15 + {}^{-}.37$ ${}^{-}.22$
11. $501 + {}^{-}372$ 129
12. ${}^{-}4.3 + 5.8$ 1.5
13. ${}^{-}20.1 + 16.7$ ${}^{-}3.4$
14. $79 + {}^{-}101$ ${}^{-}22$
15. $472 + {}^{-}378$ 94
16. $8.6 + {}^{-}3.7$ 4.9
17. ${}^{-}27.3 + 68.2$ 40.9
18. ${}^{-}.97 + .35$ ${}^{-}.62$
19. ${}^{-}46 + 31$ ${}^{-}15$
20. $7.36 + {}^{-}5.24$ 2.12
21. ${}^{-}7.6 + 3.8$ ${}^{-}3.8$
22. $6.7 + {}^{-}2.1$ 4.6
23. ${}^{-}175 + 89$ ${}^{-}86$
24. $1.18 + {}^{-}3.74$ ${}^{-}2.56$
25. $13.2 + {}^{-}4.6$ 8.6
26. $98 + {}^{-}45$ 53
27. ${}^{-}4.26 + 2.17$ ${}^{-}2.09$
28. ${}^{-}512 + 682$ 170

set G

1. ${}^{-}6 + 4 + {}^{-}9$ ${}^{-}11$
2. ${}^{-}7 + {}^{-}6 + 5$ ${}^{-}8$
3. $8 + 3 + {}^{-}4$ 7
4. $10 + {}^{-}12 + 3$ 1
5. ${}^{-}25 + {}^{-}16 + {}^{-}14$ ${}^{-}55$
6. $45 + {}^{-}29 + {}^{-}30$ ${}^{-}14$
7. ${}^{-}2 + {}^{-}4 + {}^{-}5 + {}^{-}6$ ${}^{-}17$
8. $7 + {}^{-}13 + 2 + {}^{-}1$ ${}^{-}5$
9. ${}^{-}16 + {}^{-}4 + 35$ 15
10. ${}^{-}12 + 5 + 6 + {}^{-}8$ ${}^{-}9$
11. ${}^{-}375 + 215 + 30$ ${}^{-}130$
12. ${}^{-}1.6 + {}^{-}2.4 + .8$ ${}^{-}3.2$
13. $4 + {}^{-}6 + {}^{-}9 + 10$ ${}^{-}1$
14. ${}^{-}204 + 913 + {}^{-}408$ 301
15. $2.7 + {}^{-}1.9 + .7$ 1.5
16. ${}^{-}2 + {}^{-}4 + {}^{-}5 + {}^{-}6$ ${}^{-}17$
17. ${}^{-}.6 + {}^{-}.3 + {}^{-}.8$ ${}^{-}1.7$
18. $605 + {}^{-}109 + {}^{-}576$ ${}^{-}80$
19. $.8 + {}^{-}1.2 + {}^{-}3.1$ ${}^{-}3.5$
20. $18 + {}^{-}6 + 12 + {}^{-}2$ 22
21. ${}^{-}38 + 24 + {}^{-}19$ ${}^{-}33$
22. $408 + {}^{-}965 + 126$ ${}^{-}431$
23. $.68 + .05 + {}^{-}.72$ .01
24. ${}^{-}13 + 6 + {}^{-}5 + {}^{-}2$ ${}^{-}14$
25. ${}^{-}85 + {}^{-}4 + 12 + {}^{-}3$ ${}^{-}80$
26. ${}^{-}.82 + .04 + .51$ ${}^{-}.27$
27. ${}^{-}702 + 513 + {}^{-}389$ ${}^{-}578$
28. ${}^{-}.65 + .92 + {}^{-}.14$ .13

The applications on pages 271–273 may be used anytime after this lesson.

Objective: Subtract positive and negative numbers.

Subtracting Positive and Negative Numbers

example H Writing the opposite of a given number

Name the opposite of $^{-}3$.

On a number line, a number and its opposite are equally distant from zero. Zero is its own opposite.

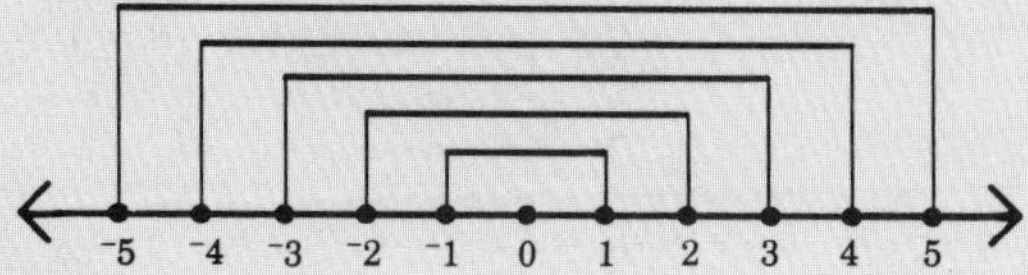

The opposite of $^{-}3$ is 3.

example I Two positive numbers

$3 - 4$

Study the pattern.

$3 - 1 = 2$	$3 + {}^{-}1 = 2$
$3 - 2 = 1$	$3 + {}^{-}2 = 1$
$3 - 3 = 0$	$3 + {}^{-}3 = 0$
$3 - 4 = {}^{-}1$	$3 + {}^{-}4 = {}^{-}1$
$3 - 5 = {}^{-}2$	$3 + {}^{-}5 = {}^{-}2$

To subtract a positive or a negative number, add its opposite.

$3 - 4 = \square$

$3 + {}^{-}4 = {}^{-}1$ Add the opposite of 4.

$3 - 4 = {}^{-}1$

example J Two negative numbers

${}^{-}6 - {}^{-}8$

${}^{-}6 + 8 = {}^{-}2$ Add the opposite of $^{-}8$.

${}^{-}6 - {}^{-}8 = {}^{-}2$

example K A negative minuend and a positive subtrahend

${}^{-}5 - 2$

${}^{-}5 + {}^{-}2 = {}^{-}7$ Add the opposite of 2.

${}^{-}5 - 2 = {}^{-}7$

example L A positive minuend and a negative subtrahend

$7 - {}^{-}4$

$7 + 4 = 11$ Add the opposite of $^{-}4$.

$7 - {}^{-}4 = 11$

example M Order of operations involving addition and subtraction

$15 - ({}^{-}8 + 2)$ First do operations inside parentheses. Then subtract.

$15 - {}^{-}6$

21

exercises

set H

Name the opposite of each number.

1. 7 $^-7$ **4.** $^-35$ 35

2. $^-6$ 6 **5.** 48 $^-48$

3. 1 $^-1$ **6.** $^-965$ 965

set I

1. $8 - 9$ $^-1$

2. $7 - 3$ 4

3. $25 - 38$ $^-13$

4. $1.7 - 1.6$ $.1$

5. $3.8 - 4.6$ $^-.8$

6. $48 - 62$ $^-14$

7. $125 - 338$ $^-213$

8. $7.9 - 12.5$ $^-4.6$

9. $824 - 931$ $^-107$

10. $3.15 - 4.24$ $^-1.09$

11. $95 - 103$ $^-8$

12. $63 - 79$ $^-16$

set J

1. $^-4 - ^-9$ 5

2. $^-5 - ^-8$ 3

3. $^-21 - ^-18$ $^-3$

4. $^-3.2 - ^-2.9$ $^-.3$

5. $^-4.9 - ^-5.6$ $.7$

6. $^-35 - ^-91$ 56

7. $^-389 - ^-462$ 73

8. $^-913 - ^-628$ $^-285$

9. $^-14.8 - ^-6.3$ $^-8.5$

10. $^-89 - ^-45$ $^-44$

11. $^-4.86 - ^-3.17$ $^-1.69$

12. $^-65 - ^-81$ 16

set K

1. $^-3 - 6$ $^-9$

2. $^-9 - 3$ $^-12$

3. $^-41 - 17$ $^-58$

4. $^-6.5 - 4.8$ $^-11.3$

5. $^-1.9 - 2.5$ $^-4.4$

6. $^-56 - 18$ $^-74$

7. $^-137 - 462$ $^-599$

8. $^-6.3 - 11.8$ $^-18.1$

9. $^-792 - 218$ $^-1010$

10. $^-1.16 - .78$ $^-1.94$

11. $^-81 - 42$ $^-123$

12. $^-.42 - 3.16$ $^-3.58$

set L

1. $9 - ^-6$ 15

2. $5 - ^-3$ 8

3. $13 - ^-12$ 25

4. $2.3 - ^-4.9$ 7.2

5. $16 - ^-12$ 28

6. $6.8 - ^-3.4$ 10.2

7. $482 - ^-186$ 668

8. $6.3 - ^-12.1$ 18.4

9. $381 - ^-469$ 850

10. $1.28 - ^-.39$ 1.67

11. $29 - ^-48$ 77

12. $.42 - ^-2.56$ 2.98

set M

1. $16 - (^-9 + ^-4)$ 29

2. $(15 - ^-8) - ^-3$ 26

3. $(^-19 + ^-3) - 16$ $^-38$

4. $(20 - ^-6) - (6 - 7)$ 27

5. $(^-3 + ^-8) - ^-9$ $^-2$

6. $26 - (39 - ^-19)$ $^-32$

7. $(^-5 - 4) - (1 - ^-2)$ $^-12$

8. $(67 + 48) - 16$ 99

9. $^-78 - (19 - ^-59)$ $^-156$

10. $^-52 - (^-98 + 65)$ $^-19$

11. $(^-8 - ^-3) - (^-4 - 5)$ 4

12. $119 - (^-34 + 102)$ 51

13. $^-48 - (14 + ^-16)$ $^-46$

14. $^-84 - (^-123 - 49)$ 88

15. $^-10 - (12 + ^-38)$ 16

16. $(19 + ^-9) - ^-16$ 26

17. $(6 + ^-9) - (5 - ^-6)$ $^-14$

18. $(28 - 7) - ^-19$ 40

19. $(^-94 + ^-6) - 100$ $^-200$

20. $936 - (21 - ^-9)$ 906

The applications on pages 274–275 may be used anytime after this lesson.

Objective: Multiply positive and negative numbers.

Multiplying Positive and Negative Numbers

example N Two positive numbers

8×6

Before developing the rules for multiplying positive and negative numbers, you may wish to have students study patterns of products.

The product of two positive numbers is positive.

$8 \times 6 = 48$

$5 \times 2 = 10$	$^{-}5 \times 2 = {}^{-}10$
$5 \times 1 = 5$	$^{-}5 \times 1 = {}^{-}5$
$5 \times 0 = 0$	$^{-}5 \times 0 = 0$
$5 \times {}^{-}1 = {}^{-}5$	$^{-}5 \times {}^{-}1 = 5$
$5 \times {}^{-}2 = {}^{-}10$	$^{-}5 \times {}^{-}2 = 10$

example O Two negative numbers

$^{-}3 \times {}^{-}4$

The product of two negative numbers is positive.

$^{-}3 \times {}^{-}4 = 12$

example P One positive and one negative number

$7 \times {}^{-}5$ $\quad$ $^{-}8 \times 6$

The product of a positive number and a negative number is negative.

$7 \times {}^{-}5 = {}^{-}35$ $\quad$ $^{-}8 \times 6 = {}^{-}48$

example Q Order of operations involving addition, subtraction, and multiplication

$6({}^{-}5) - 7({}^{-}8 + 2)$	First do operations inside parentheses.
$6({}^{-}5) - 7({}^{-}6)$	Then multiply.
$^{-}30 - {}^{-}42$	Then add or subtract.
12	

exercises

set N

1.	9×6 54	**13.**	$.7 \times .9$ .63		
2.	5×4 20	**14.**	1.6×2 3.2		
3.	7×8 56	**15.**	1.8×3 5.4		
4.	6×3 18	**16.**	7.6×10 76		
5.	2×9 18	**17.**	4×3.2 12.8		
6.	36×4 144	**18.**	9×4.5 40.5		
7.	3×25 75	**19.**	18×36 648		
8.	10×34 340	**20.**	25×48 1200		
9.	40×16 640	**21.**	$.76 \times 1.3$ .988		
10.	24×18 432	**22.**	$.89 \times .72$ .6408		
11.	12×95 1140	**23.**	105×37 3885		
12.	37×46 1702	**24.**	$.11 \times 6.2$ .682		

set O

1.	$^{-}8 \times {}^{-}4$ 32	**13.**	$^{-}18 \times {}^{-}100$ 1800
2.	$^{-}7 \times {}^{-}5$ 35	**14.**	$^{-}32 \times {}^{-}125$ 4000
3.	$^{-}9 \times {}^{-}7$ 63	**15.**	$^{-}202 \times {}^{-}68$ 13,736
4.	$^{-}6 \times {}^{-}4$ 24	**16.**	$^{-}13 \times {}^{-}2.7$ 35.1
5.	$^{-}3 \times {}^{-}9$ 27	**17.**	$^{-}1.6 \times {}^{-}2.5$ 4
6.	$^{-}2 \times {}^{-}14$ 28	**18.**	$^{-}.82 \times {}^{-}3.1$ 2.542
7.	$^{-}6 \times {}^{-}29$ 174	**19.**	$^{-}167 \times {}^{-}103$ 17,201
8.	$^{-}7 \times {}^{-}35$ 245	**20.**	$^{-}7.1 \times {}^{-}9.8$ 69.58
9.	$^{-}14 \times {}^{-}11$ 154	**21.**	$^{-}6.5 \times {}^{-}.79$ 5.135
10.	$^{-}16 \times {}^{-}98$ 1568	**22.**	$^{-}1.3 \times {}^{-}.86$ 1.118
11.	$^{-}10 \times {}^{-}72$ 720	**23.**	$^{-}45 \times {}^{-}62$ 2790
12.	$^{-}8 \times {}^{-}45$ 360	**24.**	$^{-}12 \times {}^{-}4.2$ 50.4

set P

1. $^-4 \times 7$ $^-28$
2. $8 \times {}^-3$ $^-24$
3. $2 \times {}^-16$ $^-32$
4. $^-9 \times 7$ $^-63$
5. $^-6 \times 5$ $^-30$
6. $^-2 \times .4$ $^-.8$
7. $98 \times {}^-45$ $^-4410$
8. $3 \times {}^-.16$ $^-.48$
9. $^-35 \times 21$ $^-735$
10. $71 \times {}^-83$ $^-5893$
11. $5 \times {}^-7.8$ $^-39$
12. $10 \times {}^-.95$ $^-9.5$
13. $^-7 \times 1.2$ $^-8.4$
14. $^-2.5 \times .48$ $^-1.2$
15. $.76 \times {}^-92$ $^-69.92$
16. $3 \times {}^-.124$ $^-.372$
17. $^-.8 \times .7$ $^-.56$
18. $^-68 \times 954$ $^-64{,}872$
19. $^-42 \times 36$ $^-1512$
20. $1.9 \times {}^-2.5$ $^-4.75$
21. $^-27 \times 84$ $^-2268$
22. $9 \times {}^-.9$ $^-8.1$
23. $.52 \times {}^-1.4$ $^-.728$
24. $7.8 \times {}^-9.6$ $^-74.88$
25. $^-.24 \times .39$ $^-.0936$
26. $10 \times {}^-.621$ $^-6.21$
27. $^-45 \times 251$ $^-11{,}295$
28. $^-21 \times 38$ $^-798$

set Q

1. $^-4(^-5 + 1)$ 16
2. $(1 + {}^-8)2$ $^-14$
3. $6(9) - {}^-2(7)$ 68
4. $4(^-29) + {}^-3(8)$ $^-140$
5. $^-15 + 6(7) - {}^-1$ 28
6. $^-7(^-3 + 2 + {}^-6)$ 49
7. $12 - {}^-8(2)(^-1)$ $^-4$
8. $9(^-2)(^-3) - {}^-22$ 76
9. $^-70 - 5(^-13 + 9)$ $^-50$
10. $8(^-18 + 9) - 42$ $^-114$
11. $^-5(^-3 - {}^-1)$ 10
12. $9 - (^-4 + {}^-2)$ 15
13. $2(8 - {}^-3)$ 22
14. $23 - {}^-7(2)$ 37
15. $^-2(8 - {}^-3)$ $^-22$
16. $^-10(^-3 - {}^-6 + 2)$ $^-50$
17. $^-8(^-9 - 2 - {}^-5)$ 48
18. $12(7 - 8)$ $^-12$
19. $9(^-2) + 4(3 - {}^-2)$ 2
20. $^-4(^-3) - 6(4 + {}^-1)$ $^-6$
21. $(^-9 - {}^-10) + 3(^-1)$ $^-2$
22. $8(^-7) + {}^-3(2)$ $^-62$
23. $(7 + {}^-6) - 4(^-8)$ 33
24. $39 - {}^-6(^-6)$ 3
25. $^-6(3) + (4 - {}^-9)$ $^-5$
26. $^-9(25 + {}^-38)$ 117
27. $12(19 + {}^-21) - {}^-3$ $^-21$
28. $(^-3 + {}^-8) + {}^-2(6)$ $^-23$

Find the number of triangles. 27

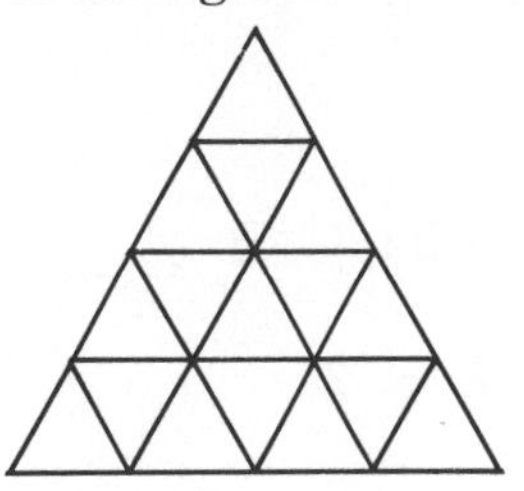

Find the number of squares. 11

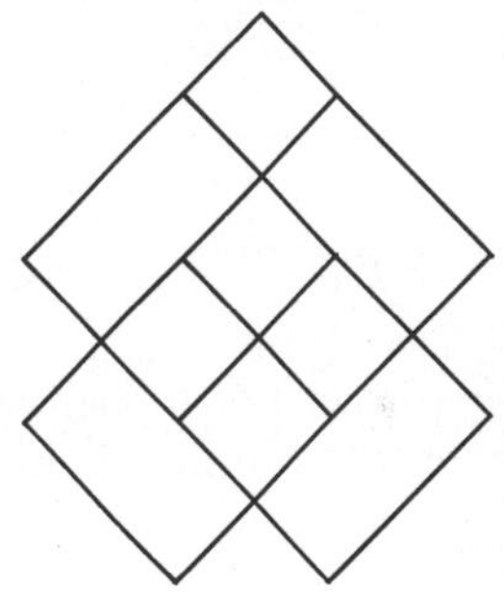

Objective: Divide positive and negative numbers.

Dividing Positive and Negative Numbers

example R

Two positive numbers

Before developing the rules for dividing positive and negative numbers, you may wish to have students study patterns relating division to multiplication.

$24 \div 6$

The quotient of two positive numbers is positive.

$5 \times 3 = 15$ | $^{-}5 \times 3 = {}^{-}15$
$15 \div 3 = 5$ | $^{-}15 \div 3 = {}^{-}5$
$5 \times {}^{-}3 = {}^{-}15$ | $^{-}5 \times {}^{-}3 = 15$
$^{-}15 \div {}^{-}3 = 5$ | $15 \div {}^{-}3 = {}^{-}5$

$24 \div 6 = 4$

example S

Two negative numbers

$^{-}14 \div {}^{-}2$

The quotient of two negative numbers is positive.

$^{-}14 \div {}^{-}2 = 7$

example T

One positive and one negative number

$^{-}56 \div 8$ $\quad$ $54 \div {}^{-}9$

The quotient of a positive number and a negative number is negative.

$^{-}56 \div 8 = {}^{-}7$ $\quad$ $54 \div {}^{-}9 = {}^{-}6$

example U

Order of operations involving addition, subtraction, and division

$\frac{8-17}{3}$ First do all operations above and below the division bar.

$\frac{^{-}9}{3}$ Then divide.

$^{-}3$

exercises

set R

1. $48 \div 6$ 8
2. $72 \div 8$ 9
3. $24 \div 4$ 6
4. $36 \div 6$ 6
5. $40 \div 5$ 8
6. $672 \div 32$ 21
7. $60 \div 12$ 5
8. $4.9 \div 7$ .7
9. $72 \div .9$ 80
10. $756 \div 28$ 27
11. $1.9 \div .05$ 38
12. $.25 \div 5$ .05
13. $.8 \div 2$ .4
14. $.56 \div .8$ .7
15. $.18 \div .03$ 6
16. $540 \div 18$ 30
17. $25 \div .5$ 50
18. $1.6 \div 16$ .1
19. $10.8 \div 12$ .9
20. $504 \div 14$ 36
21. $.4 \div .2$ 2
22. $99 \div 11$ 9
23. $4.8 \div 1.2$ 4
24. $9.3 \div 62$ .15

set S

1. $^{-}63 \div {}^{-}9$ 7
2. $^{-}21 \div {}^{-}7$ 3
3. $^{-}84 \div {}^{-}12$ 7
4. $^{-}59 \div {}^{-}1$ 59
5. $^{-}3.5 \div {}^{-}5$ .7
6. $^{-}901 \div {}^{-}17$ 53
7. $^{-}.15 \div {}^{-}.3$ .5
8. $^{-}5.6 \div {}^{-}8$ .7
9. $^{-}594 \div {}^{-}18$ 33
10. $^{-}.25 \div {}^{-}.5$ .5
11. $^{-}.81 \div {}^{-}9$ .09
12. $^{-}986 \div {}^{-}29$ 34
13. $^{-}75 \div {}^{-}5$ 15
14. $^{-}414 \div {}^{-}9$ 46
15. $^{-}124 \div {}^{-}.4$ 310
16. $^{-}.64 \div {}^{-}8$ .08
17. $^{-}162 \div {}^{-}18$ 9
18. $^{-}70.8 \div {}^{-}12$ 5.9
19. $^{-}1.96 \div {}^{-}.14$ 14
20. $^{-}.72 \div {}^{-}1.2$ .6
21. $^{-}2.52 \div {}^{-}1.8$ 1.4
22. $^{-}203 \div {}^{-}29$ 7
23. $^{-}.253 \div {}^{-}.11$ 2.3
24. $^{-}152 \div {}^{-}38$ 4

set T

1. $^{-}12 \div 6$ $^{-}2$
2. $18 \div {}^{-}3$ $^{-}6$
3. $21 \div {}^{-}7$ $^{-}3$
4. $^{-}35 \div 5$ $^{-}7$
5. $^{-}36 \div 6$ $^{-}6$
6. $42 \div {}^{-}7$ $^{-}6$
7. $^{-}1.8 \div 2$ $^{-}.9$
8. $140 \div {}^{-}7$ $^{-}20$
9. $^{-}902 \div 82$ $^{-}11$
10. $^{-}4.8 \div .6$ $^{-}8$
11. $^{-}112 \div 8$ $^{-}14$
12. $300 \div {}^{-}25$ $^{-}12$
13. $.28 \div {}^{-}7$ $^{-}.04$
14. $.144 \div {}^{-}.12$ $^{-}1.2$
15. $^{-}2.4 \div 3$ $^{-}.8$
16. $.48 \div {}^{-}4$ $^{-}.12$
17. $^{-}676 \div 26$ $^{-}26$
18. $^{-}.78 \div .6$ $^{-}1.3$
19. $^{-}.96 \div 6$ $^{-}.16$
20. $^{-}.72 \div 1.2$ $^{-}.6$
21. $345 \div {}^{-}15$ $^{-}23$
22. $4.2 \div {}^{-}3$ $^{-}1.4$
23. $^{-}176 \div 11$ $^{-}16$
24. $156 \div {}^{-}13$ $^{-}12$
25. $.48 \div {}^{-}16$ $^{-}.03$
26. $^{-}4.9 \div .7$ $^{-}7$
27. $^{-}455 \div 13$ $^{-}35$
28. $^{-}1.82 \div 14$ $^{-}.13$

set U

1. $\frac{4 - 16}{3}$ $^{-}4$
2. $\frac{^{-}28 - 14}{7}$ $^{-}6$
3. $\frac{13 - {}^{-}7}{10}$ 2
4. $\frac{25 + {}^{-}21}{^{-}4}$ $^{-}1$
5. $\frac{49 - 7}{^{-}7}$ $^{-}6$
6. $\frac{^{-}6 + {}^{-}18}{^{-}4}$ 6
7. $\frac{^{-}35 + 13}{11}$ $^{-}2$
8. $\frac{^{-}27 + {}^{-}9}{^{-}11 + 2}$ 4
9. $\frac{^{-}42 - 18}{13 + {}^{-}7}$ $^{-}10$
10. $\frac{^{-}8 - {}^{-}9}{^{-}1}$ $^{-}1$
11. $\frac{4 + 10}{^{-}1 + 3}$ 7
12. $\frac{^{-}2842}{^{-}100 + 51}$ 58
13. $\frac{102 - {}^{-}42}{^{-}56 + 8}$ $^{-}3$
14. $\frac{800 + {}^{-}464}{^{-}100 + 58}$ $^{-}8$

BREAK TIME

The number of eggs in a basket doubled every minute.

The basket was full of eggs at 3:25 P.M.

When was the basket half full?

3:24 P.M.

posttest

Number of test items - 21

Number missed	1	2	3	4	5	6	7	8	9	10
Percent correct	95	90	86	81	76	71	67	62	57	52

skill Writing and Ordering Positive and Negative Numbers pages 260–261

A Write a number for point R on the number line.

R ■ $^-2$ $^-1$ 0 1 2

$^-3$

B Use the number line in item A to compare $^-2$ and 2. Use < or >. $^-2 < 2$, or $2 > {}^-2$

C Arrange these numbers in order from least to greatest. $^-8$, 0, 4, $^-3$ $^-8$, $^-3$, 0, 4

skill Adding Positive and Negative Numbers pages 262–263

D $7 + 3$ 10 E $^-4 + {}^-5$ $^-9$ F $^-6 + 8$ 2 G $^-9 + 5 + {}^-1 + 3$ $^-2$

skill Subtracting Positive and Negative Numbers pages 264–265

H Name the opposite of $^-9$. 9 I $3 - 8$ $^-5$ J $^-2 - {}^-3$ 1 K $^-6 - 7$ $^-13$

L $6 - {}^-7$ 13 M $20 - (2 - {}^-5)$ 13

skill Multiplying Positive and Negative Numbers pages 266–267

N 7×8 56 O $^-9 \times {}^-2$ 18 P $^-6 \times 3$ $^-18$ Q $9(7) - 5({}^-2)$ 73

skill Dividing Positive and Negative Numbers pages 268–269

R $63 \div 9$ 7 S $^-48 \div {}^-6$ 8 T $12 \div {}^-2$ $^-6$ U $\frac{8 - {}^-6}{{}^-2}$ $^-7$

Objective: Solve problems involving positive and negative numbers.

In this lesson students complete score cards for a game of pinochle.

Finding Pinochle Scores

The game described is only one of several versions of pinochle.

Kristen, Ethel, and Mona played pinochle. After the cards were dealt, each girl bid the number of points that she thought could be made for the hand. Kristen was the highest bidder and named trump.

Each girl who had certain combinations of cards called meld received points. After all the cards were played, each girl counted the number of aces, kings, and tens she had taken during the play of the hand. She added these points to her meld.

Ethel melded 10 points and made 8 points for the play of the hand.

Points for meld		Points for play of hand		Total points for player
10	+	8	=	18

Ethel's score for the hand was 18 points.

Kristen had bid 20 points. She melded 4 points and made 13 points for the play of the hand, or 17 points in all. This would have been her score if she had made a bid of 17 or less.

Since she did not make her bid of 20 points, the 17 points for meld and play of hand were disregarded, and her bid became a negative score for the hand.

Kristen's score for the hand was $^{-}20$ points.

You might have students actually play several games of pinochle, keeping a running total of their scores as they do so.

Complete the score cards to find the winner.

1. Name *Kristen*

Hand	Bid	Meld	Play of hand	Score
1	20	4	13	$^{-}20$
2	—	2	8	10
3	—	6	14	20
4	—	7	9	16
5	21	11	5	$^{-}21$
			Total score	5

2. Name *Ethel*

Hand	Bid	Meld	Play of hand	Score
1	—	10	8	18
2	20	16	9	25
3	24	13	9	$^{-}24$
4	—	4	6	10
5	—	6	15	21
			Total score	50

3. Name *Mona*

Hand	Bid	Meld	Play of hand	Score
1	—	4	4	8
2	—	1	8	9
3	—	0	2	2
4	27	15	10	$^{-}27$
5	—	1	5	6
			Total score	$^{-}2$

Objective: Solve problems involving positive and negative numbers.

In this lesson students find the time and height of morning and afternoon tides.

Finding the Times and Heights of Tides

Harry Alonza likes to fish. He uses an almanac to tell when the tides are high. Then he finds the tide height.

His almanac contains complete tide tables for Boston with correction tables for other areas of the United States. Parts of these tables are shown below.

Be sure that students understand that the negative sign used with time differences refers to the entire quantity, both hours and minutes.

Tide Table for Boston

Day	Time of high tide		Tide height in meters	
	Morning	Afternoon	Morning	Afternoon
June 1	5:00	5:45	2.70	2.62
2	6:00	6:30	2.62	2.65
3	6:45	7:25	2.56	2.68
4	7:45	8:15	2.53	2.74
5	8:30	9:00	2.56	2.65
July 1	5:15	5:45	2.62	2.71
2	6:00	6:30	2.53	2.71
3	7:00	7:30	2.50	2.77
4	8:00	8:15	2.47	2.83
5	8:45	9:00	2.50	2.96
Aug. 16	7:30	8:00	2.62	3.02
17	8:30	9:00	2.59	2.99
18	9:30	9:45	2.62	3.02

16. 5:33 P.M. 2.44 m
17. 5:33 P.M. 2.53 m
18. 8:32 P.M. 5.55 m
19. 7:47 P.M. 5.30 m
20. 5:27 P.M. 1.16 m
21. 5:27 P.M. 1.47 m
22. 3:02 P.M. 1.09 m
23. 4:02 P.M. 1.15 m
24. 10:55 P.M. 0.36 m
25. 11:55 P.M. 0.48 m
26. 5:52 P.M. 1.25 m
27. 6:40 P.M. 1.34 m
28. 1:32 P.M. 8.04 m
29. 4:47 P.M. 8.35 m
30. 8:23 P.M. 2.19 m

Tide Correction Table

Location	Time difference	Height difference
MAINE		
Bar Harbor	$^{-}0$ hr. 34 min.	0.27 m
Portland	$^{-}0$ hr. 12 min.	$^{-}0.18$ m
Eastport	$^{-}0$ hr. 28 min.	2.56 m
Machias	$^{-}0$ hr. 28 min.	0.85 m
NEW YORK		
Coney Island	$^{-}3$ hr. 33 min.	$^{-}1.49$ m
Oyster Bay	0 hr. 04 min.	$^{-}0.55$ m
NEW JERSEY		
Atlantic City	$^{-}3$ hr. 56 min.	$^{-}1.68$ m
Cape May	$^{-}3$ hr. 28 min.	$^{-}1.62$ m
MARYLAND		
Havre de Grace	11 hr. 21 min.	$^{-}2.35$ m
Annapolis	4 hr. 25 min.	$^{-}2.29$ m
CALIFORNIA		
Los Angeles	$^{-}1$ hr. 33 min.	$^{-}1.43$ m
San Francisco	$^{-}0$ hr. 45 min.	$^{-}1.34$ m
ALASKA		
Anchorage	$^{-}4$ hr. 58 min.	5.33 m
Juneau	3 hr. 08 min.	1.86 m
Kodiak	1 hr. 53 min.	$^{-}0.52$ m

Harry plans to go fishing near Atlantic City, New Jersey, on June 2. He wants to know the time and height of the morning high tide.

First, he finds the time of the morning high tide in Boston on June 2. It is 6:00 A.M. Then he looks for Atlantic City in the tide correction table. The correction (time difference) is $^-3$ hours 56 minutes.

He adds to find the time.

$$\begin{array}{rcl} 6 \text{ hours } \ 0 \text{ minutes} & = & 5 \text{ hours } 60 \text{ minutes} \\ \underline{+\ ^-3 \text{ hours } 56 \text{ minutes}} & = & \underline{^-3 \text{ hours } 56 \text{ minutes}} \\ & & 2 \text{ hours } \ 4 \text{ minutes, or 2:04 A.M.} \end{array}$$

Then he computes the morning tide height for the same day. First, he finds the morning tide height for Boston on June 2. It is 2.62 meters. Then he finds the correction (height difference) for Atlantic City in the tide correction table. It is $^-1.68$ meters.

He adds to find the height.

2.62 meters + $^-1.68$ meters = 0.94 meters

Find the time and height of the morning tide for each city on the given date.

1. Portland, Maine June 1
   4:48 A.M. 2.52 m
2. Portland, Maine July 1
   5:03 A.M. 2.44 m
3. Eastport, Maine August 17
   8:02 A.M. 5.15 m
4. Eastport, Maine June 4
   7:17 A.M. 5.09 m
5. Coney Island, New York, June 5
   4:57 A.M. 1.07 m
6. Coney Island, New York, July 5
   5:12 A.M. 1.01 m
7. Cape May, New Jersey, July 2
   2:32 A.M. 0.91 m
8. Cape May, New Jersey, July 3
   3:32 A.M. 0.88 m
9. Annapolis, Maryland June 2
   10:25 A.M. 0.33 m
10. Annapolis, Maryland July 3
    11:25 A.M. 0.21 m
11. Los Angeles, California, June 3
    5:12 A.M. 1.13 m
12. San Francisco, California, June 3
    6:00 A.M. 1.22 m
13. Anchorage, Alaska July 2
    1:02 A.M. 7.86 m
14. Anchorage, Alaska August 18
    4:32 A.M. 7.95 m
15. Kodiak, Alaska July 2
    7:53 A.M. 2.01 m

16–30. Find the time and height of the evening tide for each city in exercises 1–15. See bottom of page 272.

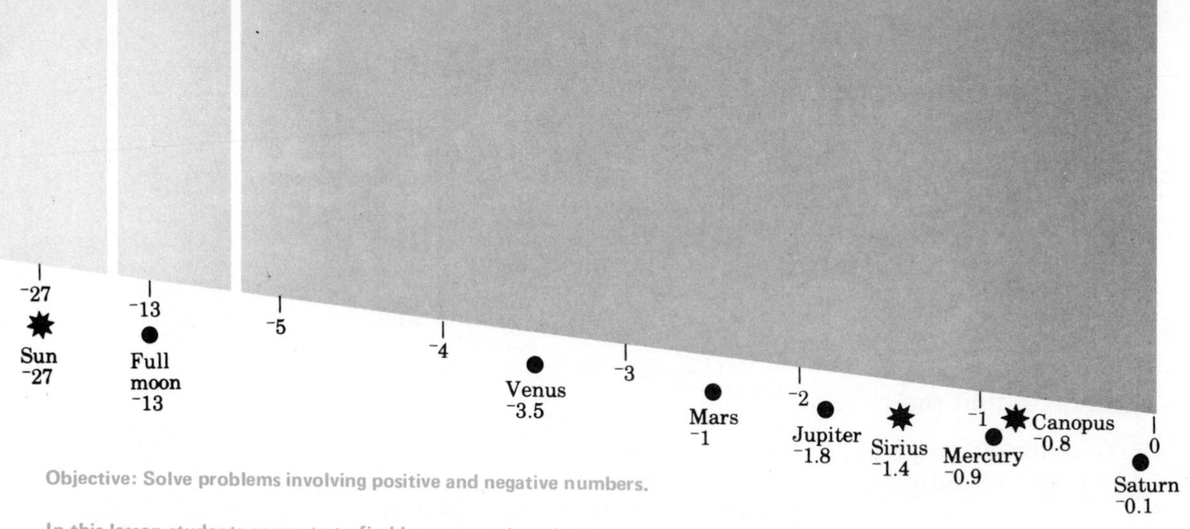

Objective: Solve problems involving positive and negative numbers.

In this lesson students compute to find how many times brighter one star or planet is than another.

Career: Astronomer

Career Cluster: Science

Barbara Huffman is an astronomer, a scientific observer of stars and planets. She uses the term **magnitude** to indicate the degree of brightness of stars and planets.

Venus has a magnitude of ⁻3.5. It is the brightest planet. Uranus has a magnitude of 5.7. This planet can scarcely be seen without using a telescope.

Barbara knows that each degree of magnitude is 2.512 (about 2.5) times brighter than the next degree. Thus, a star having a magnitude of 2 is about 2.5 times brighter than one having a magnitude of 3.

This table shows how much brighter a star or planet is than another if one knows the difference in magnitude.

Magnitude difference	Number of times brighter (nearest tenth)
1.0	2.5
1.5	4.0
2.0	6.3
2.5	10.0
3.0	15.9
3.5	25.1

Magnitude difference	Number of times brighter (nearest tenth)
4.0	39.8
5.0	100.0
6.0	251.3
7.0	631.2
8.0	1585.5
9.0	3982.7

Magnitude difference	Number of times brighter (nearest tenth)
10.0	10004.5
11.0	25131.4
12.0	63130.0
13.0	158582.5
14.0	398359.1
15.0	1000678.0

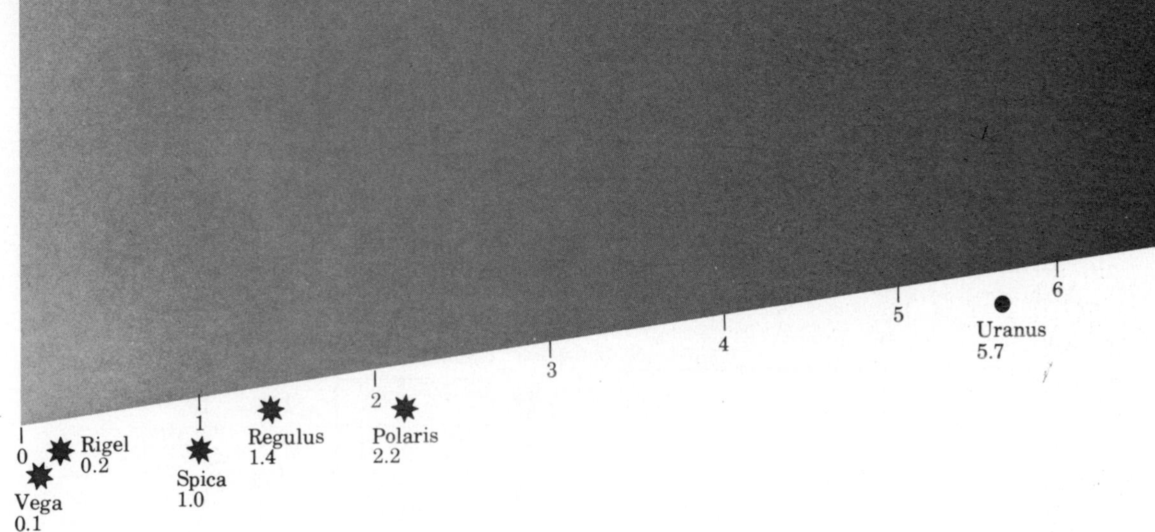

In each exercise, the brighter star or planet is underlined, and the magnitude difference is rounded to the nearest five tenths. When calculating the magnitude difference, emphasize that students *must* subtract the brightest magnitude from the dimmest magnitude, or they will obtain a negative difference.

Barbara needed to find how many times brighter Sirius was than Rigel.

First, she subtracted the magnitude of the brighter star from the magnitude of the dimmer star to find the magnitude difference. Then she rounded her answer to the nearest five tenths.

$0.2 - {}^{-}1.4 = 1.6 \approx 1.5$

Next, she located the magnitude difference of 1.5 in the table.

Sirius is about 4.0 times brighter than Rigel.

For each exercise, tell which planet or star is brighter. Then complete the table to find how many times brighter.

	Stars and planets	Magnitude difference	Number of times brighter
1.	Full Moon and Sun	14 ($^{-}13 - {}^{-}27$)	398,359.1
2.	Canopus and Polaris	3.0 ($2.2 - {}^{-}0.8$)	15.9
3.	Venus and Saturn	3.4≈3.5	25.1
4.	Spica and Vega	0.9≈1.0	2.5
5.	Regulus and Sirius	2.8≈3.0	15.9
6.	Saturn and Mars	0.9≈1.0	2.5
7.	Venus and Uranus	9.2≈9.0	3982.7
8.	Vega and Polaris	2.1≈2.0	6.3
9.	Mercury and Saturn	0.8≈1.0	2.5
10.	Mars and Venus	2.5	10.0
11.	Polaris and Sirius	3.6≈3.5	25.1
12.	Saturn and Full Moon	12.9≈13.0	158,582.5
13.	Venus and Mercury	2.6≈2.5	10.0
14.	Uranus and Saturn	5.8≈6.0	251.3

Number of test items - 29

Number missed	1	2	3	4	5	6	7	8	9	10	11	12	13	14
Percent correct	97	93	90	86	83	79	76	72	69	66	62	59	55	52

Chapter 13

A **1.** Write a number for point T on the number line.

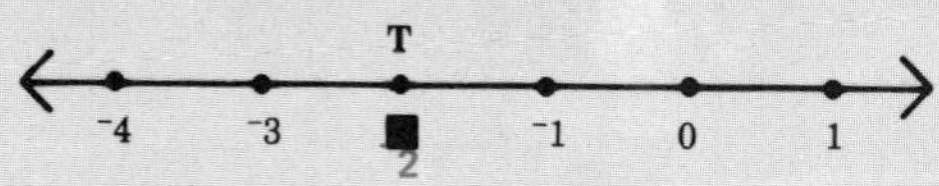

B **2.** Compare ⁻4 and 0. Use < or >. ⁻4 < 0, or 0 > ⁻4

C **3.** Arrange these numbers in order from least to greatest.

6, ⁻7, ⁻8, 9 ⁻8, ⁻7, 6, 9

D **4.** 8 + 9 17

E **5.** ⁻6 + ⁻4 ⁻10

F **6.** 7 + ⁻8 ⁻1

G **7.** 5 + ⁻7 + 6 + ⁻2 2

H **8.** Name the opposite of ⁻1. 1

I **9.** 2 − 3 ⁻1

J **10.** ⁻5 − ⁻1 ⁻4

K **11.** ⁻1 − 8 ⁻9

L **12.** 2 − ⁻9 11

M **13.** 16 − (⁻8 − ⁻3) 21

N **14.** 6 × 4 24

O **15.** ⁻5 × ⁻2 10

P **16.** 7 × ⁻4 ⁻28

Q **17.** 8(2) − 3(⁻4) 28

R **18.** 42 ÷ 6 7

S **19.** ⁻36 ÷ ⁻9 4

T **20.** ⁻28 ÷ 4 ⁻7

U **21.** $\frac{6 - {}^{-}4}{{}^{-}2 + {}^{-}3}$ ⁻2

Complete the pinochle score card.

	Hand	Bid	Meld	Play of hand	Score
22.	1	21	12	13	25
23.	2	—	8	5	13
24.	3	24	10	11	⁻24
25.	Total score				14

For items 26 and 27, use the tables on page 272.

26. Find the time of the morning tide for Annapolis, Maryland, on August 16. 11:55 A.M.

27. Find the height of the evening tide for Juneau, Alaska, on July 1. 4.57 m

For items 28 and 29, use the tables on page 274.

28. Which planet is brighter, Saturn or Jupiter? Jupiter

29. Compute to find how many times brighter Sirius is than Polaris. 25.1 times brighter

 See pages 37-38 of the *Tests and Record Forms: Duplicating Masters* for an alternate form of the Chapter 13 Test.

14

Chapter 14 Expressions and Equations

Number of test items - 14

Number missed	1	2	3	4	5	6	7
Percent correct	93	86	79	71	64	57	50

skill Evaluating Expressions pages 278-279

A Evaluate $a + 17 + b$ when $a = 3$ and $b = 6$. 26

B Evaluate $3.7 - x - z$ when $x = .9$ and $z = 2$. 0.8

C Evaluate $^{-}4sw$ when $s = 15$ and $w = {}^{-}1$. 60

D Evaluate $\frac{c}{d}$ when $c = 360$ and $d = {}^{-}60$. $^{-}6$

skill Evaluating Expressions Involving Order of Operations pages 280-281

E Evaluate $5xy + {}^{-}1$ when $x = 3$ and $y = 2$. 29

F Evaluate $\frac{2n}{.5} + 6(d - .3)$ when $n = 10$ and $d = 1.4$. 46.6

skill Solving Addition and Subtraction Equations pages 282-283

G Find r. $.83 + r = 5.7$ $r = 4.87$

H Find a. $a - .16 = .35$ $a = .51$

skill Solving Multiplication and Division Equations pages 284-285

I Find c. $^{-}6c = 420$ $c = {}^{-}70$

J Find x. $\frac{x}{^{-}4} = {}^{-}32$ $x = 128$

skill Solving Two-Step Equations pages 286-287

K Find y. $3y + 8 = 53$ $y = 15$

L Find m. $\frac{m}{7} - 1 = 8$ $m = 63$

skill Combining Like Terms to Solve Equations pages 288-289

M Find n. $4n + 3n = 63$ $n = 9$

N Find c. $12c + 3c - 7 = 68$ $c = 5$

See page T24 for additional notes on Chapter 14.

Skill

Objective: Evaluate expressions.

Evaluating Expressions

example A Involving addition

Evaluate $g + .23 + h$ when $g = 1.7$ and $h = .2$.

$g + .23 + h$

$1.7 + .23 + .2$

2.13

Substitute the given values for g and h in the expression. Then add.

example B Involving subtraction

Evaluate $n - p - 4.6$ when $n = 17.08$ and $p = .6$.

$n - p - 4.6$

$17.08 - .6 - 4.6$

11.88

Substitute the given values for n and p in the expression. Then subtract.

example C Involving multiplication

Evaluate $^{-}3ab$ when $a = {}^{-}4$ and $b = 6$.

$^{-}3ab$

$^{-}3(^{-}4)(6)$

72

Substitute the given values for a and b in the expression. Then multiply.

example D Involving division

Evaluate $\frac{51}{s}$ when $s = {}^{-}3$.

$\frac{51}{s}$

$\frac{51}{^{-}3}$

$^{-}17$

Substitute the given value for s in the expression. Then divide.

exercises

set A

Evaluate each expression when $a = .19$, $b = 4.2$, $x = {}^-6$, and $y = 57$.

1. $17 + x + 8$ 19
2. $a + 5.4$ 5.59
3. $48 + b$ 52.2
4. ${}^-60 + y$ ⁻3
5. $9.4 + a + b$ 13.79
6. $2.1 + b$ 6.3
7. ${}^-15 + x + y$ 36
8. $x + y$ 51
9. $a + 3.89 + y$ 61.08
10. $b + .08$ 4.28
11. $.71 + .053 + a$ .953
12. $105 + y$ 162
13. $22 + b + .7$ 26.9
14. $y + 21 + x$ 72
15. $b + .4 + a$ 4.79
16. $x + {}^-25$ ⁻31
17. $a + {}^-.19 + b$ 4.2
18. ${}^-98 + x$ ⁻104
19. $a + b + .99$ 5.38
20. $x + 62 + y$ 113
21. $a + 5.078$ 5.268
22. $y + 30 + b$ 91.2
23. $72.9 + b + y$ 134.1
24. $b + {}^-6.13 + a$ ⁻1.74
25. $x + x + 17$ 5

set B

Evaluate each expression when $g = 45$, $h = {}^-21$, $t = 3.7$, and $u = .9$.

1. $g - 16 - t$ 25.3
2. ${}^-36 - h$ ⁻15
3. $t - 2.5$ 1.2
4. $t - u$ 2.8
5. $2.1 - u$ 1.2
6. ${}^-45 - g$ ⁻90
7. $41.8 - 3.7 - t$ 34.4
8. $t - 1.9$ 1.8
9. $g - h$ 66
10. $g - 32 - h$ 34
11. $2.6 - t$ ⁻1.1
12. $u - t$ ⁻2.8
13. $t - 1.5 - u$ 1.3
14. $u - {}^-.3$ 1.2
15. $h - g$ ⁻66
16. $1.1 - u$ 0.2
17. $58.4 - t - g$ 9.7
18. $100.2 - u$ 99.3
19. $56 - h - g$ 32
20. $u - .005$ .895
21. $9.051 - t$ 5.351
22. $t - .06 - u$ 2.74
23. $100 - h$ 121
24. ${}^-4.51 - t$ ⁻8.21
25. $9.1 - u - t$ 4.5
26. $2000 - g - u$ 1954.1

set C

Evaluate each expression when $c = 14$, $d = {}^-90$, $k = .07$, and $n = 8.5$.

1. $26c$ 364
2. $4cd$ ⁻5040
3. ${}^-8c$ ⁻112
4. $2d$ ⁻180
5. cn 119
6. $16k$ 1.12
7. $25d$ ⁻2250
8. ${}^-7n$ ⁻59.5
9. ${}^-3d$ 270
10. $12n$ 102
11. $31k$ 2.17
12. $52c$ 728
13. ${}^-45k$ ⁻3.15
14. ${}^-10c$ ⁻140
15. ${}^-4d$ 360
16. kn .595
17. ${}^-5cd$ 6300
18. $100n$ 850
19. $2kn$ 1.19
20. $9ck$ 8.82

set D

Evaluate each expression when $m = .24$, $p = .6$, $w = {}^-5$, and $z = 50$.

1. $\frac{m}{4}$ .06
2. $\frac{m}{p}$ .4
3. $\frac{{}^-100}{z}$ ⁻2
4. $\frac{35}{w}$ ⁻7
5. $\frac{p}{3}$ .2
6. $\frac{m}{.12}$ 2
7. $\frac{w}{5}$ ⁻1
8. $\frac{z}{w}$ ⁻10
9. $\frac{z}{25}$ 2
10. $\frac{m}{{}^-.8}$ ⁻.3
11. $\frac{43.8}{p}$ 73
12. $\frac{{}^-3000}{z}$ ⁻60

Objective: Evaluate expressions involving order of operations.

Evaluating Expressions Involving Order of Operations

example E Without grouping symbols

Evaluate $\frac{45}{a} + 7k$ when $a = 15$ and $k = 4$.

$\frac{45}{a} + 7k$ Substitute the given values for a and k in the expression.

$\frac{45}{15} + 7(4)$ Do division and multiplication.

$3 + 28$ Do remaining addition.

31

example F With grouping symbols

Evaluate $\frac{x+7}{9-6} - 2(y+1)$ when $x = 26$ and $y = {}^-5$.

$\frac{x+7}{9-6} - 2(y+1)$ Substitute the given values for x and y in the expression.

$\frac{26+7}{9-6} - 2({}^-5+1)$ Do operations above and below the division bar and inside parentheses.

$\frac{33}{3} - 2({}^-4)$ Do remaining multiplication and division.

$11 - {}^-8$ Do remaining subtraction.

19

exercises set E

Evaluate each expression when $c = .3$, $s = 5.6$, $v = {}^-4$, and $y = 20$.

1. $5c + 2s$ 12.7
2. $2cs - 1$ 2.36
3. $\frac{c}{3} + 3y$ 60.1
4. $9v + 13 - {}^-2y$ 17
5. $\frac{y}{2} - \frac{16}{v}$ 14
6. $8s + 3.9$ 48.7
7. $10s - 8c$ 53.6
8. $3y + 11v$ 16
9. $7c + \frac{s}{.8}$ 9.1
10. $61 + 2v + 5y$ 153
11. $84 - 2vy$ 244
12. $\frac{180}{y} + 17c$ 14.1
13. $5s - 25c$ 20.5
14. $\frac{72}{v} + \frac{v}{4}$ ${}^-19$
15. $905c + 6.2$ 277.7
16. $10y - 30s$ 32

17. $\frac{^-2.7}{c} + {^-5}$ $^-14$

18. $^-2s - c$ $^-11.5$

Evaluate each expression when $a = 36$, $g = 50$, $h = .9$, and $k = 4.5$.

19. $\frac{k}{3} + \frac{a}{12}$ 4.5

20. $47 + \frac{100}{g}$ 49

21. $g - 30h$ 23

22. $\frac{a}{^-4} + \frac{g}{^-5}$ $^-19$

23. $\frac{h}{3} + .21$ .51

24. $40k + 7h$ 186.3

25. $\frac{k}{h} + 2.7$ 7.7

26. $3g - 2a$ 78

27. $a + g + 4k$ 104

28. $9h + \frac{k}{5}$ 9

29. $^-7g + a$ $^-314$

30. $250 + ag$ 2050

31. $ak - gh$ 117

32. $\frac{50}{g} + 5 + 2k$ 15

set F

Evaluate each expression when $b = 60$, $t = {^-8}$, $w = 3.2$, and $n = .05$.

1. $\frac{b+4}{16} + 3t$ $^-20$

2. $7w(2 + n) - 1$ 44.92

3. $\frac{b}{4} + \frac{36}{t+10}$ 33

4. $\frac{n(b+20)}{2} + w$ 5.2

5. $3(w + n) - 2wn$ 9.43

6. $\frac{488+t}{2b} - \frac{t+13}{5}$ 3

7. $\frac{95}{5} - n(23 + 6)$ 17.55

8. $\frac{22bn - 3}{w + 5.8}$ 7

9. $b(16 - 13) + 4t$ 148

10. $12(n + w) + \frac{130}{6.5}$ 59

11. $4(b + w) - 6$ 246.8

12. $8n(1.1 + w + .7)$ 2

13. $\frac{6bt}{5} + \frac{b-12}{8}$ $^-570$

14. $\frac{3t}{12} + {^-4b}$ $^-242$

15. $26n + 14(w + 1)$ 60.1

16. $n(20 - 5) + {^-.3}$ .45

17. $\frac{^-5w}{2} - 8$ $^-16$

18. $\frac{t+w}{1.2} + 2n$ $^-3.9$

Evaluate each expression when $d = 48$, $p = {^-6}$, $x = .16$, and $z = 7.2$.

19. $30xz(d - 28)$ 691.2

20. $\frac{21+p}{5} - \frac{100}{d+2}$ 1

21. $\frac{5(z+1)}{20.5} + \frac{x}{2}$ 2.08

22. $\frac{d}{3} + \frac{8(x+.3)}{4}$ 16.92

23. $\frac{15-p}{7} + d$ 51

24. $dz(14 - 7)$ 2419.2

25. $x(1 + 39) + .5z$ 10

26. $p(d - 45) - \frac{d}{16}$ $^-21$

27. $\frac{20(d+x+z)}{2}$ 553.6

28. $\frac{2p}{^-4} + \frac{p+20}{7}$ 5

29. $\frac{2z+.6}{3x+.02}$ 30

30. $\frac{dz}{3} + .2(x - {^-.01})$ 115.234

The applications on pages 292–295 may be used anytime after this lesson.

Objective: Solve addition and subtraction equations involving integers and decimals.

Solving Addition and Subtraction Equations

example G Missing addend

Find n.

$$n + 5.6 = 9.2$$

$$n + 5.6 - 5.6 = 9.2 - 5.6$$

$$n = 3.6$$

5.6 is added to n. To undo the addition, subtract 5.6 from $n + 5.6$. Also subtract 5.6 from 9.2.

Check:
Does $3.6 + 5.6 = 9.2$?
$9.2 = 9.2$ ✓

Substitute 3.6 for n in the original equation. Since the two sides of the equation are equal, n does equal 3.6.

example H Missing minuend

Find c.

$$c - 4 = {}^{-}17$$

$$c - 4 + 4 = {}^{-}17 + 4$$

$$c = {}^{-}13$$

4 is subtracted from c. To undo the subtraction, add 4 to $c - 4$. Also add 4 to $^{-}17$.

Check:
Does $^{-}13 - 4 = {}^{-}17$?
$^{-}17 = {}^{-}17$ ✓

Check by substituting $^{-}13$ for c in the original equation.

exercises set G

Find each missing number.

1. $x + 3.1 = 5.4$ $x = 2.3$
2. $b + {}^{-}7 = 18$ $b = 25$
3. $27 + a = 35$ $a = 8$
4. $1.92 + y = 2.3$ $y = .38$
5. $n + 22 = {}^{-}8$ $n = {}^{-}30$
6. $^{-}9 + c = 32$ $c = 41$
7. $51 = w + 33$ $w = 18$
8. $6.1 = d + 2.8$ $d = 3.3$
9. $z + 4.6 = 7.12$ $z = 2.52$
10. $^{-}6 + f = 15$ $f = 21$
11. $62 = t + 9$ $t = 53$
12. $9.04 + x = 31.5$ $x = 22.46$
13. $g + {}^{-}12 = {}^{-}12$ $g = 0$
14. $108 = u + 92$ $u = 16$
15. $1.15 + h = 3.06$ $h = 1.91$
16. $v + 8.4 = 9.1$ $v = .7$
17. $4 = {}^{-}13 + k$ $k = 17$
18. $41 + w = 54.9$ $w = 13.9$
19. $n + {}^{-}2 = 81$ $n = 83$
20. $3.8 + a = 7.4$ $a = 3.6$
21. $.07 + p = .38$ $p = .31$
22. $^{-}49 = d + 25$ $d = 74$
23. $r + 8.9 = 64.2$ $r = 55.3$
24. $^{-}23 + f = 73$ $f = 96$
25. $11.8 + s = 30$ $s = 18.2$

26. $h + 3.6 = 7.92$ $h = 4.32$

27. $.48 = .3 + t$ $t = .18$

28. $n + {}^{-}21 = {}^{-}6$ $n = 15$

29. $.231 + k = 1.08$ $k = .849$

30. $v + 107 = 4$ $v = {}^{-}103$

31. $3 = 11 + p$ $p = {}^{-}8$

32. $w + 26.2 = 91.2$ $w = 65$

33. $62 + a = 35$ $a = {}^{-}27$

34. $z + 4.07 = 9.3$ $z = 5.23$

35. $b + 18.2 = 31.1$ $b = 12.9$

36. $2.3 + c = 15.9$ $c = 13.6$

37. ${}^{-}41 = {}^{-}9 + y$ $y = {}^{-}32$

38. $q + 4.4 = 7.1$ $q = 2.7$

39. $49 = d + 88$ $d = {}^{-}39$

40. $h + .028 = .16$ $h = .132$

41. ${}^{-}14 + m = 26$ $m = 40$

42. $9.05 = k + 3.7$ $k = 5.35$

43. $5.5 + p = 19.4$ $p = 13.9$

44. $x + {}^{-}50 = 32$ $x = 82$

45. ${}^{-}103 = g + 6$ $g = {}^{-}109$

46. $60 + z = 31$ $z = {}^{-}29$

47. $a + 5.3 = 40$ $a = 34.7$

48. $29.2 + w = 41.8$ $w = 12.6$

49. ${}^{-}.63 + n = 1.4$ $n = 2.03$

50. $3 = c + {}^{-}12$ $c = 15$

51. $f + 91 = 156$ $f = 65$

52. $.329 + t = {}^{-}.601$ $t = {}^{-}.93$

53. $d + 1.2 = 31.7$ $d = 30.5$

54. ${}^{-}75 = z + 75$ $z = {}^{-}150$

55. $m + {}^{-}32.16 = 81.43$ $m = 113.59$

set H

Find each missing number.

1. $a - 4.1 = 2.6$ $a = 6.7$

2. $n - .25 = 1.48$ $n = 1.73$

3. $z - 7 = {}^{-}9$ $z = {}^{-}2$

4. $10 = b - 13$ $b = 23$

5. ${}^{-}8 = d - 17$ $d = 9$

6. $s - 7.08 = 1.32$ $s = 8.4$

7. $r - .8 = .09$ $r = .89$

8. $t - {}^{-}2 = 46$ $t = 44$

9. $c - 3.8 = 1.9$ $c = 5.7$

10. $f - .72 = .8$ $f = 1.52$

11. $x - 2.38 = 6.7$ $x = 9.08$

12. ${}^{-}35 = y - 14$ $y = {}^{-}21$

13. $21 = w - 98$ $w = 119$

14. $n - 3.3 = 6.06$ $n = 9.36$

15. $g - .081 = .95$ $g = 1.031$

16. $71 = k - 82$ $k = 153$

17. $3 = x - 18$ $x = 21$

18. $a - 45.92 = 6.02$ $a = 51.94$

19. $h - 8.3 = 4.77$ $h = 13.07$

20. ${}^{-}9 = m - 103$ $m = 94$

21. $2.8 = z - 5.35$ $z = 8.15$

22. $k - 8 = {}^{-}29$ $k = {}^{-}21$

23. $b - 6.2 = .49$ $b = 6.69$

24. $m - .76 = .8$ $m = 1.56$

25. $3.09 = w - 62.2$ $w = 65.29$

26. $c - 40 = {}^{-}37$ $c = 3$

27. $d - {}^{-}28 = {}^{-}74$ $d = {}^{-}102$

28. $f - 98.6 = 32.7$ $f = 131.3$

29. $p - 15 = {}^{-}64$ $p = {}^{-}49$

30. ${}^{-}19 = h - 53$ $h = 34$

31. $q - 4.04 = 30.17$ $q = 34.21$

32. $22.1 = n - 16.8$ $n = 38.9$

33. $74 = g - {}^{-}12$ $g = 62$

34. $s - 2.25 = 10.03$ $s = 12.28$

35. $5.4 = f - 9.6$ $f = 15$

36. $g - 14 = {}^{-}71$ $g = {}^{-}57$

37. $2.8 = p - 6.321$ $p = 9.121$

38. $5.1 = d - 26.4$ $d = 31.5$

39. $h - {}^{-}8 = 100$ $h = 92$

40. $17 = r - 4.5$ $r = 21.5$

41. $k - 83 = {}^{-}75$ $k = 8$

42. $t - 4.11 = 1.3$ $t = 5.41$

43. $6.6 = c - 7.9$ $c = 14.5$

44. $2 = s - {}^{-}91$ $s = {}^{-}89$

45. $m - 43.15 = 2.11$ $m = 45.26$

46. $u - {}^{-}7.7 = 40$ $u = 32.3$

47. ${}^{-}8 = t - 48$ $t = 40$

48. $n - 9 = {}^{-}10$ $n = {}^{-}1$

49. $p - 5.32 = 21.16$ $p = 26.48$

50. $v - 100 = {}^{-}4$ $v = 96$

51. $32.8 = b - .06$ $b = 32.86$

52. $q - {}^{-}19 = {}^{-}81$ $q = {}^{-}100$

53. $6 = v - {}^{-}47$ $v = {}^{-}41$

54. $w - 33.7 = 4.9$ $w = 38.6$

55. $6.2 = u - 7.06$ $u = 13.26$

56. $23 = a - {}^{-}18$ $a = 5$

57. $z - 100.17 = {}^{-}4.99$ $z = 95.18$

Objective: Solve multiplication and division equations involving integers and decimals.

Solving Multiplication and Division Equations

example I **Missing factor**

Find b.

$$^{-}30b = 240$$

$$\frac{^{-}30b}{^{-}30} = \frac{240}{^{-}30}$$

$$b = {^{-}8}$$

b is multiplied by $^{-}30$. To undo the multiplication, divide both sides of the equation by $^{-}30$.

Check:
Does $^{-}30(^{-}8) = 240$?
$240 = 240$ ✓

Check by substituting $^{-}8$ for b in the original equation.

example J **Missing dividend**

Find w.

$$\frac{w}{1.8} = 5.2$$

$$(1.8)\frac{w}{1.8} = (1.8)5.2$$

$$w = 9.36$$

w is divided by 1.8. To undo the division, multiply both sides of the equation by 1.8.

Check:
Does $\frac{9.36}{1.8} = 5.2$?
$5.2 = 5.2$ ✓

Check by substituting 9.36 for w in the original equation.

exercises

set I

Find each missing number.

1. $^{-}3w = 159$ $w = {^{-}53}$
2. $1.2a = 84$ $a = 70$
3. $^{-}63 = 7m$ $m = {^{-}9}$
4. $1.85 = .05h$ $h = 37$
5. $4d = {^{-}196}$ $d = {^{-}49}$
6. $.9x = .72$ $x = .8$
7. $3.1y = 3.1$ $y = 1$
8. $^{-}8t = {^{-}744}$ $t = 93$
9. $.62c = 4.774$ $c = 7.7$
10. $34.4 = 4.3w$ $w = 8$
11. $172.8 = 7.2g$ $g = 24$
12. $.186 = .02u$ $u = 9.3$
13. $54 = {^{-}18y}$ $y = {^{-}3}$
14. $95g = 570$ $g = 6$
15. $26k = {^{-}130}$ $k = {^{-}5}$
16. $^{-}9v = {^{-}756}$ $v = 84$
17. $^{-}561 = {^{-}33d}$ $d = 17$
18. $4.05 = 4.5y$ $y = .9$
19. $1.62 = .27q$ $q = 6$
20. $3.8c = 7.98$ $c = 2.1$
21. $^{-}3n = 120$ $n = {^{-}40}$
22. $390 = 6b$ $b = 65$
23. $70z = {^{-}5670}$ $z = {^{-}81}$
24. $21.5 = .5r$ $r = 43$
25. $10.44 = 3.6t$ $t = 2.9$

26. $9.2p = 6.44$ $p = .7$

27. $.583 = .53f$ $f = 1.1$

28. ${}^{-}17s = {}^{-}340$ $s = 20$

29. ${}^{-}80x = 1040$ $x = {}^{-}13$

30. ${}^{-}2.5w = 20$ $w = {}^{-}8$

31. $.54 = .09n$ $n = 6$

32. $.008z = .01096$ $z = 1.37$

33. $.423 = 4.7k$ $k = .09$

34. $83b = {}^{-}83$ $b = {}^{-}1$

35. ${}^{-}11u = 0$ $u = 0$

36. ${}^{-}.0588 = .98c$ $c = {}^{-}.06$

set J

Find each missing number.

1. $\frac{b}{3.4} = 1.8$ $b = 6.12$

2. $\frac{n}{{}^{-}3} = 52$ $n = {}^{-}156$

3. $.46 = \frac{a}{.7}$ $a = .322$

4. $9.1 = \frac{k}{.9}$ $k = 8.19$

5. $\frac{c}{35} = .08$ $c = 2.8$

6. ${}^{-}6 = \frac{h}{17}$ $h = {}^{-}102$

7. $\frac{g}{{}^{-}9} = {}^{-}8$ $g = 72$

8. $\frac{d}{{}^{-}5} = 75$ $d = {}^{-}375$

9. $\frac{r}{31} = 28$ $r = 868$

10. $\frac{c}{4.7} = .25$ $c = 1.175$

11. ${}^{-}1 = \frac{g}{44}$ $g = {}^{-}44$

12. $16 = \frac{b}{{}^{-}7}$ $b = {}^{-}112$

13. $.04 = \frac{s}{92}$ $s = 3.68$

14. $\frac{h}{1.9} = 2.4$ $h = 4.56$

15. $38 = \frac{a}{20.9}$ $a = 794.2$

16. $\frac{z}{{}^{-}9} = {}^{-}52$ $z = 468$

17. $\frac{t}{39} = {}^{-}3$ $t = {}^{-}117$

18. $\frac{k}{{}^{-}1} = 472$ $k = {}^{-}472$

19. $9.2 = \frac{u}{.6}$ $u = 5.52$

20. $\frac{m}{.07} = 5.3$ $m = .371$

21. $\frac{y}{.16} = .29$ $y = .0464$

22. $\frac{v}{{}^{-}18} = 34$ $v = {}^{-}612$

23. $\frac{x}{.01} = 74.9$ $x = .749$

24. ${}^{-}14 = \frac{n}{{}^{-}14}$ $n = 196$

25. $26 = \frac{w}{{}^{-}6}$ $w = {}^{-}156$

26. $\frac{p}{5.09} = {}^{-}.2$ $p = {}^{-}1.018$

27. $\frac{v}{.73} = 1.29$ $v = .9417$

28. $4.16 = \frac{q}{.27}$ $q = 1.1232$

29. $\frac{w}{{}^{-}2} = {}^{-}606$ $w = 1212$

30. $3.9 = \frac{x}{52.5}$ $x = 204.75$

31. $\frac{r}{{}^{-}3} = 70$ $r = {}^{-}210$

32. $1.25 = \frac{u}{.38}$ $u = .475$

33. $\frac{s}{{}^{-}.99} = .6$ $s = {}^{-}.594$

34. $\frac{y}{{}^{-}5} = {}^{-}400$ $y = 2000$

35. $26 = \frac{f}{{}^{-}17}$ $f = {}^{-}442$

36. $\frac{t}{{}^{-}85} = 4$ $t = {}^{-}340$

37. $\frac{d}{1.26} = {}^{-}3.05$ $d = {}^{-}3.843$

The applications on pages 291, 296–297 may be used anytime after this lesson.

Objective: Solve two-step equations.

Solving Two-Step Equations

example K Missing factor

Find n.

$$4n + 12 = 32$$

$$4n + 12 - 12 = 32 - 12$$

First find $4n$. To undo the addition, subtract 12 from $4n + 12$. Also subtract 12 from 32.

$$4n = 20$$

$$\frac{4n}{4} = \frac{20}{4}$$

Then find n. To undo the multiplication, divide both sides of the equation by 4.

$$n = 5$$

Check:
Does $4(5) + 12 = 32$?
$32 = 32$ ✓

Check by substituting 5 for n in the original equation.

example L Missing dividend

Find t.

$$\frac{t}{^-6} + 15 = 10$$

$$\frac{t}{^-6} + 15 - 15 = 10 - 15$$

First find $\frac{t}{^-6}$. To undo the addition, subtract 15 from $\frac{t}{^-6}$. Also subtract 15 from 10.

$$\frac{t}{^-6} = {}^-5$$

$$(^-6)\frac{t}{^-6} = (^-6)(^-5)$$

Then find t. To undo the division, multiply both sides of the equation by $^-6$.

$$t = 30$$

Check:
Does $\frac{30}{^-6} + 15 = 10$?
$10 = 10$ ✓

Check by substituting 30 for t in the original equation.

exercises set K

Find each missing number.

1. $3x + 1 = 13$ $x = 4$
2. $7n + 2 = 51$ $n = 7$
3. $4t + 4 = 40$ $t = 9$
4. $5a + 8 = 3$ $a = {}^-1$
5. $^-2s + 6 = 0$ $s = 3$
6. $^-9b + 2 = 56$ $b = {}^-6$
7. $10y + 3 = 83$ $y = 8$
8. $12c - 4 = 20$ $c = 2$
9. $6m + 2 = 80$ $m = 13$
10. $^-8r + 10 = {}^-30$ $r = 5$
11. $^-5d + 100 = 50$ $d = 10$
12. $1.4k + .2 = 3$ $k = 2$
13. $^-3n + 14 = 17$ $n = {}^-1$
14. $20g - 25 = {}^-25$ $g = 0$
15. $11w - 7 = 37$ $w = 4$
16. $^-4z + 12 = 32$ $z = {}^-5$
17. $2h + 8 = 11$ $h = 1.5$
18. $7s + 2 = 65$ $s = 9$
19. $30p + 10 = 340$ $p = 11$
20. $9n - 15 = 93$ $n = 12$
21. $.5x + .7 = 2.1$ $x = 2.8$
22. $2t - 13 = {}^-1$ $t = 6$
23. $8a - 12 = 124$ $a = 17$
24. $.7g + .5 = 3.3$ $g = 4$
25. $^-10k + {}^-5 = {}^-35$ $k = 3$

26. $5c - 6 = 39$ $c = 9$

27. $.03b + .08 = .14$ $b = 2$

28. $4y - 27 = 13$ $y = 10$

29. $18m + 14 = 104$ $m = 5$

30. $21h + 3 = 150$ $h = 7$

31. $^-3r + {}^-3 = {}^-30$ $r = 9$

32. $5s - 8 = {}^-23$ $s = {}^-3$

33. $^-8q - {}^-2 = {}^-38$ $q = 5$

34. $15d + 63 = 363$ $d = 20$

35. $2x + 20 = 4$ $x = {}^-8$

36. $25z - 500 = 500$ $z = 40$

set L

Find each missing number.

1. $\frac{m}{3} + 2 = 5$ $m = 9$

2. $\frac{a}{^-5} + 8 = 6$ $a = 10$

3. $\frac{x}{2} + 7 = 11$ $x = 8$

4. $\frac{n}{6} + 13 = 15$ $n = 12$

5. $\frac{t}{.7} + 9 = 10$ $t = .7$

6. $\frac{s}{^-9} + 7 = 9$ $s = {}^-18$

7. $\frac{y}{8} - 3 = 2$ $y = 40$

8. $\frac{w}{10} - 1 = 2$ $w = 30$

9. $\frac{z}{12} - 8 = {}^-4$ $z = 48$

10. $\frac{n}{^-3} + 19 = 14$ $n = 15$

11. $\frac{b}{2} - 7 = 12$ $b = 38$

12. $\frac{d}{4} - 6 = {}^-1$ $d = 20$

13. $\frac{c}{5} + 12 = 25$ $c = 65$

14. $\frac{q}{20} + 26 = 31$ $q = 100$

15. $\frac{h}{16} - 2 = 0$ $h = 32$

16. $\frac{s}{^-1} + 18 = 35$ $s = {}^-17$

17. $\frac{n}{^-8} + {}^-2 = {}^-10$ $n = 64$

18. $\frac{a}{9} - 6 = 2$ $a = 72$

19. $\frac{c}{3} - 3 = 4$ $c = 21$

20. $\frac{t}{6} - 9 = {}^-6$ $t = 18$

21. $\frac{k}{30} + 62 = 65$ $k = 90$

22. $\frac{g}{10} - 5 = 3$ $g = 80$

23. $\frac{d}{^-11} + 17 = 13$ $d = 44$

24. $\frac{h}{.4} + 2 = 11$ $h = 3.6$

25. $\frac{x}{.3} + .5 = 1.4$ $x = .27$

26. $\frac{r}{9} - 1 = 4$ $r = 45$

27. $\frac{b}{1.2} + 4.6 = 11.6$ $b = 8.4$

28. $\frac{s}{7} - 4 = 4$ $s = 56$

29. $\frac{v}{9} + 31 = 40$ $v = 81$

30. $\frac{h}{.8} + 16 = 25$ $h = 7.2$

31. $\frac{u}{9} + 6.2 = 16.2$ $u = 90$

32. $\frac{z}{13} + {}^-2 = 0$ $z = 26$

33. $\frac{c}{40} - 8 = {}^-5$ $c = 120$

34. $\frac{g}{2} - 11 = 3$ $g = 28$

35. $\frac{v}{.9} + .7 = 1.3$ $v = 1.8$

36. $\frac{d}{^-5} + 29 = 35$ $d = {}^-30$

37. $\frac{k}{6} - 8 = {}^-23$ $k = {}^-90$

Objective: Combine like terms to solve equations.

Combining Like Terms to Solve Equations

example M Missing factor, one-step equation

Find y.

$$7y + 6y = 65$$

$$13y = 65$$

$$\frac{13y}{13} = \frac{65}{13}$$

$$y = 5$$

First, combine like terms. $7y$ and $6y$ are like terms because both 7 and 6 are multiplied by y. $7y + 6y = (7 + 6)y = 13y$

Then divide both sides of the equation by 13 to find y.

Check:
Does $7(5) + 6(5) = 65$?
$65 = 65$ ✓

example N Missing factor, two-step equation

Find x.

$$8x + 18 + {}^-3x - 4 = 64$$

$$5x \quad + \quad 14 \quad = 64$$

First, combine like terms. $8x + {}^-3x = 5x$
$18 - 4 = 14$

$$5x + 14 - 14 = 64 - 14$$

$$5x = 50$$

Subtract 14 from both sides of the equation to find $5x$.

$$\frac{5x}{5} = \frac{50}{5}$$

$$x = 10$$

Then divide both sides of the equation by 5 to find x.

Check:
Does $8(10) + 18 + {}^-3(10) - 4 = 64$?
$64 = 64$ ✓

exercises set M

Find each missing number.

1. $3n + 7n = 80$ $n = 8$
2. ${}^-4x + 2x = 18$ $x = {}^-9$
3. $9z + 8z = 34$ $z = 2$
4. $a + 5a = 72$ $a = 12$
5. $2t + {}^-3t + 4t = 27$ $t = 9$
6. $14m + m = {}^-75$ $m = {}^-5$
7. $3b + 8b = 99$ $b = 9$
8. $10c - 2c = 56$ $c = 7$
9. $12p - 6p = 36$ $p = 6$
10. $r + r = 46$ $r = 23$
11. $7s + 9s = 48$ $s = 3$
12. $4v + {}^-11v = 49$ $v = {}^-7$
13. ${}^-2z + 10z = 16$ $z = 2$
14. $5d + 5d + 5d = 30$ $d = 2$
15. ${}^-3w + {}^-4w = 140$ $w = {}^-20$
16. $2y + {}^-7y = 70$ $y = {}^-14$
17. $3.1u + .2u = 6.6$ $u = 2$
18. $6x + .5x = 32.5$ $x = 5$
19. ${}^-9f + 5f = 40$ $f = {}^-10$
20. $1.8n + .7n = 10$ $n = 4$
21. ${}^-6z + 21z = 45$ $z = 3$
22. $40a - 20a = 180$ $a = 9$
23. $q + 3q + q = 135$ $q = 27$
24. $2b + 17b + b = 20$ $b = 1$
25. ${}^-4x + x - 8x = 0$ $x = 0$

set N

Find each missing number.

1. $2c + 3 + 5c = 52$ — $c = 7$
2. $n + 8n + 9 = 27$ — $n = 2$
3. $4x + {}^-9 + 3x = {}^-16$ — $x = {}^-1$
4. $9w - 2w + 10 = 31$ — $w = 3$
5. $6d - 4d - 3 = 7$ — $d = 5$
6. $7m + 25 + m = {}^-7$ — $m = {}^-4$
7. $2p - p + 1 = 10$ — $p = 9$
8. $30a + 1.6 + 1.4 + 2a = 22.2$ — $a = .6$
9. $5x + 2x - 17 = {}^-52$ — $x = {}^-5$
10. $6 + n + 3n + 9 = 47$ — $n = 8$
11. $4b + {}^-6 + 7b + b = 114$ — $b = 10$
12. $7q + 4 + {}^-3q - 7 = 13$ — $q = 4.5$
13. $19k + 8 - 6 - 12 = 560$ — $k = 30$
14. $27 + c + 11c - 15 = 96$ — $c = 7$
15. $3g + 4.6 + .7 + 13g = 11.7$ — $g = .4$
16. $t + 15 + 6t - 9 = 41$ — $t = 5$
17. $2h + 9.5 + .7 + 3 = 17$ — $h = 1.9$
18. $47 + k + 8k + {}^-6 = 68$ — $k = 3$
19. $17v + {}^-8 + {}^-11v - 2 = 20$ — $v = 5$
20. $12z - 6z + 4z - 21 = 39$ — $z = 6$
21. $8u + 70 - 4u = 30$ — $u = {}^-10$
22. $3y + 8 - y = 9$ — $y = .5$
23. $4b + b + 19 + {}^-2b - 5 = 41$ — $b = 9$
24. ${}^-17x + 2 + {}^-3x + 23 = 145$ — $x = {}^-6$
25. $4d + 1.7 + .2d + 7 = 21.3$ — $d = 3$
26. $3a + 9a + a + {}^-6 = 137$ — $a = 11$
27. $19 + s + 10s + {}^-2s + 8 = 27$ — $s = 0$
28. $1.5g + 2.5 + .8g = 2.96$ — $g = .2$
29. $53 + 6c - 2c - 1 = 80$ — $c = 7$
30. $1.6w + .7w + 9 = 9.46$ — $w = .2$
31. ${}^-4x + 32 - 5 + 8x = 7$ — $x = {}^-5$
32. $9.4a + .7a + 2.4 + 6.1 = 38.8$ — $a = 3$
33. $17k + {}^-9 - 12k + 4 = 0$ — $k = 1$
34. $12t + 8t + 44 - 36 = {}^-12$ — $t = {}^-1$
35. $g + 15 + 3g + 5g = 105$ — $g = 10$
36. $3n + 71 - 2n - 62 = 13$ — $n = 4$
37. $13 + 4p + {}^-6p + 8 = 5$ — $p = 8$
38. $5z + 52 - 47 + z = {}^-7$ — $z = {}^-2$
39. ${}^-2d + 3d + 16 - 9 = 12$ — $d = 5$
40. $3.56r + .04r + 3.9 = 11.1$ — $r = 2$

BREAK TIME

9 8 7 6 5 4 3 2 1

Place addition or subtraction signs between the digits to make a problem with an answer of 100. Do not change the order of the digits.

Here is an example that is wrong because the answer is 116.

$9 + 8 + 76 + 54 - 32 + 1 = 116$

$98 - 76 + 54 + 3 + 21 = 100$

Number of test items - 14

Number missed	1	2	3	4	5	6	7
Percent correct	93	86	79	71	64	57	50

skill Evaluating Expressions pages 278-279

A Evaluate $n + .4 + a$ when $n = .7$ and $a = 3$. 4.1

B Evaluate $b - 14 - 3$ when $b = {}^-8$. $^-25$

C Evaluate $3xy$ when $x = {}^-17$ and $y = 2$. $^-102$

D Evaluate $\frac{6.4}{m}$ when $m = 8$. .8

skill Evaluating Expressions Involving Order of Operations pages 280-281

E Evaluate $\frac{20}{c} + {}^-6d$ when $c = 4$ and $d = {}^-5$. 35

F Evaluate $3(t + .5) + \frac{9v}{2}$ when $t = 1.5$ and $v = .2$. 6.9

skill Solving Addition and Subtraction Equations pages 282-283

G Find k. $k + {}^-8 = 13$ $k = 21$

H Find g. $g - 4.3 = 17.8$ $g = 22.1$

skill Solving Multiplication and Division Equations pages 284-285

I Find w. $3.5w = 7$ $w = 2$

J Find v. $\frac{v}{9} = {}^-21$ $v = {}^-189$

skill Solving Two-Step Equations pages 286-287

K Find d. $2d - 6 = 4$ $d = 5$

L Find h. $\frac{h}{3} + {}^-6 = 19$ $h = 75$

skill Combining Like Terms to Solve Equations pages 288-289

M Find x. $6x + 2x = 96$ $x = 12$

N Find u. $13u + 8 - u = {}^-40$ $u = {}^-4$

Objective: Solve problems involving equations.

In this lesson students solve problems using the formulas $E = IR$ and $W = EI$.

Checking the Safety of Electrical Circuits

Electricity flows through circuits under a constant pressure (volts), at a certain rate (amperes), and encounters resistance (ohms). The number of volts is equal to the amperes times the ohms.

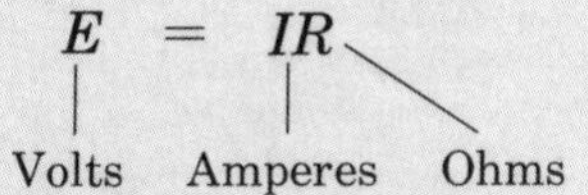

These units are given on many electrical appliances.

The amount of electrical power required to operate appliances is measured in watts. The number of watts is equal to the volts times the amperes.

$W = EI$

Watts Volts Amperes

The resistance of a radio is 60 ohms when the radio is using 120 volts. How many amperes of current is the radio drawing?

$E = IR$

$120 = I \times 60$

$\frac{120}{60} = I$

$2 = I$

The radio is drawing 2 amperes of current.

How many watts is the radio using?

$W = EI$

$W = 120(2)$

$W = 240$

The radio is using 240 watts.

An overloaded circuit could cause a fire. To check the safety of each circuit, first use the information given to find the amperes (I) and the watts (W) for each appliance on the circuit. Round your answers to the nearest tenth.

	Circuit A				
	Appliance	Ohms (R)	Volts (E)	Amps (I)	Watts (W)
1.	Toaster	22	110	5	550
2.	Percolator	20	110	5.5	605
3.	Frying pan	11	110	10	1100
4.	Clock	270	110	.4	44
5.	Doorbell	220	110	.5	55

	Circuit B				
	Appliance	Ohms (R)	Volts (E)	Amps (I)	Watts (W)
6.	Dishwasher	70	220	3.1	682
7.	Heater	55	220	4	880
8.	Dryer	25	220	8.8	1936

9. What is the total wattage of circuit A? 2354 watts

10. Circuit A can safely handle up to 1800 watts. Is circuit A safe? No

11. What is the total wattage of circuit B? 3498 watts

12. Circuit B can safely handle up to 3600 watts. Is circuit B safe? Yes

Objective: Solve problems involving equations.

In this lesson students solve problems relating to a coinsurance policy by using the formula $P = \frac{IL}{.8V}$

Interpreting a Coinsurance Clause

Some homeowner's insurance policies have an 80% coinsurance clause. This means that if the property is insured for less than 80% of its value, the insurance company will pay only part of the amount of any damages. The insurance company uses this formula to determine the amount it will pay.

$$P = \frac{IL}{.8V}$$

Point out that if the property is insured for 80% of its value or more, the entire loss would be covered by insurance, and the formula would not be used.

P is the amount paid by the company.
I is the amount of insurance carried.
L is the amount of the loss.
V is the value of the property.

Francisca's home, valued at $40,000, was damaged by fire. Francisca has a $20,000 insurance policy with an 80% coinsurance clause. The damage was $10,000. How much money would the insurance company pay Francisca?

$$P = \frac{IL}{.8V}$$

Encourage students to simplify before multiplying.

$$P = \frac{20{,}000(10{,}000)}{.8(40{,}000)}$$

$$P = 6250$$

The insurance company would pay $6250 for the damages.

How much more money would Francisca have to pay to completely repair the damages?

$$\begin{array}{r} \$10000 \\ -\quad 6250 \\ \hline \$\ 3750 \end{array}$$

Francisca would have to pay $3750.

Each of these properties is insured by a policy with an 80% coinsurance clause. Find each amount paid by the insurance company to the nearest whole dollar. Then subtract to find the amount paid by each owner.

	Value of property (V)	Insurance carried (I)	Loss (L)	Paid by insurance company (P)	Paid by owner
1.	$25,000	$18,000	$8000	$7200	$800
2.	$80,000	$40,000	$5000	$3125	$1875
3.	$10,400	$6500	$3000	$2344	$656
4.	$165,000	$130,000	$2950	$2905	$45
5.	$125,000	$85,000	$90,000	$76,500	$13,500
6.	$50,000	$30,000	$15,000	$11,250	$3750
7.	$34,500	$25,000	$25,000	$22,645	$2355
8.	$54,000	$36,000	$11,500	$9583	$1917
9.	$95,000	$47,000	$12,800	$7916	$4884
10.	$100,000	$75,000	$100,000	$93,750	$6250
11.	$72,000	$54,000	$8950	$8391	$559
12.	$46,800	$32,000	$4300	$3675	$625
13.	$37,000	$25,000	$18,400		
14.	$66,000	$50,000	$3000		
15.	$30,500	$20,000	$800		

13. $15,541, $2859
14. $2841, $159
15. $656, $144

Objective: Solve problems involving equations.

In this lesson students use the formula $P = \frac{2wh}{s+1}$ to determine the safe load for a pile that has been driven in the ground.

Career: Heavy-Equipment Operator

Career Cluster: Trades

Paul Becker is working on the construction of homes built on pile foundations. Paul operates the equipment used to drive the piles into the ground.

The pile driver drops a heavy "hammer" on the pile to push it into the ground. Paul uses this formula to determine the weight that could be supported by a pile when it has been driven into the ground (the safe load).

$$P = \frac{2wh}{s+1}$$

P is the safe load in pounds.
w is the weight of the hammer in pounds.
h is the distance in feet the hammer falls.
s is the distance in inches the pile moves under the blow.

Suppose the weight of the hammer is 3000 pounds, and when the hammer falls 10 feet, it moves the pile 2 inches into the ground. What weight could then be supported by the pile?

$$P = \frac{2wh}{s+1}$$

$$P = \frac{2(3000)(10)}{2+1}$$

$$P = \frac{60{,}000}{3}$$

$$P = 20{,}000$$

The safe load of the pile is 20,000 pounds.

For each exercise, use the values given and the formula in the example to find the safe load. Round your answers to the nearest whole number.

1. $w = 2000,\ h = 10,\ s = 1$ 20,000 pounds
2. $w = 2000,\ h = 10,\ s = 2$ 13,333 pounds
3. $w = 3000,\ h = 15,\ s = 2$ 30,000 pounds
4. $w = 2500,\ h = 7,\ s = 1$ 17,500 pounds
5. $w = 3000,\ h = 8,\ s = .5$ 32,000 pounds
6. $w = 2000,\ h = 6,\ s = .5$ 16,000 pounds
7. $w = 2000,\ h = 9,\ s = .75$ 20,571 pounds
8. $w = 2000,\ h = 15,\ s = .75$ 34,286 pounds
9. $w = 3000,\ h = 15,\ s = 1.5$ 36,000 pounds
10. $w = 3000,\ h = 12,\ s = 1.5$ 28,800 pounds

To determine what value of s will indicate a safe load of 20,000 pounds, Paul uses this formula.

$$s = \frac{2wh}{P} - 1$$

Find s if P is 20,000 pounds and these are the values of w and h.

11. $w = 2000,\ h = 15$ 2 inches
12. $w = 2500,\ h = 9$ 1.25 inches
13. $w = 3000,\ h = 20$ 5 inches
14. $w = 2500,\ h = 8$ 1 inch
15. $w = 3000,\ h = 5$ .5 inch

Objective: Solve problems involving equations.

In this lesson students find rates of vehicles in meters per second and in kilometers per hour.

Career: Police Officer

Career Cluster: Social Service

Distances are often measured between landmarks, such as overpasses, trees, culverts, and utility poles.

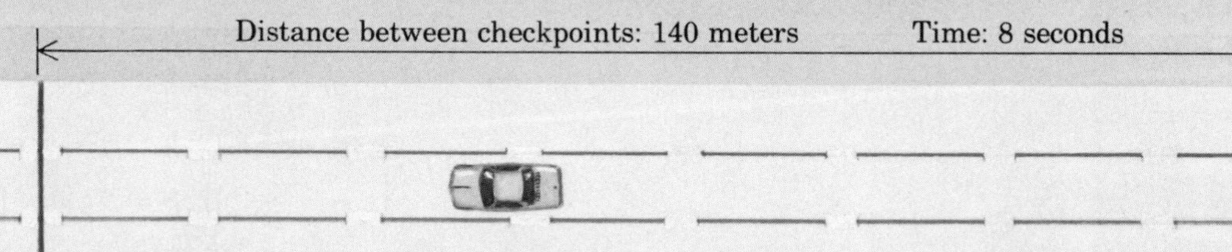

VASCAR is an acronym for Visual Average Speed Computer and Recorder.

Tracy Collier is a police officer. She uses her VASCAR equipment to time a vehicle when it passes certain checkpoints, and to measure the distance between these checkpoints. The speed of the vehicle is then computed by the equipment. If it is necessary for Tracy to appear in court, she must be prepared to explain the mathematics involved in finding the speed.

This formula is used to find speed (rate).

$$D = RT$$

Distance Rate Time

What is the speed of the automobile in the picture?

$$D = RT$$

$$140 = R \times 8$$

$$\frac{140}{8} = R$$

$$17.5 = R$$

The speed is 17.5 meters per second (17.5 m/s).

Use the formula to find each missing distance, rate, or time. Round your answers to the nearest tenth.

	Distance (meters)	Rate (m/s)	Time (seconds)
1.	250	25	10
2.	340	26.2	13
3.	185	26.4	7
4.	216	18	12
5.	73.2	12	6.1
6.	455	13	35
7.	150	15	10
8.	244	20	12.2
9.	360	14	25.7
10.	240	22.9	10.5

Officer Collier is checking speeds in an 80 kilometer per hour (80 km/h) zone. She finds that the rate of a certain vehicle is 25 m/s. Is this a violation?

To convert meters per second to kilometers per hour, multiply by 3.6.

$3.6 \times 25 = 90$

The speed of the vehicle is 90 km/h. This is a violation because it is greater than the speed limit of 80 km/h.

Complete this table. First find the rate in meters per second. Round your answer to the nearest tenth. Then find the rate in kilometers per hour and decide if the speed is a violation of the speed limit given.

	Distance (meters)	Time (seconds)	Rate (m/s)	Rate (km/h)	Speed limit (km/h)	Violation (yes or no?)
11.	200	13	15.4	55.4	60	No
12.	325	14	23.2	83.5	90	No
13.	250	10	25	90	80	Yes
14.	235	8	29.4	105.8	90	Yes
15.	450	25	18	64.8	80	No
16.	432	24	18	64.8	60	Yes
17.	360	18	20	72	65	Yes
18.	500	20	25	90	90	No
19.	1000	30	33.3	119.9	100	Yes
20.	275	15	18.3	65.9	60	Yes

Number of test items - 18

Number missed	1	2	3	4	5	6	7	8	9
Percent correct	94	89	83	78	72	67	61	56	50

Chapter 14

Evaluate each expression when $a = 5$, $b = ^{-}3$, $x = 1.8$, and $y = 90$.

A **1.** $14 + a + y$ 109

B **2.** $37.2 - x - a$ 30.4

C **3.** $2ab$ $^{-}30$

D **4.** $\frac{y}{b}$ $^{-}30$

E **5.** $2y - 3a$ 165

F **6.** $7(x + .2) + \frac{54a}{30}$ 23

Find each missing number.

G **7.** $2.5 + a = 17.1$ $a = 14.6$

H **8.** $n - 15 = ^{-}60$ $n = ^{-}45$

I **9.** $13y = ^{-}299$ $y = ^{-}23$

J **10.** $\frac{w}{.53} = 4$ $w = 2.12$

K **11.** $7c - 16 = 68$ $c = 12$

L **12.** $\frac{v}{6} + 25 = 31$ $v = 36$

M **13.** $2x + 17x = 57$ $x = 3$

N **14.** $10d + 9 - 3d = 37$ $d = 4$

15. The resistance of an iron is 20 ohms when the iron is using 120 volts. How many amperes of current is the iron drawing? 6 amperes

16. The value of a home was $40,000. The home was insured for $20,000 by a policy with an 80% coinsurance clause. If $5000 damage was done to the home, how much money would the insurance company pay the owner? $3125

17. The weight of a hammer on a pile driver is 2000 pounds. When the hammer fell 8 feet, it moved the pile 1 inch into the ground. What weight could be supported by the pile? 16,000 pounds

18. A truck traveled 220 meters in 11 seconds. What was the speed of the truck in meters per second? 20 m/s

You may wish to have students refer to the applications lessons on pages 291–297 to find the formulas needed for items 15–18.

 See pages 39–40 of the *Tests and Record Forms: Duplicating Masters* for an alternate form of the Chapter 14 Test.

pretest

Materials: Graph paper, straightedge

Number of test items - 8

Number missed	1	2	3	4
Percent correct	88	75	63	50

skill Locating Points on a Grid page 301

A Give an ordered pair for point Q. Q(3,5)

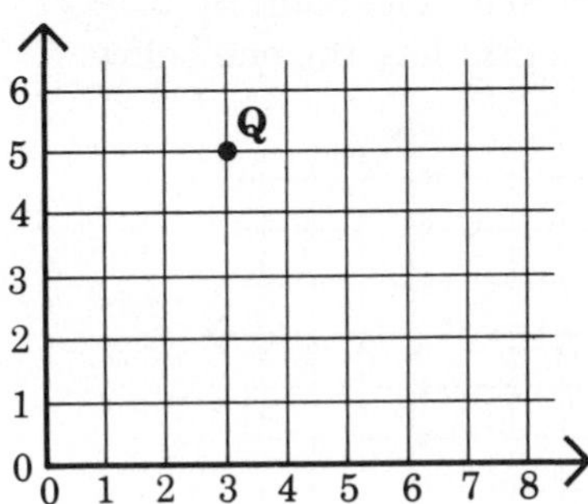

B Plot and label point R(6, 2) on a grid like the one below.

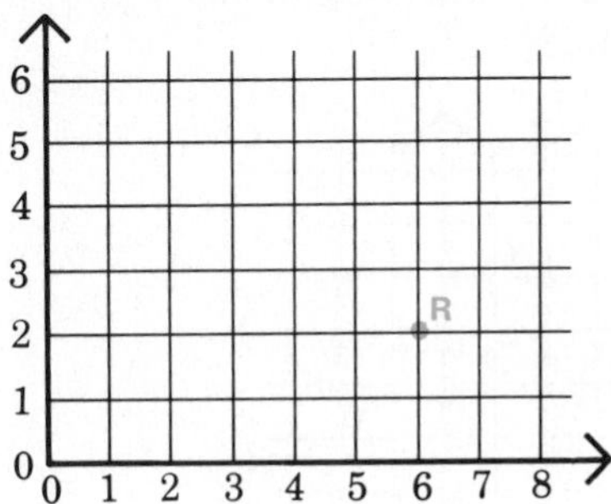

skill Reading and Making Graphs on a Grid pages 302-303

C Read the graph below to find the missing numbers in the table at the right.

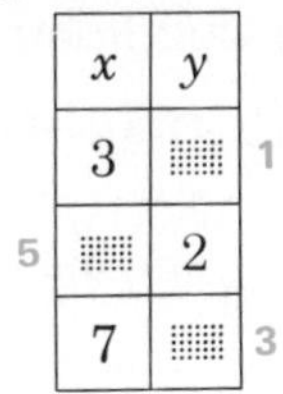

x	y
3	1
5	2
7	3

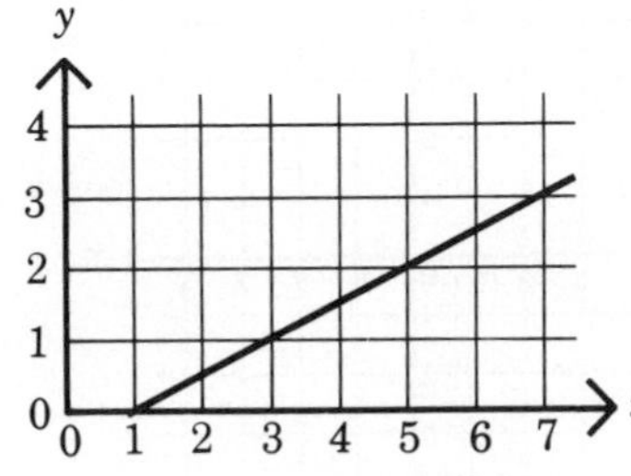

D Draw the graph of the equation $y = 2x - 2$ on a grid like the one below.

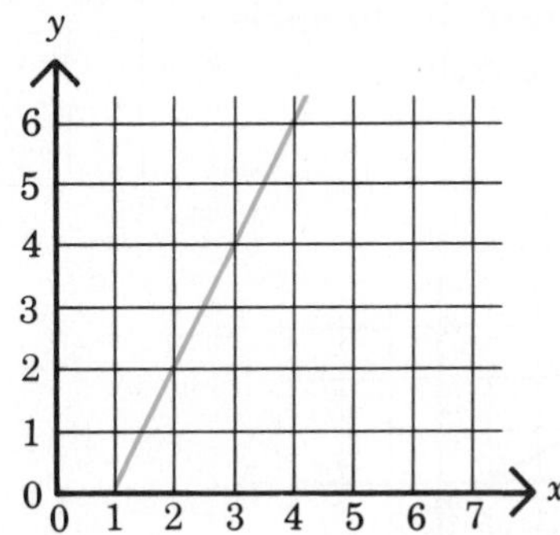

Pretest continued on page 300.

See page T25 for additional notes on Chapter 15.

Pretest continued from page 299.

Skill Locating Points in Four Quadrants pages 304–305

E Give an ordered pair for point N. N($^-2$, 1)

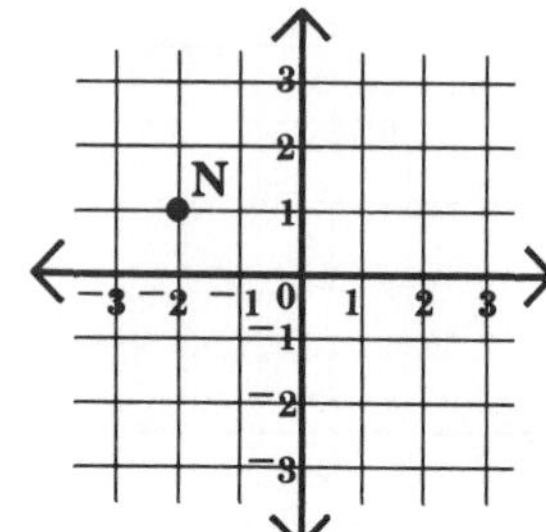

F Plot and label point T($^-2$, $^-1$) on a grid like the one below.

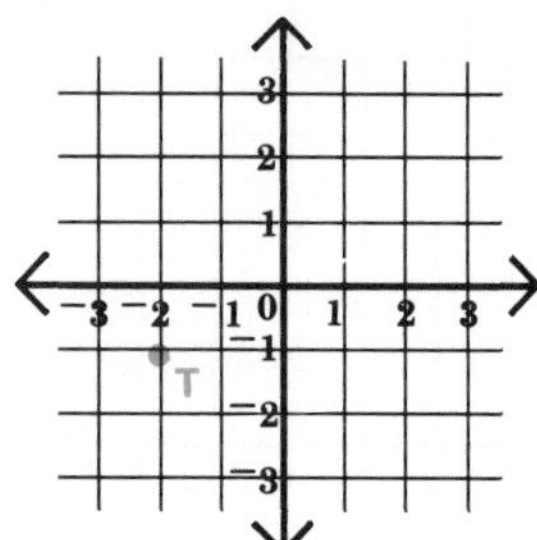

Skill Reading and Making Graphs in Four Quadrants pages 306–307

G Read the graph below to find the missing numbers in the table at the right.

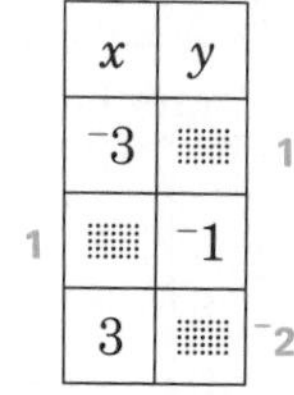

x	y
$^-3$	▦ 1
1 ▦	$^-1$
3	▦ $^-2$

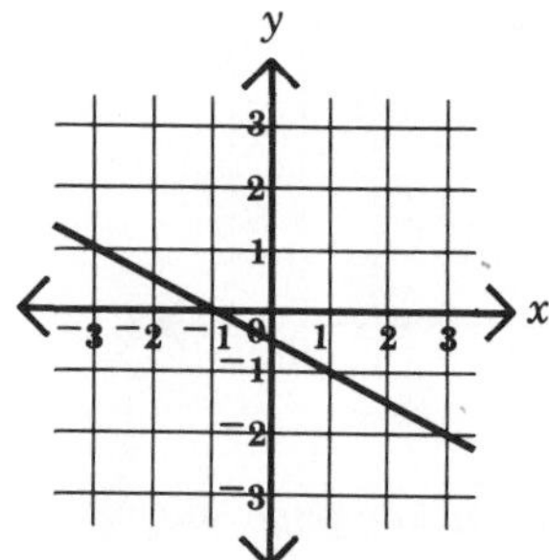

H Draw the graph of the equation $y = x + 2$ on a grid like the one below.

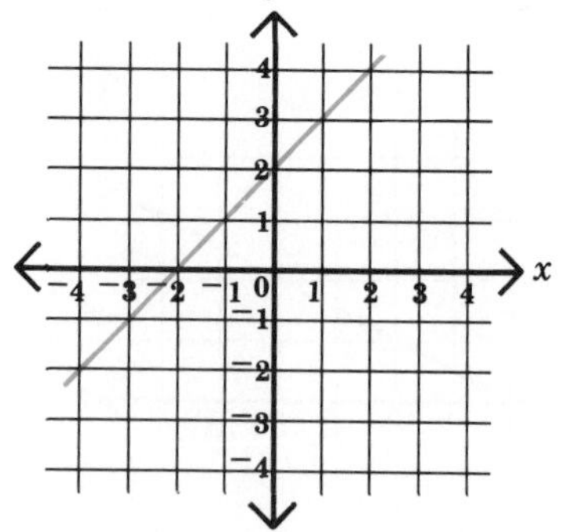

Materials: Graph paper

Objective: Give ordered pairs for points, and locate points for ordered pairs.

Locating Points on a Grid

example A Giving ordered pairs

Give an ordered pair for point A.

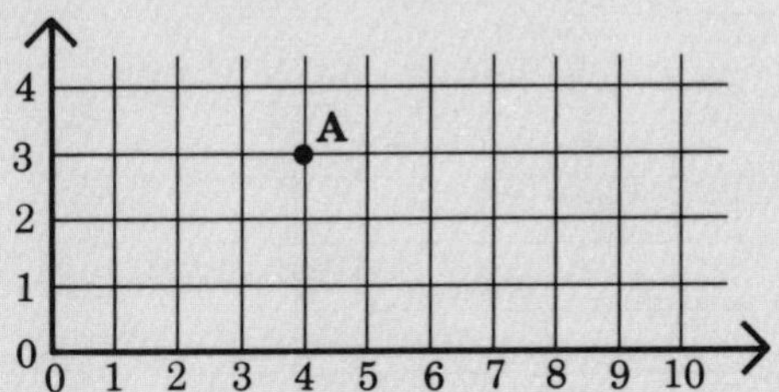

Start at the **origin** (0, 0) where the horizontal axis and the vertical axis meet.

The first number tells how many units to the right.

The second number tells how many units up.

A(4, 3)

The ordered pair for point A is (4, 3).

example B Plotting points

Plot and label point B(7, 2) on a grid like the one below.

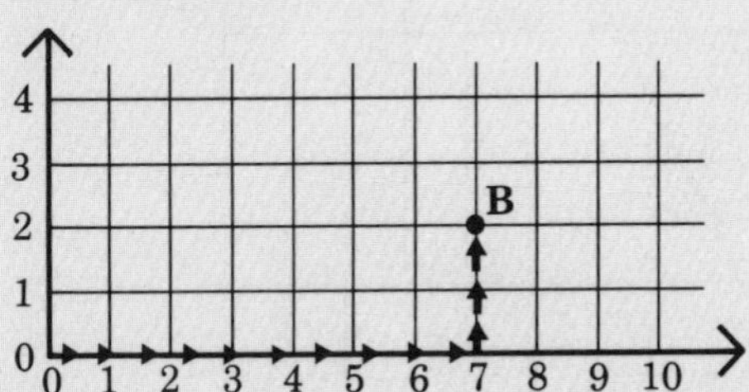

Start at the origin. Move 7 units to the right and 2 units up. Label the point B.

exercises

set A

Give an ordered pair for each point shown on the grid below.

1. Point C C(6, 4)
2. Point D D(3, 4)
3. Point E E(4, 2)
4. Point F F(0, 3)
5. Point G G(1, 5)
6. Point H H(1, 0)
7. Point I I(8, 4)
8. Point J J(10, 5)
9. Point K K(8, 2)
10. Point L L(5, 0)

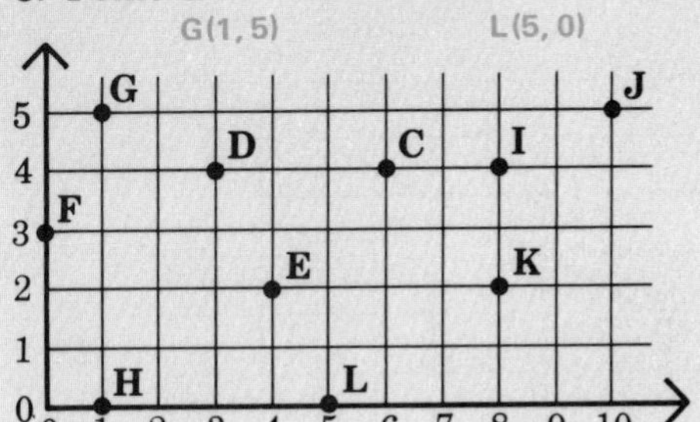

set B

Plot and label these points on a grid like the one below.

1. M(2, 5)
2. N(5, 2)
3. O(3, 3)
4. P(0, 4)
5. Q(8, 4)
6. R(9, 1)
7. S(7, 0)
8. T(2, 1)

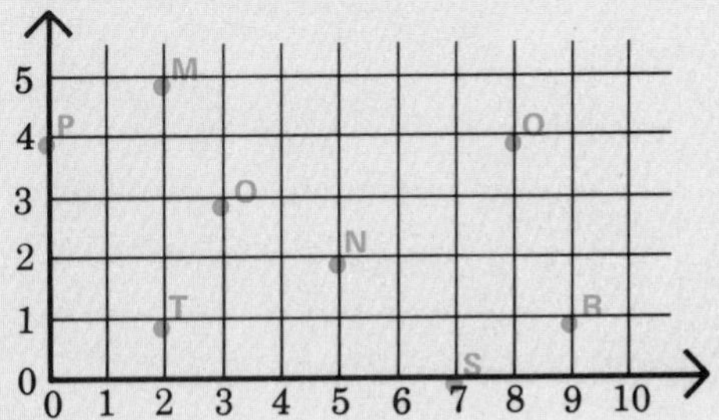

For more practice, a student could draw a simple straight-line-segment picture on a grid, write ordered pairs for points in the picture, and then give the pairs to another student to recreate the picture.

Materials: Graph paper, straightedge

Objective: Read a graph on a grid, and draw the graph of an equation.

Reading and Making Graphs on a Grid

example C Reading a graph

Read the graph below to find the missing numbers in the table at the right.

x	y
4	▒
▒	4
8	▒
▒	6

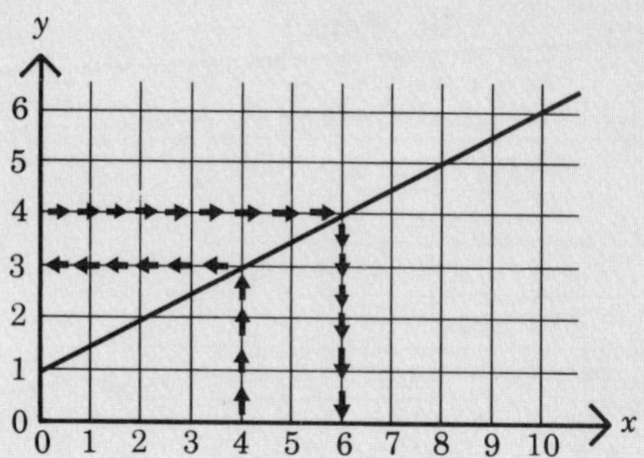

x	y
4	▒

← Find 4 on the x-axis. Move to the graph. Then move to the y-axis. The value of y is 3. (4, 3)

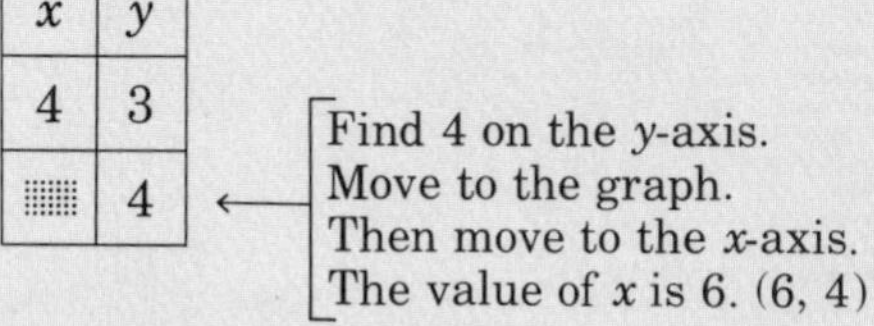

x	y
4	3
▒	4

← Find 4 on the y-axis. Move to the graph. Then move to the x-axis. The value of x is 6. (6, 4)

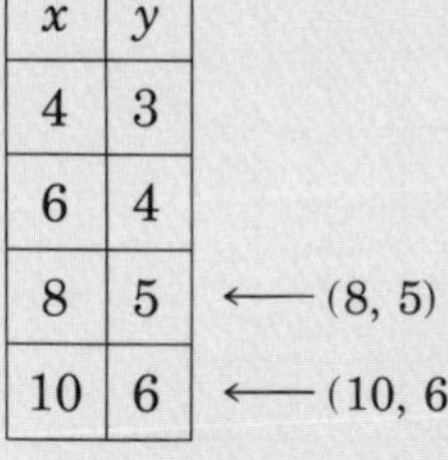

x	y	
4	3	
6	4	
8	5	← (8, 5)
10	6	← (10, 6)

example D Drawing a graph

Draw the graph of the equation $y = 2x + 1$ on a grid like the one below.

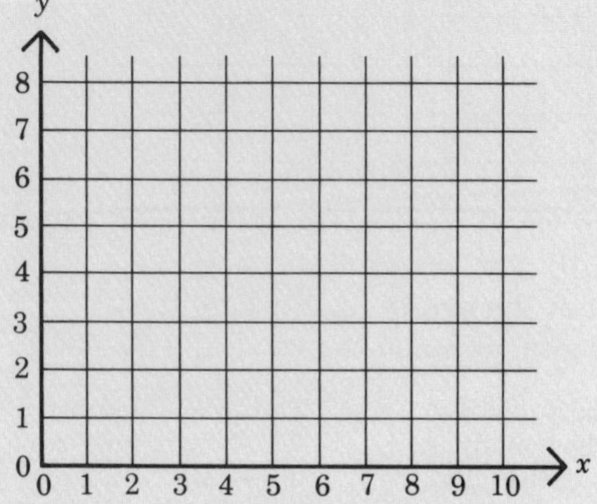

x	y	
0	1	$y = 2(0) + 1$
1	3	$y = 2(1) + 1$
2	5	$y = 2(2) + 1$
3	7	$y = 2(3) + 1$

$y = 2x + 1$

Pick some values for x. Make a table. Substitute the values for x in the equation to compute values for y.

Plot the points and connect them.

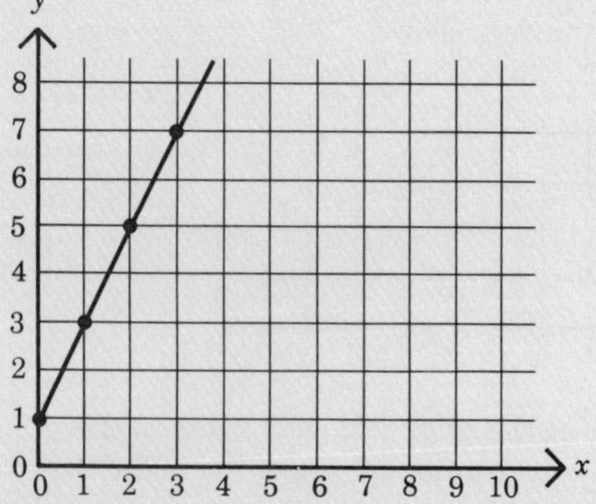

exercises

set C

Read the graphs to find the missing numbers in the tables.

1.

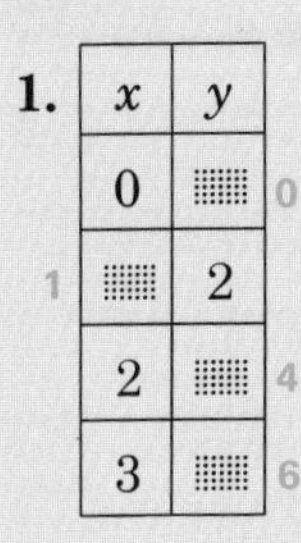

	x	y	
	0	▦	0
1	▦	2	
	2	▦	4
	3	▦	6

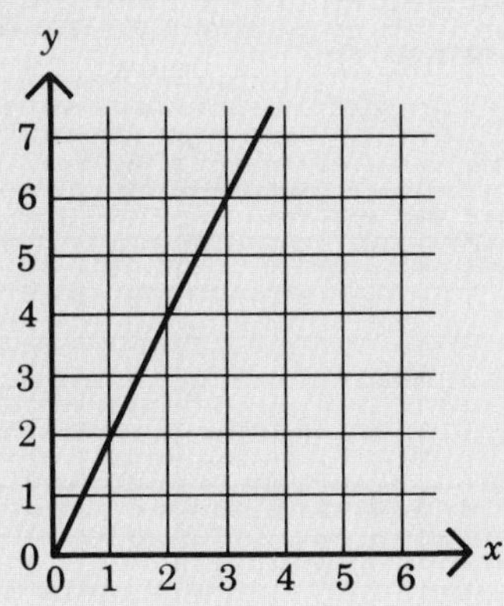

2.

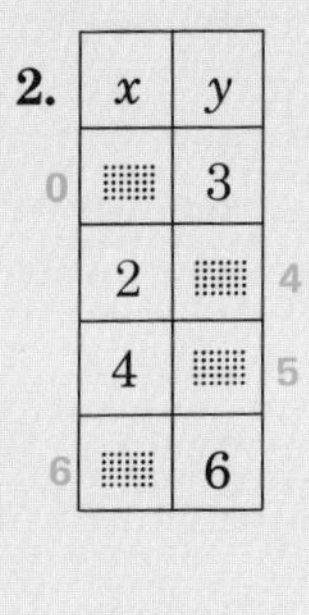

	x	y	
0	▦	3	
	2	▦	4
	4	▦	5
6	▦	6	

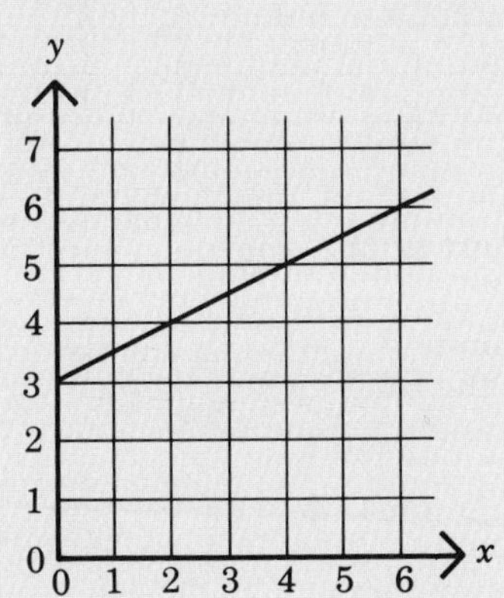

3.

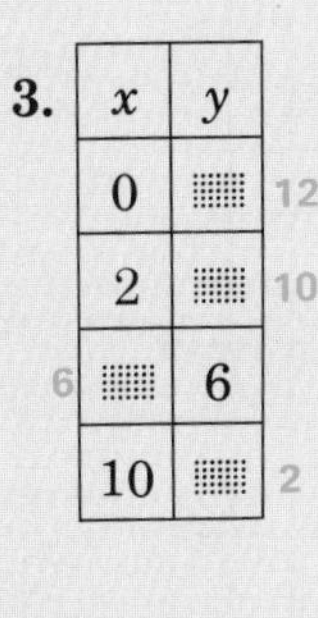

	x	y	
	0	▦	12
	2	▦	10
6	▦	6	
	10	▦	2

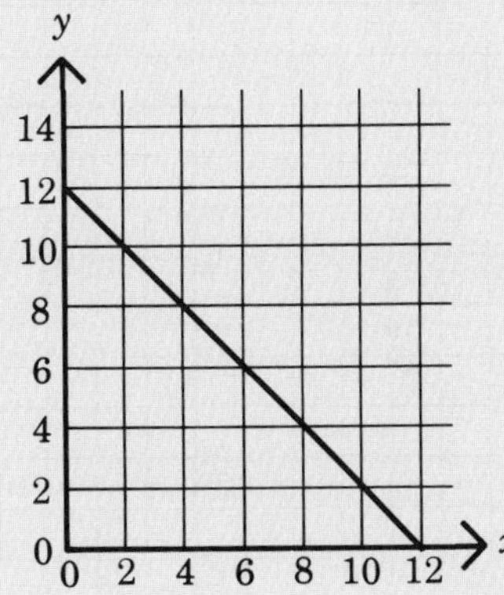

4.

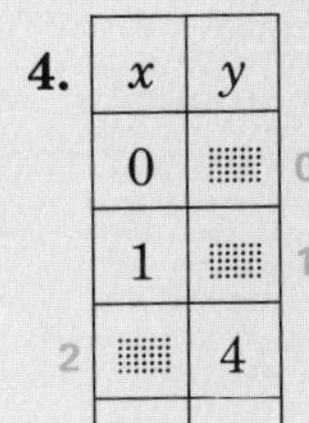

	x	y	
	0	▦	0
	1	▦	1
2	▦	4	
3	▦	9	

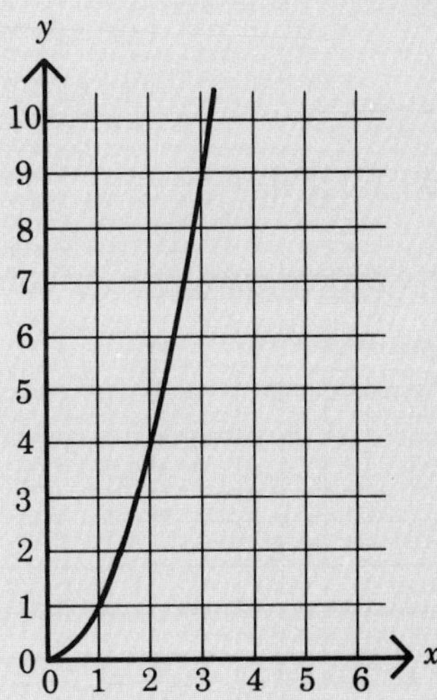

5.

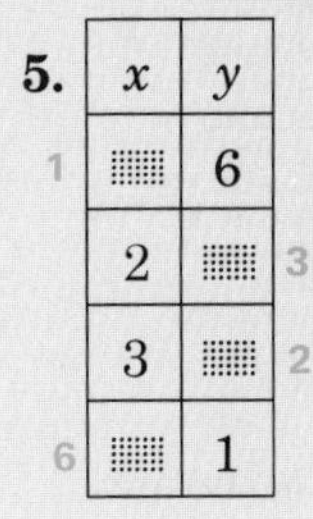

	x	y	
1	▦	6	
	2	▦	3
	3	▦	2
6	▦	1	

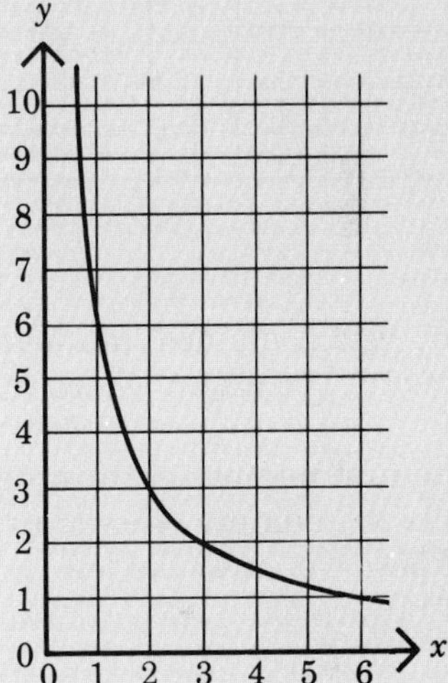

set D

See additional answers beginning on page T41.

Draw graphs of these equations on grids like the one in example D.

1. $y = x + 3$

2. $y = x - 2$

3. $y = 2x$

4. $y = 2x - 1$

5. $y = 3x - 5$

6. $y = x - 4$

7. $y = 4 - x$

8. $y = 8 - 2x$

The applications on pages 314–315 may be used anytime after this lesson.

Materials: Graph paper

Objective: Give ordered pairs of integers for points in four quadrants, and locate points for ordered pairs of integers.

Locating Points in Four Quadrants

example E Giving ordered pairs

Give an ordered pair for point R.

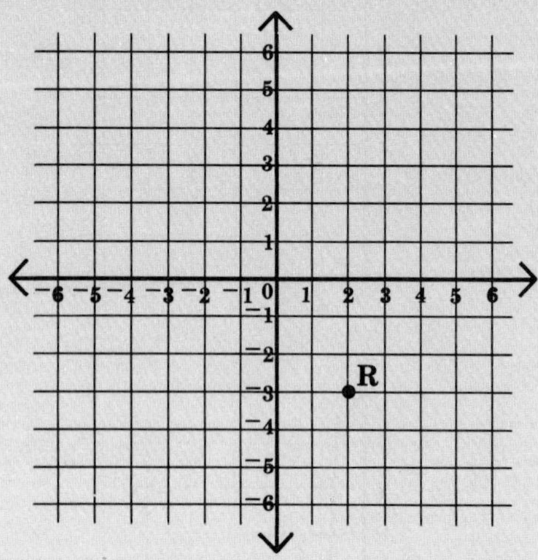

The grid is divided into four **quadrants.** Start at the origin where the axes meet.

The first number of the ordered pair tells the number of units to the right (if positive) or to the left (if negative).

The second number tells the number of units up (if positive) or down (if negative).

2 units to the right → 2; 3 units down → $^{-}3$

R(2, $^{-}3$)

The ordered pair for point R is (2, $^{-}3$).

example F Plotting points

Plot and label point V($^{-}4$, $^{-}2$) on a grid like the one below.

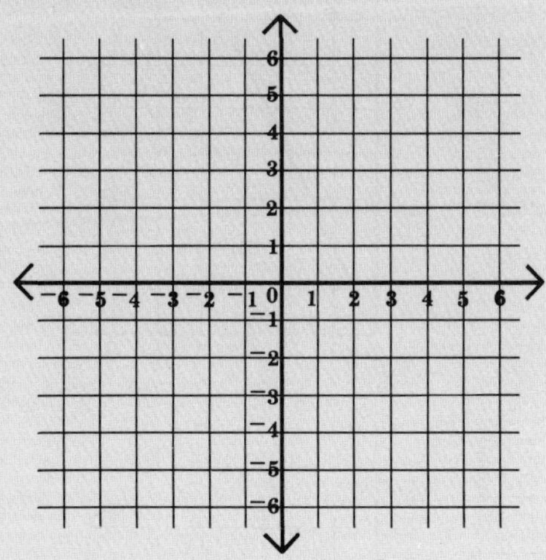

Start at the origin.

4 units to the left → $^{-}4$; 2 units down → $^{-}2$

V($^{-}4$, $^{-}2$)

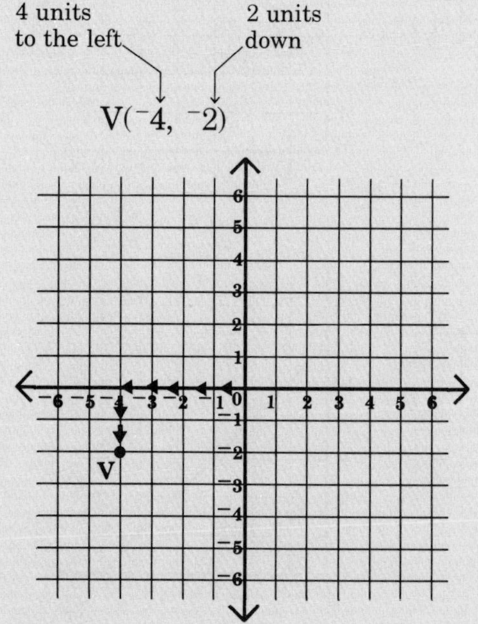

exercises

set E

Give an ordered pair for each point

1. Point A
   A($^-3$, 2)
2. Point B
   B($^-4$, 4)
3. Point C
   C(2, 4)
4. Point D
   D(0, 2)
5. Point E
   E(2, $^-3$)
6. Point F
   F($^-4$, $^-3$)
7. Point G
   G(3, 2)
8. Point H
   H($^-2$, $^-4$)
9. Point I
   I($^-3$, 0)
10. Point J
    J(4, $^-4$)

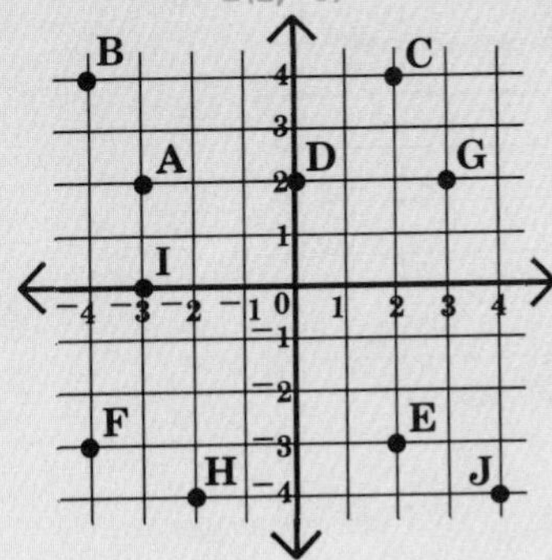

11. Point K
    K(2, 8)
12. Point L
    L($^-6$, 6)
13. Point M
    M(4, $^-4$)
14. Point N
    N($^-6$, $^-4$)
15. Point O
    O(6, 4)
16. Point P
    P(4, $^-8$)
17. Point Q
    Q($^-8$, $^-8$)
18. Point R
    R(2, 0)
19. Point S
    S($^-8$, 2)
20. Point T
    T(0, 4)

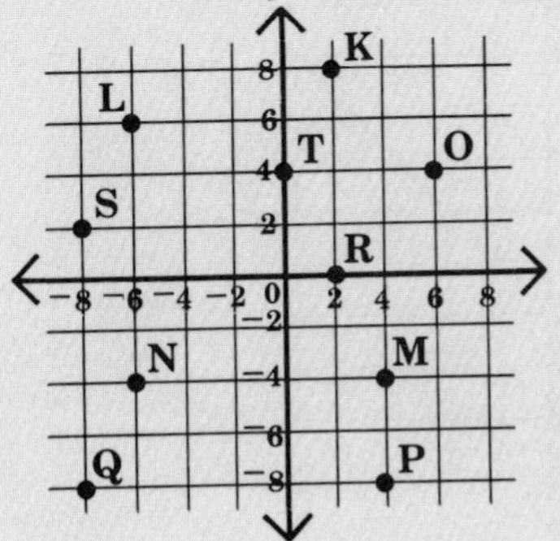

set F

See additional answers beginning on page T41.

Plot and label these points on a grid like the one in example F.

1. A(3, $^-6$)
2. B(0, 3)
3. C($^-4$, $^-3$)
4. D(4, 3)
5. E(3, $^-3$)
6. F(5, $^-4$)
7. G(1, 6)
8. H($^-3$, $^-4$)
9. I($^-4$, 3)
10. J(5, 0)
11. K(6, 5)
12. L($^-5$, 5)
13. M($^-4$, 0)
14. N($^-5$, $^-2$)
15. O($^-5$, 2)
16. P(0, $^-5$)
17. Q($^-6$, $^-6$)
18. R($^-3$, $^-6$)
19. S(2, $^-2$)
20. T(3, 2)

BREAK TIME

Copy this picture of nine dots in a square. Draw two more squares to divide the large square into nine sections with exactly one dot in each section.

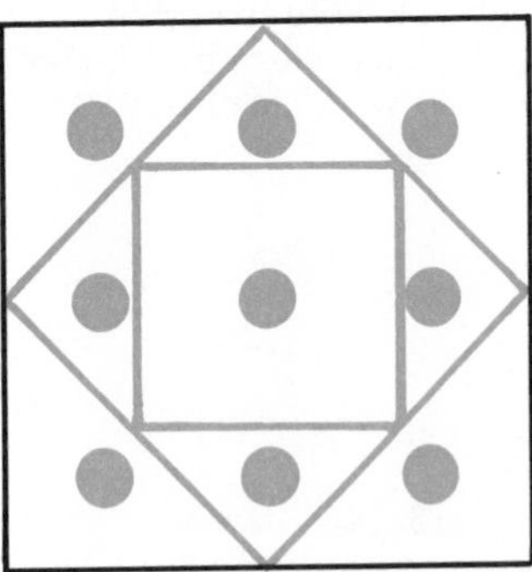

The applications on pages 312-313 may be used anytime after this lesson.

Materials: Graph paper, straightedge

Objective: Read a graph on a four-quadrant grid, and draw the graph of an equation on a four-quadrant grid.

Reading and Making Graphs in Four Quadrants

example G Reading a graph

Read the graph below to find the missing numbers in the table at the right.

x	y
$^{-}4$	
	1
2	
	$^{-}4$

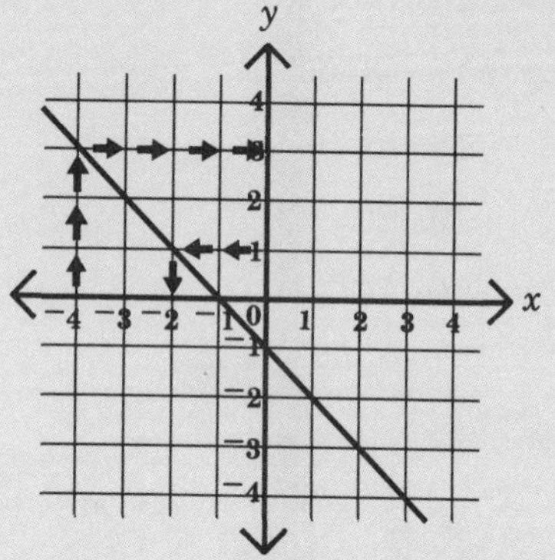

x	y
$^{-}4$	

Find $^{-}4$ on the x-axis.
Move to the graph.
Then move to the y-axis.
The value of y is 3. ($^{-}4$, 3)

x	y
$^{-}4$	3
	1

Find 1 on the y-axis.
Move to the graph.
Then move to the x-axis.
The value of x is $^{-}2$. ($^{-}2$, 1)

x	y
$^{-}4$	3
$^{-}2$	1
2	$^{-}3$
3	$^{-}4$

← (2, $^{-}3$)
← (3, $^{-}4$)

example H Drawing a graph

Draw the graph of the equation $y = x - 2$ on a grid like the one below.

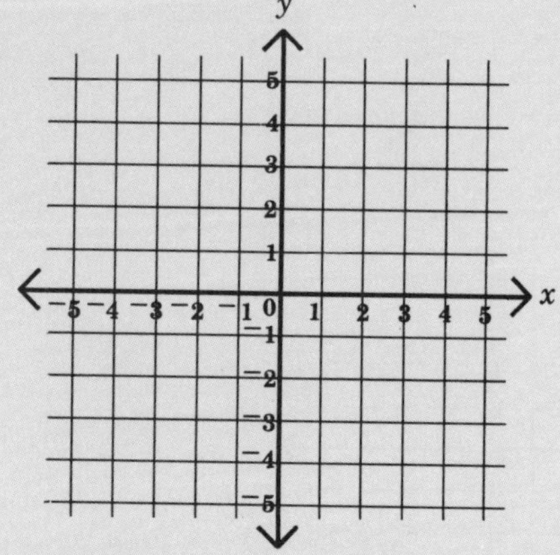

x	y	
$^{-}3$	$^{-}5$	$y = {}^{-}3 - 2$
$^{-}1$	$^{-}3$	$y = {}^{-}1 - 2$
1	$^{-}1$	$y = 1 - 2$
3	1	$y = 3 - 2$

$y = x - 2$

Pick some values for x. Make a table. Substitute the values for x in the equation to compute values for y.

Plot the points and connect them.

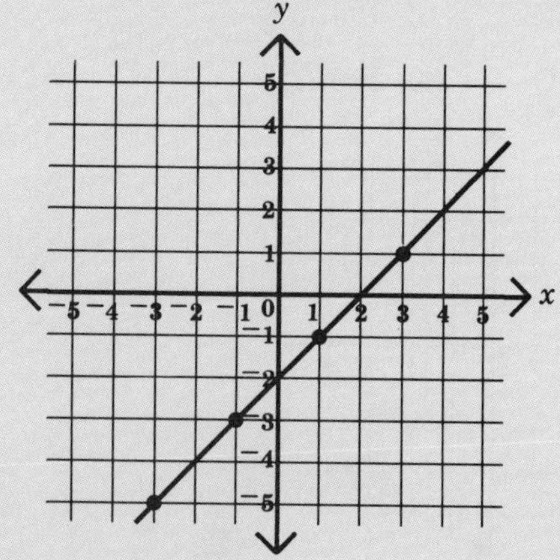

exercises

set G

Read the graphs to find the missing numbers in the tables.

1.

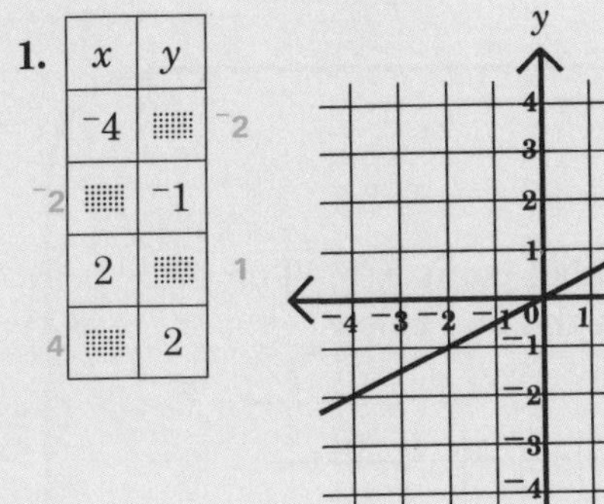

	x	y	
	$^-4$	▦	$^-2$
$^-2$	▦	$^-1$	
	2	▦	1
4	▦	2	

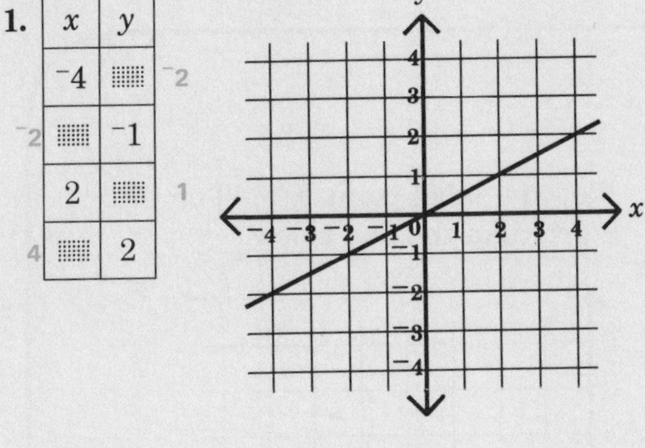

2.

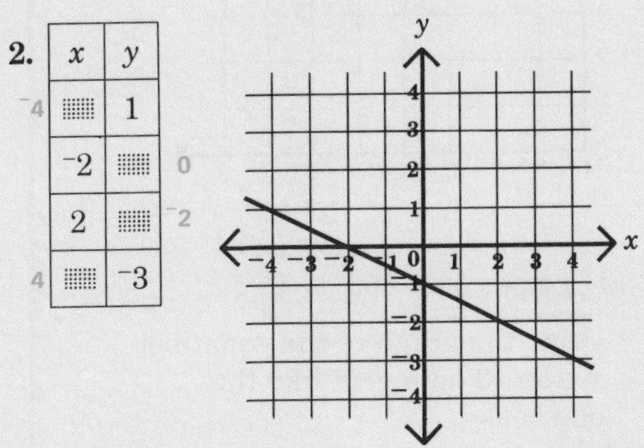

	x	y	
$^-4$	▦	1	
	$^-2$	▦	0
	2	▦	$^-2$
4	▦	$^-3$	

3.

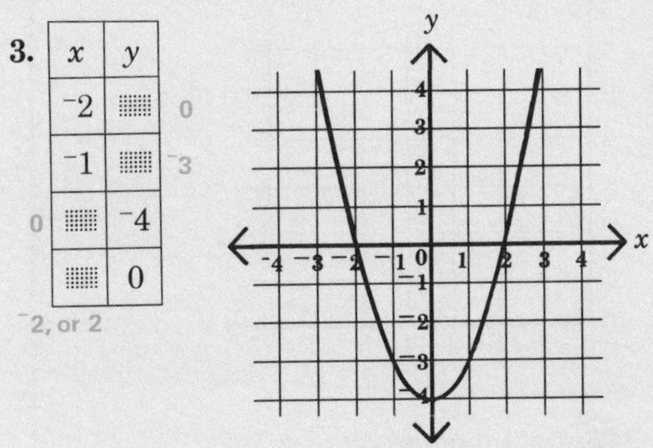

	x	y	
	$^-2$	▦	0
	$^-1$	▦	$^-3$
0	▦	$^-4$	
	▦	0	

$^-2$, or 2

4.

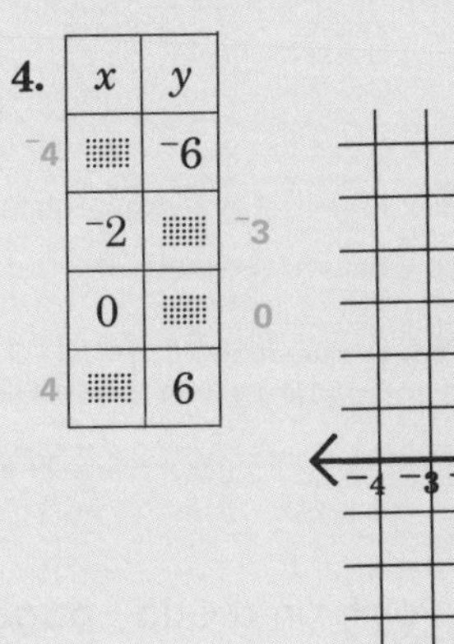

	x	y	
$^-4$	▦	$^-6$	
	$^-2$	▦	$^-3$
	0	▦	0
4	▦	6	

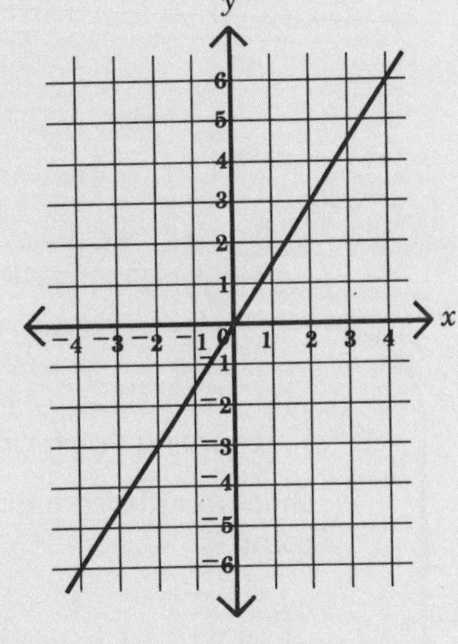

5.

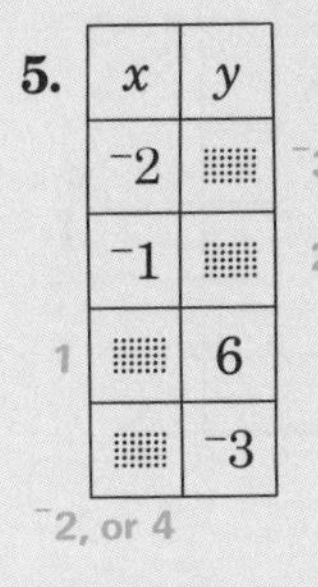

	x	y	
	$^-2$	▦	$^-3$
	$^-1$	▦	2
1	▦	6	
	▦	$^-3$	

$^-2$, or 4

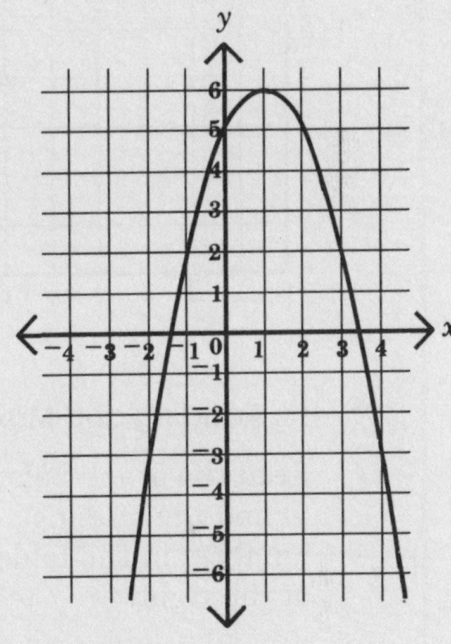

set H

See additional answers beginning on page T41.

Draw graphs of these equations on grids like the one in example H.

1. $y = x + 1$
2. $y = {}^-2x$
3. $y = x - 3$
4. $y = x$
5. $y = 2x - 1$
6. $y = {}^-2 - x$
7. $y = 3 - x$
8. $y = x + 3$

posttest

Materials: Graph paper, straightedge

Number of test items - 8

Number missed	1	2	3	4
Percent correct	88	75	63	50

skill Locating Points on a Grid page 301

A Give an ordered pair for point W. W(6, 4)

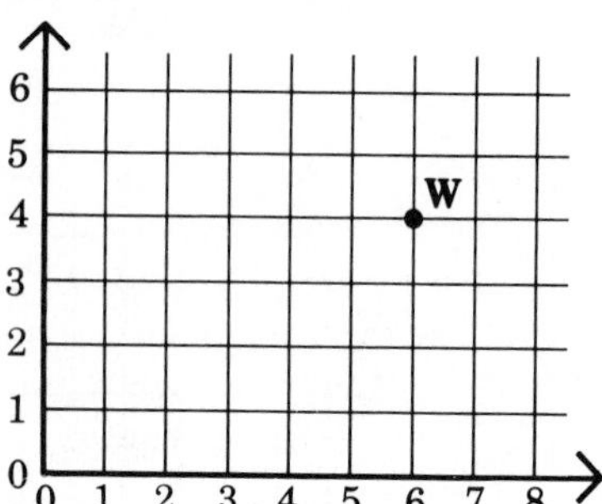

B Plot and label point K(5, 3) on a grid like the one below.

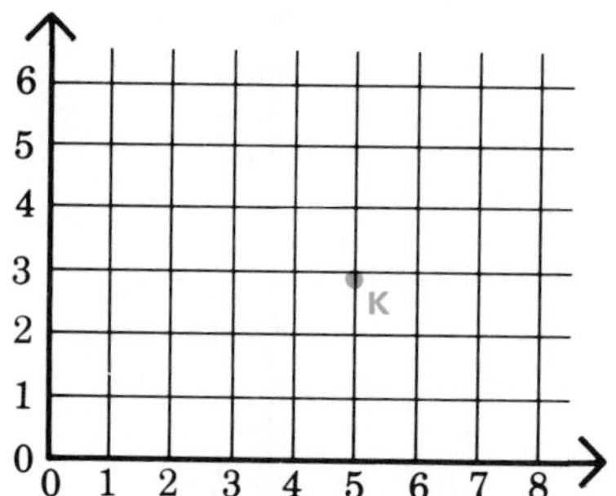

skill Reading and Making Graphs on a Grid pages 302–303

C Read the graph below to find the missing numbers in the table at the right.

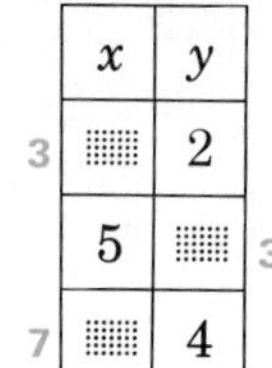

	x	y	
3	▒	2	
	5	▒	3
7	▒	4	

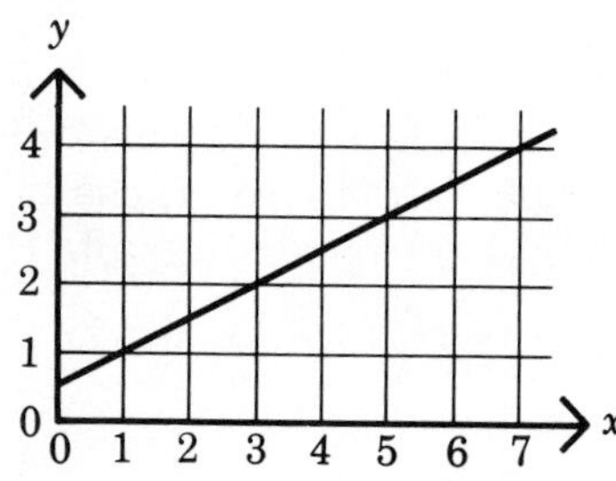

D Draw the graph of the equation $y = x - 3$ on a grid like the one below.

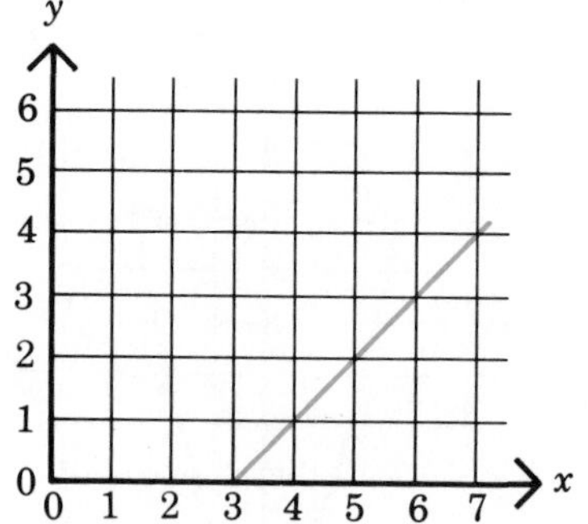

Posttest continued on page 309.

Posttest continued from page 308.

Skill Locating Points in Four Quadrants pages 304–305

E Give an ordered pair for point K. K(2, $^-3$)

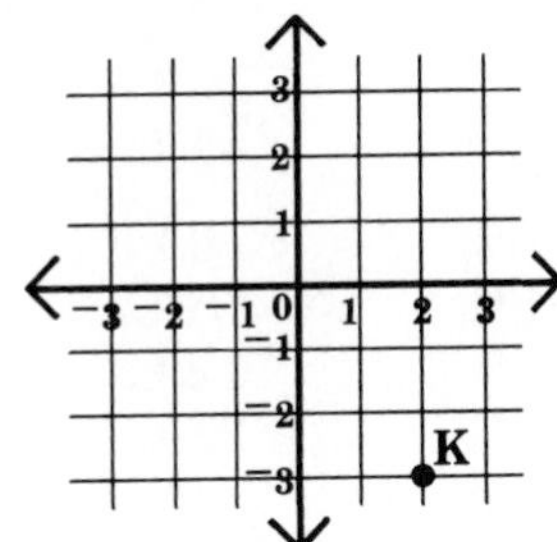

F Plot and label point M($^-3$, 1) on a grid like the one below.

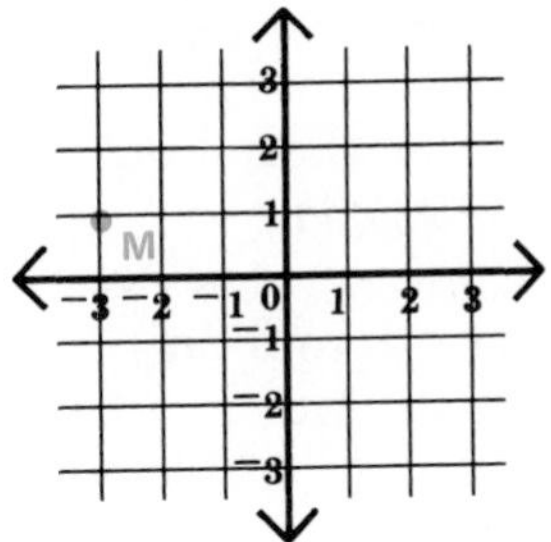

Skill Reading and Making Graphs in Four Quadrants pages 306–307

G Read the graph below to find the missing numbers in the table at the right.

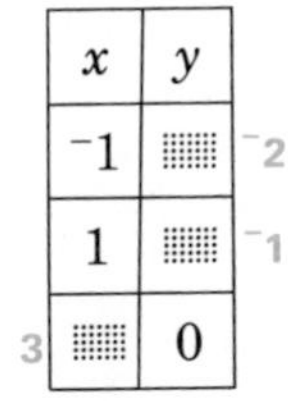

x	y	
$^-1$	▒	$^-2$
1	▒	$^-1$
▒ (3)	0	

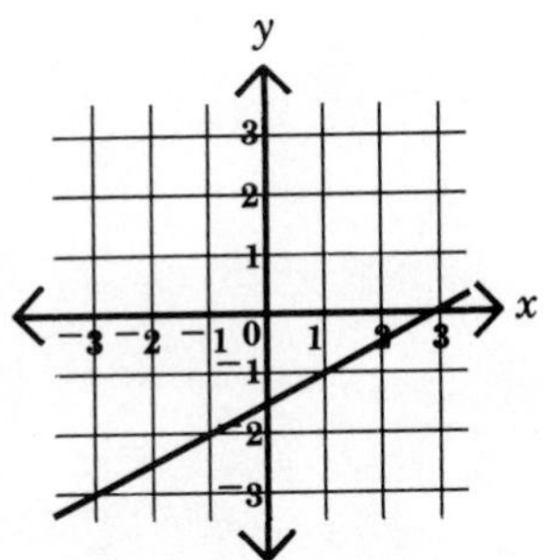

H Draw the graph of the equation $y = 2 - x$ on a grid like the one below.

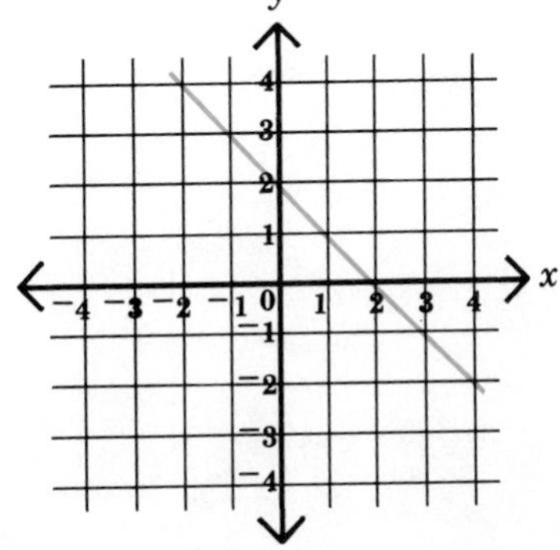

Materials: Graph paper, straightedge

Objective: Solve problems involving coordinate graphing.

In this lesson students draw graphs that show the freezing points for various concentrations of three types of antifreeze.

Buying Antifreeze

Ethylene glycol is a year-round permanent antifreeze with a boiling point of 104°C. Methanol and ethanol are non-permanent, alcohol-based antifreezes that can boil off in the summer. Their boiling points are 85°C and 84°C.

Patty Redwing needed permanent antifreeze for her car. She read an article about the types of antifreeze that she could buy.

Antifreeze is a solution of water mixed with ethylene glycol, methanol, or ethanol.

1. Use the data at the right to draw a graph for ethylene glycol. Plot points and connect them. Use a grid like the one on page 311. See page 311.

2. Draw a graph for methanol on the same grid. See page 311.

3. Draw a graph for ethanol on the same grid. See page 311.

Type of antifreeze	Concentration (percent antifreeze)	Freezing point	Ordered pairs
Ethylene glycol	0%	0°C	(0, 0)
	15%	⁻6°C	(15, ⁻6)
	32%	⁻18°C	(32, ⁻18)
	45%	⁻34°C	(45, ⁻34)
	50%	⁻40°C	(50, ⁻40)
	58%	⁻51°C	(58, ⁻51)
Methanol	0%	0°C	(0, 0)
	10%	⁻6°C	(10, ⁻6)
	20%	⁻12°C	(20, ⁻12)
	32%	⁻23°C	(32, ⁻23)
	42%	⁻34°C	(42, ⁻34)
	55%	⁻51°C	(55, ⁻51)
Ethanol	0%	0°C	(0, 0)
	18%	⁻6°C	(18, ⁻6)
	28%	⁻12°C	(28, ⁻12)
	43%	⁻23°C	(43, ⁻23)
	55%	⁻34°C	(55, ⁻34)
	81%	⁻51°C	(81, ⁻51)

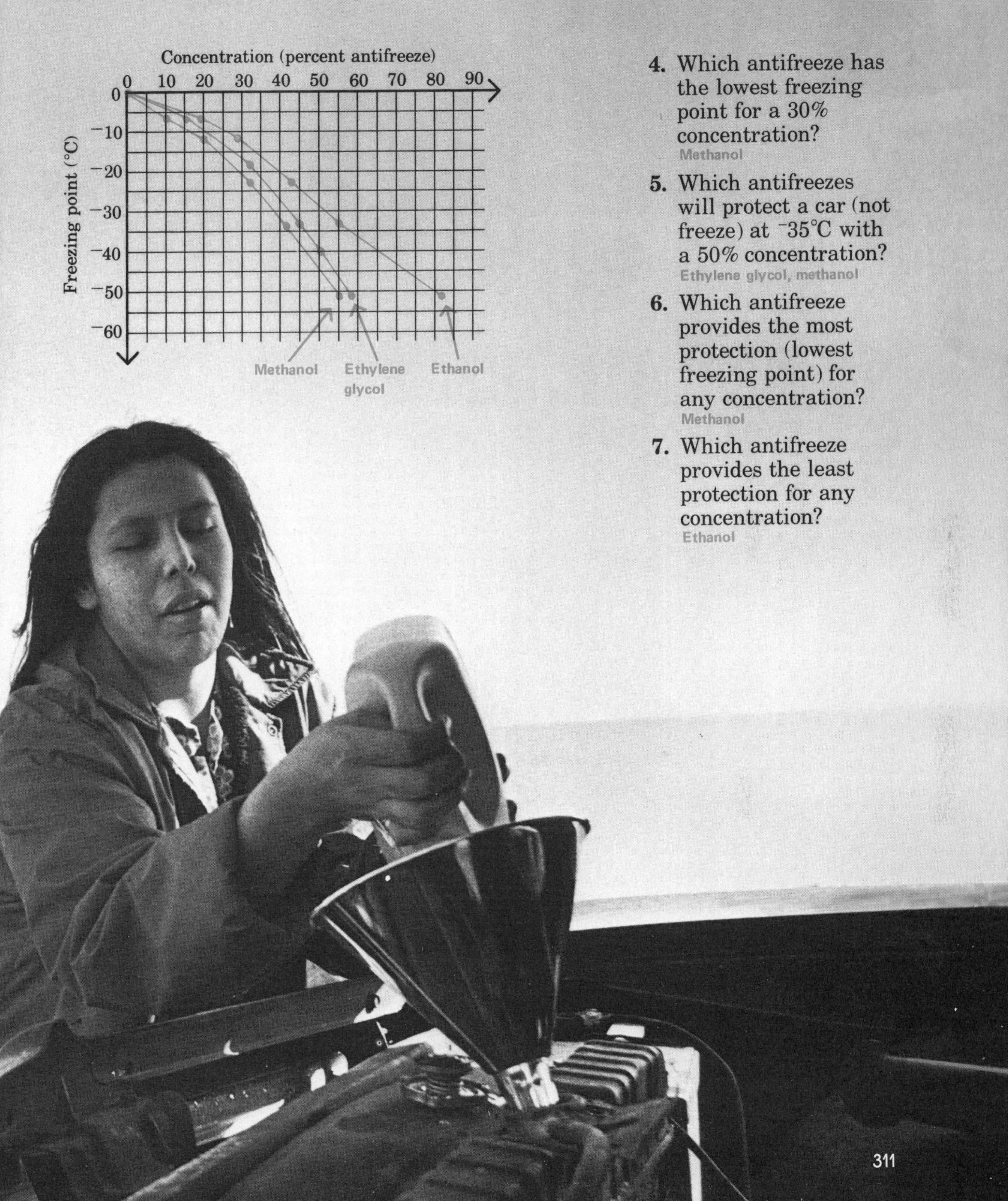

4. Which antifreeze has the lowest freezing point for a 30% concentration?
Methanol

5. Which antifreezes will protect a car (not freeze) at −35°C with a 50% concentration?
Ethylene glycol, methanol

6. Which antifreeze provides the most protection (lowest freezing point) for any concentration?
Methanol

7. Which antifreeze provides the least protection for any concentration?
Ethanol

Career: Drill-Press Operator

Career Cluster: Trades

Materials: Graph paper

Objective: Solve problems involving coordinate graphing.

In this lesson students use a grid to show the location of holes that are to be drilled by a numerical-control drill press.

Fred Willis operates a numerical-control drill press that is used in mass production.

He prepares a punched paper tape which gives instructions to a computer. The computer directs the drill to the spot where the hole is to be drilled automatically.

Each instruction tells the drill to move left (L) or right (R) and up (U) or down (D) *from the previous hole* to get to the next hole. The drill starts at the center of a grid.

Hole	Instructions	Location of hole
A	R3 U2	(3, 2)
B	L5 D6	($^-2$, $^-4$)
C	R3 U0	(1, $^-4$)

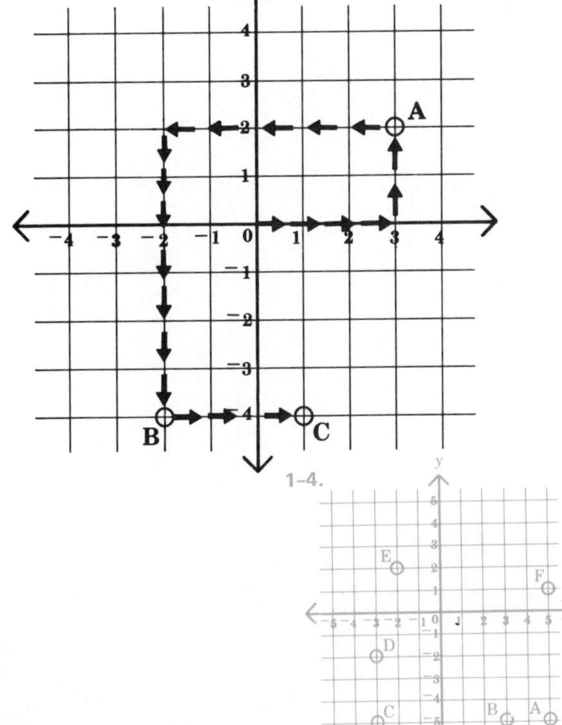

1–4.

For each table, plot and label the holes on a grid. Give the ordered pairs for the locations of the holes.

	Hole	Instructions	Location of hole
	A	R5 D5	(5, $^-5$)
	B	L2 U0	(3, $^-5$)
1.	C	L6 U0	($^-3$, $^-5$)
2.	D	R0 U3	($^-3$, $^-2$)
3.	E	R1 U4	($^-2$, 2)
4.	F	R7 D1	(5, 1)

See below left.

	Hole	Instructions	Location of hole
5.	A	L2 U1	($^-2$, 1)
6.	B	R1 U3	($^-1$, 4)
7.	C	R5 U0	(4, 4)
8.	D	L1 D3	(3, 1)
9.	E	L2 D2	(1, $^-1$)
10.	F	L4 U0	($^-3$, $^-1$)

	Hole	Instructions	Location of hole
11.	A	L2 U3	($^-2$, 3)
12.	B	R6 D2	(4, 1)
13.	C	R1 D4	(5, $^-3$)
14.	D	L7 U0	($^-2$, $^-3$)
15.	E	L3 D1	($^-5$, $^-4$)
16.	F	R0 U2	($^-5$, $^-2$)
17.	G	R1 U3	($^-4$, 1)
18.	H	L1 U3	($^-5$, 4)

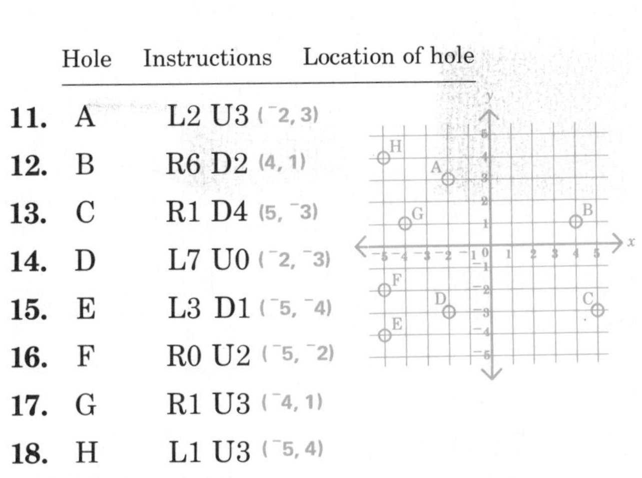

Materials: Graph paper, straightedge

Objective: Solve problems involving coordinate graphing.

In this lesson students determine the depth of various layers of rock by using graphs of data obtained from a geophone.

Career: Geologist

Career Cluster: Science

The Campbell's Stone Company bought three pieces of land. Steve Haverl, a geologist, was asked to find the depths of various layers of rock on each piece of land.

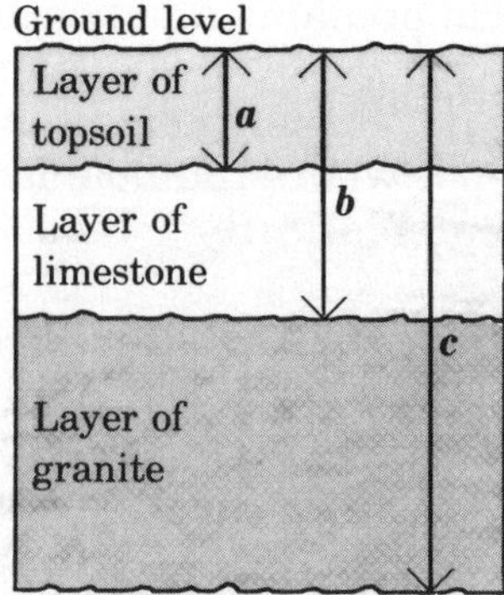

Steve set off a small charge of dynamite. He used a geophone to record how long it took the compression waves from the dynamite to travel various distances through the ground. He recorded his data on graphs like these.

Graph 1

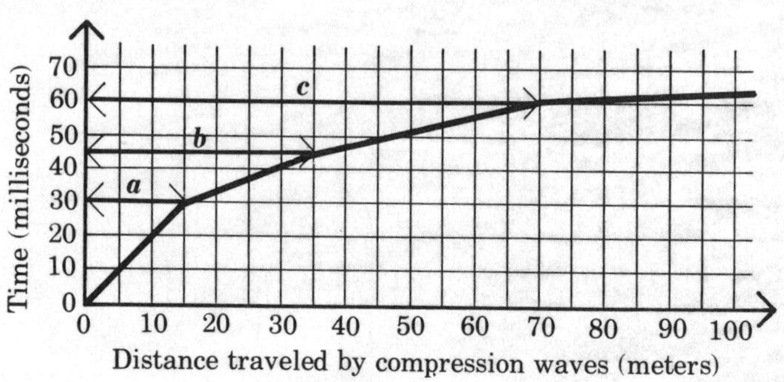

Graph 2

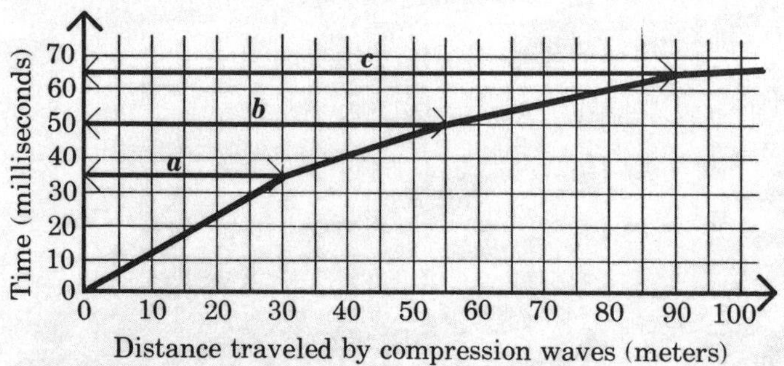

The changes in steepness, or slope, on each graph show changes in the speed of the compression waves. These changes occur where the layers end. For example, graph 1 shows that the layer of topsoil ends at 15 meters.

1. Complete the table below for graphs 1 and 2. Then do exercises 2–4 before completing the table for graph 3.

	Depth of topsoil a	Depth of bottom of limestone layer b	Thickness of limestone layer $b - a$	Depth of bottom of granite layer c	Thickness of granite layer $c - b$
Graph 1	15 m	35 m	20 m	70 m	35 m
Graph 2	30 m	55 m	25 m	90 m	35 m
Graph 3	15 m	45 m	30 m	85 m	40 m

2. Use this data to draw graph 3. (distance in meters, time in milliseconds)
(0, 0) (5, 15) (10, 30) (15, 45) (25, 55)
(35, 65) (45, 75) (65, 85) (85, 95) (125, 100) See below.

3. At what three points on your graph does the steepness, or slope, of the graph change? (15, 45) (45, 75) (85, 95)

4. Label the distances *a, b,* and *c* on your graph. See below.

5. Complete the third row of the table shown above. Use your graph. See table in exercise 1.

Objective: Solve problems involving coordinate graphing.

In this lesson students determine arrival and departure times and speeds of trains by reading a graph.

Career: Railroad Dispatcher

Career Cluster: Business Contact

Bill Locklear is a train dispatcher. He schedules trains by making graphs similar to the ones shown below.

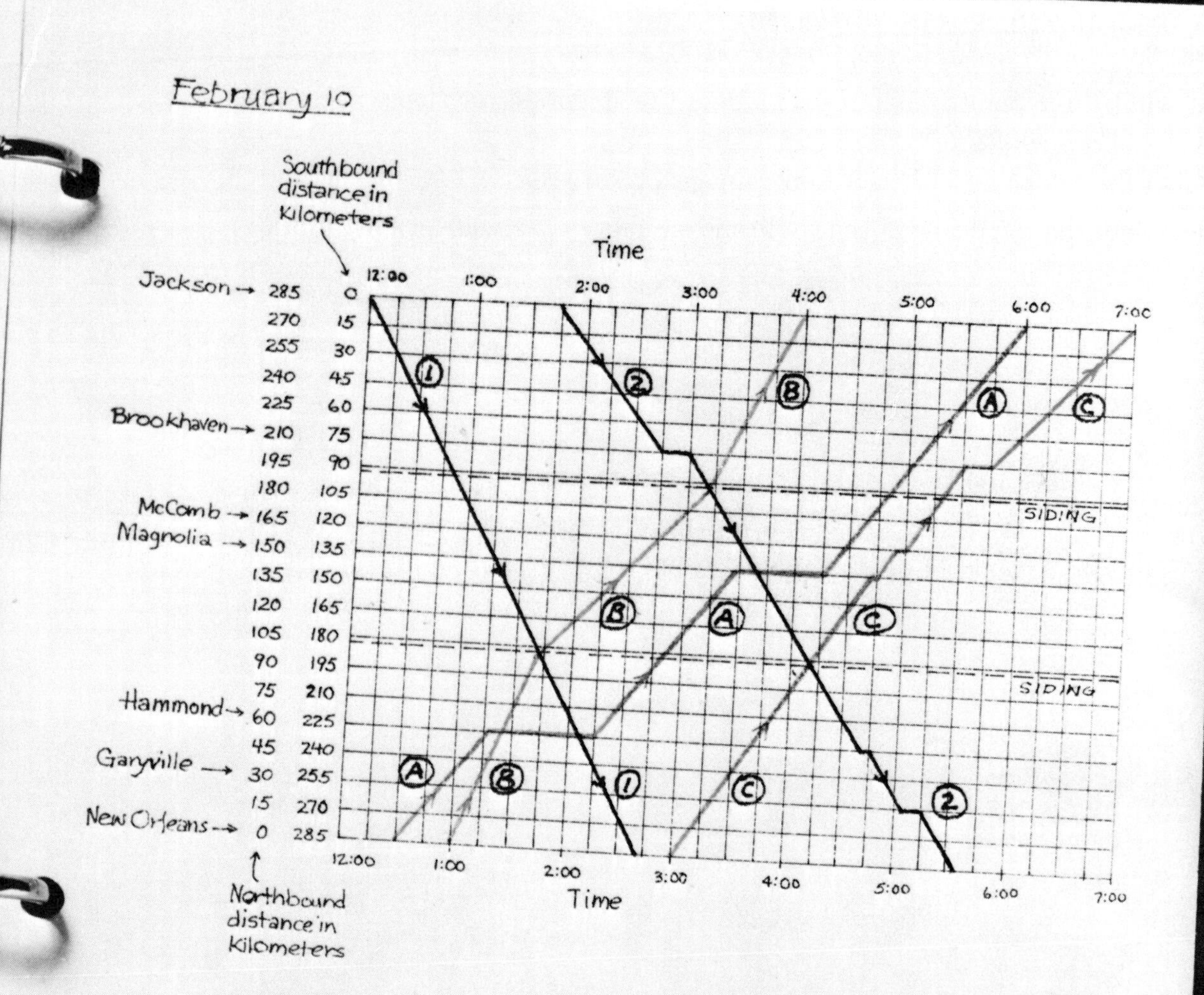

Graphs are shown for five trains that travel between Jackson, Mississippi and New Orleans, Louisiana. Trains 1 and 2 are southbound. Trains A, B, and C are northbound.

1. Train 1 is a nonstop express. Train 2 makes three stops as shown by the flat parts of its graph. In which three cities does train 2 stop? Brookhaven, Hammond, and Garyville

2. Train B passes train 1 on a siding, or sidetrack, between Hammond and Magnolia. It passes train 2 on a siding between which two cities? Brookhaven and McComb

3. Complete this timetable. Give the times that belong in the empty spaces.

Tell students to read the schedule for each train from left to right in each row before looking at the next row.

City	Train 1		Train 2		City	Train A		Train B		Train C	
	Arr.	Lv.	Arr.	Lv.		Arr.	Lv.	Arr.	Lv.	Arr.	Lv.
Jackson	▒	12:00	▒	1:45	New Orleans	▒	12:30	▒	1:00	▒	3:00
Brookhaven	▒	▒	2:45	3:00	Garyville	▒	▒	▒	▒	▒	▒
McComb	▒	▒	▒	▒	Hammond	1:20	1:15	▒	▒	▒	▒
Magnolia	▒	▒	▒	▒	Magnolia	3:27	4:15	▒	▒	4:40	4:45
Hammond	▒	▒	4:40	4:45	McComb	▒	▒	▒	▒	4:55	5:00
Garyville	▒	▒	5:05	5:15	Brookhaven	▒	▒	▒	▒	5:30	5:45
New Orleans	2:43	▒	5:35	▒	Jackson	6:00	▒	4:00	▒	7:00	▒

Be sure students understand that they only need to give times in the empty spaces. Screens are shown in spaces where times are not to be given.

To find the speed of a train, find how far it travels in one hour.

Find the speed of train 2 between Brookhaven and Hammond.

Hour interval: 3:00 to 4:00
Distance: 165 km − 75 km, or 90 km
Speed: 90 kilometers per hour

You might encourage students to use the following hour intervals for exercises 4–8:

4. 12:00–1:00
5. 1:45–2:45
6. 2:15–3:15
7. 1:45–2:45
8. 5:45–6:45

Use the graphs to find the speed of

4. train 1 between Jackson and New Orleans. 105 kilometers per hour

5. train 2 between Jackson and Brookhaven. 75 kilometers per hour

6. train A between Hammond and Magnolia. 75 kilometers per hour

7. train B after it meets train 1 and before it meets train 2. 60 kilometers per hour

8. train C between Brookhaven and Jackson. 60 kilometers per hour

Number of test items - 12

Number missed	1	2	3	4	5	6
Percent correct	92	83	75	67	58	50

Chapter 15

Materials: Graph paper, straightedge

A **1.** Give an ordered pair for point J. J(3, 2)

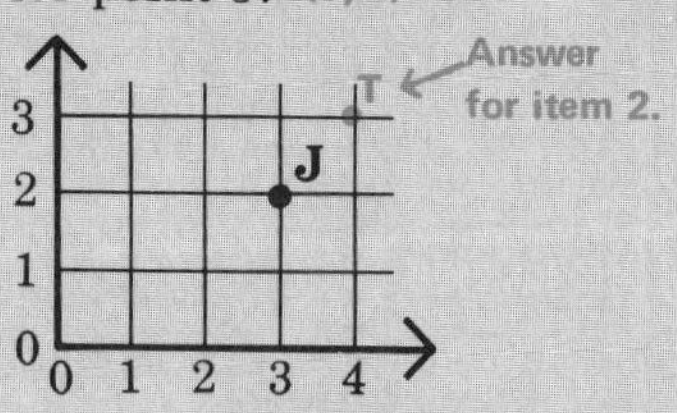

B **2.** Plot and label point T(4, 3) on a grid like the one in item 1.
See grid in item 1.

C **3.** Read the graph below to find the missing numbers in the table.

x	y
0	▒ 2
2 ▒	3
4	▒ 4

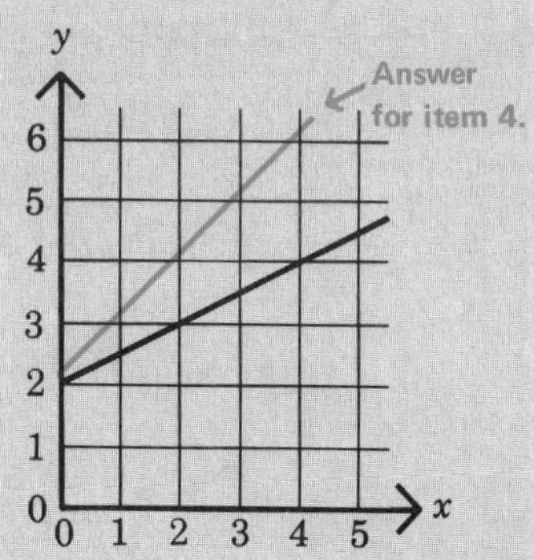

D **4.** Draw the graph of the equation $y = x + 2$ on a grid like the one in item 3.
See grid in item 3.

E **5.** Give an ordered pair for point R. R($^-3$, 2)

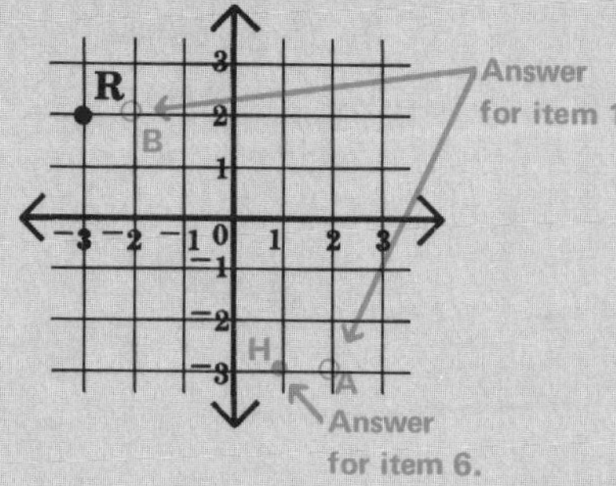

F **6.** Plot and label point H(1, $^-3$) on a grid like the one in item 5.
See grid in item 5.

G **7.** Read the graph below to find the missing numbers in the table.

x	y
$^-2$	▒ $^-3$
0 ▒	1
1	▒ 3

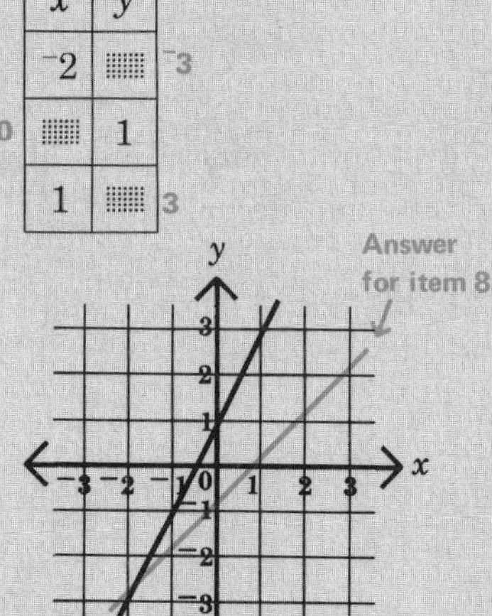

H **8.** Draw the graph of the equation $y = x - 1$ on a grid like the one in item 7.
See grid in item 7.

9. What is the freezing point for a solution that is 20% antifreeze? $^-15$°C

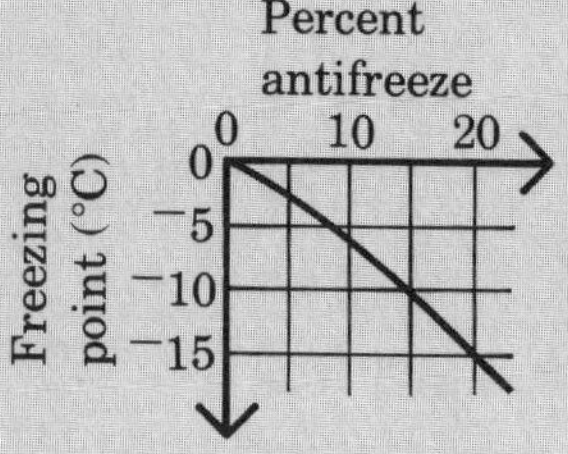

10. Plot and label holes A and B on a grid like the one in item 5. Start at (0, 0).

Hole	Instructions
A	R2 D3
B	L4 U5

See grid in item 5.

11. What is the depth of the topsoil (a)? 15 m

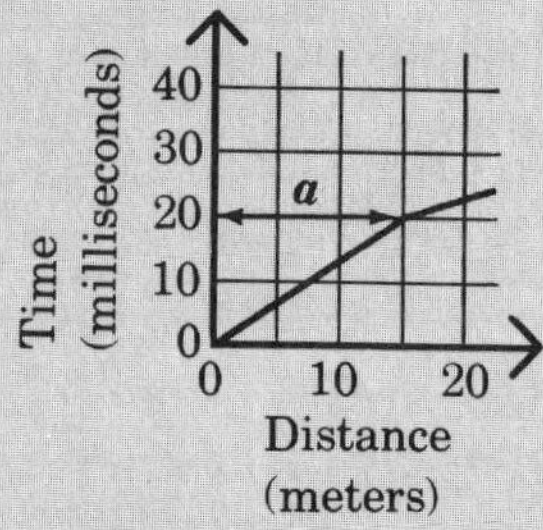

12. At what time did the train leave Kent? 12:45

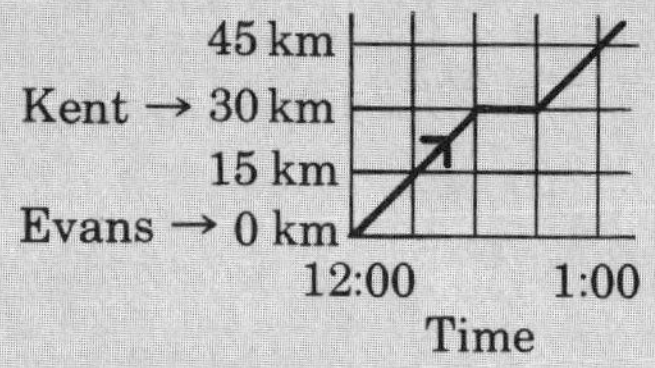

See pages 41–42 of the *Tests and Record Forms: Duplicating Masters* for an alternate form of the Chapter 15 Test.
For a test on Unit 5, see page T36 of this book and pages 43–44 of the duplicating masters.

tune-up skills

Multiplying and Dividing Fractions and Mixed Numbers, pages 131–142

1. $\frac{3}{5} \times \frac{7}{8}$ $\frac{21}{40}$
2. $\frac{4}{9} \times \frac{3}{16}$ $\frac{1}{12}$
3. $\frac{7}{12} \times \frac{3}{4}$ $\frac{7}{16}$
4. $\frac{2}{3} \times \frac{1}{2} \times \frac{3}{4}$ $\frac{1}{4}$
5. $12 \times \frac{3}{7}$ $5\frac{1}{7}$
6. $\frac{3}{4} \times 28$ 21
7. $\frac{5}{8} \times 1\frac{7}{9}$ $1\frac{1}{9}$
8. $3\frac{9}{10} \times 6$ $23\frac{2}{5}$
9. $1\frac{4}{5} \times 2\frac{7}{9}$ 5
10. $5\frac{1}{2} \times 1\frac{1}{4}$ $6\frac{7}{8}$
11. $\frac{1}{3} \times \frac{6}{7} \times 2\frac{1}{8}$ $\frac{17}{28}$
12. $7\frac{2}{5} \times \frac{5}{6} \times \frac{1}{2}$ $3\frac{1}{12}$
13. $\frac{5}{6} \times \frac{9}{16}$ $\frac{15}{32}$
14. $7 \div \frac{2}{3}$ $10\frac{1}{2}$
15. $\frac{9}{16} \div 3$ $\frac{3}{16}$
16. $7\frac{1}{2} \div 3$ $2\frac{1}{2}$
17. $1\frac{1}{4} \div 7\frac{1}{2}$ $\frac{1}{6}$
18. $3\frac{1}{4} \div 1\frac{1}{6}$ $2\frac{11}{14}$

Adding and Subtracting Fractions and Mixed Numbers, pages 151–162

1. $\frac{2}{3} + \frac{1}{2}$ $1\frac{1}{6}$
2. $\frac{7}{8} + \frac{1}{3}$ $1\frac{5}{24}$
3. $\frac{1}{3} + \frac{3}{4} + \frac{1}{12}$ $1\frac{1}{6}$
4. $\frac{2}{5} + \frac{1}{4} + \frac{1}{2}$ $1\frac{3}{20}$
5. $\frac{11}{12} - \frac{7}{12}$ $\frac{1}{3}$
6. $\frac{2}{3} - \frac{4}{9}$ $\frac{2}{9}$
7. $\frac{3}{4} - \frac{1}{5}$ $\frac{11}{20}$
8. $\frac{11}{12} - \frac{5}{8}$ $\frac{7}{24}$
9. $8\frac{3}{4} + 2\frac{3}{4}$ $11\frac{1}{2}$
10. $4\frac{3}{5} + 6\frac{7}{10}$ $11\frac{3}{10}$
11. $8\frac{1}{2} + 1\frac{1}{9}$ $9\frac{11}{18}$
12. $9\frac{2}{3} + 5\frac{7}{10}$ $15\frac{11}{30}$
13. $5\frac{3}{4} - 2\frac{1}{2}$ $3\frac{1}{4}$
14. $4\frac{5}{12} - 2\frac{7}{12}$ $1\frac{5}{6}$
15. $9 - 4\frac{7}{8}$ $4\frac{1}{8}$
16. $7\frac{1}{2} - 3\frac{4}{5}$ $3\frac{7}{10}$
17. $4\frac{1}{6} - 1\frac{5}{8}$ $2\frac{13}{24}$
18. $5\frac{3}{4} - 1\frac{5}{12}$ $4\frac{1}{3}$

Percent, pages 213–224

Write each percent as a decimal.

1. 9% .09
2. 35% .35
3. 92.1% .921
4. .35% .0035
5. 6.24% .0624
6. .1% .001
7. 27% .27
8. $5\frac{1}{4}$% .0525

Write each decimal as a percent.

9. .04 4%
10. .923 92.3%
11. $.37\frac{1}{2}$ $37\frac{1}{2}$%
12. 2.36 236%
13. .79 79%
14. .243 24.3%
15. .8 80%
16. .03 3%

Write each percent as a fraction in lowest terms.

17. 6% $\frac{3}{50}$
18. 25% $\frac{1}{4}$
19. $\frac{1}{2}$% $\frac{1}{200}$
20. 124% $1\frac{6}{25}$
21. 8% $\frac{2}{25}$
22. $66\frac{2}{3}$% $\frac{2}{3}$
23. 13% $\frac{13}{100}$
24. 75% $\frac{3}{4}$

Write each fraction as a percent.

25. $\frac{3}{5}$ 60%
26. $\frac{5}{8}$ $62\frac{1}{2}$%
27. $\frac{5}{4}$ 125%
28. $\frac{1}{200}$ $\frac{1}{2}$%
29. $\frac{4}{7}$ $57\frac{1}{7}$%
30. $\frac{9}{16}$ $56\frac{1}{4}$%
31. $\frac{3}{2}$ 150%
32. $\frac{1}{6}$ $16\frac{2}{3}$%

CALCULATOR EXERCISES

Optional

For each exercise, tell whether your calculator gives a correct answer when you use the subtraction key as a negative sign.
Yes and no answers may vary.

1. $^{-}400 + 750$ 350
2. $400 + {}^{-}750$ $^{-}350$
3. $^{-}400 + {}^{-}750$ $^{-}1150$
4. $400 - 750$ $^{-}350$
5. $^{-}400 - 750$ $^{-}1150$
6. $400 - {}^{-}750$ 1150
7. $^{-}400 - {}^{-}750$ 350
8. $^{-}400 \times 750$ $^{-}300{,}000$
9. $400 \times {}^{-}750$ $^{-}300{,}000$
10. $^{-}400 \times {}^{-}750$ 300,000
11. $^{-}9250 \div 25$ $^{-}370$
12. $9250 \div {}^{-}25$ $^{-}370$
13. $^{-}9250 \div {}^{-}25$ 370
14. If your calculator has a *change sign key* like the ones below, figure out how to get correct answers to exercises 1–13 by using that key.

Evaluate each expression when $a = 3.72$, $b = 19.63$, and $c = 7.28$.

15. $a + b + c$ 30.63
16. $4.2c + a$ 34.296
17. $8.7(b + c)$ 234.117
18. $37.4a + .7c$ 144.224
19. $\dfrac{9.5a + 14.7}{41.7}$ 1.2

Find each missing number.

20. $r + 3.65 = 19.6$ 15.95
21. $w - 14.7 = 35.1$ 49.8
22. $12.7k = 78.74$ 6.2
23. $5.4h + .8 = 8.9$ 1.5
24. $\dfrac{n}{64.78} = 197.25$ 12,777.855
25. Complete this table for the equation $y = 1.76x + 2.84$.

x	y	
0		2.84
2		6.36
4		9.88
6		13.4

Use this car rental formula to find R for the given values of d and k.

$R = 18d + .12k$

R: rental in dollars
d: days
k: kilometers driven

	d	k
26.	8 days	346 km
	$185.52	
27.	2 days	175 km
	$57.00	
28.	6 days	729 km
	$195.48	
29.	5 days	921 km
	$200.52	

Use this commission formula to find T for the given values of b and s.

$T = b + .035s$

T: total pay
b: base pay
s: sales

	b	s
30.	$329	$1417.62
	$378.62	
31.	$625	$820.14
	$653.71	
32.	$493	$2957.16
	$596.51	
33.	$515	$1073.42
	$552.57	
34.	$304	$2177.36
	$380.21	

Geometry and Right-Triangle Relations

Number of test items - 11

Number missed	1	2	3	4	5
Percent correct	91	82	73	64	55

Skill Finding Perimeter of a Geometric Figure pages 324-325

A Find the perimeter of this rectangle.

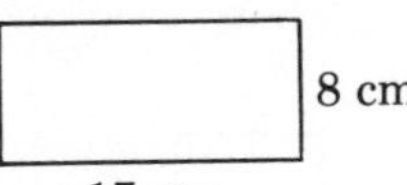

50 cm

B Find the perimeter of this polygon.

3.5 m
2 m
2.5 m
4.5 m
5 m

17.5 m

Skill Finding Circumference of a Circle pages 326-327

C Find the circumference of this circle.

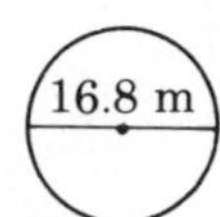

52.752 m

D Find the circumference of this circle.

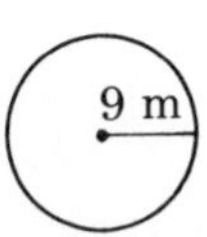

56.52 m

Skill Finding Area of a Rectangle, a Square, and a Parallelogram pages 328-329

E Find the area of this rectangle.

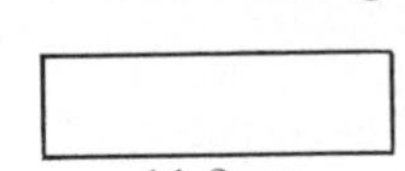

35.84 cm^2

F Find the area of this square.

4.8 mm

23.04 mm^2

G Find the area of this parallelogram.

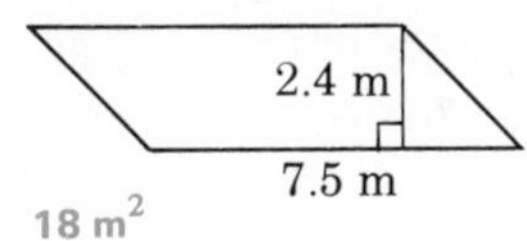

18 m^2

Skill Finding Area of a Triangle and a Trapezoid pages 330-331

H Find the area of this triangle.

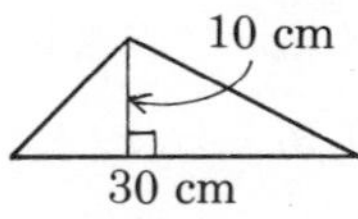

150 cm^2

I Find the area of this trapezoid.

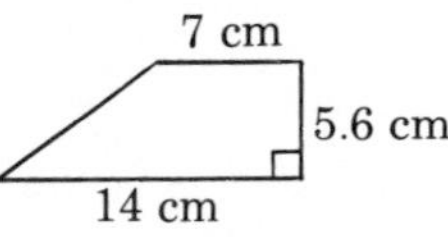

58.8 cm^2

Skill Finding Area of a Circle pages 332-333

J Find the area of this circle.

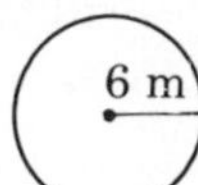

113.04 m^2

K Find the area of this circle.

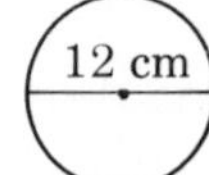

113.04 cm^2

See page T26 for additional notes on Chapter 16.

Objective: Find the perimeter of a geometric figure.

Finding Perimeter of a Geometric Figure

example A

Rectangle, when given the length and the width

Find the perimeter of this rectangle.

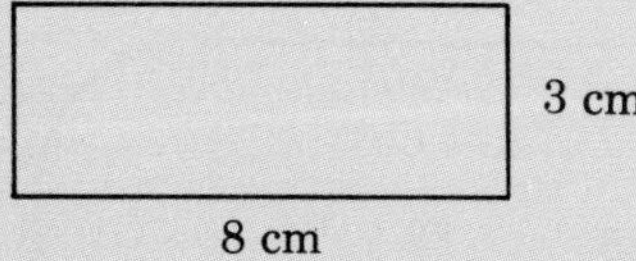

Perimeter is the distance around a polygon. The perimeter of a rectangle is twice the length plus twice the width. Use this formula.

$P = 2l + 2w$

$P = 2(8) + 2(3)$

$P = 16 + 6$

$P = 22$

The perimeter is 22 cm.

example B

Polygon, when given the measures of all sides

Find the perimeter of this polygon.

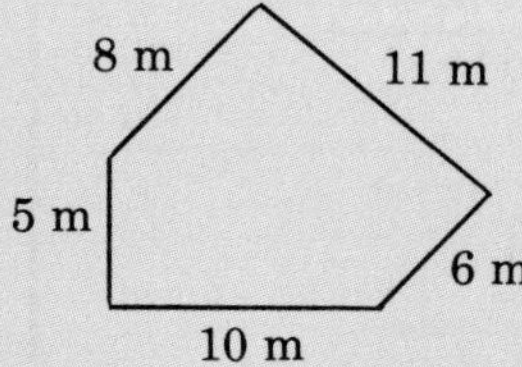

To find the perimeter of a polygon, add the lengths of the sides.

$P = 11 + 6 + 10 + 5 + 8$

$P = 40$

The perimeter is 40 m.

exercises set A

Find the perimeter of each rectangle. All measures are given in centimeters.

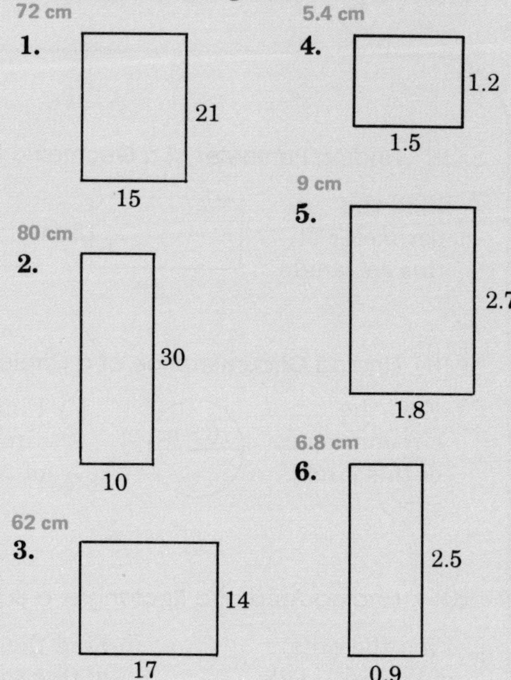

Find the perimeter of each rectangle given these dimensions.

	Length	Width	
7.	34 cm	16 cm	100 cm
8.	12.4 m	7.8 m	40.4 m
9.	38.7 m	19.4 m	116.2 m
10.	158 mm	125 mm	566 mm
11.	9.37 m	4.96 m	28.66 m
12.	17.38 m	10.05 m	54.86 m

set B

Find the perimeter of each polygon. All measures are given in centimeters.

84 cm

1.

13
25
21
15
10

63.8 cm

3.

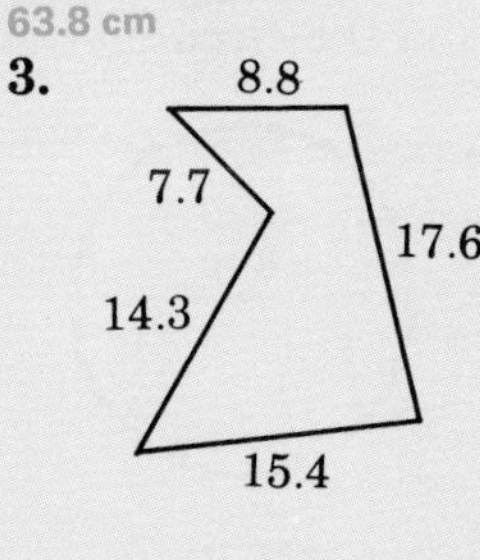

22.2 cm

2.

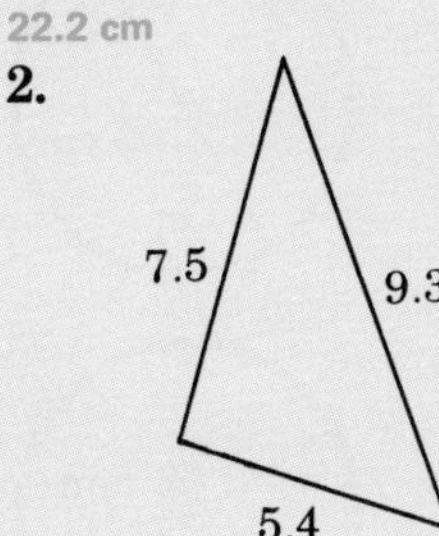

48.3 cm

4.

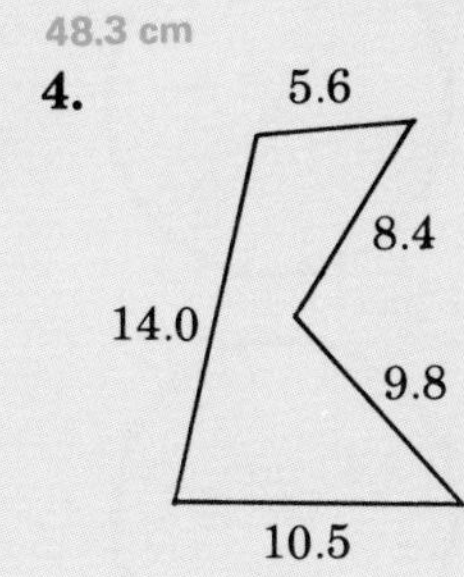

Find the perimeter of each polygon given these dimensions for the sides. All measures are given in meters.

5. 12 15 44 28 — 99 m

6. 5.6 12.0 8.8 — 26.4 m

7. 39 27 62 18 — 146 m

8. 76 42 68 35 47 — 268 m

9. 0.91 0.84 0.35 — 2.1 m

10. 5.4 9.0 4.5 7.2 9.9 — 36 m

11. 27.5 15.2 12.8 20.9 24.6 — 101 m

12. 2.17 1.93 1.85 1.94 1.79 2.06 — 11.74 m

BREAK TIME

At a track meet, Janice, Machiko, and Virginia ran a 50-meter dash.

Virginia did not come in second, and Machiko did not come in third.

Virginia's time was two seconds faster than that of the oldest girl in the race.

In what order did each girl finish the race?

First: Virginia,
Second: Machiko
Third: Janice

Objective: Find the circumference of a circle.

Finding Circumference of a Circle

example C Given the diameter

Find the circumference of this circle.

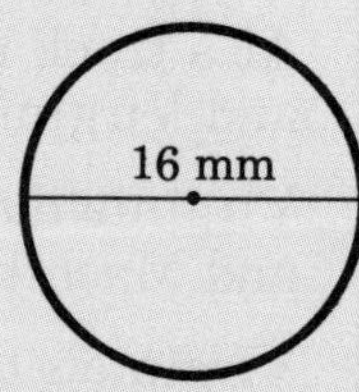

The circumference is the distance around a circle.

The circumference is π (pi) times the diameter. π is approximately equal to 3.14. Use this formula.

$C = \pi d$

$C = 3.14 \times 16$

$C = 50.24$

The circumference is 50.24 mm.

example D Given the radius

Find the circumference of this circle.

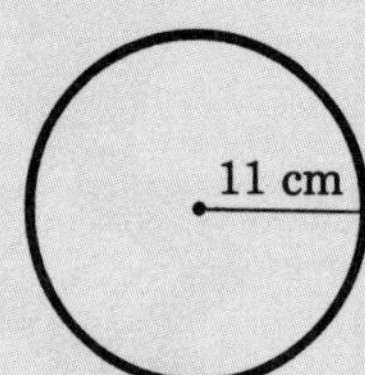

Since the diameter is twice the radius, you can also use this formula.

$C = 2\pi r$

$C = 2 \times 3.14 \times 11$

$C = 69.08$

The circumference is 69.08 cm.

exercises

set C

Find the circumference of each circle.

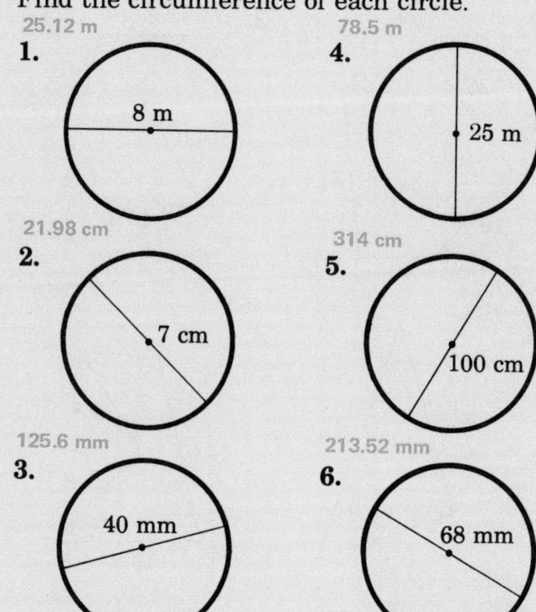

Find the circumference of each circle given these dimensions for the diameter.

7. 10 cm 31.4 cm	**17.** 42 m 131.88 m
8. 50 mm 157 mm	**18.** 61 cm 191.54 cm
9. 90 m 282.6 m	**19.** 75 cm 235.5 cm
10. 200 mm 628 mm	**20.** 22 km 69.08 m
11. 400 m 1256 m	**21.** 160 km 502.4 km
12. 700 cm 2198 cm	**22.** 280 m 879.2 m
13. 99 mm 310.86 mm	**23.** 350 cm 1099 cm
14. 15 mm 47.1 mm	**24.** 110 mm 345.4 mm
15. 37 cm 116.18 cm	**25.** 960 mm 3014.4 mm
16. 19 km 59.66 km	**26.** 570 cm 1789.8 cm

set D

Find the circumference.

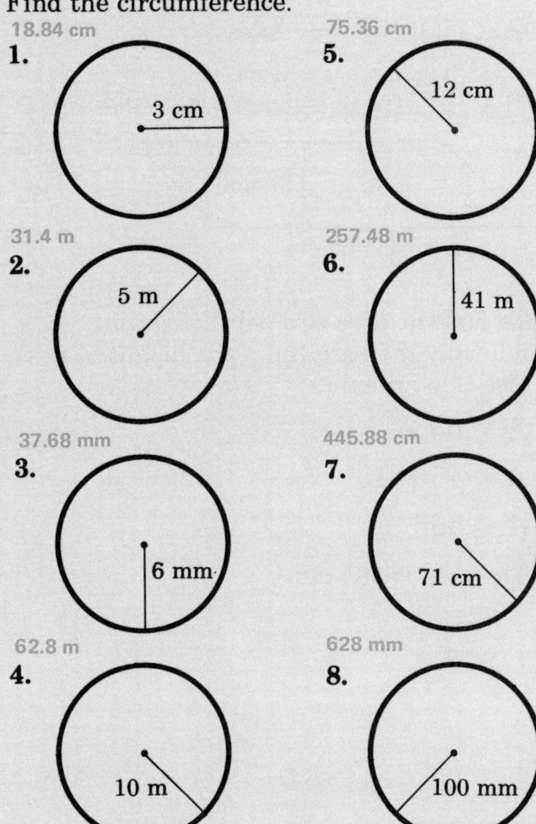

Find the circumference of each circle given these dimensions for the radius.

9. 2 m 12.56 m
10. 4 cm 25.12 cm
11. 7 km 43.96 km
12. 20 cm 125.6 cm
13. 50 m 314 m
14. 80 mm 502.4 mm
15. 90 cm 565.2 cm
16. 300 mm 1884 mm
17. 600 mm 3768 mm
18. 900 mm 5652 mm
19. 15 km 94.2 km
20. 38 cm 238.64 cm
21. 92 cm 577.76 cm
22. 120 mm 753.6 mm
23. 740 cm 4647.2 cm
24. 560 mm 3516.8 mm

BREAK TIME

Jack bought 20 magazines or books and spent a total of $60.

Each magazine cost $1.
Each paperback cost $3.
Each hardback cost $6.

How many of each could he have bought?

Possible solutions include the four shown in the table.

$1	$3	$6
12	0	8
9	5	6
6	10	4
3	15	2

The applications on pages 338–339 may be used anytime after this lesson.

Finding Area of a Rectangle, a Square, and a Parallelogram

Objective: Find the area of a rectangle, a square, and a parallelogram.

example E

Rectangle, when given the length and the width

Find the area of this rectangle.

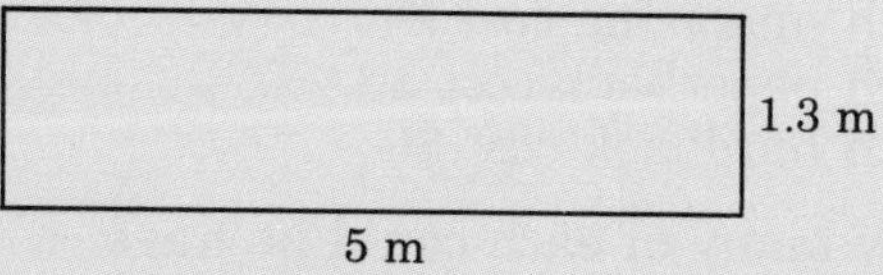

To find the area of a rectangle, multiply the length times the width. Use this formula.

$A = lw$

$A = 5 \times 1.3$

$A = 6.5$

The area is 6.5 square meters, or 6.5 m^2.

example F

Square, when given the measure of all sides

Find the area of this square.

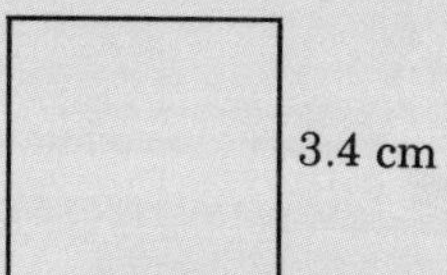

To find the area of a square, multiply the length of one side by itself. Use this formula.

$A = s^2$ s^2 is read "s squared" and means $s \times s$.

$A = (3.4)^2$

$A = 3.4 \times 3.4$

$A = 11.56$

The area is 11.56 cm^2.

example G

Parallelogram, when given the height and the base

Find the area of this parallelogram.

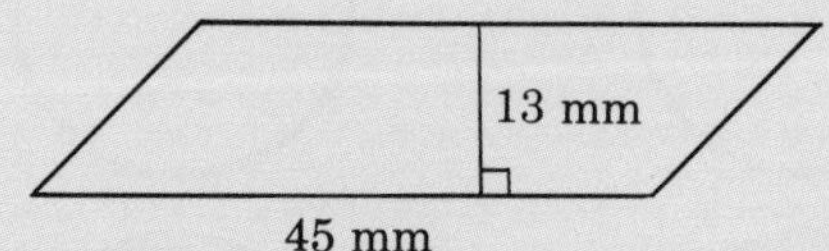

To find the area of a parallelogram, multiply the base times the height. Use this formula.

$A = bh$

$A = 45 \times 13$

$A = 585$

The area is 585 mm^2.

exercises

set E

Find the area of each rectangle.

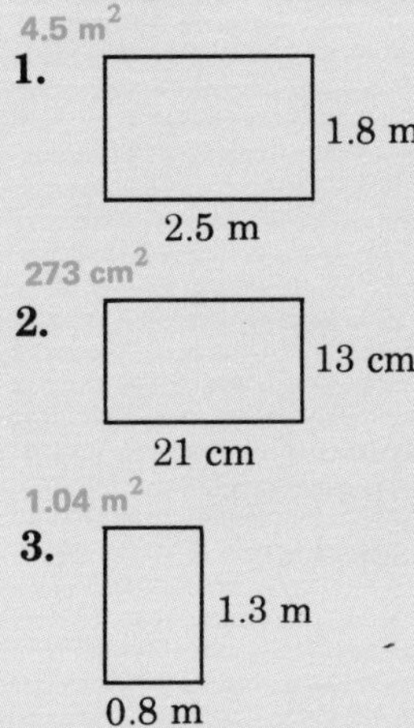

Find the area of each rectangle given these dimensions.

	Length	Width	
4.	12 mm	10 mm	$120\ mm^2$
5.	10 cm	8.4 cm	$84\ cm^2$
6.	1.5 m	0.7 m	$1.05\ m^2$
7.	2.6 cm	0.9 cm	$2.34\ cm^2$
8.	4.5 cm	3.6 cm	$16.2\ cm^2$
9.	0.52 m	0.06 m	$0.0312\ m^2$
10.	0.38 m	0.14 m	$0.0532\ m^2$
11.	1.07 m	0.96 m	$1.0272\ m^2$
12.	2.9 cm	0.7 cm	$2.03\ cm^2$
13.	4.09 cm	2.7 cm	$11.043\ cm^2$
14.	7.16 m	3.8 m	$27.208\ m^2$

set F

Find the area of each square.

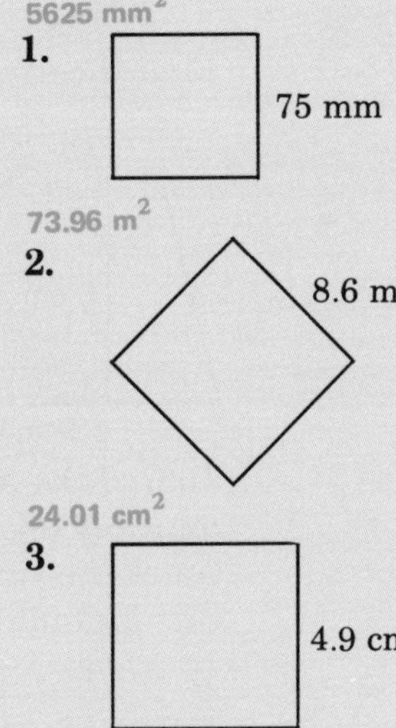

Find the area of each square given these dimensions.

	Side	
4.	10 mm	$100\ mm^2$
5.	15 mm	$225\ mm^2$
6.	1.8 cm	$3.24\ cm^2$
7.	2.5 m	$6.25\ m^2$
8.	3.8 cm	$14.44\ cm^2$
9.	12.1 cm	$146.41\ cm^2$
10.	.48 m	$0.2304\ m^2$
11.	.92 m	$0.8464\ m^2$
12.	7.6 cm	$57.76\ cm^2$
13.	4.12 m	$16.9744\ m^2$
14.	1.7 cm	$2.89\ cm^2$

set G

Find the area of each parallelogram.

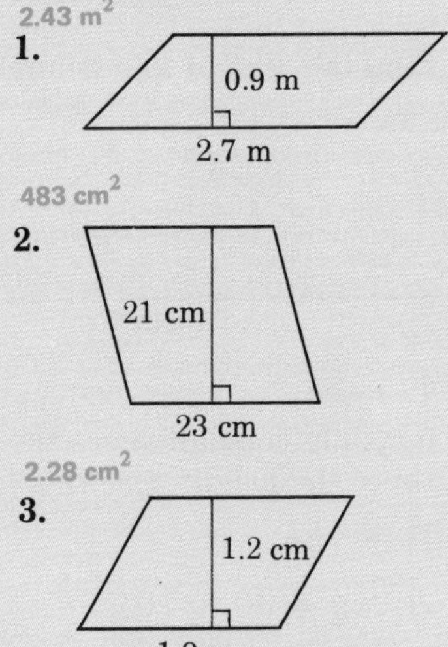

Find the area of each parallelogram given these dimensions.

	Base	Height	
4.	18 mm	10 mm	$180\ mm^2$
5.	25 mm	30 mm	$750\ mm^2$
6.	2.3 cm	0.9 cm	$2.07\ cm^2$
7.	1.7 m	0.6 m	$1.02\ m^2$
8.	0.5 m	0.8 m	$0.4\ m^2$
9.	5.8 cm	2.4 cm	$13.92\ cm^2$
10.	0.75 m	0.38 m	$0.285\ m^2$
11.	2.38 m	0.74 m	$1.7612\ m^2$
12.	1.6 m	0.8 m	$1.28\ m^2$
13.	5.49 m	2.16 m	$11.8584\ m^2$
14.	26.1 cm	18.3 cm	$477.63\ cm^2$

The applications on pages 335-337 may be used anytime after this lesson.

Objective: Find the area of a triangle and a trapezoid.

Finding Area of a Triangle and a Trapezoid

example H

Triangle, when given the height and the base

Find the area of this triangle.

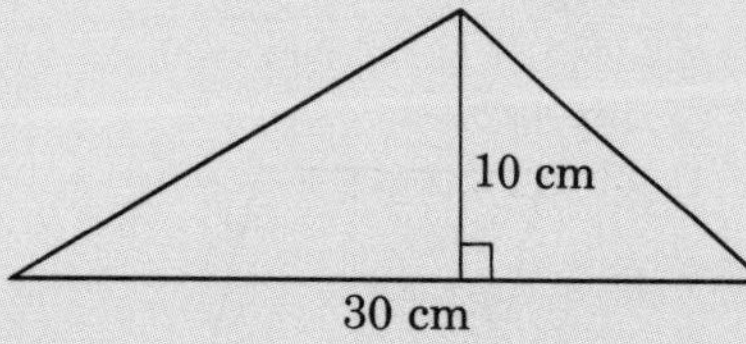

To find the area of a triangle, multiply one-half times the base times the height. Use this formula.

$A = \frac{1}{2}bh$

$A = \frac{1}{2} \times 30 \times 10$

$A = 150$

The area is 150 cm^2.

example I

Trapezoid, when given the height and the measures of the top and bottom bases

Find the area of this trapezoid.

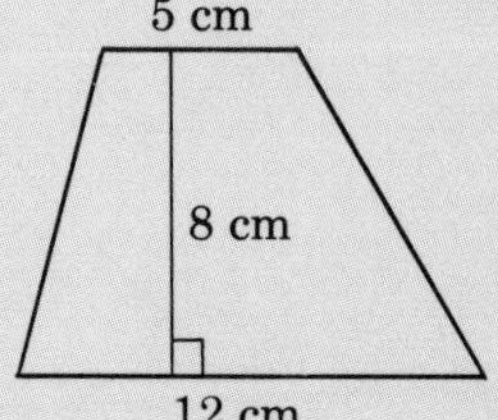

To find the area of a trapezoid, multiply one-half times the height times the sum of the bases. Use this formula.

$A = \frac{1}{2}h(a + b)$

$A = \frac{1}{2} \times 8 \times (5 + 12)$

$A = 4 \times 17$

$A = 68$

The area is 68 cm^2.

exercises

set H

Find the area of each triangle.

165 m²
1.

120 cm²
2.

180 m²
3.

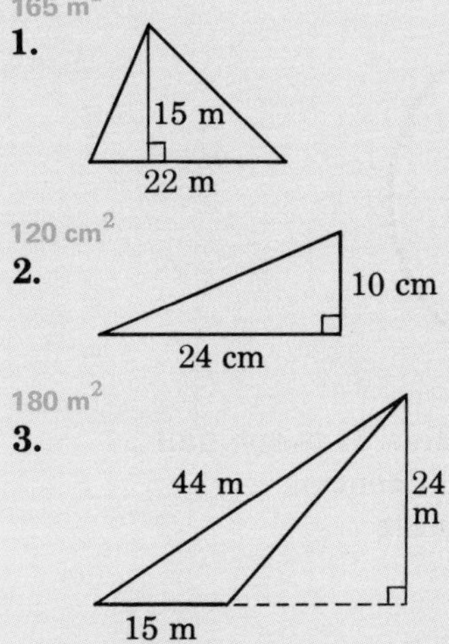

Find the area of each triangle given these dimensions.

	Base	Height	
4.	7 km	4 km	14 km²
5.	27 mm	16 mm	216 mm²
6.	1.5 cm	1 cm	0.75 cm²
7.	25 mm	11 mm	137.5 mm²
8.	3.1 m	2.5 m	3.875 m²
9.	0.36 m	0.12 m	0.0216 m²
10.	1.5 cm	2.4 cm	1.8 cm²
11.	4.4 cm	3.8 cm	8.36 cm²
12.	10.5 cm	31.5 cm	165.375 cm²
13.	34.5 m	11.5 m	198.375 m²
14.	11.2 m	6.5 m	36.4 m²

set I

Find the area of each trapezoid.

81 m²
1.

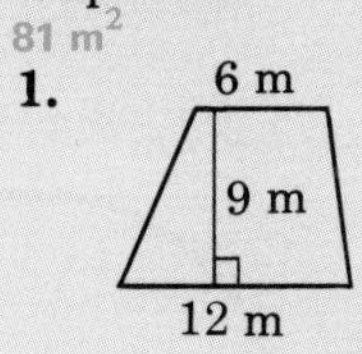

2.22 cm²
2.

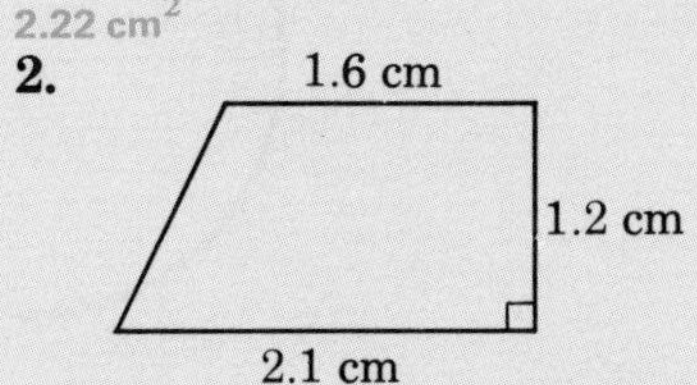

29.8 cm²
3.

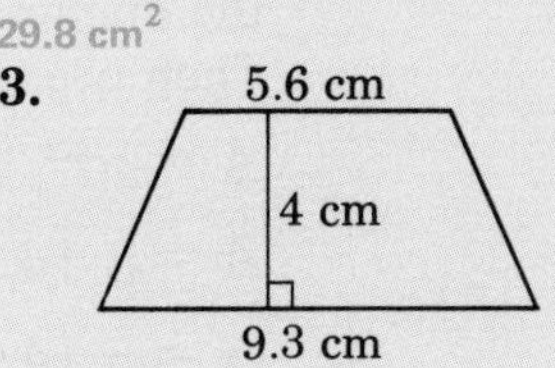

Find the area of each trapezoid given these dimensions. All measures are given in centimeters.

	Height	Base (a)	Base (b)	
4.	8	13	21	136 cm²
5.	2	1.5	2.5	4 cm²
6.	9	5.6	14	88.2 cm²
7.	6	8	19	81 cm²
8.	50	30	20	1250 cm²
9.	0.6	1.5	2.4	1.17 cm²
10.	2	2	3.5	5.5 cm²
11.	4.2	3	7.1	21.21 cm²
12.	2.5	2	4	7.5 cm²

BREAK TIME

Fill in the missing digits for each multiplication problem.

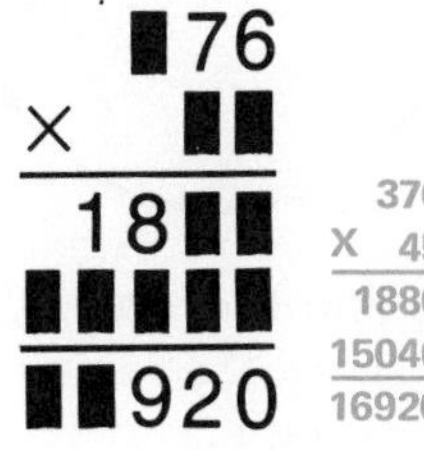

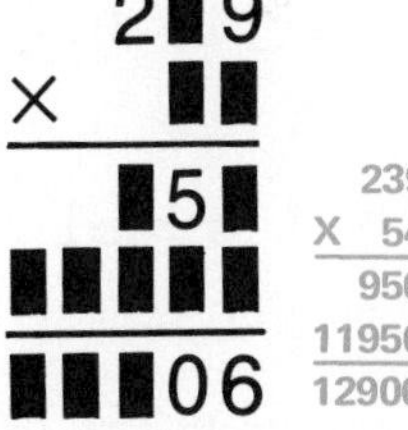

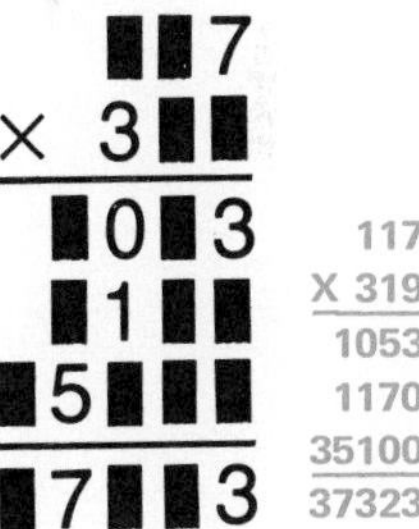

Objective: Find the area of a circle.

Finding Area of a Circle

example J Given the radius

Find the area of this circle.

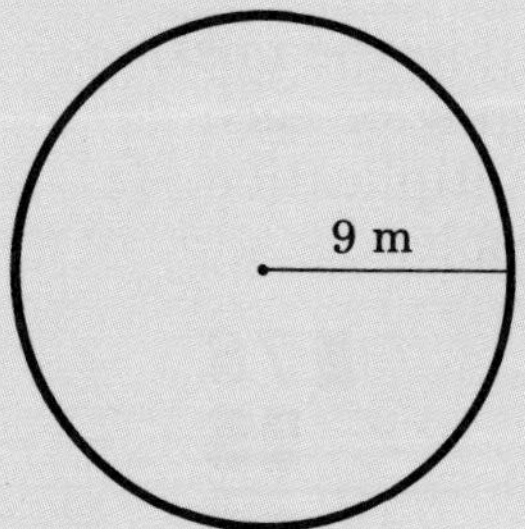

To find the area of a circle, multiply pi times the radius squared. Use this formula.

$A = \pi r^2$

$A = 3.14 \times 9^2$

$A = 3.14 \times 9 \times 9$

$A = 3.14 \times 81$

$A = 254.34$

The area is 254.34 m^2

example K Given the diameter

Find the area of this circle.

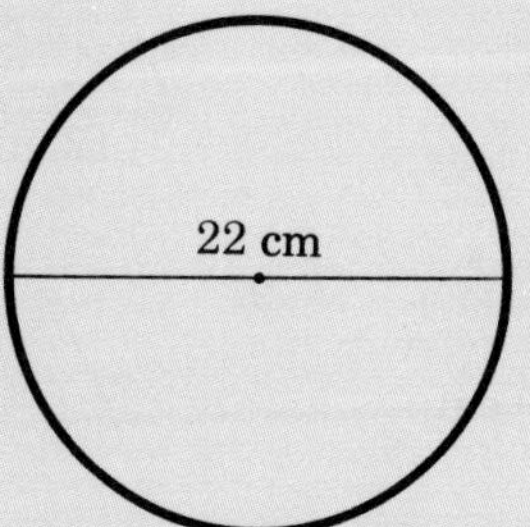

First, find the radius. It is one-half the diameter, or 11 centimeters. Then use the formula.

$A = \pi r^2$

$A = 3.14 \times 11^2$

$A = 3.14 \times 11 \times 11$

$A = 3.14 \times 121$

$A = 379.94$

The area is 379.94 cm^2.

exercises

set J

Find the area of each circle.

28.26 cm²

1.

50.24 cm²

2.

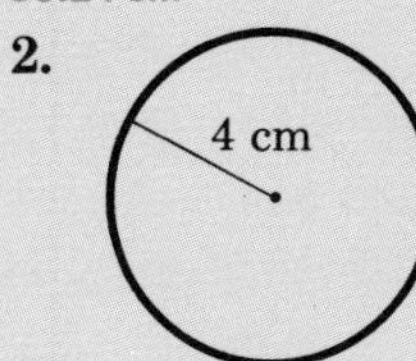

1256 mm²

3.

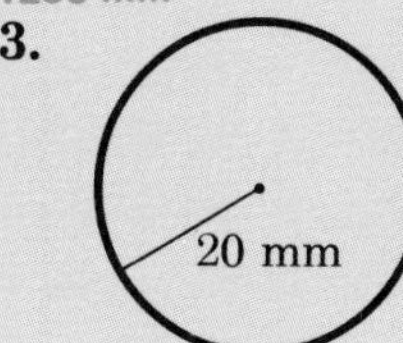

5024 mm²

4.

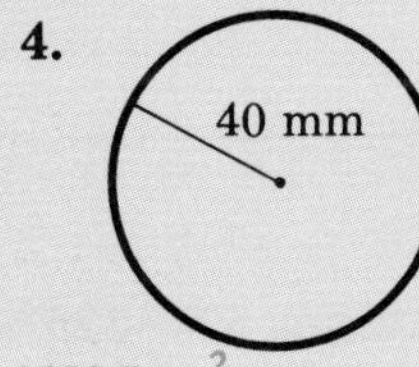

1962.5 cm²

5.

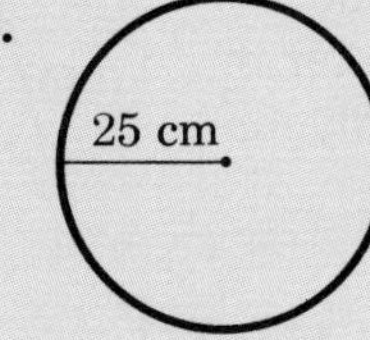

8.0384 m²

6.

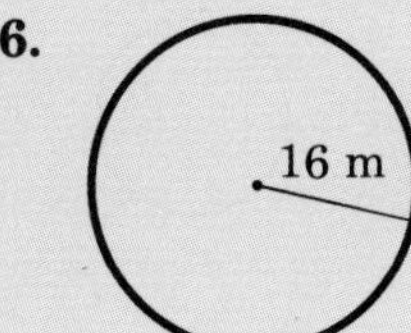

Find the area of each circle given these dimensions for the radius.

7. 6 mm
113.04 mm²

8. 5 mm
78.5 mm²

9. 2 km
12.56 km²

10. 1 km
3.14 km²

11. 7 m
153.86 m²

12. 9 cm
254.34 cm²

13. 10 mm
314 mm²

14. 100 mm
31,400 mm²

15. 80 mm
20,096 mm²

16. 90 cm
25,434 cm²

17. 40 cm
5024 cm²

18. 30 m
2826 m²

19. 60 cm
11,304 cm²

20. 25 m
1962.5 m²

21. 75 mm
17,662.5 mm²

22. 21 mm
1384.74 mm²

23. 54 mm
9156.24 mm²

24. 39 cm
4775.94 cm²

25. 78 cm
19,103.76 cm²

26. 17 m
907.46 m²

27. 32 cm
3215.36 cm²

28. 64 mm
12,861.44 mm²

set K

Find the area of each circle.

314 mm²

1.

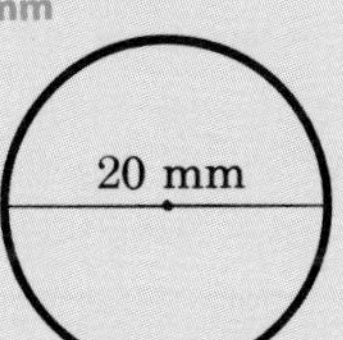

254.34 cm²

2.

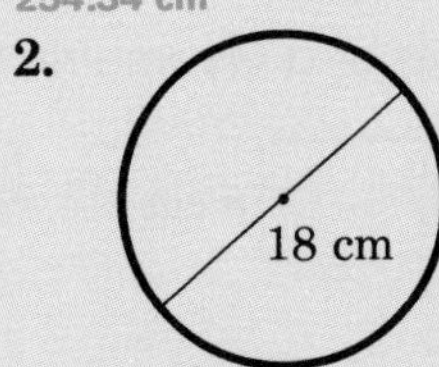

153.86 m²

3.

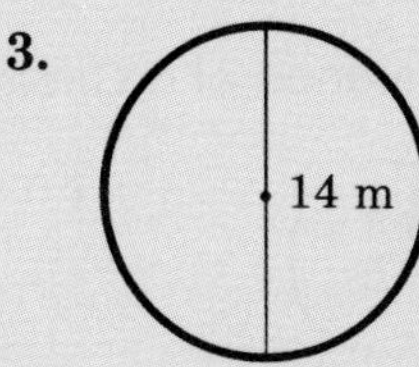

200.96 mm²

4.

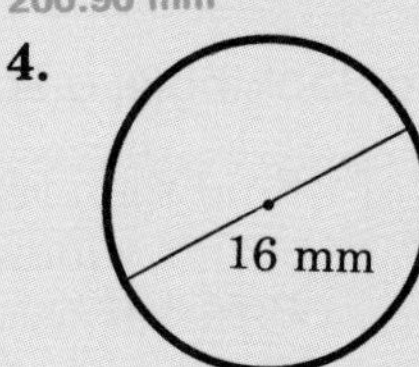

1256 mm²

5.

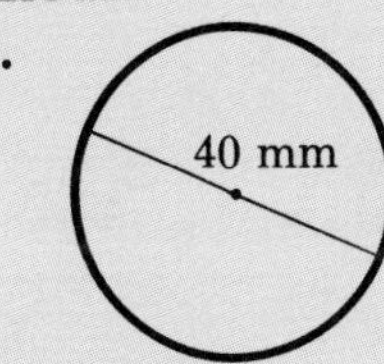

2826 cm²

6.

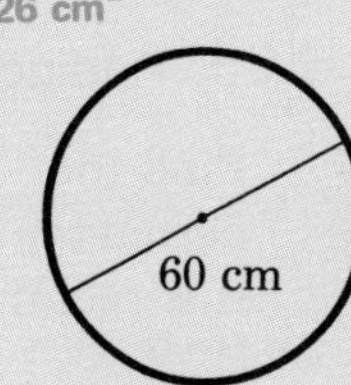

6358.5 mm²

7.

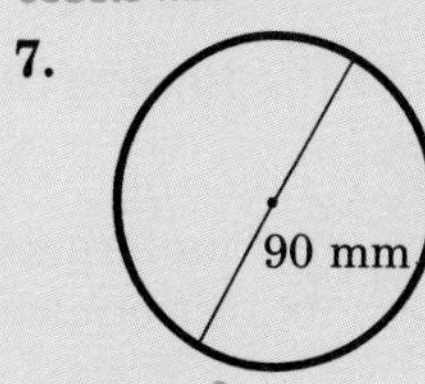

530.66 cm²

8.

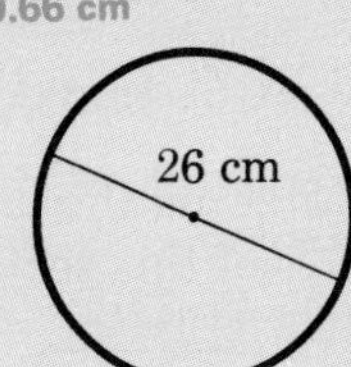

Find the area of each circle given these dimensions for the diameter.

9. 10 m
78.5 m²

10. 4 m
12.56 m²

11. 12 cm
113.04 cm²

12. 8 mm
50.24 mm²

13. 160 mm
20,096 mm²

14. 100 mm
7850 mm²

15. 200 mm
31,400 mm²

16. 80 cm
5024 cm²

17. 24 m
452.16 m²

18. 46 mm
1661.06 mm²

19. 32 cm
803.84 cm²

20. 50 cm
1962.5 cm²

21. 70 cm
3846.5 cm²

22. 28 cm
615.44 cm²

23. 36 mm
1017.36 mm²

24. 94 mm
6936.26 mm²

posttest

Number of test items - 11

Number missed	1	2	3	4	5
Percent correct	91	82	73	64	55

skill Finding Perimeter of a Geometric Figure pages 324-325

A Find the perimeter of this rectangle.
46 cm

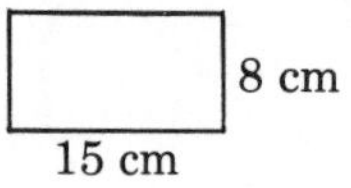

8 cm
15 cm

B Find the perimeter of this polygon.
11 m

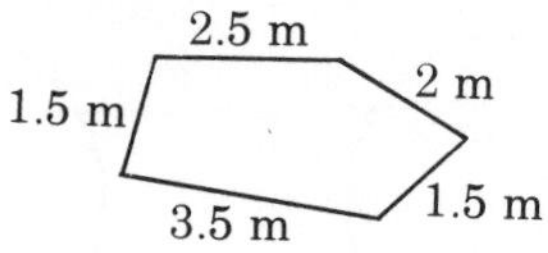

2.5 m
2 m
1.5 m
1.5 m
3.5 m

skill Finding Circumference of a Circle pages 326-327

C Find the circumference of this circle.
46.472 m

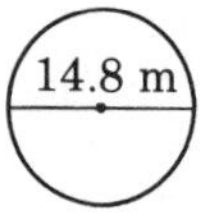

14.8 m

D Find the circumference of this circle.
43.96 m

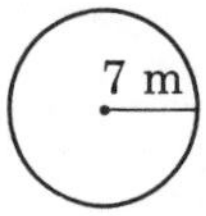

7 m

skill Finding Area of a Rectangle, a Square, and a Parallelogram pages 328-329

E Find the area of this rectangle.
46.08 cm^2

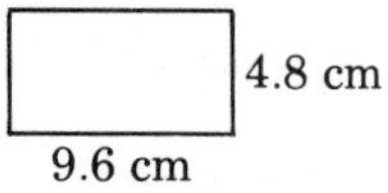

4.8 cm
9.6 cm

F Find the area of this square.
51.84 mm^2

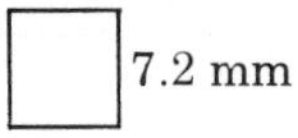

7.2 mm

G Find the area of this parallelogram.
8 cm^2

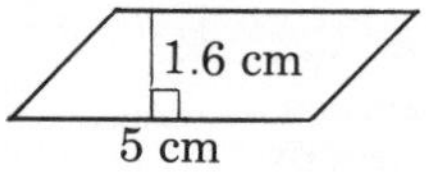

1.6 cm
5 cm

skill Finding Area of a Triangle and a Trapezoid pages 330-331

H Find the area of this triangle.
216 mm^2

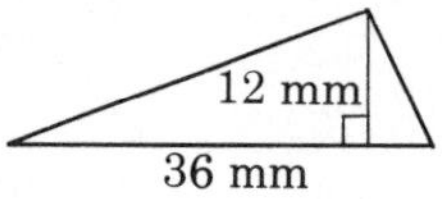

12 mm
36 mm

I Find the area of this trapezoid.
13.68 m^2

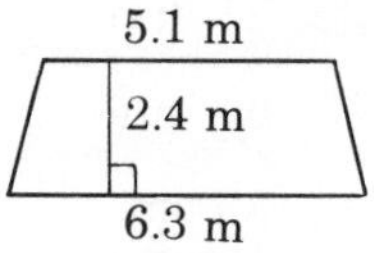

5.1 m
2.4 m
6.3 m

skill Finding Area of a Circle pages 332-333

J Find the area of this circle.
78.5 m^2

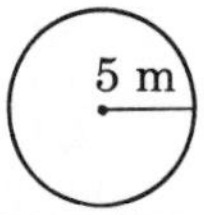

5 m

K Find the area of this circle.
176.625 cm^2

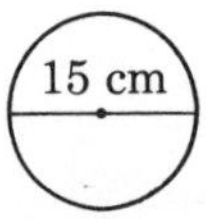

15 cm

Objective: Solve problems involving perimeter and area.

In this lesson students first find actual length and width of a room by using a blueprint, then find area of a room in square meters, and finally compute the cost of buying carpet for a room.

Buying Carpet

	Living Room	Master Bedroom	Guest Bedroom	Study
5.	$242.20	$207.60	$138.40	$110.72
6.	$279.65	$239.70	$159.80	$127.84
7.	$349.65	$299.70	$199.80	$159.84

Susan and Dave Sanner are going to put shag carpeting in their dining room.

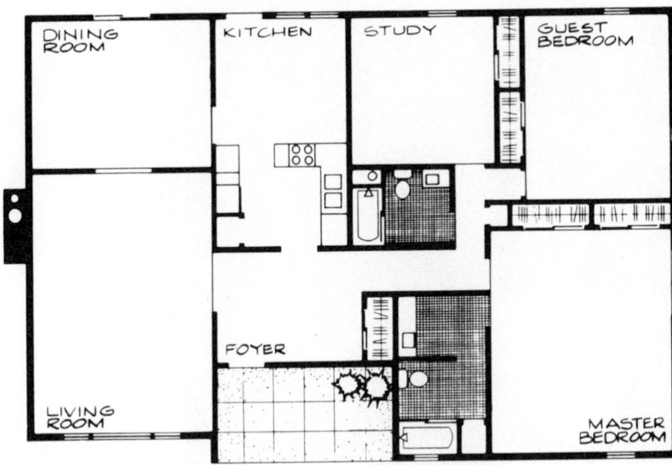

SCALE: 1 mm = 0.2 m

On this blueprint of their home, the length of the dining room is 25 millimeters, and the width is 20 millimeters. The Sanners multiplied by 0.2 to find the actual dimensions.

Actual length: 25×0.2, or 5 meters

Actual width: 20×0.2, or 4 meters

Then they multiplied the length and width to find the area, or the number of square meters.

Area: 5×4, or 20 m^2

Next, they multiplied to find the cost of carpeting the dining room at $6.92 per square meter.

Number of square meters		Price per square meter		Cost
20	×	$6.92	=	$138.40

The cost of putting shag carpeting in the dining room is $138.40.

Find the actual length and width of these rooms. Then find the area.

1. Living room 5 m by 7 m; 35 m^2
2. Master bedroom 5 m by 6 m; 30 m^2
3. Guest bedroom 4 m by 5 m; 20 m^2
4. Study 4 m by 4 m; 16 m^2

Find the cost of buying carpeting for each room in exercises 1–4 if the Sanners choose

5. shag carpeting at $6.92 per square meter. See above.
6. textured carpeting at $7.99 per square meter. See above.
7. plush carpeting at $9.99 per square meter. See above.

Caring for a Lawn

Jean Stephens works hard to make her lawn pleasing and attractive to the eye.

Objective: Solve problems involving perimeter and area.

In this lesson students find the area of the entire property, area of the house, and area of the lawn in order to compute how much fertilizer to buy for a lawn.

Jean uses this scale drawing of her property to help her find how much fertilizer she should buy for the lawn.

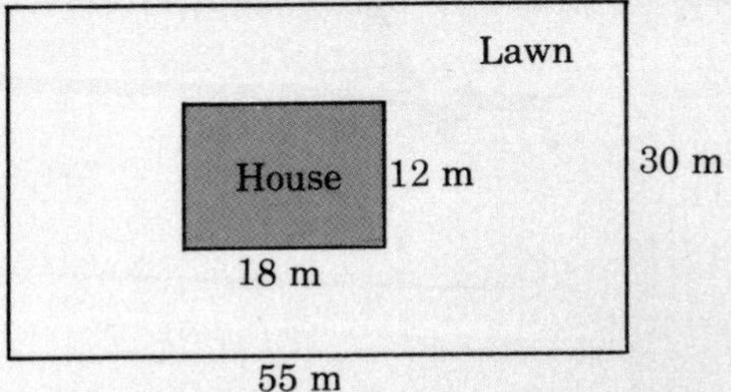

First, she must find the total area of the property and the area of the ground floor of her house.

Total area: 55×30, or 1650 m^2

Area of house: 18×12, or 216 m^2

Then she must subtract to find the area of the lawn.

Area of lawn: $1650 \text{ m}^2 - 216 \text{ m}^2 = 1434 \text{ m}^2$

Jean puts 30 kilograms of fertilizer on each 1500 square meters of lawn. So she uses this proportion to find how much fertilizer she should buy.

$$\frac{30}{1500} = \frac{n}{1434} \begin{array}{l} \longleftarrow \text{Kilograms} \\ \longleftarrow \text{Square meters} \end{array}$$

$$30 \times 1434 = 1500 \times n$$

$$43{,}020 = 1500 \times n$$

$$28.68 = n$$

Jean rounds her answer up to the next whole number. She should buy 29 kilograms of fertilizer.

The answer must always be rounded up or there will not be enough fertilizer.

Find the area of each lawn if these were the dimensions of the property and the house. All measures are given in meters.

	Property Length	Property Width	Area	House Length	House Width	Amount of fertilizer
1.	50	30	1320 m²	18	10	27 kg
2.	50	25	1090 m²	16	10	22 kg
3.	70	50	3330 m²	17	10	67 kg
4.	65	40	2360 m²	20	12	48 kg
5.	90	60	5100 m²	20	15	102 kg
6.	70	55	3584 m²	19	14	72 kg
7.	75	50	3563 m²	17	11	72 kg
8.	55	40	1996 m²	17	12	40 kg
9.	60	45	2508 m²	16	12	51 kg
10.	80	40	3002 m²	18	11	61 kg
11.	45	30	1206 m²	16	9	25 kg
12.	70	45	2814 m²	21	16	57 kg
13.	85	60	4533 m²	27	21	91 kg
14.	80	55	3963 m²	23	19	80 kg
15.	60	40	2166 m²	18	13	44 kg
16.	50	35	1465 m²	19	15	30 kg
17.	75	60	4126 m²	22	17	83 kg
18.	55	35	1621 m²	19	16	33 kg
19.	65	50	2914 m²	21	16	59 kg

20. For each of exercises 1–19, find how much fertilizer should be bought. Use 30 kilograms of fertilizer for each 1500 square meters of lawn. See above.

Objective: Solve problems involving perimeter and area.

In this lesson students find the total length of pipes used in plumbing.

Career: Plumber

Career Cluster: Trades

Oliver Graham is a plumber. He installs and repairs water pipes and fixtures in buildings. He needs to know the total length of this pipe in order to help him order materials.

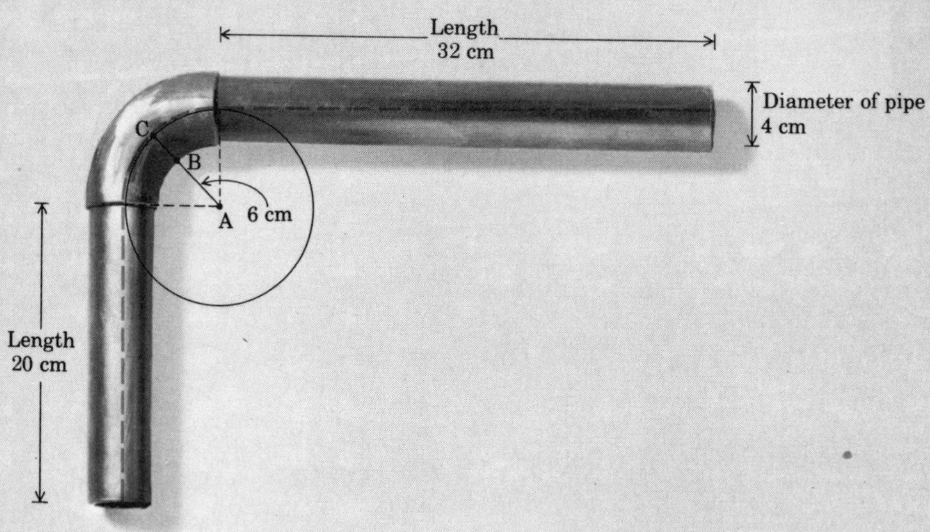

Oliver followed these steps to find the length of the curved section of pipe.

Step 1: Find one-half of the diameter of the pipe to get CB.	$\frac{1}{2} \times 4$ cm $= 2$ cm
Step 2: Add this to AB to find radius AC.	6 cm + 2 cm = 8 cm
Step 3: Find the circumference of the circle shown. Use radius AC.	$2 \times 3.14 \times 8$ cm $= 50.24$ cm
Step 4: Find one-fourth of the circumference because the bend is 90° (one-fourth of a circle). Round answer to the nearest centimeter.	$\frac{1}{4} \times 50.24$ cm $= 12.56$ cm ≈ 13 cm

The length of the curved section is about 13 centimeters.

Then Oliver found the total length of the pipe by adding the lengths of the three sections.

32 cm + 13 cm + 20 cm = 65 cm

The total length of the pipe is about 65 centimeters.

Find the total length of each pipe.

1. 69.99 cm

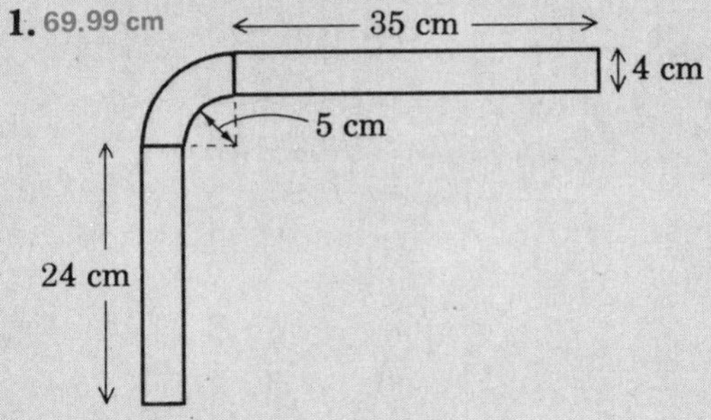

2. 97.85 cm

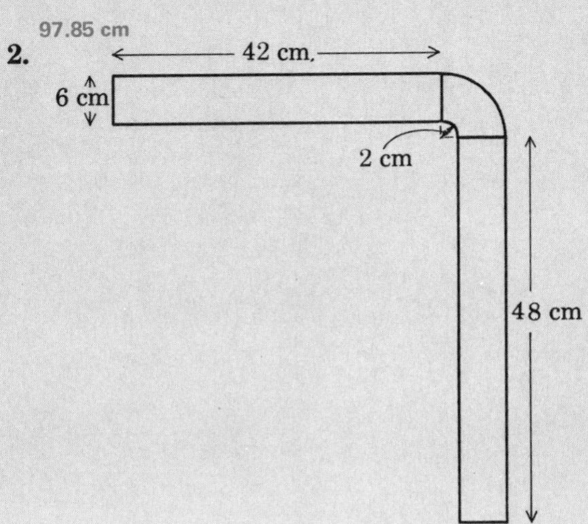

3. 93.635 cm

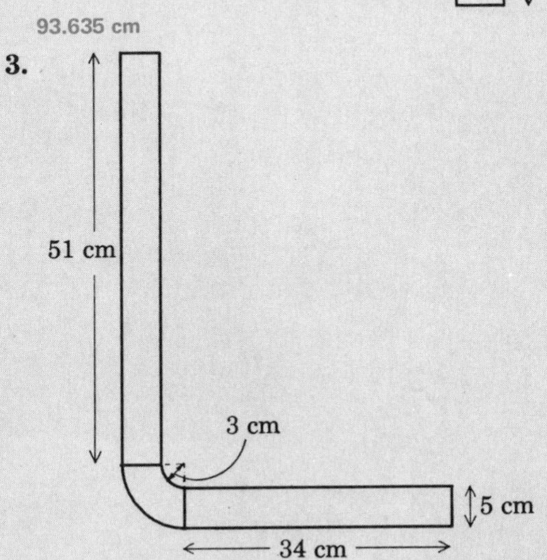

4. 87.26 cm

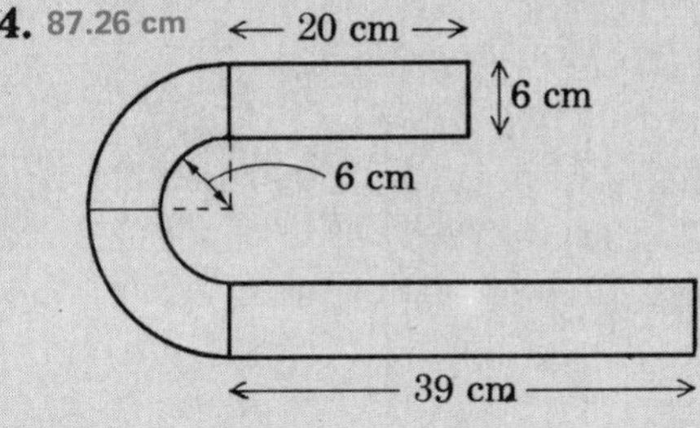

5. 133.12 cm

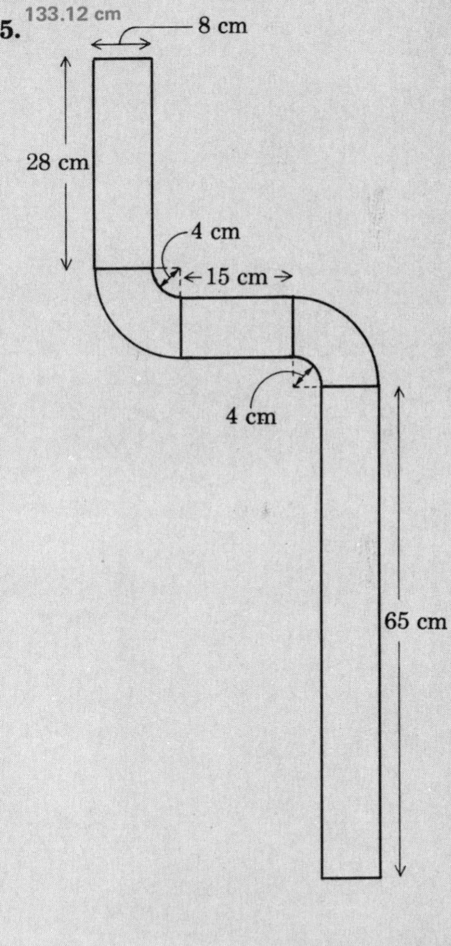

Number of test items - 14

Number missed	1	2	3	4	5	6	7
Percent correct	93	86	79	71	64	57	50

Chapter 16

Find the perimeter of each polygon.

42 m

A **1.**

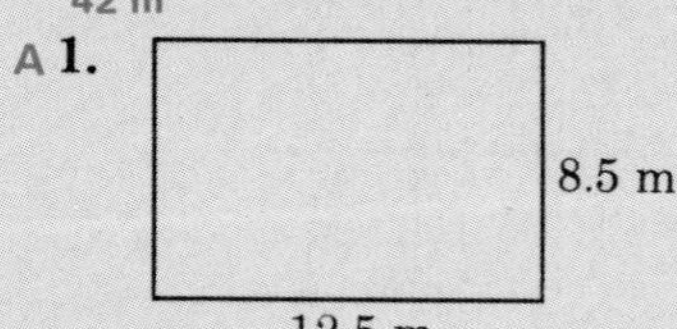

9.4 m

B **2.**

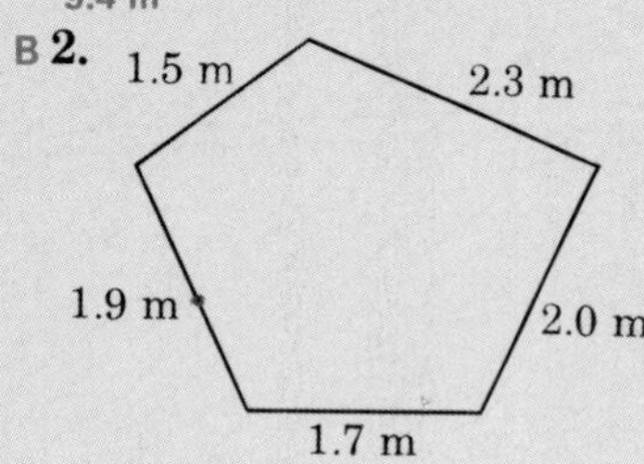

Find the circumference of each circle.

38.622 cm

C **3.**

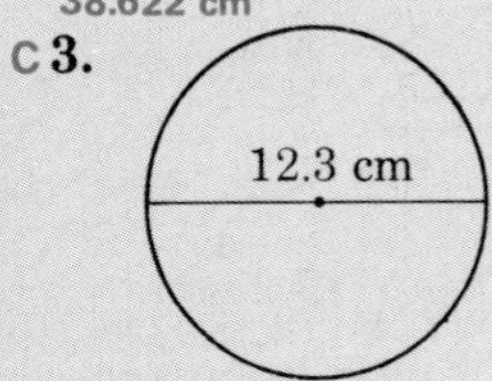

94.2 mm

D **4.**

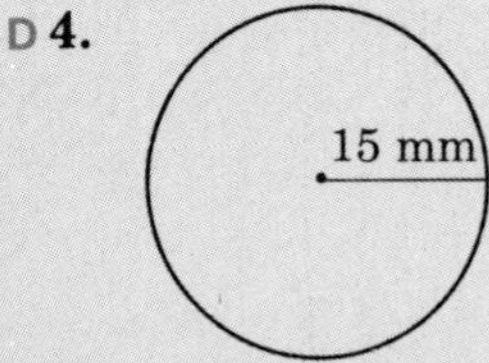

Find the area of this rectangle.

62.56 cm^2

E **5.**

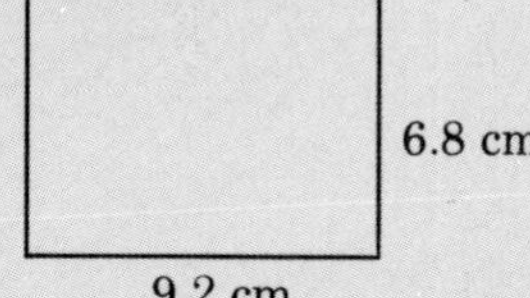

Find the area of each polygon.

32.49 mm^2

F **6.**

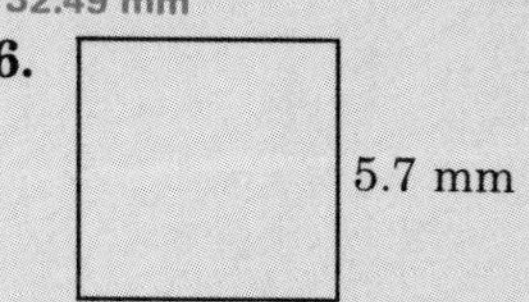

15.6 cm^2

G **7.**

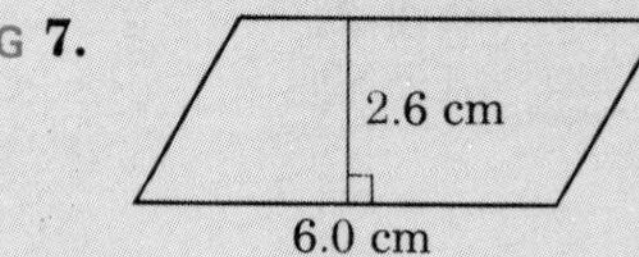

140 m^2

H **8.**

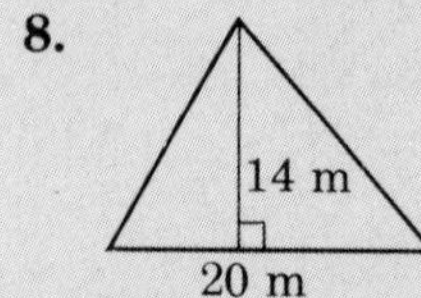

4.76 m^2

I **9.**

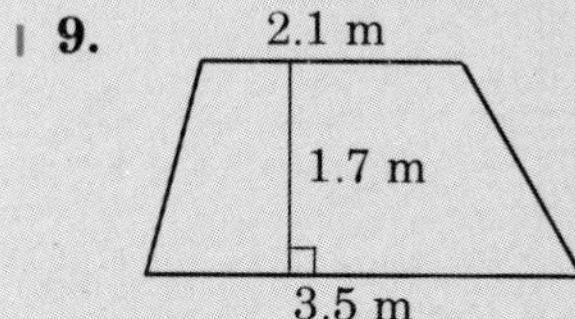

Find the area of each circle.

200.96 mm^2

J **10.**

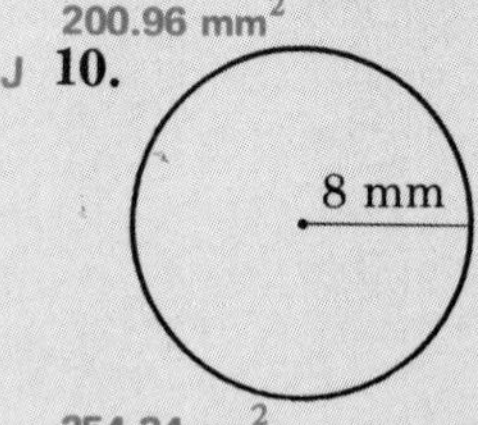

254.34 cm^2

K **11.**

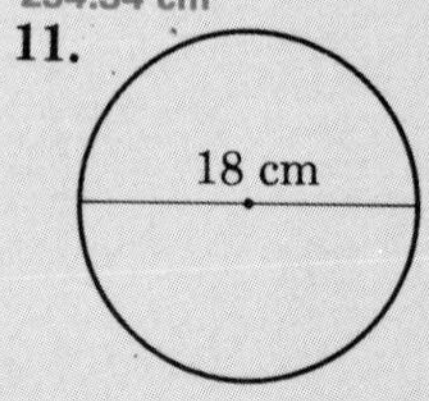

12. Plush carpeting costs $9.99 per square meter. Find the cost of carpeting a living room with these dimensions.

Length: 6 m
Width: 4 m

$239.76

13. The area of John Whitefeather's lawn is 2556 square meters. He uses 30 kilograms of fertilizer on each 1500 square meters of lawn. How many kilograms of fertilizer should he buy?

52 kg

14. Find the total length of this pipe.

65.42 cm

← 18 cm →
4 cm
4 cm
38 cm

 Use pages 45–46 of the *Tests and Record Forms: Duplicating Masters* for an alternative form of the Chapter 16 Test.

Chapter 17
Surface Area and Volume

Number of test items - 11

Number missed	1	2	3	4	5
Percent correct	91	82	73	64	55

Skill Finding Surface Area of a Rectangular Prism page 343

A Find the surface area of this rectangular prism.
550 cm^2

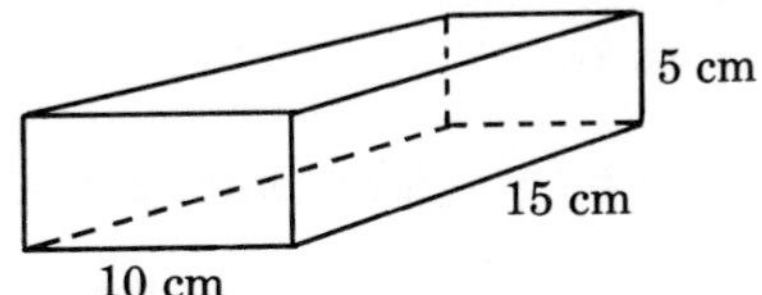

Skill Finding Surface Area of a Cube page 344

B Find the surface area of this cube.
4704 mm^2

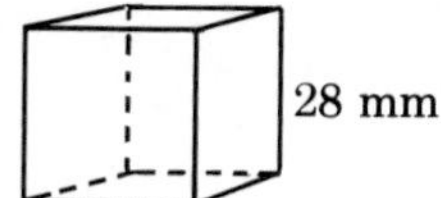

Skill Finding Surface Area of a Cylinder page 345

C Find the surface area of this cylinder.
2009.6 m^2

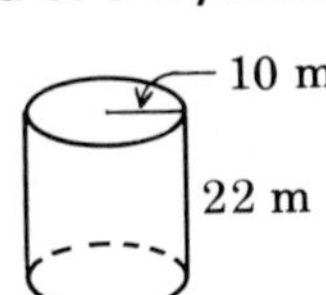

Skill Finding Volume of a Rectangular Prism and a Cube pages 346–347

D Find the volume of this rectangular prism.
4.32 m^3

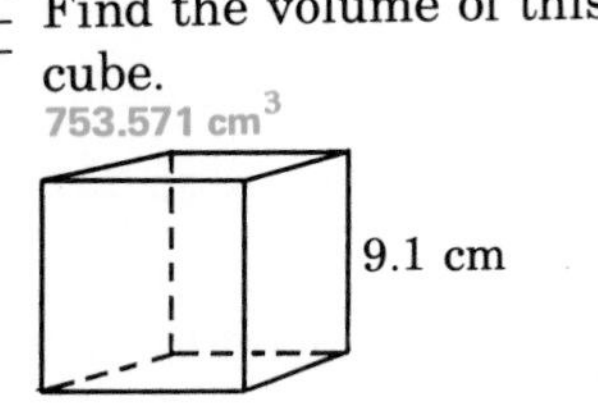

E Find the volume of this cube.
753.571 cm^3

9.1 cm

Pretest continued on page 342.

See page T26 for additional notes on Chapter 17.

Pretest continued from page 341.

skill Finding Volume of a Cylinder pages 348–349

F Find the volume of this cylinder. 314 m^3

G Find the volume of this cylinder. 763.02 cm^3

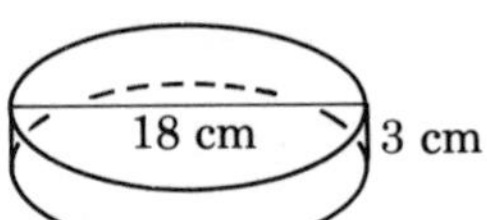

skill Finding Volume of a Pyramid and a Cone pages 350–351

H Find the volume of this pyramid with a rectangular base. 192 m^3

I Find the volume of this cone. 1186.92 cm^3

skill Finding Volume of a Sphere page 352

J Find the volume of this sphere. 14,130 m^3

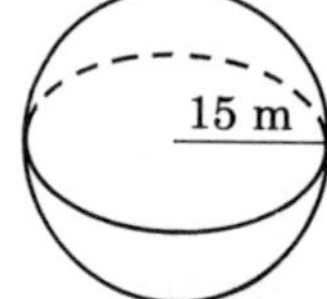

K Find the volume of this sphere. 113.04 cm^3

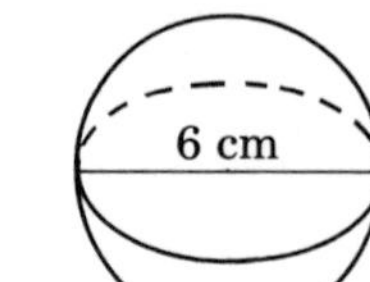

Objective: Find the surface area of a rectangular prism.

Finding Surface Area of a Rectangular Prism

example A

Given the length, width, and height

Find the surface area of this rectangular prism.

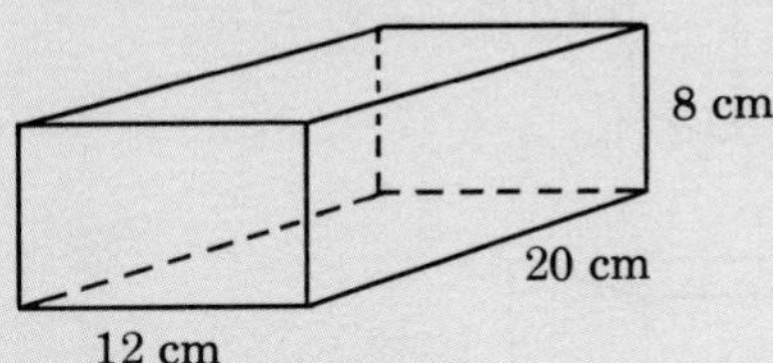

To find the surface area of a rectangular prism, add the areas of the six rectangular faces. Use this formula.

A	$=$	$2lw$	$+$	$2lh$	$+$	$2wh$
Surface area		Area of top and bottom		Area of two sides		Area of front and back

$$A = 2lw + 2lh + 2wh$$
$$A = 2(20)(12) + 2(20)(8) + 2(12)(8)$$
$$A = 480 + 320 + 192$$
$$A = 992$$

The surface area is 992 cm^2.

The formula could also be written $A = 2(lw + lh + wh)$.

4. 1090 mm^2
5. 532 cm^2
6. 10,456 cm^2
7. 138.48 m^2
8. 27,848 mm^2
9. 26.38 m^2
10. 135.98 m^2

exercises

set A

Have students identify the length, width, and height in each of the first three exercises.

Find the surface area of each rectangular prism.

490 cm^2

1.

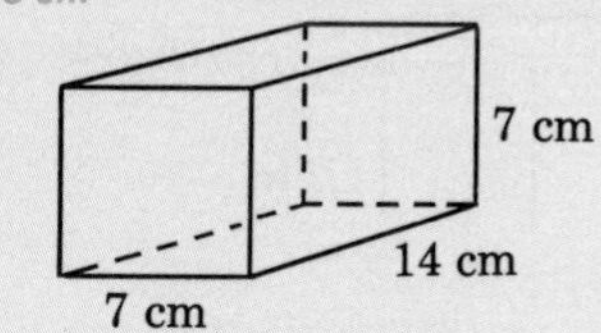

1872 mm^2

2.

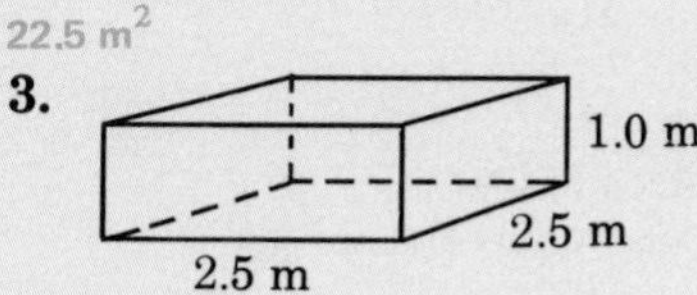

22.5 m^2

3.

1.0 m
2.5 m
2.5 m

Find the surface area of each rectangular prism given these dimensions.

	Length (l)	Width (w)	Height (h)
4.	21 mm	13 mm	8 mm
5.	43 cm	2 cm	4 cm
6.	62 cm	50 cm	19 cm
7.	8.1 m	6.4 m	1.2 m
8.	101 mm	92 mm	24 mm
9.	3.1 m	0.9 m	2.6 m
10.	5.4 m	1.3 m	9.1 m

Objective: Find the surface area of a cube.

Finding Surface Area of a Cube

example B

Given the measure of one side

Find the surface area of this cube.

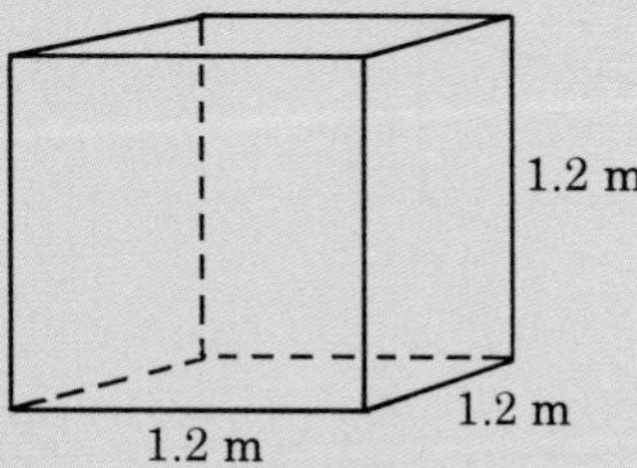

To find the surface area of a cube, find the area of one square face and multiply by six. Use this formula.

$$A = 6s^2$$

A — Surface area

$6s^2$ — Area of six square faces

$A = 6s^2$

$A = 6(1.2)^2$

$A = 6(1.44)$

$A = 8.64$

Emphasize the fact that 1.2 must be squared before it is multiplied by 6.

The surface area is 8.64 m^2.

exercises set B

Find the surface area of each cube.

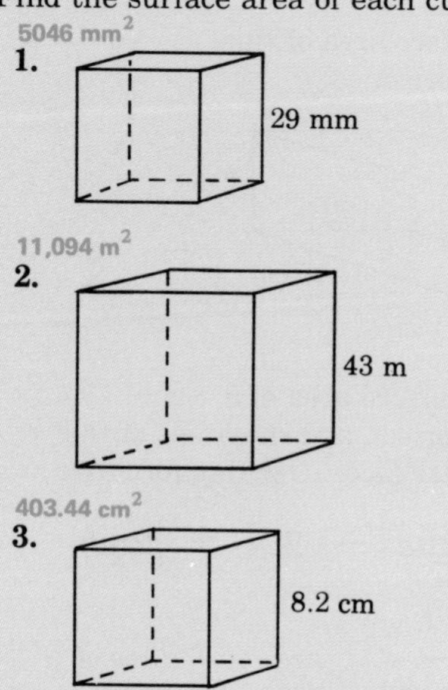

Find the surface area of each cube. The length of a side (s) is given.

4. 23 mm — 3174 mm^2
5. 1.4 m — 11.76 m^2
6. 15 cm — 1350 cm^2
7. 0.7 m — 2.94 m^2
8. 291 cm — 508,086 cm^2
9. 58 mm — 20,184 mm^2
10. 6.1 cm — 223.26 cm^2
11. 25 mm — 3750 mm^2
12. 9.2 cm — 507.84 cm^2
13. 3.5 m — 73.5 m^2
14. 48 mm — 13,824 mm^2
15. 37 m — 8214 m^2
16. 40 cm — 9600 cm^2
17. 12 m — 864 m^2
18. 0.3 m — 0.54 m^2
19. 110 cm — 72,600 cm^2
20. 41 mm — 10,086 mm^2
21. 5.3 m — 168.54 m^2
22. 50 cm — 15,000 cm^2
23. 80 mm — 38,400 mm^2
24. 6.5 m — 253.5 m^2
25. 23 mm — 3174 mm^2

Objective: Find the surface area of a cylinder.

Finding Surface Area of a Cylinder

example C

Given the radius and height

Find the surface area of this cylinder.

This flat pattern shows the surface of the cylinder. The length of the rectangle is the circumference of the circle ($2\pi r$). The width of the rectangle is the height of the cylinder.

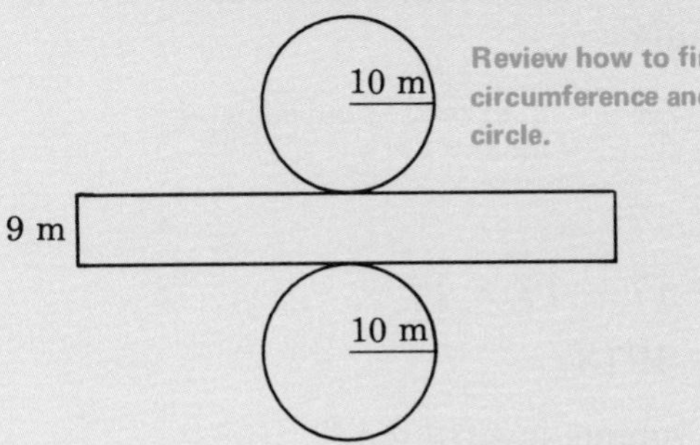

Review how to find circumference and area of a circle.

To find the surface area, add the area of the rectangle and the areas of the two circles. Use this formula.

$$A = 2\pi rh + 2\pi r^2$$

A — Surface area; $2\pi rh$ — Area of rectangle; $2\pi r^2$ — Area of two circles

$$A = 2\pi rh + 2\pi r^2$$
$$A = 2(3.14)(10)(9) + 2(3.14)(10)^2$$
$$A = 2(3.14)(10)(9) + 2(3.14)(100)$$
$$A = 565.2 + 628$$
$$A = 1193.2$$

The surface area is 1193.2 m^2.

exercises set C

Find the surface area of each cylinder.

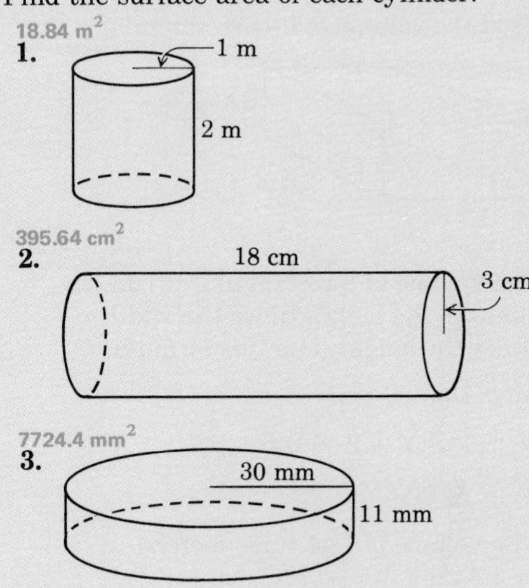

Find the surface area of each cylinder given these dimensions.

	Radius (r)	Height (h)	
4.	2 m	5 m	87.92 m^2
5.	1 cm	9 cm	62.8 cm^2
6.	30 mm	25 mm	10,362 mm^2
7.	6 cm	17 cm	866.64 cm^2
8.	4 m	3 m	175.84 m^2
9.	10 cm	18 cm	1758.4 cm^2
10.	50 mm	30 mm	25,120 mm^2
11.	5 m	14 m	596.6 m^2
12.	7 cm	8 cm	659.4 cm^2
13.	20 mm	24 mm	5526.4 mm^2

Objective: Find the volume of a rectangular prism and a cube.

Finding Volume of a Rectangular Prism and a Cube

example D

Rectangular prism, when given the length, width, and height

Find the volume of this rectangular prism.

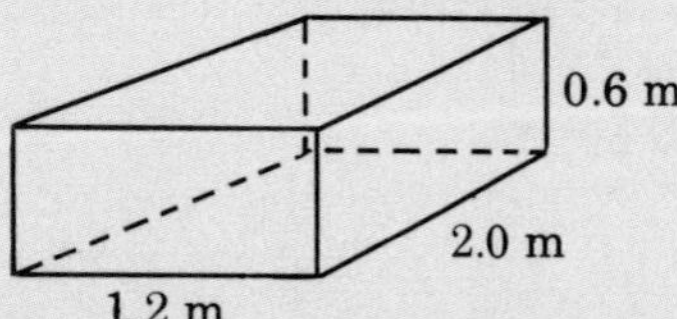

The volume of a rectangular prism is equal to the length times the width times the height. Use this formula.

$V = lwh$

$V = 2.0 \times 1.2 \times 0.6$

$V = 1.44$

The volume is 1.44 cubic meters, or 1.44 m^3.

example E

Cube, when given the measure of one side

Find the volume of this cube.

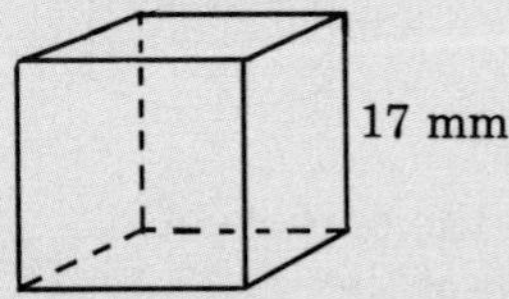

The volume of a cube is equal to the length of a side times the same length times the same length. Use this formula.

$V = s^3$ s^3 is read "*s* cubed" and means $s \times s \times s$.

$V = 17^3$

$V = 17 \times 17 \times 17$

$V = 4913$

The volume is 4913 mm^3.

exercises

set D

You might point out that the three dimensions can be multiplied in any order.

Find the volume of each rectangular prism.

256 cm^3

1.

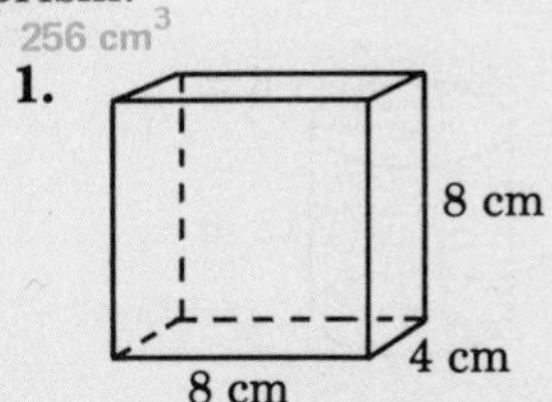

101.25 m^3

2.

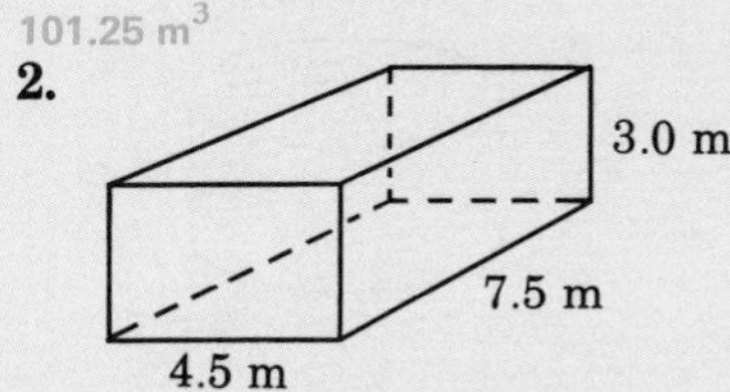

384 cm^3

3.

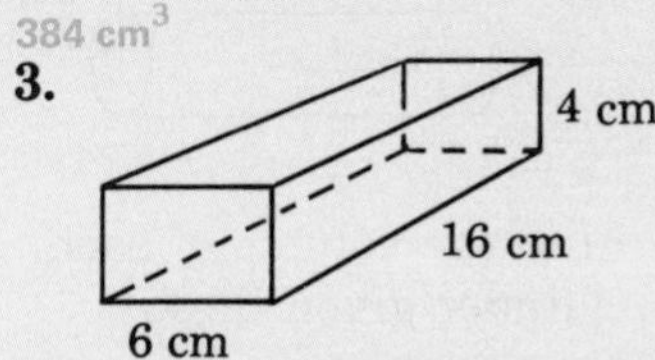

Find the volume of each rectangular prism given these dimensions.

	Length (l)	Width (w)	Height (h)	
4.	19 mm	8 mm	22 mm	3344 mm^3
5.	25 cm	13 cm	5 cm	1625 cm^3
6.	3.1 m	2.2 m	0.5 m	3.41 m^3
7.	94 cm	60 cm	45 cm	253,800 cm^3
8.	1.4 m	0.8 m	5.0 m	5.6 m^3
9.	21 cm	15 cm	34 cm	10,710 cm^3
10.	58 mm	41 mm	82 mm	194,996 mm^3

set E

Find the volume of each cube.

421,875 cm^3

1.

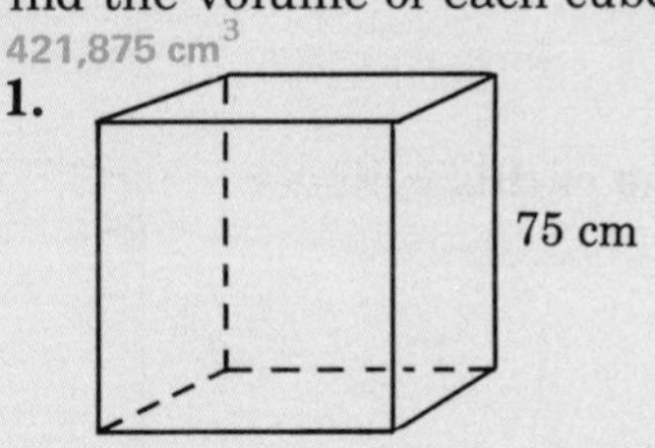

6.859 m^3

2.

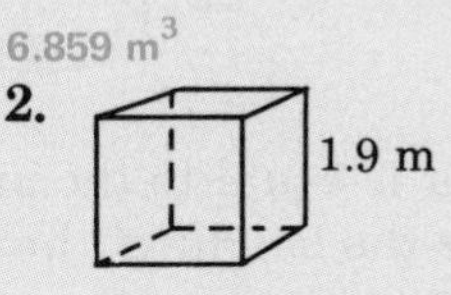

1,124,864 mm^3

3.

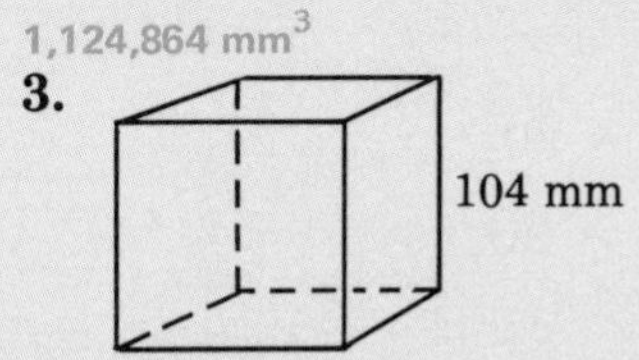

Find the volume of each cube. The length of a side (s) is given.

4. 23 m — 12,167 m^3

5. 0.4 m — 0.064 m^3

6. 81 mm — 531,441 mm^3

7. 3.7 m — 50.653 m^3

8. 48 cm — 110,592 cm^3

9. 50 cm — 125,000 cm^3

10. 1.5 m — 3.375 m^3

11. 32 cm — 32,768 cm^3

12. 10 m — 1000 m^3

13. 2.9 m — 24.389 m^3

14. 7 m — 343 m^3

15. 12.1 cm — 1771.561 cm^3

16. 56 mm — 175,616 mm^3

17. 20 m — 8000 m^3

18. 87 mm — 658,503 mm^3

19. 63 cm — 250,047 cm^3

20. 9.2 m — 778,688 m^3

21. 100 cm — 1,000,000 cm^3

22. 42 mm — 74,088 mm^3

23. 6 m — 216 m^3

24. 5.8 cm — 195.112 cm^3

25. 94 cm — 830,584 cm^3

The applications on pages 356–357 may be used anytime after this lesson.

Objective: Find the volume of a cylinder.

Finding Volume of a Cylinder

example F Given the radius

Find the volume of this cylinder.

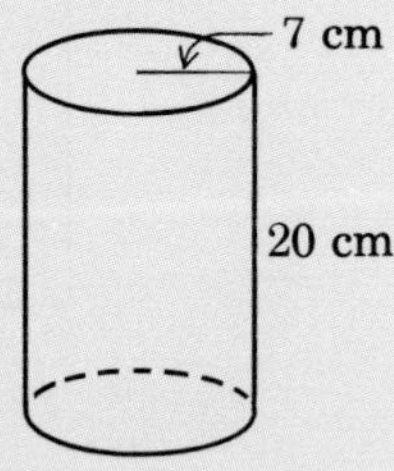

The volume of a cylinder is equal to the area of the circular base (πr^2) times the height of the cylinder. Use this formula.

$V = \pi r^2 h$

$V = 3.14 \times 7^2 \times 20$

$V = 3.14 \times 49 \times 20$

$V = 3077.2$

The volume is 3077.2 cm^3.

example G Given the diameter

Find the volume of this cylinder.

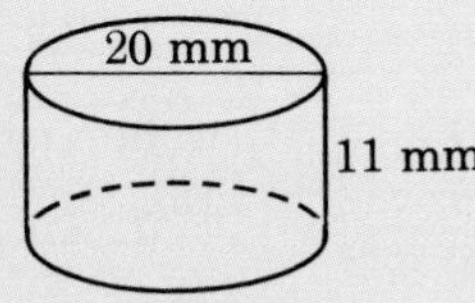

Find the radius. It is one-half the diameter, or 10 millimeters. Then use the formula.

$V = \pi r^2 h$

$V = 3.14 \times 10^2 \times 11$

$V = 3.14 \times 100 \times 11$

$V = 3454$

The volume is 3454 mm^3.

exercises set F

Find the volume of each cylinder.

1. 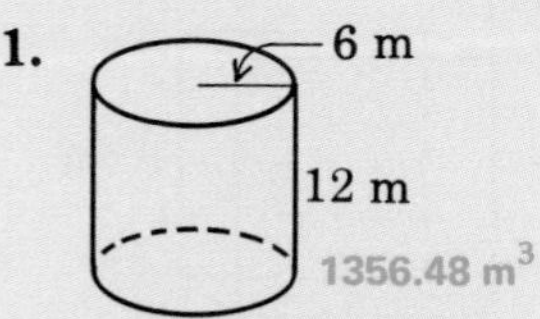

1356.48 m^3

2. 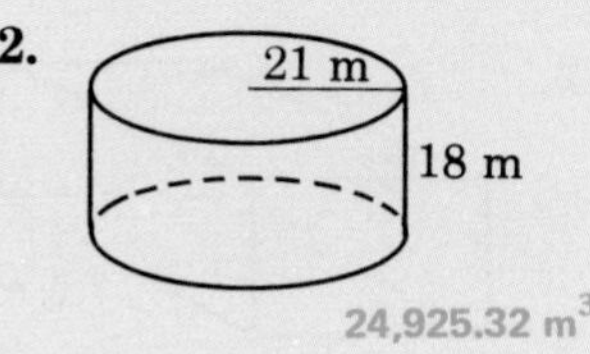

24,925.32 m^3

3. 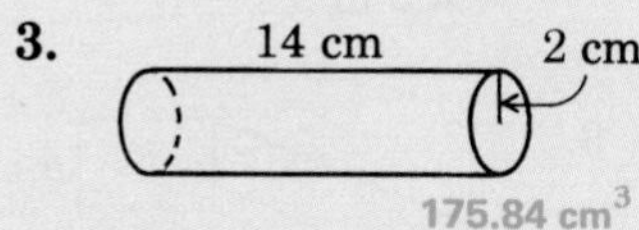

175.84 cm^3

Find the volume of each cylinder given these dimensions.

	Radius (r)	Height (h)	
4.	10 cm	13 cm	4082 cm^3
5.	8 mm	25 mm	5024 mm^3
6.	5 m	4 m	314 m^3
7.	40 cm	16 cm	80,384 cm^3
8.	9 m	8 m	2034.72 m^3
9.	26 mm	59 mm	125,235.76 mm^3
10.	38 cm	90 cm	408,074.4 cm^3
11.	3 cm	28 cm	791.28 cm^3
12.	1 m	19 m	59.66 m^3

set G

Find the volume of each cylinder.

1. 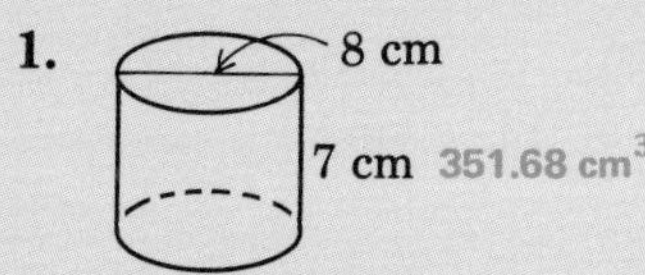

351.68 cm³

2. 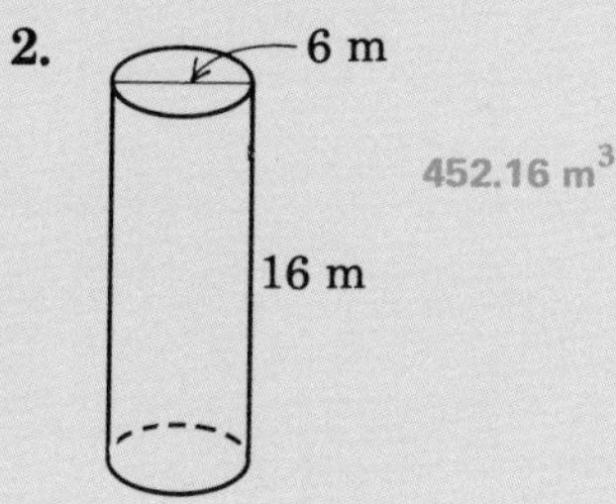

452.16 m³

3. 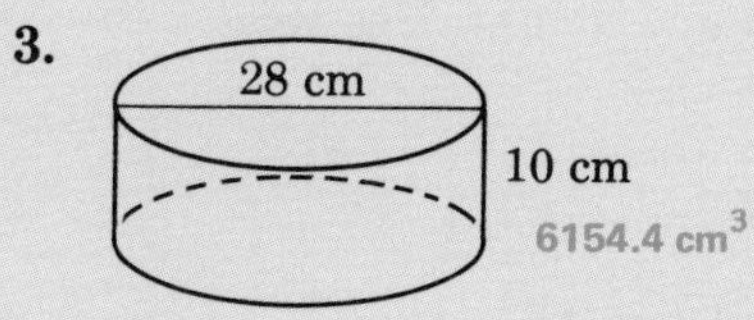

6154.4 cm³

Find the volume of each cylinder given these dimensions.

	Diameter	Height	
4.	6 m	9 m	254.34 m^3
5.	18 cm	30 cm	7630.2 cm^3
6.	10 m	8 m	628 m^3
7.	12 mm	83 mm	9382.32 mm^3
8.	4 m	19 m	238.64 m^3
9.	30 cm	20 cm	14,130 cm^3
10.	70 cm	40 cm	153.860 cm^3
11.	2 m	21 m	65.94 m^3
12.	14 cm	95 cm	14,616.7 cm^3

This is the top view of four grain elevators. When the elevators were filled, the grain overflowed to fill the space in the middle.

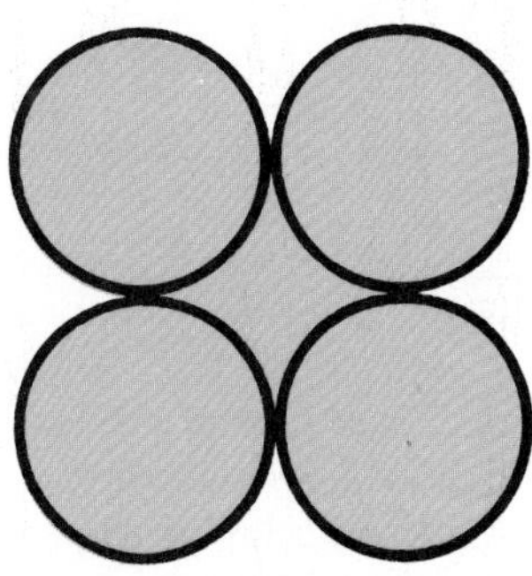

The radius of each elevator is 2 meters, and the height is 10 meters. Find the total volume of the four elevators and the space in the middle.

536.8 m^3

The applications on pages 358–359 may be used anytime after this lesson.

Objective: Find the volume of a pyramid and a cone.

Finding Volume of a Pyramid and a Cone

example H

Pyramid, when given the length, width, and height

Find the volume of this pyramid with a rectangular base.

Be sure students understand how the height is measured.

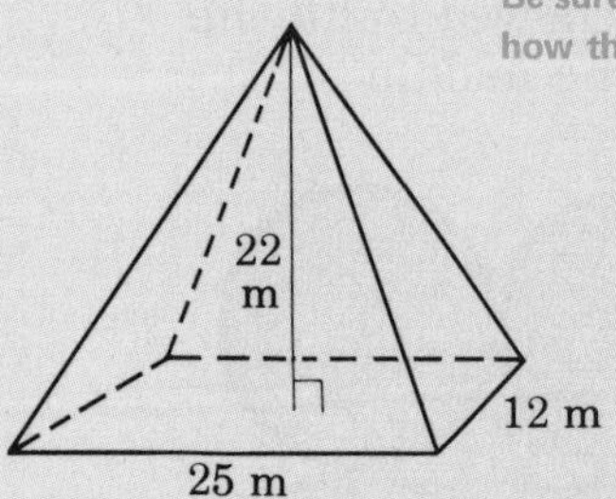

The volume of a pyramid with a rectangular base is one-third the volume of a rectangular prism with the same length, width, and height. Use this formula.

$V = \frac{1}{3}lwh$

$V = \frac{1}{3} \times 25 \times 12 \times 22$

$V = \frac{1}{\cancel{3}_1} \times \frac{25}{1} \times \frac{\cancel{12}^4}{1} \times \frac{22}{1}$

$V = 2200$

The volume is 2200 m^3.

example I

Cone, when given the radius and height

Find the volume of this cone.

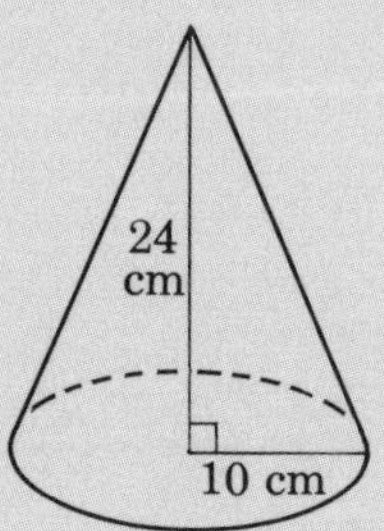

The volume of a cone is one-third the volume of a cylinder with the same radius and height. Use this formula.

$V = \frac{1}{3}\pi r^2 h$

$V = \frac{1}{3} \times 3.14 \times 10^2 \times 24$

$V = \frac{1}{3} \times 3.14 \times 100 \times 24$

$V = \frac{1}{\cancel{3}_1} \times \frac{3.14}{1} \times \frac{100}{1} \times \frac{\cancel{24}^8}{1}$

$V = 2512$

The volume is 2512 cm^3.

exercises

set H

Find the volume of each pyramid.

24 cm^3

1.

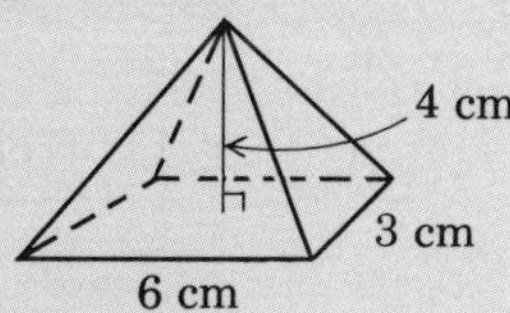

720 m^3

2.

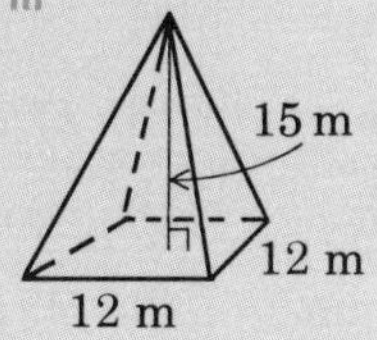

1998 cm^3

3.

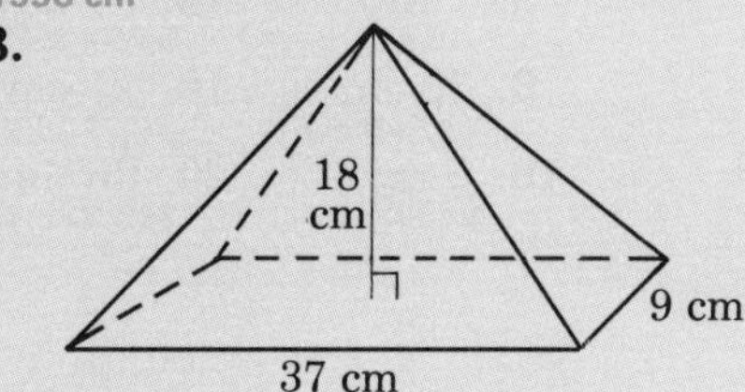

Find the volume of each pyramid given these dimensions.

	Length (l)	Width (w)	Height (h)	
4.	14 cm	8 cm	9 cm	336 cm^3
5.	20 cm	20 cm	36 cm	4800 cm^3
6.	45 mm	22 mm	15 mm	4950 mm^3
7.	17 cm	13 cm	60 cm	4420 cm^3
8.	3.2 m	3.0 m	8.5 m	27.2 m^3
9.	93 mm	87 mm	52 mm	140,244 mm^3
10.	6.0 m	2.3 m	9.2 m	42.32 m^3

set I

Find the volume of each cone.

25.12 m^3

1.

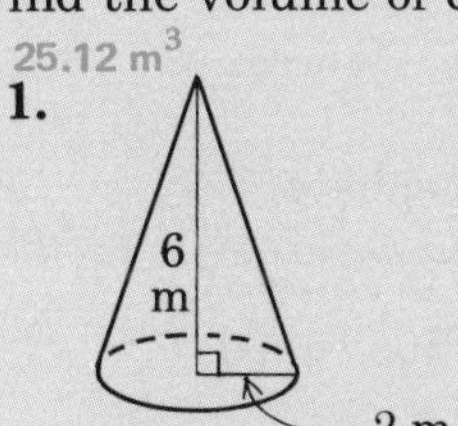

1017.36 m^3

2.

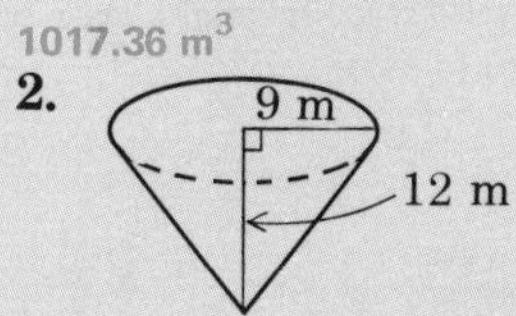

15,232.14 cm^3

3.

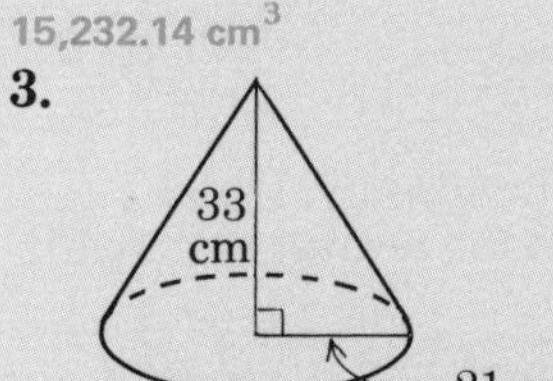

Find the volume of each cone given these dimensions.

	Radius (r)	Height (h)	
4.	3 cm	11 cm	103.62 cm^3
5.	8 cm	9 cm	602.88 cm^3
6.	5 m	3 m	78.5 m^3
7.	30 mm	43 mm	40,506 mm^3
8.	4 cm	12 cm	200.96 cm^3
9.	6 m	6 m	226.08 m^3
10.	10 cm	51 cm	5338 cm^3
11.	7 cm	18 cm	923.16 cm^3
12.	20 mm	36 mm	15,072 mm^3

Objective: Find the volume of a sphere.

Finding Volume of a Sphere

example J

Given the radius

Find the volume of this sphere.

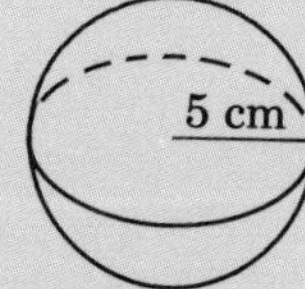

The volume of a sphere is equal to $\frac{4}{3}$ times pi times the radius cubed. Use this formula.

Some students might write 5^3 as 5 X 5 X 5 before multiplying.

$$V = \frac{4}{3}\pi r^3$$

$$V = \frac{4}{3} \times 3.14 \times 5^3$$

$$V = \frac{4}{3} \times 3.14 \times 125$$

$$V = \frac{4}{3} \times \frac{3.14}{1} \times \frac{125}{1}$$

$$V \approx 523.33$$

If necessary, round to the nearest hundredth.

The volume is about 523.33 cm^3.

example K

Given the diameter

Find the volume of this sphere.

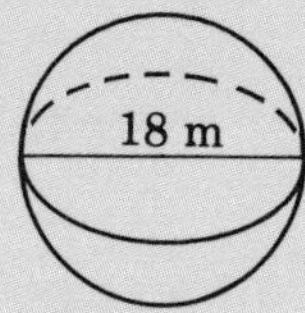

Find the radius. It is one-half the diameter, or 9 meters. Then use the formula.

$$V = \frac{4}{3}\pi r^3$$

$$V = \frac{4}{3} \times 3.14 \times 9^3$$

$$V = \frac{4}{3} \times 3.14 \times 729$$

$$V = \frac{4}{\underset{1}{\cancel{3}}} \times \frac{3.14}{1} \times \frac{\overset{243}{\cancel{729}}}{1}$$

$$V = 3052.08$$

The volume is 3052.08 m^3.

exercises

set J

Find the volume of each sphere. The radius (r) is given.

1. 3 m — 113.04 m^3
2. 15 mm — 14,130 mm^3
3. 10 cm — 4186.67 cm^3
4. 4 cm — 267.95 cm^3
5. 2 m — 33.49 m^3
6. 7 m — 1436.03 m^3
7. 40 cm — 267,946.66 cm^3
8. 1 m — 4.19 m^3
9. 30 cm — 113,040 cm^3
10. 9 m — 3052.08 m^3
11. 8 cm — 2143.57 cm^3
12. 60 mm — 904,320 mm^3
13. 100 mm — 4,186,666.67 mm^3
14. 18 cm — 24,416.64 cm^3
15. 27 mm — 82,406.16 mm^3
16. 12 cm — 7234.56 cm^3
17. 50 m — 523,333.33 m^3
18. 90 mm — 3,052,080 mm^3
19. 21 cm — 38,772.72 cm^3
20. 36 mm — 195,333.12 mm^3

set K

Find the volume of each sphere. The diameter is given.

1. 12 cm — 904.32 cm^3
2. 2 m — 4.19 m^3
3. 54 mm — 82,406.16 mm^3
4. 600 cm — 113,040,000 cm^3
5. 8 m — 267.95 m^3
6. 22 cm — 5572.45 cm^3
7. 10 m — 523.33 m^3
8. 240 m — 7,234,560 m^3
9. 66 mm — 150,456.24 mm^3
10. 90 m — 381,510 m^3
11. 6 m — 113.04 m^3
12. 102 cm — 555,365.5 cm^3
13. 30 mm — 14,130 mm^3
14. 14 m — 1436.03 m^3
15. 108 cm — 659,249.26 cm^3
16. 200 cm — 4,186,666.67 cm^3
17. 18 mm — 3052.08 mm^3
18. 180 cm — 3,052,080 cm^3
19. 96 m — 463,011.83 m^3
20. 78 cm — 248,348.88 cm^3

posttest

skill Finding Surface Area of a Rectangular Prism page 343

A Find the surface area of this rectangular prism.
42.48 m^2

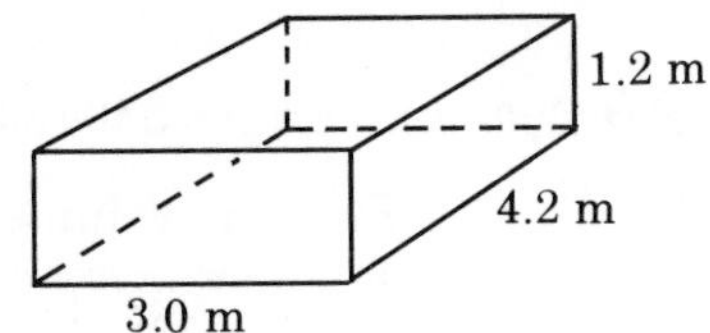

skill Finding Surface Area of a Cube page 344

B Find the surface area of this cube.
7776 mm^2

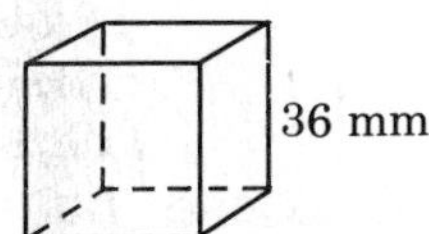

skill Finding Surface Area of a Cylinder page 345

C Find the surface area of this cylinder.
565.2 m^2

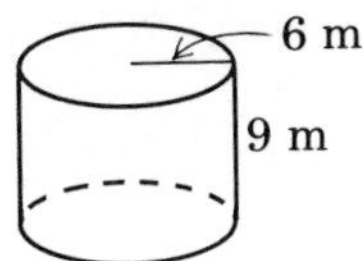

skill Finding Volume of a Rectangular Prism and a Cube pages 346-347

D Find the volume of this rectangular prism.
10,290 mm^3

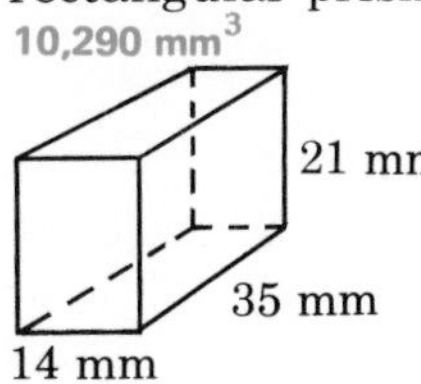

E Find the volume of this cube.
421.875 cm^3

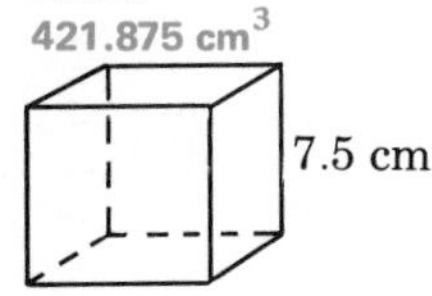

Pretest continued on page 354.

Posttest continued from page 353.

Skill Finding Volume of a Cylinder pages 348–349

F Find the volume of this cylinder. 28,260 cm^3

30 cm
10 cm

G Find the volume of this cylinder. 226.08 m^3

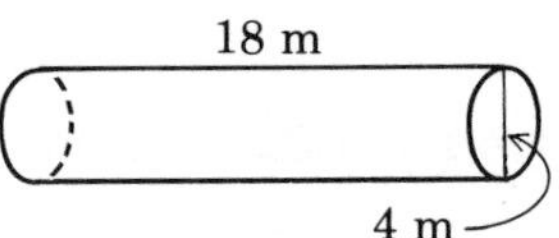

Skill Finding Volume of a Pyramid and a Cone pages 350–351

H Find the volume of this pyramid with a rectangular base. 245 m^3

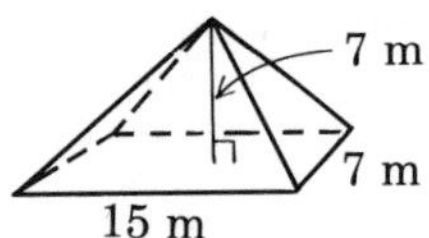

I Find the volume of this cone. 4710 mm^3

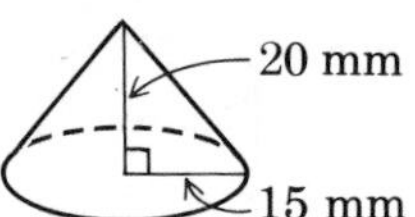

Skill Finding Volume of a Sphere page 352

J Find the volume of this sphere. 3052.08 m^3

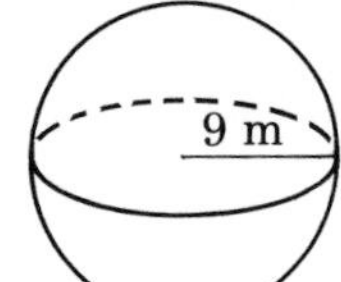

K Find the volume of this sphere. 113,040 m^3

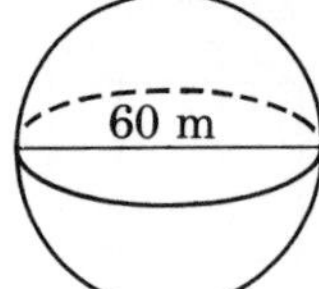

Objective: Solve problems involving volume.

In this lesson students compute the amount of wax needed to make candles.

Buying Wax to Make Candles

Mr. and Mrs. Gonzalez make candles in shapes like these as a hobby. They make several candles at a time and use them for gifts.

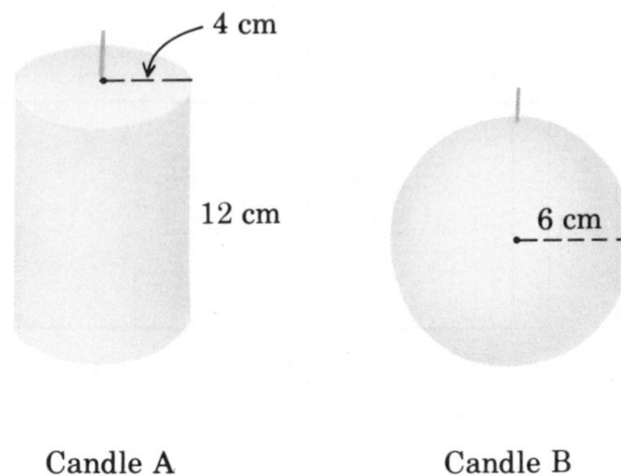

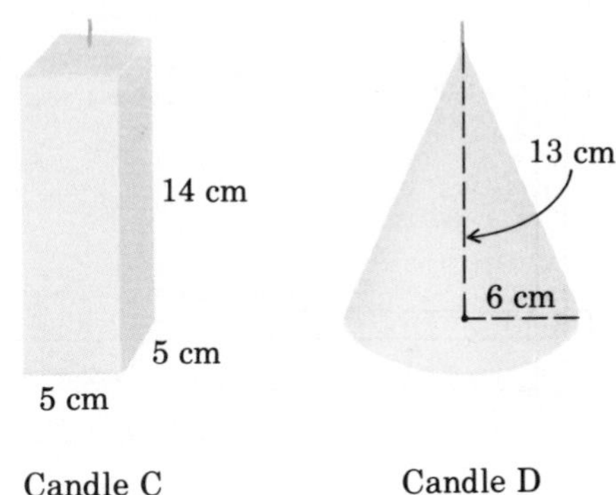

How many cubic centimeters of wax are needed to make

1. candle A? 602.88 cm^3

2. candle B? 904.32 cm^3

3. candle C? 350 cm^3

4. candle D? 489.84 cm^3

A cubic centimeter of wax has a mass of about 0.9 gram. To the nearest gram, how many grams of wax are needed to make

5. candle A? 543 grams

6. candle B? 814 grams

7. candle C? 315 grams

8. candle D? 441 grams

How many grams of wax are needed to make

9. 5 candles like candle A? 2715 grams

10. 6 candles like candle B? 4884 grams

11. 7 candles like candle C? 2205 grams

12. 4 candles like candle D? 1764 grams

13. How many grams of wax are needed to make all of the candles listed in exercises 9–12? 11,568 grams

14. How many 500-gram slabs of wax will be needed to make all of the candles listed in exercises 9–12? 24 slabs

15. A slab of wax costs $.39. How much will it cost to buy the wax to make all of the candles listed in exercises 9–12? $9.36

Objective: Solve problems involving surface area and volume.

In this lesson students estimate the cost of building a garage.

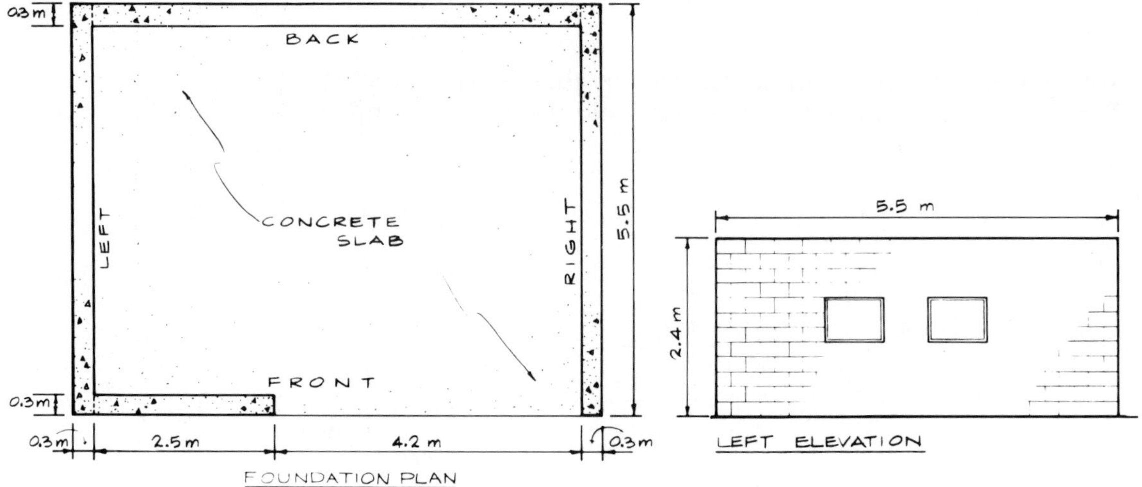

Buying Building Materials

Jeff Scott is buying materials to build a garage. First he buys concrete for the footings. Footings are trenches filled with concrete that run the length of each side and support the weight of the garage. The first picture is a top view of the footings.

The footings will be 0.9 meter deep. Other dimensions are given in the picture. Complete the table to find the amount of concrete needed for each footing.

	Footing	Dimensions (meters)	Volume (cubic meters)
1.	Front	$2.5 \times 0.3 \times 0.9$	0.675
2.	Back	$6.7 \times 0.3 \times 0.9$	1.809
3.	Left	5.5 X 0.3 X 0.9	1.485
4.	Right	5.5 X 0.3 X 0.9	1.485

5. Find the total number of cubic meters of concrete needed for the footings. Round your answer up to the next whole number. 6 m^3

6. If concrete costs \$35 per cubic meter delivered, how much will the concrete for the footings cost? \$210

7. About 4 cubic meters of concrete are needed for the floor of the garage. At \$35 per cubic meter, how much will the concrete for the floor cost? \$140

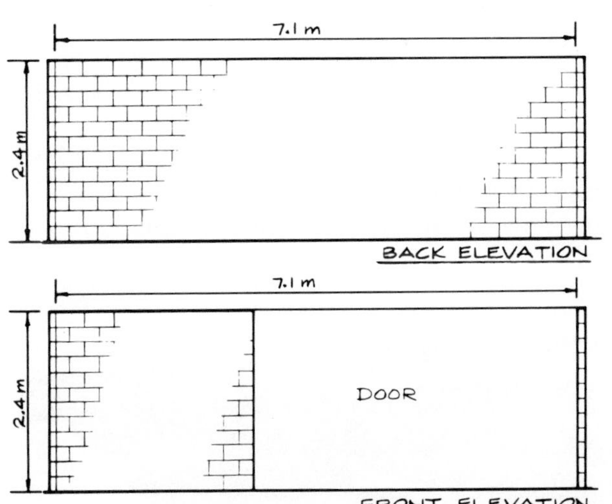

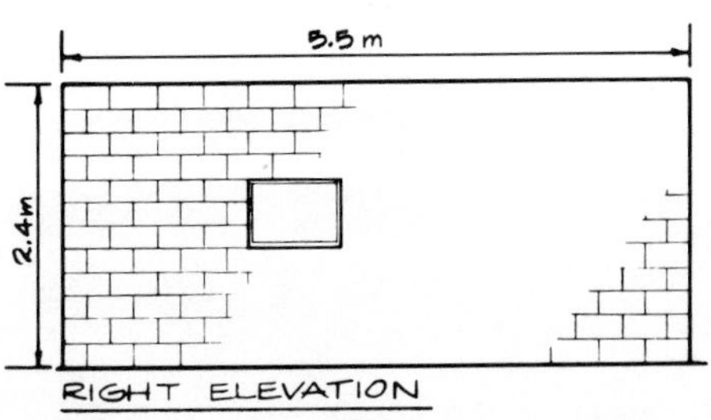

The walls of the garage will be concrete block. Use the dimensions in the four pictures of the walls to complete this table.

	Wall	Dimensions (meters)	Total area (square meters)	Area subtracted for windows or door (square meters)	Area covered with concrete blocks (square meters)
8.	Front	7.1 × 2.4	17.04	10.0 (Door)	(17.04 − 10.0) 7.04
9.	Back	7.1 X 2.4	17.04	————	17.04
10.	Left	5.5 X 2.4	13.2	1.0 (Two windows)	12.2
11.	Right	5.5 X 2.4	13.2	0.5 (Window)	12.7
12.				Total area covered	48.98

13. Write the total area to be covered in square millimeters. 48,980,000 mm^2
($1 \text{ m}^2 = 1{,}000{,}000 \text{ mm}^2$)

14. Jeff bought concrete blocks like this one. Find the area of the front face. 80,000 mm^2

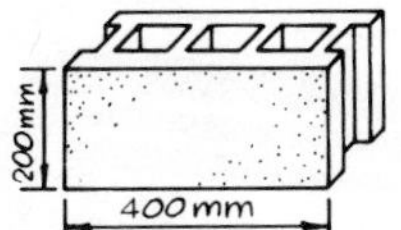

15. To find the number of concrete blocks needed, divide the total area to be covered (exercise 13) by the area of the front face of the block (exercise 14). Round up to the next whole number. 613 blocks

16. If concrete blocks cost $.58 per block, how much will the blocks for the walls cost? $355.54

17. To finish the garage, Jeff estimates he will spend $250 for the roof, $290 for the door, and $75 for all the windows. Add these amounts to the cost of the footings (exercise 6), the cost of the floor (exercise 7), and the cost of the concrete blocks (exercise 16) to estimate the total cost of the garage. $1320.54

Objective: Solve problems involving volume.

In this lesson students compute piston displacement and engine displacement.

Career: Automobile Mechanic

Career Cluster: Trades

Donna Bigeagle is an automobile mechanic. In order to repair and maintain automobiles, she must know how an automobile engine runs.

A gasoline engine works by burning a mixture of gasoline and air inside a cylinder. This causes the piston to move up and down (stroke). The piston is attached to the crankshaft and the crankshaft is connected, through a series of gears, to the rear wheels of the automobile.

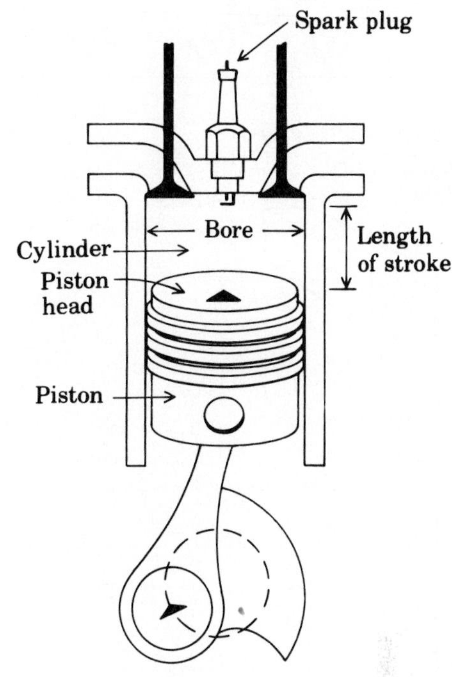

The **piston displacement** is the volume found by multiplying the area of the piston head by the length of the stroke. The greater the piston displacement, the greater the power that is obtained from the engine.

Engine displacement is found by multiplying the piston displacement by the number of cylinders in the engine. Most automobiles have an engine with either 4, 6, or 8 cylinders.

Complete this table to find the displacement for various engines.

You may wish to have students round their final answers to the nearest whole number.

	Bore (B)	Radius of piston head ($r = \frac{1}{2}B$)	Area of piston head ($A = \pi r^2$)	Length of stroke (S)	Piston displacement ($P = A \times S$)	Number of cylinders (N)	Engine displacement ($E = P \times N$)
	8 cm	4 cm	50.24 cm²	7 cm	351.68 cm³	6	2110.08 cm³
1.	10 cm	5 cm	(3.14×5^2) 78.5 cm²	5 cm	392.5 cm³	4	1570 cm³
2.	6 cm	3 cm	28.26 cm²	10 cm	282.6 cm³	6	1695.6 cm³
3.	7 cm	3.5 cm	38.465 cm²	8 cm	307.72 cm³	8	2461.76 cm³
4.	6 cm	3 cm	28.26 cm²	8.2 cm	231.73 cm³	8	1853.84 cm³
5.	5 cm	2.5 cm	19.625 cm²	8 cm	157 cm³	8	1256 cm³
6.	4 cm	2 cm	12.56 cm²	4 cm	50.24 cm³	4	200.96 cm³
7.	9 cm	4.5 cm	63.585 cm²	7 cm	445.095 cm³	6	2670.57 cm³
8.	4 cm	2 cm	12.56 cm²	5 cm	62.8 cm³	6	376.8 cm³
9.	3.8 cm	1.9 cm	11.3354 cm²	6 cm	68.0124 cm³	4	272.0496 cm³
10.	7.2 cm	3.6 cm	40.6944 cm²	8 cm	325.5552 cm³	8	2604.4416 cm³

Number of test items - 14

Number missed	1	2	3	4	5	6	7
Percent correct	93	86	79	71	64	57	50

Chapter 17

Find the surface area of each figure.

224 cm²
A **1.**

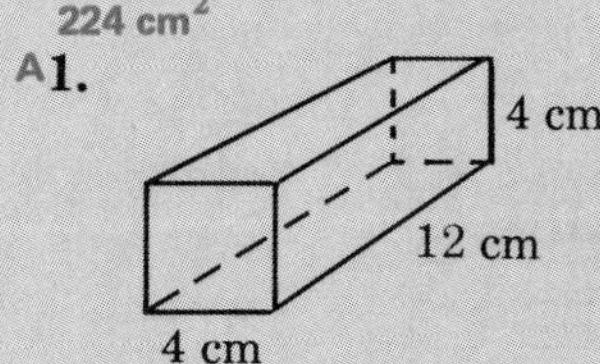

2166 mm²
B **2.**

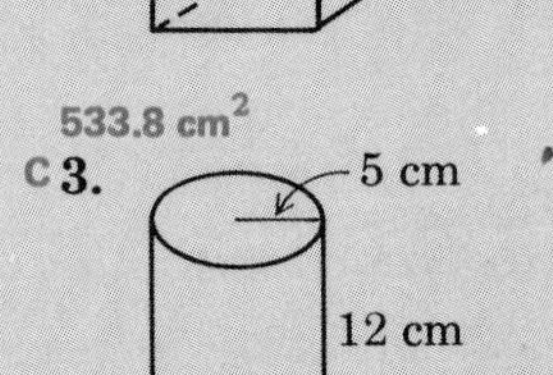

533.8 cm²
C **3.**

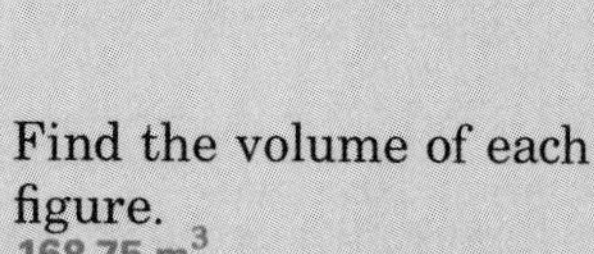

Find the volume of each figure.

168.75 m³
D **4.**

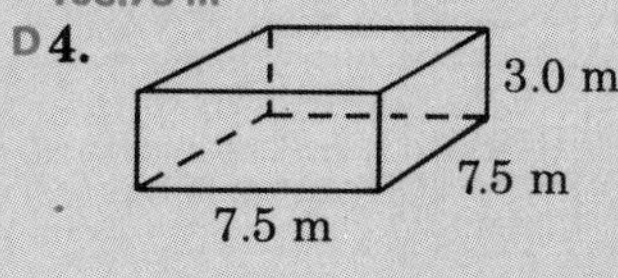

314.432 cm³
E **5.**

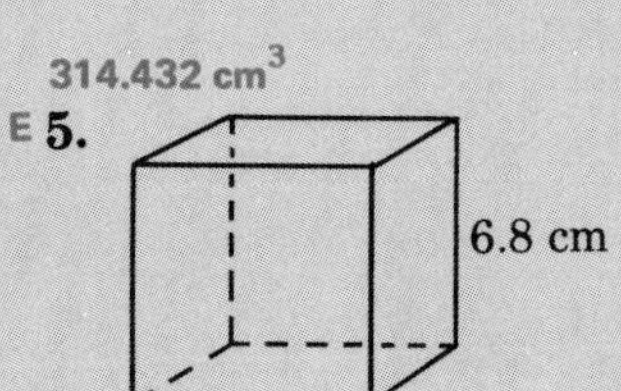

84.78 m³
F **6.**

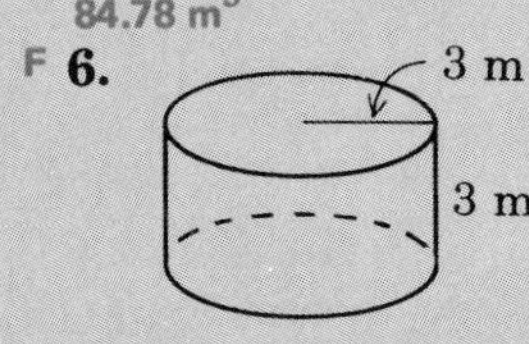

2000.18 m³
G **7.**

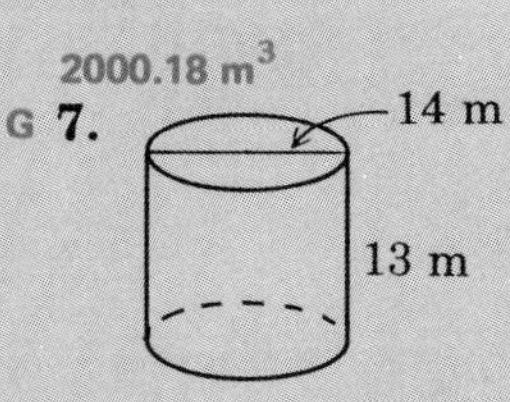

648 cm³
H **8.**

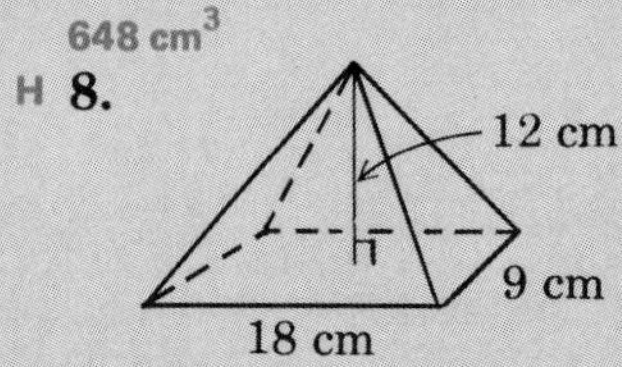

6430.72 cm³
I **9.**

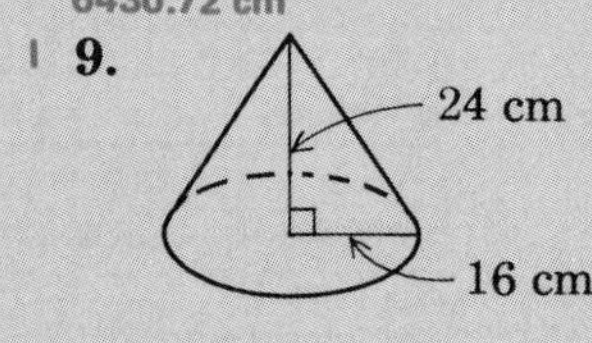

904.32 m³
J **10.**

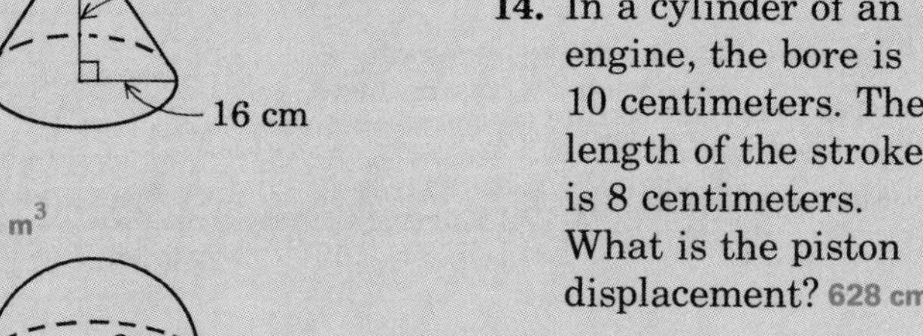

38,772.72 m³
K **11.**

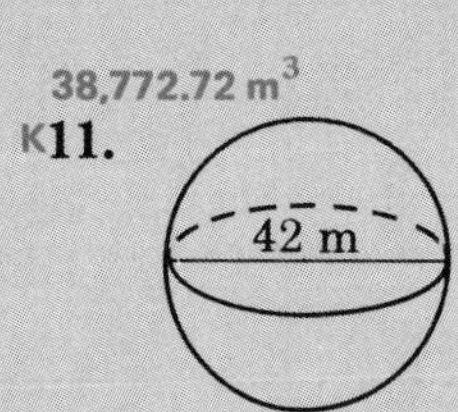

12. How many cubic centimeters of wax are needed to make this candle?

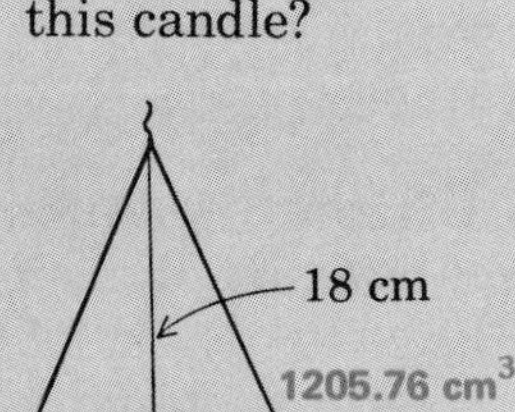

13. How many cubic meters of concrete are needed to pour a rectangular patio that measures 5 meters by 8 meters and is 0.2 meter deep? 8 m³

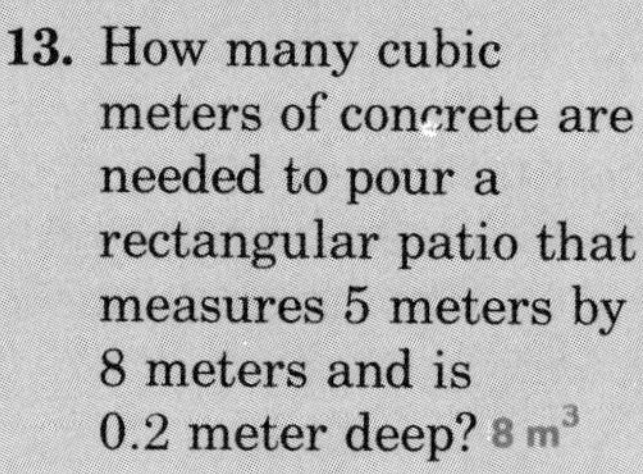

14. In a cylinder of an engine, the bore is 10 centimeters. The length of the stroke is 8 centimeters. What is the piston displacement? 628 cm³

 See pages 47–48 of the *Tests and Record Forms: Duplicating Masters* for an alternate form of the Chapter 17 Test.

Number of test items - 16

Number missed	1	2	3	4	5	6	7
Percent correct	94	88	81	75	69	63	56

skill Using Exponents and Square Roots page 363

A Compute 5^3. 125 B Find $\sqrt{64}$. 8

skill Reading a Table of Squares and Square Roots pages 364-365

C Find 35^2. Use the table on page 418. 1225

D Find $\sqrt{46}$ to the nearest tenth. Use the table on page 418. 6.7

E Find $\sqrt{7921}$. Use the table on page 418. 89

skill Using the Pythagorean Rule pages 366-367

F Use the Pythagorean Rule to find the length of the hypotenuse to the nearest tenth. Use the table on page 418. 7.8 cm

G Use the Pythagorean Rule to find the missing length. Use the table on page 418. 14 m

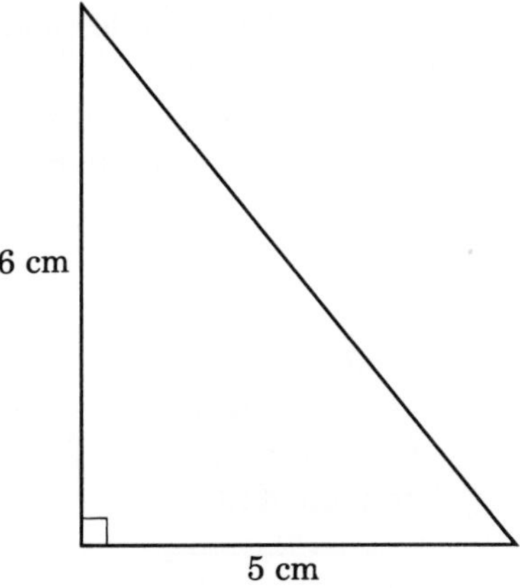

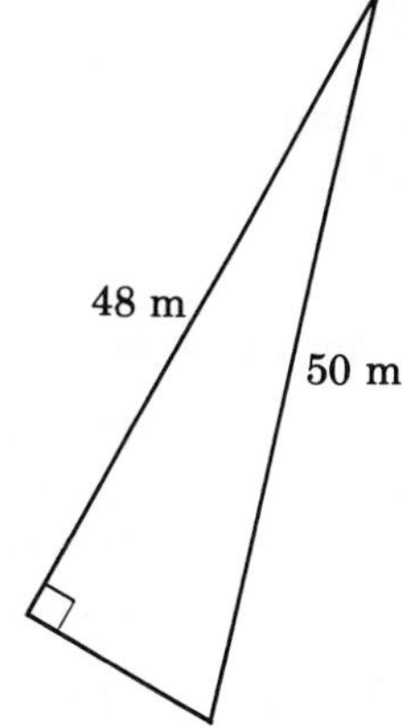

Pretest continued on page 362.

Pretest continued from page 361.

skill Writing Trigonometric Ratios pages 368–369

H Give the tangent of ∠X as a ratio and as a decimal to the nearest thousandth. $\frac{10}{24} \approx .417$

Y
26 m
10 m
X 24 m Z

I Give the sine of ∠X in item H as a ratio and as a decimal to the nearest thousandth. $\frac{10}{26} \approx .385$

J Give the cosine of ∠X in item H as a ratio and as a decimal to the nearest thousandth. $\frac{24}{26} \approx .923$

skill Reading a Table of Trigonometric Ratios pages 370–371

K Give the tangent of 18° as a decimal to the nearest thousandth. Use the table on page 419. .325

L Give the sine of 43° as a decimal to the nearest thousandth. Use the table on page 419. .682

M Give the cosine of 52° as a decimal to the nearest thousandth. Use the table on page 419. .616

skill Using Trigonometric Ratios pages 372–373

N Find n to the nearest tenth. Use the table on page 419. 19.2 cm

21°
n
50 cm

O Find t to the nearest tenth. Use the table on page 419. 5.2 cm

t
9 cm
35°

P Find y to the nearest tenth. Use the table on page 419. 37.5 m

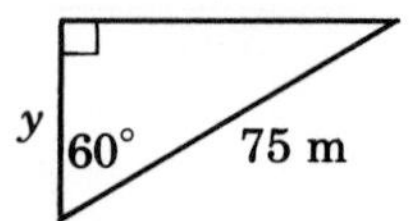

Objective: Find powers of numbers by using positive exponents, and find square roots of numbers by trial and error.

Using Exponents and Square Roots

example A Exponents

Compute 3^4.

In 3^4 the 4 is called an **exponent** or **power.** It tells how many times to use 3 as a factor.

$3^1 = 3$
Three to the first power

$3^2 = 3 \times 3 = 9$
Three squared or three to the second power

$3^3 = 3 \times 3 \times 3 = 27$
Three cubed or three to the third power

$3^4 = 3 \times 3 \times 3 \times 3 = 81$
Three to the fourth power

example B Finding square roots

Find $\sqrt{25}$.

$\sqrt{25}$ means the "**square root** of 25." The square root of 25 is a positive number that equals 25 when squared.

$25 = \square^2$	Try different numbers until you find a number that equals 25 when squared.
$25 = 5^2$	25 is 5 squared.
$\sqrt{25} = 5$	So 5 is a square root of 25.

The meaning of square root is emphasized in this lesson. A square root table is used in the next lesson.

exercises

set A

Compute each number.

1. 5^2 25	**11.** 10^1 10	**21.** 4^4 256
2. 6^3 216	**12.** 10^2 100	**22.** 18^2 324
3. 2^4 16	**13.** 10^3 1000	**23.** 1^3 1
4. 7^1 7	**14.** 10^4 10,000	**24.** $(5.1)^2$ 26.01
5. 1^7 1	**15.** 10^5 100,000	**25.** $(0.7)^2$ .49
6. 2^3 8	**16.** 10^7 10,000,000	**26.** 20^3 8000
7. 3^5 243	**17.** 10^9 1,000,000,000	**27.** 5^4 625
8. 7^2 49	**18.** 5^3 125	**28.** $(1.2)^3$ 1.728
9. 13^2 169	**19.** 4^2 16	**29.** 25^2 625
10. 2^5 32	**20.** 78^1 78	**30.** $(0.2)^4$ .0016

set B

Find each square root. Try different numbers until you find the correct answer.

1. $\sqrt{9}$ 3	**10.** $\sqrt{400}$ 20
2. $\sqrt{4}$ 2	**11.** $\sqrt{900}$ 30
3. $\sqrt{49}$ 7	**12.** $\sqrt{1600}$ 40
4. $\sqrt{100}$ 10	**13.** $\sqrt{196}$ 14
5. $\sqrt{121}$ 11	**14.** $\sqrt{2500}$ 50
6. $\sqrt{1}$ 1	**15.** $\sqrt{625}$ 25
7. $\sqrt{144}$ 12	**16.** $\sqrt{10,000}$ 100
8. $\sqrt{16}$ 4	**17.** $\sqrt{169}$ 13
9. $\sqrt{225}$ 15	**18.** $\sqrt{4900}$ 70

Objective: Find squares and square roots of numbers by reading a table.

Reading a Table of Squares and Square Roots

example C

Finding squares

Find 84^2. Use the table on page 365.

Find 84 in the column labeled "n." Read the number to the right in the column labeled "n^2."

n	n^2
84	7056

$84^2 = 7056$

example D

Finding square roots

Find $\sqrt{42}$ to the nearest tenth. Use the table on page 365.

Find 42 in the column labeled "n." Read the number in the column labeled "$\sqrt{n}$."

n	$\sqrt{n}$
42	6.481

The table gives an approximation correct to thousandths. Round to the nearest tenth.

$\sqrt{42} \approx 6.5$

example E

Finding the square root of a perfect square

Find $\sqrt{6241}$. Use the table on page 365.

$6241 = \boxed{}^2$

6241 is not shown in the column labeled "n." Look in the column labeled "n^2." 6241 is 79 squared.

$6241 = 79^2$

$\sqrt{6241} = 79$

So 79 is a square root of 6241.

exercises

set C

Find each number. Use the table on page 365.

1. 61^2 3721
2. 19^2 361
3. 87^2 7569
4. 54^2 2916
5. 38^2 1444
6. 57^2 3249
7. 30^2 900
8. 17^2 289
9. 83^2 6889
10. 21^2 441
11. 99^2 9801
12. 52^2 2704
13. 40^2 1600
14. 62^2 3844
15. 88^2 7744

set D

Find each square root to the nearest tenth. Use the table on page 365.

1. $\sqrt{15}$ 3.9
2. $\sqrt{88}$ 9.4
3. $\sqrt{40}$ 6.3
4. $\sqrt{56}$ 7.5
5. $\sqrt{2}$ 1.4
6. $\sqrt{23}$ 4.8
7. $\sqrt{59}$ 7.7
8. $\sqrt{3}$ 1.7
9. $\sqrt{64}$ 8.0
10. $\sqrt{8}$ 2.8
11. $\sqrt{39}$ 6.2
12. $\sqrt{17}$ 4.1
13. $\sqrt{49}$ 7.0
14. $\sqrt{26}$ 5.1
15. $\sqrt{75}$ 8.7

set E

Find each square root. Use the table on page 365.

1. $\sqrt{7744}$ 88
2. $\sqrt{4356}$ 66
3. $\sqrt{676}$ 26
4. $\sqrt{225}$ 15
5. $\sqrt{3481}$ 59
6. $\sqrt{2401}$ 49
7. $\sqrt{1156}$ 34
8. $\sqrt{9604}$ 98
9. $\sqrt{7225}$ 85
10. $\sqrt{484}$ 22

This table can be used with this lesson. An expanded table on page 418 can be used with subsequent lessons.

Squares and Square Roots

n	n^2	$\sqrt{n}$	n	n^2	$\sqrt{n}$
1	1	1.000	**51**	2601	7.141
2	4	1.414	**52**	2704	7.211
3	9	1.732	**53**	2809	7.280
4	16	2.000	**54**	2916	7.348
5	25	2.236	**55**	3025	7.416
6	36	2.449	**56**	3136	7.483
7	49	2.646	**57**	3249	7.550
8	64	2.828	**58**	3364	7.616
9	81	3.000	**59**	3481	7.681
10	100	3.162	**60**	3600	7.746
11	121	3.317	**61**	3721	7.810
12	144	3.464	**62**	3844	7.874
13	169	3.606	**63**	3969	7.937
14	196	3.742	**64**	4096	8.000
15	225	3.873	**65**	4225	8.062
16	256	4.000	**66**	4356	8.124
17	289	4.123	**67**	4489	8.185
18	324	4.243	**68**	4624	8.246
19	361	4.359	**69**	4761	8.307
20	400	4.472	**70**	4900	8.367
21	441	4.583	**71**	5041	8.426
22	484	4.690	**72**	5184	8.485
23	529	4.796	**73**	5329	8.544
24	576	4.899	**74**	5476	8.602
25	625	5.000	**75**	5625	8.660
26	676	5.099	**76**	5776	8.718
27	729	5.196	**77**	5929	8.775
28	784	5.292	**78**	6084	8.832
29	841	5.385	**79**	6241	8.888
30	900	5.477	**80**	6400	8.944
31	961	5.568	**81**	6561	9.000
32	1024	5.657	**82**	6724	9.055
33	1089	5.745	**83**	6889	9.110
34	1156	5.831	**84**	7056	9.165
35	1225	5.916	**85**	7225	9.220
36	1296	6.000	**86**	7396	9.274
37	1369	6.083	**87**	7569	9.327
38	1444	6.164	**88**	7744	9.381
39	1521	6.245	**89**	7921	9.434
40	1600	6.325	**90**	8100	9.487
41	1681	6.403	**91**	8281	9.539
42	1764	6.481	**92**	8464	9.592
43	1849	6.557	**93**	8649	9.644
44	1936	6.633	**94**	8836	9.695
45	2025	6.708	**95**	9025	9.747
46	2116	6.782	**96**	9216	9.798
47	2209	6.856	**97**	9409	9.849
48	2304	6.928	**98**	9604	9.899
49	2401	7.000	**99**	9801	9.950
50	2500	7.071	**100**	10,000	10.000

BREAK TIME

Ms. Whitefeather got five tires with her new car. She rotated the tires regularly. After 30,000 kilometers of driving, each tire had been used for the same number of kilometers. For how many kilometers was each tire used? **24,000 kilometers**

Each tire was used for four-fifths of the 30,000 kilometers.

$\frac{4}{5} \times 30{,}000 = 24{,}000$

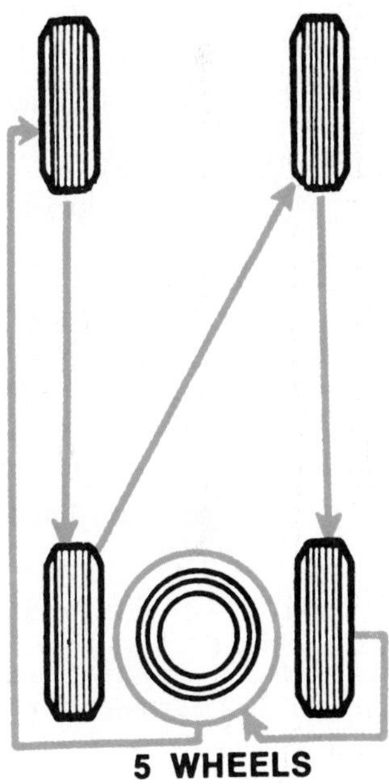

Objective: Find the length of a side of a right triangle by using the Pythagorean Rule.

Using the Pythagorean Rule

See page T27 for an activity that develops the Pythagorean Rule.

example F Finding the hypotenuse

Use the Pythagorean Rule to find the length of the hypotenuse to the nearest tenth. Use the table on page 418.

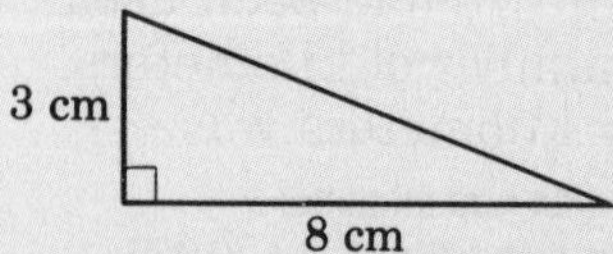

A **right triangle** has a right angle (90°). The longest side of a right triangle, opposite the right angle, is called the **hypotenuse.** The other two sides are called **legs.**

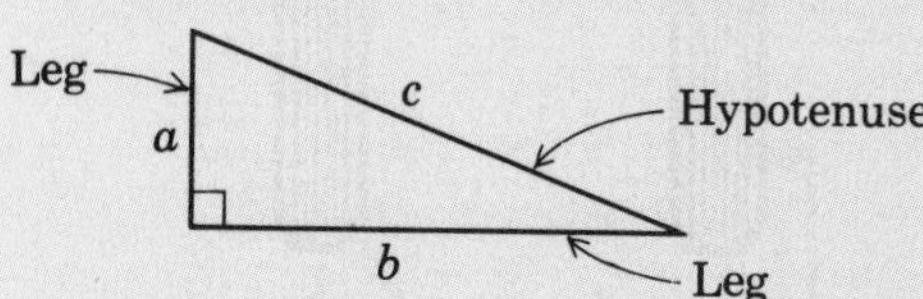

The **Pythagorean Rule** says that for any right triangle with hypotenuse of length c and legs of lengths a and b, $a^2 + b^2 = c^2$.

$a^2 + b^2 = c^2$

$3^2 + 8^2 = c^2$ Substitute 3 and 8 for a and b.

$9 + 64 = c^2$

$73 = c^2$ Since 73 is c squared, c is a square root of 73.

$\sqrt{73} = c$

$8.5 \approx c$ The table on page 418 shows that $\sqrt{73}$ is 8.544. Round 8.544 to the nearest tenth.

The hypotenuse is about 8.5 centimeters long.

example G Finding a missing leg

Use the Pythagorean Rule to find the missing length. Use the table on page 418.

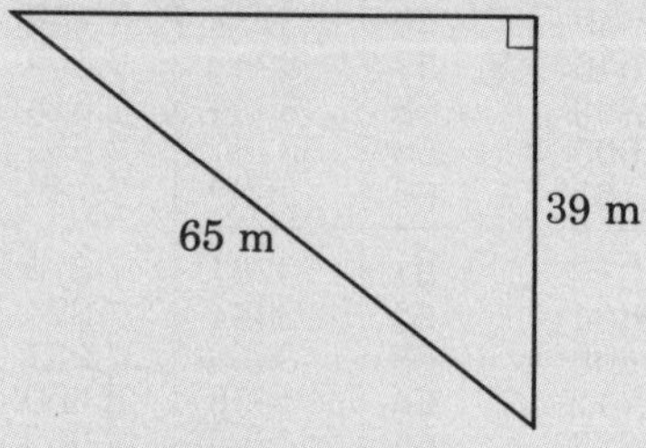

$a^2 + b^2 = c^2$

$39^2 + b^2 = 65^2$ Substitute 39 and 65 for a and c.

$1521 + b^2 = 4225$ Find 39^2 and 65^2 by multiplying or by using the table on page 418.

$b^2 = 2704$ Subtract 1521 from both sides of the equation.

$b = \sqrt{2704}$ Since 2704 is the square of b, b is a square root of 2704.

$b = 52$ The table on page 418 shows that 52^2 is 2704. So 52 is a square root of 2704.

The missing length is 52 meters.

exercises

set F

Use the Pythagorean Rule to find the length of each hypotenuse to the nearest tenth. Use the table on page 418.

1.

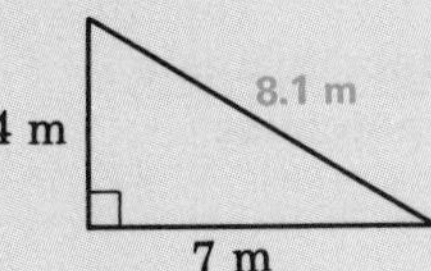

2.

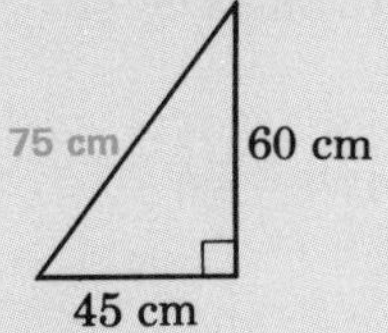

3.

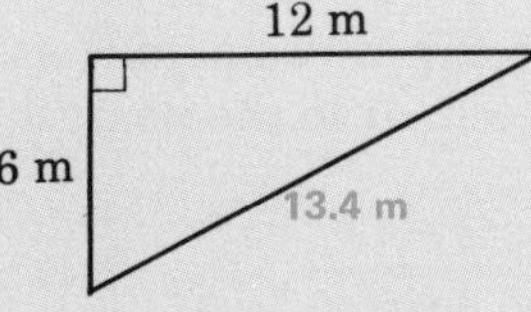

4.

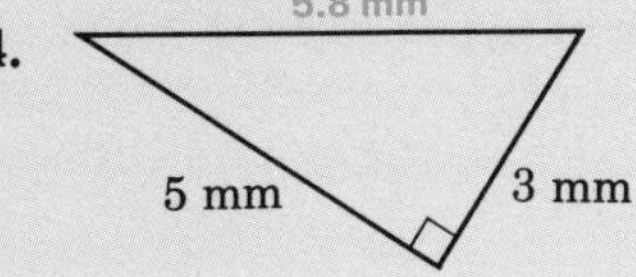

5.

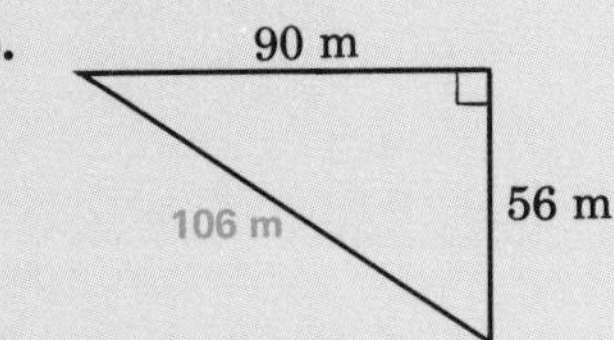

	Length in meters		
	Leg	Leg	Hypotenuse
6.	8	10	▦ 12.8
7.	40	9	▦ 41
8.	7	7	▦ 9.9
9.	11	3	▦ 11.4
10.	5	12	▦ 13
11.	6	4	▦ 7.2
12.	8	11	▦ 13.6
13.	20	21	▦ 29
14.	7	24	▦ 25
15.	10	9	▦ 13.5
16.	12	7	▦ 13.9
17.	8	15	▦ 17
18.	6	3	▦ 6.7

set G

Use the Pythagorean Rule to find each missing length to the nearest tenth. Use the table on page 418.

1.

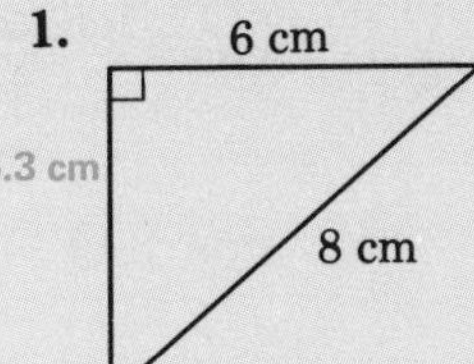

2.

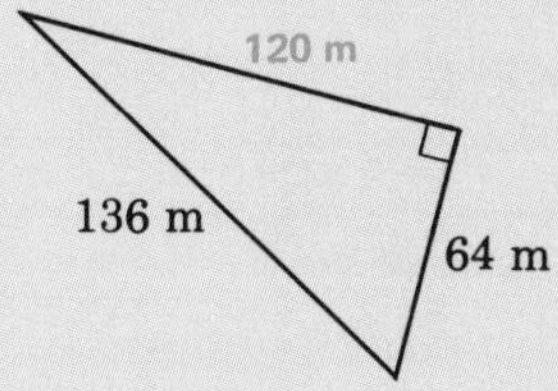

3.

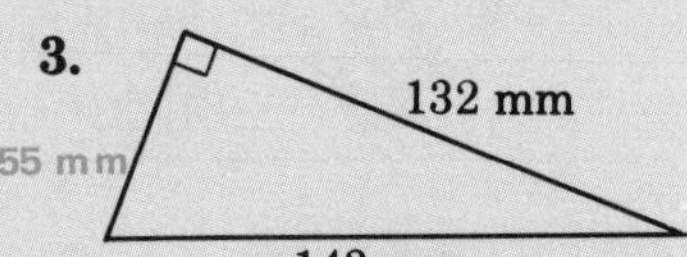

4.

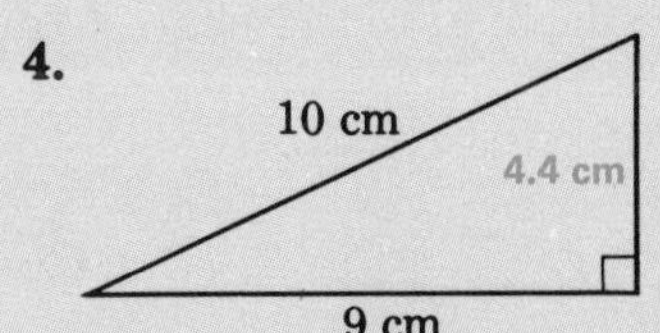

5.

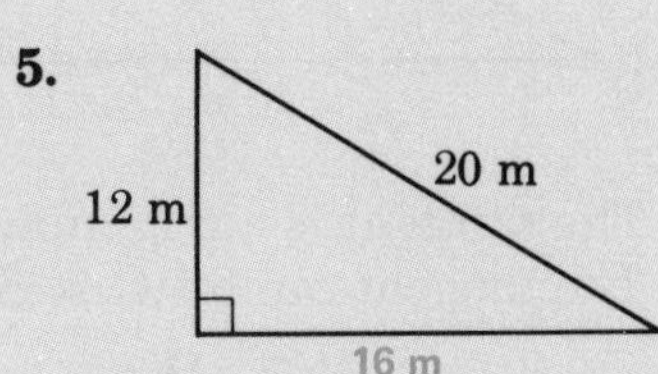

	Length in meters		
	Leg	Leg	Hypotenuse
6.	11	▦ 6.9	13
7.	▦ 40	30	50
8.	▦ 42	40	58
9.	10	▦ 13.7	17
10.	▦ 10.7	9	14
11.	84	▦ 135	159
12.	1	▦ 1.7	2
13.	▦ 72	21	75
14.	▦ 9.8	5	11
15.	18	▦ 8.7	20
16.	▦ 90	120	150
17.	41	▦ 9.1	42
18.	▦ 120	27	123

The applications on pages 376-379 may be used anytime after this lesson.

Objective: Write the tangent, the sine, and the cosine of an angle as a ratio and as a decimal.

Writing Trigonometric Ratios

example H Tangent

Give the tangent of $\angle Q$ as a ratio and as a decimal to the nearest thousandth.

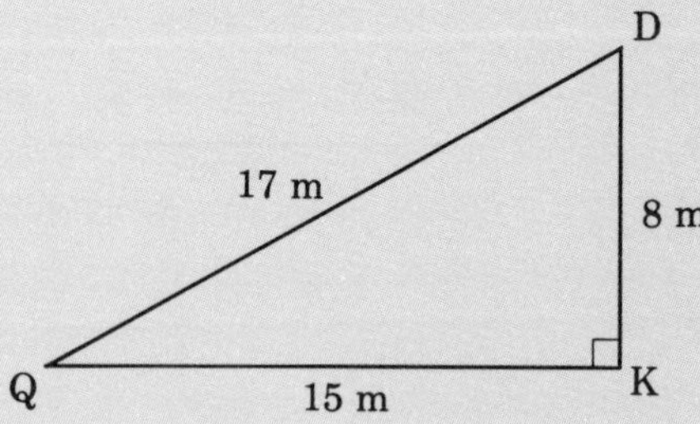

The **tangent** is a **trigonometric ratio.** The tangent can be written "tan."

$$\textbf{tan} = \frac{\textbf{length of leg opposite angle}}{\textbf{length of leg adjacent to angle}}$$

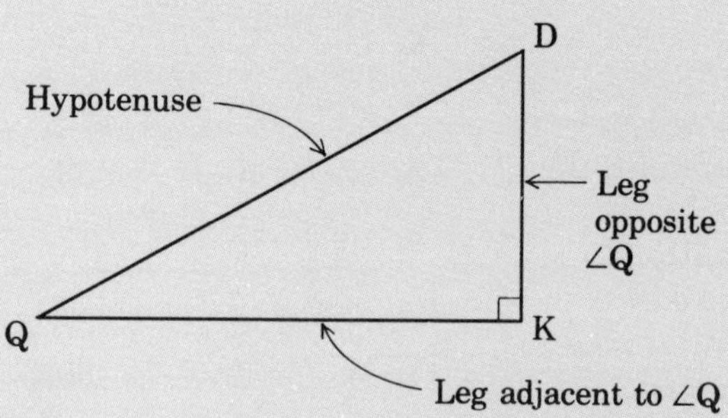

$\tan \angle Q = \frac{8}{15}$

$\tan \angle Q \approx .533$ Divide 8 by 15. Give the quotient to the nearest thousandth.

$15\overline{)8.0000}$ = .5333 ≈ .533

example I Sine

Give the sine of $\angle Q$ in example H as a ratio and as a decimal to the nearest thousandth.

The **sine** can be written "sin."

$$\textbf{sin} = \frac{\textbf{length of leg opposite angle}}{\textbf{length of hypotenuse}}$$

$\sin \angle Q = \frac{8}{17}$

$\sin \angle Q \approx .471$ Divide 8 by 17.

$17\overline{)8.0000}$ = .4705 ≈ .471

example J Cosine

Give the cosine of $\angle Q$ in example H as a ratio and as a decimal to the nearest thousandth.

The **cosine** can be written "cos."

$$\textbf{cos} = \frac{\textbf{length of leg adjacent to angle}}{\textbf{length of hypotenuse}}$$

$\cos \angle Q = \frac{15}{17}$

$\cos \angle Q \approx .882$ Divide 15 by 17.

$17\overline{)15.0000}$ = .8823 ≈ .882

This same table also appears on page 419.

Trigonometric Ratios

Measure of angle	tan	sin	cos	Measure of angle	tan	sin	cos
1°	.017	.017	1.000	**46°**	1.036	.719	.695
2°	.035	.035	.999	**47°**	1.072	.731	.682
3°	.052	.052	.999	**48°**	1.111	.743	.669
4°	.070	.070	.998	**49°**	1.150	.755	.656
5°	.087	.087	.996	**50°**	1.192	.766	.643
6°	.105	.105	.995	**51°**	1.235	.777	.629
7°	.123	.122	.993	**52°**	1.280	.788	.616
8°	.141	.139	.990	**53°**	1.327	.799	.602
9°	.158	.156	.988	**54°**	1.376	.809	.588
10°	.176	.174	.985	**55°**	1.428	.819	.574
11°	.194	.191	.982	**56°**	1.483	.829	.559
12°	.213	.208	.978	**57°**	1.540	.839	.545
13°	.231	.225	.974	**58°**	1.600	.848	.530
14°	.249	.242	.970	**59°**	1.664	.857	.515
15°	.268	.259	.966	**60°**	1.732	.866	.500
16°	.287	.276	.961	**61°**	1.804	.875	.485
17°	.306	.292	.956	**62°**	1.881	.883	.469
18°	.325	.309	.951	**63°**	1.963	.891	.454
19°	.344	.326	.946	**64°**	2.050	.899	.438
20°	.364	.342	.940	**65°**	2.145	.906	.423
21°	.384	.358	.934	**66°**	2.246	.914	.407
22°	.404	.375	.927	**67°**	2.356	.921	.391
23°	.424	.391	.921	**68°**	2.475	.927	.375
24°	.445	.407	.914	**69°**	2.605	.934	.358
25°	.466	.423	.906	**70°**	2.748	.940	.342
26°	.488	.438	.899	**71°**	2.904	.946	.326
27°	.510	.454	.891	**72°**	3.078	.951	.309
28°	.532	.469	.883	**73°**	3.271	.956	.292
29°	.554	.485	.875	**74°**	3.487	.961	.276
30°	.577	.500	.866	**75°**	3.732	.966	.259
31°	.601	.515	.857	**76°**	4.011	.970	.242
32°	.625	.530	.848	**77°**	4.332	.974	.225
33°	.649	.545	.839	**78°**	4.705	.978	.208
34°	.675	.559	.829	**79°**	5.145	.982	.191
35°	.700	.574	.819	**80°**	5.671	.985	.174
36°	.727	.588	.809	**81°**	6.314	.988	.156
37°	.754	.602	.799	**82°**	7.115	.990	.139
38°	.781	.616	.788	**83°**	8.144	.993	.122
39°	.810	.629	.777	**84°**	9.514	.995	.105
40°	.839	.643	.766	**85°**	11.430	.996	.087
41°	.869	.656	.755	**86°**	14.301	.998	.070
42°	.900	.669	.743	**87°**	19.081	.999	.052
43°	.933	.682	.731	**88°**	28.636	.999	.035
44°	.966	.695	.719	**89°**	57.290	1.000	.017
45°	1.000	.707	.707				

BREAK TIME

Each side of the square is 5 meters long. Find the circumference of each circle to the nearest tenth meter.

Smaller circle: 15.7 m
Larger circle: 22.2 m

The radius of the circle is 9 meters. Find the perimeter of each square to the nearest tenth meter.

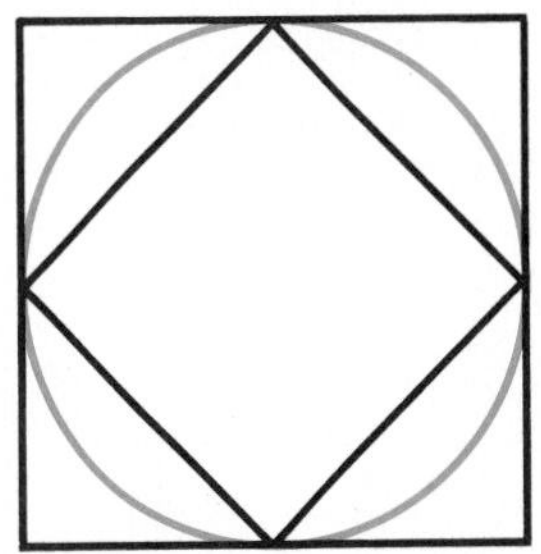

Smaller square: 50.9 m
Larger square: 72.0 m

Objective: Find the length of a side of a right triangle by using trigonometric ratios.

Using Trigonometric Ratios

example N Tangent

Find n to the nearest tenth. Use the table on page 419.

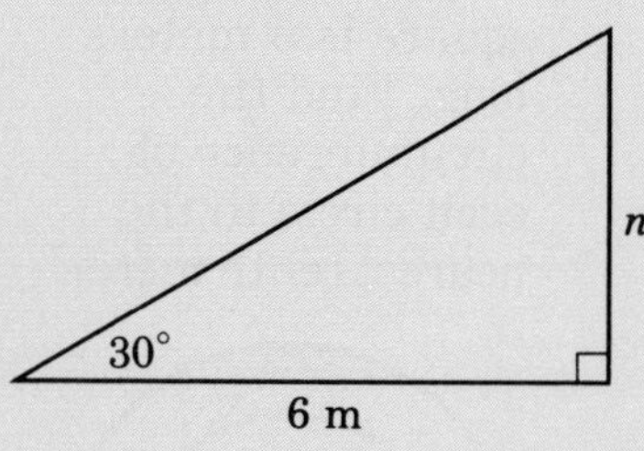

$\tan 30° = \frac{n}{6}$ Use the tangent ratio to write an equation.

$.577 = \frac{n}{6}$ Find tan 30° in the table on page 419. $\tan 30° = .577$

$3.462 = n$ Multiply both sides of the equation by 6.

$3.5 \approx n$ Round to the nearest tenth.

n is about 3.5 meters.

example O Sine

Find k to the nearest tenth.

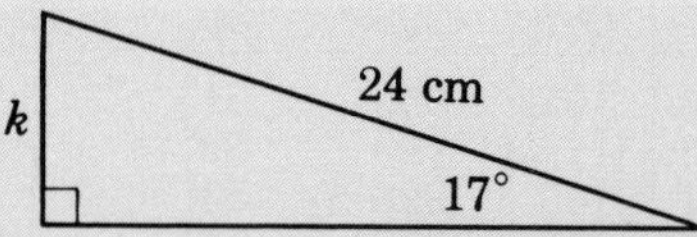

$\sin 17° = \frac{k}{24}$ Use the sine ratio to write an equation.

$.292 = \frac{k}{24}$ Use the table on page 419. $\sin 17° = .292$

$7.008 = k$ Multiply both sides by 24.

$7.0 \approx k$ Round to the nearest tenth.

k is about 7.0 centimeters.

example P Cosine

Find w to the nearest tenth.

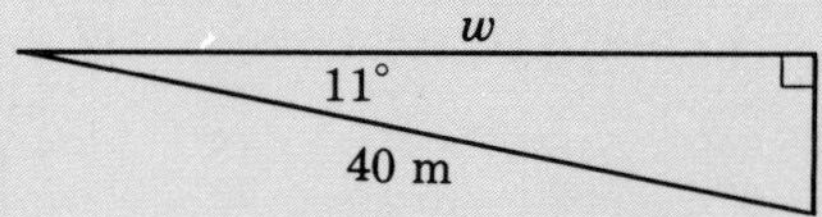

$\cos 11° = \frac{w}{40}$ Use the cosine ratio to write an equation.

$.982 = \frac{w}{40}$ Use the table on page 419. $\cos 11° = .982$

$39.280 = w$ Multiply both sides by 40.

$39.3 \approx w$ Round to the nearest tenth.

w is about 39.3 meters.

exercises

set N

Find the length of the side opposite the angle. Round to the nearest tenth. Use the table on page 419.

11.0 m

1.

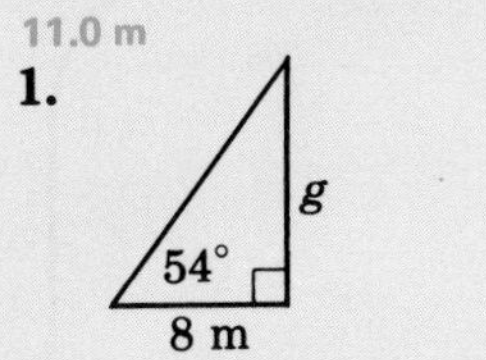

11.5 cm

2.

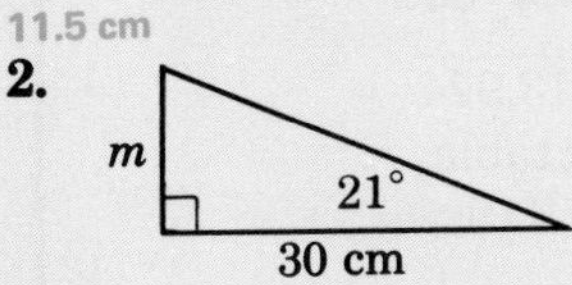

34.7 cm

3.

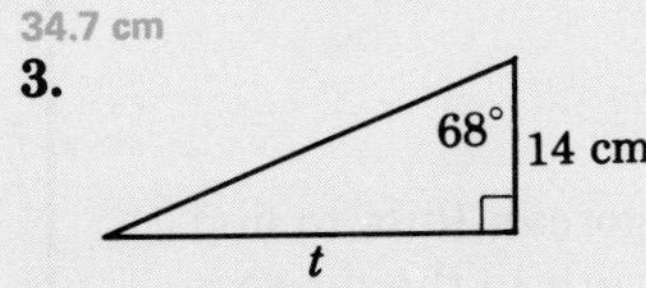

80.9 mm

4.

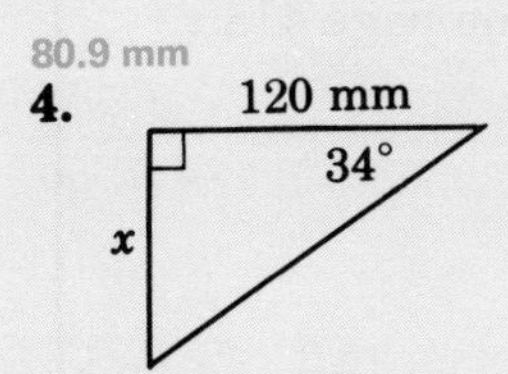

	Measure of angle	Length of side adjacent	
5.	18°	12 m	3.9 m
6.	75°	7 m	26.1 m
7.	61°	58 m	104.6 m
8.	12°	145 mm	30.8 mm
9.	37°	62 cm	46.7 cm
10.	56°	80 m	118.6 m

set O

Find the length of the side opposite the angle. Round to the nearest tenth. Use the table on page 419.

12.5 cm

1.

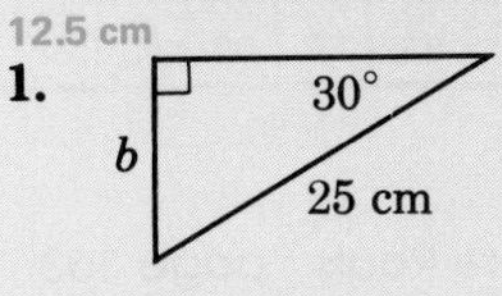

4.9 m

2.

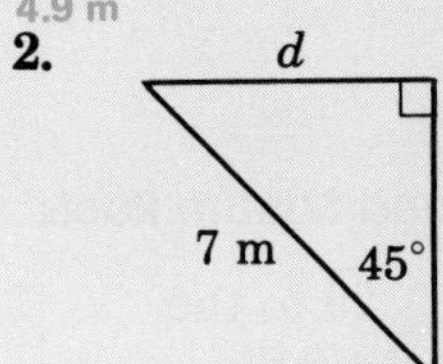

30.6 m

3.

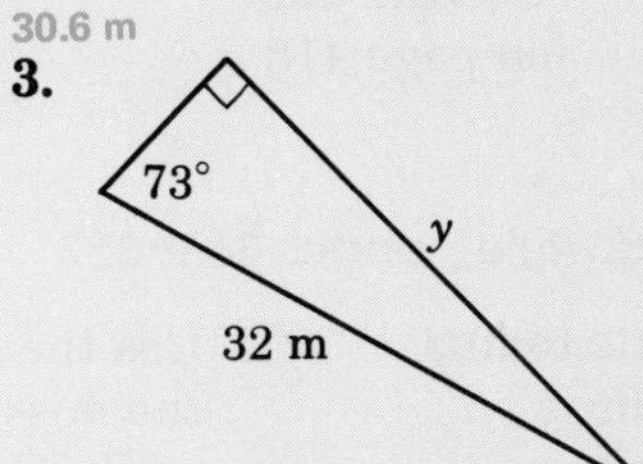

10.1 mm

4.

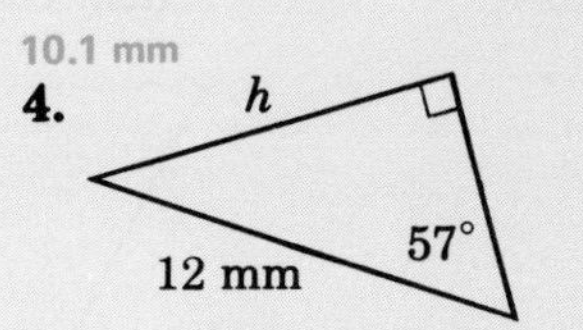

	Measure of angle	Length of hypotenuse	
5.	35°	9 cm	5.2 cm
6.	8°	28 m	3.9 m
7.	45°	12 m	8.5 m
8.	76°	3 cm	2.9 cm
9.	23°	65 mm	25.4 mm
10.	64°	200 cm	179.8 cm

set P

Find the length of the side adjacent to the angle. Round to the nearest tenth. Use the table on page 419.

13.5 m

1.

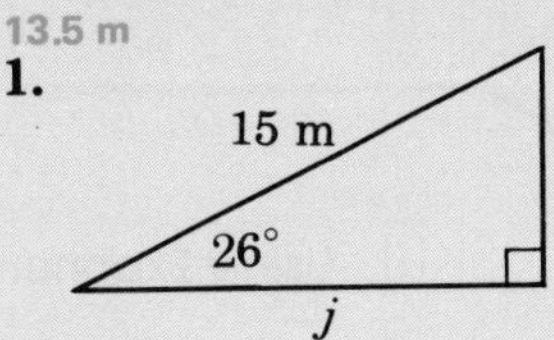

3.9 cm

2.

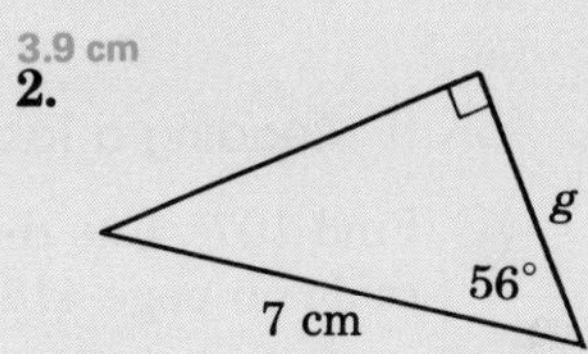

178.1 mm

3.

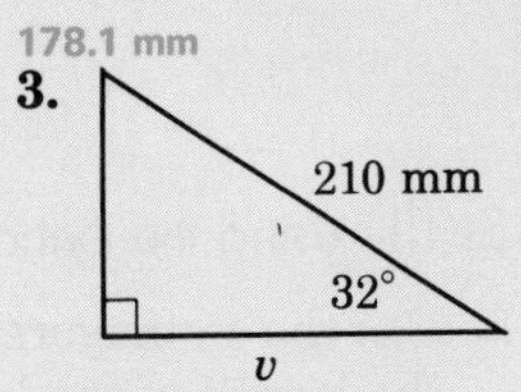

45.0 m

4.

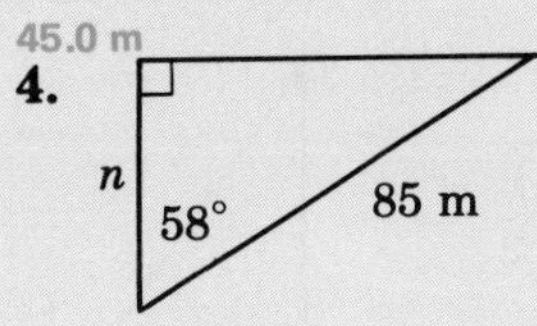

	Measure of angle	Length of hypotenuse	
5.	22°	45 cm	41.7 cm
6.	87°	16 m	0.8 m
7.	53°	70 mm	42.1 mm
8.	24°	21 cm	19.2 cm
9.	68°	150 mm	56.2 mm
10.	7°	95 m	94.3 m

posttest

Number of test items - 16

Number missed	1	2	3	4	5	6	7
Percent correct	94	88	81	75	69	63	56

skill Using Exponents and Square Roots page 363

A Compute 4^5. 1024 B Find $\sqrt{36}$. 6

skill Reading a Table of Squares and Square Roots pages 364–365

C Find 107^2. Use the table on page 418. 11,449

D Find $\sqrt{29}$ to the nearest tenth. Use the table on page 418. 5.4

E Find $\sqrt{13,924}$. Use the table on page 418. 118

skill Using the Pythagorean Rule pages 366–367

F Use the Pythagorean Rule to find the length of the hypotenuse. Use the table on page 418. 85 m

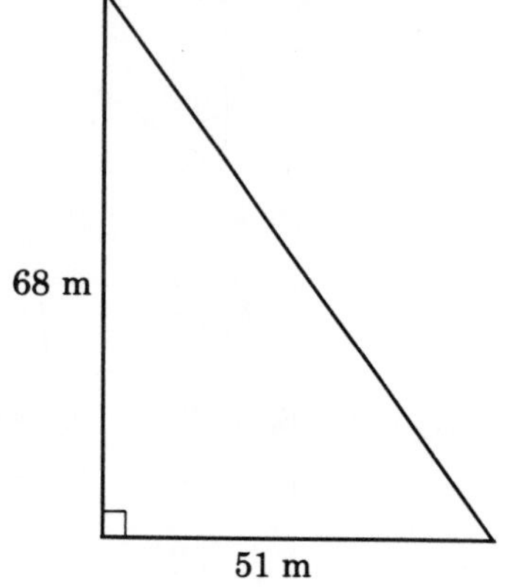

G Use the Pythagorean Rule to find the missing length to the nearest tenth. Use the table on page 418. 7.2 cm

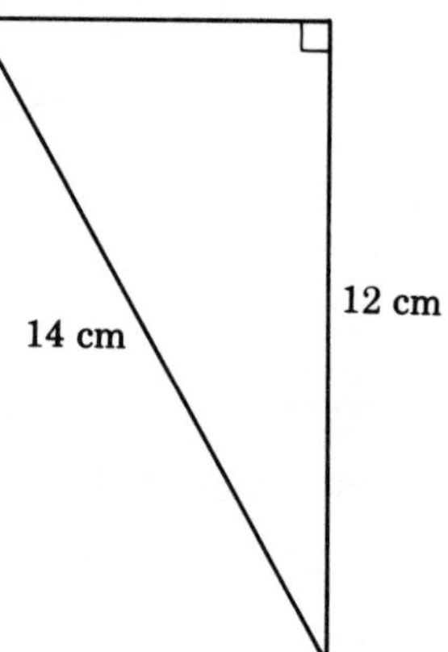

Posttest continued on page 375.

Posttest continued from page 374.

Skill Writing Trigonometric Ratios pages 368–369

H Give the tangent of ∠R as a ratio and as a decimal to the nearest thousandth. $\frac{36}{77} \approx .468$

I Give the sine of ∠R in item H as a ratio and as a decimal to the nearest thousandth. $\frac{36}{85} \approx .424$

J Give the cosine of ∠R in item H as a ratio and as a decimal to the nearest thousandth. $\frac{77}{85} \approx .906$

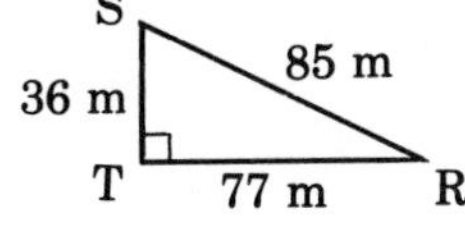

Skill Reading a Table of Trigonometric Ratios pages 370–371

K Give the tangent of 23° as a decimal to the nearest thousandth. Use the table on page 419. .424

L Give the sine of 74° as a decimal to the nearest thousandth. Use the table on page 419. .961

M Give the cosine of 19° as a decimal to the nearest thousandth. Use the table on page 419. .946

Skill Using Trigonometric Ratios pages 372–373

N Find g to the nearest tenth. Use the table on page 419. 9.9 m

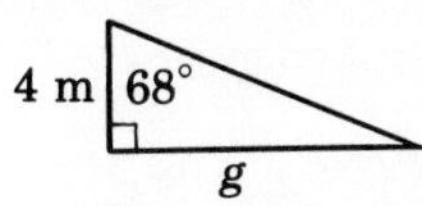

O Find w to the nearest tenth. Use the table on page 419. 12.3 cm

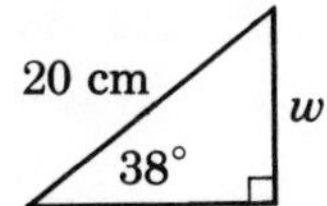

P Find k to the nearest tenth. Use the table on page 419. 6.5 cm

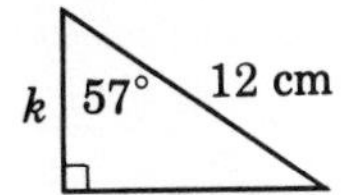

Objective: Solve problems involving the Pythagorean Rule and trigonometry.

In this lesson students tell whether a given set of lengths on a baseball field will form a right triangle at home plate, by using the Pythagorean Rule.

Laying Out a Baseball Diamond

Yvonne and her friends planned to lay out a baseball diamond in a vacant field.

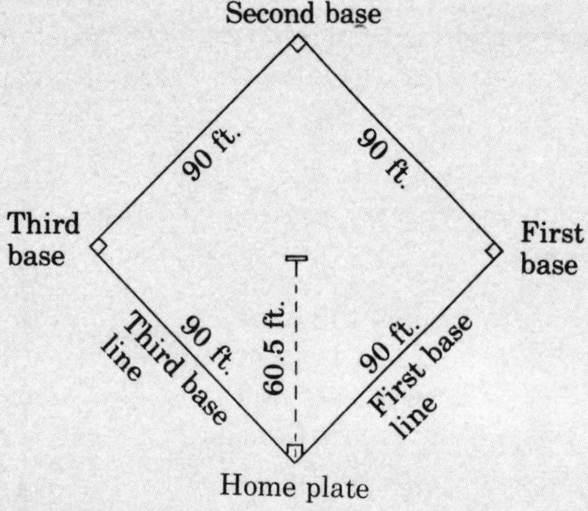

They had a tape measure, but they did not know how to check if the angle at home plate was a right angle.

Yvonne said:

"Measure 4 feet from home plate down the first base line and put a stake into the ground.

Measure 3 feet down the third base line and put a stake into the ground.

Measure the distance between the stakes. If it is 5 feet, then the angle at home plate is a right angle."

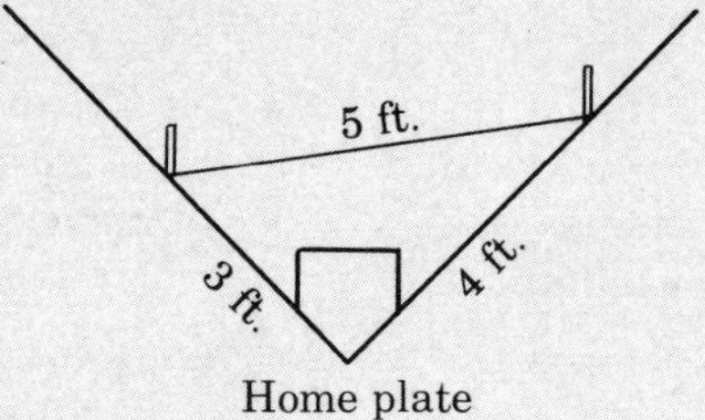

Yvonne knew that if the lengths of the sides of a triangle fit the Pythagorean Rule, then the triangle is a right triangle. She knew that sides of 3, 4, and 5 would fit the Pythagorean Rule.

$a^2 + b^2 = c^2$

$3^2 + 4^2 = 5^2$

$9 + 16 = 25$

$25 = 25$

Tell which of the distances below would form a right triangle. Check if $a^2 + b^2$ equals c^2. Use the table on page 418.

	Distance to stake on first base line (a)	Distance to stake on third base line (b)	Distance between stakes (c)	
1.	5 feet	12 feet	14 feet	No
2.	15 feet	8 feet	17 feet	Yes
3.	12 feet	36 feet	37 feet	No
4.	20 feet	28 feet	42 feet	No
5.	7 feet	11 feet	13 feet	No
6.	80 feet	18 feet	82 feet	Yes
7.	9 feet	9 feet	12 feet	No
8.	12 feet	35 feet	37 feet	Yes
9.	60 feet	63 feet	87 feet	Yes
10.	7 feet	24 feet	25 feet	Yes

Objective: Solve problems involving the Pythagorean Rule and trigonometry.

In this lesson students use the Pythagorean Rule to find the hypotenuse of a 45°-45°-90° right triangle determined by an angled pipeline, given the length of one leg, and to find the legs of a 30°-60°-90° right triangle, given the hypotenuse.

Career: Pipeline Engineer

Career Cluster: Technical

Karen Ilfeld is an engineer who designs pipelines.

Sometimes a pipeline has to be installed at an angle to avoid an obstacle. To do this, the crew connects a piece of pipe on a diagonal by using fittings called elbows.

Karen uses the Pythagorean Rule to find various distances. The offset, the run, and the diagonal shown below form a right triangle.

$$(\text{offset})^2 + (\text{run})^2 = (\text{diagonal})^2$$

$$o^2 + r^2 = d^2$$

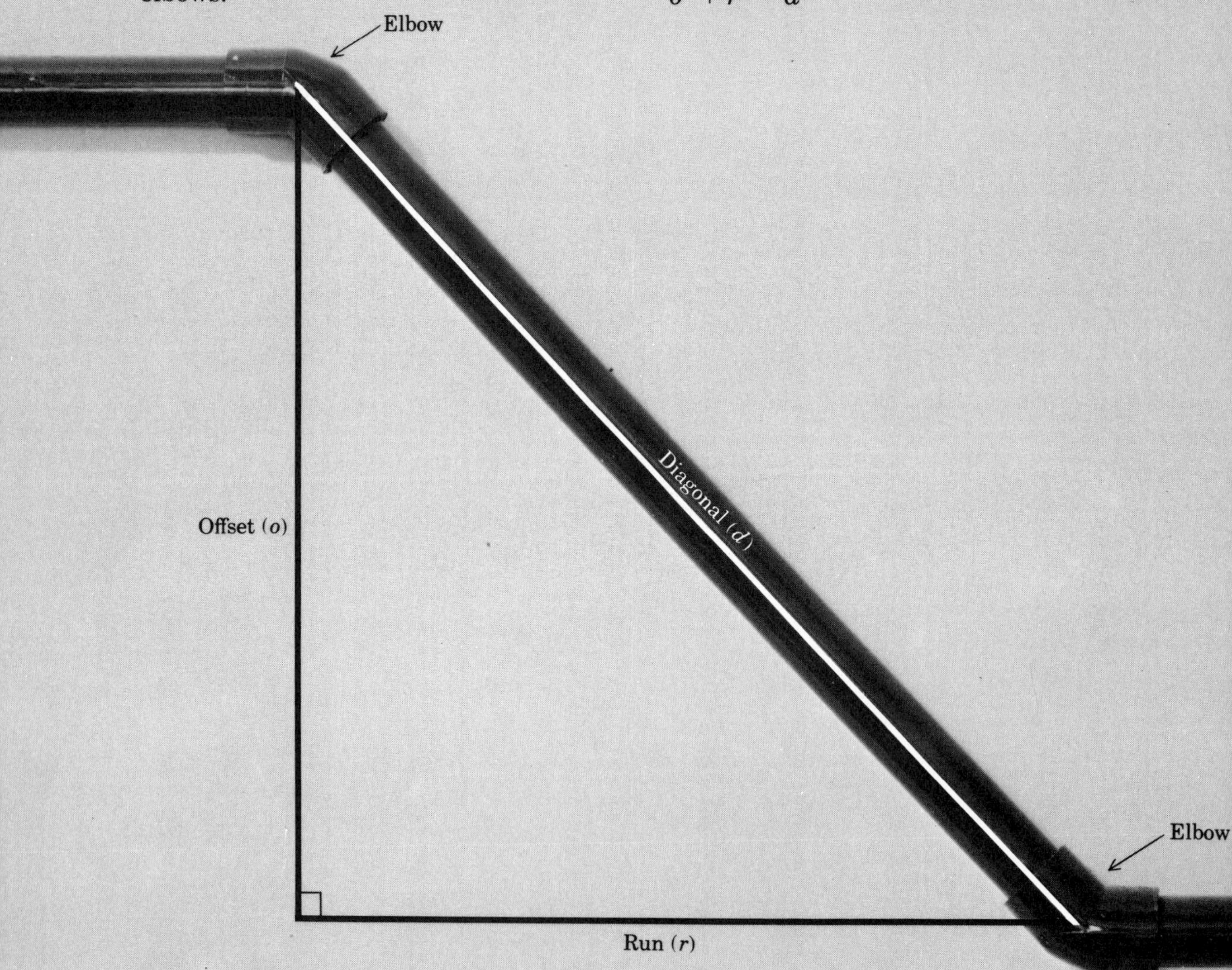

Karen planned 45° elbows for one job. She needed to find the run and the diagonal for an offset of 8 decimeters.

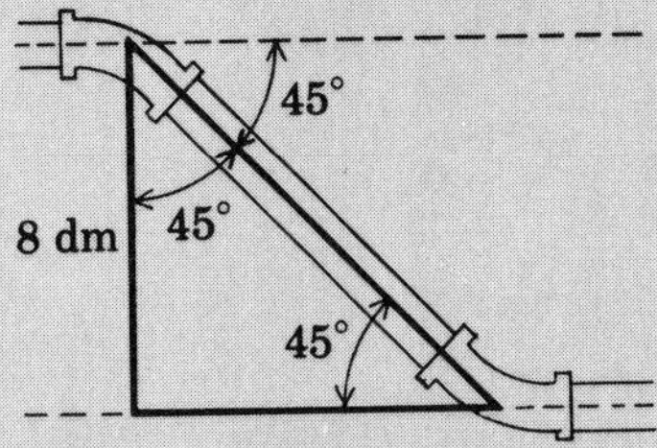

When 45° elbows are used, the offset is equal to the run. In this case, both are 8 decimeters.

$$o^2 + r^2 = d^2$$

$$8^2 + 8^2 = d^2$$

$$64 + 64 = d^2$$

$$128 = d^2$$

$$\sqrt{128} = d$$

$$11.3 \approx d$$

The run is 8 decimeters. The diagonal is 11.3 decimeters to the nearest tenth.

On another job, Karen planned for 60° elbows. She needed to find the run and the offset for a diagonal of 14 decimeters.

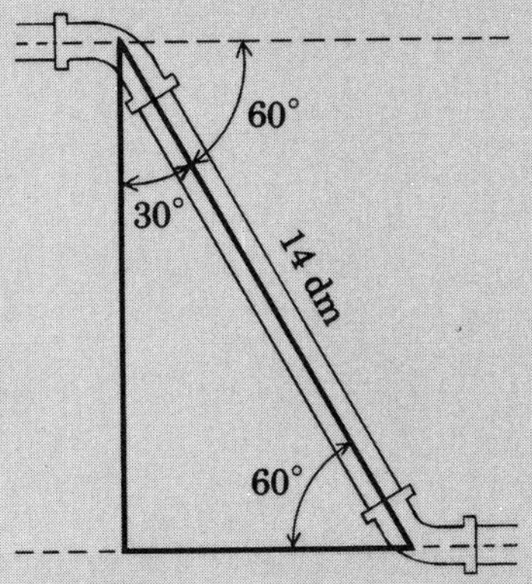

When 60° elbows are used, the run is half as long as the diagonal. The diagonal is 14 decimeters. The run is 7 decimeters.

$$o^2 + r^2 = d^2$$

$$o^2 + 7^2 = 14^2$$

$$o^2 + 49 = 196$$

$$o^2 = 147$$

$$o = \sqrt{147}$$

$$o \approx 12.1$$

The run is 7 decimeters. The offset is 12.1 decimeters to the nearest tenth.

Find the missing numbers if 45° elbows are used. Use the table on page 418. All lengths are given in decimeters. Round answers to the nearest tenth.

	Offset (o)	Run (r)	Diagonal (d)
1.	7	7	▒ 9.9
2.	4	4	▒ 5.7
3.	5	5	▒ 7.1
4.	3	▒ 3	▒ 4.2
5.	9	▒ 9	▒ 12.7
6.	10	▒ 10	▒ 14.1
7.	2	▒ 2	▒ 2.8
8.	1	▒ 1	▒ 1.4

Find the missing numbers if 60° elbows are used. Use the table on page 418. All lengths are given in decimeters. Round answers to the nearest tenth.

	Offset (o)	Run (r)	Diagonal (d)
9.	▒ 13.9	8	16
10.	▒ 10.4	6	12
11.	▒ 6.9	4	8
12.	▒ 8.7	▒ 5	10
13.	▒ 3.5	▒ 2	4
14.	▒ 5.2	▒ 3	6
15.	▒ 1.7	▒ 1	2

Objective: Solve problems involving the Pythagorean Rule and trigonometry.

In this lesson students use trigonometric ratios to find lengths of sides of right triangles in a star-shaped garden, given the measures of the angles and one side.

Career: Landscape Architect

Career Cluster: Arts

Tony Botts is a landscape architect. He designed this star-shaped formal garden for a city park.

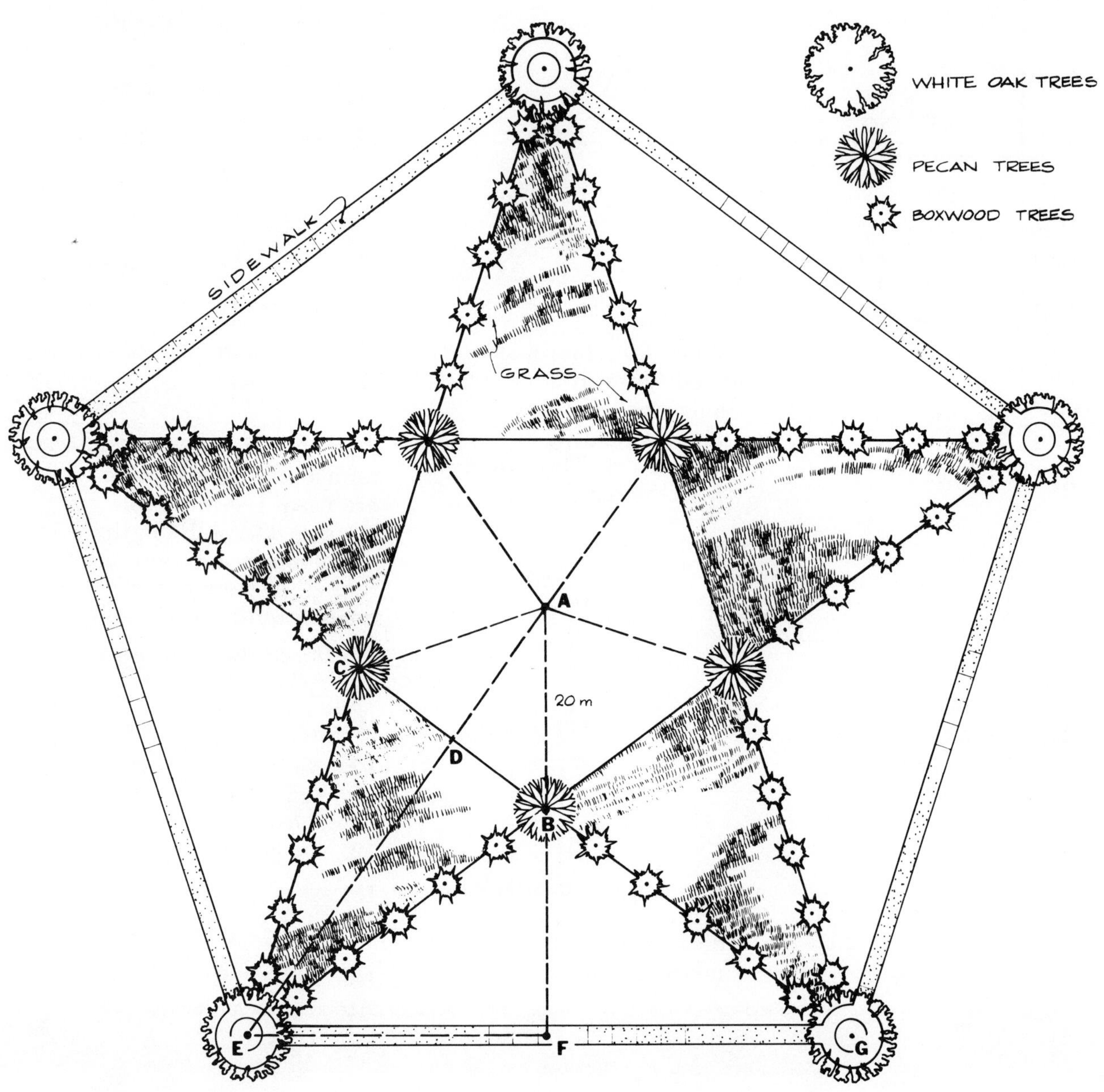

Tony knew the measures of the angles. He needed to find CB to the nearest tenth of a meter.

When the workers knew CB, they could use string and a tape measure to locate the pecan trees.

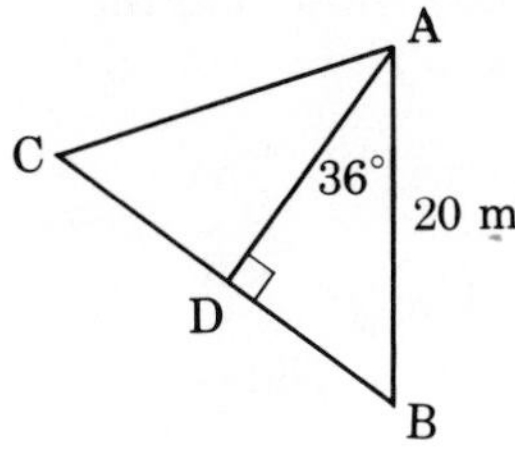

$$\sin 36^\circ = \frac{DB}{AB}$$

$$.588 = \frac{DB}{20}$$

$$11.8 \approx DB$$

CB is twice DB, or 23.6 meters to the nearest tenth.

Find CB to the nearest tenth of a meter for each of these values of AB.

1. 25 m 29.4 m
2. 14 m 16.5 m
3. 40 m 47.0 m
4. 9 m 10.6 m
5. 12 m 14.1 m
6. 27 m 31.8 m
7. 32 m 37.6 m
8. 18 m 21.2 m

	EG	Total length
18.	72.8 m	364.0 m
19.	37.2 m	186.0 m
20.	40.5 m	202.5 m
21.	30.7 m	153.5 m
22.	55.0 m	275.0 m
23.	45.3 m	226.5 m
24.	6.5 m	32.5 m
25.	51.8 m	259.0 m

Next Tony needed to find EC and EB so that the workers could locate the white oak trees.

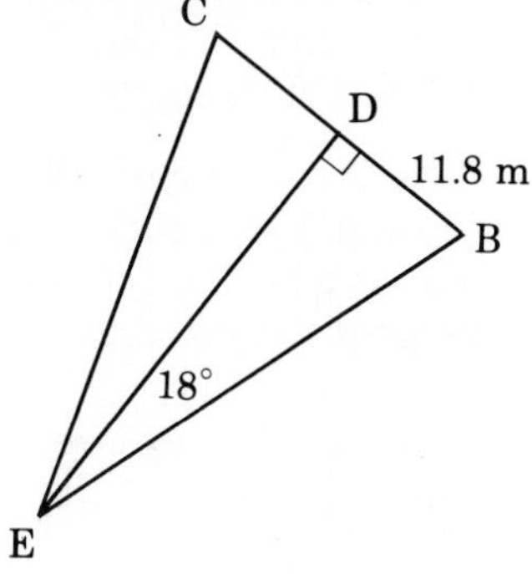

$$\sin 18^\circ = \frac{DB}{EB}$$

$$.309 = \frac{11.8}{EB}$$

$$EB(.309) = 11.8$$

$$EB \approx 38.2$$

EC and EB are 38.2 meters to the nearest tenth.

Find EB and EC to the nearest tenth of a meter for each of these values of DB.

9. 12 m 38.8 m
10. 17 m 55.0 m
11. 24 m 77.7 m
12. 8 m 25.9 m
13. 7 m 22.7 m
14. 16 m 51.8 m
15. 21 m 68.0 m
16. 10 m 32.4 m

Then Tony needed to find the distance between the boxwood trees along EB.

17. Divide EB, 38.2, by 6 to find that distance to the nearest tenth of a meter. 6.4 meters

Finally Tony needed to find EG and the total length of the sidewalk.

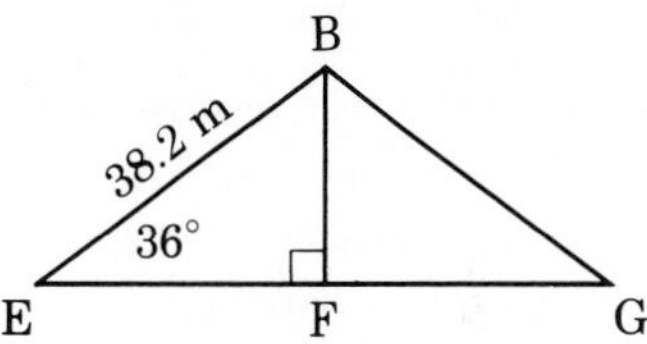

$$\cos 36^\circ = \frac{EF}{EB}$$

$$.809 = \frac{EF}{38.2}$$

$$30.9 \approx EF$$

EG is twice EF, or 61.8 meters.

The total length of the sidewalk is five times EG, or 309.0 meters.

Find EG and the total length of the sidewalk to the nearest tenth of a meter for these values of EB. See left.

18. 45 m
19. 23 m
20. 25 m
21. 19 m
22. 34 m
23. 28 m
24. 4 m
25. 32 m

Number of test items - 19

Number missed	1	2	3	4	5	6	7	8	9
Percent correct	95	89	84	79	74	68	63	58	53

Chapter 18

A **1.** Compute 2^6. 64

B **2.** Find $\sqrt{81}$. 9

For items 3–7, use the table on page 418.

C **3.** Find 153^2. 23,409

D **4.** Find $\sqrt{147}$ to the nearest tenth. 12.1

E **5.** Find $\sqrt{7396}$. 86

F **6.** Use the Pythagorean Rule to find the length of the hypotenuse to the nearest tenth. 7.6 m

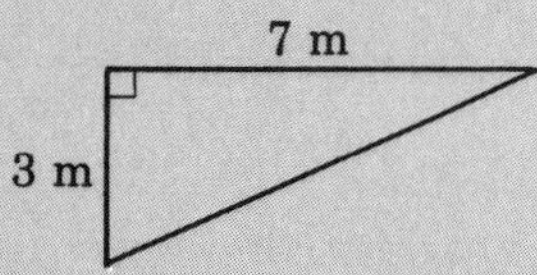

G **7.** Use the Pythagorean Rule to find the missing length. 63 m

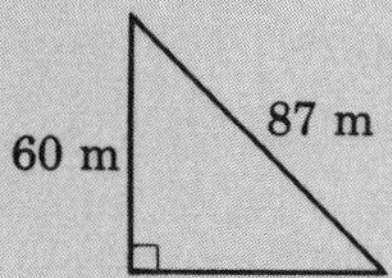

H **8.** Give the tangent of ∠W as a ratio and as a decimal to the nearest thousandth. $\frac{48}{14} \approx 3.429$

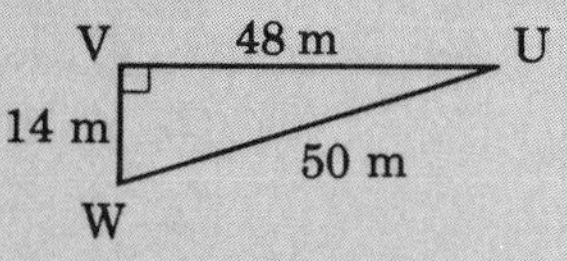

I **9.** Give the sine of ∠W in item 8 as a ratio and as a decimal to the nearest thousandth. $\frac{48}{50} = .960$

J **10.** Give the cosine of ∠W in item 8 as a ratio and as a decimal to the nearest thousandth. $\frac{14}{50} = .280$

For items 11–16, use the table on page 419.

K **11.** Give the tangent of 28° as a decimal to the nearest thousandth. .532

L **12.** Give the sine of 41° as a decimal to the nearest thousandth. .656

M **13.** Give the cosine of 67° as a decimal to the nearest thousandth. .391

N **14.** Find h to the nearest tenth. 5.6 cm

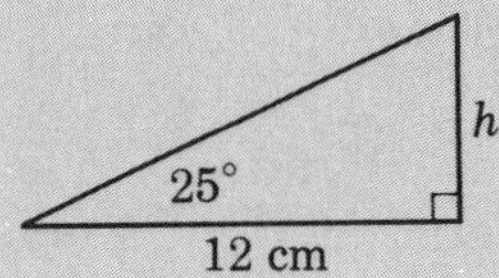

O **15.** Find d to the nearest tenth. 20.6 cm

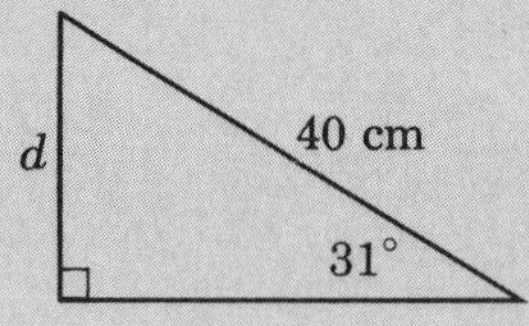

P **16.** Find b to the nearest tenth. 5.2 m

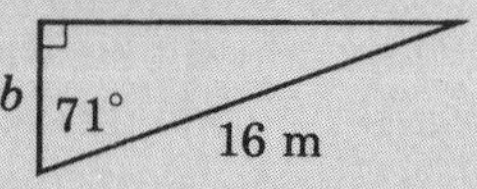

17. Would these lengths form a right triangle? No

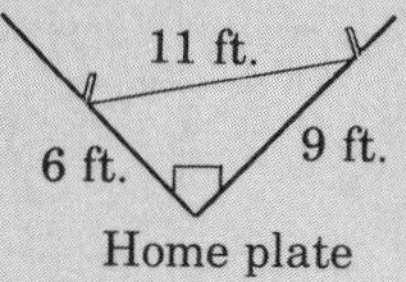

18. Find the length of the diagonal to the nearest tenth of a decimeter. Use the table on page 418. 8.5 dm

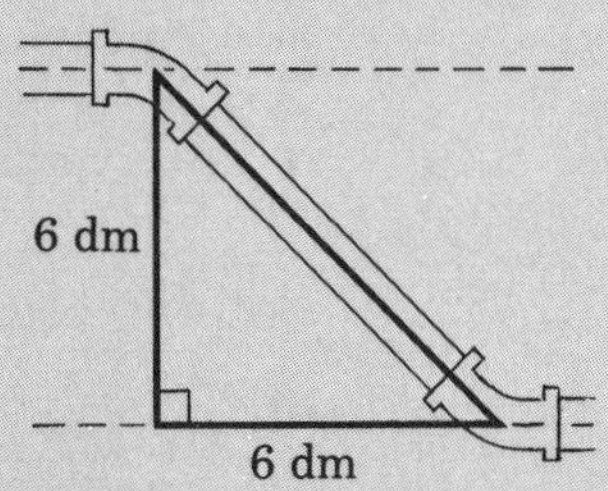

19. Find the distance between the trees, CB, to the nearest tenth of a meter. CB is twice DB. Use the table on page 419. 28.2 m

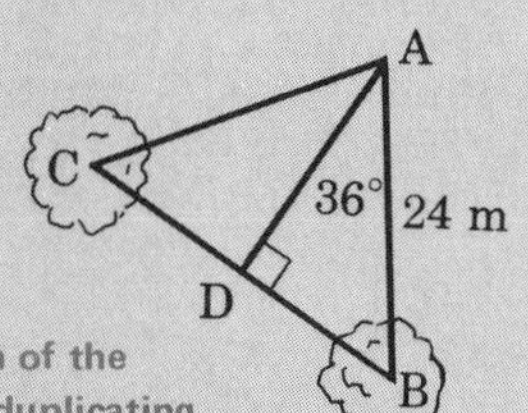

See pages 49–50 of the *Tests and Record Forms: Duplicating Masters* for an alternate form of the Chapter 18 Test. For a test on Unit 6, see page T37 of this book and pages 51–52 of the duplicating masters. For a three-part end-of-book test, see pages T38–T40 of this book and pages 53–58 of the duplicating masters.

tune-up skills

Ratio, Proportion, and Similarity, pages 195–204

Find each missing number.

1. $\frac{4}{14} = \frac{26}{n}$ $n = 91$
2. $\frac{25}{t} = \frac{20}{12}$ $t = 15$
3. $\frac{56}{48} = \frac{h}{18}$ $h = 21$
4. $\frac{30}{k} = \frac{75}{100}$ $k = 40$
5. $\frac{d}{9.1} = \frac{.4}{.7}$ $d = 5.2$
6. $\frac{2}{3} = \frac{36}{m}$ $m = 54$
7. $\frac{w}{9} = \frac{19}{57}$ $w = 3$
8. $\frac{16}{24} = \frac{a}{2.7}$ $a = 1.8$
9. $\frac{6}{10} = \frac{15}{c}$ $c = 25$
10. $\frac{f}{8} = \frac{45}{12}$ $f = 30$
11. $\frac{72}{j} = \frac{20.4}{3.4}$ $j = 12$
12. $\frac{15}{40} = \frac{m}{16}$ $m = 6$

Percent, pages 213–224

1. Find 4% of 65. 2.6
2. Find 54% of 60. 32.4
3. Find 8% of 85. 6.8
4. Find $33\frac{1}{3}$% of 63. 21
5. Find 25% of 32. 8
6. Find 125% of 40. 50
7. 27 is what percent of 45? 60%
8. 23 is what percent of 115? 20%
9. 7 is what percent of 35? 20%
10. 86 is what percent of 200? 43%
11. 5 is what percent of 12? $41\frac{2}{3}$ %
12. 7 is what percent of 84? $8\frac{1}{3}$ %
13. 4 is 8% of what number? 50
14. 57 is 60% of what number? 95
15. 99 is 30% of what number? 330
16. 4 is $16\frac{2}{3}$% of what number? 24
17. 63 is 25% of what number? 252
18. 27 is $12\frac{1}{2}$% of what number? 216

Positive and Negative Numbers, pages 259–270

1. $^-4 + 6$ 2
2. $9 + {}^-7$ 2
3. $^-18 + {}^-20$ $^-38$
4. $^-15 + 7$ $^-8$
5. $9.2 + {}^-4.7$ 4.5
6. $^-6.5 + {}^-2.4$ $^-8.9$
7. $^-8 - 3$ $^-11$
8. $7 - {}^-12$ 19
9. $^-62 - {}^-14$ $^-48$
10. $5 - 17$ $^-12$
11. $^-17.4 - 8.2$ $^-25.6$
12. $^-4.2 - {}^-3.5$ $^-.7$
13. $^-9 \times 6$ $^-54$
14. $8 \times {}^-12$ $^-96$
15. $^-25 \times 3$ $^-75$
16. $^-8 \times {}^-21$ 168
17. $2.4 \times {}^-7$ $^-16.8$
18. $^-9.5 \times 3.1$ $^-29.45$
19. $32 \div {}^-4$ $^-8$
20. $^-63 \div 3$ $^-21$
21. $^-144 \div {}^-12$ 12
22. $^-12.5 \div 5$ $^-2.5$
23. $200 \div {}^-50$ $^-4$
24. $^-13.8 \div 3$ $^-4.6$
25. $^-97 \div {}^-10$ 9.7

CALCULATOR EXERCISES

Optional In exercises 1–5, 8, 10, and 18, answers were obtained by using 3.14 for π. If students press a π button on their calculators, some of their answers will be different.

Find the circumference and area of each circle to the nearest tenth.

1. Radius: 14.2 cm
   89.2 cm; 633.1 cm^2
2. Diameter: 62.04 m
   194.8 m; 3021.4 m^2
3. Radius: 34.28 cm
   215.3 cm; 3689.9 cm^2
4. Radius: 0.43 mm
   2.7 mm; 0.6 mm^2
5. Diameter: 1.752 km
   5.5 km; 2.4 km^2

Find the surface area and volume of each figure to the nearest tenth.

6. Rectangular prism
   Length: 22.8 cm
   Width: 19.4 cm
   Height: 8.7 cm
   1618.9 cm^2; 3848.2 cm^3
7. Cube
   Side: 42.3 mm
   10,735.7 mm^2; 75,687.0 mm^3
8. Cylinder
   Radius: 9.62 m
   Height: 13.74 m
   1411.3 m^2; 3992.7 m^3
9. Rectangular prism
   Length: 20.6 mm
   Width: 18.4 mm
   Height: 12.7 mm
   1748.7 mm^2; 4813.8 mm^3
10. Cylinder
    Radius: 4.81 cm
    Height: 17.62 cm
    677.5 cm^2; 1280.0 cm^3
11. Cube
    Side: 0.75 mm
    3.4 mm^2; 0.4 mm^3

Use the Pythagorean Rule and the table on page 418 to find the length of the hypotenuse in a right triangle if the legs have these lengths.

12. 36 cm and 15 cm 39 cm
13. 55 mm and 132 mm 143 mm
14. 64 m and 48 m 80 m
15. 75 cm and 180 cm 195 cm

For each box, find the volume and then divide to find the number of cubic centimeters per dollar. Tell which box is a better buy. Giant size

16.

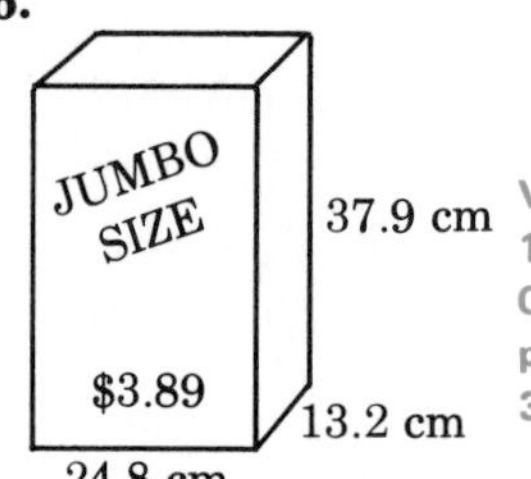

Volume ≈ 12,406.9 cm^3
Cubic centimeters per dollar ≈ 3189.4

17.

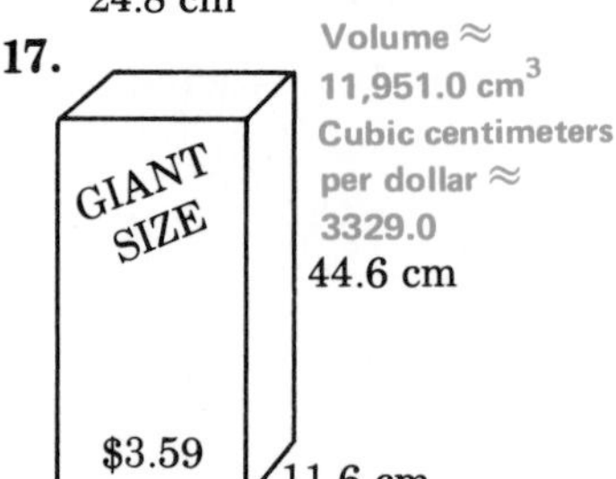

Volume ≈ 11,951.0 cm^3
Cubic centimeters per dollar ≈ 3329.0

18. Find the volume of the pot and of the can. Will the pot hold the contents of 5 of these cans? Yes

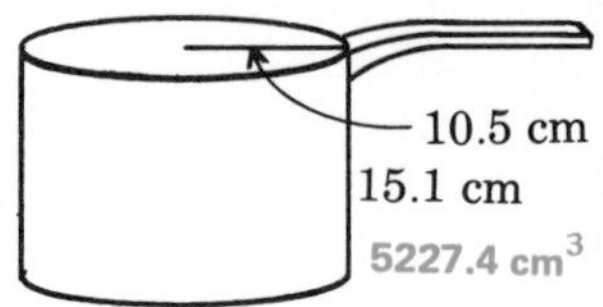

5227.4 cm^3

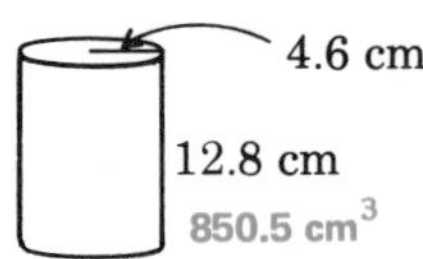

850.5 cm^3

Aviators used to find the height of the clouds at night by sighting the reflection of a strong spotlight.

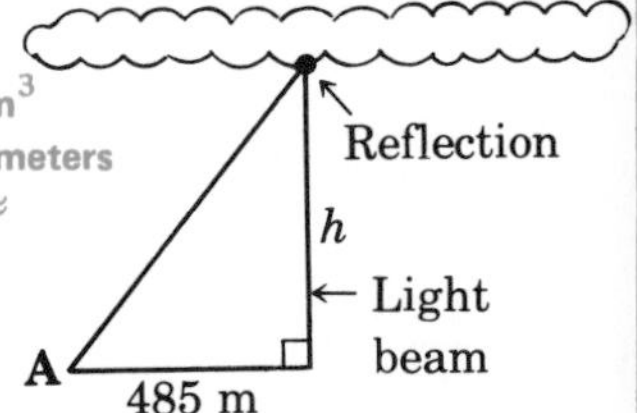

Use the tangent ratio and the table on page 419 to find h to the nearest tenth for these measures of $\angle A$.

19. 56° 719.3 m
20. 37° 365.7 m
21. 75° 1810.0 m
22. 43° 452.5 m

answers

Odd-numbered Exercises

pages 4–5

set A **1.** 86 **3.** 68 **5.** 8895 **7.** 299 **9.** 1977

set B **1.** 66 **3.** 509 **5.** 9957 **7.** 1002 **9.** 500 **11.** 1098 **13.** 2232

set C **1.** 162 **3.** 2682 **5.** 1560 **7.** 215 **9.** 159 **11.** 11,745 **13.** 3945 **15.** 979,032 **17.** 9350

set D **1.** 305 **3.** 114 **5.** 1013 **7.** 522 **9.** 27 **11.** 7268 **13.** 907 **15.** 8253 **17.** 1580 **19.** 246 **21.** 34,456 **23.** 1421 **25.** 5499 **27.** 379

pages 6–7

set E **1.** 612 **3.** 2121 **5.** 20,970 **7.** 2322 **9.** 3751

set F **1.** 888 **3.** 56 **5.** 4888 **7.** 5783 **9.** 1720 **11.** 847 **13.** 2184 **15.** 38 **17.** 2607 **19.** 3687 **21.** 317 **23.** 4611 **25.** 1679 **27.** 24,396 **29.** 3912 **31.** 19,379 **33.** 38,882 **35.** 26,346 **37.** 7564 **39.** 75,628 **41.** 295

set G **1.** 261 **3.** 4128 **5.** 4 **7.** 231 **9.** 318 **11.** 343 **13.** 5336 **15.** 4606 **17.** 7928 **19.** 31,373 **21.** 8886 **23.** 48,459 **25.** 14,758 **27.** 23,472

pages 8–9

set H **1.** 7 **3.** 25 **5.** 40 **7.** 32 **9.** 24 **11.** 40 **13.** 85 **15.** 17 **17.** 52 **19.** 9 **21.** 11 **23.** 315 **25.** 170

set I **1.** 12 **3.** 7 **5.** 53 **7.** 122 **9.** 9 **11.** 167 **13.** 28 **15.** 90 **17.** 111 **19.** 39 **21.** 162 **23.** 12 **25.** 508 **27.** 25

pages 10–11

set J **1.** $x = 35$ **3.** $n = 22$ **5.** $b = 22$ **7.** $c = 21$ **9.** $g = 65$ **11.** $h = 27$ **13.** $k = 35$ **15.** $a = 18$ **17.** $w = 13$ **19.** $x = 66$ **21.** $r = 38$ **23.** $b = 162$ **25.** $k = 1011$

set K **1.** $n = 139$ **3.** $k = 33$ **5.** $c = 83$ **7.** $v = 44$ **9.** $y = 90$ **11.** $f = 85$ **13.** $r = 58$ **15.** $s = 61$ **17.** $j = 157$ **19.** $a = 103$ **21.** $x = 885$ **23.** $z = 241$ **25.** $w = 345$

page 13 **1.** Monday's Totals: 2300; 60 Tuesday's Totals: 1436; 278 **3.** 218 grams

pages 14–15 **1.** \$283 **3.** \$249 **5.** Bus **7.** \$34 **9.** \$6 **11.** \$385 **13.** \$371 **15.** \$98 **17.** \$443 **19.** \$469 **21.** \$242

pages 16–17 **1.** \$6710; \$6300; \$5670 **3.** \$8380; \$7853; \$7068 **5.** \$10,000; \$9356; \$8420 **7.** \$11,620; \$10,859; \$9773 **9.** \$13,180; \$12,360; \$11,124 **11.** \$14,740; \$13,920; \$12,528 **13.** \$16,240; \$15,420; \$13,878

pages 18–19 **1.** 5 degree days **3.** 2 degree days **5.** 14 degree days **7.** 18 degree days **9.** 428 **11.** 207 degree days **13.** 812 **15.** 703 **17.** 1352 **19.** 972 **21.** 983 **23.** 709 **25.** 6044

pages 22–23

set A **1.** 8000 **3.** 1000 **5.** 300,000 **7.** 900 **11.** 800,000 **13.** 10,000 **15.** 4000 **17.** 40,000 **19.** 80 **21.** 600,000 **23.** 40,000 **25.** 100,000 **27.** 500 **29.** 25,000 **31.** 20,000 **33.** 3000 **35.** 2500 **37.** 40,000 **39.** 50,000 **41.** 7400 **43.** 2000 **45.** 7,000,000 **47.** 300,000 **49.** 2,000,000

set B **1.** 35,000 **3.** 7200 **5.** 32,000 **7.** 240,000 **9.** 42,000 **11.** 1800 **13.** 450,000 **15.** 210,000 **17.** 800 **19.** 24,000 **21.** 720,000 **23.** 360,000 **25.** 280 **27.** 200,000 **29.** 560,000 **31.** 490,000 **33.** 14,000,000 **35.** 12,000 **37.** 180,000 **39.** 1600 **41.** 180 **43.** 40,000 **45.** 240,000 **47.** 800,000 **49.** 35,000,000 **51.** 2,400,000 **53.** 21,000,000 **55.** 24,000,000

pages 24–25

set C **1.** 368 **3.** 128 **5.** 144 **7.** 123 **9.** 324

set D **1.** 175 **3.** 330 **5.** 329 **7.** 396 **9.** 576 **11.** 58 **13.** 161 **15.** 145

set E **1.** 45,712 **3.** 2781 **5.** 1610 **7.** 2010 **9.** 20,272 **11.** 38,812 **13.** 789,426 **15.** 181,448 **17.** 1041 **19.** 340,443 **21.** 45,591 **23.** 2708 **25.** 44,465 **27.** 588,192

set F **1.** 25,542 **3.** 2296 **5.** 603 **7.** 248,829 **9.** 19,014 **11.** 230,484 **13.** 315 **15.** 5556 **17.** 124 **19.** 563,272 **21.** 616 **23.** 526 **25.** 448 **27.** 193,146 **29.** 4824 **31.** 40,015 **33.** 186,642 **35.** 105 **37.** 4405 **39.** 33,747 **41.** 78,885 **43.** 2412 **45.** 583,515 **47.** 15,875 **49.** 118,938 **51.** 48,560 **53.** 22,974 **55.** 279,372

pages 26–27

set G **1.** 4550 **3.** 2580 **5.** 6840 **7.** 2720 **9.** 1860

set H **1.** 2436 **3.** 810 **5.** 912 **7.** 2790 **9.** 1078 **11.** 4982 **13.** 3392 **15.** 3234

set I **1.** 46,332 **3.** 329,355 **5.** 19,517 **7.** 237,276 **9.** 289,984 **11.** 14,652 **13.** 12,958 **15.** 388,606 **17.** 3,231,072 **19.** 52,461 **21.** 60,371 **23.** 15,792 **25.** 18,040,064 **27.** 8,876,276

set J **1.** 19,499 **3.** 372,070 **5.** 289,520 **7.** 457,440 **9.** 268,859 **11.** 3952 **13.** 1,122,080 **15.** 3648 **17.** 875,710 **19.** 37,800 **21.** 2,478,424 **23.** 7,263,990 **25.** 18,618 **27.** 196,992 **29.** 17,500 **31.** 11,823 **33.** 291,308 **35.** 54,360 **37.** 2,675,424 **39.** 60,560 **41.** 135,675 **43.** 7,388,550 **45.** 204,330 **47.** 49,800 **49.** 16,890 **51.** 3471 **53.** 15,120 **55.** 517,638

pages 28-29

set K **1.** 173,400 **3.** 413,500 **5.** 592,200 **7.** 494,400 **9.** 299,600

set L **1.** 204,592 **3.** 378,350 **5.** 242,004 **7.** 317,461 **9.** 207,060 **11.** 69,360 **13.** 167,634 **15.** 617,040

set M **1.** 571,250 **3.** 645,018 **5.** 633,150 **7.** 926,100 **9.** 456,615 **11.** 4,477,179 **13.** 389,872 **15.** 3,259,546 **17.** 149,490 **19.** 82,383,107 **21.** 1,584,260 **23.** 217,316 **25.** 5,119,193 **27.** 1,758,245

pages 30-31

set N **1.** 13 **3.** 26 **5.** 47 **7.** 22 **9.** 18 **11.** 54 **13.** 40 **15.** 33 **17.** 140 **19.** 19 **21.** 62 **23.** 76 **25.** 47

set O **1.** 6 **3.** 29 **5.** 30 **7.** 6 **9.** 14 **11.** 69 **13.** 48 **15.** 39 **17.** 3 **19.** 16 **21.** 14 **23.** 21 **25.** 11 **27.** 54

page 33

	Dee			Barbara		
TOTAL	52	46	81	56	58	63
Bonus	—	—	35	—	—	35
TOTAL	52	46	116	56	58	98
Lower Total	105	163	213	161	162	220
Upper Total	52	46	116	56	58	98
Combined Total	157	209	329	217	220	318
Triple Yahtzee	157	418	987	217	440	954
GRAND TOTAL		1512			1611	

pages 34-35 **1.** $320 **3.** $880 **5.** $1067 **7. a.** $1000 **b.** $2500 **c.** $1244 **d.** $6220 **e.** $5001 **9.** Mr. Diaz: $7750; Ms. Todd: $7100; Ms. Wong: $9430

pages 36-37 **1. a.** 3720ℓ **b.** 1320ℓ **c.** 5760ℓ **d.** 6960ℓ **e.** 1560ℓ **f.** 3000ℓ **g.** 1440ℓ **h.** 3960ℓ **i.** 3240ℓ **j.** 11,400ℓ **k.** 4200ℓ **l.** 11,520ℓ **m.** 6720ℓ **n.** 2520ℓ **3. a.** 279 metric tons **b.** 99 metric tons **c.** 432 metric tons **d.** 522 metric tons **e.** 117 metric tons **f.** 225 metric tons **g.** 108 metric tons **h.** 297 metric tons **i.** 243 metric tons **j.** 855 metric tons **k.** 315 metric tons **l.** 864 metric tons **m.** 504 metric tons **n.** 189 metric tons **5.** 5426 kilograms **7.** 8098 kilograms **9.** 7666 kilograms **11.** 141,372 cases **13.** $989,604

pages 38-39 **1.** 576; 768 **3.** 180; 360; 540; 720 **5.** 360; 720; 1080; 1440 **7.** 360; 720; 1080; 1440 **9.** 2100; 2200; 1900 **11.** 4200; 4400; 3800 **13.** 8400; 8800; 8300 **15.** 2800; 2880; 2770

pages 42–43

set A **1.** 7 R2 **3.** 7 R4 **5.** 7 R1 **7.** 3 R3 **9.** 6 R1

set B **1.** 19 **3.** 46 R1 **5.** 21 R1 **7.** 17 R3 **9.** 12 R1

set C **1.** 29 R3 **3.** 83 **5.** 29 R2 **7.** 271 R1 **9.** 235 R1 **11.** 285 **13.** 181 R1 **15.** 87

set D **1.** 1329 **3.** 316 R1 **5.** 115,516 R7 **7.** 7663 **9.** 1255 R5 **11.** 3255 R1 **13.** 46,568 R3 **15.** 185,484 R1 **17.** 9365 R1 **19.** 3791 R6

set E **1.** 1246 R4 **3.** 1156 R3 **5.** 26 R2 **7.** 71 R1 **9.** 1368 R3 **11.** 925 R2 **13.** 22,839 R1 **15.** 8 R1 **17.** 137 R3 **19.** 78 **21.** 728 R4 **23.** 33,627 R2 **25.** 5628 R5

pages 44–45

set F **1.** 2 R7 **3.** 1 R11 **5.** 2 R10 **7.** 1 R15 **9.** 4

set G **1.** 33 R11 **3.** 14 R59 **5.** 16 R6 **7.** 5 R85 **9.** 46 R6 **11.** 2 R61 **13.** 6 R37 **15.** 3 R23 **17.** 8 R15 **19.** 7 R4

set H **1.** 19 R2 **3.** 22 R8 **5.** 17 R39 **7.** 32 R12 **9.** 5 R18 **11.** 12 R3 **13.** 7 R74 **15.** 16 R5 **17.** 6 R20 **19.** 4 R23

set I **1.** 74 R39 **3.** 173 R15 **5.** 477 R32 **7.** 2967 R35 **9.** 291 R12 **11.** 72 R9 **13.** 2371 R38 **15.** 635 R56 **17.** 33 R66 **19.** 51 R10 **21.** 517 R36 **23.** 28,151 R6 **25.** 68,751 R24 **27.** 6982 R52

page 46

set J **1.** 305 R3 **3.** 705 R2 **5.** 2041 R6 **7.** 3602 R4 **9.** 61 R5 **11.** 604 **13.** 520 R5 **15.** 8020 R1 **17.** 4061 R4

set K **1.** 107 R8 **3.** 30 R7 **5.** 206 R2 **7.** 300 R5 **9.** 410 **11.** 109 R67 **13.** 5602 R7 **15.** 202 R13 **17.** 206 R37 **19.** 305 R33

page 47

set L **1.** 2 R297 **3.** 8 R19 **5.** 2 R264 **7.** 1 R56 **9.** 1 R106

set M **1.** 82 R219 **3.** 5 R490 **5.** 6 R147 **7.** 13 R271 **9.** 83 R389 **11.** 67 R132 **13.** 5 R115 **15.** 23 R139 **17.** 24 R241 **19.** 13 R24 **21.** 57 R376 **23.** 40 R273 **25.** 4 R474 **27.** 550 R326

pages 48–49

set N **1.** 10 **3.** 2 **5.** 27 **7.** 18 **9.** 3 **11.** 8 **13.** 0

set O **1.** 9 **3.** 3 **5.** 2 **7.** 6 **9.** 10 **11.** 13 **13.** 1

pages 50–51

set P **1.** $n=4$ **3.** $r=27$ **5.** $b=27$ **7.** $c=26$ **9.** $y=35$ **11.** $v=16$ **13.** $y=0$ **15.** $g=5$ **17.** $c=6$ **19.** $y=14$ **21.** $d=8$ **23.** $m=11$ **25.** $w=17$

set Q **1.** $x=294$ **3.** $w=169$ **5.** $k=108$ **7.** $n=75$ **9.** $t=98$ **11.** $b=217$ **13.** $n=192$ **15.** $g=432$ **17.** $s=80$ **19.** $m=90$ **21.** $d=630$ **23.** $m=92$ **25.** $t=4500$ **27.** $c=825$

page 53 **1.** $910; $210 **3.** $910; $210 **5.** $585; $135 **7.** $1118; $258 **9.** $754; $174 **11.** $1027; $237 **13.** $1157; $267 **15.** $975; $225

pages 54–55 **1.** 26¢ **3.** 17¢ **5.** 18¢ **7.** 19¢ **9.** 19¢ **11.** 33¢ **13.** 45¢ **15.** 43¢ **17.** Brand X **19.** Brand X **21.** Brand Y **23.** Brand X **25.** Brand Y **27.** Brand Y **29.** Brand X

pages 56–57 **1.** 10; 8; 18 **3.** 9; 7; 16 **5.** 26; 22; 48 **7.** 2; 2; 4 **9.** 8; 6; 14

pages 58–59 **1.** 12 **3.** 6720; 5760 **5.** 39 cases **7.** 1560 cases **9.** 134,400 cases **11.** 1,497,600 cases **13.** 30 minutes **15.** 50 minutes **17.** 90 minutes **19.** 3600 cases **21.** 2000 cases **23.** 73,000 cases

pages 60–61 **1. a.** Happ's: $19,955; Greco's: $16,653; Lee's: $17,212 **b.** Happ's: $3991; Greco's: $2379; Lee's: $4303 **c.** Happ's: 5; Greco's: 7; Lee's: 4 **3.** Greco's

page 64 **1.** 34,862 **3.** 150,862 **5.** 38,495 **7.** 14,834 **9.** 13,085 **11.** 52,539 **13.** 6,240,109 **15.** 28,036,125 **17.** 46,002,180 **19.** 88,349,680 **21.** 14,380,470 **23.** 18,467,430 **25.** 41,256 **27.** 745 **29.** 8744 **31.** 823 km; 512 km; 1608 km

page 63

Adding and Subtracting Whole Numbers **1.** 89 **3.** 760 **5.** 101 **7.** 120 **9.** 6052 **11.** 4150 **13.** 255 **15.** 62 **17.** 619 **19.** 6545 **21.** 2048 **23.** 3769 **25.** 20,157

Multiplying Whole Numbers **1.** 87 **3.** 15,500 **5.** 12,033 **7.** 81,500 **9.** 1972 **11.** 30,000 **13.** 33,522 **15.** 13,818 **17.** 1,200,000 **19.** 10,950 **21.** 106,398 **23.** 515,570 **25.** 4,119,276

Dividing Whole Numbers **1.** 181 **3.** 1812 R2 **5.** 34 R35 **7.** 600 **9.** 20,076 **11.** 8 **13.** 35 **15.** 49 R10 **17.** 90 **19.** 600 **21.** 809 **23.** 35 R313 **25.** 189

pages 68–69

set A **1.** hundredths **3.** ten thousandths **5.** thousandths **7.** hundred thousandths **9.** hundreds **11.** hundredths **13.** tenths **15.** millionths **17.** hundred thousandths **19.** ten thousands

set B **1.** .60, .600 **3.** .38, .380 **5.** .10, .100 **7.** .91, .910 **9.** .63, .630 **11.** .90, .900 **13.** 1.60, 1.600 **15.** .37, .370 **17.** .50, .500 **19.** 3.25, 3.250

set C **1.** $<$ **3.** $<$ **5.** $>$ **7.** $>$ **9.** $=$ **11.** $<$ **13.** $>$ **15.** $<$ **17.** $>$ **19.** $<$ **21.** $<$ **23.** $>$ **25.** $<$

pages 70–71

set D **1.** 18.7 **3.** 15.18 **5.** .207 **7.** 278.3 **9.** 19.857

set E **1.** .864 **3.** 1.955 **5.** 12.531 **7.** 22.253 **9.** 81.761

set F **1.** 7.9 **3.** 9.9 **5.** 1.38 **7.** 9.35 **9.** 5.71 **11.** .876 **13.** 4.723 **15.** 9.802 **17.** 1.2 **19.** 2.05 **21.** 1.928 **23.** 11.907 **25.** 2.6

set G **1.** 3.69 **3.** 2.939 **5.** 3.027 **7.** 32.93 **9.** 9.102 **11.** 1.188 **13.** 2.122 **15.** 4.153 **17.** 11.415 **19.** 8.358 **21.** 12.141 **23.** 19.23 **25.** 10.442

pages 72–73

set H **1.** 2.4 **3.** .39 **5.** 1.85 **7.** .521 **9.** .684 **11.** 3.288

set I **1.** 4.04 **3.** 3.65 **5.** 1.62 **7.** .218 **9.** .191 **11.** 4.881

set J **1.** 1.4 **3.** 3.6 **5.** .17 **7.** 2.56 **9.** 1.78 **11.** 3.87 **13.** 5.89 **15.** 8.86 **17.** .267 **19.** .889 **21.** 1.382 **23.** 4.889 **25.** 20.917 **27.** .7315

set K **1.** 6.15 **3.** 4.2 **5.** 2.15 **7.** 4.126 **9.** 2.085 **11.** 3.104 **13.** 4.266 **15.** 3.539 **17.** 2.279 **19.** 4.224 **21.** 5.175 **23.** 14.588 **25.** 12.305 **27.** .9052

page 75 **1.** $11.20 **3.** $15.55 **5.** $20.05 **7.** $30.10

pages 76–77 **1.** 101.12 **3.** 818.26 **5.** 884.96 **7.** 1193.46 **9.** 826.72 **11.** 12,318.36

pages 78–79 **1.** Nov. 8, 1976 **3.** 29.64 **5.** Dental work **7.** 176.75 **9.** 690.69 **11.** 154.64

pages 80–81 **1.** 6.426 cm **3.** 6.992 cm **5.** 3.25 cm **7.** 7.25 cm **9.** 3.342 cm **11.** 0.53 cm

pages 84–85

set A **1.** 82.08 **3.** 36.54 **5.** 4.55 **7.** 298.2 **9.** 11.256 **11.** 114.72 **13.** 7.56 **15.** 26.22 **17.** 3.978 **19.** 428.96 **21.** 132.804 **23.** 115.84 **25.** 16.252 **27.** 21.3248

set B **1.** .0603 **3.** .02212 **5.** .0234 **7.** .0002568 **9.** .028416 **11.** .00462 **13.** .0145976 **15.** .055872 **17.** .06758 **19.** .0165474 **21.** .0010778 **23.** .05076 **25.** .036381 **27.** .0052683

set C **1.** 229.77 **3.** 1.088 **5.** 9.116 **7.** 30.84 **9.** .0143 **11.** .1008 **13.** 3.246 **15.** 4.844 **17.** .7802 **19.** 2904 **21.** .2124 **23.** .3192 **25.** .0258 **27.** 12.28 **29.** .0874 **31.** .01014 **33.** .88 **35.** .1141 **37.** 18.86 **39.** 7.2 **41.** 118.8 **43.** 2.415 **45.** 2.835 **47.** 236.5 **49.** 336.8 **51.** 30.87 **53.** 3.68 **55.** 669.6

pages 86–87

set D **1.** 6.7 **3.** 4.13 **5.** 2.6 **7.** 5.22 **9.** .6587 **11.** 2.16 **13.** 3.7 **15.** .3547 **17.** 12.56 **19.** 23.4

set E **1.** .089 **3.** .0048 **5.** .08 **7.** .059 **9.** .023 **11.** .0228 **13.** .0082 **15.** .0134 **17.** .087

set F **1.** 5.39 **3.** .035 **5.** 3.42 **7.** .008 **9.** 95.9 **11.** 46.9 **13.** 6.87 **15.** .0093 **17.** 1.332 **19.** 3.04 **21.** 40.1 **23.** .0481 **25.** .119 **27.** 5.29 **29.** 6.22 **31.** .666 **33.** 47.9 **35.** .0034 **37.** .585 **39.** .008796 **41.** .29 **43.** .009 **45.** 52.4 **47.** 2.47 **49.** 45.8 **51.** 33.8 **53.** .653 **55.** 40.1

pages 88–89

set G **1.** 531.6 **3.** 168.5 **5.** 251 **7.** 3004.2 **9.** 124 **11.** 269.55 **13.** 6420.1 **15.** 1387 **17.** 5392 **19.** 7045.6 **21.** 2775 **23.** 95.33 **25.** 52,029.612

set H **1.** 560 **3.** 3740 **5.** 68,100 **7.** 21,590 **9.** 73,510 **11.** 80 **13.** 1900 **15.** 470 **17.** 2080 **19.** 930,200 **21.** 780 **23.** 738,100 **25.** 2070 **27.** 160

set I **1.** 1.25 **3.** .1943 **5.** 8.016 **7.** 5.0662 **9.** 61.5215 **11.** 6.3344 **13.** 2.64091 **15.** 5.6027 **17.** 3.4219 **19.** .45 **21.** 43.44 **23.** 63 **25.** 306.02 **27.** 52.91

set J **1.** .0346 **3.** .017 **5.** .06 **7.** .0921 **9.** .007085 **11.** .0002 **13.** .0009 **15.** .084 **17.** .0149 **19.** .000019 **21.** .04709 **23.** .03 **25.** .006 **27.** .040897

pages 90–91

set K **1.** 4.6 **3.** 5.49 **5.** 6.4 **7.** 16 **9.** 5.5 **11.** 419 **13.** 3.9 **15.** 4.1 **17.** .853 **19.** 84

set L **1.** 38 **3.** 705 **5.** 250 **7.** 800 **9.** 385 **11.** 9300 **13.** 56,080 **15.** 2940 **17.** 410

set M **1.** 5.7 **3.** 4 **5.** 8.6 **7.** 12.4 **9.** .008 **11.** 9.8 **13.** 380 **15.** .2354 **17.** .34 **19.** .021 **21.** 15 **23.** 7 **25.** 47 **27.** 54 **29.** .003 **31.** 5.8 **33.** 3.006 **35.** 5.1 **37.** 3.2 **39.** .61 **41.** 6.3 **43.** 5 **45.** 30 **47.** 75.12 **49.** 3.12 **51.** 26 **53.** .084 **55.** 500

page 92

set N **1.** 2.3 **3.** .1 **5.** 47.2 **7.** 101.3 **9.** 72.4 **11.** 27.2 **13.** .9 **15.** 12.0

set O **1.** 5.33 **3.** 12.05 **5.** 95.13 **7.** 24.05 **9.** 42.98 **11.** 4.93 **13.** 1.44 **15.** 7.50

set P **1.** .004 **3.** .285 **5.** .428 **7.** .205 **9.** 8.338 **11.** 7.253 **13.** .008 **15.** 2.436

page 93

set Q **1.** 472.3 **3.** 54.3 **5.** 6.1 **7.** .6 **9.** 1.5

set R **1.** 24.09 **3.** .37 **5.** .19 **7.** 4.24

set S **1.** .264 **3.** 1.408 **5.** 6.253 **7.** .464

page 95 **1.** $6.62 **3.** $14.58 **5.** $4.34 **7.** $4.17 **9.** $1.97 **11.** $4.47 **13.** $42.80 **15.** $24.40

pages 96–97 **1.** \$6.09 **3.** \$1.35 **5.** \$2.63 **7.** \$2.79 **9.** \$2.87 **11.** \$1.38 **13.** \$7.23 **15.** \$1.80 **17.** \$4.76 **19.** \$.62 **21.** \$5.85 **23.** \$1.89 **25.** \$15.89

pages 98–99 **1.** \$1369.71; \$6175.71; \$171.55 **3.** \$1222.83; \$5512.83; \$153.14 **5.** \$2666.61; \$12,023.11; \$333.98 **7.** \$1272.53; \$6630.53; \$221.02 **9.** \$942.25; \$4909.60; \$163.66 **11.** \$913.14; \$5719.14; \$238.30 **13.** \$815.22; \$5105.22; \$212.72 **15.** \$1777.74; \$11,134.24; \$463.93

pages 100–101 **1.** 13.5; \$.54 **3.** 12; \$.48 **5.** 9.35; \$.38 **7.** 15.75; \$.63 **9.** 280.5; \$11.22 **11.** 6.125; \$.25 **13.** 125; \$5.00 **15.** 107.35; \$4.30

pages 102–103 **1.** 36; \$117.00 **3.** 33; \$106.59 **5.** 34.5; \$163.88 **7.** 37; \$170.94 **9.** 40; \$150.40 **11.** 503; \$171.02 **13.** 467; \$158.78 **15.** 478; \$152.96 **17.** 422; \$181.46 **19.** 524; \$167.68

page 107
set A **1.** 3 cm **3.** 4 cm **5.** 2 cm **7.** 6 cm **9.** 5 cm
set B **1.** 36 mm **3.** 7 mm **5.** 46 mm **7.** 17 mm **9.** 56 mm

pages 108–109
set C **1.** 31 mm **3.** 2 km **5.** 54 mm **7.** 8 m **9.** 18 m **11.** 26 mm **13.** 10,000 m
set D **1.** 38,000 m **3.** 0.758 m **5.** 8500 mm **7.** 1.55 m **9.** 1.245 km **11.** 1650 cm

page 110
set E **1.** 8 cm^2 **3.** 13 cm^2 **5.** 8.5 cm^2
set F **1.** 800 mm^2 **3.** 1300 mm^2 **5.** 850 mm^2

page 111
set G **1.** 10 cm^3 **3.** 11 cm^3 **5.** 7.5 cm^3
set H **1.** 10,000 mm^3 **3.** 11,000 mm^3 **5.** 7500 mm^3

page 112
set I **1.** 2ℓ **3.** 235 ml **5.** 250 ml **7.** 700 ml **9.** 8ℓ **11.** 50ℓ
set J **1.** 25,000 ml **3.** 0.0827ℓ **5.** 375,000 ml **7.** 5000 ml **9.** 4.370ℓ, or 4.37ℓ **11.** 0.0834ℓ

page 113
set K **1.** 8 kg **3.** 5 g **5.** 19 kg **7.** 305 g **9.** 5 g **11.** 380 mg
set L **1.** 38,000 g **3.** 400 g **5.** 0.031 kg **7.** 7000 g **9.** 6.420 kg, or 6.42 kg **11.** 0.850 kg, or 0.85 kg

page 114
set M **1.** 30 ml; 30 g **3.** 950 ml; 950 cm^3 **5.** 63 ml; 63 cm^3 **7.** 16.3 g; 16.3 cm^3 **9.** 8.9 cm^3; 8.9 ml
set N **1.** 8ℓ; 8 kg **3.** 0.3 dm^3; 0.3ℓ **5.** 12.3ℓ; 12.3 dm^3 **7.** 85 dm^3; 85 kg **9.** 0.7 dm^3; 0.7ℓ

page 115
set 0 **1.** degrees Celsius **3.** degrees Celsius **5.** kelvins **7.** degrees Celsius **9.** degrees Celsius
set P **1.** 58°C **3.** 100°C **5.** 10°C **7.** 4°C **9.** 0°C **11.** 15°C

pages 118–119 **1.** 495 g graham cracker crumbs; 21 g baking powder; 3 eggs; 375 ml milk; 225 ml corn oil; 150 ml corn syrup; 165 g chopped pecans **3.** 340 g lasagne noodles; 2 ml oregano; 1000 g spaghetti sauce with meat; 500 ml cream-style cottage cheese; 360 g sliced mozzarella cheese **5.** 6 **7.** 0.25 kg ground beef; 15 ml finely chopped green pepper; 30 ml chopped onion; 40 ml catsup; 7.5 ml horseradish; 3.5 ml dry mustard; 1 ml salt **9.** 1 kg ground beef; 60 ml finely chopped green pepper; 120 ml chopped onion; 160 ml catsup; 30 ml horseradish; 14 ml dry mustard; 4 ml salt

pages 120–121 **1.** 0.35 m; $.62 **3.** $10.60 **5.** 0.35 m; $.60 **7.** $9.36 **9.** 1.85 m; $6.46 **11.** 1.60 m; $3.67

pages 122–123 **1.** $T = 16$ mm; $L = 25$ mm; $D = 6$ mm **3.** $T = 19$ mm; $L = 34$ mm; $D = 8$ mm **5.** $T = 25$ mm; $L = 38$ mm; $D = 11$ mm **7.** $T = 15$ mm; $L = 23$ mm; $D = 5$ mm **9.** 3.3 mm **11.** 5.0 mm **13.** 8.5 mm **15.** 14.0 mm **17.** 21.0 mm **19.** 32.0 mm

pages 124–125 **1.** 0.5 mg **3.** 20 mg **5.** 180 cm^3 **7.** 60 mg **9.** 500 mg **11.** 260 mg **13.** 500 mg **15.** 50 **17.** 200 **19.** 500

page 127

Dividing Whole Numbers **1.** 48 R1 **3.** 2 R20 **5.** 65 R7 **7.** 321 R1 **9.** 5 R260 **11.** 25 R12 **13.** 3094 R2 **15.** 130 R2 **17.** 42 R6 **19.** 31,874 R2 **21.** 6 R607 **23.** 65 R11

Adding and Subtracting Decimals **1.** 13.7 **3.** 1.20 **5.** 7.491 **7.** 10.428 **9.** 3.812 **11.** 11.423 **13.** 5.6 **15.** 20.869 **17.** 3.081 **19.** .498 **21.** 30.363 **23.** 21.44 **25.** 61.797

Multiplying and Dividing Decimals **1.** 402.04 **3.** .74 **5.** 35.67 **7.** 538.9 **9.** 12.56 **11.** .0073 **13.** 3900 **15.** .0027 **17.** 2.35 **19.** 5.43 **21.** .06 **23.** .06

page 128 **1.** 12,258.19 **3.** 16,837.92 **5.** 61.9 **7.** 87.053 **9.** 62.5583 **11.** 7855.4 **13.** 18.79092 **15.** 4015.0552 **17.** 135.828 **19.** 285.69 **21.** 2.102 **23.** .187 **25.** 1.958 **27.** $661.01 **29.** .25¢; .24¢; Brand Y **31.** .08¢; .10¢; Brand X **33.** 355 km **35.** 385 km **37.** 305 km

pages 132–133

set A **1.** $^2/_5$ **3.** $^7/_{12}$ **5.** $^5/_{10}$ **7.** $^1/_4$ **9.** $^5/_8$

set B **1.** $5\,^2/_3$ **3.** $6\,^3/_4$ **5.** $3\,^2/_5$ **7.** $2\,^1/_4$ **9.** $4\,^1/_2$

page 134

set C **1.** $^2/_3$ **3.** $^1/_2$ **5.** $^3/_4$ **7.** $^3/_5$ **9.** $^5/_6$ **11.** $^3/_{16}$ **13.** $^3/_4$ **15.** $^1/_3$

set D **1.** $21\,^4/_5$ **3.** $6\,^1/_3$ **5.** 5 **7.** 24 **9.** $14\,^2/_3$ **11.** $28\,^3/_{10}$

set E **1.** $^{43}/_3$ **3.** $^{31}/_4$ **5.** $^{97}/_{16}$ **7.** $^{23}/_9$ **9.** $^{44}/_5$ **11.** $^{85}/_8$ **13.** $^{85}/_{16}$ **15.** $^{343}/_4$

page 135

set F **1.** .25 **3.** .75 **5.** .7 **7.** .05 **9.** .5 **11.** .8 **13.** .9 **15.** .17 **17.** .0125 **19.** .4375 **21.** .55 **23.** .18

set G **1.** .333 **3.** .111 **5.** .667 **7.** .067 **9.** .833 **11.** .429 **13.** .818 **15.** .056 **17.** .556 **19.** .857 **21.** .944 **23.** .176

pages 136–137

set H **1.** $^8/_{15}$ **3.** $^5/_{18}$ **5.** $^2/_{35}$ **7.** $^7/_{48}$ **9.** $^{11}/_{48}$

set I **1.** $^3/_{10}$ **3.** $^5/_{14}$ **5.** $^5/_{18}$ **7.** $^3/_4$ **9.** $^1/_4$ **11.** $^3/_8$ **13.** $^9/_{16}$ **15.** $^7/_{15}$ **17.** $^1/_3$ **19.** $^3/_5$ **21.** $^3/_{10}$ **23.** $^1/_{12}$

set J **1.** $^8/_{15}$ **3.** $^2/_{15}$ **5.** $^9/_{40}$ **7.** $^4/_{15}$ **9.** $^1/_4$ **11.** $^1/_6$ **13.** $^2/_{21}$ **15.** $^1/_{30}$ **17.** $^5/_{21}$ **19.** $^{10}/_{147}$

set K **1.** 12 **3.** $1\,^1/_2$ **5.** $7\,^1/_2$ **7.** 24 **9.** 35 **11.** 10 **13.** 60 **15.** $3\,^3/_{10}$ **17.** $2\,^4/_5$ **19.** 35 **21.** $5\,^7/_{10}$ **23.** $20\,^1/_4$ **25.** 6 **27.** 28 **29.** $4\,^3/_8$ **31.** 100 **33.** 250 **35.** 50 **37.** 15 **39.** 4800

pages 138–139

set L **1.** $\frac{7}{8}$ **3.** $\frac{17}{30}$ **5.** 1 **7.** $1\frac{1}{9}$ **9.** $5\frac{3}{7}$ **11.** $2\frac{7}{8}$ **13.** $4\frac{1}{2}$ **15.** $7\frac{13}{20}$ **17.** 1

set M **1.** 33 **3.** $21\frac{1}{3}$ **5.** 27 **7.** 99 **9.** $22\frac{3}{4}$ **11.** $13\frac{2}{3}$ **13.** 146 **15.** 370 **17.** 18 **19.** 33

set N **1.** $4\frac{7}{8}$ **3.** 12 **5.** $4\frac{1}{5}$ **7.** $24\frac{2}{5}$ **9.** 6 **11.** $2\frac{1}{2}$ **13.** $13\frac{3}{4}$ **15.** $18\frac{3}{4}$ **17.** $6\frac{7}{8}$ **19.** 10

set O **1.** $8\frac{3}{4}$ **3.** $\frac{17}{28}$ **5.** 16 **7.** 25 **9.** $3\frac{1}{12}$

pages 140–141

set P **1.** $\frac{4}{3}$ **3.** $\frac{9}{1}$ **5.** $\frac{1}{6}$ **7.** $\frac{5}{4}$ **9.** $\frac{100}{7}$ **11.** $\frac{4}{29}$ **13.** $\frac{7}{34}$ **15.** $\frac{16}{7}$ **17.** $\frac{8}{29}$ **19.** $\frac{4}{63}$

set Q **1.** $\frac{7}{10}$ **3.** $1\frac{1}{2}$ **5.** $1\frac{1}{2}$ **7.** $1\frac{1}{4}$ **9.** $14\frac{2}{7}$ **11.** $1\frac{1}{4}$ **13.** $\frac{11}{16}$ **15.** 32 **17.** 1000 **19.** $\frac{27}{40}$ **21.** $11\frac{1}{3}$ **23.** $\frac{7}{10}$ **25.** 1 **27.** 60 **29.** $7\frac{1}{3}$

set R **1.** $\frac{3}{16}$ **3.** $\frac{2}{15}$ **5.** $\frac{3}{16}$ **7.** $\frac{1}{20}$ **9.** $\frac{2}{21}$ **11.** $\frac{1}{10}$ **13.** $\frac{5}{6}$ **15.** $\frac{3}{20}$ **17.** $\frac{1}{45}$ **19.** $\frac{1}{100}$ **21.** $\frac{7}{16}$ **23.** $\frac{1}{100}$ **25.** $\frac{7}{30}$ **27.** $\frac{3}{4}$ **29.** $\frac{5}{16}$

set S **1.** $\frac{39}{56}$ **3.** $\frac{8}{9}$ **5.** $\frac{1}{6}$ **7.** $\frac{3}{26}$ **9.** $\frac{1}{14}$ **11.** $1\frac{3}{7}$ **13.** $\frac{2}{5}$ **15.** $1\frac{3}{5}$ **17.** 1 **19.** $\frac{3}{8}$ **21.** $2\frac{1}{2}$ **23.** $1\frac{1}{2}$ **25.** $2\frac{11}{14}$ **27.** $2\frac{2}{7}$ **29.** $\frac{5}{28}$

page 143 **1.** $4\frac{1}{2}$ min. **3.** 18 min. **5.** $8\frac{5}{8}$ min. **7.** 4 laps **9.** $8\frac{1}{2}$ laps **11.** $8\frac{1}{2}$ min. **13.** $10\frac{5}{8}$ min. **15.** $2\frac{1}{8}$ min. **17.** 5 laps **19.** 3 laps

pages 144–145 **1.** $\frac{1}{2}$ in. **3.** 1 in. **5.** $\frac{1}{3}$ in. **7.** $\frac{7}{12}$ in. **9.** $\frac{7}{9}$ in. **11.** 27 turns **13.** $13\frac{1}{2}$ turns **15.** 15 turns **17.** 9 turns **19.** 36 turns

pages 146–147 **1.** $1\frac{3}{16}$ in. **3.** $\frac{7}{8}$ in. **5.** $\frac{11}{16}$ in. **7.** $1\frac{3}{8}$ in. **9.** $\frac{1}{2}$ in. **11.** $1\frac{1}{8}$ in. **13.** $\frac{3}{4}$ in. **15.** $1\frac{7}{8}$ in. **17.** $1\frac{1}{2}$ in.; $\frac{15}{16}$ in. **19.** $\frac{3}{4}$ in.; $\frac{15}{32}$ in.

pages 148–149 **1.** $7\frac{1}{2}$ in.; 28; 84 **3.** $10\frac{1}{2}$ in.; 6; 12 **5.** $11\frac{1}{4}$ in.; 10; 10 **7.** $15\frac{3}{4}$ in.; 12; 24 **9.** $62\frac{1}{2}$ hours

page 152

set A **1.** $\frac{9}{12}$, $\frac{4}{12}$ **3.** $\frac{5}{8}$, $\frac{2}{8}$ **5.** $\frac{3}{6}$, $\frac{2}{6}$ **7.** $\frac{10}{15}$, $\frac{9}{15}$ **9.** $\frac{15}{20}$, $\frac{8}{20}$ **11.** $\frac{12}{15}$, $\frac{5}{15}$ **13.** $\frac{10}{16}$, $\frac{3}{16}$ **15.** $\frac{9}{12}$, $\frac{2}{12}$ **17.** $\frac{9}{24}$, $\frac{14}{24}$ **19.** $\frac{20}{30}$, $\frac{21}{30}$

set B **1.** $\frac{4}{6}$, $\frac{5}{6}$, $\frac{3}{6}$ **3.** $\frac{5}{10}$, $\frac{6}{10}$, $\frac{9}{10}$ **5.** $\frac{6}{10}$, $\frac{5}{10}$, $\frac{9}{10}$ **7.** $\frac{15}{24}$, $\frac{6}{24}$, $\frac{15}{24}$ **9.** $\frac{9}{12}$, $\frac{8}{12}$, $\frac{2}{12}$ **11.** $\frac{24}{30}$, $\frac{20}{30}$, $\frac{21}{30}$

page 153

set C **1.** $>$ **3.** $>$ **5.** $<$ **7.** $>$ **9.** $<$

set D **1.** $>$ **3.** $<$ **5.** $>$ **7.** $<$ **9.** $<$

set E **1.** $<$ **3.** $>$ **5.** $=$ **7.** $<$ **9.** $>$

pages 154–155

set F **1.** $1\frac{2}{5}$ **3.** 1 **5.** $1\frac{2}{3}$ **7.** $1\frac{1}{2}$ **9.** $1\frac{1}{3}$

set G **1.** $1\frac{1}{8}$ **3.** $1\frac{1}{4}$ **5.** $1\frac{3}{16}$ **7.** $1\frac{1}{3}$ **9.** $1\frac{1}{10}$ **11.** $1\frac{1}{5}$ **13.** $1\frac{1}{12}$ **15.** $1\frac{1}{12}$ **17.** $1\frac{3}{10}$ **19.** $1\frac{7}{15}$ **21.** $1\frac{7}{20}$ **23.** $1\frac{5}{24}$ **25.** $1\frac{1}{18}$ **27.** $1\frac{5}{14}$ **29.** $1\frac{7}{40}$ **31.** $1\frac{1}{30}$ **33.** $1\frac{1}{10}$ **35.** $1\frac{1}{20}$ **37.** $1\frac{7}{12}$ **39.** $1\frac{7}{18}$ **41.** $1\frac{5}{18}$

set H **1.** $1\frac{2}{7}$ **3.** $1\frac{1}{4}$ **5.** $1\frac{1}{6}$ **7.** $1\frac{3}{10}$ **9.** $1\frac{5}{24}$ **11.** $1\frac{1}{5}$ **13.** $1\frac{1}{16}$ **15.** $1\frac{1}{4}$ **17.** $1\frac{3}{20}$

pages 156–157

set I **1.** $\frac{1}{3}$ **3.** $\frac{3}{7}$ **5.** $\frac{1}{2}$ **7.** $\frac{3}{5}$

set J **1.** $\frac{1}{6}$ **3.** $\frac{1}{4}$ **5.** $\frac{1}{4}$ **7.** $\frac{5}{12}$ **9.** $\frac{7}{12}$

set K **1.** $\frac{1}{5}$ **3.** $\frac{1}{3}$ **5.** $\frac{1}{2}$ **7.** $\frac{2}{3}$ **9.** $\frac{1}{2}$ **11.** $\frac{1}{4}$ **13.** $\frac{1}{8}$ **15.** $\frac{2}{9}$ **17.** $\frac{3}{4}$ **19.** $\frac{1}{6}$ **21.** $\frac{5}{12}$ **23.** $\frac{1}{10}$ **25.** $\frac{7}{15}$ **27.** $\frac{1}{24}$ **29.** $\frac{11}{20}$ **31.** $\frac{17}{40}$ **33.** $\frac{13}{30}$ **35.** $\frac{7}{12}$ **37.** $\frac{11}{30}$ **39.** $\frac{7}{24}$

pages 158–159

set L **1.** $7\frac{3}{5}$ **3.** $11\frac{3}{4}$ **5.** $15\frac{5}{6}$ **7.** $14\frac{11}{12}$ **9.** $7\frac{9}{10}$

set M **1.** $5\frac{1}{2}$ **3.** $9\frac{2}{5}$ **5.** $4\frac{3}{8}$ **7.** $10\frac{1}{4}$ **9.** $8\frac{1}{3}$ **11.** $10\frac{5}{8}$ **13.** $6\frac{3}{7}$ **15.** $5\frac{8}{9}$ **17.** $2\frac{1}{2}$ **19.** $10\frac{1}{6}$ **21.** $5\frac{5}{6}$ **23.** $3\frac{4}{5}$

set N **1.** $5\frac{1}{8}$ **3.** $16\frac{3}{10}$ **5.** $6\frac{1}{6}$ **7.** $15\frac{1}{20}$ **9.** $5\frac{1}{12}$ **11.** $9\frac{1}{14}$ **13.** $13\frac{5}{24}$ **15.** $12\frac{9}{20}$ **17.** $7\frac{11}{20}$ **19.** $9\frac{13}{24}$

set O **1.** 10 **3.** 15 **5.** $11\frac{1}{2}$ **7.** $13\frac{1}{2}$ **9.** $11\frac{2}{3}$ **11.** $13\frac{1}{4}$ **13.** $8\frac{1}{8}$ **15.** $12\frac{1}{8}$ **17.** $10\frac{1}{3}$ **19.** $18\frac{1}{4}$ **21.** $11\frac{1}{6}$ **23.** $15\frac{1}{12}$ **25.** 11 **27.** $8\frac{13}{24}$ **29.** $16\frac{3}{14}$ **31.** $8\frac{5}{24}$ **33.** $8\frac{7}{30}$ **35.** $8\frac{19}{40}$ **37.** $9\frac{13}{40}$ **39.** $10\frac{1}{24}$

pages 160–161

set P **1.** $5\frac{1}{4}$ **3.** $4\frac{1}{2}$ **5.** $5\frac{1}{5}$

set Q **1.** 5 **3.** 4 **5.** 13

set R **1.** $2\frac{3}{5}$ **3.** $5\frac{1}{3}$ **5.** $1\frac{1}{2}$ **7.** $2\frac{3}{5}$

set S **1.** $3\frac{7}{12}$ **3.** $2\frac{5}{6}$ **5.** $2\frac{5}{12}$ **7.** $7\frac{19}{24}$

set T **1.** $2\frac{3}{5}$ **3.** $3\frac{1}{4}$ **5.** $3\frac{1}{6}$ **7.** $2\frac{2}{5}$ **9.** $\frac{1}{3}$ **11.** $3\frac{1}{6}$ **13.** $4\frac{1}{8}$ **15.** $1\frac{5}{6}$ **17.** $5\frac{5}{12}$ **19.** $2\frac{7}{12}$ **21.** $1\frac{23}{24}$ **23.** $1\frac{3}{10}$

page 163 **1.** 27 hr.; \$81 **3.** 39 hr.; \$117 **5.** 33 hr.; \$99

pages 164–165 **1.** $2\frac{3}{4}$ dollars **3.** $\frac{7}{8}$ dollar **5.** $\frac{5}{8}$ dollar **7.** $2\frac{3}{8}$ dollars **9.** $\frac{3}{8}$ dollar **11.** $\frac{7}{8}$ dollar **13.** $\frac{7}{8}$ dollar **15.** $27\frac{7}{8}$ dollars **17.** $2\frac{1}{8}$ dollars **19.** $5\frac{6}{8}$, or $5\frac{3}{4}$ dollars **21.** $4\frac{6}{8}$, or $4\frac{3}{4}$ dollars

pages 166–167 **1.** 8¢ **3.** $11\frac{3}{8}$¢ **5.** $18\frac{5}{8}$¢ **7.** $38\frac{3}{8}$¢ **9.** $37\frac{4}{8}$, or $37\frac{1}{2}$¢ **11.** Toyparts Company **13.** $36\frac{3}{8}$¢ **15.** $61\frac{3}{8}$¢

pages 168–169 **1.** 20 sec. **3.** $9\frac{3}{10}$ sec. **5.** 930 sec., or $15\frac{1}{2}$ min. **7.** $18\frac{19}{20}$ sec. **9.** $19\frac{7}{20}$ sec. **11.** $17\frac{73}{80}$ sec.

pages 172–173

set A **1.** $\frac{1}{6}$ **3.** $\frac{1}{6}$ **5.** $\frac{1}{6}$

set B **1.** $\frac{2}{6}$, or $\frac{1}{3}$ **3.** $\frac{1}{6}$ **5.** $\frac{2}{6}$, or $\frac{1}{3}$ **7.** $\frac{5}{6}$ **9.** $\frac{1}{7}$ **11.** $\frac{2}{7}$ **13.** $\frac{3}{7}$ **15.** $\frac{1}{11}$ **17.** $\frac{2}{11}$ **19.** $\frac{3}{11}$

set C **1.** 1 **3.** 4 **5.** 15 **7.** 4 **9.** 7 **11.** 14 **13.** 6 **15.** 16 **17.** 28

pages 174–175

set D Tree diagram will vary. **1.** The 6 outcomes are 1) yellow, gray; 2) yellow, green; 3) yellow, brown; 4) orange, gray; 5) orange, green; and 6) orange, brown. **3.** The 4 outcomes are 1) head, head; 2) head, tail; 3) tail, head; and 4) tail, tail. **5.** The 8 outcomes are 1) true, true, true; 2) true, true, false; 3) true, false, true; 4) true, false, false; 5) false, true, true; 6) false, true, false; 7) false, false, true; and 8) false, false, false.

set E **1.** $\frac{1}{4}$ **3.** $\frac{2}{4}$, or $\frac{1}{2}$ **5.** $\frac{3}{4}$ **7.** $\frac{3}{8}$ **9.** $\frac{1}{8}$ **11.** $\frac{4}{8}$, or $\frac{1}{2}$ **13.** $\frac{3}{8}$ **15.** $\frac{1}{8}$

pages 176–177

set F **1.** 10 **3.** 100,000 **5.** 4 **7.** 16 **9.** 64 **11.** 36 **13.** 24 **15.** 1728

set G **1.** $\frac{1}{100}$ **3.** $\frac{3}{100}$ **5.** $\frac{9}{100}$ **7.** $\frac{2}{1000}$, or $\frac{1}{500}$ **9.** $\frac{100}{1000}$, or $\frac{1}{10}$ **11.** $\frac{1}{10000}$ **13.** $\frac{99}{10000}$ **15.** $\frac{2}{100000}$, or $\frac{1}{50000}$

pages 178–179

set H **1.** $\frac{2}{156}$, or $\frac{1}{78}$ **3.** $\frac{1}{156}$ **5.** $\frac{2}{156}$, or $\frac{1}{78}$ **7.** $\frac{1}{156}$ **9.** $\frac{1}{156}$ **11.** $\frac{6}{1716}$, or $\frac{1}{286}$ **13.** $\frac{6}{1716}$, or $\frac{1}{286}$ **15.** $\frac{12}{1716}$, or $\frac{1}{143}$ **17.** $\frac{2}{1716}$, or $\frac{1}{858}$ **19.** $\frac{6}{1716}$, or $\frac{1}{286}$ **21.** $\frac{6}{90}$, or $\frac{1}{15}$ **23.** $\frac{6}{90}$, or $\frac{1}{15}$ **25.** $\frac{3}{90}$, or $\frac{1}{30}$ **27.** $\frac{2}{90}$, or $\frac{1}{45}$ **29.** $\frac{3}{90}$, or $\frac{1}{30}$ **31.** $\frac{6}{720}$, or $\frac{1}{120}$ **33.** $\frac{6}{720}$, or $\frac{1}{120}$ **35.** $\frac{6}{720}$, or $\frac{1}{120}$ **37.** $\frac{9}{720}$, or $\frac{1}{80}$ **39.** $\frac{3}{720}$, or $\frac{1}{240}$

pages 180–181

set I **1.** $\frac{4}{16}$, or $\frac{1}{4}$ **3.** $\frac{9}{36}$, or $\frac{1}{4}$ **5.** $\frac{18}{28}$, or $\frac{9}{14}$ **7.** $\frac{18}{60}$, or $\frac{3}{10}$ **9.** $\frac{8}{34}$, or $\frac{4}{17}$ **11.** $\frac{33}{90}$, or $\frac{11}{30}$ **13.** $\frac{21}{81}$, or $\frac{7}{27}$ **15.** $\frac{26}{68}$, or $\frac{13}{34}$ **17.** $\frac{75}{150}$, or $\frac{1}{2}$ **19.** $\frac{45}{125}$, or $\frac{9}{25}$ **21.** $\frac{16}{83}$

set J **1.** 7 **3.** 18 **5.** 15 **7.** 8 **9.** 14 **11.** 35 **13.** 40 **15.** 84 **17.** 24 **19.** 18 **21.** 28 **23.** 63 **25.** 15 **27.** 25 **29.** 50 **31.** 50 **33.** 72 **35.** 52 **37.** 102

page 183 **1.** 6,760,000 **3.** $\frac{2}{6760000}$, or $\frac{1}{3380000}$ **5.** $\frac{676}{6760000}$, or $\frac{1}{1000}$ **7.** $\frac{676000}{6760000}$, or $\frac{1}{10}$ **9.** $\frac{7000}{6760000}$, or $\frac{7}{6760}$

pages 184–185 **1.** 2; 3 **3.** 8; 5; 1; 14 **5.** 11; 2; 2; 15 **7.** $^{3}/_{42}$, or $^{1}/_{14}$ **9.** $^{12}/_{42}$, or $^{2}/_{7}$ **11.** $^{14}/_{42}$, or $^{1}/_{3}$ **13.** $^{15}/_{42}$, or $^{5}/_{14}$ **15.** $^{3}/_{42}$, or $^{1}/_{14}$ **17.** 10 sections **19.** 32 sections **21.** A net loss of 11 chips **23.** A net loss of 7 chips **25.** A net loss of 6 chips

pages 186–187 **1.** 62; 91; 124; 143; 195 **3.** $^{14}/_{124}$, or $^{7}/_{62}$ **5.** $^{20}/_{91}$ **7.** $^{28}/_{195}$ **9.** $^{50}/_{195}$, or $^{10}/_{39}$ **11.** $^{19}/_{195}$ **13.** 72 **15.** 129 **17.** 49 **19.** 8ℓ **21.** 13ℓ **23.** 5ℓ

pages 188–189 **1.** $^{15}/_{9912}$, or $^{5}/_{3304}$ **3.** $^{17}/_{9665}$ **5.** $^{38}/_{9173}$ **7.** $^{303}/_{4130}$ **9.** $^{107}/_{468}$ **11.** Ages 7–12 **13.** Age 99 **15.** $^{2626}/_{7699} \approx .34$ **17.** $^{9480}/_{9743} \approx .97$ **19.** $^{1311}/_{2626} \approx .50$

page 191
Multiplying Whole Numbers **1.** 608 **3.** 1950 **5.** 7284 **7.** 12,258 **9.** 28,000 **11.** 41,402 **13.** 40,000 **15.** 17,444 **17.** 3008 **19.** 16,000,000 **21.** 385,088 **23.** 612 **25.** 5,880,984
Multiplying and Dividing Decimals **1.** 125.86 **3.** .0782 **5.** .00021 **7.** 5400 **9.** .0001 **11.** 3.3 **13.** .08 **15.** .05 **17.** 62.1 **19.** .47 **21.** 14.37 **23.** 68.77
Multiplying and Dividing Fractions and Mixed Numbers **1.** $^{2}/_{9}$ **3.** 25 **5.** $^{7}/_{12}$ **7.** $8\,^{1}/_{6}$ **9.** 28 **11.** $^{2}/_{3}$ **13.** 8 **15.** $^{1}/_{6}$ **17.** $^{5}/_{19}$

page 192 **1.** .7143 **3.** .5833 **5.** .2656 **7.** .0528 **9.** 59.5625 **11.** .090909 **13.** .272727 **15.** .454545 **17.** .636363 **19.** .818181 **21.** $70\,^{3}/_{8}$ **23.** $44\,^{5}/_{16}$ **25.** $12\,^{47}/_{56}$ **27.** $403\,^{1}/_{3}$ **29.** $55\,^{11}/_{15}$ **31.** $330\,^{3}/_{4}$ **33.** .0129 **35.** .0153

pages 196–197
set A **1.** $\frac{100}{12}$ **3.** $\frac{100}{1}$ **5.** $\frac{21}{60}$ **7.** $\frac{4}{7}$ **9.** $\frac{340}{5}$ **11.** $\frac{35}{15}$ **13.** $\frac{2}{75}$ **15.** $\frac{9}{14}$ **17.** $\frac{3}{7}$
set B **1.** $\frac{8}{60}$ **3.** $\frac{28}{76}$ **5.** $\frac{20}{15}$ 7. $\frac{32}{20}$ **9.** $\frac{100}{64}$ **11.** $\frac{12}{18}$ **13.** $\frac{75}{65}$

pages 198–199
set C **1.** 30×12; 9×40; equal **3.** $.6 \times 2.0$; $.8 \times 1.5$; equal **5.** 15×16; 10×20; not equal **7.** 4×56; 7×32; equal **9.** 3×27; 8×10; not equal **11.** 40×30; 160×8; not equal **13.** 8×45; 30×12; equal **15.** 1.1×12; $.3 \times 44$; equal **17.** 9×130; 15×81; not equal **19.** 2.8×3.5; 4.5×2.1; not equal **21.** $.3 \times 4.5$; $.5 \times 3.0$; not equal **23.** 12×15; 21×10; not equal **25.** 18×42; 14×54; equal
set D **1.** $n = 45$ **3.** $t = 35$ **5.** $c = 45$ **7.** $s = 13$ **9.** $h = 15$ **11.** $a = 20$ **13.** $f = 2.7$ **15.** $s = 18$ **17.** $t = 13$ **19.** $z = 36$ **21.** $c = 3$ **23.** $d = 6$ **25.** $g = 1$ **27.** $n = 15$

pages 200–201

set E **1.** b **3.** c **5.** b **7.** a

set F **1.** ∠D and ∠A, ∠M and ∠J, ∠R and ∠E; $\overline{DM}$ and $\overline{AJ}$, $\overline{DR}$ and $\overline{AE}$, $\overline{MR}$ and $\overline{JE}$ **3.** ∠N and ∠B, ∠L and ∠V, ∠R and ∠Y; $\overline{LR}$ and $\overline{VY}$, $\overline{LN}$ and $\overline{VB}$, $\overline{NR}$ and $\overline{BY}$ **5.** ∠T and ∠L, ∠B and ∠J, ∠E and ∠W; $\overline{TB}$ and $\overline{LJ}$, $\overline{TE}$ and $\overline{LW}$, $\overline{EB}$ and $\overline{WJ}$

pages 202–203

set G **1.** 15; 12 **3.** 150; 90 **5.** 216; 180 **7.** 9.0; 5.4 **9.** 130; 50

set H **1.** $\frac{92}{138}=\frac{80}{n}$; $n=120$ m **3.** $\frac{50}{20}=\frac{15}{n}$; $n=6$ m **5.** $\frac{10.5}{7.5}=\frac{6.3}{n}$; $n=4.5$ m **7.** $\frac{140}{252}=\frac{45}{n}$; $n=81$ m **9.** $\frac{25}{7.5}=\frac{60}{n}$; $n=18$ m

page 205 **1.** 8.7 hr. **3.** 7.5 hr. **5.** 7.6 hr. **7.** 6.0 hr. **9.** 3.8 hr. **11.** 5150 km **13.** $575

pages 206–207 **1.** 12.8 m **3.** 27.2 m **5.** 10.5 m **7.** 37.8 m **9.** 80 paces; 64 m **11.** 120 paces; 96 m **13.** 180 paces; 144 m **15.** 100 paces; 80 m

pages 208–209 **1.** 3 cm^3 **3.** 17 tablets **5.** 25 cm^3 **7.** 12 tablets **9.** 42.5 ml **11.** 30 tablets **13.** $3.75 **15.** $4.10 **17.** $5.84 **19.** $3.44 **21.** $19.13 **23.** $14.53

pages 210–211 **1.** 8640 m **3.** 5760 m **5.** 2880 m **7.** 12,000 m **9.** 8000 m **11.** 18,000 m **13.** 12,000 m **15.** 6000 m

pages 214–215

set A **1.** .096 **3.** .02 **5.** 2.7 **7.** .32 **9.** .01 **11.** .95 **13.** .085 **15.** .127 **17.** .804 **19.** 8.00, or 8 **21.** .41 **23.** .0513 **25.** 1.47 **27.** 1.005 **29.** .8 **31.** .0125 **33.** .14 **35.** .025 **37.** .0092 **39.** .009 **41.** .0725 **43.** 3.00, or 3 **45.** .919 **47.** .095 **49.** .0021 **51.** .0525 **53.** .0625 **55.** .82 **57.** .081 **59.** .05 **61.** .008 **63.** .015 **65.** .005 **67.** .072 **69.** .0035 **71.** .0875 **73.** .006 **75.** 9.00, or 9

set B **1.** 62% **3.** 80% **5.** 17% **7.** .5% **9.** 37% **11.** 501% **13.** 28% **15.** 79% **17.** 8.2% **19.** 73.1% **21.** $37\frac{1}{2}$% **23.** .9% **25.** .8% **27.** 73% **29.** 50% **31.** 51% **33.** 8% **35.** 84% **37.** 3% **39.** 91% **41.** 492% **43.** 41% **45.** 9% **47.** 77% **49.** $55\frac{5}{9}$% **51.** 55.1% **53.** 650% **55.** 99% **57.** 7% **59.** 88% **61.** 99.9% **63.** .7% **65.** 18% **67.** 46.4% **69.** 62.6% **71.** 40% **73.** 1% **75.** 150%

pages 216–217

set C **1.** 7/100 **3.** 1/10 **5.** 7/10 **7.** 67/100 **9.** 13/100 **11.** 71/100 **13.** 1/200 **15.** 1/3 **17.** 2/25 **19.** 31/100 **21.** 3/2, or 1 1/2 **23.** 3/8 **25.** 1/100 **27.** 43/100 **29.** 19/100 **31.** 3/1, or 3 **33.** 27/100 **35.** 11/10, or 1 1/10 **37.** 3/5 **39.** 7/20 **41.** 81/100 **43.** 1/9 **45.** 1/11 **47.** 5/6 **49.** 3/400

set D **1.** 50% **3.** 40% **5.** 14 2/7% **7.** 88 8/9% **9.** 53 11/13% **11.** 95% **13.** 62 1/2% **15.** 57% **17.** 90% **19.** 11 2/3% **21.** 87 1/2% **23.** 75% **25.** 125% **27.** 66 2/3% **29.** 80% **31.** 56 1/4% **33.** 23% **35.** 34 4/9% **37.** 56 2/3% **39.** 1/2%

pages 218–219

set E **1.** 5.4 **3.** 1.74 **5.** .078 **7.** 1.26 **9.** 20.13 **11.** 7.9 **13.** 6.82 **15.** 1.53 **17.** 31.2 **19.** 8.52 **21.** 9.3 **23.** 4.05 **25.** 2.35 **27.** 12 **29.** 10.92 **31.** 47 **33.** 11.04 **35.** 115.36 **37.** 60.8 **39.** 3.968 **41.** 35.88 **43.** 44.8 **45.** 22.5 **47.** 11.02 **49.** 30.6 **51.** 1.71 **53.** 578.4 **55.** .5673

set F **1.** 20 **3.** 30 **5.** 9 **7.** 100 **9.** 60 **11.** 40 **13.** 188 **15.** 4 **17.** 9 **19.** 6

set G **1.** .38 **3.** 1.68 **5.** .08 **7.** .18 **9.** .24 **11.** .19 **13.** .05 **15.** .04 **17.** .25 **19.** .09 **21.** .15 **23.** 1.11 **25.** .07

pages 220–221

set H **1.** 25% **3.** 75% **5.** 40% **7.** 300% **9.** 94% **11.** 125% **13.** 32% **15.** 50% **17.** 8% **19.** 70% **21.** 250% **23.** 135% **25.** 15% **27.** 50% **29.** 1% **31.** 75% **33.** 16% **35.** 100% **37.** 2% **39.** 50% **41.** 25%

set I **1.** 12 1/2% **3.** 41 2/3% **5.** 88 8/9% **7.** 71 3/7% **9.** 37 1/2% **11.** 116 2/3% **13.** 22 2/9% **15.** 85 5/7% **17.** 86 2/3% **19.** 13 1/3% **21.** 103 1/8% **23.** 43 3/4% **25.** 85 5/7% **27.** 83 1/3% **29.** 85 5/7% **31.** 5 1/2% **33.** 16 2/3% **35.** 112 1/2% **37.** 16 2/3% **39.** 55 5/9% **41.** 14 2/7%

pages 222–223

set J **1.** 45 **3.** 20 **5.** 50 **7.** 50 **9.** 88 **11.** 116 **13.** 800 **15.** 140 **17.** 24 **19.** 600 **21.** 40 **23.** 330 **25.** 156 **27.** 525 **29.** 18 **31.** 100 **33.** 3000 **35.** 30 **37.** 3200 **39.** 150

set K **1.** 18 **3.** 282 **5.** 36 **7.** 24 **9.** 600 **11.** 48 **13.** 360 **15.** 24 **17.** 120 **19.** 124 **21.** 460 **23.** 486 **25.** 112 **27.** 12 **29.** 112 **31.** 111 **33.** 728

page 225 **1.** Amount saved $4.30; Sale price $17.20 **3.** Amount saved $1.20; Sale price $6.79 **5.** Amount saved $8.99; Sale price $35.96 **7.** Amount saved $5.69; Sale price $13.29 **9.** Amount saved $7.49; Sale price $22.46

pages 226–227 **1.** Interest $25.80; Total amount $240.80 **3.** Interest $3.57; Total amount $122.57 **5.** Interest $74.88; Total amount $386.88 **7.** Interest $5.25; Total amount $180.25 **9.** Interest $25.83; Total amount $312.83 **11.** 1.5% **13.** 1.25% **15.** 2.25% **17.** 1.75% **19.** 2%

pages 228–229 **1.** $1213.50; $12.14; $1225.64 **3.** $1086.40; $936.40; $9.37; $945.77 **5.** $803.73; $653.73; $6.54; $660.27 **7.** $515.38; $365.38; $3.66; $369.04 **9.** $221.24; $71.24; $.72; $71.96 **11.** $71.96

pages 230–231 **1.** 0.17 ±10%; 0.153 to 0.187 **3.** 97,000,000 ±10%; 87,300,000 to 106,700,000 **5.** 660 ±10%; 594 to 726 **7.** 2100 ±5%; 1995 to 2205 **9.** 70,000,000 ±5%; 66,500,000 to 73,500,000 **11.** 1.4 ±2%; 1.372 to 1.428 **13.** 41,000 ±10%; 36,900 to 45,100 **15.** 990 ± 10%; 891 to 1089

page 235
set A **1.** 8 **3.** 247.3 **5.** 8.3 **7.** 71 **9.** 15.7 **11.** 83.2 **13.** 118.3 **15.** 247.3 **17.** 17.1 **19.** 137.6

pages 236–237
set B **1.** 6 **3.** 5 **5.** 16 **7.** 358 **9.** 24 **11.** 176 **13.** 9 **15.** 77 **17.** 3189 **19.** 15 **21.** 19 **23.** 32 **25.** 8718
set C **1.** 1 and 7 **3.** 3 **5.** 16 **7.** 359 **9.** 12 **11.** 178 **13.** 9 **15.** 76 **17.** 3213 **19.** 12 **21.** 19 **23.** 29 **25.** 8791

pages 238–239
set D **1.** 150 tapes **3.** 140 tapes **5.** 155 tapes **7.** Monday, Tuesday, Wednesday, Friday **9.** Thursday **11.** Tuesday, Thursday **13.** Tuesday
set E **1.**

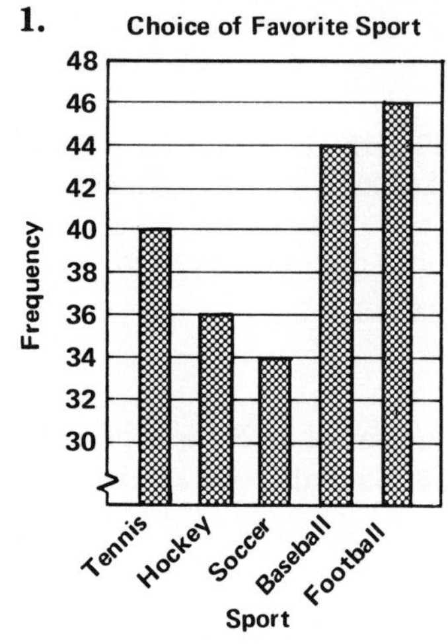

3.

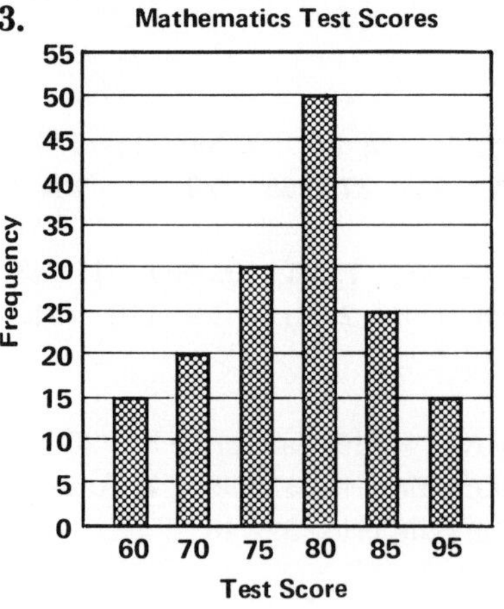

pages 240–241

set F **1.** May, June, July, August, September **3.** May, June, July, August, September **5.** January, December **7.** April, May, June, July, August, September, October **9.** May **11.** June **13.** January 550 min.; February 600 min.; March 675 min.; April 750 min.; May 850 min.; June 900 min.; July 900 min.; August 875 min.; September 800 min.; October 700 min.; November 625 min.; December 550 min.

set G **1.** **3.**

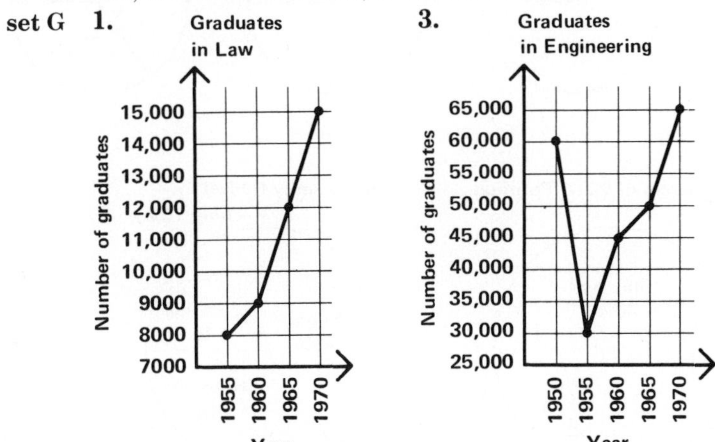

pages 242–243

set H **1.** Muscle **3.** Bone **5.** Muscle, Fat, Bone **7.** Muscle **9.** Muscle **11.** Fat

set I **1.** a. 18 kg; b. 16.2 kg; c. 45 kg; d. 10.8 kg **3.** a. 16.4 kg; b. 14.76 kg; c. 41 kg; d. 9.84 kg **5.** a. $168; b. $480; c. $432; d. $360 **7.** a. $621; b. $189; c. $540; d. $486; e. $405

pages 244–245
set J

1.

3.

5.

90°

7.

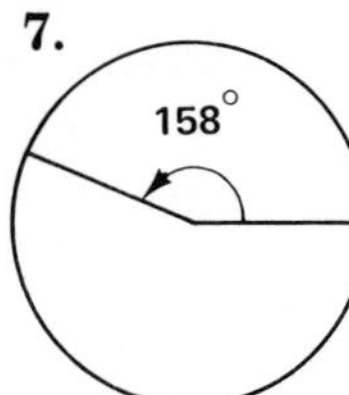

9.

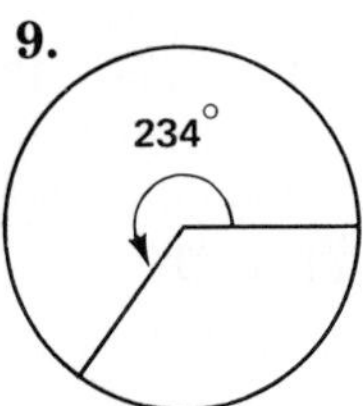

set K

1. Elements of Human Body

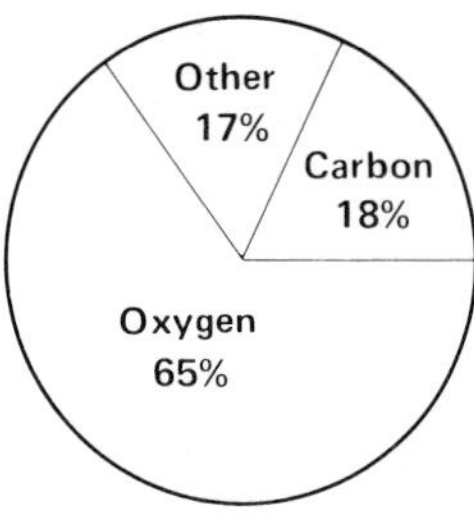

3. Sources of Water Polution

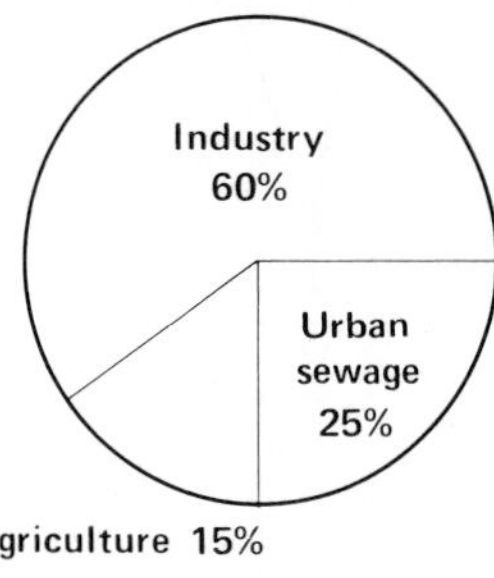

5. Family Budget

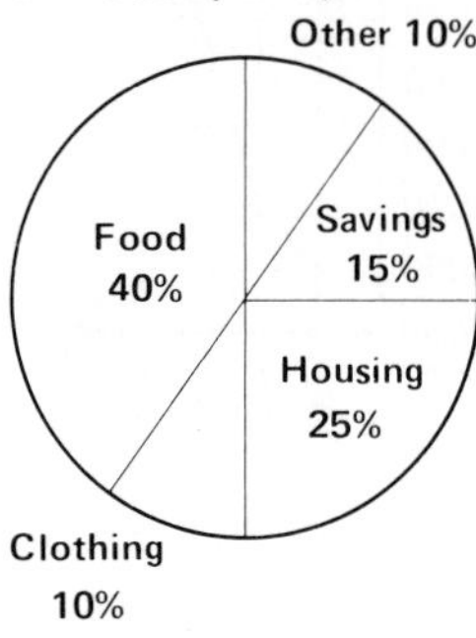

7. Earth's Land

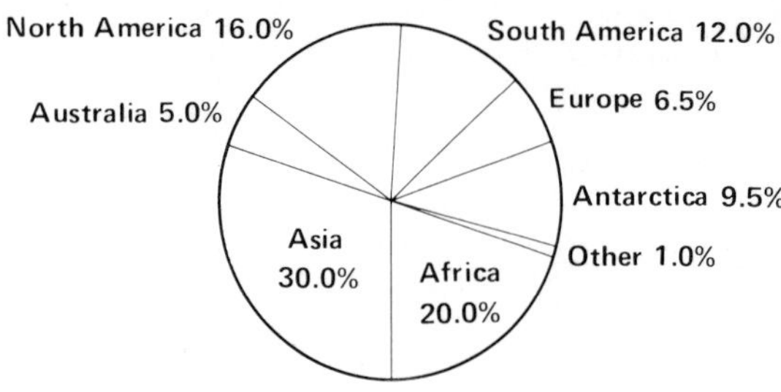

pages 248–249 **1.** March through October **3.** January, February, March, April, October, November, December **5.** January, February, March, September, October, November **7.** April through October **9.** May through October **11.** May through October **13.** January \$50; February \$60; March \$35; April \$25; May \$20; June \$15; July \$10; August \$15; September \$15; October \$25; November \$45; December \$65 **15.** January \$130; February \$135; March \$105; April \$90; May \$50; June \$45; July \$45; August \$40; September \$45; October \$65; November \$80; December \$120 **17.** \$35.42 **19.** High 1975 \$130; Low 1968 \$50; Difference \$80 **21.** High 1975 \$90; Low 1969 \$20; Difference \$70 **23.** High 1975 \$40; Low 1968 \$15; Difference \$25

pages 250–251 **1.** Asheville 14°C; Birmingham 17°C; Dodge City 13°C; New York 12°C; Miami 24°C; Honolulu 25°C **3.** Asheville 9.6 cm; Birmingham 11.2 cm; Dodge City 4.3 cm; New York 8.9 cm; Miami 12.7 cm; Honolulu 4.9 cm

pages 252–253 **1.**

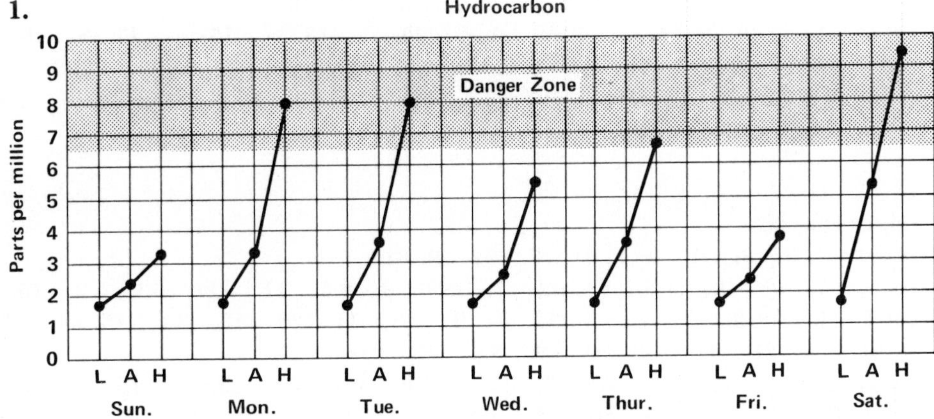

3.

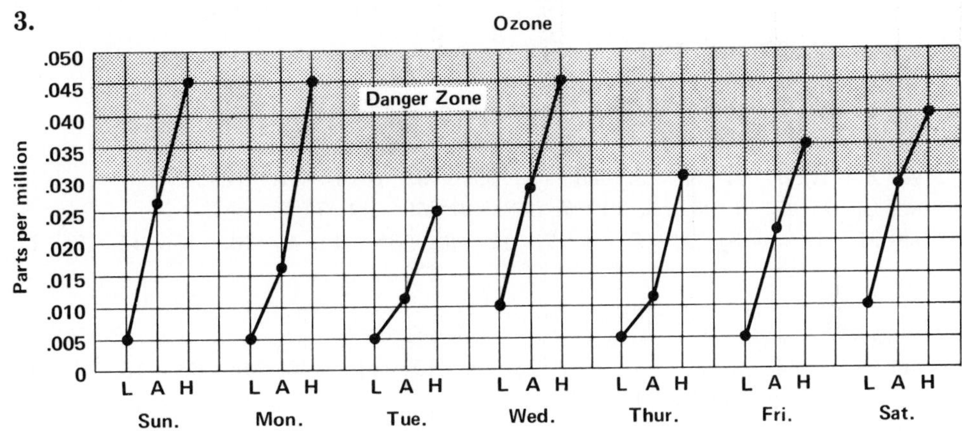

5. Monday: C; Tuesday: B, C

page 255

Adding and Subtracting Whole Numbers **1.** 97 **3.** 384 **5.** 98,220 **7.** 160 **9.** 241 **11.** 156 **13.** 22 **15.** 109 **17.** 88 **19.** 8861 **21.** 2248 **23.** 4838 **25.** 45,388

Adding and Subtracting Decimals **1.** 12.9 **3.** 1.09 **5.** 8.961 **7.** 1.591 **9.** 5.692 **11.** 10.213 **13.** 24.17 **15.** .59 **17.** 2.181 **19.** .476 **21.** 28.41 **23.** 8.261 **25.** 5.399

Adding and Subtracting Fractions and Mixed Numbers **1.** $1\frac{1}{10}$ **3.** $1\frac{1}{2}$ **5.** $10\frac{7}{12}$ **7.** $7\frac{1}{3}$ **9.** $5\frac{11}{12}$ **11.** $4\frac{1}{2}$ **13.** $3\frac{7}{12}$ **15.** $3\frac{17}{24}$ **17.** $1\frac{5}{7}$

page 256 **1.** $n = 1072.1$ **3.** $n = 735.9$ **5.** $n = 10{,}235.0$ **7.** 834.632 **9.** 1199.298
11. $21,037.78 **13.** $2406.25 **15.** $2042.50 **17.** $7290.00 **19.** $281.78 **21.** $564.51
23. $505.92 **25.** $903.33

pages 260–261
set A **1.** $^{-}1$, 2, 6 **3.** $^{-}5$, $^{-}4$, 4 **5.** 22, 25 **7.** $^{-}50$, $^{-}48$
set B **1.** $<$ **3.** $>$ **5.** $>$ **7.** $<$ **9.** $<$ **11.** $<$ **13.** $>$ **15.** $<$ **17.** $>$ **19.** $>$
set C **1.** $^{-}4$, $^{-}1$, 3, 6 **3.** $^{-}5$, $^{-}3$, 7, 9 **5.** $^{-}30$, $^{-}10$, 25, 40 **7.** $^{-}9$, $^{-}8$, $^{-}7$, 0, 8
9. $^{-}9$, 0, 7, 8, 9 **11.** $^{-}16$, $^{-}14$, 0, 8, 13 **13.** $^{-}7$, $^{-}5$, $^{-}1$, 1, 5, 7 **15.** $^{-}10$, $^{-}7$, $^{-}2$, 6, 10
17. $^{-}28$, $^{-}21$, $^{-}9$, $^{-}5$, 14, 16 **19.** $^{-}9$, $^{-}5$, $^{-}4$, $^{-}2$, 4, 6, 9

pages 262–263
set D **1.** 9 **3.** 4.4 **5.** 11.31 **7.** 462 **9.** 81
set E **1.** $^{-}11$ **3.** $^{-}12.3$ **5.** $^{-}8.2$ **7.** $^{-}193$ **9.** $^{-}9.5$ **11.** $^{-}111$ **13.** $^{-}5.2$ **15.** $^{-}1724$
set F **1.** $^{-}4$ **3.** $^{-}12$ **5.** 15 **7.** $^{-}.5$ **9.** $^{-}2.3$ **11.** 129 **13.** $^{-}3.4$ **15.** 94 **17.** 40.9
19. $^{-}15$ **21.** $^{-}3.8$ **23.** $^{-}86$ **25.** 8.6 **27.** $^{-}2.09$
set G **1.** $^{-}11$ **3.** 7 **5.** $^{-}55$ **7.** $^{-}17$ **9.** 15 **11.** $^{-}130$ **13.** $^{-}1$ **15.** 1.5 **17.** $^{-}1.7$ **19.** $^{-}3.5$
21. $^{-}33$ **23.** .01 **25.** $^{-}80$ **27.** $^{-}578$

pages 265–266
set H **1.** $^{-}7$ **3.** $^{-}1$ **5.** $^{-}48$
set I **1.** $^{-}1$ **3.** $^{-}13$ **5.** $^{-}.8$ **7.** $^{-}213$ **9.** $^{-}107$ **11.** $^{-}8$
set J **1.** 5 **3.** $^{-}3$ **5.** .7 **7.** 73 **9.** $^{-}8.5$ **11.** $^{-}1.69$
set K **1.** $^{-}9$ **3.** $^{-}58$ **5.** $^{-}4.4$ **7.** $^{-}599$ **9.** $^{-}1010$ **11.** $^{-}123$
set L **1.** 15 **3.** 25 **5.** 28 **7.** 668 **9.** 850 **11.** 77
set M **1.** 29 **3.** $^{-}38$ **5.** $^{-}2$ **7.** $^{-}12$ **9.** $^{-}156$ **11.** 4 **13.** $^{-}46$ **15.** 16 **17.** $^{-}14$ **19.** $^{-}200$

pages 267–268
set N **1.** 54 **3.** 56 **5.** 18 **7.** 75 **9.** 640 **11.** 1140 **13.** .63 **15.** 5.4 **17.** 12.8
19. 648 **21.** .988 **23.** 3885
set O **1.** 32 **3.** 63 **5.** 27 **7.** 174 **9.** 154 **11.** 720 **13.** 1800 **15.** 13,736 **17.** 4
19. 17,201 **21.** 5.135 **23.** 2790
set P **1.** $^{-}28$ **3.** $^{-}32$ **5.** $^{-}30$ **7.** $^{-}4410$ **9.** $^{-}735$ **11.** $^{-}39$ **13.** $^{-}8.4$ **15.** $^{-}69.92$ **17.** $^{-}.56$
19. $^{-}1512$ **21.** $^{-}2268$ **23.** $^{-}.728$ **25.** $^{-}.0936$ **27.** $^{-}11{,}295$
set Q **1.** 16 **3.** 68 **5.** 28 **7.** $^{-}4$ **9.** $^{-}50$ **11.** 10 **13.** 22 **15.** $^{-}22$ **17.** 48 **19.** 2
21. $^{-}2$ **23.** 33 **25.** $^{-}5$ **27.** $^{-}21$

pages 268–269

set R **1.** 8 **3.** 6 **5.** 8 **7.** 5 **9.** 80 **11.** 38 **13.** .4 **15.** 6 **17.** 50 **19.** .9 **21.** 2 **23.** 4

set S **1.** 7 **3.** 7 **5.** .7 **7.** .5 **9.** 33 **11.** .09 **13.** 15 **15.** 310 **17.** 9 **19.** 14 **21.** 1.4 **23.** 2.3

set T **1.** $^{-}2$ **3.** $^{-}3$ **5.** $^{-}6$ **7.** $^{-}.9$ **9.** $^{-}11$ **11.** $^{-}14$ **13.** $^{-}.04$ **15.** $^{-}.8$ **17.** $^{-}26$ **19.** $^{-}.16$ **21.** $^{-}23$ **23.** $^{-}16$ **25.** $^{-}.03$ **27.** $^{-}35$

set U **1.** $^{-}4$ **3.** 2 **5.** $^{-}6$ **7.** $^{-}2$ **9.** $^{-}10$ **11.** 7 **13.** $^{-}3$

page 271 **1.** 10; 20; 16; $^{-}21$; 5 **3.** 8; 9; 2; $^{-}27$; 6; $^{-}2$

pages 272–273 **1.** 4:48 A.M.; 2.52 m **3.** 8:02 A.M.; 5.15 m **5.** 4:57 A.M.; 1.07 m **7.** 2:32 A.M.; 0.91 m **9.** 10:25 A.M.; 0.33 m **11.** 5:12 A.M.; 1.13 m **13.** 1:02 A.M.; 7.86 m **15.** 7:53 A.M.; 2.01 m **17.** Portland July 1 5:33 P.M.; 2.53 m **19.** Eastport June 4 7:47 P.M.; 5.30 m **21.** Coney Island July 5 5:27 P.M.; 1.47 m **23.** Cape May July 3 4:02 P.M.; 1.15 m **25.** Annapolis July 3 11:55 P.M.; 0.48 m **27.** San Francisco June 3 6:40 P.M.; 1.34 m **29.** Anchorage August 18 4:47 P.M. 8.35 m

pages 274–275 **1.** Sun; 14; 398,359.1 **3.** Venus; 3.4 ≈ 3.5; 25.1 **5.** Sirius; 2.8 ≈ 3.0; 15.9 **7.** Venus; 9.2 ≈ 9.0; 3982.7 **9.** Mercury; 0.8 ≈ 1.0; 2.5 **11.** Sirius; 3.6 ≈ 3.5; 25.1 **13.** Venus; 2.6 ≈ 2.5; 10.0

pages 278–279

set A **1.** 19 **3.** 52.2 **5.** 13.79 **7.** 36 **9.** 61.08 **11.** .953 **13.** 26.9 **15.** 4.79 **17.** 4.2 **19.** 5.38 **21.** 5.268 **23.** 134.1 **25.** 5

set B **1.** 25.3 **3.** 1.2 **5.** 1.2 **7.** 34.4 **9.** 66 **11.** $^{-}1.1$ **13.** 1.3 **15.** $^{-}66$ **17.** 9.7 **19.** 32 **21.** 5.351 **23.** 121 **25.** 4.5

set C **1.** 364 **3.** $^{-}112$ **5.** 119 **7.** $^{-}2250$ **9.** 270 **11.** 2.17 **13.** $^{-}3.15$ **15.** 360 **17.** 6300 **19.** 1.19

set D **1.** .06 **3.** $^{-}2$ **5.** .2 **7.** $^{-}1$ **9.** 2 **11.** 73

pages 280–281

set E **1.** 12.7 **3.** 60.1 **5.** 14 **7.** 53.6 **9.** 9.1 **11.** 244 **13.** 20.5 **15.** 277.7 **17.** $^{-}14$ **19.** 4.5 **21.** 23 **23.** .51 **25.** 7.7 **27.** 104 **29.** $^{-}314$ **31.** 117

set F **1.** $^{-}20$ **3.** 33 **5.** 9.43 **7.** 17.55 **9.** 148 **11.** 246.8 **13.** $^{-}570$ **15.** 60.1 **17.** $^{-}16$ **19.** 691.2 **21.** 2.08 **23.** 51 **25.** 10 **27.** 553.6 **29.** 30

pages 282–283

set G **1.** $x = 2.3$ **3.** $a = 8$ **5.** $n = {}^{-}30$ **7.** $w = 18$ **9.** $z = 2.52$ **11.** $t = 53$ **13.** $g = 0$ **15.** $h = 1.91$ **17.** $k = 17$ **19.** $n = 83$ **21.** $p = .31$ **23.** $r = 55.3$ **25.** $s = 18.2$ **27.** $t = .18$ **29.** $k = .849$ **31.** $p = {}^{-}8$ **33.** $a = {}^{-}27$ **35.** $b = 12.9$ **37.** $y = {}^{-}32$ **39.** $d = {}^{-}39$ **41.** $m = 40$ **43.** $p = 13.9$ **45.** $g = {}^{-}109$ **47.** $a = 34.7$ **49.** $n = 2.03$ **51.** $f = 65$ **53.** $d = 30.5$ **55.** $m = 113.59$

set H **1.** $a = 6.7$ **3.** $z = {}^{-}2$ **5.** $d = 9$ **7.** $r = .89$ **9.** $c = 5.7$ **11.** $x = 9.08$ **13.** $w = 119$ **15.** $g = 1.031$ **17.** $x = 21$ **19.** $h = 13.07$ **21.** $z = 8.15$ **23.** $b = 6.69$ **25.** $w = 65.29$ **27.** $d = {}^{-}102$ **29.** $p = {}^{-}49$ **31.** $q = 34.21$ **33.** $g = 62$ **35.** $f = 15$ **37.** $p = 9.121$ **39.** $h = 92$ **41.** $k = 8$ **43.** $c = 14.5$ **45.** $m = 45.26$ **47.** $t = 40$ **49.** $p = 26.48$ **51.** $b = 32.86$ **53.** $v = {}^{-}41$ **55.** $u = 13.26$ **57.** $z = 95.18$

pages 284–285

set I **1.** $w = {}^{-}53$ **3.** $m = {}^{-}9$ **5.** $d = {}^{-}49$ **7.** $y = 1$ **9.** $c = 7.7$ **11.** $g = 24$ **13.** $y = {}^{-}3$ **15.** $k = {}^{-}5$ **17.** $d = 17$ **19.** $q = 6$ **21.** $n = {}^{-}40$ **23.** $z = {}^{-}81$ **25.** $t = 2.9$ **27.** $f = 1.1$ **29.** $x = {}^{-}13$ **31.** $n = 6$ **33.** $k = .09$ **35.** $u = 0$

set J **1.** $b = 6.12$ **3.** $a = .322$ **5.** $c = 2.8$ **7.** $g = 72$ **9.** $r = 868$ **11.** $g = {}^{-}44$ **13.** $s = 3.68$ **15.** $a = 794.2$ **17.** $t = {}^{-}117$ **19.** $u = 5.52$ **21.** $y = .0464$ **23.** $x = .749$ **25.** $w = {}^{-}156$ **27.** $v = .9417$ **29.** $w = 1212$ **31.** $r = {}^{-}210$ **33.** $s = {}^{-}.594$ **35.** $t = {}^{-}442$ **37.** $d = {}^{-}3.843$

pages 286–287

set K **1.** $c = .4$ **3.** $t = 9$ **5.** $s = 3$ **7.** $y = 8$ **9.** $m = 13$ **11.** $d = 10$ **13.** $n = {}^{-}1$ **15.** $w = 4$ **17.** $h = 1.5$ **19.** $p = 11$ **21.** $x = 2.8$ **23.** $a = 17$ **25.** $k = 3$ **27.** $b = 2$ **29.** $m = 5$ **31.** $r = 9$ **33.** $q = 5$ **35.** $x = {}^{-}8$

set L **1.** $m = 9$ **3.** $x = 8$ **5.** $t = .7$ **7.** $y = 40$ **9.** $z = 48$ **11.** $b = 38$ **13.** $c = 65$ **15.** $h = 32$ **17.** $n = 64$ **19.** $c = 21$ **21.** $k = 90$ **23.** $d = 44$ **25.** $x = .27$ **27.** $b = 8.4$ **29.** $v = 81$ **31.** $u = 90$ **33.** $c = 120$ **35.** $v = 1.8$ **37.** $k = {}^{-}90$

pages 288–289

set M **1.** $n = 8$ **3.** $z = 2$ **5.** $t = 9$ **7.** $b = 9$ **9.** $p = 6$ **11.** $s = 3$ **13.** $z = 2$ **15.** $w = {}^{-}20$ **17.** $u = 2$ **19.** $f = {}^{-}10$ **21.** $z = 3$ **23.** $q = 27$ **25.** $x = 0$

set N **1.** $c = 7$ **3.** $x = {}^{-}1$ **5.** $d = 5$ **7.** $p = 9$ **9.** $x = {}^{-}5$ **11.** $b = 10$ **13.** $k = 30$ **15.** $g = .4$ **17.** $h = 1.9$ **19.** $v = 5$ **21.** $u = {}^{-}10$ **23.** $b = 9$ **25.** $d = 3$ **27.** $s = 0$ **29.** $c = 7$ **31.** $x = {}^{-}5$ **33.** $k = 1$ **35.** $g = 10$ **37.** $p = 8$ **39.** $d = 5$

page 291 **1.** 5; 550 **3.** 10; 1100 **5.** .5; 55 **7.** 4; 880 **9.** 2354 watts **11.** 3498 watts

pages 292–293 **1.** \$7200; \$800 **3.** \$2344; \$656 **5.** \$76,500; \$13,500 **7.** \$22,645; \$2355 **9.** \$7916; \$4884 **11.** \$8391; \$559 **13.** \$15,541; \$2859 **15.** \$656; \$144

pages 294–295 **1.** 20,000 pounds **3.** 30,000 pounds **5.** 32,000 pounds **7.** 20,571 pounds **9.** 36,000 pounds **11.** 2 inches **13.** 5 inches **15.** .5 inch

pages 296–297 **1.** 25 m/s **3.** 26.4 m/s **5.** 73.2 m **7.** 10 sec. **9.** 25.7 sec. **11.** 15.4 m/s; 55.4 km/h; No **13.** 25 m/s; 90 km/h; Yes **15.** 18 m/s; 64.8 km/h; No **17.** 20 m/s; 72 km/h; Yes **19.** 33.3 m/s; 119.9 km/h; Yes

page 301

set A **1.** (6, 4) **3.** (4, 2) **5.** (1, 5) **7.** (8, 4) **9.** (8, 2)

set B

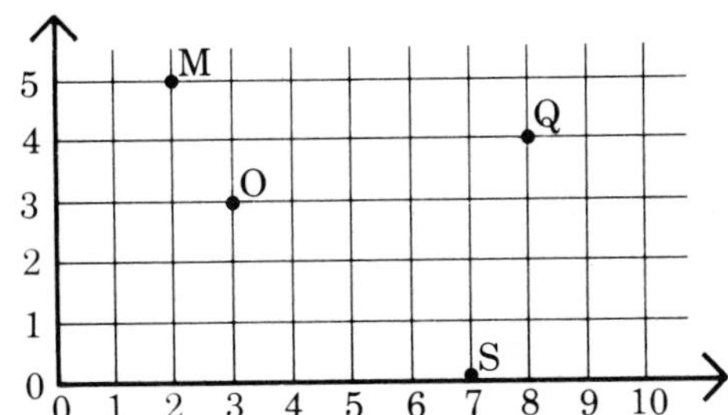

pages 302–303

set C **1.** 0; 1; 4; 6 **3.** 12; 10; 6; 2 **5.** 1; 3; 2; 6

set D **1.** $y = x + 3$ **5.** $y = 3x - 5$

3. $y = 2x$ **7.** $y = 4 - x$

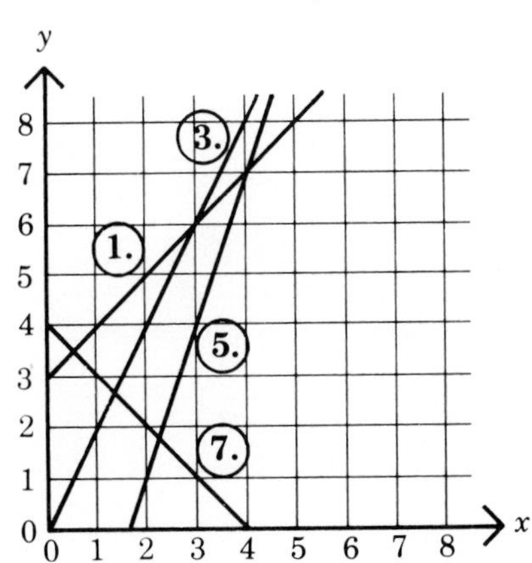

pages 304–305

set E **1.** ($^-3$, 2) **3.** (2, 4) **5.** (2, $^-3$) **7.** (3, 2) **9.** ($^-3$, 0) **11.** (2, 8) **13.** (4, $^-4$) **15.** (6, 4) **17.** ($^-8$, $^-8$) **19.** ($^-8$, 2)

set F

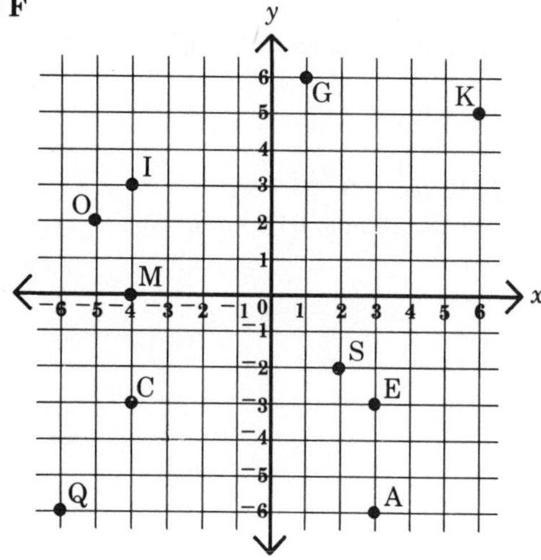

pages 306–307

set G **1.** $^-2$; $^-2$; 1; 4 **3.** 0; $^-3$; 0; $^-2$, or 2 **5.** $^-3$; 2; 1; $^-2$, or 4

set H **1.** $y = x + 1$ **5.** $y = 2x - 1$

3. $y = x - 3$ **7.** $y = 3 - x$

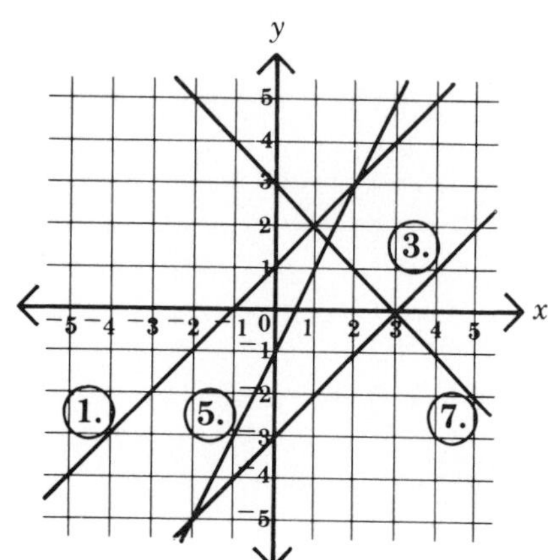

pages 310–311

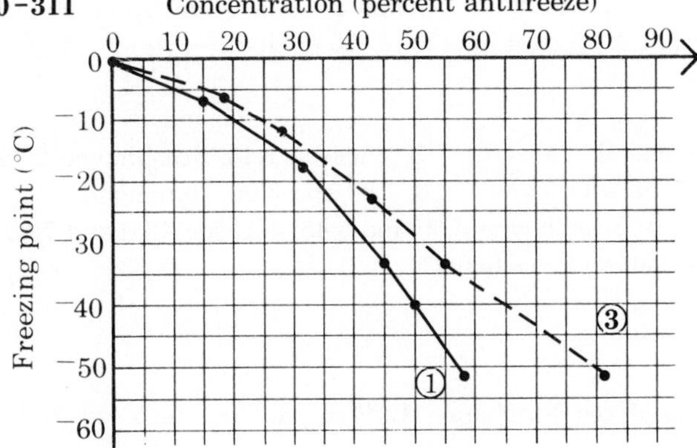

5. Ethylene glycol, Methanol
7. Ethanol

pages 312–313 **1 and 3.**

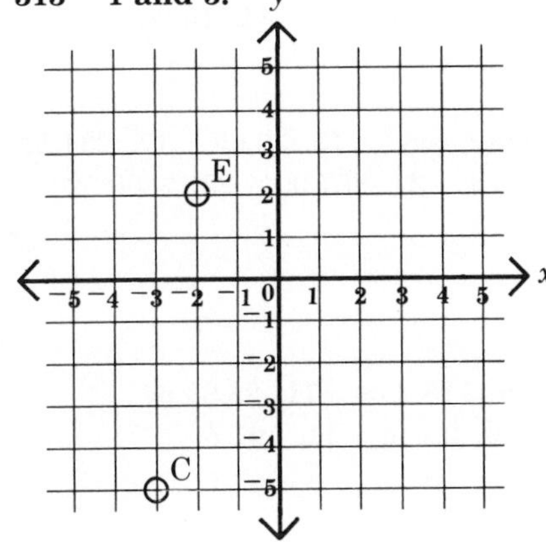

5, 7, and 9.

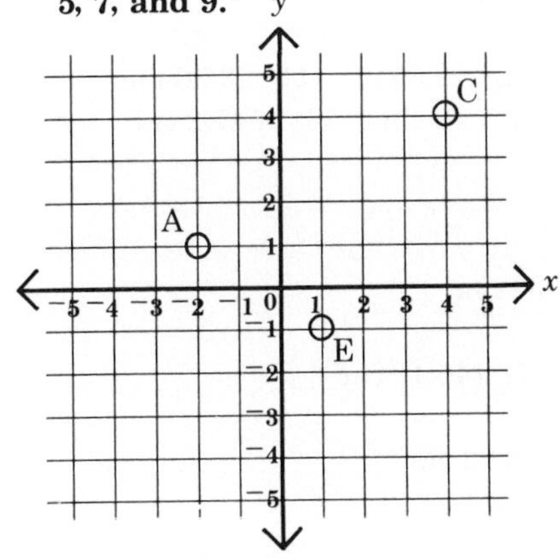

11, 13, 15 and 17.

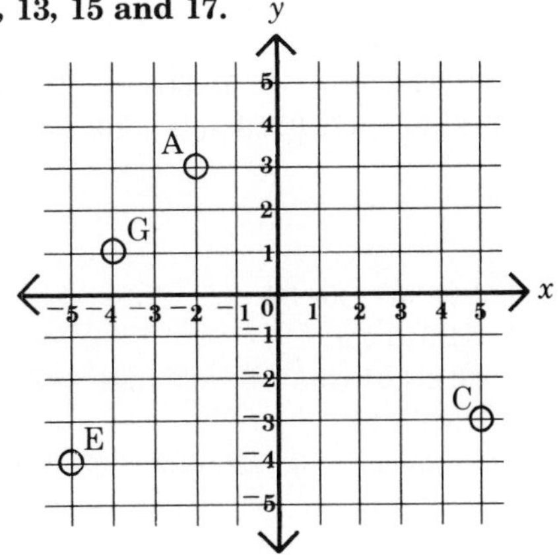

pages 314–315 **1.** Graph 1: 35 m; 20 m; 70 m; 35 m Graph 2: 30 m; 55 m; 25 m; 90 m; 35 m **3.** (15, 45) (45, 75) (85, 95) **5.** Graph 3: 15 m; 45 m; 30 m; 85 m; 40 m

pages 316–317 **1.** Brookhaven, Hammond, Garyville **3.** Jackson 1:45; Brookhaven 2:45 and 3:00; Hammond 4:45; Garyville 5:15; New Orleans 12:30, 1:00 and 3:00; Hammond 1:15; Magnolia 4:15 and 4:45; McComb 5:00; Brookhaven 5:30 and 5:45; Jackson 4:00 and 7:00 **5.** 75 kilometers per hour **7.** 60 kilometers per hour

page 319

Multiplying and Dividing Fractions and Mixed Numbers **1.** $\frac{21}{40}$ **3.** $\frac{7}{16}$ **5.** $5\frac{1}{7}$ **7.** $1\frac{1}{9}$ **9.** 5 **11.** $\frac{17}{28}$ **13.** $\frac{15}{32}$ **15.** $\frac{3}{16}$ **17.** $\frac{1}{6}$

Adding and Subtracting Fractions and Mixed Numbers **1.** $1\frac{1}{6}$ **3.** $1\frac{1}{6}$ **5.** $\frac{1}{3}$ **7.** $\frac{11}{20}$ **9.** $11\frac{1}{2}$ **11.** $9\frac{11}{18}$ **13.** $3\frac{1}{4}$ **15.** $4\frac{1}{8}$ **17.** $2\frac{13}{24}$

Percent **1.** .09 **3.** .921 **5.** .0624 **7.** .27 **9.** 4% **11.** $37\frac{1}{2}$% **13.** 79% **15.** 80% **17.** $\frac{3}{50}$ **19.** $\frac{1}{200}$ **21.** $\frac{2}{25}$ **23.** $\frac{13}{100}$ **25.** 60% **27.** 125% **29.** $57\frac{1}{7}$% **31.** 150%

page 320 **1, 3, 5, 7, 9, 11, 13.** Yes and No answers may vary. **15.** 30.63 **17.** 234.117 **19.** 1.2 **21.** 49.8 **23.** 1.5 **25.** 2.84; 6.36; 9.88; 13.4 **27.** $57.00 **29.** $200.52 **31.** $653.71 **33.** $552.57

pages 324–325

set A **1.** 72 cm **3.** 62 cm **5.** 9 cm **7.** 100 cm **9.** 116.2 m **11.** 28.66 m

set B **1.** 84 cm **3.** 63.8 cm **5.** 99 m **7.** 146 m **9.** 2.1 m **11.** 101 m

pages 326–327

set C **1.** 25.12 m **3.** 125.6 m **5.** 314 cm **7.** 31.4 cm **9.** 282.6 m **11.** 1256 m **13.** 310.86 mm **15.** 116.18 cm **17.** 131.88 m **19.** 235.5 cm **21.** 502.4 km **23.** 1099 cm **25.** 3014.4 mm

set D **1.** 18.84 cm **3.** 37.68 cm **5.** 75.36 cm **7.** 445.88 cm **9.** 12.56 m **11.** 43.96 km **13.** 314 m **15.** 565.2 cm **17.** 3768 mm **19.** 94.2 km **21.** 577.76 cm **23.** 4647.2 cm

pages 328–329

set E **1.** 4.5 m^2 **3.** 1.04 m^2 **5.** 84 cm^2 **7.** 2.34 cm^2 **9.** 0.0312 m^2 **11.** 1.0272 m^2 **13.** 11.043 cm^2

set F **1.** 5625 mm^2 **3.** 24.01 cm^2 **5.** 225 mm^2 **7.** 6.25 m^2 **9.** 146.41 cm^2 **11.** 0.8464 m^2 **13.** 16.9744 m^2

set G **1.** 2.43 m^2 **3.** 2.28 cm^2 **5.** 750 mm^2 **7.** 1.02 m^2 **9.** 13.92 cm^2 **11.** 1.7612 m^2 **13.** 11.8584 m^2

pages 330–331

set H **1.** 165 m^2 **3.** 180 m^2 **5.** 216 mm^2 **7.** 137.5 mm^2 **9.** 0.0216 m^2 **11.** 8.36 cm^2 **13.** 198.375 m^2

set I **1.** 81 m^2 **3.** 29.8 cm^2 **5.** 4 cm^2 **7.** 81 cm^2 **9.** 1.17 cm^2 **11.** 21.21 cm^2

pages 332–333

set J **1.** 28.26 cm^2 **3.** 1256 mm^2 **5.** 1962.5 cm^2 **7.** 113.04 mm^2 **9.** 12.56 km^2 **11.** 153.86 m^2 **13.** 314 mm^2 **15.** 20.096 mm^2 **17.** 5024 cm^2 **19.** 11,304 cm^2 **21.** 17,662.5 mm^2 **23.** 9156.24 mm^2 **25.** 19,103.76 cm^2 **27.** 3215.36 cm^2

set K **1.** 314 mm^2 **3.** 153.86 m^2 **5.** 1256 mm^2 **7.** 6358.5 mm^2 **9.** 78.5 m^2 **11.** 113.04 cm^2 **13.** 20,096 mm^2 **15.** 31,400 mm^2 **17.** 452.16 m^2 **19.** 803.84 cm^2 **21.** 3846.5 cm^2 **23.** 1017.36 mm^2

page 335 **1.** 5 m by 7 m; 35 m^2 **3.** 4 m by 5 m; 20 m^2 **5.** Living room \$242.20; Master bedroom \$207.60; Guest bedroom \$138.40; Study \$110.72 **7.** Living room \$349.65; Master bedroom \$299.70; Guest bedroom \$199.80; Study \$159.84

pages 336–337 The first answer is the area of the lawn; the second answer is the amount of fertilizer that should be bought for exercise 20. **1.** 1320 m^2; 27 kg **3.** 3330 m^2; 67 kg **5.** 5100 m^2; 102 kg **7.** 3563 m^2; 72 kg **9.** 2508 m^2; 51 kg **11.** 1206 m^2; 25 kg **13.** 4533 m^2; 91 kg **15.** 2166 m^2; 44 kg **17.** 4126 m^2; 83 kg **19.** 2914 m^2; 59 kg

pages 338–339 **1.** 69.99 cm **3.** 93.635 cm **5.** 133.12 cm

page 343

set A **1.** 490 cm^2 **3.** 22.5 m^2 **5.** 532 cm^2 **7.** 138.48 m^2 **9.** 26.38 m^2

page 344

set B **1.** 5046 mm^2 **3.** 403.44 cm^2 **5.** 11.76 m^2 **7.** 2.94 m^2 **9.** 20,184 mm^2 **11.** 3750 mm^2 **13.** 73.5 m^2 **15.** 8214 m^2 **17.** 864 m^2 **19.** 72,600 cm^2 **21.** 168.54 m^2 **23.** 38,400 mm^2 **25.** 3174 mm^2

page 345

set C **1.** 18.84 m^2 **3.** 7724.4 mm^2 **5.** 62.8 cm^2 **7.** 866.64 cm^2 **9.** 1758.4 cm^2 **11.** 596.6 m^2 **13.** 5526.4 mm^2

pages 346 - 347
set D **1.** 256 cm^3 **3.** 384 cm^3 **5.** 1625 cm^3 **7.** 253,800 cm^3 **9.** 10,710 cm^3
set E **1.** 421,875 cm^3 **3.** 1,124,864 mm^3 **5.** 0.064 m^3 **7.** 50.653 m^3 **9.** 125,000 cm^3
11. 32,768 cm^3 **13.** 24.389 m^3 **15.** 1771.561 cm^3 **17.** 8000 m^3 **19.** 250,047 cm^3
21. 1,000,000 cm^3 **23.** 216 m^3 **25.** 830,584 cm^3

pages 348 - 349
set F **1.** 1356.48 m^3 **3.** 175.84 cm^3 **5.** 5024 mm^3 **7.** 80,384 cm^3
9. 125,235.76 mm^3 **11.** 791.28 cm^3
set G **1.** 351.68 cm^3 **3.** 6154.4 cm^3 **5.** 7630.2 cm^3 **7.** 9382.32 mm^3
9. 14,130 cm^3 **11.** 65.94 m^3

pages 350 - 351
set H **1.** 24 cm^3 **3.** 1998 cm^3 **5.** 4800 cm^3 **7.** 4420 cm^3 **9.** 140,244 mm^3
set I **1.** 25.12 m^3 **3.** 15,232.14 cm^3 **5.** 602.88 cm^3 **7.** 40,506 mm^3
9. 226.08 m^3 **11.** 923.16 cm^3

page 352
set J **1.** 113.04 m^3 **3.** 4186.67 cm^3 **5.** 33.49 m^3 **7.** 267,946.66 cm^3 **9.** 113,040 cm^3
11. 2143.57 cm^3 **13.** 4,186,666.67 mm^3 **15.** 82,406.16 mm^3 **17.** 523,333.33 m^3
19. 38,772.72 cm^3
set K **1.** 904.32 cm^3 **3.** 82,406.16 mm^3 **5.** 267.95 m^3 **7.** 523.33 m^3 **9.** 150,456.24 mm^3
11. 113.04 m^3 **13.** 14,130 mm^3 **15.** 659,249.26 cm^3 **17.** 3052.08 mm^3 **19.** 463,011.83 m^3

page 355 **1.** 602.88 cm^3 **3.** 350 cm^3 **5.** 543 g **7.** 315 g **9.** 2715 g **11.** 2205 g
13. 11,568 g **15.** $9.36

pages 356 - 357 **1.** 0.675 m^3 **3.** $5.5 \times 0.3 \times 0.9$; 1.485 m^3 **5.** 6 m^3 **7.** $140
9. 7.1×2.4; 17.04 m^2; 17.04 m^2 **11.** 5.5×2.4; 13.2 m^2; 12.7 m^2 **13.** 48,980,000 mm^2
15. 613 blocks **17.** $1320.54

pages 358 - 359 **1.** 78.5 cm^2; 392.5 cm^3; 1570 cm^3 **3.** 3.5 cm; 38.465 cm^2; 307.72 cm^3; 2461.76 cm^3
5. 2.5 cm; 19.625 cm^2; 157 cm^3; 1256 cm^3 **7.** 4.5 cm; 63.585 cm^2; 445.095 cm^3; 2670.57 cm^3
9. 1.9 cm; 11.3354 cm^2; 68.0124 cm^3; 272.0496 cm^3

page 363

set A **1.** 25 **3.** 16 **5.** 1 **7.** 243 **9.** 169 **11.** 10 **13.** 1000 **15.** 100,000 **17.** 1,000,000,000 **19.** 16 **21.** 256 **23.** 1 **25.** .49 **27.** 625 **29.** 625

set B **1.** 3 **3.** 7 **5.** 11 **7.** 12 **9.** 15 **11.** 30 **13.** 14 **15.** 25 **17.** 13

pages 364–365

set C **1.** 3721 **3.** 7569 **5.** 1444 **7.** 900 **9.** 6889 **11.** 9801 **13.** 1600 **15.** 7744

set D **1.** 3.9 **3.** 6.3 **5.** 1.4 **7.** 7.7 **9.** 8.0 **11.** 6.2 **13.** 7.0 **15.** 8.7

set E **1.** 88 **3.** 26 **5.** 59 **7.** 34 **9.** 85

pages 366–367

set F **1.** 8.1 m **3.** 13.4 m **5.** 106 m **7.** 41 m **9.** 11.4 m **11.** 7.2 m **13.** 29 m **15.** 13.5 m **17.** 17 m

set G **1.** 5.3 cm **3.** 55 mm **5.** 16 m **7.** 40 m **9.** 13.7 m **11.** 135 m **13.** 72 m **15.** 8.7 m **17.** 9.1 m

pages 368–369

set H **1.** $\tan \angle J = \frac{20}{21} \approx .952$ **3.** $\tan \angle M = \frac{5}{12} \approx .417$ **5.** $\tan \angle K = \frac{24}{7} \approx 3.429$

7. $\tan \angle X = \frac{12}{35} \approx .343$ **9.** $\tan \angle D = \frac{45}{28} \approx 1.607$ **11.** $\tan \angle P = \frac{40}{9} \approx 4.444$

13. $\tan \angle G = \frac{72}{154} \approx .468$ **15.** $\tan \angle F = \frac{16}{63} \approx .254$

set I **1.** $\sin \angle J = \frac{20}{29} \approx .690$ **3.** $\sin \angle M = \frac{5}{13} \approx .385$ **5.** $\sin \angle K = \frac{24}{25} = .960$

7. $\sin \angle X = \frac{12}{37} \approx .324$ **9.** $\sin \angle D = \frac{45}{53} \approx .849$ **11.** $\sin \angle P = \frac{40}{41} \approx .976$

13. $\sin \angle G = \frac{72}{170} \approx .424$ **15.** $\sin \angle F = \frac{16}{65} \approx .246$

set J **1.** $\cos \angle J = \frac{21}{29} \approx .724$ **3.** $\cos \angle M = \frac{12}{13} \approx .923$ **5.** $\cos \angle K = \frac{7}{25} \approx .280$

7. $\cos \angle X = \frac{12}{37} \approx .946$ **9.** $\cos \angle D = \frac{28}{53} \approx .528$ **11.** $\cos \angle P = \frac{9}{41} \approx .220$

13. $\cos \angle G = \frac{154}{170} \approx .906$ **15.** $\cos \angle F = \frac{63}{65} \approx .969$

pages 370–371

set K **1.** .158 **3.** 3.732 **5.** 1.483 **7.** 14.301 **9.** 28.636

set L **1.** .946 **3.** .500 **5.** .995 **7.** .755 **9.** .276

set M **1.** .946 **3.** .643 **5.** .857 **7.** .530 **9.** .707

pages 372–373
set N **1.** 11.0 m **3.** 34.7 cm **5.** 3.9 m **7.** 104.6 m **9.** 46.7 cm
set O **1.** 12.5 cm **3.** 30.6 m **5.** 5.2 cm **7.** 8.5 m **9.** 25.4 mm
set P **1.** 13.5 m **3.** 178.1 mm **5.** 41.7 cm **7.** 42.1 mm **9.** 56.2 mm

pages 376–377 **1.** No **3.** No **5.** No **7.** No **9.** Yes

pages 378–379 **1.** 9.9 **3.** 7.1 **5.** 9; 12.7 **7.** 2; 2.8 **9.** 13.9 **11.** 6.9 **13.** 3.5; 2 **15.** 1.7; 1

pages 380–381 **1.** 29.4 m **3.** 47.0 m **5.** 14.1 m **7.** 37.6 m **9.** 38.8 m **11.** 77.7 m **13.** 22.7 m **15.** 68.0 m **17.** 6.4 m **19.** 37.2 m; 186.0 m **21.** 30.7 m; 153.5 m **23.** 45.3 m; 226.5 m **25.** 51.8 m; 259.0 m

page 383
Ratio, Proportion, and Similarity **1.** $n = 91$ **3.** $h = 21$ **5.** $d = 5.2$ **7.** $w = 3$ **9.** $c = 25$ **11.** $j = 12$
Percent **1.** 2.6 **3.** 6.8 **5.** 8 **7.** 60% **9.** 20% **11.** $41\frac{2}{3}$% **13.** 50 **15.** 330 **17.** 252
Positive and Negative Numbers **1.** 2 **3.** $^{-}38$ **5.** 4.5 **7.** $^{-}11$ **9.** $^{-}48$ **11.** $^{-}25.6$ **13.** $^{-}54$ **15.** $^{-}75$ **17.** $^{-}16.8$ **19.** $^{-}8$ **21.** 12 **23.** $^{-}4$ **25.** 9.7

page 384 **1.** 89.2 cm; 633.1 cm^2 **3.** 215.3 cm; 3689.9 cm^2 **5.** 5.5 km; 2.4 km^2 **7.** 10,735.7 mm^2; 75,687.0 mm^3 **9.** 1748.7 mm^2; 4813.8 mm^3 **11.** 3.4 mm^2; 0.4 mm^3 **13.** 143 mm **15.** 195 cm **17.** 11,951.0 cm^3; 3329.0; better buy **19.** 719.3 m **21.** 1810.0 m

Measures, Symbols, and Formulas

Metric System

Length

10 millimeters (mm) = 1 centimeter (cm)
10 centimeters, 100 millimeters = 1 decimeter (dm)
10 decimeters, 100 centimeters = 1 meter (m)
1000 meters = 1 kilometer (km)

Area

100 square millimeters (mm^2) = 1 square centimeter (cm^2)
10,000 square centimeters = 1 square meter (m^2)
100 square meters = 1 are (a)
10,000 square meters = 1 hectare (ha)

Volume

1000 cubic millimeters (mm^3) = 1 cubic centimeter (cm^3)
1000 cubic centimeters = 1 cubic decimeter (dm^3)
1,000,000 cubic centimeters = 1 cubic meter (m^3)

Mass

1000 milligrams (mg) = 1 gram (g)
1000 grams = 1 kilogram (kg)
1000 kilograms = 1 metric ton (t)

Capacity

1000 milliliters (ml) = 1 liter (ℓ)
1000 liters = 1 kiloliter (kl)

United States Customary System

Length

12 inches (in.) = 1 foot (ft.)
3 feet, 36 inches = 1 yard (yd.)
1760 yards, 5280 feet = 1 mile (mi.)
6076 feet = 1 nautical mile

Area

144 square inches (sq. in.) = 1 square foot (sq. ft.)
9 square feet = 1 square yard (sq. yd.)
4840 square yards = 1 acre (A.)

Volume

1728 cubic inches (cu. in.) = 1 cubic foot (cu. ft.)
27 cubic feet = 1 cubic yard (cu. yd.)

Weight

16 ounces (oz.) = 1 pound (lb.)
2000 pounds = 1 ton (T.)

Capacity

8 fluid ounces (fl. oz.) = 1 cup (c.)
2 cups = 1 pint (pt.)
2 pints = 1 quart (qt.)
4 quarts = 1 gallon (gal.)

Symbols

$\approx$	approximately equal to
$\overline{AB}$	segment AB
$\angle G$	angle G
45°	45 degrees
∟	right angle
$\sqrt{25}$	square root of 25

Geometric Formulas

Perimeter
rectangle $P = 2l + 2w$

Circumference
circle $C = \pi d$ or $C = 2\pi r$

Area
rectangle $A = lw$
square $A = s^2$
parallelogram $A = bh$
triangle $A = \frac{1}{2}bh$
trapezoid $A = \frac{1}{2}h(a + b)$
circle $A = \pi r^2$

Surface area
rectangular prism $A = 2lw + 2lh + 2wh$
cube $A = 6s^2$
cylinder $A = 2\pi rh + 2\pi r^2$

Volume
rectangular prism $V = lwh$
cube $V = s^3$
cylinder $V = \pi r^2 h$
rectangular pyramid $V = \frac{1}{3}lwh$
cone $V = \frac{1}{3}\pi r^2 h$
sphere $V = \frac{4}{3}\pi r^3$

Squares and Square Roots

n	n^2	$\sqrt{n}$
1	1	1.000
2	4	1.414
3	9	1.732
4	16	2.000
5	25	2.236
6	36	2.449
7	49	2.646
8	64	2.828
9	81	3.000
10	100	3.162
11	121	3.317
12	144	3.464
13	169	3.606
14	196	3.742
15	225	3.873
16	256	4.000
17	289	4.123
18	324	4.243
19	361	4.359
20	400	4.472
21	441	4.583
22	484	4.690
23	529	4.796
24	576	4.899
25	625	5.000
26	676	5.099
27	729	5.196
28	784	5.292
29	841	5.385
30	900	5.477
31	961	5.568
32	1024	5.657
33	1089	5.745
34	1156	5.831
35	1225	5.916
36	1296	6.000
37	1369	6.083
38	1444	6.164
39	1521	6.245
40	1600	6.325
41	1681	6.403
42	1764	6.481
43	1849	6.557
44	1936	6.633
45	2025	6.708
46	2116	6.782
47	2209	6.856
48	2304	6.928
49	2401	7.000
50	2500	7.071

n	n^2	$\sqrt{n}$
51	2601	7.141
52	2704	7.211
53	2809	7.280
54	2916	7.348
55	3025	7.416
56	3136	7.483
57	3249	7.550
58	3364	7.616
59	3481	7.681
60	3600	7.746
61	3721	7.810
62	3844	7.874
63	3969	7.937
64	4096	8.000
65	4225	8.062
66	4356	8.124
67	4489	8.185
68	4624	8.246
69	4761	8.307
70	4900	8.367
71	5041	8.426
72	5184	8.485
73	5329	8.544
74	5476	8.602
75	5625	8.660
76	5776	8.718
77	5929	8.775
78	6084	8.832
79	6241	8.888
80	6400	8.944
81	6561	9.000
82	6724	9.055
83	6889	9.110
84	7056	9.165
85	7225	9.220
86	7396	9.274
87	7569	9.327
88	7744	9.381
89	7921	9.434
90	8100	9.487
91	8281	9.539
92	8464	9.592
93	8649	9.644
94	8836	9.695
95	9025	9.747
96	9216	9.798
97	9409	9.849
98	9604	9.899
99	9801	9.950
100	10,000	10.000

n	n^2	$\sqrt{n}$
101	10,201	10.050
102	10,404	10.100
103	10,609	10.149
104	10,816	10.198
105	11,025	10.247
106	11,236	10.296
107	11,449	10.344
108	11,664	10.392
109	11,881	10.440
110	12,100	10.488
111	12,321	10.536
112	12,544	10.583
113	12,769	10.630
114	12,996	10.677
115	13,225	10.724
116	13,456	10.770
117	13,689	10.817
118	13,924	10.863
119	14,161	10.909
120	14,400	10.954
121	14,641	11.000
122	14,884	11.045
123	15,129	11.091
124	15,376	11.136
125	15,625	11.180
126	15,876	11.225
127	16,129	11.269
128	16,384	11.314
129	16,641	11.358
130	16,900	11.402
131	17,161	11.446
132	17,424	11.489
133	17,689	11.533
134	17,956	11.576
135	18,225	11.619
136	18,496	11.662
137	18,769	11.705
138	19,044	11.747
139	19,321	11.790
140	19,600	11.832
141	19,881	11.874
142	20,164	11.916
143	20,449	11.958
144	20,736	12.000
145	21,025	12.042
146	21,316	12.083
147	21,609	12.124
148	21,904	12.166
149	22,201	12.207
150	22,500	12.247

n	n^2	$\sqrt{n}$
151	22,801	12.288
152	23,104	12.329
153	23,409	12.369
154	23,716	12.410
155	24,025	12.450
156	24,336	12.490
157	24,649	12.530
158	24,964	12.570
159	25,281	12.610
160	25,600	12.649
161	25,921	12.689
162	26,244	12.728
163	26,569	12.767
164	26,896	12.806
165	27,225	12.845
166	27,556	12.884
167	27,889	12.923
168	28,224	12.961
169	28,561	13.000
170	28,900	13.038
171	29,241	13.077
172	29,584	13.115
173	29,929	13.153
174	30,276	13.191
175	30,625	13.229
176	30,976	13.266
177	31,329	13.304
178	31,684	13.342
179	32,041	13.379
180	32,400	13.416
181	32,761	13.454
182	33,124	13.491
183	33,489	13.528
184	33,856	13.565
185	34,225	13.601
186	34,596	13.638
187	34,969	13.675
188	35,344	13.711
189	35,721	13.748
190	36,100	13.784
191	36,481	13.820
192	36,864	13.856
193	37.249	13.892
194	37,636	13.928
195	38,025	13.964
196	38,416	14.000
197	38,809	14.036
198	39,204	14.071
199	39,601	14.107
200	40,000	14.142

Trigonometric Ratios

Measure of angle	tan	sin	cos	Measure of angle	tan	sin	cos
1°	.017	.017	1.000	**46°**	1.036	.719	.695
2°	.035	.035	.999	**47°**	1.072	.731	.682
3°	.052	.052	.999	**48°**	1.111	.743	.669
4°	.070	.070	.998	**49°**	1.150	.755	.656
5°	.087	.087	.996	**50°**	1.192	.766	.643
6°	.105	.105	.995	**51°**	1.235	.777	.629
7°	.123	.122	.993	**52°**	1.280	.788	.616
8°	.141	.139	.990	**53°**	1.327	.799	.602
9°	.158	.156	.988	**54°**	1.376	.809	.588
10°	.176	.174	.985	**55°**	1.428	.819	.574
11°	.194	.191	.982	**56°**	1.483	.829	.559
12°	.213	.208	.978	**57°**	1.540	.839	.545
13°	.231	.225	.974	**58°**	1.600	.848	.530
14°	.249	.242	.970	**59°**	1.664	.857	.515
15°	.268	.259	.966	**60°**	1.732	.866	.500
16°	.287	.276	.961	**61°**	1.804	.875	.485
17°	.306	.292	.956	**62°**	1.881	.883	.469
18°	.325	.309	.951	**63°**	1.963	.891	.454
19°	.344	.326	.946	**64°**	2.050	.899	.438
20°	.364	.342	.940	**65°**	2.145	.906	.423
21°	.384	.358	.934	**66°**	2.246	.914	.407
22°	.404	.375	.927	**67°**	2.356	.921	.391
23°	.424	.391	.921	**68°**	2.475	.927	.375
24°	.445	.407	.914	**69°**	2.605	.934	.358
25°	.466	.423	.906	**70°**	2.748	.940	.342
26°	.488	.438	.899	**71°**	2.904	.946	.326
27°	.510	.454	.891	**72°**	3.078	.951	.309
28°	.532	.469	.883	**73°**	3.271	.956	.292
29°	.554	.485	.875	**74°**	3.487	.961	.276
30°	.577	.500	.866	**75°**	3.732	.966	.259
31°	.601	.515	.857	**76°**	4.011	.970	.242
32°	.625	.530	.848	**77°**	4.332	.974	.225
33°	.649	.545	.839	**78°**	4.705	.978	.208
34°	.675	.559	.829	**79°**	5.145	.982	.191
35°	.700	.574	.819	**80°**	5.671	.985	.174
36°	.727	.588	.809	**81°**	6.314	.988	.156
37°	.754	.602	.799	**82°**	7.115	.990	.139
38°	.781	.616	.788	**83°**	8.144	.993	.122
39°	.810	.629	.777	**84°**	9.514	.995	.105
40°	.839	.643	.766	**85°**	11.430	.996	.087
41°	.869	.656	.755	**86°**	14.301	.998	.070
42°	.900	.669	.743	**87°**	19.081	.999	.052
43°	.933	.682	.731	**88°**	28.636	.999	.035
44°	.966	.695	.719	**89°**	57.290	1.000	.017
45°	1.000	.707	.707				

Tangent

$$\frac{\text{length of side opposite angle}}{\text{length of side adjacent to angle}}$$

Sine

$$\frac{\text{length of side opposite angle}}{\text{length of hypotenuse}}$$

Cosine

$$\frac{\text{length of side adjacent to angle}}{\text{length of hypotenuse}}$$

See note on page 421.

Careers Chart

This four-page chart gives information about jobs in eight career clusters: Trades, Technical, Science, Health, Arts, Social Service, Business Contact, and Business Detail.* These clusters cover most of the occupations and educational programs which people enter.

The following code is used under the heading "Qualifications."

C 4 years or more of college required
S Special training required (technical or vocational school, junior college, or apprenticeship)
— No college or special training required

Trades	Qualifications	Estimated employment in 1970	Average annual openings to 1980
Air-conditioning, refrigeration, or heating mechanic	S	115,000	7900
Aircraft mechanic	S	140,000	6000
Appliance service person	—	220,000	11,000
Assembler	—	865,000	44,000
Automobile mechanic	—	610,000	23,300
Bricklayer	S	175,000	8500
Carpenter	S	830,000	46,000
Electrician (construction)	S	190,000	12,000
Industrial machinery repair person	S	180,000	9000
Inspector	S	665,000	29,700
Instrument repair person	S	95,000	5900
Machine tool operator	—	425,000	9600
Machinist	S	530,000	16,600
Maintenance electrician	S	250,000	11,000
Meatcutter	S	190,000	5000
Millwright	S	80,000	3100
Painter or paperhanger	—	390,000	22,000
Plumber or pipefitter	S	350,000	20,000
Power truck operator	—	200,000	5100
Supervisor	S	1,488,000	56,500
Television or radio service technician	S	132,000	4500
Tool and die maker	S	165,000	4700
Truck and bus mechanic	—	115,000	5200
Welder or oxygen and arc cutter	—	535,000	22,000

*Cluster titles are from the American College Testing Career Planning Profile, 1971. Information about jobs is from the "Occupational Outlook Handbook in Brief," *Occupational Outlook Quarterly,* vol. 16, no. 1, Spring, 1972 and the *Occupational Outlook Handbook, 1974–75 Edition.*

The eight career clusters are first mentioned in career lessons on pages 18-19, 36-37, 38-39, 58-59, 124-125, 148-149, 186-187, and 250-251. When a cluster is first mentioned, you might have the students turn to this chart and read the data for the jobs listed in that cluster. Ask for highest and lowest employment in 1970 and highest and lowest average annual openings to 1980. Remind students that employment prospects depend on other factors as well such as number of people seeking employment in a particular career. Students can write down jobs they might want and then look up additional information about the jobs, including salaries, in the *Occupational Outlook Handbook* in the library or the guidance office.

Technical

Technical	Qualifications	Estimated employment in 1970	Average annual openings to 1980
Aerospace engineer	C	65,000	1500
Air traffic controller	C	20,000	800
Chemical engineer	C	50,000	1700
Civil engineer	C	185,000	10,000
Drafter	S	310,000	16,300
Electrical engineer	C	235,000	12,200
Engineering and science technician	S	650,000	33,000
Forester	C	22,000	1000
Industrial engineer	C	125,000	8000
Mechanical engineer	C	220,000	10,100
Pilot or copilot	S	49,000	4800
Technical writer	C	20,000	1000

Science

Science	Qualifications	Estimated employment in 1970	Average annual openings to 1980
Chemist	C	137,000	9400
Economist	C	33,000	2300
Geologist	C	23,000	500
Home economist	C	105,000	6700
Life scientist	C	180,000	9900
Mathematician	C	75,000	4600
Physicist	C	48,000	3500

Health

Health	Qualifications	Estimated employment in 1970	Average annual openings to 1980
Dental assistant	—	91,000	9200
Dentist	C	103,000	5400
Dietitian	C	30,000	2300
Medical assistant	—	175,000	20,000
Medical laboratory worker	C	110,000	13,500
Pharmacist	C	129,000	5100
Physician	C	305,000	22,000
Radiologic technologist	S	80,000	7700
Registered nurse	S,C	700,000	69,000
Surgical technician	—	25,000	2600
Veterinarian	C	25,000	1500

Arts	Qualifications	Estimated employment in 1970	Average annual openings to 1980
Commercial artist	S	60,000	2500
Dancer	S	23,000	1500
Musician or music teacher	S,C	210,000	11,100
Photographer	—	65,000	2000
Radio or television announcer	—	17,000	1000
Singer or singing teacher	S,C	75,000	4300

Social Service

Automobile parts stock clerk	—	68,000	2600
Automobile sales agent	—	120,000	4300
Barber	S	180,000	7700
Bartender	—	160,000	8700
Building custodian	—	1,110,000	70,000
College or university teacher	C	336,000	22,000
Cook or chef	—	740,000	49,000
Cosmetologist	S	484,000	43,000
Firefighter	—	180,000	11,800
Gasoline service station attendant	—	410,000	13,300
Guard	—	200,000	15,700
Hospital attendant	—	830,000	111,000
Kindergarten or elementary school teacher	C	1,260,000	52,000
Lawyer	C	280,000	14,000
Librarian	C	125,000	11,500
Licensed practical nurse	S	370,000	58,000
Model	—	58,000	1900
Personnel worker	C	160,000	9100
Police officer (municipal)	—	332,000.	17,000
Private household worker	—	1,558,000	16,000
Real estate sales agent or broker	S	226,000	14,800
School counselor	C	54,000	5200
Secondary school teacher	C	1,015,000	38,000
Social worker	C	170,000	18,000
State police officer	—	41,000	2900
Taxi driver	—	100,000	1800
Telephone operator	—	420,000	28,000
Waiter or waitress	—	1,040,000	67,000

Business Contact	Qualifications	Estimated employment in 1970	Average annual openings to 1980
Advertising worker	C	141,000	5400
Bank clerk	—	510,000	29,600
Bank officer	C	174,000	11,000
Bank teller	—	153,000	14,700
Conductor (railroad)	—	37,500	1200
Local truckdriver	—	1,200,000	35,000
Manufacturers sales representative	—	510,000	25,000
Marketing research worker	C	23,000	2600
Motel manager or assistant	C	195,000	14,400
Public relations worker	C	75,000	4400
Purchasing agent	C	167,000	5400
Retail sales worker	—	2,500,000	131,000
Securities salesworker	S	200,000	11,800
Shipping and receiving clerk	—	379,000	12,000
Stock clerk	—	500,000	23,000
Supervisor of newspaper carriers	—	240,000	2600
Traffic agent or clerk (civil aviation)	—	45,000	4800
Truck driver, over-the-road	—	665,000	21,000
Wholesale trade salesworker	—	539,000	27,700

Business Detail	Qualifications	Estimated employment in 1970	Average annual openings to 1980
Accountant	C	491,000	31,200
Bookkeeping worker	—	1,340,000	74,000
Cashier	—	847,000	64,000
Electronic computer operator	—	200,000	34,200
File clerk	—	169,000	15,300
Front office clerk (hotel)	—	61,000	4500
Industrial traffic manager	C	18,000	700
Office machine operator	—	365,000	20,800
Programmer	S,C	200,000	34,700
Receptionist	—	298,000	23,500
Systems analyst	S,C	100,000	22,700
Stenographer or secretary	—	2,833,000	247,000
Typist	—	671,000	61,000

Brief descriptions of terms are listed in this glossary. These descriptions need not be considered definitions.

acute angle
Any angle whose measure is less than 90 degrees.

addend
One of the numbers used in addition. In $25 + 37 = 62$, 25 and 37 are addends.

adjacent side
Side AB is next to, or adjacent to, angle A

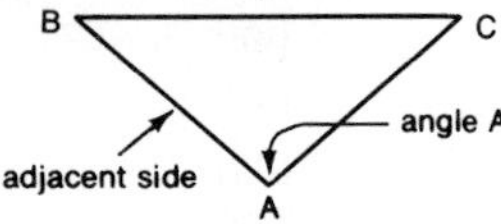

angle
Two rays with the same endpoint. The measure of an angle is given in degrees.

annual
For one year or 12 months.

area
The measure, given in square units, of an amount of surface inside a closed, plane figure.

average
A number obtained by dividing the sum of the addends by the number of addends.

axis
A horizontal or vertical line used for reference on a grid.

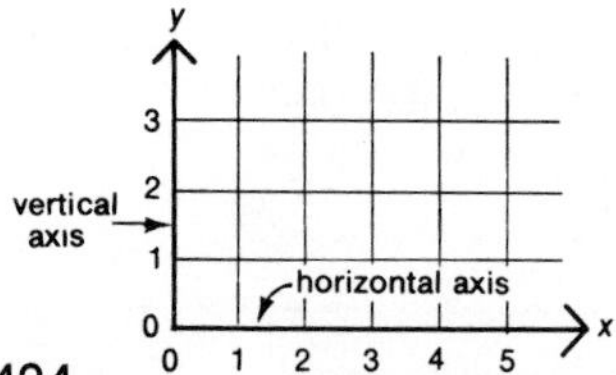

calorie
Unit of energy supplied by food.

capacity
The greatest number of units a container can hold. The capacity of a gas tank is 17 liters.

central angle
An angle whose vertex is the center of a circle.

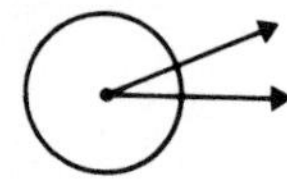

checking account
An account into which money is paid (deposited). The money is taken out (withdrawn) by using forms called checks.

circle
A closed curve in a plane. Each point on the circle is the same distance from the center.

circumference
The measure of the distance around a circle.

common denominator
A common multiple of two or more denominators. A common denominator for $\frac{3}{4}$ and $\frac{5}{6}$ is 12.

common factor
A number that is a factor of two or more numbers. 2 is a common factor of 6 and 14.

common multiple
A number that is a multiple of two or more numbers. 18 is a common multiple of 3, 6, and 9.

cone
A space figure shaped like the one shown below.

corresponding angles or sides
The matching angles or sides in similar figures.

cosine
For a given acute angle in a right triangle, the ratio:
$\frac{\text{length of adjacent side}}{\text{length of hypotenuse}}$

cross-products
The cross-products for the ratios below are 3×8 and 4×6. Two ratios are equal if their cross-products are equal.
$\frac{3}{4} = \frac{6}{8}$ because $3 \times 8 = 4 \times 6$.

cube
A rectangular prism with all square faces (sides).

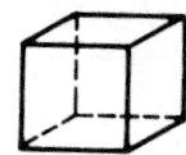

cylinder
A space figure shaped like the one shown below.

data
Information such as scores, measurements, and values.

decimal
A decimal point and place value are used to write decimals, such as 3.8, .015, and 8.00.

denominator
In the fraction $\frac{7}{8}$, 8 is the denominator.

diameter
Segment of a circle. It passes through the center and has its endpoints on the circle.

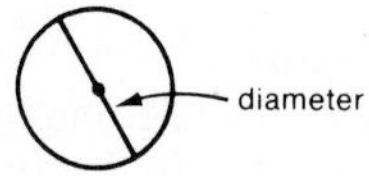

difference
The answer in a subtraction problem. In $88 - 23 = 65$, 65 is the difference.

digits
One of the symbols used to show numbers. In base ten, the digits are 0, 1, 2, 3, 4, 5, 6, 7, 8, and 9.

discount
Amount deducted from list price to obtain sale price; a percent of the list price.

dividend
In $450 \div 25 = 18$, 450 is the dividend.

divisor
In $450 \div 25 = 18$, 25 is the divisor.

equal fractions
Fractions that name the same number, such as $\frac{2}{3} = \frac{6}{9}$.

equal ratios
Ratios that indicate the same rate or comparison. The cross-products of equal ratios are equal.

equation
A mathematical sentence that uses the equals sign (=), such as $5 + 6 = 11$ and $14n = 98$.

exponent
In 4^3, 3 is the exponent. It tells that 4 is to be used as a factor three times.
$4^3 = 4 \times 4 \times 4 = 64$

face
A plane region of a space figure.

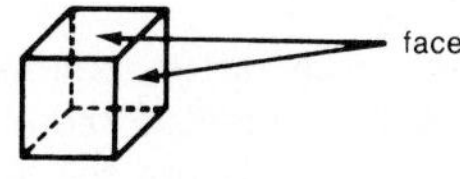

factor
A number used in multiplication. In $14 \times 8 = 112$, 14 and 8 are factors.

finance charge
A fee paid for buying an item on credit or on an installment plan.

fraction
Any number of the form $\frac{2}{3}$, $\frac{8}{8}$, $\frac{9}{5}$, or $\frac{4}{7}$.

frequency
The number of times an outcome or event occurs.

frequency table
A listing of data and how many times each item of the data occurred.

graph
A picture used to show data. The picture could be a bar, line, or circle graph, or a pictograph. It might also be points on a grid matched with given ordered pairs.

greater than (>)
An inequality relation between two numbers, such as $51 > 15$, $9 > 1.4$, and $\frac{1}{3} > \frac{1}{5}$.

gross income
Income before any deductions are made.

gross profit
The amount left after the expenses and costs are deducted from the selling price.

hypotenuse
The side opposite the right angle of a right triangle.

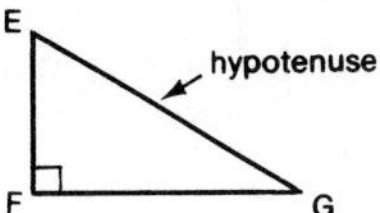

inequality
A mathematical sentence that uses >, <, or ≠, such as $9 > 4$, $.53 < .7$, and $3(5) \neq 9$.

integer
A number such as ⁻83, ⁻52, 0, 106, or 14,679.

interest
An amount paid for the use of money, usually a percent of the amount invested, loaned, or borrowed.

inventory
A detailed list of articles, usually with their estimated values.

lease
The right to use property for a given length of time. Money (rent) is usually paid for the use of the property.

less than (<)
An inequality relation between two numbers, such as $15 < 51$, $1.4 < 9$, and $\frac{1}{5} < \frac{1}{3}$.

list price
Original or regular price before subtracting the discount.

loan
An amount of money borrowed for a certain period of time. Interest is usually paid for the use of the money.

lowest terms
A fraction is in lowest terms if the only common factor of the numerator and denominator is 1. $\frac{1}{5}$, $\frac{8}{3}$, and $\frac{4}{7}$ are in lowest terms.

mass
The measure of quantity of matter an object contains.

mean
Another name for average. The mean of 1, 5, and 6 is $12 \div 3$, or 4.

median
The middle number in a series of numbers when the numbers are in order. The median of 2, 2, 3, 4, and 5 is 3.

mixed number
Any number of the form $15\frac{3}{7}$, $7\frac{9}{10}$, or $34\frac{1}{2}$.

mode
The number occurring most often in a series of numbers. The mode of 1, 1, and 3 is 1.

multiple
The product of a given number and a whole number. Multiples of 5 are 5, 10, 15, 20, 25, and so on.

multiplier
One of the factors in a multiplication problem.

negative number
A number less than zero, such as $^-8$, $^-15$, and $^-96$.

net gain
Actual profit after expenses have been deducted from gross income; expenses are less than income.

net income
Income remaining after deductions are made.

net loss
Actual losses after expenses have been deducted from gross income; expenses are greater than income.

numerator
In the fraction $\frac{7}{8}$, 7 is the numerator.

operation
Addition, subtraction, multiplication, and division are examples of operations.

opposites
Two numbers whose sum is zero. 9 and $^-9$ are opposites because $9 + {^-9} = 0$.

ordered pair
Two numbers used in a certain order, such as (4, 0).

origin
On a grid, the point (0, 0). The two number lines, or axes, meet at this point.

parallel lines
Lines in the same plane and do not meet.

parallelogram
A four-sided polygon whose opposite sides are parallel.

percent
A fraction whose denominator is 100. Percent means "hundredths" or "out of 100." $\frac{4}{100} = .04 = 4\%$

perimeter
The measure of the distance around a closed figure.

pi (π)
The ratio of the circumference to the diameter of a circle. Approximately equal to 3.14.

place value
The value a digit has because of its position. In 78, the 7 has a value of 7(10), or 70, and the 8 has a value of 8(1).

polygon
A closed figure made up of segments.

positive number
A number greater than zero, such as 9, 146, and 32,508.

principal
Amount of money upon which interest is computed.

prism
A space figure with two parallel faces (bases) that have the same measure.

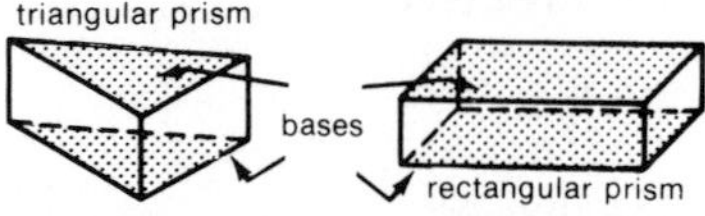

probability
A number that tells how likely it is that a certain event will happen. Expressed as $\frac{\text{number of favorable outcomes}}{\text{number of possible outcomes}}$

product
The answer in a multiplication problem. In $35 \times 26 = 910$, 910 is the product.

proportion
A statement that two ratios are equal.

pyramid
A space figure with one base. All sides are triangles.

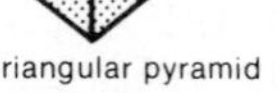
triangular pyramid

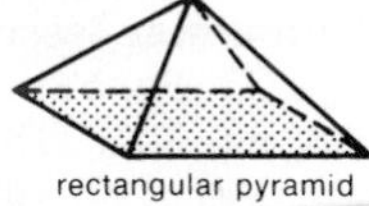
rectangular pyramid

quadrant
The axes separate a grid into four sections. Each section is a quadrant.

quotient
In $450 \div 9 = 50$, 50 is the quotient.

radius
A segment of a circle. One endpoint is the center and the other is on the circle.

ratio
A pair of numbers that expresses a rate or a comparison.

ray
Part of a line that has one endpoint and extends in one direction.

reciprocals
Two numbers whose product is 1. $\frac{3}{4}$ and $\frac{4}{3}$ are reciprocals because $\frac{3}{4} \times \frac{4}{3} = 1$.

rectangle
A parallelogram with four right angles.

rectangular prism
See prism.

remainder
When 15 is divided by 6, the remainder is 3.

$$6\overline{)15}\ \text{ = 2 R3}$$

right angle
An angle whose measure is 90 degrees.

right triangle
A triangle with one right angle.

salary
Money paid to a person for work completed. It is usually paid weekly, twice a month, or monthly.

sale price
The price after the discount is subtracted from the list price; also called net price.

segment
Part of a line, which includes two endpoints.

share of stock
One unit of ownership in a company or corporation. Shares are traded (bought or sold) through a business called a stock exchange.

similar figures
Figures having the same shape but not necessarily the same size.

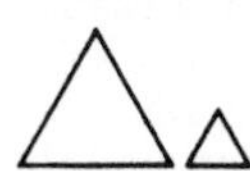
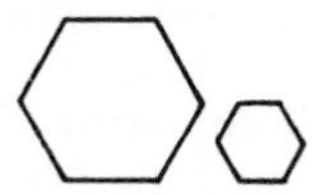

sine
For a given acute angle in a right triangle, the ratio: $\frac{\text{length of opposite side}}{\text{length of hypotenuse}}$

sphere
A round space figure shaped like a basketball. All points on a sphere are the same distance from the center.

square
A rectangle with four sides having the same measure.

square root
One of two equal factors of a number. 5 is the square root of 25 because $5 \times 5 = 25$.

sum
The answer in an addition problem. In $76 + 48 = 124$, 124 is the sum.

surface area
The total area of all the faces of a space figure.

tangent
For a given acute angle in a right triangle, the ratio: $\frac{\text{length of opposite side}}{\text{length of adjacent side}}$

trapezoid
A four-sided polygon with one pair of parallel sides.

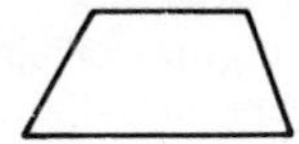

triangle
A polygon with three sides.

trigonometric ratios
See cosine, sine, tangent.

volume
The measure, given in cubic units, of an amount of space inside a space figure.

whole number
Any number in the set 0, 1, 2, 3, 4, 5, and so on.